MW01089172

Manhattan Projects

Manhattan Projects

The Rise and Fall of Urban Renewal
in Cold War New York   **Samuel Zipp**

OXFORD
UNIVERSITY PRESS

Happy reading!
Compliments of
Wisconsin Public Radio
www.wpr.org

OXFORD
UNIVERSITY PRESS

Oxford University Press, Inc., publishes works that further
Oxford University's objective of excellence
in research, scholarship, and education.

Oxford   New York
Auckland   Cape Town   Dar es Salaam   Hong Kong   Karachi
Kuala Lumpur   Madrid   Melbourne   Mexico City   Nairobi
New Delhi   Shanghai   Taipei   Toronto

With offices in
Argentina   Austria   Brazil   Chile   Czech Republic   France   Greece
Guatemala   Hungary   Italy   Japan   Poland   Portugal   Singapore
South Korea   Switzerland   Thailand   Turkey   Ukraine   Vietnam

Published by Oxford University Press, Inc.
198 Madison Avenue, New York, New York 10016
www.oup.com

First issued as an Oxford University Press paperback, 2012.

Portions of chapter 5 appeared in "The Battle of Lincoln Square: Neighbourhood Culture
and the Rise of Resistance to Urban Renewal," *Planning Perspectives*, 24, 4 (October 2009):
409–33. Reproduced by permission of Planning Perspectives/Taylor and Francis.

Library of Congress Cataloging-in-Publication Data
Zipp, Samuel.
Manhattan projects : the rise and fall of urban renewal
in cold war New York / Samuel Zipp.
p. cm.
Includes bibliographical references and index.
ISBN: 978-0-19-532874-5 (hardcover); 978-0-19-987405-7 (paperback)
1. Urban renewal—New York (State)—New York—History—20th century.
2. Manhattan (New York, N.Y.)—Social conditions—20th century.   I. Title.
HT177.N5Z57 2010
307.3'416097471—dc22   2009049007

1 3 5 7 9 8 6 4 2

Printed in the United States of America
on acid-free paper

To the memory of
HARRIET VERMILYA ZIPP,
city planner, librarian,
and mother.

Acknowledgments

One of the unexpected rewards of otherwise solitary intellectual work is the interest that others take in one's ideas and progress. Over the years I've lived with *Manhattan Projects,* I have been continually surprised and rejuvenated by the attention and generosity of a host of family members, friends, colleagues, and strangers. I am happy to get the chance to discharge just a little of the debt I've accrued and thank some of them here.

In the American Studies Program at Yale University, I had the good fortune to study intellectual and cultural history with Jean-Christophe Agnew. One of the great gifts of my time in New Haven was the opportunity to try to climb inside Jean-Christophe's mind and figure out how he puts ideas together. I owe the title of the book and much else to his wide-ranging intellect, generous mentorship, illuminating commentary, and simple confidence in my ability to make it all work. Whatever credibility I may have as a scholar of the built environment should be credited to Dolores Hayden, whose forthright and bracing critiques taught me much about the virtue of precision and helped to reel in some of my more abstract excesses. I am grateful also to Matt Jacobson for his encouragement and several sets of thoughtful and perceptive comments. I have the dim sense that I am lifting this wholesale from one of my predecessors' acknowledgments, but that echo should only reinforce its accuracy: Michael Denning did me the favor of genially disagreeing with much of what I said to him during my years in graduate school, and I can only hope that this book is a little better for having brushed up against his iconoclastic and expansive mind.

I am indebted to a number of other current or former Yale faculty members. Mary Lui read the finished dissertation and prepared a helpful and perceptive reader's report. Laura Wexler, Charles Musser, Dudley Andrew, and Max Page critiqued seminar papers that eventually found their way into the book in one form or another. Though they may not realize it, Paul Gilroy, Nancy Cott, Steve Pitti, John Demos, and Alan Trachtenberg each provided intellectual resources without which this book would be far poorer. I could not have made it through without the friendship and wise counsel of Vicki Shepard.

At George Washington University, where I began my graduate work, Howard Gillette schooled me in the fundamentals of urban history. Melani McAlister trusted that I would make a promising student and, by way of both careful instruction and personal example, opened my mind to whole new realms of intellectual inquiry. I'm grateful for the faith she showed in me then and the friendship and intellectual challenges she continues to offer me today. I hope she sees something of her influence in this book. Similarly, I hope that Carl Smith, Michael Sherry, and Terry Mulcaire, each of whom tried to teach me how to write and think in college, feel that this book represents something of a return on their investment of time and effort.

I've had the opportunity to present portions of this project at various conferences, symposiums, and lectures, where I've been lucky to get good advice and criticism. Mike Wallace has been a great source of encouragement. His readings of the manuscript and invitations to several events and seminars hosted by the Gotham Center for New York History, particularly the Seminar on Postwar New York, have been a great boon to this book. Three of his students—Mei-Ling Israel, Emily Pecora, and Hillary Miller—offered useful critiques of the manuscript. Hilary Ballon included me in the major conference she organized on Robert Moses at Columbia. Her support and thoughtful critiques have made this a better book. At these and other events over the years, I've been thankful also to Robin Bachin, Penny Von Eschen, Edward Dimendberg, Nina Silber, Charles Capper, Bruce Schulman, Marilyn Halter, Julian Zelizer, Rob Snyder, Marci Reaven, Peter Eisenstadt, Suzanne Wasserman, Josh Freeman, Rich Greenfield, Stephen Petrus, Aaron Gurwitz, Vicky Nunez, Ella Howard, Pedro Pedraza, Robert Fairbanks, Nick Bloom, John Bauman, Casey Nelson Blake, Connie Rosenblum, Thomas Sugrue, Bob Lockhart, Ian Williams, Brad Lander, and Charlie McGovern for their comments, criticism, and support.

This project has benefited, directly and indirectly, from the support of a number of people in the places I've taught. I thank Brett Mizelle and Sarah Schrank at Cal State, Long Beach, for encouragement and friendship. Jon Wiener, Laura Mitchell, and Vicki Ruiz helped me to feel welcome during my one-year stint in the History Department at University of California, Irvine. I am lucky to have landed in American Civilization and Urban Studies at Brown, where Elliott Gorn, Patrick Malone, Vernon Henderson, Marion Orr, Jim Morone, Tamar Katz, Susan Smulyan, Bob Lee, Ralph Rodriguez, Beverly Haviland, Rich Meckel, Steve Lubar, Rhacel Parrenas, Robert Self, Seth Rockman, Tara Nummedal, Jean Wood, Rosanne Neri, Isabel Costa, and Heather Parker have all been models of collegiality and offered crucial advice and support as I navigated the first few years in Providence. I am grateful that John Logan saw fit to include me in the Spatial Structures in the Social Sciences Initiative, and I am thankful also to him and Seth Spielman for their conversations with me about mapping. Robert Self offered a valuable intervention in the last stages, subjecting my introduction and conclusion to a close reading that saved me from some not inconsequential errors. I thank him for that and for his general intellectual camaraderie.

Several generous grants and fellowships allowed me to complete research tasks and to prepare the final manuscript. A publication and presentation grant from the Graham Foundation for Advanced Study in the Fine Arts helped to secure the images and artwork. A Rockefeller Archive Research Grant gave me several days of productive work in the archives at Sleepy Hollow. At Yale, an Enders Research Fellowship and the generous Franke Interdisciplinary Fellowship supported my early work on the dissertation. At Brown, awards from the Dean's Office Humanities and Social Sciences Research Fund allowed me to undertake some final research trips.

Like all travelers in the world of the past, I am indebted to the keepers of numerous historical archives. For particular assistance beyond the call of duty, I thank Daniel May at the Met Life Archives; Jon Giman, former manager of Stuyvesant Town; Judith Johnson at the Lincoln Center, Inc., Archives; Chris Hagedorn and Al Zezula at *Town and Village;* and the staff of the La Guardia and Wagner Archives in Queens, particularly Joe Margolis, Douglas DiCarlo, and Maureen Drennan. Howard Marder of the New York City Housing Authority generously allowed me to use photographs from the agency's collection. Also helpful were Pedro Pedraza and Mario Ramirez of the Centro de Estudios Puertorriquenos at Hunter College, Inna Guzenfeld of the Avery Architectural and Fine Arts Library at Columbia, Marleen Buelinckx, Marvin Cordova, and Shelley Lightburn of the United Nations Archives, the staff of Yale's Sterling Memorial Manuscripts and Archives, Jeff Bridgers at the Library of Congress Prints and Photographs Division, Andrea Felder at the New York Public Library, Hannah Marcus and Wesley O'Brien at the New York City Planning Department, and Michele Hiltzik at the Rockefeller Archive Center. Archivists and librarians at the Municipal Archives, the Citizens Housing and Planning Council, the National Archives and Records Administration in College Park, and the New-York Historical Society helped me to find some obscure records during research visits. The staff of the New York Public Library Manuscripts and Archives Division, Performing Arts Library, and Schomburg Center for Research in Black Culture and the staff of the Columbia University Archives and Rare Book and Manuscript Library all provided extended help over periods of days and weeks. At Irvine, Kay Collins helped me with census data. Anne Dodge, Rosemary Cullen, and Holly Snyder of Brown's John Hay Library have helped me to unearth important resources. Bart Hollingsworth made key interventions in the home stretch to secure images through interlibrary loan. Ben Tyler, of Brown Libraries Digital Initiatives, has gone out of his way to prepare images for publication. My thanks to all of them.

Students in my postwar New York seminars at Yale and Brown produced interesting work that helped me to see this period in fresh light. Abigail Cook-Mack, a history major at Yale when I was just getting going on all this, bequeathed me some of the fruits of her senior thesis research on Lincoln Square. Harris Present, Martha Seidman, Pamela Long, and Lee Lorch all shared their memories of various aspects of these events with me; I hope I've done their stories justice. Several works of New York literature have proved invaluable, so much so that they deserve a mention here. All students of the New York cityscape owe a debt to Robert A. M. Stern and his co-authors; *New York 1960* was something of a bible for me. In *The New York Approach,* the late Joel Schwartz uncovered the buried political history of urban renewal. Finally, I owe a great debt to Marshall Berman, whose *All That Is Solid Melts into Air* first fired my imagination long ago.

It's often said that one learns the most from one's friends. At Yale, I was lucky to fall in with Aaron Sachs, Scott Saul, and Andrew Friedman. Some of my happiest memories of those times involve the semester we spent reading nonfiction and talking about writing. Aaron is an unfailing source of intellectual and personal generosity. I count on his wisdom and support. Scott has never ceased to amaze me with the depths of his enthusiasm and encouragement for my work. Andrew walked many of the streets and plazas of this book with me during our time in New York, all the while offering his sense of justice, his impatience with settled thought, and his off-kilter passion for connection and inspiration. Those were difficult years for both of us and for the city; I'm glad we all made it to the other side. I also thank other friends from the American studies and history communities at Yale for things big and small and too numerous to mention: Brenda Carter, Adriane Smith, Tucker Foehl, Josh Guild, Annemarie Strassel, Mark Krasovic, Amy Reading, Mark Greif, Roxanne Willis, Elaine Lewinnek, Brian Herrera, Ferentz Lafargue, Catherine Whalen, Joseph Entin, Tavia N'yongo, and Amy Chazkel. In Washington, P. J. Brownlee, Derek Miller, Jon Cox, and Paul Gardullo held down the homefront.

In New York, Rosten Woo and Damon Rich gave me the sense that this work could matter beyond the academy. "The City without a Ghetto" and other public projects they launched under the auspices of the Center for Urban Pedagogy rejuvenated my sense that there were new and revelatory aspects of urban renewal out there to be uncovered. The city books-and-burgers club that Rosten, Jake Barton, and (for a time) Jonathan Ringen convened each month was a rare gift: a regular chance for urbanists of different stripes to sit together and trade ideas, gossip, and general banter. Rosten Woo and Andrea Meller, Konrad and Angelika Buehler, Nathaniel Frank, and Najib Majaj have provided convivial places to stay on my return visits to New York, making it possible for me to finish my research.

This book would not exist without some ineffable sources of inspiration and motivation from several long-time friends for whom much of this book may still be a mystery. First among these is Eric Wilson. Over almost 30 years, Eric has offered me hilarity, unfiltered intelligence, innumerable provocations, and countless lessons on how to think on one's feet. It might be hard for him to see his mark here, but I could not have become the writer and thinker I am without him. Tony Ross and Cosby Hunt have been there just as long, and I count on their steadfast loyalty. Mark Goble has offered the quiet example of his wit, intelligence, and prose. Pete Coviello actually has read a piece of this book; and despite that fact he still reminds me, from time to time, that I am, indeed, a writer. Without the light and heat cast from his burning pursuit of prose, poetry, music, conversation, and comradely affection, I'd have much less of a reason to want to write in the first place.

I would have had much more trouble bringing this all together if not for Sarah Seidman, who gave a summer of her graduate education to expertly masterminding the campaign to secure image reproductions and permissions. I've made Lynn Carlson's life difficult over the past few months, but the maps she put together really make the book. My greatest editorial debt is to Susan Ferber at Oxford University Press. Susan has been an unfailing supporter of this book and very patient with my many requests and worries. I am thankful to her for her efforts to shape the manuscript and for her careful edits of each chapter. Thanks also to Jessica Ryan and Merryl Sloane at Oxford for their efforts in shepherding the book into print.

My father, Stephen J. Zipp, and my sister, Holly Zipp, have been as steadfast and caring as ever. Day to day, the burdens of this project have fallen most heavily on Ilona Miko. She's never wavered, offering fierce love and moral support, technological and intellectual advice, and a recurrent and affectionate editorial refrain: "Why so many words?" This couldn't have happened without her. My mother, Heidi Zipp, passed away just before I began *Manhattan Projects,* but I like to think it would have pleased her. I have dedicated it to her memory.

Contents

Manhattan Projects

Introduction

Looking back on his arrival in New York, Claude Lévi-Strauss recalled the discovery of a fantastic metropolis. It was 1941, he remembered, and like so many Jewish migrants in those days, the anthropologist was escaping the terror of Nazi-occupied France. And like the generations that preceded him through the "golden door" of New York harbor, he greeted New York as a city "where anything seemed possible." But most surprising and "enchanting" was the fact that Manhattan defied his expectations. New York was "not the ultra-modern metropolis" he had been given to expect. The city seemed not modern—not new at all, in fact—but archaic, a jumbled hodgepodge of the old-fashioned and the exotic sifted in with the contemporary.

In New York, the past seemed everywhere present. "Doorways" opened "in the wall of industrial civilization" onto "other worlds and other times." In "the back rooms of second-hand shops" lurked sixteenth-century Tuscan sideboards; a wary dealer in "South American knickknacks" cautiously revealed a midtown courtyard shed "crammed with Mochica, Nazca and Chimu vases piled on shelves towering to the ceiling." Everywhere, the city yielded classical European artifacts or the booty of colonialism that had once confirmed the Continent's sway over the globe. New York appeared to Lévi-Strauss as a kind of frontier trading post, ready to "bear witness among us to the still real presence of a lost world." European folklorists could find traditional tales, presumed long forgotten in the old country, being told "among their immigrant compatriots," while Lévi-Strauss himself went to work everyday beneath the neoclassical arcades of the New York Public Library's American room, only to find himself sitting near an original American: "an Indian in a feather headdress and a beaded buckskin jacket—who was taking notes with a Parker pen."

To his eyes, the very streets and buildings of the city itself appeared "an immense horizontal and vertical disorder attributable to some spontaneous upheaval of the urban crust rather than to the deliberate plans of builders." If some of the new "ultra-modern" towers of Wall Street and the Chrysler and Empire State buildings had been thrown up early in the 1930s, the building bust of the Depression had left them gleaming over a cityscape that was ever eroding and crumbling, revealing the past sedimented beneath a shroud of modernity. One could read the city's built history in the "vacant lots, incongruous cottages, hovels, red-brick buildings"—the "still visible remnants" that emerged from the clamor and smoke "like witnesses to different eras." Lévi-Strauss also discovered New York as an "agglomeration of villages," a succession of ethnic enclaves in which "one changed countries every few blocks." Endowed with energetic cycles of newness, obsolescence, and decay, New York was a place where history and difference survived. It was open and available, a livable city. Away from the skyscrapers, "the web of the urban tissue was astonishingly slack." New York was "a city where one could breathe easily."

However, Lévi-Strauss delivered this rhapsody with the grim knowledge that the city was on the cusp of a remarkable transformation. "Naturally," he writes—and we feel his chest tighten in grief even across the years—"all these relics were being assaulted by a mass culture that was about to crush and bury them." Peruvian antiquities would give way to hi-fi sets and televisions; the courtyards of midtown would be razed and great steel and glass towers rise from the rubble. New Yorkers had long been forced to put up with the loss of their past, but previous remakings in their city's churning history had happened building by building, lot by lot. The change Lévi-Strauss feared was something else altogether. Twenty years after he disembarked, New York would be seen by many as the capital of the world, an impression due in no small part to the fact that its physical landscape would be replaced block by block and neighborhood by neighborhood. Gone would be the old cottages and hovels as well as many of the tenements and stone and iron buildings once thought of as "skyscrapers." In their place would rise rows of shining office towers, apartment buildings, hospitals, universities, and, most consequential for the livable, breathing city Lévi-Strauss remembered, spare, geometric forests of housing projects.

Lévi-Strauss recalled that, in 1941, his beloved red-brick buildings—warehouses, factories, armories, tenements—were "already empty shells slated for demolition." This old city would fall victim to a many-faceted and pervasive program of slum clearance and urban renewal designed to clear decrepit building stock and remake the city along modern lines. City officials, aided by national legislation, subsidies, and funds, replaced the old buildings with what they understood to be modern, efficient "machines for living," the inspiration and designs for which, ironically, were derived in part from the Europe Lévi-Strauss had left behind. Many New Yorkers—official, elite, and ordinary—felt that they lived in a city where one could *not* breathe, where light and air had no chance of reaching people sealed away in tightly packed tenements with narrow air shafts and dingy, weed-choked backyards. So, just as Lévi-Strauss's Indian scholar took up his "Parker pen," the builders took up their "deliberate plans"—the emblematic tools of an orderly modernity—and began to sweep away the old and bring forth the new.[1]

This book is a cultural history of the urban transformations that Lévi-Strauss lamented, an account of Manhattan's experience with urban renewal. Urban renewal was a vision for remaking the industrial cities of the North and Midwest that flourished and fell in the 30 years after World War II. Proponents of urban renewal had a number of practical goals for what I call their "benevolent intervention" in the cityscape. They intended to use the powers of eminent domain (the legal doctrine that gives governments the right to take private property for public purposes), slum clearance, modern architecture, and rational city planning to sweep away the built environment of the nineteenth century and replace it with a new cityscape. They hoped to clear away "slums" and "blight," rationalize traffic patterns, free city-dwellers from the environmental hazards of industry and the rigid lot and block configuration of the real estate market, bring middle-class shoppers and residents back to the central city in an age of suburbanization, and rehouse the urban poor in modern apartments with amenities and community facilities.

But in New York, Manhattan's renewal boosters—led by Committee on Slum Clearance chair Robert Moses and a host of allies from the broad front of urban liberalism—also saw modern rebuilding projects as a way to make Manhattan a symbol of American power during an age of metropolitan transformation and the Cold War. Urban renewal, they believed, could deliver the proper cityscape of a world-class city, underwrite the city's status as an icon of global power, and make it, quite literally, the capital of international modernity. A renewed Manhattan could project an image of modernization and prosperity to compete with the equally grandiose vision of progress simultaneously motivating the Soviet Union.

And yet, closer to home, these grand plans sparked no small amount of reaction to their overweening impositions on the lives of ordinary New Yorkers. The vigorous accumulation of doubts, critiques, reformulations, and resistance that greeted urban renewal were remarkable for the way they, too, engaged with the rhetoric of the Cold War. Ordinary New Yorkers argued about whether or not the effects of slum clearance and the new plazas and towers were evocative of freedom and democracy, the fabled American way that would vanquish Soviet Communism. While some made their peace with the new city spaces, others described urban renewal's techniques and results as a top-down, mass replacement of an older, more historical, lived cityscape. They saw urban renewal's spatial intervention as total and absolutist, its architecture regimented and alienating, and the displacement it required a travesty of democracy; its entire social and aesthetic profile seemed more suited to a totalitarian regime rather than to the United States. If proponents had envisioned urban renewal as a Cold War bulwark, shoring up the nation's domestic readiness for John F. Kennedy's "long twilight struggle," those who had to live with its interventions increasingly saw it as a liability in that contest precisely because they came to associate it with their fears about the Cold War enemy. These objections to urban renewal's ostensibly benevolent intervention eventually led to the remaking of urban renewal itself and the first inklings of a new brand of urbanism.

This history explores how the vision of urban renewal formed, how it was put into practice in remaking actual Manhattan places, and how it was undone by the experiences and critiques of those living in the places it left in its wake. In keeping with the Cold War context—in which battles were so often fought in the symbolic realm, with images and ideas as much as brute firepower or military maneuver—we must see that this transformation was cultural as much as political, a matter of meaning as much as movements. It was the result of a contest to win the right to determine what this new mode of city rebuilding meant. Was it development? Was it destruction? Or was it something in between, something more complex? Riffing on some lines from Willa Cather, the literary historian Carlo Rotella suggests that there is a "city of feeling" and a "city of fact." Cities of fact, "material places assembled from brick and steel and stone, inhabited by people of flesh and blood," inspire cities of feeling, but are also given shape and meaning by ideas and representations. Urban renewal projects and other like-minded attempts at city remaking on a grand scale are first imagined, designed, planned, and built. But then they are represented and used, and thus reimagined, and so, in a symbolic sense, rebuilt. Most important, the way they are reimagined gives impetus and shape to future efforts at designing, planning, and building, so that new cityscapes of fact can emerge from the old. If postwar cities were formed by explicitly political and social contestation—policy initiatives, struggles between political coalitions, electoral decisions, and street-level conflicts over racial and class boundaries—they were also subject to symbolic and imaginative struggle, attempts to give various cityscapes of feeling purchase in the actual cityscape of fact. These symbolic acts amounted to a fight for the right to give imaginative shape to the city—to describe the character and nature of urban life—and to make that conception natural or normal, the common-sense, shared understanding of that place. In the postwar years urban renewal became the object of just such a struggle, one that was waged with both facts and feelings, to determine the terms, methods, and principles by which cities would be remade. The social and political battles over urban renewal reveal a deeper disturbance in the realm of meaning, a contest to shape the "structure of feeling"—the arrangements of sentiment, allegiance, and belief—that could justify one mode of city shaping over another.[2]

If urban renewal itself rose and fell with the symbolic swells of the Cold War's domestic political culture, in the long run it played a crucial role in shaping the fate of postwar Manhattan. Urban renewal's fraught vision of how to rebuild Manhattan in an age of Cold War and modernity had a crucial hand in creating a divided cityscape. Ultimately, urban renewal reveals how New York, too, was rising and falling: simultaneously climbing to become the political, cultural, and financial capital of the world and dropping deeper into what, by the mid-1960s, would be known as the "urban crisis."

Of course, at the most basic level, urban renewal was a solution to physical and economic problems, a matter of urban politics and policy. Faced with the suburban flight of capital and people in the postwar era, city officials, as historian Jon Teaford has put it, tried to "beat suburbia at its own game." Much municipal activity of the era was directed toward basic infrastructure upgrades—reducing air and water pollution or renovating sewer systems, for instance. But city officials also invested in great highway, slum clearance, and rebuilding projects designed to preserve the profitability of city property and to attract new private capital investment. Such new investment aimed to underwrite higher land values, increased tax revenues, new jobs, and overall prosperity and economic growth. For those officials, big projects and increased prosperity meant more votes on election day. Urban renewal was the latest technique by which city officials and their allies in downtown businesses, urban planning agencies, civic organizations, and neighborhood groups—the constituents of what are often called urban "growth coalitions"—cooperated to keep urban space profitable and their city competitive in regional and national markets.[3]

These policy initiatives had a social goal as well: highway and clearance projects sought to lure white, middle-class residents and shoppers—particularly women—back downtown. Many promoters of urban renewal were motivated by the fear that downtowns would become "Negro shopping districts." As a campaign to bring order to the built environment, it is no surprise that urban renewal also sought to reinforce "orderly" relations between peoples. Influenced by modern planning theory, which prescribed specific and separate zones in the cityscape for disparate uses, urban renewal policies served to perpetuate inequitable patterns of race and gender and to preserve white middle- and upper-class power in central cities.[4]

Title I of the 1949 U.S. Housing Act mobilized the federal government's growing capacity for the physical manipulation of cities. "Urban redevelopment" looked to subsidize local rebuilding campaigns. (It wasn't until 1954 that revisions to the Housing Act introduced the term "urban renewal.") Washington's subsidies came in response to years of halting, largely unsuccessful efforts by city governments to clear slums and rebuild. Cities like New York had used New Deal funds to build some public housing during the 1930s, but it was difficult to attract private builders to risk capital on high-priced slum land close to the downtown core without significant government help. The 1949 act was the most successful of President Harry Truman's domestic Fair Deal policies, providing federal subsidies for municipal purchases of built-up urban land acquired through eminent domain and giving cities the financial leverage to prepare tracts of cleared land for either privately backed redevelopment or new public housing.[5]

And yet, urban renewal was more than a set of policies or economic transactions. It was a vision, a symbolic and cultural undertaking that both shaped and was shaped by urban policy. During the 20 years after World War II, "urban renewal" emerged as a highly contested phrase, one that grabbed the public's imagination in a way that "redevelopment" never did. Across the United States and the globe, the term came to be understood, by both its proponents and its critics, as symbolic of the way that planning and architecture were remaking the daily lives of city-dwellers. It signified a new, emerging mode of city living, a controversial vision of how to see postwar cities in an age of modernity and Cold War. This was nowhere more true than in New York, where the intellectual, architectural, design, arts, and media communities had ample opportunity to reflect on the reshaping of the metropolis. As a center for the various international communications and cultural industries in the postwar years, New York— and Manhattan in particular—became both actor and stage in the great urban dramas of the age.[6]

If proponents of urban renewal pitched projects as cures for urban obsolescence and as symbols of a new city, other New Yorkers received them as fundamental and sometimes unwelcome reorderings of the experience of city life. Their complaints and critiques echoed Claude Lévi-Strauss's lament for his lost city. A diverse cast of characters—planners and architects, city officials, businesspeople, bankers, tenant activists, social workers, housing reformers, journalists, photographers, filmmakers, artists, and residents of both the old industrial and tenement landscape and the new world of towers and superblocks—competed with one another to represent the experience of clearance or the new spaces ushered in by modern urban planning practices. As they shaped, depicted, and protested the new urban forms that renewal provided, they struggled to claim the power to describe the impact that urban renewal was having on the city.

On the one hand, "urban renewal" was shorthand for an entire ideal and practice of spatial transformation that employed characteristic aesthetic forms—modern architecture and superblock urban planning—to sweep away the nineteenth-century street grid. Shared and practiced by a broad coalition of interested parties in both the public and private sectors—including architects, planners, city and federal officials, businesspeople, bankers, housing reformers, social workers, union officials, and even tenant organizers—this vision propelled efforts to reclaim city life from housing deterioration, "irrational" industrial uses in residential districts, traffic congestion, and dangerous health conditions—a complex of problems summed up by the terms *slums* and *blight*.

If urban renewal was at root a practical, market-minded attempt to restore order and prosperity to cities, many of its proponents were also inspired and motivated by the more abstract sense that it was "modern." Confident of its appeal to contemporary visions of progress and newness, urban renewal's most idealistic supporters shared the assumption that it was modern in three senses: it advocated the economic modernization of cities, employed the arts and practices of aesthetic modernism, and stood for a new time and space of urban modernity. All three components pointed toward the creation of living and working spaces on a mass scale for an emerging mass society. This new built infrastructure of everyday life was to be, in and of itself, an emblem of that modern, mass society.

Public housing and urban renewal functioned as a kind of domestic counterpart to the modernization theory that liberal American planners and social scientists recommended for nations emerging from colonialism. Faith in economic growth through technological proficiency, administrative efficiency, and government spending would usher developing nations into modernity and affluence; urban renewal offered a similar program for what Congressman Byron Rogers called "the underdeveloped areas at home." Also appealing was urban renewal's aesthetic affiliation with modernism in the arts, its resemblance to a three-dimensional form of modern art. The design idioms of modern architecture and superblock planning were nothing if not forward-looking. They treated traditional city forms like modern painting did the conventions of figure, line, and depth. Slum clearance scoured away the old cityscape and its traditional, sedimented urban patterns. Then, the clean, progressive rationality of the towers and plazas rose over the ruins. City blocks were literally uprooted, broken down, and reconstructed in geometric arrangements that produced a new, unfamiliar sense of order and a remade experience of urban space. Urban renewal's modernism was one propelled by the spirit of "creative destruction" that Joseph Schumpeter and Karl Marx found at the heart of capitalism and the modern age. This faith in the creative powers of destruction was at root an embrace of modernity, of the necessity and promise of living in an age of progress and newness. Proponents of urban renewal assumed that its built environment—its cleared, open superblocks and austere towers—was a self-evident symbol of a new kind of time and space. These built forms stood for the very idea that it was necessary and possible to do away with the old city, for the faith that tradition had to be displaced, for the belief that city building had to reveal time rolling ever forward, leaving outmoded ways of life behind.[7]

Supporters of renewal turned their lofty beliefs toward grand goals. The chaos of progress and newness could be harnessed, they believed, in a rational effort to plan for the future of cities. According to planning theory, modern architecture and superblock urban planning provided the necessary and proper forms for the orderly and healthy development of cities threatened by poverty, decay, war, urban migration, and overcrowding. Designed as responses to the need to think beyond building only for individuals and single families, they would remake postwar cities for an emerging mass society by bringing industrial standardization and functionalist architecture to the building industry. Over the course of the postwar era, modern towers and open, park-like plazas came to represent a new approach to city life that was emerging worldwide. Their shapes and images stood for what it meant to live in the time of the all-conquering now, when past urban worlds were being relentlessly churned up, readying the old soil of the city for new built forms.[8]

Of course, these grand ambitions floated high above the lived reality of the city. It was not long before urban renewal also came to be seen as a force for turning working-class neighborhoods over to private developers, destroying neighborhoods, dislocating people, and implanting a foreign, imposed landscape. Clearance site evacuees, cast out by the destructive energies of progress, were said to resemble the displaced persons of postwar Europe. To many of the people caught in its path, urban renewal earned the popular sobriquet "Negro removal," because it continually targeted poor African American and Puerto Rican enclaves for destruction. For them, it was simple expropriation, another instance in which public authority combined with private wealth to uproot people with little power from land with much potential value, not unlike American Indian removal or other cases of historic racial displacement. With its open plazas and modern towers erected over the ruins of old neighborhoods, urban renewal appeared as a vast apparatus for replacing the horizontal relations of neighborhoods with the vertical authority of "projects." For some, the new modern spaces of urban renewal marked the arrival of the dark side of mass society, bringing with it all the anomie and isolation that term seemed to threaten.

Although resistance to renewal is most often identified with the writer Jane Jacobs and her 1961 book, *The Death and Life of Great American Cities*, a closer look at the story of urban renewal reveals that dissent was actually present all along. Currents of critique and unrest surfaced in urban renewal's infancy and matured alongside it, developing out of the same liberal and left coalition backing renewal itself. From the moment that privately backed urban renewal debuted at Stuyvesant Town in 1943, a relative handful of doubters—dissident liberal housing experts, tenant movement radicals, crusading lawyers, unorthodox planners and architects, social workers working in the new public housing—began to gradually and haltingly separate themselves from modernist orthodoxy. Urban renewal, they argued, uprooted stable neighborhoods, fed the creation of new slums, perpetuated deindustrialization, and redoubled racial segregation.

Here were the first glimmerings of a new kind of urban vision, one drawn from the intricate social connections fostered by old city neighborhoods rather than from the principles of modern planning practice. Here was an insurgent urbanism from below based on the street, stoop, and sidewalk instead of the superblock, tower, and plaza. Jacobs and other supporters of what would come to be called *advocacy planning* drew upon, extended, and refined these critiques, forging a movement to end urban renewal. Over some 25 years, this resistance unmade Robert Moses's liberal coalition around renewal, while simultaneously unmaking urban renewal itself as the dominant conception of urban building and rebuilding.[9]

One must be careful to specify how these struggles matter. Urban renewal's failures should not be ascribed solely to the impact of modern architecture and planning. The greatest troubles for public housing resulted from declining maintenance budgets, incompetent management, deepening racial segregation, and the overwhelming influx of dislocated tenants from renewal, highway, and other clearance projects.[10] But people caught in the turmoil of urban renewal reacted to the character of the new cityscape; they delivered judgments on the forms of urban renewal's city-rebuilding efforts as well as its effects. So while urban renewal's vast ambitions were not inherently productive of the social chaos charged to its account, its all-or-nothing city-rebuilding strategies and austere, utopian design visions did set the stage for its fall. "Benevolent intervention" in the cityscape had unforeseen consequences. They arrived in the form of struggles over what that intervention meant. People did learn to adapt to these new spaces and transform them for their own ends (particularly in middle-income projects where the social problems of public housing were rarer), but it was the imaginative struggle with the spatial transformation wrought by new projects and resistance to clearance that undid urban renewal. As a vision of city remaking, urban renewal rose and fell on the terms in which it was originally conceived. People who lived with its remade world went on to turn its lofty vision inside out.

To understand that movement requires moving beyond some convenient fictions. The story of urban renewal has often been loosely described via a familiar dichotomy. The "planners" versus the "walkers," the "view from the tower" versus the "view from the ground," even "Moses" versus "Jacobs"—all these oppositions capture in concepts what was actually a historical process. On the one hand were the planners, the removed apostles of what James Scott calls "authoritarian high modernism," who descended from on high to wipe away history, street life, and the day-to-day patterns of working-class neighborhood life in the interests of administrative order. On the other were the walkers, whose peregrinations represented an entirely different city, a reservoir of affiliations and attachments that the view from on high surveyed and even controlled, but did not under-stand. These oft-repeated metaphorical figures describe accurate tendencies, but employed in accounts of actual events they become static placeholders rather than active navigators reacting to events in the flow of time. They are fixed and frozen outside of history.[11]

What if, instead, we put the planners and walkers back into the flow of his-tory? Their struggle was never as simple as the dichotomy presupposes. Over time, former advocates of renewal joined the resistance, critics looked for reform rather than abolition of renewal, some resisters made their peace with clearance if it meant new housing, and some residents embraced or accommodated them-selves to modernist spaces. In the long run, the vision of urban renewal was not simply undone; Manhattan also absorbed its urban interventions and made them a part of its cityscape.

The reformist vision that Jacobs and other '60s era activists would make the new commonsense lingua franca of post-renewal urbanism was not something entirely apart from the city-remaking principles it displaced. Jacobs's critique emerged directly from close, lived experience with the top-down vision of Cold War era urban renewal and its ideal scenarios for the built environment of a mass society. The rise and fall of urban renewal was part of a glacial shift within the broad front of post–World War II urban liberalism as it confronted the domestic political culture of the Cold War. The story told here reveals not only urban renewal's transformation, but also the transformation of New York itself as it simultaneously underwent both a fall into urban crisis and a rise to world city status.

Urban renewal and its characteristic instrumental forms—modernist archi-tecture and superblock planning—were the product of a half-century's worth of efforts by housing reformers and modern planners to improve urban life. Their most immediate sources were the movement for modern housing and the drive for slum clearance, two campaigns born in the great cities of Europe and North America and raised through a process of transatlantic intellectual exchange over the course of the first four decades of the twentieth century. A wide range of housing reformers, social workers, urban businesspeople, crusading politicians, journalists, intellectuals, and urban professionals of various stripes, particularly architects and city planners, founded these two movements and made them into a widespread ethos of urban reform.

Housing reformers like Jacob Riis, Lawrence Veiller, Edith Elmer Wood, and Mary Simkhovitch came to the ideal of slum clearance through several decades' worth of campaigns against the "tenement evil." Inspired by the belief that the deteriorating urban environment was at the root of poverty, family instability, crime, and other social problems, they provided the intellectual arguments for an uneasy alliance of tenement reformers, city politicians, urban planners, and businesspeople with interests in downtown property values. This group had divergent goals—the reformers wanted to improve working-class housing conditions, alleviate the social problems caused by "slums," and encourage the poor to be better citizens; the city politicians wanted to clear slums by whatever means possible; the planners hoped to launch balanced programs of comprehensive land use planning by both private and public forces; and the business interests wanted to get rid of economic "blight" and free up urban land for profitable development—but they all gradually converged around the tactic of slum clearance as a way to ease the problems of the inner city. Over the first few decades of the twentieth century, they moved from trying to reform and enforce building codes and zoning rules to envisioning the wholesale destruction of tenement districts and the creation of new neighborhoods for the poor.

Modern housing, on the other hand, was a particularly European-inspired vision of how to remake cities and the entire social shape of shelter. Its advocates— housing reformers, architects, planners, and other left-leaning urbanists—offered

I.1. Design for Living? This image of children playing around a smoldering pile of rags in a tenement yard opened housing reformer Edith Elmer Wood's pamphlet on slum conditions across the country. The caption captured the spirit of more than a half-century of reformist zeal and suggested both the threats to conventional domestic life posed by unchecked urban real estate speculation and the readiness of reformers to supply a more healthful, family-friendly design for living through slum clearance and modern housing construction. From Wood, *Slums and Blighted Areas in the United States* (Washington, DC: U.S. Government Printing Office, 1935), frontispiece.

new, avant-garde forms of architecture and city planning for a new mass society. Inspired by European modernists like Le Corbusier, Walter Gropius, Ludwig Hilberseimer, and Ernst May, their designs featured low (and later, high-rise) multifamily modernist dwellings with ample communal amenities sited in open green space. Envisioning the built environment as the fundamental interface between humanity and nature, the "housers" promised to use building as a way to bring the two into balance and order after decades of chaotic urban development. They saw the territory of modern housing's operations as potentially limitless, unbounded by the constraints of geography, tradition, or national borders. If advocates of slum clearance offered a practical, high-handed, even ruthless distaste for the slums born of middle-class Victorian values, modern housing's partisans contributed a progressive and idealistic but no less overweening appeal to reforming the lives of the poor. The alliance between the two laid the groundwork for a set of philosophies, practices, and principles that we can call the "ethic of city rebuilding."[12]

Advocates of modern housing and slum clearance had linked aspirations. However, they were often at odds over how to achieve the ordered metropolis. The thinkers behind the modern housing movement—particularly its chief advocate, Catherine Bauer—were often leery of slum clearance. They abhorred the idea of paying slumlords' trumped-up prices for cleared land, and they worried that the city planners and businesspeople who favored clearance would work—as they did—to turn land over to private development rather than create low-income housing. Many of them felt that the only way to get vast amounts of new housing built cheaply—as well as in an environment befitting proper moral and community life—was to create new developments on the outskirts of the existing city. But a significant portion of modern housing's advocates eventually did come to back the slum clearance ideal, if only because of public pressure to do something about the age-old scourge of slums.

The Depression and World War II, with their weighty combinations of privation, suffering, and expectation, brought a mounting sense of urgency to the cause and gave impetus to a process of intellectual compromise and political opportunism. After 1937, when the New Deal committed significant funds to public housing, housing reformers could finally clear and build on densely packed land at the heart of the city. They paired government subsidies for clearance with an adaptive and practical approach to the aesthetic and social visions of modern housing. The merger between the slum clearance and modern housing traditions emerged most palpably in New York, under the auspices of the New York City Housing Authority (NYCHA), where planners and housers worked together to meld modernism in housing and planning with the power of government-backed slum clearance. Architecturally, NYCHA married modern functionalism and American garden apartment traditions to pioneer its own brand of cruciform-shaped, red-brick-clad modern towers. Most important, NYCHA brought into wide usage a planning innovation crucial to the elaboration of urban renewal: the "superblock." Both European and American reformers agreed that, in order to be successful, city rebuilding had to launch a sizable intervention in the old city fabric. New housing, they believed, had to arrive in such quantity that it would not be overwhelmed by the old tenement district; it had to form the basis for what planners and housers called a self-contained "neighborhood unit"—an urban intervention big enough to survive, but small enough to nurture community life. By taking large tracts through eminent domain, closing streets, and putting up modern, tower-block housing on cleared green space, new superblock housing projects would ensure their own economic survival, offer the ideal environment for proper family and community life, disrupt the old speculative street grid, and return light, air, and open space to city-dwellers. NYCHA built a handful of these projects before the war. The early projects were walk-ups of 4 stories, but increasingly NYCHA built taller towers to bring light and air to more people. In 1941, a few months before Pearl Harbor, NYCHA built East River Houses in East Harlem, with 6-, 10-, and 11-story towers that provided a blueprint for the physical shape of a new urban world.

Advocates of slum clearance and modern housing may have found a measure of common ground, but they could not have knocked down any tenements or built any new projects without World War II. The war brought slum clearance and most housing construction to an abrupt halt, but provided time and inspiration in their place. The war's vast scale, with its mass mobilization of industry and population, required unprecedented planning at all levels of society. The devastation of European cities left cleared ground for rebuilding, inspiring hope that a new urban world could emerge from the charred remains. In the United States, untouched by bombing, hope sprang from expected postwar affluence, modernization, and economic growth, forces that could sweep away old city forms just as effectively—and, it would later be revealed, nearly as ruthlessly—as bombing. City planners, architects, housing experts, and government officials used the war years to lay plans for a broad-based campaign of urban redevelopment. Guided by visions of modern housing and its urban innovations, they foresaw a widely expanded campaign of urban rebuilding. New Deal economist and housing policy expert Leon Keyserling offered a comprehensive vision for what he called "cities in modern dress," a strategy to rehouse the poor, stabilize the dwindling middle class, and restore order to the cityscape with modern city-planning principles. Rebuilding, he said, should be undertaken "in accord with a master city plan" and "should include the assembly and clearance of slums

I.2. East River Houses, New York City Housing Authority, 1941. East River was NYCHA's first true tower-in-the-park project. This government photo gives a glimpse of the world that the project displaced in the right foreground. Public Works Administration and U.S. Housing Authority Collection, National Archives and Records Administration, photo no. NWDNS-196-HA-NY-05–05-S2664.

and blighted areas, and their rebuilding for a variety of purposes—including privately financed housing for upper income and middle income groups, public housing for families of low income, commercial projects, recreational facilities, parks and playgrounds." This was the city-rebuilding ethic in full flower and the set of principles that would serve as the early ideological armature of New York's campaign to remake itself as a metropolis fit for the title of capital of the world.[13]

In 1940, New York's City Planning Commission produced a plan for putting these principles to work. As part of its master planning process, the commission drew up a map for postwar rebuilding of "appropriately located obsolescent areas." This map identified areas suitable for "clearance" and "replanning" and called for their use for "low rent housing." Like Keyserling, the commissioners suggested in their accompanying report that, "in some of these districts, very high rent housing would not be inappropriate." Thus, "the sections shown on the map will not and should not be rebuilt exclusively with subsidized low rent projects. They will logically include housing developments for many different income groups." On the one hand, this was a progressive vision of a renewed city for all: "The City can become a place of light and beauty and hope that all would be proud to have fostered—a city without slums, where the only difference between the houses of the very rich and the very poor would be the number and size and furnishing of the rooms they live in." On the other, it did not offer low-income public housing pride of place; redevelopment by private capital was equally if not more important. As it happened, the Board of Estimate never formally ratified the plan; Robert Moses, suspicious of the ideological goals behind master planning, made sure that the plan was never officially adopted. Still, the map retained a kind of unofficial power, and even Moses used it to legitimate both public and private projects that he negotiated with NYCHA and individual renewal sponsors. The CPC replanning scheme provided a glimpse of what the city-rebuilding ethic might accomplish, but its poor political fortunes foreshadowed how that ethic would be transformed into the policy of urban renewal in the early years of the Cold War.[14]

Manhattan Projects begins in the period during and just after World War II, when the struggle to define urban renewal began in earnest. It continues through the two decades after the war—when the debates over clearance, dislocation, and the character of the new modern spaces were fully joined—and comes to a close in the late 1960s. By then, urban renewal had remade significant chunks of Manhattan, but had also been discredited and largely undone as both policy and vision. The main characters in this story are four iconic Manhattan projects, each a prime example of the efforts by liberals in the public and private sphere to save the city from slums and blight and to assure Manhattan's image as a center of global influence: the UN headquarters complex, Metropolitan Life's housing development Stuyvesant Town, the Lincoln Square urban renewal plan that gave New York the Lincoln Center performing arts complex, and the vast belts of public housing that the New York City Housing Authority erected in East Harlem. Analyses of the physical and cultural construction of each place are paired with accounts of how the projects were received, the better to reveal how those who experienced the tumultuous interventions of renewal elaborated various responses—from accommodation and negotiation to critique and resistance—to the arrival of the bulldozers, plazas, and towers.

If the years before World War II saw the elaboration of an ambitious ethic of city rebuilding, aspirations for urban reconstruction acquired their most trenchant symbol in the years immediately after the war, when the United Nations buildings went up on the East Side of Manhattan. The UN headquarters was not a true urban renewal project. John D. Rockefeller bought a few acres of

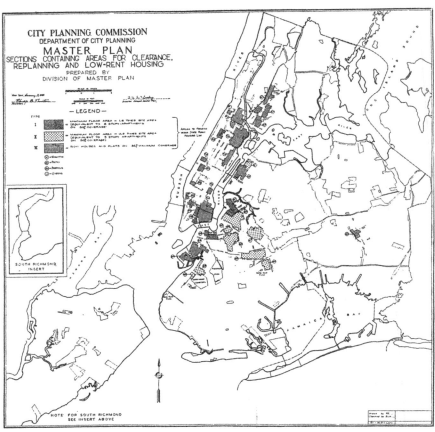

I.3. New York's vision for postwar slum clearance and new housing construction designated areas of slums and blight around the city's historic core, but it left open what sort of new uses would take over the land. The plan, never formally ratified, became a flexible, easily modified guide to renewal for Robert Moses after the war. City Planning Commission of New York City, Department of City Planning, Master Plan: Sections Containing Areas for Clearance, Replanning and Low-Rent Housing, January 3, 1940. Used with permission of the New York City Department of City Planning. All rights reserved.

slaughterhouses along the East River from real estate mogul William Zeckendorf and made a gift of them to the United Nations. Robert Moses arranged the necessary permits and rights-of-way, but no federal or state monies provided for its construction. But the fact that a few acres of slaughterhouses were transformed into one of the central icons of the postwar world had great significance for the era of rebuilding to come.

With the war over and the United States victorious, relatively unscathed, and ready to assume the mantle of global leadership, many elite observers and civic leaders predicted that New York was poised to become the political and cultural capital of the world. But in order for the city to leap into the first rank of what would later be called "global cities," they believed that the metropolis needed to undertake a grand scheme of city remaking, one that was symbolic and imaginative as well as physical. The city-rebuilding ethic was harnessed to this greater vision of urban myth making. It would function as the infrastructural nuts and bolts of an imaginative project that required the actual rebuilding, in concrete, glass, brick, and steel, of an outmoded cityscape along modern lines. With their modern design, the UN buildings offered not only a new architectural ideal for great buildings, but an entire program of city remaking that placed the visions offered by slum clearance and modern housing front and center. These urban rebuilding techniques, the United Nations demonstrated, were the key to restructuring the entire city in the United Nations' image: a city of towers and open space, free of the smoke and soot of industry and the hampering confinement of nineteenth-century blocks and lots. In the United Nations' progressive design and its campaign for world peace lay a new vision of global and urban harmony, one that was dependent on the principles of order offered by the city-rebuilding ethic.

Meanwhile, just 20 blocks south of the UN site, the city-rebuilding ethic was in the process of being transformed. Stuyvesant Town was a city- and state-financed "blueprint" for the federal policy of urban redevelopment launched by the 1949 Housing Act. In putting together the deal, Robert Moses and Metropolitan Life head Frederick Ecker collaborated on a new public/private mechanism for renewal, which drew on the aesthetic forms of the city-rebuilding ethic but rewrote its social ambitions to support their primary goals of clearing slums and shoring up middle-class life in the central city. The company offered Stuyvesant Town as a public good, but controlled it as private space. As such, Stuyvesant Town was a model for not only the policy, but also the culture of post-1949 urban renewal.

Met Life's "suburb in the city" was a modernist-inspired, whites-only housing reserve at the northern end of the Lower East Side. Opponents, led by Harlem civil rights groups and dissident liberals like Stanley Isaacs and Charles Abrams, called it a "walled city" for the white middle class. Residents, meanwhile, had to figure out how to live in its novel kind of urban space. Left-wing tenants affiliated with the American Labor Party worked to desegregate the complex from the inside, while others concentrated on fulfilling the promise of its marketing as a suburb in the city. They laid claim to the new postwar family-centered, middle-class ideal. They hoped to build that vision in the city, but struggled with the contradictions that Met Life's authority and the project's mass form posed. The conflicts at the heart of Stuyvesant Town life, conflicts between the freedom and hope that rebuilding brought and the sense of authority and regimentation that the new spaces of renewal seemed to inspire, would echo throughout the history of urban renewal.

Stuyvesant Town demonstrated that, if urban renewal began as a set of ideas offered by housing reformers and advocates of slum clearance, the latter eventually got the upper hand. It showed how housing reform efforts were appropriated by city planners and downtown real estate and business interests and then codified in a policy—the Housing Act of 1949—that employed federal subsidies to destroy slums, revitalize central business districts, and bring the middle class back downtown. Met Life's alliance with Robert Moses was the first in a long line of local, liberal, urban growth coalitions that later backed and implemented federal policies. These coalitions embraced the idea of slum clearance, seeing renewal first and foremost as a tool to preserve the profitability of urban land. The campaign to create livable, publicly funded communities for low-income urbanites survived, but as an afterthought. As policy, urban renewal became an attempt to prop up property values, stave off downtown decline, and attract white middle-class people back to cities that were becoming poorer and darker-skinned in an age of urban migration, deindustrialization, and suburbanization.[15]

This denouement was not ushered in all at once with the 1949 Housing Act; the political maneuvering over the fate of the city-rebuilding ethic had started years before and its effects only gradually became apparent thereafter, playing out in a series of Cold War–inflected compromises and struggles over the shape and vision of particular projects. By 1949, the campaign for slum clearance and modern housing had made its social and cultural vision the dominant intellectual and practical approach to city rebuilding. The result of political compromise and struggle, however, was a practical, money-minded urban renewal policy for the middle classes and downtown business districts carried out with the forms, aesthetics, and rhetoric of utopian modernism in planning and architecture.

Lincoln Square was the height of Robert Moses's urban renewal efforts in Manhattan. The project cleared 48 acres of the urban grid for luxury slab-block tower housing, facilities for the Red Cross and Fordham University, and its much-heralded centerpiece, Lincoln Center for the Performing Arts. It expressed the highest ambitions of Manhattan's urban renewal vision, trading blocks and blocks of tenements, warehouses, factories, and storefronts for a world-class, modern performing arts complex that capped New York's campaign to become the cultural capital of the world. Lincoln Center's backers, like chair John D. Rockefeller III, hoped it would provide the nation with an image of cultural maturity and urban resurgence that could be brandished in the Cold War with the Soviet Union. At the same time, the project revealed the fault lines at the heart of urban renewal. The organized resistance to relocation at Lincoln Square, which rallied around liberal lawyer Harris Present, brought growing discontent with Robert Moses's all-or-nothing bulldozer clearance practice of urban renewal—until then led mainly by left-wing tenant radicals—to the attention of a citywide audience. The resistance furthered the critique begun by the opponents of Stuyvesant Town, showing how urban renewal fostered divisions along lines of class and race, uprooted stable neighborhoods, perpetuated racial segregation and deindustrialization, and fed the creation of new slums. Perhaps most important, the resistance revealed a vision of urban culture that was diametrically opposed to that on offer at Lincoln Center; instead of a new modern cityscape for a world city delivered from on high, the residents and businesspeople of Lincoln Square defended the complex social world of their old neighborhood.

Urban renewal rose and fell in tandem with public housing. Between 1941 and 1961, the New York City Housing Authority put up 10 percent of all the public housing built in New York City in East Harlem. Cold War–inflected conflict in the U.S. Congress ensured that the 1949 Housing Act left public housing a poor stepchild to urban redevelopment, with its social vision straitened and its numbers depleted. And yet, in East Harlem and elsewhere in the city, NYCHA clung tenaciously to the ideals of the city rebuilding ethic, trying to put up as much housing possible for as many people as possible.

The authority succeeded in transforming East Harlem, but the results were not universally welcomed. Some appreciated the new, clean housing, but by the mid-1950s, East Harlemites, led by a coalition of social workers, started a campaign to reenvision public housing. Drawing on the talents of planner Albert Mayer and editor and writer Jane Jacobs, they produced a series of redesigned plazas and housing plans set into rather than on top of the urban fabric of the neighborhood. They worked to undo the practice of bulldozer renewal, to encourage more community-friendly planning, and to ease racial tension by bringing neighborhood groups together in community organizations and redesigned urban spaces. In the process, they offered one of the first full critiques of modernist urbanism and what they called its "mass way of life." Their attempts to rethink urban renewal from the same neighborhood perspective that Lincoln Square residents had championed laid the groundwork for the undoing of urban renewal.

Whatever the fate of urban renewal itself, it had deep and lasting effects on Manhattan, the entire city of New York, and American political culture. At first glance, this seems improbable. Compared to the private real estate market, urban renewal built comparatively little. Between 1949 and the early 1960s, Robert Moses built 16 privately backed projects in Manhattan and the boroughs.

NYCHA added scores of public projects—152 by 1965—in the years between the New Deal and President Richard Nixon's embargo on public housing construction in the early 1970s. And yet, this impact pales beside the dubious gift to the city's built environment left by the combined, uncoordinated efforts of thousands of builders, developers, and real estate schemers who remade New York in the postwar era. As impressive as Stuyvesant Town, Lincoln Center, and the rows of public projects lining the East River Drive may be, today they are swallowed up by the city—each one an almost indistinguishable set of towers amid the jumble. By the 1970s, all of midtown had been remade by glass-curtain skyscrapers; First, Second, and Third avenues were lined from 20th Street to Harlem with apartment towers. But the impact of urban renewal cannot be measured in numbers of buildings put up or acres cleared and re-covered with towers and open space. Its effects were both subtler and deeper. While it obviously never succeeded in wholly rebuilding the island of Manhattan, nor in remaking the entire built environment of the nation's great metropolis, it did play a crucial role in the history of New York and the postwar United States. Urban renewal's significance was not simply in its raw power to transform the city, but in the far greater influence it had over the terms by which cities were understood and in the fact that it called forth a series of public controversies in which New Yorkers and other Americans debated the impacts of modernism, progress, public and private power, and Cold War ideology on culture, politics, and social life.

No doubt, the greatest fact of postwar American life was unprecedented economic prosperity. This newfound plenty was underwritten by a particular approach to political economy, one that, like urban renewal, was jump-started during World War II. Advocates of economic growth—emboldened by a wartime spending boom that dispelled fears of economic stagnation lingering in the wake of the Great Depression—guided the nation toward a policy of expanded government spending to stoke the fires of private production and consumption. This "politics of growth," as sociologist Alan Wolfe has called it, sought to update the domestic policies of the New Deal to fit the so-called American century, that era of American cultural and political dominance over the world heralded by Time-Life publisher Henry Luce. According to Luce, the United States, flush with cash, militarily superior, possessed of a wealth of commodities for which the world longed, should be both powerful and good. "For every dollar we spend on armaments, we should spend at least a dime in a gigantic effort to feed the world," he wrote.[16]

Policymakers like Leon Keyserling, the New Deal housing economist who became head of the Council of Economic Advisers under President Truman, offered an economic policy that could underwrite this mission. They believed that increased government spending and private consumption would ward off another depression and push the economy to ever-higher levels of growth. The unprecedented tax revenue surpluses such growth produced, Keyserling suggested, could be reinvested in the social programs that had previously been underwritten by direct federal spending during the New Deal. In the formulation offered by Henry Luce, dollars for armaments would produce dimes for feeding the poor.[17]

The success of economic growth policies was measured in a number of ways. Abroad, it showed in military might, the informal empire of international economic influence, the global proliferation of images of rising postwar prosperity and affluence. At home, the rising capacity of ordinary spenders to drive the nation's economic and cultural engines seemed to confirm these policies' wisdom. As such, their crowning domestic glory was the spread of the developer-built communities of single-family homes that collected outside cities and seemed to represent freedom, abundance, and happiness to a generation of Americans seeking respite from two decades of depression and war. Suburban growth and the decline of industrial cities were at the heart of the American century and the era of economic growth. Despite the democratic rhetoric of equal benefits for everyone that accompanied the politics of growth, the affluence the United States enjoyed in the postwar years was a product of urban decline. As historian Robert Beauregard has argued, economic growth policies made places profitable by shifting capital from cities to suburbs and the Sunbelt. "To achieve prosperity and dominance," he writes, "the United States had to sacrifice its industrial cities."[18]

However, the campaign to rebuild American cities along modern lines was a no less crucial part of an urban politics of growth. Urban renewal may appear now as simply a hopeless rearguard action, but at the time it seemed the best hope to return the central city to its former glory and to extend to city-dwellers the abundance promised by the idea of the American century. The 1949 Housing Act enacted a historic compromise between conservative realtors and downtown business interests and progressive supporters of public housing, in the process solidifying a pro-growth coalition of urban liberals, planners, developers, business interests, and housing reformers that supported the reclaiming of the central city. This compromise was hailed as the high tide of postwar urban liberalism. The act ushered in a new urban age, a time that the housing reformer Elizabeth Wood called "an era of urban renewal and high employment," when general prosperity, it was hoped, would underwrite the salvation of cities.[19]

Urban renewal's central role in growth policies prepared it to play an equally significant part in the great political drama of the era. It emerged as a battleground on the domestic front of the Cold War, appearing first as a weapon and then as a hazard for the United States. In the late 1940s and '50s, renewal—more market-minded than ostensibly "socialistic" public housing—was drafted into service as evidence that the United States was meeting its internal challenges. As time went by, however, renewal's impact began to rankle, its association with the idea of a mass society narrowed the perceptual gap between it and public housing, and it would prove more of a liability in the struggle of images and ideas waged for hearts and minds.

In 1946, when the American diplomat George Kennan sent his famous "long telegram" back to Washington from Moscow, warning his colleagues of the threat posed by the Soviet Union, he made sure to stress the importance of putting the homefront in order. Calling Communism a "malignant parasite which feeds only on diseased tissue," Kennan advised that "every courageous and incisive measure to solve internal problems of our own society, to improve self-confidence, discipline, morale, and community spirit of our own people, is a diplomatic victory over Moscow worth a thousand diplomatic notes and joint communiqués." A few years later, the authors of the highly influential national security document NSC 68 adopted the spirit of Kennan's warning by recommending that massive conventional military rearmament be supported by pro-growth policies, with the inevitable surpluses funding abundance at home. As the foundations of Cold War policy and the link between Keyserling's growth initiatives and the Cold War effort, these documents suggested how urban renewal, like other pro-growth policies, could function as a key component of a domestic containment effort to secure an orderly and prosperous homefront and complement containment of the Soviet Union on the international level.[20]

The climate of urgency generated around the domestic front of the Cold War in the late 1940s and 1950s reverberated in the fields of housing and urban renewal. "We have been told that we must gather our strength for the long pull," said NYCHA executive director Gerald J. Carey in a 1951 speech before the National Association of Housing Officials, attacking proposed cuts in funds for public housing. "The struggle is one not alone of force, but of ideologies," he continued. Public housing may not be "the one weapon, or even the most important weapon, with which we will defeat Communism in general, or the Soviet Union in particular," he said, but "the strength that comes from unity of purpose and equality of sacrifice is needlessly sapped" when public housing funds are cut.[21]

For some, both public housing and urban renewal appeared to be handy weapons in this war of images and impressions because slums and urban decay were seen as a threat to domestic tranquility. Advocates of clearance had long said that slums needed to be cut out like cancers that undermined healthy city life. In the postwar period, they became, in Kennan's terms, "diseased tissue" of another kind: food for parasitic Communism, a dangerous weakness in the domestic bulwark against socialism and collectivist social philosophies. For instance, the famous educator and Cold Warrior James Conant warned of the dangers of metropolitan inequity. "What can words like 'freedom,' 'liberty,' and 'equality of opportunity' " mean for inner-city children? he asked. Their upbringing, he feared, left them with few resources to withstand "the relentless pressures of communism."[22]

While some housing advocates saw public housing as a weapon in beating back the Communist threat, many Americans saw it as socialistic and un-American. Public/private urban renewal, on the other hand, could operate as a potential immunization against the threat, a way to beat the Soviets at their own game. Urban renewal was at the heart of what historian Nicholas Dagen Bloom calls the "businessman's utopia," the arrangement by which urban business interests walked a tightrope between federal and private power, trying to save the inner city through publicly subsidized private initiatives rather than outright state direction of the housing market. This effort was a competitive response to the gains in urban social welfare demonstrated in Western Europe and the Soviet Union. Businesspeople who supported Federal Housing Administration policies and urban renewal thought that American cities could be reclaimed more efficiently through private enterprise than through state activism of either the social democratic or Communist variety. But they feared the apparent successes of socialist urbanism, and knew that if business could not clear the slums and rehouse their residents in new, modern communities, more state-friendly schemes might be given room to try.[23]

Urban renewal would represent, like racial desegregation in the same years, an effort to contain the infelicities of American life for Cold War onlookers abroad. By alleviating inequities, urban renewal would promote the idea that cities were entering a new era of abundance and rational modernity for all. Cities would become true partners with the "sitcom suburbs" in the triumphal progression of American postwar prosperity.

And yet, urban renewal did not so much contain as uproot and transform. Not only did it start to become clear that urban renewal deepened rather than ameliorated racial segregation and urban poverty, it also began to appear that its supposed advances in housing and planning undermined American ideals. In fact, urban renewal itself would be undermined by the extent to which its new cityscape began to seem just as regimented and anonymous as public housing—the landscape of a new "mass society." Its urban interventions could appear—and feel, as its new residents testified—authoritarian and imposed, rather than open and available as it seemed on the planners' drawing boards and in modernist visions. If urban renewal had initially represented all for which the United States fought in the Cold War, it increasingly resembled just what the country was mobilized to resist. By the late 1950s and early '60s, slum clearance and modern planning had joined public housing in the public eye as a threat to abundance and prosperity, a national symbol of the failure of postwar urban liberalism to master the turbulence of cities. Slum clearance evacuees and modern housing towers evoked the divided urban landscape—suburban plenty at the fringe and urban deprivation at the core—that marked the dawning age of "urban crisis."[24]

Urban renewal in New York, however, had a somewhat subtler impact. In the city, and in Manhattan in particular, urban renewal was key to understanding not only the split between city and suburb, but also the divided landscape of the city itself. Like all the other industrial cities of the North and Midwest, New York faced powerful economic challenges in the postwar era, when federal housing and highway policy underwrote the suburbanization of homes, industry, and commerce, pulling jobs and capital to the edges of the city. As early as the 1950s, just as Robert Moses's projects began to sprout, the city was already feeling the early effects of this decentralization. And yet, these were boom years for Manhattan as well, a period when the city was enjoying its resounding power as the capital of modernity and culture, the headquarters of global capitalism, and a symbol of American power during the Cold War. Urban renewal arrived at Manhattan's moment of triumph, offering to renovate the city in line with the metropolis's mythic postwar image of itself. In the end, it would inaugurate forces that heralded both New York's descent into the urban crisis and its rise to world city status.

New York's postwar prosperity and cosmopolitan élan owed much more than is commonly understood to its unique, small-scale, intricate, working-class, industrial economy and culture. The city was not dominated by one major industry like Pittsburgh or Detroit, with their steel mills and car factories. Its dense mixture of industry and commerce; the preponderance of small workplaces; a diverse, highly skilled workforce; custom or "small-batch" production; less developed divisions of labor; and versatile but densely communal industries (like the garment trade) gave the city a resilience that other industrial monocultures did not have. Still, during the postwar decades, many manufacturing jobs decamped to the suburbs and to the new, centerless, sprawling urban areas of the South and West. Federal, state, and city policymakers did little to discourage the choices made by managers looking for larger, more modern plants, easier access to national transportation networks, lower taxes, and more pliant, non-union workforces. In fact, most contemporary social policy and urban planning doctrines suggested that overall metropolitan economic development would be best served by perpetuating the decentralization of industry and that white-collar opportunities should replace departing factory jobs at the urban core. Corporate managers in the financial, real estate, and entertainment sectors were happy to oblige, leveraging their power through various foundations, public/private partnerships, and commissions to rezone the center of Manhattan for white-collar uses, further hastening the displacement of New York's industry. Meanwhile, Robert Moses's system of federally subsidized postwar expressways pushed the city farther into its hinterlands and made a regional metropolis out of the old centered city. White ethnic workers could now join jobs and the middle class in an intensifying exodus to the far reaches of Queens and the suburbs, where they enjoyed federal subsidies for whites-only homeownership. At the same time, just as jobs, capital, and white residents departed, New York attracted thousands of African American and Puerto Rican migrants. These new arrivals transformed the complexion and culture of New York's working class, but they also increased the burdens on the city's elaborate social welfare system, filled public housing, and made up the majority of those who were displaced by slum clearance.[25]

Twenty years after the close of World War II, New York's prestige and influence would not be entirely diminished, but by 1965 it had become clear to most Americans that something had gone terribly wrong. Despite years of national economic prosperity, New York was beset by a host of social ills stemming from industrial job loss and the tide of new migrants, conditions that appeared in the form of deepening poverty, entrenched segregation, racial strife, and rioting in a series of long hot summers, accelerating white flight, the apparent failure of public housing, and the mounting displacements of slum clearance. Observers of city life began to talk about an urban crisis or "a city destroying itself"; many bemoaned a loss of civility and worried for the viability of urban life in New York and other cities.[26]

Urban renewal was initially thought of as a way to offset the deleterious effects of decentralization, an attempt to keep investment, wealth, and the middle class downtown. But urban renewal exacerbated the process of deindustrialization and decentralization, replacing factories and warehouses with apartment towers, university buildings, hospital complexes, and cultural institutions. It also heightened and perpetuated the emerging social and class divisions, renovating and upscaling some formerly downtrodden neighborhoods, but displacing poor populations into nearby slums or into public housing, thereby reinforcing the racial segregation and ghetto boundaries that clearance had hoped to disperse. In New York, as in other older northeastern and midwestern cities, the urban crisis and "second ghetto" of the 1960s and '70s had its roots not in the liberal government social policies of the 1960s—which were said to encourage lawless behavior and a lack of personal responsibility—but in the vast transformations wrought by public/private urban renewal and public housing policies starting in the '40s and '50s.[27]

Alongside crisis and decline, however, went triumph and glory. Postwar New York was at the heart of the American century, the home of modernity and the preeminent American Cold War city. On Manhattan island, captains of finance and industry bucked the suburban trend under way across much of the nation. Instead, they expanded their central office operations on the island, making the city into the nation's preeminent "headquarters town" and the center of an emerging global economy. All over midtown and Wall Street sprouted new glass- and steel-skinned skyscrapers, the ultimate symbols of modernity, tangible examples of the payoff provided by modernization and growth. While the actual political and diplomatic course of the Cold War was established in Washington, it was Manhattan's banks, corporate directors, and foreign policy elite that directed the expansion of the Cold War national security state, while its growing social welfare provisions put the surpluses of the pro-growth economy to work ensuring the livelihoods of ordinary citizens. The city also housed the headquarters of the world's most powerful makers of opinion, news, and entertainment and provided offices for the theater, publishing, advertising, and magazine industries. The island's painters, dancers, musicians, and poets were the world's foremost modern artists; their movements and aesthetics, particularly abstract expressionism in painting, were often depicted in Cold War terms as exemplars of American freedom, despite the fact that more conservative elements saw them as dangerously cosmopolitan and even subversive of common sense and rationality. The city seemed, in other words, to be the summation of the new and the font of postwar power.[28]

Urban renewal assumed an important but little appreciated role in these triumphal undertakings. In New York, it not only helped to cause the urban crisis, it also preserved and enhanced the city's claim to be the capital of the world by providing it with the institutional infrastructure to actually become the world city it appeared to be at the close of the war, when the United Nations went up on Turtle Bay. Urban renewal, in many ways, served to jump-start the Manhattan boom years of the late '40s and '50s. Robert Moses and his urban renewal allies took many of the initial risks required to underwrite the spread of white-collar culture. Their projects made room in the city grid for research medicine, high culture, and higher education; they cleared away industry and working-class neighborhoods; they set down islands of middle-income and luxury housing in seas of tenements; they established beachheads for profitable investment in urban land in neighborhoods like the Gas House District and Lincoln Square that were removed from the towers of midtown and long abandoned by private capital; they gave spark to short-term, neighborhood-level real estate booms; they prepared the ground for the long, slow waves of gentrification that have waxed and waned for a half-century right down to our own time. Urban renewal was a first step, faltering perhaps, but first nonetheless, in an epochal transformation that continues to remake Manhattan and all of New York in the twenty-first century.

In the end, urban renewal came and went as a way to remake cities, but its checkered career provides us with an opportunity to look anew at the postwar years in New York. The 1960s in the city are often seen as a tragic fall from the glorious heights of the '40s and '50s, a long slide from, as architectural historian Robert A. M. Stern has put it, "world capital to near collapse." However, the lens of urban renewal helps us to see how these two seemingly disparate developments—the rise of a world city and the decline into urban crisis—were coterminous and mutually dependent. Together, they worked to create the distinct profile of modern, late twentieth-century Manhattan, with its bifurcated landscape of shimmering towers and stark ghettos. New York's decline was actually a transformation, announcing not only the descent into urban crisis but also the rise of a white-collar world city. Urban renewal was at the heart of this transformation, remaking the very space of the city as it gave rise to the upheavals at the root of the city's power and shame.[29]

United Nations

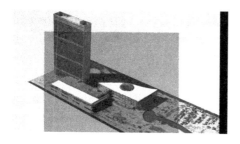

CHAPTER 1

CLEARING
THE SLUM
CALLED WAR

This Island Fantasy

It used to be that the Statue of Liberty was the signpost that proclaimed New York and translated it for all the world. Today Liberty shares the role with Death. Along the East River, from the razed slaughterhouses of Turtle Bay, as though in a race with the spectral flight of planes, men are carving out the permanent headquarters of the United Nations—the greatest housing project of them all. In its stride, New York takes on one more interior city, to shelter, this time, all governments, and to clear the slum called war.
—E. B. White, *Here Is New York*, 1948

For a few days in the summer of 1948—"during a hot spell," he said—the essayist E. B. White returned to his old home of Manhattan on assignment for the up-market travel magazine *Holiday*. The result was a piece—later published as a little book called *Here Is New York*—that stands as one of the great and lasting accounts of New York. In it, White ranges across a broad swath of Manhattan, accounting for the island's habits and manners; noting its desires, dangers, and joys; and sorting out its natives, commuters, and seekers. He finds that all of these collect and mingle under the sway of three intimately entwined but contradictory elements of New York life. First is the city's imperturbable, anonymous nature, its ability to "absorb almost anything that comes along" while still bestowing the "queer prizes" of privacy and loneliness. Then there is the compensation it offers for those dubious gifts: as the "greatest human concentrate on earth" and a "permanent exhibit of the phenomenon of one world," New York "makes up for its hazards and its deficiencies by supplying its citizens with massive doses of a supplementary vitamin—the sense of belonging to something unique, cosmopolitan, mighty and unparalleled." Like Claude Lévi-Strauss, White celebrates the medium in which loneliness and worldly belonging are reconciled: the city's series of "countless small neighborhoods," each with its own "little main street," its customs, and its diurnal patterns not unlike those practiced by country villagers. These in combination give the city its unequaled sense of congeniality, longing, and promise.

But then, as he draws his essay to a close, White interrupts his reverie. Among the back and forth of late '40s Manhattan, he is struck by the hint of something dark and worrisome. He notices a new menace, one that is drawn by the city's cosmopolitan singularity, but might threaten to shatter its inviolability, privacy, and neighborliness:

> The subtlest change in New York is something people don't speak much about but that is in everyone's mind. The city, for the first time in its long history, is destructible. A single flight of planes no bigger than a wedge of geese can quickly end this island fantasy, burn the towers, crumble the bridges, turn the underground passages into lethal chambers, cremate the millions.

Yet, even in the face of the new atomic threat, all hope is not lost. White was a proponent of what he called "federal world government," and he warily notes that the United Nations, arising "from the razed slaughterhouses of Turtle Bay," offers the promise of turning back "the spectral flight of planes" and nudging the world toward peace and away from war. Not only that, but the arrival of the United Nations in Manhattan brings to a head New York's role as the icon of its age. The city, he writes,

> at last perfectly illustrates both the universal dilemma and the general solution, this riddle in steel and stone is at once the perfect target and the perfect demonstration of nonviolence, of racial brotherhood, this lofty target scraping the skies and meeting the destroying planes halfway, home of all people and all nations, capital of everything, housing the deliberations by which the planes are to be stayed and their errand forestalled.

If the United Nations can succeed in its mission, White implies, and keep the towers from burning and the bridges from crumbling, then it will not only usher in world peace and preserve "this island fantasy," but also triumphantly cap the postwar ascendance of New York and the United States to the world stage. The city, he writes, is not "a national capital or a state capital," but now "capital of the world" and, in fact, the "capital of everything." White was giving voice to a common trope among liberal internationalists and New York boosters in those days. New York's vision of itself as the cultural capital of the world—solidified 20 years later with the building of Lincoln Center—begins with the arrival of the United Nations in the late '40s. But White's musings also suggest that the United Nations can help to underwrite New York's capital city status in a more unexpected way as well.

In a telling association, White describes the United Nations as "the greatest housing project of them all" whose purpose it is to "clear the slum called war." On its face, White's offhand association between the UN headquarters and a

1.1. The UN Secretariat building going up on Turtle Bay, as seen by Mrs. James Rath from the old world of the tenements just to the west across First Avenue on September 16, 1949. © Bettmann/CORBIS.

housing project is simply aesthetic, a response to the fact that the UN plans called for modernist architecture, for buildings that looked to him like "cigar boxes set on end." But their "clean modern look," as the *New York Times* put it in early 1947, was not merely a matter of style. White's aside reveals the way that the United Nations represented a particular social and urban vision, one that would have symbolic consequences in the cityscape beyond its ostensible roles in forestalling another world war or ratifying the city's emergence as the first postwar "global city." It implies that the progressive campaigns for slum clearance, public housing, and international cooperation for peace complemented one another. Securing the city's global profile would depend on dispersing the urban "concentration"—to use White's term—of the Turtle Bay slaughterhouses. Clearing the actual slums would set the stage for clearing "the slum called war." The United Nations was a vision of not just a new world order but a new urban order as well. Like the housing projects springing up around the city at the same time, the United Nations' modern architecture and urban plan provided a blueprint for a new kind of city, one that was cleansed of all the urban impurities—overcrowding, disease, poverty—that had so long preoccupied housing reformers and advocates of slum clearance.[1]

Reading between the lines of White's essay reveals that the United Nations should, as he put it, "stick in all our heads" as both symbol and inspiration for a campaign of city remaking. Designed by a committee of modernist architects in 1947, the complex on the East River at Turtle Bay featured the first "international style" skyscraper built in Manhattan. But if the Secretariat has been seen, then and now, as a landmark moment in the arrival of glass-skinned skyscraper modernism on U.S. shores, the entire complex's importance as an icon of modernist urbanism and city reshaping has been somewhat less well understood. Like the postwar urban renewal projects it prefigured, the headquarters was built on a superblock assembled from the Manhattan street grid and reclaimed from industrial, commercial, and residential uses. White's essay reminds us that the United Nations' seemingly separate symbolic roles—as a vision of both internationalist politics and modern city rebuilding—were intricately linked.

For a moment in the late 1940s, the concerns of liberal internationalism and urban renewal dovetailed, providing a link between the state of world affairs and the urban situation. Slums and urban disorder seemed analogous to the unsure, chaotic, and menacing postwar geopolitical scene. In this context, the UN complex rising on Turtle Bay acquired a double symbolism as a blueprint for both a new, ordered international terrain and a new, ordered city. First, the United Nations was legally lifted out of the bedrock of New York, becoming a kind of international territory, considered inviolable under U.S. law, and figuratively, politically, and aesthetically belonging to no one nation. In keeping with the United Nations' particular mission, the headquarters complex design deliberately lacked any national or local aesthetic context; it represented a new kind of international or, as one of the design committee architects put it, "un-national" structure that would serve to encapsulate in physical form the United Nations' ideals. Second, such a design scheme required a complementary urban plan, one that was abstracted from the old city's industrial era streetscape, but that would also serve as a model for what that old city could become. In a sense, then, New York's unprecedented role as the capital of international modernity depended on the precedent and inspiration laid out in the abstraction and purity of the United Nations' avant-garde glass-curtain walls and the open greenswards of its superblock plaza.

The United Nations was the most apt crystallization of the ideals behind New York's ambitious ethic of city rebuilding precisely because it supported Manhattan's claim to world capital status. In Manhattan, the United Nations supplied the ideals of urban renewal with loftier goals than in other cities. Not only would the city-rebuilding ethic clear slums, rehouse the poor, and attract new uses to the city center, but it would also remake the cityscape in the image of the United Nations, implanting in the island's schist a new urban form that would give all of Manhattan a profile equal to its title as capital of the world.

Finding the World Capital

We in New York, with our mingling of many races, colors, and creeds, have long had our own "United Nations." We know that with a firm determination to exercise tolerance and reasonableness men can live and work together for the common good. —"A Sacred Ceremony," New York Times, April 13, 1947

The United Nations came to New York in the last days of 1946, but it was not a given that it would have its home there. For more than a year, officials of the fledgling world body had been engaged in the hunt for a permanent headquarters. The United States' postwar prominence and power ensured that the new organization would look there, away from the European conflicts and entanglements that had doomed the old League of Nations, but still at the center of a world system dominated by Western capitalism and empire. The UN planners entertained proposals from a number of major U.S. cities and towns, seriously considering bids from Boston; Westchester County, New York; Fairfield County, Connecticut; Philadelphia; and San Francisco, where the United Nations' founding conference had been held. New York, under the guidance of construction coordinator Robert Moses and Mayors Fiorello La Guardia and William O'Dwyer, offered the 1939 World's Fair grounds at Flushing Meadows in Queens, which was already in use as a temporary meeting place for the UN General Assembly. The United Nations captured O'Dwyer's imagination, and he was determined to make it part of his legacy. "I felt," he later remembered, "that this was the one great thing that would make New York the center of the world."[2]

The delegates and staff of the United Nations favored a New York location. Meeting in the temporary facilities at Flushing Meadows and Lake Success, on Long Island, they discovered that they really wanted to be, as Robert Moses would later put it, "in mid-Manhattan, with the restaurants, hotels, and the flesh-pots, and all the rest of it." But New York's attractions were not enough to sway the UN site committee to choose the Flushing Meadows site, which they considered both technically problematic—there were said to be difficulties in drilling foundations there—and isolated in the midst of a residential borough. By December 1946, the committee was on the verge of selecting a site near Philadelphia. That prospect excited no one save Philadelphia's boosters; the old Quaker city was seen as too close to Washington to be independent from influence and too close to New York to hold its own as a new center for world organization. Many feared that all the UN politicking would be done in Washington and the socializing in New York, leaving the new UN complex a redundant ghost town.[3]

A last-minute offer saved the day for New York. John D. Rockefeller Jr. proposed to buy 18 acres of land on the East River in midtown Manhattan from realtor William Zeckendorf and deed it to the United Nations. Zeckendorf had bought the site—six blocks of warehouses, factories, slaughterhouses, and tenements east of First Avenue between 42nd and 48th streets—in late 1945. He had planned to raze the site and erect a massive commercial, residential, and office complex he called "X-City," for which he had already retained Rockefeller Center architect Wallace K. Harrison as master planner. But with the UN site question so unsettled so close to the deadline, Zeckendorf suggested to Mayor O'Dwyer that X-City might become the UN headquarters, saying that he'd offer the site "at any price" the United Nations wished to pay. In conversations with UN secretary general Trygve Lie, who had always favored a New York location, O'Dwyer found that he and Robert Moses had discussed that very site as a backup for Flushing Meadows. Now, they just needed a way to pay for it. They contacted Nelson Rockefeller, who had been instrumental in the founding of the world body. In an eleventh-hour family meeting the night before the United Nations was expected to ratify Philadelphia, the Rockefellers first considered donating family land in Westchester County. Nelson realized, however, that only the in-town site could sway the United Nations back to New York. His father agreed to offer $8.5 million, the sum for which Wallace Harrison believed that X-City could be had. At 10:30 the night before the vote, Harrison was dispatched to get Zeckendorf's consent. He found the realtor in the midst of a banquet at the Monte Carlo Hotel, where they drew up an impromptu contract on a city map of the site. The offer came as a relief to Lie and the UN Headquarters Committee, and they unanimously approved it the next morning. With this hastily assembled deal, a year's worth of searching was abruptly ended in little more than a week.[4]

If the selection of the East River site was a relief to the United Nations, to many elite New Yorkers it seemed a welcome but overdue confirmation of the city's status. As early as July 1945, the *Times* was pushing New York as the proper and fitting home of the United Nations; in early 1946, the editors assured readers—under the headline of an editorial called, simply, "The Capital of the World"—that the choice of New York or its suburbs was "logical and even inevitable." New York had all the material advantages: it was the center of finance, opinion, and communication; the home of superior recreational and cultural resources, including unparalleled research institutes and libraries; and the hub of a vast transportation network reaching all over the country and the globe. Beyond these matters of fact were more abstract concerns. New York, a host of commentators agreed, deserved its status as capital of the world in large part due to its "cosmopolitan population, itself a cross-section of the United Nations." The city, the *Times* explained, "provides a unique environment for a World Capital in which nobody need feel strange, and is at the same time a living monument to harmony between many nationalities."[5]

Everyone involved in the UN deal struck this note again and again. "We in New York," intoned the *Times* editorial page in noting the ceremonial transfer of the site to the United Nations, "have long had our own 'United Nations.'" For John D. Rockefeller Jr., New York was "a center where people from all lands have always been welcomed." Mayor O'Dwyer cited New York as proof that the United Nations could succeed in its mission; it was a kind of living laboratory where, as the *Times* put it in reporting his speech, "people of all races and nations can live together peacefully." The New York State Senate gave its official imprimatur to these popular notions in a largely symbolic resolution assuring "the delegates and staff of the United Nations" that in New York they would "find a practical demonstration that tolerance and good will can erase artificial hatreds and bigotry, and that millions of people of diverse races, colors, religious and economic beliefs can live and work in harmony, a lesson that might well be applied on the international level."[6]

Officials of the United Nations expressed their own enthusiasm for the city's democratic and cosmopolitan qualities. Trygve Lie kept, in a personal file, his own set of "general arguments for New York," including New York's institutions, leaders, and infrastructure. Most important, it was "vital and dynamic and truly inspiring." Not only "a great American city," it was "a great world city." As "a crossroads of civilization and culture from its earliest days," it was home to "peoples of many races and nationalities from all over the whole wide world."[7]

These proclamations masked a more complicated reality. In part, such sentiments were predictable public relations boilerplate, convenient celebrations on the part of elites and officials. The truth was that, in postwar New York, people of color—whether they were Americans or not—faced entrenched segregation and discrimination in public accommodations, real estate, employment, and schools. Ludlow W. Werner, the editor of the African American newspaper the *New York Age,* noted how the United Nations' arrival made the city's racial divides all too apparent. Writing to Mayor O'Dwyer about the UN dedication ceremonies, he said he was "thrilled" to hear the speeches celebrating New York's racial harmony, but disappointed to see no "representatives of the Negro population on the program." This omission "slight[ed] the Negro citizens who have contributed more than their share to the culture and life of New York City" and made all the rhetoric about racial fellowship in the city ring quite hollow.[8]

Nonwhite UN diplomats and staff confronted this reality daily, mostly when trying to eat in restaurants or to rent apartments. One Haitian staff member, weary with sitting "unnoticed" in New York restaurants, hoped that "some day the United States will be as democratic as Europe." Some diplomats—accustomed to all the privileges of their station—suffered humiliating racial abuse or intimidation by white Americans when they crossed geographic boundaries known all too well by American blacks. Over the years, these slights, indignities, and even outright violence led some in the United Nations to wonder if the United States had been such an ideal site for the world capital after all.[9]

Ironically, the U.S. government was itself divided over the value of the United Nations. President Truman was thrilled to have the opportunity to make good on Woodrow Wilson's failed experiment and saw it as something between a twist of fate and destiny that he presided over installing it on U.S. shores. He had famously carried folded in his wallet since boyhood lines from Tennyson's "Locksley Hall," including its ardent hopes for world organization:

> Till the war-drum throbbed no longer, and the battle flags were furl'd
> In the Parliament of Man, the Federation of the World.
> There the common sense of most shall hold a fretful realm in awe,
> And the kindly earth shall slumber, lapt in universal law.

Others, however, found "the common sense of most" more common than sense. Truman's secretary of state, Dean Acheson, thought that the bulk of the United Nations' time was spent posturing for domestic political audiences, purposes entirely at odds with the proper conduct of diplomacy and strategy. Acheson preferred that the UN be headquartered anywhere but the United States. The organization's irrelevancy to the real conduct of foreign affairs was only compounded by the fact that, as he later put it, "the misplaced generosity of the Rockefeller family" placed the United Nations "in a crowded center of conflicting races and nationalities." Acheson's casual recognition of New York's racial problems did not inspire him to believe that the United Nations might help

New Yorkers to address those conditions. Meeting in New York, he thought, would only further belabor the already pointless back and forth in the United Nations' assemblies and council chambers.[10]

Yet the sentiments of Lie and the others, however naïve, were indicative of widespread geopolitical and urban optimism, a faith in the value of both the United Nations and New York. People everywhere looked to the new assembly as a source of inspiration in much the same way that Americans, during World War II, had embraced the abstract goals of President Franklin Roosevelt's "four freedoms": freedom of expression and religion and freedom from want and fear. In fact, the United Nations' ideals were derived from the Allies' aims in the war. Like E. B. White, the United Nations' global constituency viewed its vision of internationalism and peace as a natural extension of the battle against fascism, the chief support for democracy and freedom in a world menaced by the atomic bomb and a brewing Cold War between the United States and the Soviet Union. One of the chief planks in this set of ideals was racial equality, an ideal the United Nations expressed by way of its mandate to protect human rights.

Likewise, a number of advances in race relations got under way in the United States just as the United Nations landed in New York. These included the establishment of antidiscrimination legislation in several states, the desegregation of baseball, a number of federal initiatives to curb racial discrimination—including the Fair Employment Practices Commission, Truman's desegregation of the armed forces, and the Supreme Court's 1948 ruling against restrictive covenants in housing—and the beginning of citizens campaigns to end segregation in public accommodations. New York's civil rights organizations were at the forefront of these campaigns, and despite the indignities noted by UN staff and continuing inequality, the city gained a justifiable reputation as the home of the newly rejuvenated drive for racial equality. For a moment in the late '40s, the color line that had so long undermined American democracy seemed to be weakening, and New York and the United Nations both appeared as symbolic representatives of the campaign to make the principles of wartime progressivism a reality in the United States and abroad.[11]

Perhaps the most underappreciated effects of the United Nations' arrival were on the urban front. The vision of international peace and security, domestic racial harmony, and urban progressivism that briefly flourished in the late '40s would have its most important effects not in a transformed racial order— although the United Nations' presence in New York did serve as a source of moral authority for the city's African Americans in their campaigns for racial justice—but as a catalyst for a transformed built environment in New York. The *Times* boasted that the city's "heaven-rearing skyscrapers will become the fitting symbols of the high aspirations out of which the United Nations Organization was born." But in order to do so, the buildings would have to be remade to live up to the image of the United Nations itself. Accordingly, when UN officials turned toward building a fitting home for the world body, they undertook a design and plan that would fulfill the lofty hopes placed in both their organization and its host city. The headquarters would be a skyscraper—"a new concept" in monumental buildings, admitted Trygve Lie, because "vertical architecture has been more closely associated in recent years with commercial enterprises." But, as E. B. White noted, it was not only to office buildings that the proposed UN complex gestured, but also to housing projects. The new skyscraper headquarters could take its place among the other "heaven-rearing skyscrapers" of midtown in symbolizing the drive for world peace and become what the *Times* editors called "hallowed ground." But that would be achieved, they implied in early 1947, not only when the United Nations could "maintain peace in a world that has never long known peace," but also when the site at Turtle Bay was "supporting its future skyscrapers but affording also an occasional glimpse of the green earth." This impulse, that the new UN headquarters appear as a model for urban as well as political transformation, remained implicit in most commentary in the early postwar years, but it would grow as the world body went to work designing its new home.[12]

An Un-National Workshop for Peace

A capital city is a symbol. National capitals embody the spirit of nations. A World Capitol [*sic*] should embody the spirit of mankind. New York already stands as an embodiment of many of modern civilization's finest manifestations, and it can inspire others. We cannot disregard symbols. The spirit as well as the purposes and functions of an age usually finds [*sic*] expression in architectural and civic forms.
—Cleveland Rodgers and Rebecca Rankin, *New York: The World's Capital City,* 1948

Building the UN headquarters was an immense physical challenge. The technical dilemmas involved in putting up a clutch of modern buildings in Manhattan's dense urban jumble were legion. But the symbolic dimensions of the headquarters construction, the problems of meaning associated with building for the new world body, were equally complicated and far more visible to the public. The United Nations' weighty mission demanded what city planner Cleveland Rodgers and municipal librarian Rebecca Rankin called "architectural and civic forms" capable of "embody[ing] the spirit of mankind." As a result, the symbolic burden that Rodgers and Rankin urged New York to shoulder fell first and heaviest on the headquarters' physical designers. Charged with finding a physical shape for a political body expected to ensure global peace in the wake of world war, they would make decisions with ramifications for the geopolitical and urban futures of the city, the nation, and the world. Headquarters planners, UN officials, and commentators in the press all agreed that the headquarters' physical shape should have some universal or broadly humanistic appeal, but it took a good deal of debate among the United Nations' panel of architects to settle on the specific idea that the headquarters should evoke the spirit of collaboration and solidarity hoped for from the United Nations itself. These qualities first marked the purely architectural significance of the complex, but as the team of designers elaborated a modernist idiom equal to the United Nations' mission, it became clear that the same source from which the architecture flowed would feed the complex's impact on urban design and planning as well.

Working under intense public scrutiny, Trygve Lie determined to move quickly in order to avoid the controversies and delays that had dogged the United Nations' predecessor, the League of Nations. He directed the UN Headquarters Planning Committee to appoint as its director of planning Wallace K. Harrison, the architect who had been slated to design the X-City project. The Rockefeller family's architect had intimate knowledge of the site, extensive experience with large building projects, a temperament suited to leading and organizing groups of designers, architects, and engineers, and an affinity for forward-looking yet practical design. Most important, he was a well-established figure; he had close acquaintance with the chief players, particularly Robert Moses, and connections in Washington.

Harrison presided over the selection of an international panel of architects, planners, and engineers drawn from UN member nations. The primary Board of Design was made up of 10 architects, the most well known of whom was Le Corbusier of France. Harrison directed their efforts, soothed egos, and tried to forge agreement. The initial design process involved a series of 45 meetings, lasting from February to June 1947, in which the Board of Design worked through the complexities of shaping the headquarters. Much of the discussion revolved around the arrangement of the buildings on the site. The architects sketched out interior arrangements, architectural details, and technical specifications, but largely left them to be finalized later. They had quickly settled on the three primary structures—Secretariat, Council building, and General Assembly Hall— but their effort was expended in figuring out the sizes, shapes, functions, and floor plans of the buildings and the arrangement of the buildings, in relation both to one another and to the confines of the East River site. They progressed through a series of possible design schemes proposed by one or more of the team, looking to narrow the possibilities while still incorporating the input of all. Harrison did not seek formal consensus, but instead hoped to forge an informal balance between forward progress and equal involvement that would produce a superior design. He guided the process by soliciting opinions, telling a *New York Post* reporter, "if you put a group of composers together to write a symphony there are bound to be some discordant notes. We must bring the differences out in the open." He offered no design schemes of his own, but reserved the right to bring his own inclinations into play in order to supersede creative stalemate, a right he rarely exercised. Despite a number of heated disagreements between shifting factions on the board, the end result was, as Harrison put it, "a U.N. job—a collaborative job."[13]

The final design scheme, submitted to the United Nations and the public in July 1947, was derived from a plan drawn up by Le Corbusier, which had been modified and adapted by contributions from others, particularly his young Brazilian disciple Oscar Niemeyer. The site limitations required a skyscraper, and as early as 1946, in a study he offered to Trygve Lie, Corbusier had first envisioned the thin, slab-block,

1.2. Members of the UN Board of Design pose with preliminary models of the headquarters complex, April 1947. Notable members include Sven Markelius (*first from left*), Le Corbusier (*second from left*), Ssu-Ch'eng Liang (*fourth from left*), Wallace Harrison (*fifth from left*), Oscar Niemeyer (*sixth from left*), Nikolai Bassov (*eighth from left*), and Max Abramovitz (*behind Bassov*). UN Photo by unknown photographer.

office building form for the Secretariat. This vision, which became something of an assumption for the Board of Design early in its process, differentiated the UN complex from Rockefeller Center, its most recent nearby predecessor and presumed influence. He also came up with the informal openness of the grounds and the buildings' basic locations, shapes, and profiles. However, it took a new plan from Niemeyer and suggestions from others to get the Council Chamber building placed in one low block along the river and to arrange a harmonious relation between the General Assembly Hall and the Secretariat. This negotiated collaboration produced a striking, yet harmonious and functional, link between the headquarters' two primary elements. The horizontal, curving Assembly Hall—the heart of the world body—was brought forward into pride of place and then, as Wallace Harrison's deputy George Dudley put it, "counterpoised" on a "clear plane" with the broad, reflective, 39-story vertical face of the aluminum- and glass-walled Secretariat, which was recessed to

1.3. The General Assembly Hall and Secretariat from the northwest. Ezra Stoller specialized in capturing the clean lines and austere shapes of modern architecture. His photos, which frame buildings as works of art, give the viewer a good sense of the way that modern structures like the Secretariat and General Assembly Hall were understood by both their creators and the public as symbols of newness, freed from all historic and spatial context. Ezra Stoller © Esto.

the background, where it opened up the grounds and gave the entire complex a focal point that functioned as both efficient landmark and austere backdrop.[14] This is particularly evident in the architectural photography of Ezra Stoller, whose spare, elegant images of the complex highlight its pure, interrelated structural forms.

The General Assembly building did not open to delegates until October 1952, but between the summer of 1947, when designs for the complex were first released, and the fall of 1950, when UN staff went to work in the newly completed Secretariat, accounts of the headquarters' architectural forms grabbed public attention. The *Times*, giving voice to conventional wisdom, heralded the arrival of the headquarters design as a "bold thrust into the future, for nothing quite like it has ever before been conceived." The Secretariat—a "massive vitreous structure," the newspaper called it—was the largest glass-walled skyscraper built to date. Others appreciated the simplicity of its design, particularly the way its uniform exterior appearance both expressed the modular, efficiency-based design of its interior offices and revealed the structure of its steel skeleton. While some avant-gardists found the design predictable, *Architectural Forum* greeted its "vast marble frame for two mirrors" as an attempt to "answer more burning architectural questions than had been answered in any other large building constructed in the 20th Century." Since then, its full-glazed slab fronts have been widely credited as precursors to the many other international-style office blocks built across the United States in its wake. But beyond purely "architectural questions," beyond the technical details of design, engineering, architecture, and even site planning, was a debate about the headquarters' meaning and influence. What, it was asked, did these modern structural forms mean?[15]

At issue was an ongoing controversy over modernism's capacity to capture the true significance of buildings entrusted with such a solemn mission. The opposed positions became apparent from the moment that Harrison accepted his appointment. Warren Austin, the U.S. representative to the United Nations, chair of the Headquarters Advisory Committee, and a key behind-the-scenes player in securing the New York site, took the opportunity of Harrison's appointment to lay out a daunting task for the designers:

> We are going to inscribe in stone and steel the achievements of the human race up to this time. To us falls the task of making the headquarters of the United Nations an appropriate presentation of the progress of history and a promise for the future that will be constantly telling mankind that we are working in harmony; that we are maintaining unity.[16]

Harrison, however, was inclined to disavow such "symbolism" altogether. He was not interested, *Times* reporter Gertrude Samuels reported, in trying to "symbolize the United Nations in some highly imaginative design." Following

Harrison's lead, the Board of Design chose not to follow historical precedent. Wanting to avoid what its members considered to be the ponderous monumentalism of the League of Nations building in Geneva; the great marble edifices of official Washington, DC; or, worst, the staggering buildings of totalitarian Germany, they opted instead for a purely utilitarian structure. In keeping with modernist ideals, its form would follow its function, and it would simply be a good place for people to work and meet. The design board intended to "accommodate human beings in a complex civilization," not a "Greek god" in "some phony Greek temple." Working from the inside out, rather than from extraneous ideals, would reveal the necessary design. "The work to be done inside a building," wrote Samuels after spending some time with the Board of Design, "must alone determine the height, arrangement and form of it; character, they argue, will automatically grow out of its perfect working order."[17]

Nikolai Bassov, the Soviet representative to the Board of Design, considered symbolism "unnecessary." With time, all symbols "grow out of date," he said, leaving the architecture to look "ridiculous." Corbusier wondered what there was to symbolize. "The U.N. simply does not exist yet," he said. "The nations are not united. The U.N. is not proved." He did not think they were designing a "world capital, or a temple of peace," but rather what he called "a poste de combat—a battle post." Corbusier's martial metaphor—he seemed to see the United Nations as an outpost on a hostile shore, a bastion of order amid "the violence of New York"—perhaps mischaracterized his ultimate vision, however. "I see it as a meeting center," he continued, "as office buildings efficient to the last detail, for conference meetings, for the preservation of documents, with air, space and gardens around for perfect working conditions. There is no symbolism in all that." Wallace Harrison famously summed up the design approach in unveiling the plans. "The world hopes for a symbol of peace," he said. "We have given it a workshop for peace."[18]

Predictably, many architects and commentators were dismayed that Harrison and company had missed the opportunity to deliver more resounding and solemn affiliations. A group of traditional architects surveyed by the *New York Herald Tribune* agreed that symbolism and monumentality had been deftly avoided, but saw no virtue in that fact. The plan's practicality earned their scorn, while its claims to novelty spurred their outrage. One remarked that the design "seems more like a diabolical dream of an engineer where stark efficiency has given way to the beauty that architecture represents." Another thought it simply "looked like a sandwich on edge and a couple of freight cars." Always an iconoclast, the *New Yorker* columnist Lewis Mumford had no desire to see "a group of temples and basilicas," but he agreed that the buildings had failed to "proclaim with a single voice that a new world order, dedicated to peace and justice, is rising on this site."[19]

Others, however, felt that Harrison and company had not avoided symbolism at all. They saw the building's functionalism as its true representational significance: as an expression of the absolute limit in technological and organizational achievement. And yet, their seemingly objective, technocratic avant-gardism took on a particularly nationalist cast, drafting the Secretariat into an argument for American power and influence. The editors of *Architectural Forum,* for instance, heralded the Secretariat—which they argued was the complex's central element—as "plastically a work in the manner of Le Corbusier." But it was "technologically, and as an organizational feat, an American product." For them, the true hero of the hour was Wallace Harrison. He had managed to bring out the "American architectural tradition" of technological achievement that made Corbusier's advances possible. In Harrison, "America had produced an architect in its own great tradition, capable of fusing the esthetic accomplishments of international modern architecture with the technological accomplishments which made it livable." They recognized the complex as a fragment of "the vertical city" Corbusier had first proposed in his paper utopias of the 1920s, but the editors stressed the way that the union of European and American genius had resulted in two essentially technical marvels. They hailed the Secretariat as a work of art, a "shimmering fabric" for the play of light and shadow, surface and depth, but stressed the way such aesthetic pleasures were indebted to the engineering prowess necessary to erect a glass skyscraper. They applauded its "free-hanging glass-and-metal curtain wall" as a fitting sheath for the work of a modern bureaucratic corporation because the flexible, open floor spaces gave managers ample freedom to arrange office spaces to reflect a company's hierarchical management structure. The Secretariat appeared as the built representation of U.S. capitalism's technological advancement, organizational sophistication, and global hegemony; American ingenuity and engineering sophistication were the practical fulfillment of European artistry, invention, and social idealism—the culmination of the entire modernist tradition in building.[20]

For some, however, this American achievement was more ironic than triumphant. The architect Henry Churchill noted that the Secretariat had become, against its designers' will, the true spirit of the age:

> It is somehow fitting that the Secretariat should become the symbol of the U.N.—an up-ended filing case for human beings, their hopes, their fears and their aspirations for a steady job. That is the new American Dream, a steady job, that is what we hope a United World will bring us, in the terms of peace and security; and of that the Secretariat is a just, if unconscious, expression.

As a three-dimensional representation of managed bureaucracy and the promise of white-collar prosperity, Churchill found, the Secretariat worked quite well.

From this perspective, the ideology of the American century—prosperity and security guaranteed by the power of rational efficiency—underwrote both the United Nations' political mission and its architectural symbolism. The Secretariat overwhelmed and stood in for the rest of the complex and its more participatory functions. The tower was, in a hopeful sense, a "filing case," or more nefariously, a "warren of bureaucratic offices." But as *Architectural Forum* had intimated, it was largely a confirmation of U.S. ingenuity and influence.[21]

Yet this verdict was not the only register in which the UN building's symbolism and influence were expressed. From the earliest days of the design process, there was another conception of the project's significance that predicted a very different legacy. Some members of the design team hoped to found an equally collaborative and universal design, one that would supersede not only the traditional vision of a building as the product of individual artistic genius, but also all purely national characteristics, allowing it to symbolize, through its purity of abstraction, the possible and necessary solidarity of all the world's peoples. The architects were encouraged by legal precedent: U.S. law would see to it that the site itself was "inviolable"—the equivalent of a foreign embassy. But they considered the 18-acre site to be home to no one government, no one place. Ironically, in working through this collaborative universalism, the Board of Design created a plan that was more symbolic of the United Nations' ideals, functions, and promise than any monumental pile could have ever been.

Key members of the design board intended to dispense with all the grandiose ideals, expectations, and preconceptions that had already been draped on the United Nations' shoulders. In the spirit of modernism, their design would acquire its meaning and its form not only in its function, but from the very process of its making. The finished product would reveal and comment upon, in its shape and form, the collaborative process through which it came to be. Given the nature of their "client," they would take it one step further. Not only would their plan reveal the conditions of its making, but their process and the plan it produced would reflect and give inspiration to the world body for which they were designing it.

The public information officers for the United Nations pitched the deliberations of the design board as efforts to create the unanimous product of an international consensus, a living embodiment of the "one worldist" ideals that floated the United Nations. Whatever the truth behind this PR campaign—and there was no small amount of discord among the architects—it's clear that some of the participants did see their process as a kind of analogue to the United Nations' efforts, one that they believed didn't so much synthesize as transcend national influences. For instance, Ssu-Ch'eng Liang, the Chinese delegate to the design committee, told a reporter that "this group of buildings should be not only international in character, but un-national—expressing no country's characteristic but expressive of the world as a whole." In a "declaration" that Le Corbusier wrote up and read aloud for the group, he said that the "World Team of the United Nations" was "laying down the plans of a world architecture, *world*, not *international*," he stressed, "for therein we shall respect the human, natural and cosmic laws." Blithely ignoring any disagreement between his fellows, Corbusier declared, "We are a homogeneous block. There are no names attached to this work.... there is simply discipline." By "discipline," he seemed to mean the discipline of modern architecture and urbanism, which, in its fealty to "human, natural and cosmic laws," was greater than any one person or any international collection of national contexts. It was "the standard of measurement" that "alone is capable of bringing order" and through which "modern civilization will establish its equilibrium."[22]

With their rhetoric of collaboration and universalism, the planners hoped that the character of this un-national collaborative process would provide a model of cooperation and solidarity for the United Nations' deliberations. Harrison proclaimed that he and his fellow architects were building for "the people who have lived through Dunkerque, Warsaw, Stalingrad and Iwo Jima." He hoped that they would "build so simply, honestly and cleanly that it will inspire the United Nations, who are today building a new world, to build this world on the same pattern." Of course, the "pattern" was for not only a new political world of un-national collaboration, but a new urban world as well. With its un-national design, the UN complex symbolized a sense of order rescued from disorder, a will toward aesthetic purity and political security that symbolized an abstract universal urban ideal and a world political vision beyond national divisions, one that foresaw a joint utopia of renewed cities and world peace.[23]

Garden City of the World

Not since Lord Carnarvon discovered King Tut's Tomb in 1922 had a building caused such a stir. Just as Carnarvon's discovery influenced everything from cigarettes to women's skirts, so the new Secretariat would change the face of every city in the Western World.
—*Architectural Forum*, November 1950

When the editors of *Architectural Forum*, modernism's leading American champion, compared the Secretariat to King Tut's tomb, with its inordinate influence on the patterns of Jazz Age mass culture, they were more right than even they knew. Their comments accurately predicted the rise and proliferation of a new, repeatable, mass-produced form for glass-skinned, steel skeleton office buildings—in other words, a new kind of international mass culture of corporate modernism birthed from the high art of modernist architecture. This was the tradition that led to Lever House, the Seagram Building, and the other glass boxes lining Park and Sixth avenues; it was the vision that sent hundreds of towers hurtling skyward from open plazas; it was the form codified by the 1961 zoning law that gave Manhattan's business districts a new building style to replace the setbacked stone piles of the pre–World War II era. But the entire headquarters complex offered inspiration to urban planning as much as to architecture. It represented the arrival of a new approach to city rebuilding on a mass scale, a new international—or, more accurately, un-national—mass culture fit to renew cities worldwide.[24]

Whatever its novelty, as a piece of urban planning the UN complex was the realization of a particular prewar tradition: the slum clearance and housing-derived, modernist, city-rebuilding ideal. Of course, one could search in vain for any reference to the planning of modern housing—the associations with public housing offered by E. B. White notwithstanding—in the comments and narratives of the design team. And yet, the modern housing tradition made itself felt indirectly through the example of Le Corbusier himself, as the UN complex is the realization of a fragment of one of his 1920s planning utopias like the Plan Voisin or Ville Contemporaine.[25] At first glance, the complex's considerable architectural achievement—the austere, abstract, functionalist lines of the Secretariat's façade and the entire complex's aesthetic of universalist collaboration—provided a symbolic backdrop for what seemed to be more prosaic site-planning goals. But as an early deployment of the city-rebuilding ideal, the UN complex acquired its own symbolic role for urban planning.

Of course, the United Nations' intervention in the Manhattan grid was not only symbolic; it was quite real. The headquarters complex's eventual imaginative influence on urban renewal began with its own slum clearance program, which close cooperation with the city of New York ensured would be carried out in accordance with modern urban planning principles. In March 1947, a few months after the Rockefellers turned the six-block site over to the United Nations and just as the design board was getting to work, Robert Moses delivered a roster of municipal incentives to the fledgling world body. Moses, who had been included in the site deliberations from the beginning, believed that the provisions necessary to protect the United Nations' investment—tax exemption for the site and street closures needed to form a superblock—would be the same minimum incentives necessary to encourage the private clearance and rebuilding of expensive in-town land for urban renewal projects to come. In addition to closing 43rd through 47th streets between the East River and First Avenue, the city, Moses pledged, would extend a tunnel under First Avenue to guide traffic away from the site, widen First Avenue and 42nd Street to further remove the

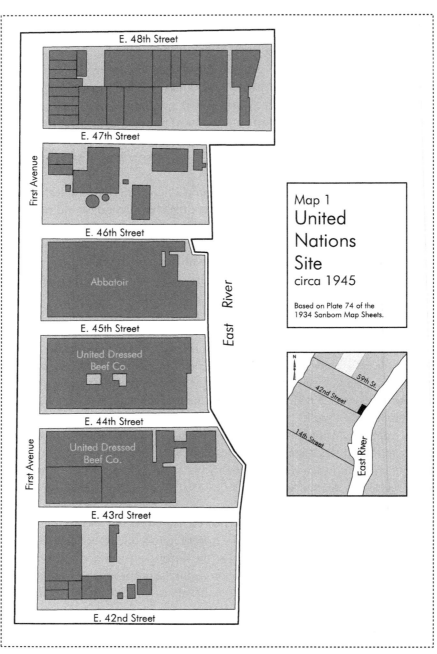

E. 48th Street

E. 47th Street

First Avenue

E. 46th Street

Abbatoir

E. 45th Street

United Dressed
Beef Co.

E. 44th Street

First Avenue

United Dressed
Beef Co.

E. 43rd Street

E. 42nd Street

East River

Map 1
United
Nations
Site
circa 1945

Based on Plate 74 of the
1934 Sanborn Map Sheets.

59th St.

42nd Street

14th Street

East River

Maps 1 and 1a. The UN site and the United Nations.

52

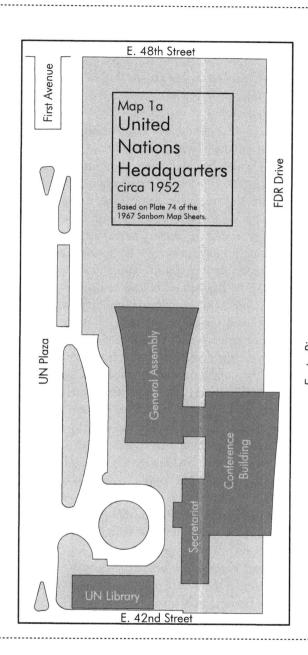

E. 48th Street

First Avenue

Map 1a
United
Nations
Headquarters
circa 1952

Based on Plate 74 of the
1967 Sanborn Map Sheets.

FDR Drive

East River

UN Plaza

General Assembly

Conference Building

Secretariat

UN Library

E. 42nd Street

UN complex from the city around it, and change zoning regulations to ban tall buildings, industrial uses, and billboard advertising in the immediate area of the site. There would be some disagreement as to whether these measures were enough to protect the integrity of the site, and some saw the plot as entirely too small—Lewis Mumford referred to it as a mere "fleabite" of land—but there was little doubt that the UN site-planning process offered the chance to demonstrate how cities ought to be rebuilt.[26]

Before construction could get under way, city officials and UN planners had to confront the neighborhood the headquarters buildings would replace. Between the spring of 1947 and September 1948, when construction got under way, the city worked to implement the UN-funded removal and relocation of residential and commercial tenants. The process, while relatively uncontroversial, provided a glimpse of struggles between new and old, modern order and multiplicitous urban jumble, future promise and storied neighborhood life, struggles that would echo down through the years as New Yorkers encountered many more demands that they abandon their neighborhoods and make way for progress.

The area alongside Turtle Bay had no official name. It was a low-rise, motley expanse of four-, five-, and six-story industrial buildings, clustered in ungainly array between the river and the hill rising above First Avenue. There were a few seven-story buildings, and one that reached nine, but on balance it was a few blocks of tumbledown garages, warehouses, storefronts, and the odd apartment building dominated by the slaughterhouses and meatpacking plants that had given the neighborhood its prime industry and culture for several generations. Animals bound for the killing floors were routinely herded through the streets; one could often see packs of doomed sheep being led to slaughter by an old goat that local wags called Judas. This world had long been considered an unsightly and noisome plague on what was an otherwise fetching stretch of Manhattan real estate; the impulse to replace these particular buildings appeared uncontroversial to almost everyone. And, in truth, site demolition turned out to be a relatively hassle-free process for the United Nations compared to the disruptions and displacements put in motion by the contemporary plans for Stuyvesant Town or by federally backed housing and redevelopment projects in later years.

This was in large part because few people actually lived there anymore. A municipal survey found that there were only 8 apartment buildings on the site, and just 2 of them were occupied, housing 53 families or about 150 people. There were, by contrast, 51 commercial buildings housing 72 businesses. The relocation problems multiplied somewhat when one took into account the extra territory needed to widen the surrounding streets; those operations would bring the total number of endangered commercial tenants to 102 and the total number of families needing relocation to 179. Still, this seemed a manageable task to city

1.4. A view of the industrial buildings on the future UN site from the window of the Tudor City apartment complex, looking north along First Avenue, with the Queensboro Bridge in the background. Serge Wolffe Collection, Image S-0593–0006, United Nations Archive.

officials. With UN funds, they renovated several nearby apartment buildings for the affected families and made provisions for the remainder in city-owned buildings or with cash grants to help them relocate themselves.[27]

The process was not nearly so easy for the commercial tenants. They were given less help, financial or otherwise, and often had to fend for themselves once their premises were given to the United Nations. There was some resistance among business owners, particularly from those outside the immediate UN-owned footprint, who questioned the city's right to take their property for the purposes of mere street widening. A furniture maker and a local Catholic church mounted a campaign to have this displacement halted, claiming that the financial and social hardships would put them out of business. Their entreaties fell on deaf ears. Deputy Mayor John J. Bennett lectured the furniture maker on his civic responsibilities in the face of "one of the greatest honors paid our City in its long history," and Robert Moses advised city relocation officials to see the archbishop rather than waste time with the parish priest, "who does not get the whole picture." In the end, businesses caused minor delays in the clearance schedule, but they never sought to stop the project. There were some recalcitrant holdouts, and according to UN officials it was "necessary to cajole and frighten" at least one businessman with legal proceedings. Historian Joel Schwartz has estimated that 2,600 commercial and industrial jobs were relocated from Manhattan by the UN clearance efforts. These losses hardly registered in the overall Manhattan economy, but they set a precedent for the aggressive attitude that redevelopment policies would take against neighborhoods like the slaughterhouse district. In an era when "deindustrialization" was a hope not a threat, neighborhoods like that, along with the lives and culture they supported, didn't stand much of a chance. The "whole picture" was too big and too bright to deny.[28]

Depictions of the future UN site painted a dismaying picture. Here, it appeared, were six blocks of truly outmoded cityscape. The *Times* reported that this "dead-end" neighborhood—so christened because each of its east-west streets came to rest at a municipal Dead End sign at the riverbank—had the "heaviest sootfall" in the entire city, a fact conveyed by the alarming figure of 150 tons per square mile each year. From the planners' clinical perspective, these blocks were an irrational use of space, taking up land that would be better occupied by so-called higher residential or commercial uses. This was an economic argument of sorts, seeking the highest return for the municipal dollar, as well as a social one, looking for the most efficient distribution of residences and workplaces to support high land values and the fluid transportation of people and goods. But these arguments avoided the place itself, and the categories that planners usually marshaled to justify clearance did not quite fit. It was not wholly accurate to call the area a "slum"—few people lived there and there were few severe social problems or dangers outside of the inordinate air pollution (which choked the entire city)—and it was not really "blighted" either: land prices were quite low, but most of the industries were going concerns, not just shells on vacant lots failing to pay taxes or to put people to work.[29]

Ultimately, the justifications for clearance of the area did not rest on planning theory, but on what appeared to be common sense. In truth, no justification was needed, only a story that laid out a clear and meaningful progression from one kind of neighborhood to another. The slaughterhouse district was seen as unsightly, distasteful, and noxious in comparison to the refined precincts of Sutton Place and Tudor City hard by its northern and eastern borders. But what really did in the neighborhood was the sense that it was ultimately unimportant in light of the world historic splendors planned to replace it.

As a photo essay in the independent magazine *United Nations World* put it, the "rectangle between First Avenue and the river is a dead end in the traffic sense, and a dead end to life itself." An inefficient area for proper municipal circulation, yes, but its real failing was that "people long ago deserted its tenements. Activity died except in the slaughterhouses. Only grimness and neglect—grimy abbatoirs, decayed buildings and refuse dumps—were left. Time long ago passed the area by. It is a place where ghosts of the past still tread their old familiar haunts." The place was "a graveyard, all right," a cop from the local precinct reported. "Nothing ever happens here anymore." Everything that had happened in the neighborhood had happened in the past. The reporter found that "chats in dim taverns go back to before World War I, antedating not only the UN but the League of Nations." The local workers "speak of the First Avenue horse-drawn trolley as though they were still pursuing it in sneakered feet and patched pants." They remembered wrestling matches in the back of Hackenschmidt's bar; their "fight talk dwells on figures like Jess Willard, Harry Greb and Jack Johnson." These piquant observations not only locked the place in the past, but depicted it as a place outside of time, peopled by denizens of a perpetual world apart, moored to their archaic precinct, unconnected to the larger city and the passage of time itself. The commentary was interspersed with a series of grim photos: a Stop, Dead End sign; an abandoned tenement foregrounded by a shadowy piece of debris in the shape of a cross; boarded-up storefront windows which "made a gruesome showcase for garish movie posters"; the World Cafeteria (whose name was "strictly a coincidence"); a parade of slaughterhouse-bound sheep; and a one-eyed man holding an old wagon wheel.

The final photo in the series was a bit different, however. It was a nocturnal view of the East Side skyline from the river in which the blank darkness of the future UN site "sits huddled and invisible at the feet of the mighty glittering skyscrapers of midtown New York." However, this dark spot would soon be gone, and "where the crumbling, reeking buildings of the river side now stand, will rise new skyscrapers, dedicated to the welfare of mankind....Instead of dumps and wreckage, spacious lawns and tree-lined paths are likely to fringe the UN site along the busy river." Just as that final photo represented the culmination of the narrative of inevitable progress and succession, the blank spot in the skyline suggested that the culmination of the neighborhood's history was as a place that has disappeared, a literally "dead" spot on the map, existing only as an opportunity for another, more glorious future. Who, the essay implied, could in good conscience stand in the way of a world capital sweeping away a few stinking abbatoirs?[30]

The UN site did offer a good case for "benevolent intervention" in the cityscape. Trading slaughterhouses for the United Nations was an easy decision. On the other hand, we now know that this was an opening episode in a decades-long attack on industry and blue-collar life in Manhattan on the part of urban

THE wide doors of the slaughterhouses are open most of the day and you can see dirty sheep huddled in nearby pens. If you wait around, Judas (he may be a goat or an old sheep, depending on which slaughterhouse employs him) shambles into the pen accompanied by a Negro with a sort of razor strop. The driver probably calls him Joe. Outsiders have named him Judas, for it's the goat who leads the mob of sheep, like lost legions in an unfriendly land, into "sheep-kill alley", where the villain neatly sidesteps into freedom and his followers go to their doom. The slaughterhouse men have gruesome anecdotes. In the early 20th century the poor came with cups to drink the warm blood of killed animals, because they thought it would make them healthy.

Those were the days, too, when liver could be had for the asking. "Why, they would hit you in the face with the stuff." said a truck driver . . . "Hell, they don't throw anything away today. Look at the ox tails, etc."

THERE is even a broken-down blacksmith's shop complete with smithy, in the UN site. A slaughterhouse built thirty-five years ago is still known as "the new slaughterhouse." Even the talk of the slaughterhouse workers is pitched in the era of long ago. They speak of the First Avenue horse-drawn trolley as though they were still pursuing it in sneakered feet and patched pants. As though it were yesterday, they revel in the memories of the back of Hackenschmidt's bar, where wrestling matches were on view for the price of a few beers. Their fight talk dwells on figures like Jess Willard, Harry Greb and Jack Johnson.

Chats in dim taverns go back to before World War I, antedating not only the UN but the League of Nations.

1.5. Photo essay from "UN Site—Symbol of UN Job," *United Nations World* (April 1947). This photo essay indulged in local color to demonstrate that the slaughterhouse district was a remnant of the city's past. Image courtesy of United Nations Archives.

redevelopment policies. The industrial and commercial jobs lost on the UN site were part of a vital and endangered urban cultural ecology and economy. Out of that context, the munificence of the deal seems obvious. What the seeming singularity of the UN site conceals is the assumptions that drove this campaign against industry. Planners and other officials believed that industry—and the neighborhoods, cultures, and institutions that supported it—were archaic, dead, and outmoded in Manhattan. This story—which is both narrative and judgment—delivered a ready-made picture, a transportable image, of the supposedly irrefutable benefits of cityscape upgrade, which could be transferred to any neighborhood certified as potentially dodgy by planners, developers, or word-of-mouth. It could be grafted onto facts, figures, and images to convince the public that future interventions would be benevolent as well. Here, the slum clearance ideal could be reduced to its purest logic, but it would be much more complicated when applied elsewhere in the years to come.[31]

If the UN site represented the highest fulfillment of the logic of replacement and progress behind slum clearance, it also represented the possibility and promise of the city-rebuilding ethic for Manhattan. "There is startling and ironical symbolism" in the fact that the United Nations would rise from an old, outmoded industrial area, *United Nations World* announced. "For by chance, the UN skyscraper capital will rise upon a site that in many ways represents all the human, economic, and material woes of the world at large." That the Turtle Bay neighborhood was not nearly so destitute as this account suggested hardly mattered. The site "symbolizes the very job of the UN itself." Likewise, the world body would measure its success in international affairs by its putative success in urban reconstruction. "The aim of the UN," the magazine concluded, "will be to make its achievements in world security and rehabilitation as impressive as its capital—the HQ of 55 or more nations." The United Nations' mission appeared here as a dual endeavor: international security first and foremost, but also the kind of urban "rehabilitation" that its "spacious lawns and tree-lined paths" would bring to the "dumps and wreckage" of the industrial cityscape.

Planners and architects ratified this symbolic linkage, claiming that overcoming urban disorder was not just a matter of city rebuilding, but analogous to the United Nations' fundamental mission. Modern city-planning principles, two New York Congress of Industrial Organizations (CIO) housing consultants told the City Planning Commission, could provide a "physical environment...which symbolizes the hopes men and women have placed in the United Nations." War and international strife were likened to what Le Corbusier called the "invading and hostile confusion" of unchecked urban development and decay. The United Nations would relegate all of that old menace to the dustbin of history. The "site control" provisions of the modern urbanist practice that Corbusier had long championed would establish a "protective zone" around the United Nations, "bar[ring] the way of disorder" and offering "protection, reassurance, security" from an always encroaching city in the same way the United Nations itself would offer security and reassurance to a troubled world.[32]

As the site-planning process went forward, the UN planners and other urbanists offered this symbolic vision of urban rehabilitation as a model for the city beyond the six blocks on Turtle Bay. This was true as early as 1946, when the critic Lewis Mumford saw in the UN headquarters planning process the opportunity to found "a new kind of urban community" in the form of the dispersed garden cities he had long advocated. Of course, this was when everyone assumed that the United Nations would select a large, rural site, but as it became more likely that the United Nations would land inside a city, Mumford adapted his ideas. A new city, he suggested, could be carved out of an older metropolis "by a large-scale process of slum clearance, removal, and rebuilding, financed wholly by the United Nations." One could still found a garden city, but now the headquarters could have an even greater mandate. The UN headquarters could be a demonstration in urban space of the "very methods of cooperation we must now apply throughout the planet to preserve order, to keep the peace, to establish a decent minimum of living, and to make the maximum human use of the energies man now commands." With so much at stake, Mumford somewhat blithely suggested, "it would not be difficult to find plenty of land, on the scale of two to three thousand acres, whose gradual clearance for a world center would immensely revitalize the whole city."[33]

Rockefeller's 18-acre gift forced UN planners to make the liability of a much smaller site into an opportunity. Abandoning the grandiose site-planning goals Mumford had advocated, they embraced the chance to model in miniature the particular kind of slum clearance and redevelopment he suggested. Le Corbusier particularly came to envision the UN site as a potential validation of his utopian urban visions. When he was picked for Harrison's team, he too hoped that the site would be a rural one. He had never liked New York and its crowded, piecemeal, market-driven cityscape and he had long campaigned to have urban conglomerations like Manhattan erased and replaced with great swaths of towers, parks, and highways. In his first report to the United Nations, delivered in July 1946, he had caustically dismissed the idea of putting the United Nations in the city, calling New York a "terrifying city." "For us," he warned, "it is menacing. We are not wrong in keeping at a distance." But after the site committee made its choice, he reversed his verdict, seeing the opportunity to prove on a truly world stage his modern planning ideals. Here was the chance to embrace a "new conception" in city building unlike "anything ever built before," with its "many green spaces" providing relief and open vistas to "visitors who come out of the very tight streets

1.6. *The United Nations and the City of New York* (November 1951), cover. This booklet, published by Robert Moses and the Manhattan Borough President's Office, visually demonstrates the relations between the city and the world body. The United Nations, with its superblock and tower, fills a cleared spot in the midst of the jumble, implanting a new spatial model in the fabric of the old metropolis. Avery Architectural and Fine Arts Library, Columbia University.

around the site." He expected that his conception of the United Nations would "bring to a head New York's long expected crisis, through which New York will find the ways and means to resolve its urbanistic deadlock, thus effecting upon itself a startling metamorphosis." "The United Nations [will] settle on the East River," predicted Corbusier, and "the whole East River will be brought to life, will awaken"—and here he explicitly invoked the influential modern utopias he had envisioned in the 1920s—"and will thrive as a 'Radiant City.' "[34]

Wallace Harrison agreed, and he put Corbusier's lofty abstractions in terms anyone could understand. New York, he told a *Post* reporter, was not as it should be. His ideal city, the journalist related, "would be a green city, each skyscraper surrounded by parks and gardens and all the buildings linked by modern express highways." The UN headquarters, Harrison said, would be an opening salvo in the campaign for such a city. "While the site is now the home of gas stations and slaughter houses," Harrison said in early 1947, "it will one day be a garden city of the world."[35]

The UN planning team adopted these ideals and made their plans a self-conscious attempt to reenvision New York's urban fabric. The site, said Glen E. Bennett, secretary of the UN planning office, "permits planning different from the general disorder and confusion of Manhattan." By building the Secretariat as a tower block, reducing ground coverage, and collecting the buildings in the southern half of the site, the planners left "most of the ground space free and unobstructed." They filled that space with plazas, open gardens, and a broad walkway along the river with a series of benches. By orienting the Secretariat on a north-south axis, they kept its shadow off the bulk of the site. This provided what Bennett called "ample light, space and garden—three elements which are lacking in most of New York's business district." "The people of the city," he said, "long accustomed to dark, high-walled streets, will be surprised to discover this midtown zone of open, radiant space." In the UN plan, "tension and chaos give way to calm and order."[36]

Like Bennett, UN secretary general Trygve Lie had been inspired by Corbusier's vision of a "radiant city." He championed "the fundamental elements of modern urbanism—sunlight, space, and verdure"—at work on the site. He thought the architecture and site planning formed a gratifying and propitious partnership. "Rarely," he wrote in his report to the General Assembly on the headquarters development, "has such an opportunity been presented to bring into a harmonious whole masses of such significance and on such an imposing scale; to establish, after a century of mounting urban disorder, a landmark of order in the heart of a great city." Like the others, Lie believed that the UN headquarters would have a sweeping influence on postwar New York and on international urban culture in general:

1.7. The grounds of the UN headquarters, "a landmark of order in the heart of a great city," according to the first UN secretary general, Trygve Lie. This is a view from the north showing the open lawns, the north face of the General Assembly Hall and its entry plaza, and the marble profile of the Secretariat. Stoller gives the serene complex the overhanging blessing of a tree and sets off its new marble facings against three soot-blackened smokestacks from the Consolidated Edison plant just to the south. Similarly, he lets the General Assembly building's linear grill push the Tudor City apartment complex and the city beyond it to the edge of the frame in the right background. Ezra Stoller © Esto.

Cities do renew themselves, contrary to the belief of those who flee them. The United Nations headquarters site project, itself a small scale prototype of sound urban planning can become part of a redevelopment and thus serve as the precipitating cause of a long-range transformation of the City around it, and perhaps of other cities throughout the world.[37]

Public and professional reaction to the UN site plans echoed these concerns. Most critics and commentators agreed that the plans offered what the *Architects' Journal* called "a lead to the future development of New York City" and a display of state-of-the-art urbanism, but some were not sure they did quite enough to advance the cause. Architect Morris K. Ketchum hailed the United Nations' superblock arrangement as a step up from the outmoded "horse and buggy" pattern of market-driven, block-by-block city development. City planning commissioner Newbold Morris declared that the site would be the "focal point of the entire rehabilitation of the East Side from the Battery to Harlem." But if this was the opportunity that the United Nations offered, it was also a dilemma. For some observers, like Lewis Mumford, the UN site was too small to accomplish its ambitious goals. The surrounding streets still "offer a field day to speculation and architectural chaos," commented the planner Hugh R. Pomeroy. Some felt that the answer was a monumental approach, something to give the complex a more dignified setting. A group of planners and influential elites, led by William Zeckendorf, led a campaign to transform 47th Street into a broad ceremonial boulevard, but the project was deemed too expensive. Another group of planners and architects, working under the aegis of the New York chapter of the American Institute of Architects, offered a comprehensive plan for "East midtown Manhattan" that would cut a new approach to the United Nations through the blocks between 46th and 47th streets between Park and First avenues, further upgrade zoning in the district, and plan for the rebuilding of the entire area. The City Planning Commission undertook perhaps the most ambitious effort to extend the United Nations' example, voting in 1950 to mark the surrounding area as "suitable for planning and redevelopment." This change to the city's unofficial master plan was largely symbolic—it simply gave official approval to any large-scale public or private interest that wanted to begin a process of redevelopment on modern lines—but it demonstrated the inspirational role the United Nations played in spurring schemes for redevelopment.[38]

The fact that none of these efforts actually bore fruit demonstrates that the United Nations' influence was more symbolic than direct, but also that it extended far beyond the complex's immediate neighborhood. The United Nations may not have had any direct "urbanistic radioactivity" to "sterilize slums"—as planner Hugh Pomeroy put it—but it did serve as a symbol of what such power could do. The Citizens Housing Council declared, "As the home of the United Nations, New York was to be the center of the new 'one World,'" but unfortunately, the city's housing conditions jeopardized this standing. In order to be a "worthy world headquarters," New York had to "take the leadership in providing all of its citizens with decent, safe, and adequate homes." Overall, the UN headquarters existed as a goad to planners, officials, and urbanists, a reason to work toward a rebuilt city that would be truly worthy of the title of world capital, and an example in miniature of what such a renewed city would look and feel like.[39]

Just as clearance and construction got under way, this vision reached a city- and nationwide audience. In their 1948 book, *New York: The World's Capital City*, Cleveland Rodgers and Rebecca B. Rankin traced the history of their city

1.8. This image predicts the likely influence of the United Nations—early designs for which are depicted at the upper right—on the complex's immediate neighborhood. Part of the deliberations over how to create a fitting ceremonial approach to the United Nations along 47th Street, it reveals how some hoped that the United Nations would provide a new planning template for remaking Manhattan with a cityscape fit for the capital of the world. Artist: Earl Purdy. Lincoln Center for the Performing Arts, Inc., Archive.

from "trading post to world capital." Echoing E. B. White's essay that same year, they viewed the arrival of the United Nations in New York as the crowning event in the city's history and as a signpost for the future. What the city needed, they remarked, was "to evolve a comprehensive plan, both for midtown and for Greater New York, in which the United Nations will become part of a modern integrated community." They felt sure that the United Nations guaranteed "the complete rebuilding and transformation of Manhattan's frontage on the East River from Brooklyn Bridge to the Harlem River and on up to the Hudson." With Stuyvesant Town and Peter Cooper Village going up and a vast plan for public housing starting up in East Harlem and the Lower East Side, these goals appeared to be within reach. But "rehabilitation of the center of the island" was still in the offing, they said.

The true problem was that "the power, resources, and techniques for replanning New York as a World Capital still wait to be merged by popular demand." What city planners had not yet mastered was "the more difficult and realistic problem of replanning old cities to make them more livable, while preserving the manifest advantages of centralization." But the tools were available. New York had already embraced the power to condemn property, which "removed the first barrier to better housing and to the redevelopment of many sections of New York on a new and greatly improved pattern." Rodgers and Rankin were confident that "this new kind of city, with new designs for urban living, is rapidly coming into being." Now, the United Nations gave this ethic of city rebuilding symbolic purpose and a widened field of operations.[40]

Perhaps the most succinct depiction of the United Nations' promise for urbanism in New York arrived in early 1949 from the drawing board of Hugh Ferriss, the renowned architectural draftsman whose visions of imagined modern cityscapes had long captivated the public. A "visual consultant" to the United Nations, he was asked by the New York Times Magazine to contribute to an article predicting the fate of New York in 1999. All the other contributors (Robert Moses, Wallace Harrison, the architect Eliel Saarinen, and the director of planning for the United Nations, Harvey Wiley Corbett) envisioned a range of practical or visionary advances—from better parking, housing, and parks to the end of slums, crosstown expressways, and a metropolitan region divided into a series of decentralized communities "enclosed in a spacious green-belt system"—but it was Ferriss's contribution that best captured the United Nations' conceptual influence on the age of modern rebuilding to come. His drawing showed a vast city of glass towers, green plazas, and swift highways. At the center of the image, recessed into the background with the remade city radiating out toward the viewer, was the UN headquarters. "Fifty years from now," Ferriss said, "New York will be a capital city in a united world. A city of several levels, of glass and light, with building masses set wide apart and separated by tree lined malls. It will, I hope, be run by atomic power, working for peace, not war. That of course, is the hope on which the future of the city, and the world, depends." In Ferriss's estimation, then, the United Nations inspired a comprehensive vision for replanning New York as a glorious new metropolis where everyone, rich and poor alike, would live and work in soaring towers and open spaces. The new metropolis's built qualities would be underwritten by a social vision of equality, security, and justice inspired by the ideals for which the United Nations quite literally stood, both as an institution and as an artifact of visionary urban planning.[41]

All these visions revealed a particular symbolic current running through American culture in the late 1940s. During these years, the United Nations and the ethic of city rebuilding stood together in the minds of progressives and liberals. Both were legacies of Franklin Delano Roosevelt's political idealism—one a mainstay of his domestic New Deal and the other of his democratic internationalism. Both seemed to many liberals to be the fruits of the struggle in World War II; replanned and rejuvenated cities went hand in hand with a world free from war and strife. Both, too, were imperiled, potential casualties of the dawning Cold War and the compromises that

1.9. The cartoonist Herblock depicted the linked fates of modern housing reform and the United Nations, each a progressive effort to renew the world, in the unsure summer of 1948. "Did They Fool You on Housing, Too?" *Washington Post*, June 28, 1948. Copyright by the Herb Block Foundation.

Truman accepted for his Fair Deal. In the summer of 1948, both the United Nations and impending housing and redevelopment legislation seemed to be on the rocks. The United Nations needed a loan of $65 million from the United States to finish its new headquarters complex, while the housing bill that would eventually become the 1949 Housing Act had failed to get a majority of votes in Congress. In the *Washington Post,* cartoonist Herblock depicted the sorry state of these linked concerns. Two bureaucrats, one a UN diplomat and the other a U.S. housing official, sit forlornly on the doorstep of a ruined tenement with a caved-in door, each clutching torn copies of their bills. They are surrounded by trash and refuse; a cluttered slum skyline looms above them. In the distance is the U.S. Capitol with a Gone Home sign slung over its dome. "Did they fool you on housing, too?" says the housing man to the diplomat, lamenting the political impasse that prevented them both from getting to work on the urban ills that surround them.[42]

In time, the United Nations got its loan and finished its headquarters. The Housing Act won enough votes and gave federal imprimatur and subsidies to city redevelopment projects. But in Herblock's cartoon, the final fate of these linked ambitions lay in the unpredictable future, each of them potential institutions of progressive political endeavor, each one drawing symbolic sustenance from the other in their allied campaigns for better urban and international worlds. Despite these momentary defeats and a mounting tide of reaction, victory, it seems, might still be snatched from the teeth of defeat. E. B. White's "greatest housing project of them all" might yet shoot up along the East River; the United Nations would no doubt get to work on "clearing the slum called war"; and it might yet serve as an inspiration to those planning to clear the real slums and build more housing projects for everyone.

The United Nations provided a glimpse of New York after the age of urban renewal, a white-collar city of modern towers and open spaces that had banished what E. B. White called "the unexpungeable odor of the long past" lingering in its streets.[43] Despite the cool assurance of the headquarters design and the confident benevolence that launched the United Nations' interventions into the cityscape, this legacy would turn out to be more ambivalent than triumphant. The UN model of a modern, global city for all would, like the world body's own mission of world peace, be considerably complicated by the Cold War that was arriving just as the headquarters buildings went up on Turtle Bay. Looking back to this moment, one wonders whether it is a blessing or a lost opportunity that New York was never able to remake itself entirely in the image of the United Nations. But vast swaths of the city did face the wrecking ball and the rebuilders in the years after the UN headquarters went up on Turtle Bay. In those places, people had to reckon with the complex legacy of its shining idealism and progressive modernity. The story of this ambivalent legacy continues 20 or so blocks south, where another massive development was under way in these early years of the Cold War, one that promised to extend the vision offered by the United Nations and the modern housing movement, to redeem the city for the middle classes, and to become the prototype for federal city-rebuilding policies.

II Stuyvesant Town

The View from the Tower

The Metropolitan Life Insurance Company has just announced plans for another of its great housing projects, which not only gives an outlet for millions of dollars of its policyholders' funds on an economically sound basis, but also meet[s] a great social need for modern housing.
—A. L. Kirkpatrick, *Chicago Journal of Commerce*, April 1943

Sometime in the spring of 1942, a newspaperman by the name of A. L. Kirkpatrick climbed up to the tower of the Metropolitan Life Insurance Company's home office building. From this high perch—45 stories and some 600 feet above the corner of Madison Avenue and 23rd Street on Manhattan's East Side—he looked out over all of Manhattan to the Narrows, the harbor and Staten Island, the Hudson and New Jersey, the East River, and Brooklyn and Queens beyond. North and west loomed the spires of midtown, with Metropolitan Life's skyline partners, the Empire State and Chrysler buildings, pushing out high above the stacked blocks of setback piles. But the other way, down the island, the view was clear; there was nothing but air all the way to the financial district and its familiar array of Gothic towers.

Down below where Kirkpatrick stood lay the vast reaches of what was then considered the Lower East Side. South of the 20s and east of Third Avenue, row upon row of tenements, factories, warehouses, vacant lots, and churches clustered in an unruly jumble. Atop the tower that day, Kirkpatrick and a Metropolitan official surveyed these blocks with concerned eyes. How, Kirkpatrick's guide wondered aloud, could anyone be expected to live in the Lower East Side when "they could get decent quarters at a reasonable price elsewhere"? As if to prove the logic of his point, the Metropolitan's man swept his hand across the whole of the Lower East Side and remarked with, as Kirkpatrick noted, "some exaggeration for emphasis," that it was "almost all vacant." Evidently, Kirkpatrick was doubtful, but "looking down closer to us," he admitted, "we could see that many of the surrounding buildings were not at all well occupied."[1]

Indeed, to the money-minded, the Lower East Side was not merely the slum it might appear to be to housing reformers and others concerned about the welfare of tenement-dwellers. After 20 years of depopulation, its crumbling tenements were still a threat to public health, but now they also appeared to Kirkpatrick to more closely resemble open land vacant of both population and economic or human value. Somehow, these "old rundown city areas" seemed to represent possibility more than tragedy. To the capable minds at Met Life, the Lower East Side was not merely a fiscal and human wasteland; it was also, and equally, an opportunity for a corresponding economic and social investment.

Kirkpatrick recalled this visit to the tower a year later, after the Metropolitan announced a plan, backed by the city and state governments, to clear 18 of those Lower East Side blocks of tenements, stores, and warehouses and replace them with a new residential community. Stuyvesant Town was to be 35, entirely "modern," 13-story brick apartment buildings set in open parkland with, a Metropolitan press release boasted, "an atmosphere of trees and paths such as many suburbs do not possess."[2] Standing between Avenue A on the east, 14th Street on the south, Avenue C and the East River Drive on the east, and 23rd Street on the north, Stuyvesant Town and its slightly more upscale companion to the north, Peter Cooper Village, would replace an old section of the Lower East Side known with both affection and notoriety as the Gas House District. Subsuming all the area's north-south avenues and east-west streets in its superblock, Stuyvesant Town would invade and displace the Manhattan street grid that had been virtually inviolable since 1811. Clearance and construction on this unprecedented project began soon after the close of World War II. Stuyvesant Town welcomed its first families in August 1947 and was finished and fully occupied less than two years later, on June 1, 1949. Little more than five years after Kirkpatrick went up the Metropolitan tower, the view from its heights was irrevocably transformed. Stuyvesant Town not only replaced 18 blocks of nineteenth-century cityscape, but also provided the economic, social, and cultural blueprint for the many like-minded interventions in the Manhattan grid to come in the age of urban renewal.

Stuyvesant Town, Kirkpatrick assured his readers, would be a "sound investment." Unlike so much of the "social planning" undertaken by naïve but well-meaning reformers and do-gooders, he opined, this project was being undertaken by people who understood the "idea of trusteeship for the funds which they are spending." He had it on record from Frederick H. Ecker, chair of the Metropolitan board, that the company would "restore the residential values that lie in the land," which were now going to waste as the neighborhood lay "blighted." But Met Life was not interested in merely mining the city for profit. Met Life was no U.S. Steel or General Motors, and the streets of New York not merely a resource. The company was in the business of life insurance, so while it had to be sure that its investments would pay sufficient returns to justify the use of policyholders' funds, it also made it part of its business to underwrite public welfare. By 1943, according to *Business Week,* "about one U.S. city dweller in three" was insured by Met Life, so the "provision of better living conditions for city folks must accordingly improve the company's mortality experience and annual earnings." It was quite simple, opined a *New York Times* reporter: "People in non-slum areas live longer and continue to pay insurance premiums. It's a purely self-interested proposition." Restoring an empty, depleted cityscape to economic health could be profitable and a source of greater good.[3]

For years, Met Life officials had brought visitors, particularly groups of social work students, up to the tower. From the commanding heights of its Italianate campanile—symbolic of the company's commitment to the ideals of public service and civic engagement found in the Italian republics from which architects N. LeBrun and Sons had drawn inspiration—they could look out over the tene-

2.1. Architect Richmond Shreve, Metropolitan Life vice president George Gove, and Chairman Frederick Ecker (*left to right*) review a model for Stuyvesant Town and its intervention in the dense urban fabric of the Lower East Side. © 2009 Metropolitan Life Insurance Company. All rights reserved.

ments where Met Life sold many of its policies and, as historian Olivier Zunz puts it, "appraise the field of their future work." This ritual revealed the Metropolitan's social and financial interest in the "field" beneath its tower walls; the company surveyed the cityscape not simply with the cold eye of authority, but with the reserve of a patron or guardian. The tower had long stood as a symbol of Met Life's parental fortitude and social concern to the city and the world. Within, the company's fathers—stern, removed, unerringly rational officials with their actuarial tables and calculations of health rates and birth and death statistics—oversaw a vast fleet of white-collar women workers. These clerks, typists, stenographers, switchboard jockeys, and social workers brought a respectable, reassuring, and domestic air to the particularly maternal tasks of managing the fates of the company's wards—its majority working- and lower middle-class policyholders, many of whom filled the streets around the tower.[4]

But now, rather than simply overseeing the welfare of the toilers in the tenements and avenues from on high, the Metropolitan sought to remake the field of the company's work with a new spatial form. The company looked to transform those streets with modern architecture and garden city design, a new urban landscape where what they considered to be proper family life would flourish. Coming down from their removed watchtower, the company's managers looked not to preserve the tenements nor simply to supervise the lives lived there, but to uproot them and transform the cityscape. They planned to rescue a portion of the "rundown city" for white, middle-class family life, decrease insurance premiums for their policyholders, and secure the health of the public and their own social and economic investment in Manhattan real estate. In the process, they took on the largest slum clearance job to date, pioneered the effort to rethink the ethic of city rebuilding as urban renewal, and created what one historian has called "the prototype" for the "bulldozer redevelopment" that would so transform New York in the quarter-century after A. L. Kirkpatrick glimpsed the future city from the Met Life campanile.[5]

Stuyvesant Town was not merely a set of buildings, but an intensely charged and controversial political and cultural space. Throughout the project's early life, from its first announcement by Mayor Fiorello La Guardia, a bevy of competing interests vied to shape the project's material and human complexion and supply the terms by which the public might understand this new East Side agglomeration of brick, steel, concrete, grass, and trees. Civil rights groups protested Met Life's policy of racial segregation. Some dissident liberals, particularly City Council member Stanley Isaacs and the housing reformer Charles Abrams, objected to the project's overwhelming intervention in the cityscape and its public/private form for slum clearance. Residents and businesspeople protested the clearing of the Gas House District. Residents of the new complex worked to both desegregate the project and adjust to its new kind of urban space. These conflicts became referendums on the physical and social character of later city-wide efforts at urban redevelopment, giving Stuyvesant Town a predictive power far beyond its share of acreage in the Manhattan schist.

The Metropolitan intended Stuyvesant Town, quite explicitly, as a suburb in the city. Early on, while plans were still before the City Planning Commission, Frederick Ecker Jr., son of the chairman and president of the company, claimed that in Stuyvesant Town, "the whole scheme is life in the country in the heart of the city." City Council member Stanley Isaacs, in a turn of phrase that would haunt the project for years to come, replied that the project "will be a medieval walled town in the middle of the City of New York."[6] This war over the shape of 18 blocks, fought in symbols and metaphors as well as with political rhetoric and policy, was joined on many sides. The immediate contest was a skirmish within the broad front of urban liberalism, pitting Met Life and its backers in city government, particularly Robert Moses, against a host of protestors from civic groups, tenants in the Gas House District, labor organizations, and civil rights groups. The lines of battle were not orderly, however, and criticism of the city and company's plans never fully coalesced around one issue or ideological position. Later, after the new tenants moved in, they engaged in a series of struggles with Met Life and among themselves over desegregation and the larger shape of mass, urban, middle-class housing.

Stuyvesant Town's journey from drawing board to living community raised such a ruckus because it had major symbolic importance for postwar New York. An antidote to years of war and depression, the towers' clean lines and blank faces seemed somehow immune to the cares of the past; burdens would dissipate in this new place, swept away like the dingy streets and tenements that sagged and buckled with the accumulated weight of the old troubles: poverty, crime, congestion, ill health. Such simple dreams were dashed, of course, and Stuyvesant Town acquired a more complex legacy. In its design and social shape, in its ambitions and the conflicts it created, Stuyvesant Town helped to foretell the world that urban renewal would make.

Creating Urban Redevelopment: Retooling the Ethic of City Rebuilding

Like New York, all big cities are back to work, more or less, on their common chronic ailment, which might be described as degeneration of the heart, geography-wise.
—Clarence Judd, "For Rent: Sunlight and Fresh Air," Steelways, March 1947

By the early 1940s, Metropolitan Life was the largest private corporation in the United States. With assets totaling close to $6 billion at the end of 1942, the insurance giant had actually grown during the Depression. But with so much money held in securities and government bonds whose interest rates had fallen during the long economic malaise, the company was looking for secure and profitable investment outlets for its policyholders' funds. The company's head, Frederick Ecker, turned to one of his long-time interests: housing.[7]

Met Life had been involved in housing and other reform efforts in New York since the turn of the century. As with other Progressive Era campaigns, these endeavors were rooted in more than just altruism. For Met Life, the interest was purely financial. Early in the century, Met Life officials had recognized that, in the words of historian Thomas C. Cochran, "the physical welfare of the people of the United States was closely geared to the financial welfare of the Metropolitan." The company imagined a range of privately sponsored social welfare initiatives that amounted to "social democracy administered by business trustees." By the 1940s, however, the plan had been largely abandoned, as unions and the New Deal had stepped in to provide much of that social infrastructure.[8]

With housing, however, the attempt to marry philanthropy and business remained active throughout the 1920s and '30s. The company believed, as a matter of business faith, that "public health and welfare are dependent on proper housing." Most private philanthropic efforts in the housing field strove to show that private interests could build decent housing for the working poor without government subsidies and still make a reasonable profit. Before Met Life, such efforts had provided decent apartments on a small scale, but their primary function was as an inspirational lesson to commercial builders. Frederick Ecker set out to make the mass housing game safe for private money. Unlike his predecessors, he would not be so leery of public aid; in fact, he would demand it, and in quantity sufficient enough to guarantee the safety of the long-sought vision of private redevelopment through eminent domain.[9]

The Metropolitan began by building a small group of apartment buildings in Queens in the 1920s. From there, it expanded quickly, getting a number of planned communities under way across the country in the years before the United States entered World War II. Parkchester, the largest housing development in the United States to date, rose on 129 acres of Bronx fields in 1941 as an entirely private undertaking. A "Middletown-on-the-Subway," according to the *Christian Science Monitor,* it was designed to appeal to those in the middle class who longed for the affordability and community life of a small town, but couldn't bring themselves to abandon the convenience of urban life. But Parkchester was really a suburban development, built on open land at the end of the subway lines. It did little to answer a more pressing set of questions. What about those parts of the metropolis now called the "inner city," those downtown areas where dense and uneven private market development had left a vexing combination of poverty, substandard housing, high real estate values and no open land? What could or should be done there?[10]

Ecker and Met Life found themselves faced with this old, timeworn urban question at a propitious moment. By the late 1920s, a construction boom, rising real wages, and plentiful mass transit had allowed many workers to escape lower Manhattan. The Lower East Side lost half its population in the '20s, considerably reducing overcrowding and demand for housing. The Gas House District, the area A. L. Kirkpatrick surveyed that spring day in 1942, was no exception. In 1910, at the height of immigration from Southern and Eastern Europe, the district's population was about 23,000 and overcrowded, like the rest of the Lower East Side. Ten years later, it was 21,000. During the '20s, when immigration was all but cut off, thousands more were able to move to upper Manhattan or the outer boroughs. By 1930, the population stood at about 13,500, and the 1940 Census registered only about 12,150 people. With many of the neighborhood's young men off at war, the population might have been as low as 11,000. The movement of commerce and industry uptown and the creep of population to the boroughs had, as historian Anthony Jackson puts it, "turned the Lower East Side into a backwater." With the neighborhood in decline, property owners lost money on their rentals and looked to unload unprofitable real estate, freeing up land for potential redevelopment.[11]

The real estate was available, but it still would not come cheap. Private interests could not afford to buy acres of tenements at still-inflated prices. Bankers and corporate directorships would never back such a risky scheme. Who could afford to clear these depleted and seemingly unwanted districts? New York, of course, was the cradle of the slum clearance and housing movement. By the 1940s, the loose alliance of reformers, social workers, developers, architects, and city planners who called themselves "housers" had developed a substantial vision and practice of tenement destruction and housing construction. This ethic of city rebuilding had resulted in the New York City Housing Authority's New Deal–backed program of slum clearance and public housing and an ambitious vision for remaking cities along modern lines. Meanwhile, small businesspeople or developers in a few neighborhoods had also used New Deal monies to combat the decline of their immediate areas. Still, there was no policy mechanism by which private interests could enter the rebuilding field en masse.

Ecker was not alone in his ambitions. Robert Moses was also troubled by the fact that large private interests remained shy about pitching in to rebuild the city. He believed that only "great reservoirs of private capital," backed by government power and subsidies, could take on large clearance and building projects and stop the spread of slums. By the outbreak of the war, Moses had carried out an unprecedented public works program, creating parks, beaches, bridges, and roadways in his capacity as parks commissioner, but had only dabbled in housing and slum clearance. Having convinced Mayor Fiorello La Guardia and many reformers that his expertise in providing recreation should be tied to finding sites for new housing, Moses began to cast about for large institutions to sponsor projects on the Lower East Side.[12]

After negotiating with a number of insurance companies, most of which refused to commit assets to what they believed to be a risky venture, Moses turned to Frederick Ecker in late 1942. Ecker's interest in the social benefits of housing, his need to find profitable investments for the Metropolitan's assets, and his desire to protect the company's existing investment in downtown Manhattan made him the perfect candidate. In fact, he had already discussed with Mayor La Guardia an East Side project that would not only clear acres of tenements, but in his words, "have an additional value in helping to anchor population in Manhattan." Both Moses and Ecker later claimed to have had the idea of Stuyvesant Town first, and each had slightly separate, but linked motives.[13] Ecker wanted to promote social health (and build another profitable investment) by stemming the tide of economic blight, while Moses looked to clear slums in the most economically efficient manner.[14] Ecker's sense of remunerative social concern aligned neatly with Moses's pragmatic planning ambitions. With La Guardia's blessing, they entered into negotiations, forging an unprecedented mechanism for public support of private reuse of urban land claimed by eminent domain. Their arrangement laid the groundwork for a modification of the ethic of city rebuilding, one that would provide mass housing for the middle class rather than the so-called worthy poor served by public housing, but would still appear, in its intentions at least, to share the spirit of benevolent intervention in the urban landscape that motivated the ethic in the first place.

On February 1, 1943, Ecker, Moses, city comptroller Joseph McGoldrick, and Met Life's general counsel sat down in Mayor La Guardia's office and signed an agreement for "the redevelopment of a blighted area of eighteen city blocks comprehended by 14th and 20th Streets and First Avenue and Avenue C." By the terms of the agreement, Metropolitan Life would "provide all money necessary to execute the project." The company would buy as much of the area as it could, and the city would step in to acquire the rest through its powers of eminent domain and then sell it to Met Life at cost. The city would give Met Life "all lands in streets closed under the plan" and the company would give the city back any land for new streets, as well as land needed for street widening. Met Life would build access roads, paths, landscaping, and buildings that could cover up to 28 percent of the land and reach "a height sufficient to produce not less than 32,000 rooms and not more than 34,000 rooms." No parks or schools were thought necessary because East River Park was a few blocks away, and the city promised to build a new school nearby to replace one that would be demolished. To sweeten the deal, the city guaranteed that, for 25 years after completion of the project, Met Life's tax bill would remain fixed, based on the value of the property before redevelopment, meaning that the project's new buildings would be altogether exempt from taxation for that duration. Rents would be capped at $14 per month per room for the first 5 years of tax exemption. If Met Life felt that this restriction hampered its ability to realize "a reasonable return" on its investment—Ecker later put the necessary figure at 6 percent—then the company could petition the city's governing body, the Board of Estimate, to raise the rent ceiling. Finally, the parties agreed that the project should be seen as serving the "public purpose" that state laws demanded redevelopment projects must serve.[15]

Unfortunately, the benevolent intervention they imagined wasn't legal yet. The 1942 Redevelopment Companies Law, the most recent in a series of state laws granting eminent domain to municipalities and partial tax exemption to builders, allowed insurance companies and savings banks to invest in or found limited-dividend companies for the purpose of slum clearance, but still provided less public subsidy and more public control than private interests could stomach. Ecker was wary about proceeding if Moses and La Guardia could not get the law to conform to their agreement, so Moses set out to do just that. He had already launched a campaign to get the state law amended, and now he identified legislators who might introduce a bill and drafted a letter to go out under Ecker's name, notifying them that Met Life would be "seriously interested in helping to solve the problem" of "housing in slum areas." Moses goosed the process as best he could: in addition to having his office oversee the writing of a new law, he started work on a formal contract, worked with Met Life on a memo with a schedule for municipal approval of the project, wrote to Governor Thomas Dewey urging him to sign the bill, and stood "ready to stake my personal reputation" on the fact that the changes to the bill would be in the public interest.[16]

Moses supported public housing, but he believed most of all in clearing slums. "Certain specific agencies," he wrote to the governor, are "interested in public housing and obsessed with the idea that only public housing is the answer to slum clearance." There were, as he would tell the Board of Estimate a few weeks later, after the amended bill had already passed, "captious critics and wiseacres" who made "projects of this kind a battleground for the vindication of social objectives." They might claim that "a private project is in fact a public project," but they were just "looking for a political issue and not for results in the form of actual slum clearance." There were also "some pretty mean critics on the outside—the real radical housing boys," he warned La Guardia, who didn't want "private capital horning into their field" and might drag the whole thing into the courts.[17] Anticipating the opposition and their tactics, Moses worked to convince Dewey and La Guardia that slum clearance by any means necessary was the primary objective, not low-income housing, and that in order to get it moving, they had to provide a warm welcome to private capital. This was a key moment in the history of urban renewal, because amending the 1942 law allowed private interests not only to clear the land, but to redevelop it on their own terms without having to build the low-income housing that had accompanied earlier public slum clearance efforts.[18]

Not surprisingly, the new bill adhered exactly to the terms laid out in the agreement that Met Life and the city had signed two months earlier. It even sweetened the deal for Met Life by dropping the earlier version's requirement that the redeveloper make adequate provision for displaced tenants, and it defined condemnation for redevelopment as a "superior public use," thereby setting an invaluable precedent for private redevelopment efforts. In signing the Hampton-Mitchell Redevelopment Companies Law on March 30, Governor Dewey explained to the public that there were some provisions about which he was "doubtful," but the need for housing was so dire that it required both public and private resources. Unlike Moses, he said that "the purpose of the bill" was to provide housing, and he reassured the public that "the immediate practical problem is housing or no housing. The answer is in favor of housing." Dewey made sure to mention public housing in his announcement, but the bill he signed didn't simply, as he said, "permit and encourage the entrance into the housing field of life insurance companies." It set the stage for the rise of private-led rebuilding efforts that would eventually eclipse public housing authorities as the primary coordinators of replanning efforts and rewrite the city-rebuilding ethic as the policy of urban redevelopment.[19] Defenders of low-rent public housing protested the arrangement, horrified by, as one somewhat overheated critic put it, "a vision of tomorrow's boodler, who sneers at yesteryear's picayune franchise grabs and exhibits a fat sheaf of gilt-edged housing projects." But with the sure, respected hand of the Metropolitan at the helm and the universally popular Robert Moses on deck as well, fears that the state was subsidizing slumlords fell on deaf ears.[20]

La Guardia took to the airwaves on Sunday, April 18, with Ecker by his side, leading off his weekly radio address from City Hall with the announcement that Met Life and the city would throw in together to build Stuyvesant Town. "18-Block East Side 'Suburbia' for 30,000 to Be Built after War," announced the *World-Telegram*. This "suburb in [the] city," as the *Times* headline called it, was, according to Met Life's press release, "a step in the direction of the new Manhattan…one in which wholesomeness of residential environment will combine with existing convenience to 'anchor' families, especially those with children, to this borough." Met Life sold Stuyvesant Town as a blueprint for a new kind of urban landscape, where neither "wholesomeness" nor "convenience" needed to be sacrificed, and New Yorkers could recover the light and air offered by suburban escape and even the organic, natural qualities of rural living. At once romantic and modern, the development was a bid to save the city from suburbanization by introducing the appeal of suburbia into the city itself.[21]

This language established the terms by which Met Life hoped Stuyvesant Town would be understood, but it also revealed the pervasive effect that Stuyvesant Town would have on the ethic of city rebuilding. In repeating Ecker's hope that the development would "anchor" families in the bedrock of Manhattan, the company's press release showed that the company's social ideals were rooted in financial realism. To the company, the Gas House District was hemorrhaging population and tax revenues due to its mix of "indiscriminately mingled" buildings and uses. Reconstruction would bring families, investment, and tax dollars back to the "blighted" area. Stuyvesant Town would be a model of how to prevent capital flight and commercial decentralization. Forcefully intervening in what the *Saturday Evening Post* called "the hampering, blight-making gridiron of streets" and their inevitable "ruinously high real-estate taxes," Stuyvesant Town's superblock swath of landscaped greenery and modern architecture would provide construction jobs for returning soldiers, clear away a "slum," and build new housing, but its primary motivation was to protect the central city for investment and urban, middle-class living. To Met Life, economic blight was the real problem, and the answer to the social problems brought on by slum conditions was, as *Business Week* put it, to halt "the process of decentralization which has been undermining the financial soundness of every major city in the United States." Grafting social concern to strict economic principles, Stuyvesant Town was a crucial moment in the process by which downtown business interests transformed the housing reform movement into an effort to offset decentralization and promote the central business district.[22]

Out of the Past and into the Gas House District

The Gashouse District wasn't just a geographical location; it was primarily a bad smell, and secondarily an attitude of mind. Gas, leaking from the tanks, made the immediate neighborhood as near an imitation of what hell must smell like as you could find on earth. —Tom O'Connor, *PM*, March 1945

Before Met Life could put this blueprint to work, the company had to confront the neighborhood that Stuyvesant Town was intended to replace. The Gas

House District, like the slaughterhouse district that the United Nations displaced, was little more than an afterthought for most New Yorkers. Few people other than some of its beleaguered residents and a handful of social workers thought it worth saving, or that its dense streetscape of tenements, storefronts, warehouses, small manufactories, and gas works compared favorably with the vision of Stuyvesant Town. Still, if the clearance of the Gas House District was only nominally opposed, the process gave New Yorkers an early indication of the ambiguous social and cultural transformations that urban renewal would bring to the city. While many observers depicted life in the Gas House District as a kind of antediluvian specimen, the process of clearance itself indicated that there might be more than memories and crumbling buildings in that old streetscape. It suggested that the specter of loss could accompany the bright, ambitious visions of urban renewal.

The moment word went out that the Gas House District was not long for the world, reporters fanned out into Stuyvesant Town's 18-block footprint, eager to tell the neighborhood's story. In the two years before the Metropolitan began razing the district, newspapers near and far provided a narrative floated by equal parts fond nostalgia and breathless disgust. Their memorializations of the area's long-gone heyday depicted it as a place with a romantic past, full of legends and mythic characters, but no possible future. It was an "old hotbed of Tammany rule." It was the "stamping ground [sic] of Charlie Murphy, the Tammany chieftain and many other Tiger leaders," or it "once rang with the bully cries of Charlie Murphy's bright lads and the turtle-neck sweater boys." Of course, since it was "traditionally associated with beer bottle fights and frequent murder," it had also been home to much less savory characters. "For over 50 years," one reporter noted, "footpads of the Gashouse gang terrorized the neighborhood, taking their place with such other murder-and-larceny societies as the Gophers and the Hudson Dusters." Their "playmates were 'the girls with the swinging handbags,' celebrated in the old song 'The Belle of Avenoo A.'"[23]

The Gas House District, reporters found, remained an ethnic neighborhood, bearing the legacy of generations of European immigration. For the *World-Telegram,* it was "truly a melting pot," and for the *Daily Mirror* and *Herald Tribune,* there was a feeling of "clannishness" among the people. But whether they aspired to modern habits or clung to their old ways, all the Poles, Germans, Russians, Hungarians, Italians, leftover Irish, Czechs, and assorted others shared an American, up-and-comer's sense of self-sufficiency, nurtured in the days when, as 73-year-old Marion Dillon put it, they had turf wars with the "rich bugs" across Stuyvesant Square. "We could take care of ourselves then. We'll have to do it again," he said defiantly upon hearing of the Metropolitan's plans. With its ancient populations and storied streets, the Gas House District appeared in these accounts as an isolated, plucky little burg tucked away in an underused corner of the island.[24]

More celebrated writers joined the ink-stained wretches, finding the district alternately alluring and repelling. Despite his distaste for the "insensate industrial town," Lewis Mumford found in the Consolidated Edison gas works themselves a kind of fading romance: "Their tracery of iron, against an occasional clear lemon-green sky at sunrise, was one of the most pleasant esthetic elements in the new order." This early exercise in industrial chic aside, the gas tanks remained a menace. "Towering above the town, polluting its air, the gas tanks symbolized the dominance of 'practical' interests over life-needs." Novelist Thomas Wolfe agreed. He remembered the Gas House District's brutal glamour, calling it a place of "powerful ugliness and devastation…with its wasteland rusts and rubbish, its slum-like streets of rickety tenement and shabby brick, its vast raw thrust of tank, glazed glass and factory building…lifted by a powerful rude exultancy of light and sky and sweep and water such as is found only in America." Majestic or tawdry, sublime or shabby, the place had a storied past, but a grim, lifeless present and little future. Any future it might have, these sorts of accounts agreed, belonged to Stuyvesant Town.[25]

There was no lack of raw material from which to spin these twin stories of industrial deprivation and tenement romance. In 1940, the unemployment rate in the district had been high: 25 percent compared to a citywide average of 15 percent. The war had largely taken care of that problem, though, and a 1945 survey by the Community Service Society (CSS), a local social work agency, found that no employable person was out of work. The neighborhood remained decidedly working class, with most residents working in unskilled or semi-skilled occupations. Between 15 and 25 percent worked in shipyards and other defense industries, suggesting that postwar cutbacks might hit the area hard. Out of the 836 families surveyed, a quarter of them earned under $100 a month and about 70 percent under $200 a month. Only 300 out of 3,400 families were on welfare. The neighborhood's aristocracy was its local merchant class. They employed local residents, often lived nearby, and depended on neighborly patronage for their livelihood.

Housing conditions were less than ideal. Three-quarters of the apartment buildings went up in the nineteenth century, and only 5 percent had been built since 1920. There were about 400 residential buildings on the site, most of them old-law tenements and converted one-family houses. As many as 42 percent of them were in need of repair, three-fourths had no central heat, two-thirds were without bathrooms, and one-fifth had no private toilets. Only 330 of them were occupied at the time of the CSS survey, and most of those had vacancies. The 1940 Census found a residential vacancy rate of 20 percent. Of the people still

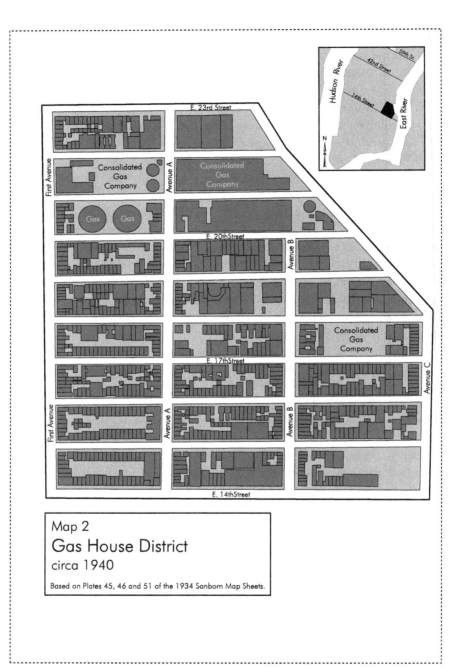

Map 2
Gas House District
circa 1940

Based on Plates 45, 46 and 51 of the 1934 Sanborn Map Sheets.

Maps 2 and 2a. The Gas House District and Stuyvesant Town

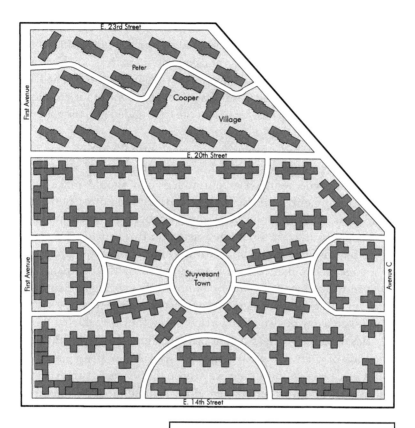

E. 23rd Street

Peter

First Avenue

Cooper

Village

E. 20th Street

First Avenue

Stuyvesant
Town

Avenue C

E. 14th Street

Map 2a
Stuyvesant Town
and
Peter Cooper Village
circa 1950

Based on Plates 45, 46 and 51 of the 1967 Sanborn Map Sheets.

living there, about 90 percent paid under $30 a month in rent, and the average rent per room was $5.90. During the New Deal, federal housing inspectors from the Home Owners Loan Corporation had given the area their lowest rating—"fourth grade" or "D"—thereby guaranteeing that it would get little mortgage support from banks. A "D" rating indicated that a neighborhood was no longer a "desirable" place to live and was a poor investment for mortgage lenders. There was no firm set of criteria for this grade, only a broad set of attributes to guide investigators, which identified poor housing conditions and nonhomogeneous or "undesirable" populations as an investment risk. Oddly, the area had not been included in the City Planning Commission's 1940 blueprint for rebuilding, but Moses made sure that a special session of the CPC added it to the rolls of slums fit only to be cleared.[26]

For some, this catalog of deprivation was cause for action, not romance. In a January 1945 photo essay, Met Life's supporters at the *World-Telegram* argued that the tenements were "outmoded" and should make way for a "modern development" to be built, they said, cribbing directly from a Metropolitan press release, "along lines almost suburban." Even nostalgia, the editors seemed to suggest, would be wasted on this squalor. This argument was made by way of visual comparison. Three photographs filled the top half of a page, accompanied by a map, supplied by the company, showing the stages in which tenants would be removed that spring and summer. The photos seem to be almost calculated to cast the district in the worst light possible. Taken a day or two after a heavy snow, they reveal what looks to be a nearly deserted and lifeless neighborhood. Plows had been through, and gray mounds of dirty snow envelop the curbs. A few people are here and there, and just two cars pick their way through the slushy streets. The tenements look dark and weather-stained, almost abandoned. The pictures make for a grim contrast to the simple efficiency of the map. It divides the blocks into three sections—one white, one cross-hatched, and one black—designating the orderly procession in which the area would be divested of the little life it seemed to have left. In the last of the three pictures, a young boy, bundled in coat, hat, woolens, and knickers, stands in the slush and piled snow in front of his stoop. He stands to the right, in the relative brightness of the snowy sidewalk, looking curious but immobilized, while the building looms from the left; dark window panes and sills topped with snow fill the frame. The eye immediately finds the boy in the right foreground, and then, equally, on the left, a clutch of topless, overflowing, upended garbage cans spilling out onto the sidewalk toward his feet. "Sights such as the above," the caption concludes about this parable of endangered childhood, "will not be seen in the ultra-modern Stuyvesant Town."[27]

2.2. This photograph was used in a *New York World-Telegram* photo essay that juxtaposed a map showing the schedule of demolition with scenes of wintry desolation. New York World-Telegram Photograph Collection, Library of Congress.

For Met Life, the official verdict was perhaps more clinical, but little different. The Gas House District, the company announced, had "slowly lapsed into obsolescence." Frederick Ecker told the Annual Conference of Mayors that the neighborhood was a "blighted, run-down, dilapidated area." Just like the UN planners, Met Life regularly invoked a seductive rhetoric of obsolescence to describe the area. Its appeal echoed long-standing alarm over the spread of "slums," but was largely shorn of the explicit moral concerns characteristic of housing reform. The Metropolitan avoided the messy specifics of life in the neighborhood and focused squarely on restoring economic value to the blighted land. Invoking what historian Alison Isenberg calls the "comforting inevitability of organic decline," the company gestured most forcefully to the bright future. It was quite prescient: by the 1950s, this argument would become the dominant mode of rhetorical persuasion for backers of urban renewal across the nation. And yet, despite the fact that Met Life labeled the Gas House District blighted, it strove by other means to show that it was simultaneously a social, and not merely an economic, problem. Just as the *World-Telegram* editors had called on an image of imperiled youth to bring home their message, the Metropolitan also used photography to argue for the beneficial social impact of its project.[28]

To the casual observer, it may have seemed that the Metropolitan took almost no interest in the fate of the Gas House District. The neighborhood appears as little more than an afterthought in official proclamations, but even as the company prepared to erase the district's actual buildings and streets from city maps, company officials took steps to preserve the district, or at least a two-dimensional facsimile of it. In fact, the Gas House District still exists today in one frozen, virtual form: a collection of photographs owned by Metropolitan Life. This ghostly archive is a careful visual account of every building, storefront, corner, vacant lot, sidewalk, and billboard in the 18 blocks bounded by First Avenue, 14th Street, 20th Street, and Avenue C as they looked in the spring and summer of 1943, just after Met Life announced that it would raze it all for Stuyvesant Town.[29]

The unknown photographer or photographers who made these images were after coverage, not art. For the most part, the images are a prosaic succession of streetscapes, shot head-on from the street or opposite sidewalk; some are turned at an angle to capture as much frontage as possible in one frame. They resemble both portraits and backdrops. Buildings appear as a long series of faces or as stages for lost and forgotten dramas. But largely missing are the players in these performances. People appear as afterthoughts, as blurry movement interrupting the stillness. Their lives or concerns are beside the point. The images do not make use of angles, light, or distance to reveal disjuncture, loss, or novelty. One by one, frame by frame, they seem to display only the facts of their contents. Similarly, the archive as a whole is like a visual ledger book. Within a few months after the city condemned the properties and the wreckers arrived, the company would own all of it. The photos operate like a visual analogue of that mastery, a record to equal and buttress those stored in the company's rent rolls, record books, and actuarial tables. The neighborhood is caught and held in the stasis the company and most of the public imagined for it; all possibility of change, save for its destruction, of course, permanently arrested by the camera's light transfer.

Because the images are artless and appear to be without agenda, they worked well as evidence of the neighborhood's decline. The company used individual images for selected publications and promotional materials, in order to contrast the old tenement neighborhood and the new towers to come. Like a latter-day Jacob Riis, the photographer also ventured off the streets, into the backyards and crumbling, largely abandoned rear tenements of the neighborhood to find trash-strewn yards, children playing in rubble and abandoned buildings, flapping laundry, and a bum sleeping it off in a doorway. Sometimes these images were sent out for public use, and they did more than the innocuous streetscapes to naturalize the inevitable logic of Met Life's benevolent intervention. For

2.3. In 1943, Metropolitan made a photographic record of every block in the Stuyvesant Town clearance site. Along 15th Street, the camera caught a series of rowhouses and a patriotic banner saluting the neighborhood "boys" serving in World War II. © 2009 Metropolitan Life Insurance Company. All rights reserved.

instance, one of these photos of a tenement backyard was given the caption "A dirty and unsightly tangle of tenements," on a page titled "Time moves on and a city grows," in a promotional booklet distributed to Stuyvesant Town residents. It assured readers that, as the booklet said, "possessed of few of the assets which modern housing standards require, the neighborhood slowly settled into obsolescence."[30] Embedded in the rhetoric of inevitable progress, these photos spoke volumes about the social improvements Met Life promised to bring to the city. The Gas House District, the photos assured viewers, should and would inevitably give way to the ordered world of Stuyvesant Town.

2.4. Corner of 16th Street and Avenue B, 1943. © 2009 Metropolitan Life Insurance Company. All rights reserved.

However, had people been allowed to view Metropolitan's entire collection, they'd have seen a record of the neighborhood's lingering vitality, not merely its arrested development. The photos do confirm A. L. Kirkpatrick's vision from the tower and the numbers in the 1940 Census: the streets, while not deserted, have a lonely feel; there are few cars; and pushcart vendors and horse-drawn wagons are not uncommon. Still, the neighborhood is not dead. The six or seven blocks in the northeastern corner, those with the highest concentration of small industrial

2.5. Rear of buildings on First Avenue and 402 E. 16th Street. © 2009 Metropolitan Life Insurance Company. All rights reserved.

shops, car yards, and abandoned lots, have a desolate feel to them, but the businesses are largely functioning and active. The other two-thirds of the neighborhood may not be bustling, but much of it looks almost prosperous. Many of the four- and five-story tenements that line the streets look kept up, as do other odd, older houses mixed in. There are at least two theaters, a Murrays five-and-dime chain store, numerous ornate churches, and two schools. Billboards advertise

2.6. Front of rear building on Avenue A. This image, intended to reveal the Gas House District's physical obsolescence and social ills, echoes the visual vocabulary of several generations of housing reform images dating back to the late nineteenth century.

war loans; American flags hang from fire escapes; many families have service stars in their windows; and the camera catches the bottom half of a banner strung across 15th Street: "God Bless Our Boys."

In fact, the Metropolitan's photos reveal that not everyone found the neighborhood to be outmoded. On the corner of 15th Street and First Avenue, the photographer caught a man bent at the knee, examining a sign in the window of Williams Furniture Shop. "Tenants, Owners, Business Men," reads a notice from the Peter Stuyvesant Landowners Group, "Do you want to stay in your neighborhood? Go to the public hearing against Metropolitan." Hanging next to it is a clipping from the May 27, 1943, issue of the news magazine *PM*, headlined "Shocked Experts Call for Brakes on Fantastic 'Met Life' Housing."[31] A day later, *PM* ran its own photo essay surveying the neighborhood, entitled "The Vanishing Scene of Old New York: These Must Give Way when 'Walled City' Moves In." Rather than finding images of squalor, it countered the *World-Telegram* and Met Life's brash vision of progress with depictions of neighborhood institutions soon to be lost. There was a 75-year-old bar at 18th and C whose owner stood in the doorway looking solemnly into the camera, and a small church, St. Mary

Magdalene, built in 1873. There was the "village blacksmith," Bernard Clark, who testified, "I love the District," beneath a picture of himself in a black tank top at his anvil. He had lived there 40 years and wanted to move somewhere nearby when the project arrived. Contradicting the headline and reducing the impact of the montage, the largest picture was not of the Gas House District at all, but of the "non-fireproof" school somewhere nearby that would have to make up for the lack of a school in Stuyvesant Town. Poking above the building, dead center in the frame, was the Met Life tower's campanile. Not much for subtlety, *PM* directed its readers to "Note Metropolitan's tower looming in background," despite the fact that the company posed no threat to the actual street and buildings in the image.[32]

Indeed, many Gas House District residents were not willing to accept the official story about their neighborhood. Some reporters who fanned out into the district found a living neighborhood. Like Clark the blacksmith, residents viewed the place with simple affection, despite poverty and a declining population. The neighborhood was the setting for the great events of ordinary life and had become as precious to them as the people with whom they had shared their lives. "My husband died here," lamented Mrs. Concetta Tornabene to a *Herald Tribune* reporter, "and I want to die here too." "It hurts when you pass by and see it," another woman said of the ruins left in the wake of the early demolition, "like a knife stabbing your heart."

Stuyvesant Town was set to intrude upon a complex social world, one characterized by sophisticated and cosmopolitan familial arrangements. For instance, Mary Kenney, a 59-year-old Irishwoman who worked as a matron on Welfare Island, lived across the hall from Vito Cali, an Italian widower. They each had a four-room, cold-water flat with a common toilet in the hallway. But despite the neighborhood's supposed "clanishness," the doors were always open, and Mary Kenney considered Cali's three sons and one daughter her own children. "I only hope we can stay here 'til our son comes back," she said, referring to Vito Jr., who was a mechanic with the U.S. Army Air Force in India.[33]

Those sorts of cross-ethnic liaisons and improvisatory rearrangements of gender norms and family structure reflected not only wartime upheaval, but also strategies of sociability for getting by that were peculiar to working-class neighborhoods. Stuyvesant Town would uproot such long-established patterns, habits, and community networks. For instance, the Tarantinos, Lafiandras, and Alleluias, family groups headed by two sisters and a brother from Naples, had met the Raposkys, a Lithuanian family, in 280 Avenue A, a building within Stuyvesant Town's footprint. Rather than be separated, they decided to move together to the best place they could find: a dilapidated five-story house on East 27th Street. Mrs. Angelina Tarantino reported that nobody liked it there. They

Vanishing Scene of Old New York:

hese Must Give Way When 'Walled City' Moves In

Clark has been "village black-
in the Gas House District for
years. He'll move—but not very
cause "I love the District."

This 88-year-old non-fireproof school is one of the schools in the "undeveloped" areas around the proposed Metropolitan Life Insurance Co. "walled city" which will have to absorb children from the project. This is PS 50, built in 1855.
(Note Metropolitan's tower looming in background).

This bar has served the Gas House District for 75 years. It stands on the corner
of 18th St. and Ave. C, but will be torn down. Owner is Matthew Clark.

Church of St. Mary Magdalen, built in 1873 and rebuilt in 1934, will be torn
down. There will be no churches in Stuyvesant Town.

2.7. The left-wing daily *PM* offered a different view, which highlighted the loss of a
particular neighborhood character. Not much for subtlety, the photographer placed the
Met Life office tower front and center in the upper right image, and the editors reminded
the viewer to "Note Metropolitan tower looming in background." "These Must Give Way
When 'Walled City' Moves In," *PM*, May 28, 1943.

couldn't get water in the top-floor toilet or sink, and she had to come downstairs to her sister's apartment to wash her face. But it wasn't just the bad conditions in the new place; they were sorry to have left the Gas House District behind. This street and neighborhood, she said, were "too dead." Many of their neighborhood friends were now scattered across the city. Nunzio, her 12-year-old nephew, remarked, "Over there we knew everyone on three blocks; we played baseball together. Now most of us go to different schools." They had to go to a new church now too, but Mrs. Tarantino couldn't get used to the stores in her new neighborhood. She still took the bus down First Avenue to her old 10th Street market.[34]

There were those, mostly the young, who praised the decision. One of the Tornabenes' neighbors, Anthony Rotundo, thought it "a damn good thing. . . . It's the only way we'll ever get out of this place." Some others accepted it with grim resignation and vowed to move without help, despite the fact that everyone they knew seemed to be having trouble finding new apartments. On the whole, though, the CSS social workers found that the most common feeling was "open resentment against the Stuyvesant Town project and their necessity to move." Even those who thought the district should be improved were incensed that their homes and businesses would be destroyed "so that richer people can move in." "Stuyvesant Town is not for working people like us," said one resident. It was all about "putting the poor people out," said another. Met Life threatened informal economic and social interconnections built over time, such as landlords who cut long-standing tenants slack on the rent in difficult times and older people who depended on neighbors' help for day-to-day tasks. The "whole neighborhood," one woman reported, came to console her when she heard the news that her son had died in battle. Residents, the social workers concluded, felt "a tenacious attachment to the neighborhood and a sense of belonging together, a feeling of solidarity which made them in fact a real community."[35]

"I was amazed to hear that the City of New York has declared the area . . . substandard and unsanitary and a slum," said Mary Murray, a landlord in the district. She and other property owners filed suit against the city to stop condemnation, but the state supreme court turned it back in December 1943. Meanwhile, the Stuyvesant Tenants League, a local affiliate of the citywide United Tenants League (UTL), began to organize for the residents' rights. The UTL, like most liberal and leftist groups, supported slum clearance and even private-led urban redevelopment as both part of the domestic front of the war and "essential to meet our postwar needs." It hoped that Met Life would simply go slower and make adequate provisions for displaced tenants. The group held a series of meetings, passed resolutions, and lobbied La Guardia to support a bill delaying removals until six months after the war. Barring that, they tried to make the exodus of Gas House District residents as painless as possible, discouraging militancy among the tenants and settling for assurances from La Guardia that displaced tenants could find homes in public housing. Former area congressman Jim Fay made more noise than the entire tenants league, comparing the Metropolitan to the "Gestapo" and the removals to events in Nazi Germany. He also intervened with the company on behalf of some individual tenants, but was not able to slow or halt the plans. In the end, most of the potential organized tenant opposition believed that the benefits of Stuyvesant Town outweighed the survival of the Gas House District as a community. Hamstrung by their long-term political allegiances, tenant groups sacrificed the neighborhood for the promise of new low-income housing to come with redevelopment.[36]

The people of the Gas House District were left with few options. Their complaints registered as isolated voices; they appeared as unfortunate casualties of progress rather than as representatives of an alternative urban vision. They were unable to show how relocation, demolition, and clearance knocked down more than investment-killing housing stock, how it leveled the little-understood horizontal relations of kinship, friendship, and commerce that come to characterize a neighborhood over time. These affiliations—the building blocks of just such an urban vision—would go all but unnoticed until the years after the 1949 Housing Act. In the short run, widespread support for urban redevelopment cleared the way for Met Life to act.

During 1943 and 1944, *Fortune* reported, Met Life "had quietly bought up certain parcels" of land in the Gas House District "through intermediaries" in order to establish "reasonable condemnation values." It was often able to get properties and mortgages for below market value, and by November 1943 the company owned 117 parcels in the neighborhood. In one mass purchase on May 8, 1944, the Stuyvesant Town Corporation took title to 135 properties. Little by little, the company bought additional individual parcels and properties. When the city condemned the entire 18-block area late that year, Met Life took control of the entire site and began to collect rents from its new tenants.[37]

The 1942 Redevelopment Companies Law did not require Metropolitan to make provisions for rehousing tenants, but the company accepted the responsibility of doing so. Careful to avoid a public relations disaster, Met Life assured the city government, the public, and the tenants of the Gas House District that nobody would be forcibly evicted and that new homes would be found for all. The company hoped that "gradual clearance of the area" could happen "with a minimum of hardship and discomfort." With that in mind, the company opened a Tenant Relocation Bureau on 14th Street headed by realtor James Felt. The bureau gathered vacancy information, kept apartment listings, inspected vacant apartments, interviewed tenants about their housing needs in their native languages, and took people around in a station wagon to see prospective apartments. Dividing the area into three sections, each of which had a moving deadline, the bureau offered a rebate of one month's rent for those tenants who met the deadlines for their area. The process began in mid-January 1945, when Met Life sent out notices to residents telling them that their neighborhood was slated for demolition.[38]

Interviewed tenants reported that it was hard to find apartments by themselves. Many said they had no time or energy to look. Fathers worked, mothers had children to care for, and many sons and husbands were away in the armed forces. Others were willing to move, but only if it would boost their station in life. One mother who paid $26 a month for a four-room, cold-water flat could pay up to $35 a month, but wanted heat and a private bath for her two children and her husband, who was away working on the Alcan Highway: "We don't want to move if we just go into another cold-water house with no bath of our own." Still, by March 15, about 550 people had managed to leave the area. Felt had registered 1,885 tenants out of the roughly 3,000 families and 11,000 individuals on the site. He had 8,207 vacancy listings, but fewer than 6,000 were viable options because about 2,400 had only cold water, no private toilet, or both. By October, he had listed 14,249 apartments and registered 2,322 families. Met Life encouraged recalcitrant tenants to move by serving them with dispossession proceedings and then eviction notices. None were actually evicted though, and by November 1945 only 77 families remained.[39]

This official account obscured a more complicated reality. In late 1944, a city survey found that there were 683 vacant apartments with heat on the Lower East Side, and 1,204 families on the Stuyvesant Town site with heat. There were about 2,000 vacancies without central heat. The report therefore suggested that one-third of the tenants would have to move to the West Side between Chelsea and Columbus Circle or above 23rd Street on the East Side. Robert Moses was livid at the idea that the city might force many tenants to move to the West Side slums or to nearby substandard housing, no matter "what kind of cold-water rat traps many of these people are living in at present." Such a suggestion would be "positively harmful if it became public," Moses warned. Instead, he forced a law through the state legislature providing tax exemption for the rehabilitation of substandard apartments, hoping that enough landlords would take advantage of the subsidy to provide those whom Stuyvesant Town displaced with adequate housing. Rehabilitation, however, proved to be a false hope. Wartime prices were far too high for landlords to make improvements and still keep rents affordable. Not a single apartment, James Felt observed in early 1946, was made available under the terms of the law in all of 1945.[40]

The June 1945 CSS study determined that no more than 3 percent of the 3,000 Gas House District families would be able to afford Stuyvesant Town, and only about 22 percent would be eligible for public housing. About 2,250 families had incomes that were too high for public housing but too low for Stuyvesant Town. They would have to do exactly what Moses feared or leave Manhattan. For instance, John Russon, the manager of a roofing company, had lived in the neighborhood all his life. Fourteen dollars a room in Stuyvesant Town, he told a *Post* reporter, was "no break for the people living around here." Rents were "$6 to $7 a room." The CSS study found that 59 percent hoped to stay nearby. Hard statistics were never released, but in the end, Felt estimated, most of the families moved to the surrounding neighborhoods of the Lower and Middle East sides. Some found their way to the East 50s and 60s, and many went to Brooklyn or the Bronx. Few would move to the West Side; it was considered a step down from the Gas House District. Ultimately, the tenant bureau thought the effort a success. Felt believed that residents who had acted quickly and moved before July—about 2,000 families—had on the whole been able to find better accommodations than those they had left. But nobody could say for sure what effect all those new residents would have on the surrounding neighborhood. Felt was well aware that, "by forcing people from one slum area into another, the basic ills of most urban low-rent housing will merely be shifted to a different location." With perhaps

2.8. The remains of the Gas House District during clearance for Stuyvesant Town in 1945. Observers often likened clearance sites to images they had seen of bombed cities during World War II, which had ended only months earlier. New York World-Telegram Photograph Collection, Library of Congress.

7,500 people squeezing into the tenements of the already ailing Lower East Side during a severe housing shortage, Edwin S. Burdell of the CSS remarked, the Stuyvesant Town relocation was not "slum clearance" but "slum displacement." Felt's doubts about the efficacy of clearance policies would only grow over the next decade, and by the mid-1950s, as a city planning commissioner, he would lead efforts to reform urban renewal.[41] Meanwhile, in the fall of 1945, demolition of the Gas House District got under way. By June 1946, Met Life was taking applications for apartments, and by the next summer the first families had moved into the first building. Of course, the journey from drawing board to construction site to move-in day was not so simple or so smooth. Stuyvesant Town sparked a firestorm of controversy, but the clamor over the loss of the Gas House District was only a brushfire among the larger conflagration. The most immediate and long-lasting struggles were joined over the social shape of the project itself, not the supposedly outmoded world it had replaced.

Suburb in the City or Medieval Walled Town? The Design of the Business Welfare State

Jeeps will be harnessed to the plow; London and Coventry will be rebuilt with slums eliminated. In these practical ways the better world that is in the making takes form; and New York City is peering ahead to plan a post-war city and ascertain the place private capital will have in its building. . . . Unpolitical private enterprise for the common good—*that* can go far in saving our post-war economy.
—"Housing without Strings," *America* magazine, May 1943

Both novel and controversial, Stuyvesant Town attracted global attention and intense interest around the United States. The notices began the day after La Guardia's radio announcement and continued while the Gas House District was cleared and Stuyvesant Town built and occupied. The vast bulk were favorable, commending New York and the Metropolitan's efforts. Some outlets, like the *New York World-Telegram,* were downright boosterish in their praise. "Stuyvesant Town: Where Hard Heads Made Dream True," blared one of the paper's headlines, which was followed by an equally grandiose subhead: "Giant Housing Project Which Wiped Out Slum a Masterpiece of Capital." Others were more measured, picking up on the widespread hope of "re-centralization" and observing that the project represented "one of the coming methods for putting human as well as financial values back into city areas."[42]

It is hard now to recall the downright eventfulness of Stuyvesant Town's arrival on the Lower East Side. The "best known housing project in the nation"—as one radio commentator had it—the complex was eminently visible, appearing on tourist maps and in books, magazines, and newspapers all over the world.

Time magazine, outlining what might happen if a Soviet bomber dropped its solitary nuclear payload over Manhattan at Union Square, made sure to mention that among other "obliterated" landmarks "struck by a giant fist" would be "the teeming cliff dwellings of Peter Cooper Village and Stuyvesant Town." The *Herald Tribune,* reporting on a high-altitude, transcontinental, Air Force photo reconnaissance mapping mission, even noticed that "from eight miles up" Stuyvesant Town was Manhattan's most noticeable feature, standing out in the dark sooty jumble as a chunk of bright new construction along the island's right flank. Stuyvesant Town made headlines because it represented more than just new housing or a wise investment; it became a symbol of the postwar world to come, standing for the promise of a new, modern, more humane way to live in cities that would transform old, seemingly outmoded nineteenth-century urban space. It represented one of the first tangible rewards of the war effort, a political, economic, social, and aesthetic symbol of what the United States was fighting for in the war. And it was also a step forward, out of war and into peace, out of old troubles and into new prosperity.[43]

Closer to the ground, however, Stuyvesant Town provoked as much controversy as awe. Announcement of the plans in 1943 touched off an interlocking set of controversies whose fire would not abate until the mid-1950s. A diverse group of interests offered significant challenges to Met Life's plans. Architects and planners found fault with the design. Housing reformers and liberal civic groups lined up at a series of municipal hearings to condemn the project for its density, the lack of a school, and inadequate community facilities. African Americans and their white allies in civil rights groups and left-wing unions, some of whom were activists with the Communist-influenced American Labor Party, led a decade's worth of sustained attacks on Met Life's policy of racial segregation.

The battles over Stuyvesant Town were so bitter and long lasting in large part because they were a kind of civil war among like-minded partisans. A confusing array of organizations and constituencies dogged Stuyvesant Town's progress through three court cases, several municipal hearings, and its construction and occupancy. Still, almost everyone involved on both sides—from Robert Moses to the Citizens Housing Council to the tenant leagues—agreed that Manhattan needed slum clearance and new housing. In the long run, this basic agreement ensured that Stuyvesant Town would weather these storms relatively untouched. The most powerful of its critics—liberal civic groups, housing reformers, and a few city officials—formed a kind of "go-slow" opposition looking to amend the project on a handful of issues. But they were not willing to halt the progress of clearance and new housing construction.

Still, Stuyvesant Town caught them by surprise. The Metropolitan's benevolent intervention in the Gas House District provided them with the first glimpse of urban renewal's linked promise and peril. On the one hand, it was an unprecedented attempt to better the lives of city-dwellers, but on the other, it revealed both the overwhelming nature of the ethic of city building's potential physical and social impact on the old cityscape and its economic transformation into urban redevelopment—a publicly subsidized campaign to build private housing and amenities for the middle class.

Stuyvesant Town's critics challenged its immediate impact on the urban fabric and its larger economic and political implications. They rejected Met Life's description of the project as a "suburb in the city" and embraced City Council member Stanley Isaacs's rejoinder: "medieval walled town" was more like it. At the same time, they were stunned by the efficiency with which Moses had laid the groundwork for public/private redevelopment policy. On this score, they claimed that Stuyvesant Town was the first step toward, in housing reformer Charles Abrams's phrase, a "business welfare state." Public/private cooperation in the Stuyvesant Town mold was a smokescreen, they charged, for public subsidy of private profit. The project, Abrams wrote, was "a spearhead for the effort to shift governmental powers from the public to the private domain." It was cut from the same cloth, he felt, as the New Deal's Federal Housing Administration and the Home Owners Loan Corporation, which underwrote not only private profit at the expense of cities, but racial discrimination as well. Stuyvesant Town, he thought, would do to downtown the same thing that FHA and HOLC policies did in the suburbs.[44]

As Stuyvesant Town's critics groped to understand the project, it became increasingly clear to them that its social and urban shape was intimately linked to its innovations in political economy. Stuyvesant Town's massive intervention in the cityscape—as well as the uninspired architecture, congestion, class and ethnic divisions, and racial segregation they feared would come with it—was a necessary precondition for attracting Met Life's investment. The social vision of the project—massive superblocks to offset the rot of slums—was also the economic measure by which Met Life intended to protect its investment. For the project's critics, the built representation of a "business welfare state" was a "walled town" in the heart of the metropolis.

Abrams, Isaacs, and company had at least one thing right: Stuyvesant Town was an overwhelming intervention in a neighborhood of 5- and 6-story tenements. On the 18 city blocks that the city reclaimed for Met Life, the company built a 61-acre superblock development with 35 12- and 13-story buildings. The buildings covered 25 percent of the land (down from 69.3 percent in the Gas House District), leaving the rest for lawns, pathways, and playgrounds. There were 8,755 apartments—one-, two-, and three-bedroom models—housing just over 24,000 people by 1949. The apartments were of three, four, five, and seven rooms, making for 4,535 one-bedrooms, 3,729 two-bedrooms, 452 three-bedrooms, and 39 five-bedrooms—a fact that troubled those who wondered how many families with more than one child would fit into the project. There were six underground parking garages for 1,500 cars and off-street parking for another 400 cars. At street level on 14th Street, 20th Street, and First Avenue, the project featured 1,000 feet of retail space.[45]

Met Life assembled a Board of Design, led by the Empire State Building designer, Richmond Shreve, and his chief architect, Irwin Clavan, to plan Stuyvesant Town. The board delivered a no-frills design, directly inherited from the New York City Housing Authority's "red-brick modernism." Stuyvesant Town's interiors were considerably less spartan than public housing, but like many of NYCHA's New Deal era projects, the development was composed of simplified brick boxes, non-descript and unadorned at their base or roof line, with blank façades broken only by regular rows of single windows. Each building was composed of from one to five standardized core units—various groupings of crosses and L-shapes—that joined in a number of different combinations and footprints.

These units were arranged in an urban plan that, like the architecture itself, gestured toward the influence of sophisticated European modernism, but took its cues from New Deal era adaptations of continental innovations. True to its roots in the continental modern housing movement, each Stuyvesant Town unit was placed at least 60 feet from its nearest neighbor, and most apartments had multiple exposures to ensure healthful quantities of light and air. However, the plan took the open "tower in a park" form derived from European progressive ideals and rearranged the tower units in a symmetrical, ordered, and almost pastoral array that recalled the Beaux Arts landscaping traditions of the turn-of-the-century City Beautiful movement; it even included a ceremonial fountain. The hillocks, curving pathways, and playgrounds, however, tempered any tendency toward grandiosity and gave the project its somewhat superficial resemblance to a suburb in the city. The planners shrouded the project's forward-looking engineering in a romantic, naturalist plan. Something of an old-fashioned romantic next to its European precedents, Stuyvesant Town tried to mask its mass character with bucolic decoration. Like many of New York's pre-war public projects, Stuyvesant Town preserved an echo of the enclosed garden apartment tradition, striving for its own sense of internal harmony rather than stentorian Beaux Arts grandeur or modernist rationality. No doubt, this befitted a middle-class preserve in the midst of a working-class enclave; the order carved out of the nineteenth-century jumble served a nostalgic, comforting purpose, especially compared to the frank, pure, assuredly progressive yet impersonal modernism of the public housing towers built to house those relocated in the wake of later urban renewal projects.[46]

The historian Richard Plunz has suggested that the symmetrical array of buildings was less an aesthetic strategy than one of security, allowing for panoptic surveillance of the grounds. The security patrol booth just below the fountain appeared to command a view of the entire grounds, and on paper the project does radiate from this center point. But on the ground, with the tall buildings arranged around the oval and the hilly, almost pastoral landscaping, there was no commanding central point. Sight lines were continually blocked by the buildings themselves or by the generous contours of the project's carefully arranged hillocks and serpentine pathways. The Metropolitan's Board of Design, wrote Lewis Mumford, "contrived to accentuate the stereotyped character of these buildings by so placing them that one cannot anywhere find a vista that is not quickly blocked by thirteen stories of brick and glass." In Stuyvesant Town, one was more likely to feel lost than watched. Security guards patrolled its grounds, but the warren of building walls, pathways, entrances, and playgrounds seemed designed to enclose rather than expose. What was at first unnerving or confusing—and stories abound about early residents returning home to strangers' apartments in the look-alike towers—became comforting and protecting with a little experience negotiating the place.[47]

Of course, this was no mistake. That sense of comfort was provided by the project's size. Its bulk ensured isolation from the outside streets it was designed to replace. With its 35 13-story brick towers arranged on a superblock, the development's sheer mass contained and protected the relaxed flow of its green space. Early in its life, the project seemed stark and empty; the towers shot straight and squat out of the mud and grass and seemed to blot out the stunted landscaping. Over the years, however, as its trees have grown to mature size and enveloped the buildings, Stuyvesant Town has become less, not more open, and the foliage and façades have joined to form a series of interconnected, dappled, and protected grottoes. It has a lulling, not unpleasant, enveloped air. Many residents down through the years have remarked that it feels like an "oasis" removed from the rest of the city.

Stuyvesant Town's combination of nostalgia and modernism provoked contradictory responses from planners, architects, and urbanists. Seeing the plans just weeks after they were released, architect William Lescaze commented to the editors of the *New York Sun* that "here the statistics dictated the design, and not the experts." He was an avid modernist, but felt that "where boldness was required we got timidity. Where variations and rhythms were wanted we got regimentation and monotony." In the *New Yorker*, Lewis Mumford appreciated the "rhythms" Lescaze missed, finding them in the "handsome plantings" and the "pool of quiet green" at the center, but he regretted that these benefits were overwhelmed by the asphalt playgrounds, increased congestion, and "inhuman scale of the architecture."

2.9. This 1951 photograph shows how Stuyvesant Town's landscaping gave the project an enclosing, protective feel designed to mimic the pastoral landscape of middle-class suburbia. Gottscho-Schleisner Collection, Library of Congress.

Mumford was disturbed by the towers' lack of ornamentation, particularly when they came in such numbers. "Though the buildings are not a continuous unit," he wrote, "they present to the beholder an unbroken façade of brick, thirteen stories high, absolutely uniform in every detail, mechanically conceived and mechanically executed, with the word 'control' implicit in every aspect of the design." Met Life's benevolent intervention was nothing but grim oppression. Stuyvesant Town represented "the architecture of the Police State, embodying all the vices of regimentation one associates with state control at its unimaginative worst." His review was titled "Prefabricated Blight." For Mumford, Stuyvesant Town was ultimately little different from the neighborhood it had replaced. Inhuman design ensured eventual obsolescence.[48]

Mumford's dire review brought into sharp relief the first objection of many critics: the Stuyvesant Town plan created unwarranted population congestion. "Once the decision was made to house twenty-four thousand people on a site that should not be made to hold more than six thousand," Mumford suggested, "all the other faults followed automatically." Despite appearances, too many people were packed onto the project's acreage. Whether they were crowded into tenements or stacked in modern boxes, they lived at "slum densities."[49] Other architects, planners, and municipal officials had raised the alarm about density as well. Just before Stuyvesant Town went before the City Planning Commission for approval in the spring of 1943, 23 leading architects and planners sent the body a letter decrying "the fact that there are just too many people to use too little space" and calling the density "inhuman, anti-social and uneconomic." Commissioner Lawrence Orton, in his dissent to the commission's report, observed that the bulk of the buildings, measured by the floor area ratio, was almost double that of the allowable figure, despite the fact that the population density was within the commission's limits. This made for tall buildings and a "tight site plan," which would result in just what the planners and architects feared: a lack of sunlight, restricted recreational areas, and no space for essential features, most important a school and community facilities.[50]

That summer, the Citizens Housing Council (CHC), the liberal reform group that led the go-slow opposition, prepared a full report on Stuyvesant Town. It demonstrated that, even in terms of population, the project would have unlawful, not to mention unacceptable, congestion. By including the interior street areas in its calculations, Met Life had reached a figure of 397 persons per acre, which was far too high, but below the legal threshold of 416 per acre that the City Planning Commission had established for the project. With the street areas left out, the figure jumped to 594 persons an acre—a more accurate, and alarming, representation of the amount of people grouped on the site. As Stanley Isaacs noted, this was at least 170 people per acre more than any public or private project yet built.[51]

Moses and Met Life responded to these criticisms by reminding the public and city officials that the population of the area had been steadily declining. Moses assured readers of the *New Yorker* that, with the postwar housing shortage, the area would have returned to its older population levels. At least now, he said, the 24,000 residents of the area had decent, roomy apartments with "sunlight and air." The company was dealing with expensive slum land, and while it would rather build smaller, it had to recoup its investment. The project had rooms one and a half times the size of those of any public project, Moses lectured the critics, and a slum had been cleared.[52]

Stuyvesant Town's critics also objected to the relationship the project's design appeared to invite with the surrounding neighborhood. They were concerned that Stuyvesant Town's 12- and 13-story towers turned their backs to First Avenue and 14th Street, forming a blank, uninviting wall to passersby and a looming, alien presence in an area of 4- and 5-story tenements and storefronts. The CHC, for instance, noted in its study that the project's bulk threatened to overwhelm the neighborhood. Its buildings, parking garages, and commercial space, the CHC observed, "combine to form an enclosure completely obstructing the public view of the project except for partial glimpses at the eight entrances, each of which is to be marked 'private street.'" For the CHC reformers, Stuyvesant Town seemed designed not to keep its people in, like a panoptic prison, but to keep other people out, some of whom would have been displaced to make way for the project in the first place.[53]

The idea that Stuyvesant Town was a walled town gained significant currency among the go-slow opposition. Architects, planners, social workers, the CIO, civil libertarians, and civil rights activists all latched onto Stanley Isaacs's phrase. The architect Henry Churchill wrote to *Architectural Forum* to complain that Stuyvesant Town was a "walled city, a medieval enclave" whose "13-story structures" made "an almost solid wall" designed to "prevent a view of the great interior park." The CIO Council of New York picked up on the same objection, urging its 500,000 members to oppose the project and joining the CHC in appealing to Mayor La Guardia to slow the process of municipal approval. Met Life's suburb in the city was not benevolent and forward-looking, the opposition claimed; it was instead a return to a divisive and best-forgotten spatial arrangement wholly out of place in a democratic city. Stuyvesant Town was not an icon

2.10. The Citizens Housing Council's critique of Stuyvesant Town stressed the way that the development walled itself off from the surrounding city physically, socially, and mentally. Citizens Housing Council, *CHC Housing News*, June–July 1943, Marian Sameth Archival Library, Citizens Housing and Planning Council.

of progress or modernity, they implied, but an evocation of feudalism. That the metaphor did not play out entirely was of little consequence to the protestors; it was an effective way of demonstrating that, if Stuyvesant Town represented something new, it was not progress, but a new way of reinforcing divisions and inequality in the cityscape. The image of a walled town provided a symbol for their take on Stuyvesant Town's social and economic impact. It offered a way to understand the visible immensity of the project's physical plan, one that suggested that Stuyvesant Town secured its "suburban" air by sealing itself off from and perpetuating the supposed disorder beyond its walls.[54]

Whether the metaphor worked or not, the critique struck home because it offered a partisan reinterpretation of Met Life's economic and social aims. After all, as *Fortune* magazine reported in 1946, the Metropolitan had a "recipe for safe-investment housing." This recipe was in large part a rudimentary adaptation of modern city-rebuilding ideals. "The best protection against obsolescence," Frederick Ecker told the Annual Conference of Mayors in 1948, "is light and air." Stuyvesant Town preserved the urban population densities required by the high cost of land, but provided light and air by reducing the coverage of buildings on the land, setting them far apart, and building straight up. "Doubling the height of the buildings," he said, "will permit the housing of the same population and leave half of the area free for landscaping and recreation." Interchangeability of fixtures and standardized floor plans, parts, and appliances saved further money and made it simpler to do repairs and upkeep on a mass scale. For the Metropolitan, the development's modern design was not only a social good, but a wise fiscal investment.[55]

Preventing obsolescence required not only proper site planning and architecture, but an overwhelming intervention in the cityscape. The project had to be large enough to be its own community. Stuyvesant Town, one sympathetic journalist wrote, "was made so large that it would create its own social and economic climate."[56] Large-scale development—planning not in terms of individual houses or streets but in terms of neighborhood-size chunks of cityscape—had been an ideal since the early part of the century. "Piecemeal" rehabilitation of slums or blighted areas was doomed for failure, planners argued, because a single good building or street would never constitute enough of a beachhead to attract further rehabilitation or renewal. This ideal had remained only a vision until the 1930s, when slum clearance came into its own; now, after the war, Met Life was uniting slum clearance and neighborhood-scale intervention in the name of private sector urban redevelopment.[57] In order to offset the spread of blight, large-scale development had to intervene in and disrupt the gridiron of the city streets. In order, in Ecker's own words, to "be planned on a scale sufficient in size to create and to conserve its own environment," Stuyvesant Town had to be on the largest urban superblock yet planned, isolated from the street grid it interrupted. Trading the "super-block for slums," as New York comptroller Joseph McGoldrick put it, would insulate Stuyvesant Town from the remaining slums it had obliterated and prevent the project from lapsing into the obsolescence Lewis Mumford predicted for it.[58]

Some of Met Life's critics saw this merging of social and economic aims as little more than a naked land grab. "The density, bulk and site arrangement" of Stuyvesant Town, wrote the architect Simon Breines, "stem not so much from functional and social reasons as from considerations of economics." The project's design, in Breines's mind, was intended solely to serve Met Life's investment. But as reductive as it was when he claimed that "the outstanding feature of Stuyvesant Town, the 'medieval' wall itself, is part of the deep compulsion to protect the investment," Breines had hit on a truth about what he called "the relationship between architecture and the social premises it serves." If Stuyvesant Town's design and social ideals were, as Ecker demonstrated, intended to shore up its economic fortunes, the opposite was true as well: the Metropolitan's need to protect its investment through public works was its social and cultural ideal.[59]

In the end, the controversy over the project revealed that the social and economic aims of this new form for city remaking were deeply entangled. Whether

2.11. This view of the completed project, from the southeast, demonstrates the unprecedented innovation of Met Life's intervention in the old cityscape and the immensity of the project in comparison with the city around it. By Thomas Airviews, in the Collection of the New-York Historical Society.

one thought of Stuyvesant Town's design as beneficial and attractive or regimented and exclusive, it was pioneering a new form for the social and economic restructuring of the postwar city. The images of the "walled town" and the "suburb in the city" were symbolic positions, partisan engagements with the implicit social objectives of Stuyvesant Town's urban intervention and economic innovation. They were attitudes taken toward the built form of Ecker's and Moses's real undertaking: founding a public/private arrangement with which to remake the city for middle-class residents and transform the ethic of city rebuilding into the policy of urban redevelopment.

This public/private compact led Met Life's critics to contend that Stuyvesant Town would have a more pronounced effect than anyone had yet imagined. "The shadow-boxing about the merits of Stuyvesant Town as a piece of architecture has only obscured the main issue," wrote Charles Abrams about the semi-public feud between Robert Moses and Lewis Mumford over Mumford's *New Yorker* review. "If Stuyvesant Town were an architectural dream-town," continued Abrams, "it would still be a financial nightmare, an unforgivable imposition on NYC's taxpayers." For Abrams, an activist lawyer and housing expert, the campaign to amend Stuyvesant Town was an opportunity to name the set of political and economic arrangements that made this new urban policy possible. For Abrams, the danger of this "walled city" was its subsidy by public monies and powers. He viewed the catalog of incentives that the Metropolitan received as a public investment in private gain, a subsidy for inequality and racial discrimination.[60]

Abrams and other critics did not fear private power. They lamented the fact that public power was being put in private hands without even the pretense of the safeguards and restraints that were intended to hold public power accountable to standards of justice and equality. Freedom, Abrams maintained, survived not only because of the separation of powers, but because of the separation of government and business. Of course, these sorts of public/private arrangements had long propelled the American economy, and the most pervasive example of this compact—federal subsidies for suburban homeownership—was getting under way even as Abrams wrote. Still, Abrams was sensing the emergence of a new tendency in an old pattern. As the country turned from fighting a war to preserving domestic prosperity, the New Deal welfare state was being transformed into a "pro-growth" regime in which public subsidies for private efforts became the primary method of carrying out social goals. Supporters of this compact saw it as the most efficient way for a democratic, capitalist society to compete with the social provisions offered by European social democracy and Soviet Communism. Abrams and other critics thought that it put democracy at the mercy of capitalism. New Deal social welfare provisions, they maintained, had been intended to increase individual and collective freedoms in an age of corporate capitalism by guaranteeing economic self-sufficiency for a wider spectrum of citizens. But in a new, emerging "business welfare state," Abrams explained, the "government is being called upon to pump the funds authorized under the newly expanded welfare programs into certain private pipe-lines." Business beneficiaries of these new revenue streams expected to retain "the same immunity from regulation they enjoyed before they drew upon the government's purse and the government's powers." They insisted, in other words, on the freedom to act privately with public legitimacy. Thus, the business welfare state eroded the "insulation" between government and business, and allowed urban redevelopment—and other public/private schemes—to become a way for private enterprise to avoid maintaining equality under the law.[61]

Ultimately, it was "Stuyvesant Town the precedent, rather than Stuyvesant Town the project," Abrams wrote, "that loom[ed] so large as a threat to the American way of life." Met Life's suburban intervention in the Gas House District may have been as benevolent as its public relations literature boasted, but it was the form that intervention took that disturbed Abrams and the go-slow opposition. Of course, in the years to come, this public/private form would be among urban renewal's most attractive qualities for American city officials and planners. Not only did it give them a policy tool with which to steer capital back downtown, but with the onset of the Cold War—just dawning as Abrams penned his critiques—it gave them a market-friendly alternative to European social democratic and Soviet Communist city-remaking models.[62]

Abrams may have ridiculed the idea that the Stuyvesant Town controversy was about mere "architecture," but the complex did give the business welfare state an innovative physical shape and urban plan. Indeed, the large-scale urban intervention Ecker and Moses required relied on this emergent economic and political arrangement, and the opposition warned that this policy underpinned a newly divisive urban form. With the image of the "walled town," Stuyvesant Town's critics offered an early, embryonic preview of the revolt against urban renewal, objecting to the divisions of race and class it would institute on the Lower East Side. Such skepticism would be renewed in the years after 1949, when the federal government gave its imprimatur to the urban policy and planning forms pioneered by Met Life at Stuyvesant Town. Meanwhile, the most tangible impact of this new urban policy and form would be felt in the social and cultural experience of the new space. Conflicts over who could inhabit whites-only Stuyvesant Town and how those inhabitants adapted to their new home gave the initial critiques new emphases. When unease about the character of project life joined a sense of newfound value for whom and what had been displaced and lost in the tide of clearance and rebuilding, the lineaments of the revolt against urban renewal would be fully elaborated.

Despite all the controversy over its urban plan and its political economy, there was unprecedented demand for Stuyvesant Town apartments, particularly during the immediate postwar housing shortage. Bad as the shortage was nationwide—one estimate put the deficit at 3.2 million units—it was particularly acute in New York. The 1950 Census found that only eight-tenths of 1 percent of the city housing stock was available for rent; New York, one analysis estimated, needed 430,000 housing units. It was the worst shortage in the city's recorded history. Met Life was deluged with applicants: 325 letters arrived on the very day in June 1946 that the first rental ads appeared in the morning and evening newspapers; there were 7,000 only a day later. Most were from veterans, to whom the company had announced it would give preference. The letters, Met Life observed, painted "a picture of acute and stark distress." The Metropolitan's correspondents, many of them veterans, complained of living with parents and in-laws, squeezing their young families into studio apartments, delaying their marriages, sleeping in living rooms, and facing eviction. For thousands of war-torn home seekers, Stuyvesant Town represented the means by which they would be delivered from the strife and instability of the war years. One native of the Gas House District tried to parlay his emotional ties to the old homestead into a convincing pitch for an apartment in the new development, writing, "while I shed a furtive tear when I saw the pile I had the consolation to know that a thing of beauty will rise in its place."[63]

But this "thing of beauty" remained only a picture in people's minds, little more than a set of plans and an idea of the future. At first, Stuyvesant Town seemed to offer only a blank slate given vague social shape by the fact of the Metropolitan's enlightened stewardship—a vertical relationship of private, paternal, reputedly munificent authority slated to replace the Gas House District's horizontal linkages of kinship, friendship, and commerce. Stuyvesant Town's residents would have to work to make lives there. Met Life's vision of the "suburb in the city" described the project's amenities, provided a symbolic representation of urban redevelopment's benevolent aims, and set the standard by which Stuyvesant Town's new residents would approach it. However, in looking to fulfill those terms, the new residents ended up adapting them to their own situations as much as confirming the Metropolitan's expectations. In the struggles over those ideals—played out around segregation, the mass character of the project, the availability of middle-class amenities, and Met Life's authority—residents discovered some of the questions and dilemmas that would haunt urban renewal in the years to come.

CHAPTER 3

THE MASS HOME IN THE MIDDLE-CLASS CITYSCAPE

Middle Class Beachhead on 14th Street

Two or three minutes from Union Square and the offices of *The Daily Worker*, as the bus flies, the middle classes are all set for a smashing victory. Battle is to be joined the minute our previous commitments with Hitler and Hirohito are brought to a satisfactory conclusion.
—"Fourteenth Street Bourgeoisie," *New York Times*, 1943

Stuyvesant Town, the *Times* blithely implied in 1943, was a form of class warfare. "It would be going a bit far," continued this breezy piece in the "Topics of the Times" section, "to say about this new housing enterprise, Silk Stockings Oust Gas House.... But, all in all, it will be a middle-class community." Metropolitan Life's "new tenants will have either a middle-class income or a middle-class mentality, or both." This was reassuring to the Grey Lady because not so long before, there had been no shortage of loose talk—"here and there"—about the end of the war bringing not only an end to fascism, but "the liquidation of the middle classes" as well. Stuyvesant Town, it seemed, was doing its part to put a cap on all that; now, "most of the former critics of the middle classes" could be sure that the middling sorts were "serving a useful purpose in defending Democracy. This good opinion may persist for some time after the job of mopping up the Totalitarians has been finished." What better way to ensure a noble civic role for the middle class than to carve out and eliminate 18 blocks of working-class life, build new modern apartments, double the rent, and replace the old dusty streets with a cheerful middle-class cityscape?[1]

The *Times*'s casual assurances aside, Stuyvesant Town's benevolent intervention was a bold piece of grand strategy. Even if it were not, as the newspaper hinted, calculated to beat the proponents of "people's war" at their own game and win the peace for bourgeois respectability, the project did imagine a postwar city remade for a higher tax bracket. And with the slum clearance ideal at work, it managed this task by enlisting the cautious support of the traditional habitués of Union Square for the idea of redevelopment, if not the particulars of Stuyvesant Town itself. Still, we shouldn't counter the *Times*'s smug affirmation with compensatory scorn. The new, modern, organic ideal—the suburb in the city—succeeded; it worked because of its modernity, its newness, and its wholesale displacement of a working-class world few were willing to defend.

It would be too simple to condemn Stuyvesant Town as a characterless nowhere, simply a bland, petit bourgeois barracks paved over the vital slums. Some portion of Stuyvesant Town life was dedicated to carefully distinguishing itself from the world it had displaced and which still surrounded it on the Lower East Side. Fundamentally, though, Stuyvesant Town was an experiment in middle-class living on a mass, urban scale. Although it was full of people with a "middle-class income," the character of their "middle-class mentality" was far from assured. Stuyvesant Towners transformed the project from a set of plans handed down by the Metropolitan to an actual lived place in ways the *Times* would never have predicted; they made the project an arena for their own struggles to define the culture and character of a new mass middle-class cityscape. The development's early history is the story of how its residents remade this new cityscape, of how they drew up a blueprint not only for the policy of bulldozer redevelopment, but also for the conflicted "structure of feeling" that urban renewal would underwrite in the years to come.

Back in 1943, when City Council member Stanley Isaacs called Stuyvesant Town a "walled town," he also worried that it would become "just a series of homes," not a real community.[2] Both Metropolitan and the new residents of Stuyvesant Town worked hard, and sometimes at cross-purposes, to ensure that Isaacs's judgment of the plans would not fit the actual project. If Stuyvesant Town had been a contested space on the drawing board, life in the realized project was marked by further argument over what kind of community it would be. Throughout the late 1940s and '50s, early Stuyvesant Towners were continually forced to negotiate among three uncomfortably linked understandings of their new home. First was their hope that the development could be just what the company had said it was, a suburb in the city providing a haven from the pressures of urban routine and a landscape of prosperity equivalent to the suburbs Met Life evoked in its promotional rhetoric. However, this notion ran headlong into the second conception: the development's suburban character depended on exclusionary designs and policies that sought to seal residents away from all difference and urban mixture between classes and races. Finally, there was the idea, mostly offered by outsiders, that Stuyvesant Towners lived in a regimented enclave, an icon of the "mass society" that intellectuals of the era imagined imperiled American freedom. By these lights, Stuyvesant Town—and public housing, for which it was often mistaken—was the equivalent in the built environment of the mass culture that was so often said to threaten the autonomy necessary to preserve American individualism in the dawning years of the Cold

War. To some, it seemed a place in which residents would themselves reflect the mass production techniques employed to build their apartments. Assembly-line homes, it was thought, would attract or even produce automatons. Many Stuyvesant Towners, walking a fine line among these conceptions of their home, hoped to achieve the first desire while dispelling the fact of the second and the impression of the third.

Early Stuyvesant Towners confronted a series of troubles provoked by the controversial character of their new home. These conflicts pitted residents against the company, but also against each other. The first was over desegregation. Like most other major housing developers of the era—urban or suburban—the Metropolitan believed that renting to blacks or Puerto Ricans would endanger its investment. The company argued that, despite the public subsidies involved in clearing the Gas House District and the municipal tax deal the development enjoyed, it was private housing and thus free from the purview of antidiscrimination laws. Stuyvesant Town's critics disagreed, and beginning in 1943 they waged a campaign to open the project to blacks. They made little headway, however, until the project was finished and a group of Stuyvesant Town residents joined with black New Yorkers in civil disobedience and direct action. This effort dramatized many Stuyvesant Towners' commitment to making Stuyvesant Town open to all who could afford it. By framing Met Life's refusal to admit blacks as an unnecessary stain on the fabric of American democracy, the residents affirmed their sense that making the development an open neighborhood was necessary in order to realize the good society of postwar America for which Stuyvesant Town claimed to stand, the very society all Americans were being called to defend in the dawning Cold War.

While some residents tried to desegregate the project, many—and sometimes they were the same people—also spent time living up to the company's claim that the project was a suburb in the city. Postwar marketers and retailers confirmed Met Life's pitch to potential residents, and Stuyvesant Town residents, with help from the company and the renewed postwar consumer economy, worked to make the project into an in-town relative of Levittown or one of the other mass-produced suburban communities. They expected the same level of convenience, livability, comfort, and consumer abundance from their rental apartments that suburban pioneers did from tract houses bought with GI Bill loans on easy terms underwritten by the Federal Housing Administration. This was the Stuyvesant Town that the writer Corinne Demas remembers in her memoir of her childhood there: "a utopia of the Fifties" and "a way of life."[3]

Of course, these were not new single-family homes on private plots of land, and Stuyvesant Towners didn't own their apartments. These facts introduced a note of dissonance into the sunny picture of the development as a downtown

Levittown. Residents were continually troubled that many people continued to think that they lived in a regimented "barracks" sealed away from the outside world. In addition, the company's role as landlord was not always congruent with its role as the benevolent provider of the suburb in the city. Both tenants and landlord had their own, sometimes conflicting visions of the pastoral order Stuyvesant Town promised. These conflicts were not nearly as visible or heated as those over desegregation—they involved quarrels over regulations, rent hikes, infrastructure for television and air conditioning—but tenants' attempts to push the boundaries of the company's influence over their lives helped to define what it meant to live urban middle-class life on a mass scale. Most important, these struggles over the character of life in Stuyvesant Town foreshadowed the issues that would haunt urban renewal throughout the 1950s and into the '60s as its city-remaking visions were elaborated, realized, critiqued, and then undone.

"Within the Very Shadow of the United Nations": Desegregating the Walled Town

Negroes and whites don't mix. Perhaps they will in a hundred years, but not now. If we brought them into this development, it would be to the detriment of the city, too, because it would depress all the surrounding property.
—Frederick H. Ecker, *New York Post,* May 1943

Hettie Jones moved to the south side of East 14th Street, just west of First Avenue, in late 1960. She and her husband, LeRoi, were unconventional, even for the northern fringes of downtown bohemia. She was white, Jewish, Queens-bred, a part-time manager and sometime copyeditor at *Partisan Review,* and mother to their little girl, Kellie. He was from Newark, black, a poet and essayist, a happy father, and, as it turned out, a part-time husband to Hettie. She remembers that their Jamaican nanny, Clotelle Bailey, took Kellie down to Stuyvesant Town for organized playground activities for toddlers. After a week or so of games, "Miss Bailey was asked to take her child and leave." Bailey, who "didn't cotton to divisions," was furious and mystified. All the other nannies had been black, of course. But for Jones, philosophical perhaps about the fortitude needed to live "mixed" in a city and country where, as Frederick Ecker put it, "Negroes and whites don't mix," it was less surprising. The Stuyvesant Towners could plainly see that her daughter couldn't possibly live there. According to Jones, Bailey remained nonplussed, but defiant. She was sure they did it "because Kellie kept winning the games."[4]

Stuyvesant Town's own residents noticed injustices as well. "The other day," began a 1959 letter to the editor in the *New York Post,* "for the first time my pride at being a resident of Stuyvesant Town and of New York City was replaced by indignation and shame." The writer had watched as Stuyvesant Town security officers forced two boys, "quiet, well-behaved—and Puerto Rican," off a Stuyvesant Town bench and, the writer implied, out of the project. "How really poor are we of Stuyvesant Town and of New York City, too," the writer asked, "that we can't share a bench with two boys?" The *Post*'s editor, sensitive to the territorial issues at stake in such everyday negotiations over urban space, gave the letter the headline "Stay in Your Own Turf."[5]

In the 20 years after Stuyvesant Town had its debut, these and other New Yorkers noticed that, if the project was a walled town, it was guarded most closely along lines of color. Indeed, race was the hole in the heart of Met Life's benevolent intervention. Until 1952, Stuyvesant Town was whites-only. But even in the late 1950s and '60s, almost a decade after Met Life had bowed to growing civil rights pressure and nominally opened the project to nonwhites, Stuyvesant Town was commonly understood as segregated housing. The few African American families admitted made only shallow inroads in the project's de facto segregation well into the 1970s. Since its private playgrounds and walkways were not technically open to the public, blacks, Puerto Ricans, or other dark-skinned people, unlikely to be residents in the eyes of officials, could easily be ushered off the property.[6]

When Frederick Ecker came out of the City Planning Commission hearings in late May 1943 and told an inquiring *Post* reporter that "Negroes and whites don't mix," he thought himself well within his rights. He believed the company was building private housing and could control tenant selection as it saw fit. Ecker assumed that, just as in suburban postwar housing developments like Levittown and other segregated, FHA-sponsored tracts, his project's economic success depended on racial homogeneity.[7] But his comments provoked outrage among African Americans, civil rights advocates, and their allies among New York's varied and powerful liberal and leftist communities, who saw Stuyvesant Town as a product of what Charles Abrams called the "business welfare state"—a quasi-public facility subject to the equal protection clause of the Constitution. A campaign to desegregate the project was born almost right away. This initial effort, carried out by way of petitions, pickets, protests, testimony at municipal hearings, insider politicking, mass rallies, and courtroom challenges, was led by blacks (joined by liberal allies like Charles Abrams and the reformers of the Citizens Housing Council), who made desegregation of Stuyvesant Town a key part of the wartime Double-V campaign to wipe out fascism and racism abroad and at home.

When these efforts had little effect, the cause was taken up by residents of Stuyvesant Town themselves—many of them left-wing unionists and American Labor Party (ALP) activists—who added a domestic form of civil disobedience to the roster of tactics, inviting black allies to move into their own apartments. These activists portrayed segregated Stuyvesant Town as an affront to national ideals. They pressed for desegregation as a form of true Americanism and a chance for Met Life and New York to live up to the ideals for which the war had been fought and the peace won. These tactics succeeded because Stuyvesant Town appeared to so many as the realization in brick and mortar of postwar prosperity and equality; it was at the heart of New York's and the nation's plans for modern rebuilding, a domestic counterpart to the Marshall Plan, and, fundamentally, a form of hope. Of course, as emblems of U.S. modernity and prosperity, Stuyvesant Town and the urban redevelopment policies it prefigured became tools in the Cold War struggle between freedom and totalitarianism. Only a few years later, by the mid-1950s, the poor public relations image that segregation offered abroad would force some national policymakers to entertain and even encourage desegregation; at Stuyvesant Town, liberals and the Left rehearsed tactics designed to force this geopolitical deal, painting Met Life as un-American and a threat to the liberty that the United States—blacks and whites—had defended in World War II.[8]

The desegregation campaign influenced many Stuyvesant Town residents' attempts to shape the middle-class mentality of the project. They challenged the dominant patterns of market-based, government-subsidized racism in housing, demanding that Met Life's suburb in the city not replicate the racially exclusionary patterns of federally insured suburbs that catered to homeowners. While white homeowners argued that open neighborhoods jeopardized their property values, and thus their piece of the American dream, white Stuyvesant Town activists countered that living in a mixed community was a fundamental part of that American dream, and the company's policies were inhibiting their right to the pursuit of happiness. The activists offered a rebuke to the pervasive sense that the "middling sorts" were always and everywhere complacent or bigoted. Their vision of a democratic, middle-class cityscape, open to all regardless of color, defied the political culture of "white flight" that was beginning to reshape American metropolitan areas in these years.[9]

The effort to desegregate Stuyvesant Town was an important episode in the northern civil rights movement. It was initiated by black organizations in Harlem and their liberal allies as part of the wartime and postwar civil rights ferment in the North that predated the *Brown v. Board of Education* decision in 1954. Largely an effort to achieve equal treatment in public accommodations, this early phase of civil rights struggle chipped away at entrenched discrimination in public life across the North. The campaign to desegregate Stuyvesant Town would launch a fair housing movement in New York State that led to municipal and state laws banning racial discrimination first in projects backed by Title I funds, then in publicly assisted private housing, and eventually in all private housing.[10]

The 1940s were the scene of a great upheaval in race relations. An antifascist war, massive migrations of southern blacks to the North and West for war work, and the beginning of desegregation campaigns in public accommodations promised to undo, or at least weaken, the color line that had undermined American democracy since its beginnings. Pluralism thrived, as both rhetoric and reality, for ethnic immigrants, who were now thought to have all but assimilated and no longer appeared threatening to national cohesion. Blacks, however, still stood outside the national consensus forged by wartime ideals. But in those years, Roosevelt established the Fair Employment Practices Commission, and many states—including New York—passed antidiscrimination legislation. Major league baseball opened to blacks, President Harry Truman desegregated the armed forces, and in 1948 the Supreme Court outlawed restrictive covenants in housing. On the one hand, leftist campaigns for economic justice and political freedom were diluted by suburbanization's subsidy of white privilege and deferred by Cold War red-baiting. And yet, the cause at Stuyvesant Town might have been lost without a generation of Communist or Communist-friendly activists, black and white, who, facing a growing Red Scare that would disable the Old Left, scored a considerable triumph at a moment when their larger fortunes appeared quite grim.[11]

The controversy over segregation stretched from 1943 to 1952; it was the longest lasting and the most heated of all the issues that dogged Stuyvesant Town's early years. Met Life first came under fire for its unwillingness to admit blacks at the Board of Estimate hearings on June 3, 1943, a few days after Ecker made his comments about race mixing. Twenty civic organizations lined up to testify against the project, 14 of which made discrimination their chief complaint. Despite these objections, support for the principle of urban redevelopment, and even private involvement, was nearly unanimous. Nobody doubted that the Board of Estimate would give its go-ahead, and it did, approving the plan 11–5. Two months later, the Citizens Housing Council and other civic groups sponsored a taxpayer's lawsuit (*Pratt v. La Guardia*), seeking public controls on the publicly subsidized project. Their complaint cited racial discrimination, but the court dismissed that claim in March 1944. Met Life had yet to build or rent out the apartments, so racial discrimination, the decision said, applied to "future uncertainties."[12]

While the appeal was under way, Robert Moses and the Metropolitan looked to head off their attackers, announcing that the company intended to build Riverton, a 1,232-apartment project in Harlem. From their perspective, Riverton secured "equal protection" for blacks under the 14th Amendment in an "equal, or substantially equal facility." This, Charles Abrams wrote, was Metropolitan's "master-stroke": "There would now be one project for whites and one for Negroes—on the Southern pattern." The *Amsterdam News* agreed: "The pulse-beat of the average Harlemite is geared to a belief that the Riverton proposal is merely a discriminatory 'sop' tossed in their direction." Still, Met Life professed its good intentions. Riverton, it said, was simply more housing for the black citizens of Harlem, an effort the company saw as entirely consistent with its right to control tenant selection at both projects and guarantee the "safety" of the two investments. With the *Pratt* action dismissed as premature and Riverton under way, the Metropolitan was free to clear the Gas House District, build the project, and select tenants.[13]

In June 1947, several black veterans sued Met Life's subsidiary, the Stuyvesant Town Development Corporation, for residency in the project. The first of Stuyvesant Town's buildings was about to open, and Met Life had accepted no black tenants. Charles Abrams, arguing *Dorsey v. Stuyvesant Town* for the plaintiffs, renewed the argument that Stuyvesant Town was as much a public endeavor as a private one. It was the latest in a string of devices that, while intended to improve cities, were perverted to prevent minorities from "infiltrating" white neighborhoods.[14] Stuyvesant Town, Abrams argued, was made possible through exclusive state powers, and it was thus also an instance of "state action" and subject to the equal protection clause of the 14th Amendment. As veterans, the plaintiffs should have the right to the same preferential consideration as white veterans.[15]

For its part in the case, Met Life maintained that there was no "state action" involved in building and running Stuyvesant Town. The state and city had offered indirect inducements to get the project started, but it remained a private housing complex. The state courts agreed, and through two years and two appeals, continued to find that the "public use and purpose involved terminates when the work of redevelopment is completed." The court hadn't budged from *Pratt v. La Guardia*: the public subsidy was for slum clearance, not housing. The state had no part in the operation of housing created by urban redevelopment and thus had no constitutional obligation to admit the plaintiffs.[16]

Meanwhile, a new challenge emerged from within the project itself. In October 1948, a group of Stuyvesant Town and Peter Cooper Village residents formed the Town and Village Tenants Committee to End Discrimination in Stuyvesant Town. As an inaugural act, they took a poll of 105 Stuyvesant Town residents, 62 percent of whom favored admitting blacks. They reported their findings in the independent newspaper *Town and Village*. The editors received a volley of outraged protest mail doubting the findings, suggesting the committee members move to Harlem or Riverton, and resisting all integration, but when the paper ran its own poll, it found that a two-to-one majority of 551 residents polled supported integration. Buoyed by these results, the tenants committee grew steadily, representing at its peak about 1,800 tenants. Led by Paul L. Ross, former city rent commissioner and former administrative secretary to Mayor William O'Dwyer, the tenants committee circulated a petition asking the mayor to intervene with the company and get the ban removed. The petition asked that the city "take all the necessary steps... to open the still unrented apartments in Stuyvesant Town to Negro tenants who otherwise meet eligibility qualifications applied to other tenants." O'Dwyer appeared sympathetic and regretted the deal his predecessor had made, but told the petitioners that his hands were tied by the existing contract.[17]

After the mayor's rebuff and *Dorsey v. Stuyvesant Town*'s defeat in the New York State Court of Appeals, the committee decided to change its tactics. In the summer of 1949, Jesse Kessler, a white organizer with Local 65 of the Wholesale and Warehouse Workers, invited a black member of his union to stay with his family in their apartment at 1 Stuyvesant Oval. Hardine Hendrix; his wife, Raphael; and their son, Hardine Jr., moved in while the Kesslers were away for the summer. That fall, Dr. Lee Lorch, a recently dismissed mathematics professor at CCNY who was headed for Penn State, offered the Hendrixes his family's Stuyvesant Town apartment for the year.[18] Stuyvesant Town regulations prohibited the subletting of apartments, but both Kessler and Lorch had avoided the rule by inviting the Hendrixes as guests. Despite a few hostile remarks and phone calls, the Hendrixes reported feeling welcome, and the *Times* found that only 3 of 15 residents the paper interviewed objected to the family's presence.[19]

In June 1950, just after the U.S. Supreme Court refused to hear *Dorsey v. Stuyvesant Town,* City Council members Earl Brown and Stanley Isaacs introduced a bill making discrimination in housing a misdemeanor. In 1944, the city had passed a law making discrimination in all future publicly assisted projects illegal; the Brown-Isaacs bill sought to make this constraint retroactive and thus include Stuyvesant Town. With this threat looming, and the continued activism of the tenants committee unsettling day-to-day operations in the project, Met Life made a sudden and surprising announcement: it would lease "some" apartments to qualified "Negro families." There had been no basic change in policy, the management said. The company still reserved the right to select tenants as it saw fit. Demanding a change in company policy, not merely an informal promise, Brown and Isaacs pushed forward with their bill. Despite widespread red-baiting in the more conservative dailies, the bill passed unanimously in the City Council and by a 12–1 margin in the Board of Estimate. The new mayor, Vincent Impellitteri, signed it into law in March 1951.[20]

This was not the end, however. Even before the Metropolitan made concessions to ease public pressure, it had moved to evict 35 families connected with the tenants committee. For almost two years, the families, including the Rosses, Kesslers, and Lorches, fought the evictions in the courts and legislatures, seeking to prove that they were a reprisal for activism. Politicians, unions, and liberal civic groups—even some of those who had found the tenants committee too radical for their taste in the past—rallied to their side. Each time Met Life prepared to serve eviction papers on the families, the tenants committee and the New York State Committee on Discrimination in Housing (NYSCDH)—an umbrella group set up to represent the tenants—mounted a public pressure campaign and forced the company to delay the notices. Finally, City Council head Rudolph Halley agreed to moderate negotiations between the NYSCDH and the company. After a few days, Halley emerged with a compromise: the Metropolitan would relent, the residents regarded as the most troublesome—including the Lorches, Kesslers, and Rosses—would relocate voluntarily, and the company would accept the Hendrixes as tenants. Meanwhile, Harlem residents had launched an organized effort to apply for apartments in the project, and Met Life officials gave NYSCDH officials Hortense Gabel and Algernon Black assurances that the company was acting to process the applications of several black families.[21]

A closer look at the rhetoric surrounding the desegregation struggle reveals how the political culture of the dawning Cold War shaped the conflict. Radical tenants—wary of red-baiting—appealed to true Americanism while liberals invoked the need to protect the nation's image abroad. The tenants offered themselves and the integrated project they imagined as representatives of democracy and postwar hope. Extending the wartime argument that a segregated Stuyvesant Town gave comfort to the fascist enemy, their rhetoric appropriated images of postwar suburban family life, depicting integration as entirely congruent with American ideology. Integration, they suggested, was a necessary component of the middle-class prosperity and domesticity promised to everyone in the postwar era.[22] Meanwhile, the liberals in NYSCDH complemented this affirmative vision with a warning: segregation in Stuyvesant Town was an unacceptable blot on the nation's image when its ideals were being tested in the dawning Cold War.

Robert Moses and Met Life tried to ignore these geopolitical questions, viewing them as political pandering and demagoguery. Moses scorned all the high-minded talk as little more than the "rotten eggs and abuse of irresponsible people." "The colored issue," he wrote to a concerned citizen in 1943, "has been dragged in by the hair. There are no colored people in the neighborhood today, and never have been any." Blacks, he felt, had no prior claim to the Gas House District, so why should anyone expect them to be represented in Stuyvesant Town? Both Moses and Met Life had little patience with what the commissioner called "long range social objectives" like opening the entire city to

a landlord vs. the people...

3.1. The cover of a pamphlet distributed by the Committee to End Discrimination in Stuyvesant Town defending desegregation activists against evictions. Courtesy of Amy Fox.

discrimination-free housing. They had always warned that too much contro-versy at Stuyvesant Town might jeopardize future redevelopment funds. Now, they simply stressed that Stuyvesant Town was a much-needed postwar project. It would help to alleviate the inevitable housing shortage, stoke the municipal economy, give a jolt to the local building industry, and do its part to head off the return of economic doldrums with postwar jobs. The opposition agreed with these prosaic concerns, but saw the project's postwar impact in broader terms. Their success in forcing the issue showed how Moses and Met Life had failed to understand the importance of Stuyvesant Town's new social and imaginative world to postwar peace, prosperity, and democracy.[23]

The color line at Stuyvesant Town, *The New Republic* had editorialized in 1943, "is a question of national—even of international—importance, because the housing project will be built after the war, and must therefore be regarded as a part of our plans for the post-war world." Similarly, architect Simon Breines observed, "[T]he feeling runs strong that out of the struggle must come a new world.... Post-war planning must embody the ideals for which our brothers and friends are giving their lives." But "if the plans we make now" undermine the fight against a "totalitarian world, with its theory of racial superiority and its practice of economic and social oppression ... we may defeat the enemy and lose the war." Stuyvesant Town stood as a symbol of the entire nation's disposition toward the world after the war. Approval of a segregated Stuyvesant Town, a biracial citizens group told La Guardia, would "establish inequality and intoler-ance in the very fabric of the postwar world."[24]

The Town and Village activists agreed. Most of the men in the group were vet-erans and took wartime pluralist ideals seriously. For them, fighting against dis-crimination was continuing the fight against fascism by other means. "Many of us have taken our share of hard knocks in the past few years," one veteran told the *Times*. "We've learned that it's up to us all to live together the best way we can. We have problems enough without worrying about color lines." Jesse Kessler, remark-ing on his motives for taking in the Hendrixes, said that his union "practiced the democratic principle that Negro and white can live and work side by side." Met Life was the "un-American" force at work here, the protestors contended. Mrs. Frances Smith, a neighbor and former member of Kessler's union, remarked that the company's policies put it outside the mainstream of American life and dehu-manized everyone involved. Kessler's invitation, she enthused, "gives the rest of us a chance to feel like human beings again. Stuyvesant Town will be a part of America someday, just wait and see."[25]

Despite their appeals to true Americanism, the tenants committee was attacked as a Communist front group from the moment of its inception. Writing to *Town and Village*, S. Kasper of 19 Stuyvesant Oval believed that "the strongest force behind the present movement is the Communist Party." One reader who wished to remain anonymous assured the editors that "we personally have nothing against the colored people and in fact some of them are better than those Communists and minorities stirring up this trouble." Much of the red-baiting moved by rumor and veiled innuendo. When letter writers lamented that a noble ideal had been perverted for "political" purposes, the word *political* functioned as code for *Communist*. For instance, Isidore Sapir of East 20th Street reassured the editor that "most of us who are against bias and discrimination will continue to carry on the fight the right way without trying to connect the fight to any political group."[26]

Met Life, too, kept a close watch on the "political" interests of the tenants committee. Daniel B. English, a Met Life employee sent by the firm to observe a mass meeting welcoming the Hendrixes to Stuyvesant Town, reported back that the meeting was "intended as a device, primarily, for building up the political fortunes of the Leftist parties, with especial attention to Marcantonio's ambitions to become mayor of New York." Vito Marcantonio, the congressional representative from East Harlem, was the American Labor Party candidate for mayor in 1949, and Paul L. Ross accompanied him on the ticket as the ALP choice for comptroller. English, unfamiliar with left-wing politics, did not understand the connection between the ALP electoral campaign and the antidiscrimination drive. He seemed most concerned with proving to his employers that "politics"—meaning the ALP and, presumably, Communists' ambitions for elected office—had been brought into the desegregation efforts. He reported that desegregation had become a secondary concern for the audience, most of whom "seemed to [him] of Jewish appearance," and that the movement was turning toward getting Marcantonio to City Hall. That these were linked strategic goals was lost on him, even as he reported that Ross called for an escalation of the desegregation campaign. While "the fight would be continued in the courts," Ross said, "it must be directed now against the city government."[27]

Meanwhile, *Town and Village* supported the desegregation efforts and cautiously endorsed the tenants committee. "There can be no compromise with prejudice," announced a 1948 editorial headlined "The Color Line." "We believe this yelling 'Red' has gone a bit too far," the editor continued. "Of course, there are undoubtedly some people on that resident Provisional Committee who could be accused of having leftist, even communistic leanings. But let's not fall into the error of immediately decrying a decent American motive, just because leftists climb on the bandwagon." It would be interesting, the editor thought, to follow "a movement by American citizens trying to insure that other American citizens be allowed to enjoy the benefits of that citizenship." Almost two years later, after Met Life refused to renew the leases of committee members, the paper again sided with the tenants, saying that, if the accusations were true, Met Life would be guilty of "committing an undemocratic act in American life." Since they were strictly "matters of American principle," the editor demanded that his views not be "interpreted as aid or comfort for the Communists and their contemptible fellow travelers."[28]

All along, the activists downplayed the red-baiting, preferring to wrap themselves in the American flag. They refused to discuss the charges of subversion and Communist influence, hoping to use their loyalty to the nation and its ideals to weather the mounting anti-Communist tide. As Paul Talbot, a Stuyvesant Town resident, tenants committee and Liberal Party member, and potential evictee, put it, Met Life was squandering "an opportunity for a big American corporation—operating almost within the very shadow of the United Nations building—to act in an American way. Think of what the Voice of America could have done with Stuyvesant Town if it had developed into a real symbol of the democratic way of life." Cleaving to Americanism allowed the activists to preserve their effectiveness, joining liberals in putting pressure on Metropolitan Life to live up to democratic ideals.[29]

In early 1951, as the Brown-Isaacs bill made its way through the legislative mill, these controversies began to attract citywide attention, bringing the conflict to a head. Charles Abrams noted in a letter to the *Times* that "it is being whispered that Communist-front groups are behind the bill." Trying to distance "seven years" of liberal effort in the courts from what he depicted as the more recent interest of Communist front groups, he claimed they had been "outmaneuvered in their efforts, and it is playing into their hands to give them credit for the fight."[30] Meanwhile, Met Life continued to see the bill as a serious threat to its investment. Friendly editors at the *Daily News, Mirror,* and *World-Telegram* ran editorials and stories attacking the desegregation campaign. "The dope," wrote the *Daily News,* "is that some of our Councilmen have allowed themselves to become so intimidated by Commie pressure that they're actually contemplating voting for the current irresponsible measure." C. Frank Leavis, a Metropolitan lawyer, testifying at the Board of Estimate hearings on the bill, charged that it "stems right out of the Communist line" and would "open the gates to race hatred." But Stanley Isaacs countered by reading segregation right out of the national consensus. Holding up the *Daily News,* he noted that its editorial had ended by demanding to know: "what goes on in this supposedly American city?" "Let me say what goes on," responded Isaacs, "it is the elimination of a blot upon the City that wasn't American in its origin."[31]

After the Brown-Isaacs bill passed, Met Life had little left with which to fight. Its late attempt at containment had fallen flat—"as few such charges have in recent years," remarked the *Nation* of times that also saw the trials of Alger Hiss and the Rosenbergs—and the liberal coalition felt safe enough to support the leftist tenants committee in its battle against the evictions. Their shared principles of democracy, open housing, and Americanism were both municipal law and, it appeared, popular opinion. In the dawning Cold War, pluralism and racial justice could set the United States apart from its Soviet rival. Unfortunately, as NYSCDH secretary Hortense Gabel wrote to Mayor Vincent Impellitteri, Met Life was using its power "to suppress expressions of democratic ideals which our nation itself has adopted and for which it is the most powerful exponent throughout the free world."[32]

Under the sign of Cold War Americanism, the old Popular Front cooperation between anti-Communist liberals and leftist activists prevailed, surviving just long enough to end segregation in Stuyvesant Town. While the liberals never could have brought Met Life to the table without the tenants committee, the ALPers and their allies had to bow to the use of Cold War pressure on Met Life. "New York City," Gabel wrote, "is a prime example of how peoples of all races with different ideas and opinions can live peacefully together and enjoy the freedom of our democracy. It would be unfortunate, especially now when the American ideals are being tested in a worldwide struggle for the minds of men, to have this record tarnished." Met Life's discrimination had become a national and municipal liability in the "worldwide struggle for the minds of men," and the liberals of the NYSCDH, using the terms of that Cold War struggle, forced Met Life to compromise its authority and autonomy to safeguard its power and standing. By making the city and Met Life live up to "American" ideals—and thereby inoculating the project against the charge that it besmirched the nation's global image—the campaigners helped to erect Stuyvesant Town and, more deeply, federally funded urban renewal as vital bulwarks in the domestic front of the Cold War. Stuyvesant Town was a model for a city ready to be remade by Cold War liberalism.[33]

Actual integration came slowly to Stuyvesant Town, so the victory over desegregation seemed a symbolic one in the short term. Only a small number of blacks and Puerto Ricans lived in Stuyvesant Town over the next 10–15 years. Met Life did little to encourage applications, but what was most surprising to those who had led the charge for desegregation was that few African Americans, it turned out, wanted to live in such a bastion of whiteness. Beyond activists like Raphael and Hardine Hendrix, few families were interested in such an uncomfortable vanguard experiment. That started to change in the '60s, and the 1970 Census counted 641 "nonwhites," up from only 90 in the Census 10 years earlier. It took a 1968 suit by the New York City Commission on Human Rights to prod Met Life into actively pursuing integration.[34]

In the long run, the New York campaign for "inclusive urbanization," as historian Martha Biondi calls it, was less successful in securing actual integration in the new spaces created by urban renewal than in simply pioneering legislation. In part, this was because the new laws were selectively enforced, but it was also because urban renewal projects, both Title I redevelopment projects and Title III public housing, while nominally color-blind spaces, ultimately reinforced already existing patterns of de facto residential segregation. Title I projects, used to reclaim desirable neighborhoods for white-collar uses, provided bastions of middle-class urban affluence for primarily white populations, while public housing, often put down on cheaper land within existing ghettos, became overwhelmingly black and Puerto Rican.[35] Hettie Jones's experience of Stuyvesant Town predicted a deeper and less encouraging future for the new divided cityscape of urban renewal.

New Mass Homes

Have You Studied the New Mass Homes?...How can you, as a retailer, help make these new minimum space homes more comfortable and functional?
—*Home Furnishings Merchandiser*, July 1947

If Met Life fought to keep Stuyvesant Town all white, it worked equally hard to ensure that the project would have the proper cultural and class composition. According to one estimate, the Metropolitan spent close to $100 million securing the 18 blocks of the Gas House District, removing the tenants, and building the project. With such a massive investment at stake, the company undertook a careful tenant selection process. Interviewers gave applicants lengthy surveys and often visited their homes to ensure they possessed the proper domestic skills. According to Gustave Zismer, head of housing projects for the company in the early 1950s, the Metropolitan looked for "families of moderate to middle income" of "good character" who were from "that large group of the population which lies between those families who can afford to pay prevailing rentals and those who can only afford to live in government or public housing."[36]

Whether or not they quite fit Zismer's impressionistic prescription, there's no doubt that most Stuyvesant Towners—those who desegregated the project and those who opposed opening the project to blacks, those with Communist sympathies and those without—were among the middle classes. In one company sample of 3,349 families who entered the project in the early years, the average head-of-family income was $4,192 a year. With "other income" added (from unspecified sources but probably including investments and women's work outside the home), the average yearly income was $5,356, quite a bit higher than the 1950 Manhattan median income of $2,347. "Stuyvesant Town," Corinne

Demas remembers, "was a middle-class community where little girls took piano lessons and were expected to go to college. If our fathers weren't doctors or dentists, lawyers or school principals, they worked in offices." Martha Seidman, a "pioneer" in the project, worked as a high school librarian, while her husband was a social worker in the city's Department of Welfare. Their neighbors were a school secretary and a teacher. Across the way, in the slightly more affluent Peter Cooper Village, Pamela Long's uncle was a radio engineer at ABC; she remembers a psychiatrist, two social workers, a police officer, a lawyer, an accountant, an obstetrician, and the actor Karl Malden living nearby in the late '40s and '50s. Some of these early residents were the first in their families to go to college, wear a white collar, or work in the professions rather than the trades or factories, and most were young veterans just starting out in their careers, but they were all able to afford Met Life's rents.[37]

However, for reasons not purely financial, many middling New Yorkers didn't quite fit Met Life's demographic of "in-between families with incomes neither large nor small." The company's criteria were economic, but as Zismer's language of "character" suggests, they were also cultural, and the extensive interview process was designed to select tenants who could demonstrate their fealty to proper norms of middle-class family life. As one "perplexed veteran" who had been turned away from both Stuyvesant Town and NYCHA's Amsterdam Houses told the *Sun,* he made $3,044 a year, too much for public housing, but had his application for a four-room apartment in Stuyvesant Town rejected because he and his wife had a boy and a girl who could not be allowed to share a bedroom. Unfortunately, the company informed him, he didn't make enough for a five-room apartment.[38] Frederick Ecker had often stressed that one of Met Life's interests was to "anchor" families in the bedrock of Manhattan; the company's practices suggested that any minor deviation from narrow conceptions of middle-class family ideals could disqualify applicants.

If the company saw this careful policing of family composition as another tool to protect its investment, then it was also a way of ensuring that the vision of Stuyvesant Town as a suburb in the city survived. Met Life hoped that the project would be seen in the same light as houses in the suburbs. Ecker assured the 1948 Conference of Mayors that a Stuyvesant Town apartment was "the ideal in housing for the average person of limited means" and "as healthful as a detached dwelling." The company took great pride in the extensive landscaping and planting, the serenity of the central oval, and the quiet escape it provided from city noise. No doubt, some residents—committed urbanites who had chosen an apartment in the city over the lure of the suburbs—were somewhat less invested in this ideal. Still, many appreciated and often praised their surroundings. Pamela Long, who grew up in the project, still thinks of it as "idyllic." "It's beautiful, with the greenery," she says, "and you come into the grounds after walking uptown and it's ten degrees cooler." Likewise, in a letter to *Town and Village*, Mrs. C. C. Robinson responded to Lewis Mumford's critique of the project, asking "where else in New York can one step from the door of one's home, without landing on a sidewalk full of noise and scurrying people?" Martha Seidman remembered that "the space between the buildings... was eye opening." For residents, the innovations of modern planning made Stuyvesant Town into something of a hybrid form between the city and the suburb, a kind of "middle landscape" that promised equal parts urban convenience and suburban remove.[39]

Yet, as Ecker's interest in families suggested, Stuyvesant Town's "suburban" character depended on a particular social structure as much as its design features. In the immediate postwar years, suburbs were not only imagined as places of "livability," "comfort," and "convenience," but as places that encouraged strictly defined gender roles. In this set of ideals, men inhabited public life, most often commuting to the city for work. Women stayed at home, where they performed the unpaid domestic work of the private sphere that underwrote and made possible men's participation in public life.[40] In keeping with Met Life's vision of the development as a place where residents could "enjoy quiet suburban living in a busy city," this ideology was at work in Stuyvesant Town as well. Stuyvesant Town's women—like their sisters nationwide—embraced motherhood. The early residents of the project—a vast majority of whom were young couples— did their part for the baby boom, producing kids at an astonishing rate. Some even called it "Rabbit Town" for the exuberance with which Stuyvesant Towners procreated. In October 1948, there were 1,663 children in the project. A year later, with all the buildings occupied, there were 3,208, and by 1950 one estimate put the number at 5,500. In 1957, the Census Bureau counted 6,609 children under the age of 19 in Stuyvesant Town.[41]

In addition, it appeared that families that moved to Stuyvesant Town relied less on women's income once they were there. While income was up 3.84 percent by late 1950, and head-of-family income went up 14.5 percent, the "other income" category decreased by 34.5 percent. So while family incomes rose, male breadwinners spurred the bulk of that increase, which suggests that female contributions—some undetermined portion of "other income"—actually shrank as a proportion of the whole after families moved to Stuyvesant Town. Of course, there were probably quite a few Stuyvesant Town women who worked outside the home on top of their unpaid housework, and perhaps they did so in increasing numbers as women's paid employment continued to rise in the postwar era. But the women of Stuyvesant Town, like suburban women, were particularly subject to the domestic ideals and pressures that had captured the national imagination. For instance, Corinne Demas remembered, "if our mothers worked at all, they were teachers." Her mother, a biology teacher before they came to Stuyvesant Town, tried to return to teaching when Corinne was a toddler, but the experiment proved short-lived. Nursemaids were unreliable, and Corinne's father, like many other American men, "believed mothers should stay home and take care of their children; he also felt that my mother's working made it seem as if he was an insufficient provider." The various practical and societal pressures proved too much, and Electra Demas abandoned teaching for a decade, resuming it only when Corinne was in junior high school. Martha Seidman, too, stopped working when her kids were born and then returned to her librarian job when they were teenagers. In part, these uneven work patterns were the result of the few childcare options available. Like its suburban counterparts, Stuyvesant Town was in many ways designed to be a group of self-contained homes. There was a recreation staff that offered games for kids, but no formal childcare or preschool services, making it more difficult for women to commit to full-time careers.[42]

The postwar mass consumption economy helped Met Life and Stuyvesant Towners alike to negotiate these domestic ideals. Postwar domestic ideology charged women with overseeing the family's consumption habits. Men ultimately controlled the family's purchasing power, but advertisers appealed to women as the keepers of the hearth. They became the conduit through which dollars would flow and postwar prosperity and abundance would be secured. Or, as Corinne Demas put it, "Shopping was the province of women. That was the way it was in my family, and in all the other families I knew. Women shopped for the food, the clothes, the furniture. If men bought anything, it was the family car." Postwar retailers capitalized on this ideology, using its imagery and rhetoric to sell to Stuyvesant Town residents.[43]

Women were, as a 1946 ad for Sachs Quality Stores that featured Stuyvesant Town put it, "our homemakers of tomorrow." Above a picture of a Stuyvesant Town model, the ad announced that the department store chain was "Looking Forward to Our Second Half-Century of Service to an Even Greater New York." The project—lit in bright white to stand out from the darkened tenements around its flanks—was "a brave new world in old Manhattan . . . bringing the promise of better living to thousands of home-hungry New Yorkers. Stuyvesant Town will be a far cry from the crammed, crowded tenements that teemed through the 'Gay Nineties,' when Sachs-Quality first began serving New York." The ad was the first in a series "dedicated to the homes that make New York the biggest Home Town in America," identifying Stuyvesant Town with the middle-class ideal of the hometown, now made possible in the midst of a tenement district. It represented the "glowing future," modern living, and hope for the postwar era. And it stood for community, family, home, and the carefully delineated gender roles these domestic ideals represented.[44]

Marketers sold this complex of affiliations by suggesting that Stuyvesant Town stood at the heart of postwar culture. Retailers should realize, the ads suggested, that these sorts of powerful associations could take root in Manhattan, that the island was not simply Park Avenue and a swarm of tenements, but one big "Home Town." For instance, the *New York Journal-American* used Stuyvesant Town to sell advertisers its services in *Advertising Age*. "This Is New York," it announced above a photo of the towers in mid-construction. In Stuyvesant Town and Peter Cooper Village, the ad proclaimed, "37,000 people of moderate income will realize the finest in modern living in 56 highly desirable apartment buildings." Advertisers, it said, wanted to "sell New York." The newspaper could deliver buyers, particularly the "*Journal-American*'s predominant family audience," which was soon to be living in apartments like Stuyvesant Town that were "highly desirable" both for residents and as target markets. This is where the new postwar mass markets would be, the ad implied, and advertisers needed the *Journal-American* to get them in the door.[45]

"Have You Studied the New Mass Homes?" asked a headline in the trade journal *Home Furnishings Merchandiser* for July 1947. The journal's editors had undertaken an informal, "superficial," yet "eye-opening" survey about where the new female buyers were living and what the floor plans looked like. They provided a chart with room measurements from "typical development houses" across the country. They featured unnamed developments in Detroit, Kansas City, and Seattle; they had Kaiser homes in Los Angeles; and they had eight developments from Long Island, including Levittown. In addition, listed by name were Stuyvesant Town and Peter Cooper Village. With comparable room dimensions and similarly compact layouts, Stuyvesant Town, the journal demonstrated, should be thought of as part of the same mass market as the suburban housing developments. Likewise, an article in *Fashion Trades,* a garment industry trade journal, detailed the ways that new housing projects were "particularly attractive to retail enterprises." Due to the projects' stable income level and selective tenant admissions, retailers did not have to worry about an adequate customer base; in fact, "the project itself acts to enforce this condition." Urban mass housing, these accounts agreed, was a critical part of the burgeoning postwar mass market.[46]

Stuyvesant Town had its debut outside the realm of municipal politics in these kinds of ads. If the Gas House District had been consigned to the literal rubbish heap of history in part by the power to deploy explicitly visual, photographic evidence, Stuyvesant Town was made visible and understandable in the public's mind by images as well, resolving in ads like these from the blocky shapes of an architect's plans into aerial photographs and close-ups of furnishings and details. Shaped as an imaginative phenomenon as much as a physical one by these sometimes subtle, sometimes brazen appeals to the postwar promise of better living, the development appeared exactly as Met Life envisioned it: an emblem of future prosperity. In these ads, the austere forms of modern architecture begin to take on a new set of associations; they appear not only forward-looking, clean, efficient, and functional but comfortable, familiar, and suitable for traditional homemaking.

Department stores, newspapers, and magazines took up and expanded this project in Stuyvesant Town's early years, portraying the development much the way they did suburban tract housing. This campaign was, of course, more localized than the national suburban fascination, and Stuyvesant Town did not signify quite the same compact of heady ideals that Americans associated with the detached house in the suburbs. Stuyvesant Town, while sold as a "home," did not evoke the same combination of independent ownership, individualistic self-reliance, rooted permanence, pastoral ease, and healthful vitality that investment in a house and yard invariably signified.[47] Stuyvesant Town pioneered a different but related set of associations about what a proper middle-class home should be. The project was designed to "domesticate" not potato fields, but the wild Lower East Side of Manhattan; it was urban and middle class, the built embodiment around which the culture of urban renewal would evolve.

In addition, these accounts addressed themselves to the particular problems of what *Home Furnishings Merchandiser* called the "new, minimum space homes." Stuyvesant Town apartments had modern layouts with combined dining and living rooms, but unlike many of their suburban contemporaries, which were squares or rectangles with rooms arranged around a central core, they were often arranged in a strip so as to better fit into the various H-, T-, and cross-shaped building forms that made up the Stuyvesant Town towers. One most often entered into a little hallway that opened onto a foyer and dining area next to the kitchen. This foyer flowed seamlessly into the living room, and the bedrooms were almost always laid out along a hallway leading off the far end of the living room. The bathroom was at the end of the hallway. Many—but not all—apartments had corner bedrooms with two windows. Overall, Stuyvesant Town apartments compared favorably with their suburban competition. At about 12 feet by 18 feet, 7 inches, the typical Stuyvesant Town living room was larger than the living rooms in many of the suburban tract homes, including the Kaiser homes and many of the Long Island developments. Stuyvesant Town bedrooms were also comparable, ranging from 140 to 180 square feet. Nevertheless, the department stores, home magazines, and other marketers realized that these were all "mass homes" made for economy. The main problem would be overcoming their "minimal" and repetitive spaces—a design dilemma that came to stand in for the larger symbolic problem of managing the cultural implications of living in these mass homes.

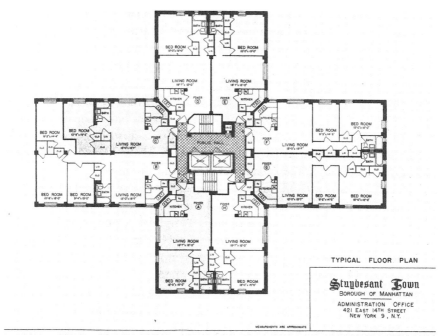

Stuyvesant Town's plan placed particular demands on the project's home-makers. Wrote residents Milton and Mildred Lewis in the *Herald Tribune:*

For the woman of the house,...development living presents a real challenge. It's hard enough in any average home to create attractive surroundings, as there's usually an unsightly beam or an odd-shaped window to cope with. But try it for size in a layout identical with thousands of others, where the long walls, the short walls, and even the electrical outlets practically dictate the placing of furniture. The very efficiency of the space planning (none of the waste of a suburban home) works against you. And yet originality can be accomplished; the ingenuity of a determined woman becomes a charming thing to behold.

Faced with the standardized spaces of the new mass homes, women's "ingenuity" took on an enhanced role. When it was so much more difficult to make a place "charming," this Stuyvesant Town couple told their female reader that she must redouble her efforts, make the process *and* herself charming, and thereby make a real home for herself and her grateful husband and children.[48]

The department store chain Hearns put the most effort into solving these problems. In June 1947, the chain's flagship location at 14th Street and Fifth Avenue debuted a showroom replica of a Stuyvesant Town apartment. Two years in the making, it copied every detail of a two-bedroom project apartment and featured specially designed, sized, and standardized furnishings, accessories, and fixtures. A few months later, after the first residents of Stuyvesant Town had moved in, the replica was redecorated, this time in "modern style" to spark the interest of newly arrived residents. Wallpaper in "beige flecked with brown, gold and coral" complemented coral sectional loveseats; coral, brown, and green draperies; and blond oak sectional cabinets. Blond oak furniture in the master bedroom nicely offset the peach and green plaid bedspread and matching tie-back shower curtains in the bathroom. All these tropical colors might have been better suited to a subdivision on the fringes of Miami, but Hearns's president felt sure that "emphasis has been placed upon the functional properties of furniture and the color harmony of fabric and accessories." All efforts, he said, had been made "to provide the tenants of the new housing development with a tasteful and artistic sample of decoration in contemporary design." As a final touch, the store provided a selection of "modern prints" framed particularly for the "Stuyvesant Towner Collection."[49]

The store took out a full-page ad in *Town and Village* to announce the redesign. "Hearns Designs for Your Individual Needs: A Newly Redecorated Typical Apartment of Stuyvesant Town," it trumpeted. The "you" for whose needs Hearns designed appears as a drawing of a young, prim, blonde woman—a wife-to-be or a recent arrival in Stuyvesant Town perhaps. She is looking excitedly away from the reader, but as if through a window in the page and into a Stuyvesant Town bedroom, marveling at the peach and green plaid water-repellent bedspread. Below her is a photograph of the requisite Stuyvesant Town model, but this time an oversized floor plan of the project's two-bedroom apartment has been affixed to the model's north end, as if a giant floor plan had subsumed Peter Cooper Village and the East River shore much the same way Stuyvesant Town replaced the Gas House District. Here, Stuyvesant Town's apartments are imagined to be individually domesticating the East Side of Manhattan home-maker by homemaker, not merely collectively as an entire development. One's "individual needs"—or, as the ad visually implies, desires—can contribute to Stuyvesant Town's overall campaign to domesticate the inner city. The ad's text suggests why modern design might suit this project. The "young in spirit" who love "*good* 'modern'" can fill in the empty space of that floor plan with the "new look" in home furnishings, just as the "good modern" of Stuyvesant Town gave the Lower East Side a "new look." Similar to Stuyvesant Town's modern design itself, the ad implies, Hearns's furnishings are "fashioned for *function*" and convey a sense of "effortless luxury, the handsome simplicity that's derived from uncluttered lines." And, of course, all this simple luxury is affordable: Hearns offered a "convenient" 15-month payment plan with no down payment on furniture and rugs. This melding of populist appeal and affordable luxury for everyday life promised suburban-style comfort in an apartment carved right out of the city streets.[50]

These ads and images also suggested that homemakers had to domesticate the austere, limited spaces of their new modern apartments. If clearance and rebuilding had provided ample space for middle-class life in the midst of a tenement district, it was up to Stuyvesant Town's new residents to adapt the modern spaces of the project to contemporary middle-class ideals. Stuyvesant Town and the other postwar mass homes were not palatial, *Home Furnishings Merchandiser* reminded retailers. The rooms had to serve multiple purposes. Dining areas were just alcoves; living rooms were small, but had become "more than a place to converse." Bedrooms had to be for more than sleep. They had to function as a place of "study or work or relaxation" as well. There was little storage space for "all those necessary implements to contemporary living…tennis rackets, overshoes, golf clubs, skis, vases, variety in table wares and hostess aids." "Designing for today's living" meant providing both economy in space and versatility in design, which required leaving behind "conventional furniture design" for more streamlined, modern designs. Furniture dealers and manufacturers, the journal believed, could tap the emerging markets of the postwar housing developments by helping consumers to make "these new, minimum space homes more comfortable and functional." By "finding out what the consumer wants and then giving it to her," the furniture business could enjoy the same prosperity as the homemakers it hoped to attract. All in all, the journal suggested that the home furnishings business had to strike a balance between cramped quarters and the variety and munificence expected of "contemporary" middle-class living. This, it suggested, was the industry's chief dilemma, which applied to urban as well as suburban projects.[51]

Retailers followed the trade journals' lead. Other New York department stores joined Hearns in pitching their home furnishings to Stuyvesant Towners explicitly, offering a number of different services to help buyers outfit their apartments. They approached women shoppers or young couples in particular, addressing the need to find a balance between comfort and ease and compact space and value.

Ludwig Baumann—"Homemaker to Millions"—offered consumers the LB Housing Center, a full-service section of its Eighth Avenue store where residents

3.3. Hearns department stores made a big pitch for customers from Stuyvesant Town. The chain built a replica of a Stuyvesant Town apartment in its 14th Street branch and offered continuously updated design and decoration ideas pitched to a middle-class audience trying to make homes in the new standardized project. Hearns Stuyvesant Town advertisement, *Town and Village*, November 1947. Hagedorn Communications.

of all the new housing projects, public and private, could come for help in furnishing their new spaces. The store ran a newspaper ad for it, too, naming all the recently built or soon-to-be-finished projects and featuring the familiar image of the Stuyvesant Town model. The model was pictured in context—surrounded on all sides by replicas of the crowded buildings of the Lower East Side—a tactic that served to highlight its open spaces and clean lines. Hovering over the balsa-wood cityscape was a line drawing of a young, conservatively dressed white couple, intently surveying the project with an air of considered satisfaction. Ludwig Baumann promised this young family "complete blueprints of the apartments, the exact room measurements, the layouts." The store had "unusual color themes" and "new furniture planning" offered by "professional decorators, color stylists and designers," who could "plan dramatic window treatments" and "work out stunning space-saving, space-making arrangements." LB offered to initiate project-dwellers into the pleasures of the domestic arts, suggesting that housing project apartments, with all their bothersome "light, space and exposure problem[s]," could become "your lovely new home" with the proper planning.[52]

Gimbels teamed up with *McCall's* magazine to demonstrate how to dispel the "institutional look" associated with Stuyvesant Town apartments. They redecorated Mr. Wyeth Ramsay's apartment, a duplicate of which went on display at the store. "Solid blond maple" furniture, "fashioned along clean, modern lines," complemented a living room done in beige, brown, green, blue, and yellow; a four-piece sectional sofa was covered in "a textured plaid in green, yellow and brown." There was a lightweight aluminum lamp "finished in a lovely dull beige," and the double bed in the master bedroom featured a "maple-framed headboard," which could be covered in "fabric or in plastic leather." All such details were intended to spare the budget, but not at the expense of modern, "attractive" design.[53]

In September 1948, *House and Garden* gave Stuyvesant Town its imprimatur, portraying the development as a "first real home" with "a country air." The story—called "They Live in Stuyvesant Town"—profiles Doris and Jack Landman, who, after the "uncertain, nomadic war years," are "really settling down to stay put." Jack is a teacher and Doris a mother of two. Since they have "endured all sorts of conditions of furniture and accessories," they prefer modern design. Using affordable "modular units" from Macy's, the Landmans conquer the classic Stuyvesant Town dilemma: lack of space and a modest budget. They make decisions as a family unit, but the story portrays Doris as the frontline consumer, choosing the storage units and selecting fabrics "which she and her husband both liked." She does much of the sewing and he the painting. This modern apartment, so cleverly appointed for contemporary living, is an equitable, comfortable space, with just the right amount of traditionalism to be a proper home. The piece opens with an aerial photo of Stuyvesant Town. But in

3.4. This department store ad situated Stuyvesant Town as one among many new housing projects, most of which were public housing. In this early postwar moment, public and private mass housing were understood as part of the same market, and each could be depicted as objects of middle-class desire. Ludwig Baumann advertisement, *New York Journal-American*, October 24, 1947.

order to emphasize that the project can be a "real home," the magazine super-imposed a two-bedroom floor plan over the East River. An arrow connects the disembodied floor plan to the Landmans' window in the labyrinth of towers, revealing how the decoration schemes on offer in the article can domesticate and individualize the project's repetitive enormity. Stuyvesant Town is a real home, the article seemed to say, because one could enjoy its amenities while learning how to humanize its impersonal scale.[54]

It's impossible to know whether Stuyvesant Town residents rushed to Hearns and Gimbels or took specific tips from the Landmans. But they did participate in their own, local communal forum for comparing and inspiring interior decoration. Every week, *Town and Village* featured a design column called "The House I Live In," which highlighted one Stuyvesant Town apartment and the design and furnishing choices of its inhabitants.[55] Each tour of a neighbor's apartment was a quick lesson in the domestic arts. The columns were illustrated with artist Edward Caswell's renditions of the living room, and his line drawings were titled by family name: "The Home of the Shepard Kurnits" or "The Home of George and Magda White." Like the mass media articles and department store ads, the column focused on style, color, materials, and efficient use of space. It recounted the process by which the family had made their decisions and gave a few details about the family's life. Both husbands and wives contributed to the design projects. But with only a few exceptions, the men confirmed women's opinions and executed the plans. They built the shelves and storage space, while women selected fabrics and styles. Invariably, it was women who led the reporter around the apartment, narrating the decision-making process and explaining the various problems she and her husband confronted and overcame. Except where husbands were industrial designers, architects, or the like, "The House I Live In" was largely women's space. The column was written by female interior decorators and featured a series of wives displaying their domestic spaces for the envy, critique, or imitation of their neighbors. These women were the frontline troops, converting Stuyvesant Town's space limitations and rigid, repeated plans into comfortable, livable spaces. The column was based on the idea that each family had its own well-considered style. Each week, the form was the same—the 220-square-foot living room—but the content was different. The authors stressed variation and, most important, practical and inventive methods of solving the usual space problems. As a group of buildings Stuyvesant Town may have been a series of boxes, susceptible to the "institutional look," but the real life of the place, the column suggested, was in its people and their individual stylistic improvisations. They made the development's repeated geometric structures into just what Stanley Isaacs had predicted it could never be, while the column itself provided a sense of shared endeavor in making the "series of homes" into a functioning community.

Bed Room
15' x 12'

Bed Room
9' x 14'

Living Room
12' x 18'

Dining

Kitchen

Scale In Feet   0   5   10   15   20   25

3.5. *House and Garden* and postwar retailers helped residents to adapt to the enormity of the project, showing how one unit in a vast housing complex could be made a "home." "They Live in Stuyvesant Town," *House and Garden* (September 1948). Photographs by Kurt Miehlmann and Haanel Cassidy, text by Irwin Clavan. © Condé Nast Publications.

They live in Stuyvesant Town

How a young couple, furnishing their first real home, used paint
and pretty materials to stretch their limited decorating budget

TENANT JACK LANDMAN helps daughter Leslie off the slide in one of the many playgrounds.

JUNGLE GYMS for youngsters to climb form an intricate pattern.

TREES AND GRASS outside the Landmans' apartment add a country air.

D ORIS and Jack Landman were married in 1943, the week after he got his wings at Pensacola. Five years (and a number of rented houses and apartments) later, they are really settling down to stay put. The intervening years have added a daughter, Leslie, now three-and-a-half, and Susan, who is brand new, to the family. Mr. Landman has a job as a teacher, and an apartment in one of New York's housing developments, Stuyvesant Town. Getting this particular apartment was a stroke of good fortune they appreciate to the full. The rent is reasonable ($76.50 a month) and the sunny playgrounds, with their jungle gyms and protected areas for skating, hopscotch and other games, are grand for children. The apartment, though it is not large, has two bedrooms, and presents few decorating problems because of the intelligent placement of windows, the generous lengths of wall which are convenient for storage units. In addition, community spirit runs high. As a matter of common consent, neighbors keep an eye on each other's children, take telephone messages and help out with the marketing. (Continued on the next page)

Opposite:
THE VAST BEEHIVE of the housing development called Stuyvesant Town overlooks New York's East River, when finished will comprise 8,755 apartments. The one whose plan is at the top is rented by the Landmans, a family of four.

Page 6 STUYVESANT TOWN & COOPER VILLAGE, NEW YORK, N. Y. November

The House I Live In

Mr. Shepard Kurnit of Apartment 4A, 635 East Fourteenth Street is a twenty-three year old commercial artist and an interior decorator who believes in modern design. And naturally, when it came to furnishing his four room apartment, all his knowledge, taste, and prejudices in art were put to good use.

Furnishing a home well when your furniture budget runs high in the four figures is relatively simple, both Mr. Kurnit and his young wife, Jean agree. But when economy is definitely an item, ingenuity pays off.

T A apartments in 635 are unique for Stuyvesant Town in that they all have a dining alcove that is walled on three sides completely separate from the living room. This makes the living room a separate unit and therefore a slightly different designing problem.

The living room is modern, very simple, and warm. Solid colors are prevalent, and the fabrics, in the modern school, are bright rough weaves. The couch on the left wall is actually two sectional pieces in dubonnet. The lamp at its far end is a good example of Mr. Kurnit's strong desire to keep his apartment functional, without of course losing any necessary warmth. It is solid gray, and in the position illustrated, serves as an excellent reading lamp since it casts its light on the couch below the eye level. But when the flexible coil that makes up a good part of its length is bent upward to a vertical position the reflector becomes inverted, making it a desirable reflector lamp.

The rug, again in the modern school, is a very inexpensive coarse-weave cotton and jute rug that according to Mr. Kurnit has only one disadvantage — its gets dirty quickly. But were it darker, its good looks and functional value to Mr. Kurnit would make it an ideal buy. A nine by twelve of this type sells for only $39.

On the right side of the room, contrasting beautifully with the gray rug and dubonnet couch, are two "Eames" chairs. Made of plywood molded to fit body contours, these chairs have had quite a brilliant career. Before they were sold to the general public, they were exhibited at the Museum of Modern Art as a good example of function and beauty combined. While on exhibit an Eames chair was put into a revolving barrel similar to those at Coney Island, and left there for three months. The tremendous abuse it underwent hardly scratched the surface of this structurally perfect piece.

The Home of the Shepard Kurnits

Underneath the moulded seat and behind the back rest, the designer has inserted rubber foam cushions which make this black-lacquered wooden chair feel like an armchair.

An artist himself, Mr. Kurnit considers a good many artists are worthy of occupying some space on his walls. But like most every appreciative person, any single painting becomes a bit tiring after a while. To solve this problem, and at the same time save the prohibitive cost of a good many wood frames, Mr. Kurnit has built a two-sided frame (top and bottom) nine feet long. In it are eight 12 by 18 inch units covered by the same size window glass sheets 12 by 18 cost $.25 at most any hardware [illegible]. At this moment Picasso, Renoir, Van Gogh and other less celebrated moderns grace this wall. But the very-modern Steinberg may soon find himself having a one-man show at the Kurnits, and Shepard says he also has plans for photographic exhibits etc.

The beam-to-beam A apartments in 635 also have two beams in the far wall drapes. They are a solid green, again in rough-textured fabric. In the illustration they have been pulled to cover the casement.

The problems of attractive modern yet inexpensive dinette chairs, has been solved by Mr. Kurnit in a very satisfactory and inexpensive manner. He designed and made them himself. Using a friend's workshop and birch plywood, Mr. Kurnit made both chairs (left foreground of the illustration) and then webbed them himself. The last of the webbing, in fact, was just completed this past Saturday.

Before they moved in, ever-the-artist Kurnit had ideas about repainting one wall chocolate brown, but the service department soon dissolved his desires. Mr. Kurnit, however, is compensating spectacularly. Between the foyer and the living room, to make for an interesting division, he has plans for a box suspended in mid air by four or five parallel ropes from ceiling to floor. The box will be illuminated within by three fluorescent tubes, covered on both sides by frosted glass interrupted only by twelve open sections. In these open sections, Mr. Kurnit intends to insert kodachrome transparencies (he's also a camera fiend), and photo reproductions of paintings. Like his walled art gallery, the transparencies would be changed often.

The far side of the room (not illustrated) will contain a wall-size bookcase, record, radio, and phonograph unit that he has designed and which will be built by a cabinet maker. The deep-set bookcases will hold two books in depth, and a back platform, raised above the lower one will keep the back set of books partially exposed.

From the description, it seems to be a one-man show, but Mrs. Kurnit really doesn't object. She thinks her husband has lots of ideas.

Browsing In the Shops

At Fred Leighton Inc., 15 East 8th Street, you will find inexpensive peasant furniture, informal cooking pottery, hand-blown glassware, lamps and rugs — a shop full of colorful, useful "South of the Border" crafts. Ideal for gifts and for home decorations. Open Wednesday and Friday until 10 p. m.

Library Invites Residents To New Child Book Show

A special invitation "to the young mothers of the city's two newest communities," was extended this week by Anna L. Glantz, administrative assistant, to attend the 35th annual exhibition of "Children's Books Suggested As Holiday Gifts" at the New York Public Library, 5th Avenue and 42nd Street.

The exhibition opened last Tuesday afternoon in the Central Children's Room with a celebration attended by authors, illustrators, editors, critics, teachers and librarians.

The more than 100 books exhibited represent a selection of the outstanding children's books published during the year. Featured are five books which are considered by Mrs. Frances Clarke Sayers, the Library's Superintendent of Work with Children, "to be especially noteworthy of their illustrations and text."

These books are "White Snow Bright Snow," "Pancakes-Paris," "Big City," "Return to the Level Land," and "The Quest of Johnny Longfoot."

Observe Meatless Tuesday.
Observe Eggless Thursday.
Back the food-saving program.

3.6. "The House I Live In," a regular column in the neighborhood newspaper *Town and Village,* provided a communal public forum for personalizing the institutional form of the generic Stuyvesant Town living room. The column's title, taken from the popular Frank Sinatra song celebrating pluralism and inclusion, revealed the progressive democratic spirit embraced by some of the residents, particularly in their campaign to desegregate the project. "The Home of the Shepard Kurnits," *Town and Village,* September 9, 1948. Hagedorn Communications.

As "The House I Live In" indicated, community was always possible among people who shared similar or complementary experiences and tastes. The column gave residents a chance to glimpse their neighbors' particular takes on solving the inherent problems of Stuyvesant Town living, while also providing a forum for both imagined and actual community. The column could provide an invisible connection between strangers who shared similar circumstances and backgrounds, while readers also knew that they were sharing actual, defined, physical space with those strangers, the inclusive boundaries of which indicated that anonymous neighbors could easily become friends. Unlike in much home marketing and design media, the column's appeal was never based on property envy; everyone began on a level playing field, with the same physical space, and anybody could create the designs on display each week or, better, their own personal version of them. Mildly voyeuristic, but always tasteful and careful to balance modernity and tradition in matters of culture, the column offered residents the chance to participate in a democratic, widely shared, available world of popular taste and refinement governed by women. The column's name, taken from Frank Sinatra's 1945 anthem of wartime pluralism and inclusion, said it best. The very apartments of Stuyvesant Town were imbued with the ethic that had inspired so many of the young families headed by veterans: equality, tolerance, and forward-looking modernity, a kind of tasteful, progressive, democratic spirit. The private, domestic space of Stuyvesant Town should, according to *Town and Village,* stand for these public ideals. Stuyvesant Town's "houses" should be just like the "house" of the nation—dedicated to equality, pluralism, and a comfortable, secure way of life. Of course, in segregated Stuyvesant Town the column's title was something of a provocation as well. If the song's most controversial lyric—"All races and religions / That's America to me"—had been excised from Sinatra's popular short-film version, the message remained widespread as an ideal even in the early Cold War years. Considering the paper's liberal editorial policy—pro-integration but anti-Communist—it seems likely that the editor didn't know the song's Popular Front origins (or that its writers, Earl Robinson and Lewis Allan, were left-wing songwriters close to the Communist Party) but believed that its economic populism and racial pluralism should be the social contents of Stuyvesant Town's many "houses."[56]

Regimentation or Freedom?

You live *there*? It looks like a barracks...all those identical apartments and all that regimentation. And you *like* it?
—Anonymous comments on Stuyvesant Town, *New York Herald Tribune,* December 1956

While many Stuyvesant Towners embraced the project as a new landscape for urban middle-class life, there was no getting around the fact that it had what Gimbels called an "institutional look." At first glance, remembered Martha Seidman, it was "mammoth, big, unattractive." Proper attention to domestic ideals would help to offset this problem, but residents' working relationship with postwar marketers and retailers could not allay all the fears that Stuyvesant Town resembled a barracks. Concerns about the "regimented" character of Stuyvesant Town living went beyond aesthetic questions of interior decoration.

Savvy domestic decision making could do little to change the fact that the public often thought of Stuyvesant Town as less like a suburban home and more like the New York City Housing Authority's public projects. The unornamented red-brick façades, superblock siting, and blocky lines of the towers looked almost identical to the public housing that was going up around the city and nearby on the Lower East Side. Met Life itself admitted that, "from time to time, Stuyvesant Town has mistakenly been referred to as if it were a public housing project." Even residents casually called their home "the project." As the Ludwig Baumann Housing Center ad demonstrated, listing Fresh Meadows (built by New York Life Insurance in Queens), Riverton, and Stuyvesant Town along with the Jacob Riis, Abraham Lincoln, Brownsville, and James Weldon Johnson projects made it seem that public and private developments were in the same class of housing, with residents who had similar spatial and lifestyle needs. Over the years, Met Life worked hard to dispel this notion, going to some lengths to show that public projects, although "well-run," were "not comparable to Stuyvesant Town."[57]

Most of the differences, the company said, were physical. Stuyvesant Town rooms were 40 percent larger, while public housing had no plaster on its ceilings or columns, just painted concrete. Public projects had "asphaltic tile" instead of oak flooring and steel bathroom fixtures instead of porcelain. The most austere public housing in the late 1940s had no doors to the kitchen or closets, and what doors it did have were wood, not fireproof steel. Project elevators often stopped only at every other floor; there was even exposed plumbing in the bathroom ceilings. By the late '50s, as public housing declined, urban troubles deepened, and the suburban exodus of industry and residents grew, the differences appeared to be social and cultural as well. For Town and Village in 1957, it was lamentable that its beat "might outwardly resemble" public housing, because the paper's editors saw little similarity. "Public mismanagement," they said, voicing a growing consensus, had made public projects "as lawless as jungles" with a "lurid record of brutality, terror, perversion and juvenile crime."[58]

Fears about crime and disorder in public housing were, to a certain degree, displaced concerns about the world outside the Stuyvesant Town superblock. Residents were ambivalent about the surrounding neighborhood, which seemed to present just such a contrast with the restrained confines of the project. "When you stepped across First Avenue," Demas writes:

> you were in another culture. There were crowds and bustle and disorder, dogs and cats who may not have belonged to anyone in particular, and litter of all varieties. In the gutter there were broken bottles and decayed fruit, and once I saw a mouse, not-quite-dead, in a discarded trap. The sidewalk was uneven and punctuated by cellar doors, often flapped open to reveal the catacombs of shops below....And the smells! Baking bread, garlic, garbage, paint, the sweat of people.

Outside the "walled town" was a visual and olfactory jumble it had been designed to supersede, a world apart that upended the conventions on which the development itself was predicated. One resident, for instance, was wandering around east of First Avenue one day in 1949. He'd heard that somewhere on 17th Street was the house where Antonín Dvořák had composed the *New World Symphony*. When he couldn't find it, he asked a local resident. "Who?" she asked. He explained that he meant the composer. She shrugged and told him, with disdain for his lack of street savvy, "Why don'tcha check the mail boxes." This little vignette, told for the amusement of *Town and Village* readers, gave them a concrete example, through the language of class and taste, of just how different the "culture" out there was supposed to be.[59]

Of course, some Stuyvesant Town residents had grown up in neighborhoods like that, and so the surrounding blocks represented something from which they had escaped. The Lower East Side was not quite foreign, but rather a place that was back in time as much as over there, across First Avenue or 14th Street. That may have meant looking across the borders of the development in horror or in fondness, but always with concern. For instance, in July 1948, *Town and Village* ran an exposé on sanitary conditions in stores on First Avenue and 14th Street. Seymour Roman, of 4 Stuyvesant Oval, wrote in to castigate the editors for their snobbery. He did not "accept" the paper's "proposition that these conditions should be corrected because we who live in Stuyvesant and Cooper patronize those stores. Please remember that the sanitary faults you point out affect all people in this neighborhood....The idea that Stuyvesant and Cooper residents are a people apart is abhorrent." While he was sure that the problems should be corrected, there and elsewhere in the city, he asked the editor to recall that everyone in the project had been the victim of the housing shortage. They were all lucky, and "your paper," he wrote, "would be helpful if it rallied former victims of the housing shortage to the aid of the present victims." He and his fellow Stuyvesant Towners "do not exist in a vacuum," he concluded.[60]

And yet perhaps the most widespread and recurring concerns for Stuyvesant Towners were their own struggles with the idea that the project was too orderly, that its austere design reflected the supposedly somnolent mass character of their lives. Outsiders charged that it was regimented or a barracks. Lewis Mumford was most notorious among Stuyvesant Towners for this view. "As things go nowadays one has only a choice of nightmares," wrote Mumford in his 1948 *New Yorker* review:

> Shall it be the old, careless urban nightmare of post–Civil War New York.... Or shall it be the new nightmare, of a great superblock, quiet, orderly, self-contained, but designed as if the fabulous innkeeper Procrustes had turned architect—a nightmare not of caprice and self-centered individualism, but of impersonal regimentation, apparently for people who have no identity but the serial numbers of their Social Security cards?

Stuyvesant Towners Milton and Mildred Lewis found these sorts of comments "patronizing," and many other residents reacted angrily to Mumford's attack, but that was in part because it represented their own fears.[61] The bland, standardized physical structure of the buildings was thought to mirror or, worse, even cause regimentation among its inhabitants. As William Cole sneered in a 1967 *New Yorker* poem called "Conformity":

> On any summer morning,
> With all the windows open,
> At exactly 7:30
> Stuyvesant Town
> Rings.

Regimentation, it seemed, even overwhelmed the project grounds. The landscaping, Demas remembers, was "regulated and manicured. Order always prevailed." The playgrounds, for instance, were fenced in, and "the children inside the playgrounds looked like zoo animals, caged in." "Forces of men in brown uniforms"—the project's maintenance staff—"were perpetually sweeping the sidewalks."[62]

Concerns about the "men in brown uniforms" abounded. The "guards," as Martha Seidman put it, "were ubiquitous." No small part of residents' anxiety about living in a regimented environment came from their conflicts with Met Life itself. Mumford had called Stuyvesant Town "the architecture of the police state," and if residents resented the idea that this described them, the idea that the physical design communicated something about the builder's intentions seemed not so far off the mark. While many, like Seidman and Pamela Long, appreciated the safety the guards provided, some believed that they were there to police them and their behavior as much as that of outsiders. "The threat 'I'll report you,'" Demas remembers, "was always in the air in Stuyvesant Town." Residents lived in fear that neighbors would report them to the management for rule violations. "Any infraction, any misbehavior, any straying from the norm," she writes, "could result in the penalty all residents lived in fear of: eviction." Rules abounded in Stuyvesant Town, and they made a deep impression on people. One mother, lamenting the lack of sandboxes in the playgrounds, expressed her concern. She had taken her son to the beach, and every time he saw a man, "whether he was in uniform or not," he had asked his mother "whether he should stop digging."[63]

Many residents believed that the Metropolitan had rigid ideas about community standards. Although these strictures were apparently vague and undefined, rumor was that they extended to the mundane details of domestic life. Residents particularly worried that Met Life would inspect their apartments and report them for violations. They heard that hanging pictures was forbidden; they heard that the company had men who patrolled the grounds looking for apartments where tenants had left the lights on while out. These men, it was said, had master keys and would enter apartments to turn lights out. Even more fantastic was the rumor that, if a resident had a party and then went out leaving dishes in the sink, the company had someone who would come up, wash the dishes, and leave the tenants a bill for services rendered.[64]

Met Life was hardly the authoritarian power of Mumford's hyperbole or residents' rumors, but the company was vigilant about the norms of its community. Management preferred paternal munificence to outright autocracy. It sent out pamphlet after pamphlet—often with the rent bill—advising tenants on the rules and regulations of Stuyvesant Town living, while also instructing them on the proper etiquette of middle-class project life. The company told residents how to avoid overloading the electric circuits and how to wash their windows; encouraged them to vote in national elections; gave them a map of the project so that their visitors wouldn't get confused in the labyrinth of towers; warned them to watch out for pedestrians when on their bikes and in their cars; told them to stay off the grass and not to litter; offered technical assistance on making their open windows safe for babies; tutored them in the patriotic history of nearby locales; instructed them in the use and care of their refrigerators and in elevator etiquette; warned kids about the perils to innocent passersby of rambunctious play; advised them on Christmas tree disposal; suggested rugs to cut down on noise and a quiet tone of voice for summer nights when all the windows were open; and instructed them in proper incinerator etiquette. These notices, couched in terms of friendly advice and illustrated with lighthearted cartoons, appealed to the idea of shared community, while consistently reminding residents what was expected of them as individual members of that community.[65]

Of course, the company did, as some feared, monitor the residents' behavior. As a part of ensuring the livability of the community and the profitability of its investment, the management made reports for its files on all sorts of tenant activities. Looking at one year of reports reveals a vast assortment of incidents judged worthy of official notice, from serious crimes like robberies, burglaries, sexual assaults, and car thefts (mostly by nonresidents against tenants), to less serious violations of domestic regulations. These include kids' pranks, illegal alterations of electrical wiring discovered while making repairs, parking violations, disorderly and dirty apartments, children loitering at building entrances, an unsanitary refrigerator discovered while it was being repaired, elevator tampering, a woman who fed a cat on the lawn, and another resident's ill-tempered cat that scratched two workmen.[66] Various kinds of behavior, both dangerous and seemingly inconsequential, were grounds for a report and, as tenants suspected, potential eviction. During the struggle over the evictions of the antisegregation activists, George Gove, stonewalling on the question of whether the activists were being evicted for their political activities, told an official at the Citizens Housing Council that the company never told residents the reasons for their evictions. "You can't give the real reasons," he said. "Some are persistently drunk; some may be dirty housekeepers. They are the kind of tenants who will never be part of the community. They will never be absorbed into the community." Met Life, Gove admitted, was prepared to evict residents for their failures as housekeepers. The norms of this private middle-class community were internal and domestic, designed to ensure residents' own propriety, as much as they were defensive and exclusive, designed to keep outsiders out. Residents—insiders—could become outsiders if they did not observe these norms.[67]

Met Life was not alone in policing the boundaries of propriety. Stuyvesant Towners themselves kept a steady stream of complaints flowing to management, many of which became official reports. They complained when the company provided inefficient or slow service, particularly when it came to cleaning the halls and repairing damage to apartments. But residents, as Demas remembered, were just as likely to report their neighbors for violations as the company was to discover them on their own. Stuyvesant Towners reported on their neighbors most often for small nuisances, such as welcome mats or garbage left in the hall, minor vandalism, obscene graffiti, littering, "destructive irresponsible children," excessive noise, "obstreperous teenage activity," boys playing ball on the lawn, and "inconsiderate and loud-mouthed people." Some residents of Stuyvesant Town thought that the main threat to the project's middle-class standards came from the residents themselves. As one anonymous and particularly disturbed letter writer said to the resident manager about all the littering and noise:

> It is time that the residents of Stuyvesant Town are explicitly told what is expected of them, and if there are any rules or regulations they should be strictly enforced—without excepting anyone—and on a steady basis, not just for a few weeks or months.... Perhaps plain-clothes men from time to time would be the answer to bring things under control.... many residents beside myself are deeply distressed and concerned that the beauty, peace and cleanliness of the community is [*sic*] being destroyed.[68]

Of course, the letter writer, like most Stuyvesant Towners, appreciated his "lovely apartment at such a very reasonable rent." Residents complained to the company about service or about their neighbors precisely because they believed, as Met Life did, that it was a place of "beauty, peace and cleanliness." In fact, Stuyvesant Towners' biggest gripes were about the limitations of project living for middle-class aspirations. They had bought into the ideal, now they wanted to fulfill it. As more and more of them bought cars, they complained that there was never enough parking; the once-empty streets of the Gas House District were filled not only by modern towers and verdant landscaping, but also with too many cars for too few spaces. As more and more of them bought televisions, they complained about reception; Met Life was slow in putting up central antennas on each building, and as a result Stuyvesant Towners could get few channels. And as they watched their suburban compatriots across the country expanding into the hotter climes of the South and West, they too wanted to be able to conquer sweltering summer days with air conditioning. But Stuyvesant Town wasn't wired for that much voltage, and it would be years before residents could have their own window units. Stuyvesant Town's limitations only served to heighten residents' desires for the expected consumer accoutrements of postwar middle-class life. The disjuncture between these shortcomings and the domestic ideals of the postwar market that Met Life had embraced to sell the project encouraged many residents to complain that the company had failed to live up to its own vision of the project.[69]

The biggest challenge to the viability of middle-class life in Stuyvesant Town, however, was Met Life's first proposed rent increase in early 1952. Pitting residents squarely against their munificent landlord, the conflict over the rent hike symbolized the character of this middle-class community. When Metropolitan, citing soaring costs and returns below its guaranteed 6 percent, went before the Board of Estimate in May 1952 to request a $7.87 per room monthly increase, more than 600 Stuyvesant Towners packed the chamber to protest. Calling upon that familiar rhetorical specter of New York politics, the "vanishing middle class," residents and others looked to protect and conserve their experiment in urban mass housing. If a housing development designed particularly for the middle class could not preserve middle-class rents, they asked, then how could middle-class life survive on the island of Manhattan? "This is supposed to be a middle-class project," said Mrs. Shirley Rosner. "If this increase goes through all the middle-class people will have to move out."

According to the *Herald Tribune,* Rosner was the "wife of a salesman and mother of two young children." About 90 percent of the 600 protestors at City Hall that day were women, homemakers like Rosner who had come on 16 special buses with their children. Making the private public, temporarily shedding their domestic roles to protect the sanctity of that station, these women thought it worth stepping outside of respectable norms to protect the privileges of comfort, order, and ease they enjoyed as tenants in Stuyvesant Town. The sight of mothers feeding children and babies in strollers in the chambers of government was a dramatic demonstration of what the rent hike would imperil. Met Life, they demonstrated, was putting the squeeze on the very middle-class ideal the city had intended Stuyvesant Town to underwrite. Homemakers, mothers, and babies, the backbone of this ideal, would be the primary victims of the rent increase. Losing them would mean losing stable family life and with it the middle-class identity around which the project was organized. The organization that tenants displayed on this occasion yielded mixed results—they were only able to turn back the increase temporarily—but it revealed perhaps the most concrete demonstration of their shared sense of community.[70]

Can we definitively describe the character of the shared middle-class life Stuyvesant Town residents defended? Perhaps not; the conflicts surveyed here distilled no coherent identity from a varied population. Better, then, to see that life as shaped by a series of negotiations over the various possibilities and limits offered by Stuyvesant Town living. Of course, residents undertook these transactions in the face of the very definite visions offered by their landlord. Met Life hoped that Stuyvesant Town's open spaces, trees, and garden city landscaping approximated suburban remove, security, and ease. At the same time, the project's neighborhood-unit scale and the company's cheery prescriptions for behavior and community togetherness sought to encourage the spontaneous, face-to-face connection thought to inhere in urban or even small town, village life. The top-down delivery of these homilies and the Metropolitan's carefully guarded behavioral norms, however, suggested that community by bureaucracy was a fraught goal. Whether they welcomed or resented Met Life's attentions, residents made the project their own arena for enacting a middle-class life carved from the working-class tenement grid. Accepting or disputing the company's guidance as they saw fit, Stuyvesant Towners walked a narrow path between suburban exclusivity and urban heterogeneity, segregation and open housing, humble origins and elevated postwar prospects, consumer freedom and rejuvenated gender roles, and individuality and regimentation, all the while working out their own takes on what it meant to be middle class in mass housing.[71]

The most sustained tension in the development was between individual liberty—most often figured in the idiom of consumer freedom—and the institutional sameness prescribed by the project's architecture and its watchful landlord. Most Stuyvesant Towners, even those who fought to turn back the rent increase or desegregate the project, seem to have embraced the overall terms under which the project was advertised and planned. But even when they shared the company's ideals and goals, they often resisted the sense that it knew what was best for them. Wanting the private autonomy that middle-class life was thought to embody, but not wanting to lose the convenience and urbanity of city life, residents were both welcoming and distrustful in the face of Met Life's removed and paternal authority. Some feared that the company had the power, which it did, to invade and disrupt their homes, while others fretted that the company did too little to protect and guard the "public" areas of the development it owned. This tension, between autonomy and authority, provided the frame in which this private project, built in the name of the public good, was seen in its early years.

After 1949, when New York and other cities looked to the federal government to help fund private redevelopment of the inner city for middle-class life, this conflict would be magnified. Urban redevelopment's mass intervention in the cityscape, seeking a wholesale transformation of urban experience in the name of middle-class standards, would continue to be dogged by the difficulties Stuyvesant Towners faced. In the coming years, however, the tension would increasingly be figured in terms supplied by the domestic political culture of the Cold War. If the fate of desegregation at Stuyvesant Town was determined by the degree to which civil rights appeared all-American, the career of urban renewal itself would be shaped by a related rhetorical debate. Slum clearance and modern rebuilding would be hailed where it appeared to underwrite supposed American virtues—individualism, prosperity, homefront security—and decried where it seemed to herald the arrival of social characteristics more commonly associated with the Cold War enemy: regimentation, mass scale, anonymity, and unchecked power over individual lives.

In 1950, *Town and Village* asked the "noted artist" Reginald Marsh for his opinion of the new project. Marsh, the newspaper reported, was a neighbor. He lived just west of Stuyvesant Town on 15th Street and had a studio on Union Square. Unfortunately, Marsh was none too fond of Stuyvesant Town. "Each window looks like its neighbor," he said. "It's too big. Too uninteresting." Marsh, the reporter said, preferred "places where people congregate, such as Coney Island, busy tenement streets, docks and parks," and thought that the only "dynamic, really alive picture" in the new development was "the children romping in the playgrounds." Marsh was an urban realist, known for his depictions of the jostling to and fro of working-class city life, the play of glances and bodies in New York's theaters, subways, and streets. His sketchy, earthy watercolors and engravings shared subject matter with 1930s social realism, but dispensed with radical urgency in favor of gritty romance. "When it comes to a choice between a Third Avenue derelict and a business man," he told the *Town and Village* reporter, "I'll take the derelict any time." Stuyvesant Town, having cleared away all the ingredients of his art, was almost unrepresentable for him. "There's no picture in a Stuyvesant Town husband going to work in the morning." Marsh found something menacing in the project's blank façades and its straight, high towers. Stuyvesant Town was just another step toward what he called an "invisible abstract world."

Marsh could think of only one way to make a "picture" out of Stuyvesant Town. "From the Brooklyn shore," he said, "with the surrounding skyline as background," the "invisible abstract world" of the Stuyvesant Town towers "would make a fine cubist painting." Practically unrepresentable as realism, with seemingly no dramatic human subject matter worth recording—Marsh seems to have missed the ongoing clamor over desegregation—Stuyvesant Town was imaginable only from a distance as a set of shapes and forms disrupting the space and time of the old city's "surrounding skyline." This, after all, was the ambition at the heart of the ethic of city rebuilding. Now that it had been realized in brick, steel, and glass, the visions of that ethic could seem less profound and more overwhelming. In the long run, Stuyvesant Town was a success for Met Life and for most of its residents. But over the next decade, as the ethic of city rebuilding was replaced by the practice of urban renewal, New Yorkers would begin to wonder whether this new form of mass culture, this new "invisible abstract world" ushered in by further efforts in building new mass homes for urban living, was worth the costs it seemed to entail. If they at first welcomed urban renewal's efforts to remake the cityscape, they began to question the way it uprooted communities and replaced them with overwhelming, seemingly anonymous new urban spaces. These tensions blossomed in the controversies surrounding New York's most well-known urban renewal project: Lincoln Square, home of the Lincoln Center for the Performing Arts.[72]

NEW YORK STATE THEATER

Lincoln Square

CHAPTER 4

CULTURE AND COLD WAR IN THE MAKING OF LINCOLN CENTER

Another West Side Story

Out of the most barren wastes, as poets since Chaucer have observed, come the most beautiful flowers. A barren urban waste is the Lincoln Square area on the west side of midtown New York. Old-law tenements stand, blowsy and run-down, in silent shoulder-to-shoulder misery, full of filth and vermin.... Out of it will rise the Lincoln Center for the Performing Arts, a cultural fairyland.
—Harold C. Schonberg, *New York Times*, May 1958

There is a scene early in the film version of *West Side Story* that provides a dramatic encapsulation of the intermingled hope and violence at the heart of urban renewal. As the overture crashes to its end, the screen blooms with a helicopter's-eye-view of lower Manhattan. The camera moves into the metropolis from over the harbor in short takes, backed by the high, distant roar of the city, an echoing whistle, and periodic, insistent conga drums. It ghosts over bridges and docked ocean liners, pausing slightly to take in iconic vistas of Battery Park and Wall Street, Rockefeller Center and the Empire State Building. It jumps uptown, making sure to survey the new blocky forms of the United Nations and Stuyvesant Town in its impromptu tour of Manhattan at midcentury. Slowly, the music gathers force, and the familiar thrill of this skyline panorama is undercut by mounting tension. Then, the camera slides off the end of Central Park, hops over to Broadway, and abruptly drops down to street level and into a West Side playground ruled by a finger-popping street gang. The Jets. They are white ethnic immigrant kids, those whom Arthur Laurents, in his book for the original 1957 play, labeled "an anthology of what is called 'American.'"[1]

The Jets are detached and distant, appearing to care even less for the camera than they do the mute parade of monuments just gone by. Their insouciance, their blank allegiance to the world of asphalt and chain-link fence before them, betrays no awareness of that other New York. But this is a musical, so the Jets' insouciance promptly gives way to exuberance. They take the camera's bait; the streets become a stage they turn to their own ends. Grabbing us and dancing us over their turf to Leonard Bernstein's rushing score, the Jets leap and pirouette over their gang name chalked across the street, laying claim to what's theirs. Then, all of a sudden, they are brought up short by the Sharks, their Puerto Rican antagonists. As outsiders in both neighborhood and nation, the Sharks don't own the turf or the choreographic focus. Their dance is brasher and less assured, but more daring. They lure the Jets through the streets, conducting ambushes and guerrilla raids on land not theirs, rushing in from beyond the frame to claim their own name in the street. The resolutely local world their dance reveals seems only distantly related to the monumental city the camera surveyed on its way down to these streets. The symbols of New York's financial, political, and cultural sway over the globe at midcentury appear inconsequential to the decisive, life-or-death geopolitics of these few blocks. Who owns the street, not the world, is the question that shapes these lives.

But then, just before the scene's climax, the walls and streets part, and we get a view of the world beyond. One of the Sharks goads three Jets into a rubble-strewn lot. He leads them up and over a head-high pile of broken concrete and into a hail of vegetables, eggs, and rocks thrown by his lurking comrades. And there, as the camera follows them to the top of the demolition pile, is a sudden vista of a huge modern apartment building hovering over the rubble. It's little more than a glimpse of the world beyond the few blocks over which the gangs fight, but it serves as a brief reminder that the urban world of *West Side Story*'s skirmishes—the streets in their nineteenth-century grid, the dark, hovering tenements, the gangs with their all-consuming struggles—is doomed, slated to go under the bulldozer and be replaced by the new forms ushered in by Stuyvesant Town and the United Nations. It's the most blatant display of the most obvious of *West Side Story*'s narrowly sociological lessons. In its depiction of juvenile delinquency, gangs, and Puerto Rican immigrants, the film showed what was "wrong" with the city and why those neighborhoods would be leveled to make way for a new, modern cityscape. Seen by millions, *West Side Story* was a "blockbuster" in two senses of the word.

This opening scene was partly filmed on location in and around West 67th and 68th streets between Amsterdam and West End avenues in the late summer of 1960. By 1961, when the film reached theaters, those blocks no longer existed. They had been bulldozed and cleared of tenements, warehouses, and stores, made ready to be replaced by the Lincoln Square urban renewal project and its headline-grabbing centerpiece, Lincoln Center for the Performing Arts. Those particular blocks of 67th and 68th streets were subsumed into the superblock layout of developer William Zeckendorf's Lincoln Towers: eight 28-story luxury apartment buildings affixed to the northern end of the project in an effort to attract middle-class residents to the new performing arts district.[2]

And yet, against that foreboding glimpse of urban destruction, the careening playfulness of the dance introduces a contrapuntal note of possibility, one that seems to emerge from the same energies that will transform the old cityscape. The film's producers encouraged this notion, echoing and amplifying the fleeting impression from the film's early moments with a striking promotional image that ran in the issue of *Life* magazine that hit newsstands the week the film debuted. Taking half of a full two-page spread announcing an article titled "Explosion on the West Side," the image shows an exuberant Jet in the midst of a spread-eagle leap. Behind him, flames burst from a pile of debris and a bright, modern tower-block apartment shoots up in the distance. The caption reads, "Against smoldering rubble of New York slum clearance project Jet leader Riff (Russ Tamblyn) leaps in pride. The Jets, he sings, are kings of the world." With its frisson of urban dissolution and rebirth, this promotional image trades on the social imagination underlying urban renewal. The past, it suggests, lies burning before us while the future sweeps up from behind, shimmering with promise in the fire's roaring sheen. Like the modern tower itself, Riff springs from the revivifying fire of slum clearance.[3]

If *West Side Story* seems at first to offer a purely negative lesson about the benefits of urban renewal—depicting it as an effort to rid the city of accumulated ills—it also gestures at urban renewal's promise. The film advertises its own authentic eruption from the crucible of urban decay and slum clearance by reference to the power of what Lincoln Center construction director Otto Nelson called the "painful surgery" that "a virile and vast program of urban renewal" would bring to Manhattan. As the largest, most ambitious, far-reaching, and idealistic of New York's urban renewal efforts, the Lincoln Square project that replaced *West Side Story*'s real sets and imaginative setting was the most likely project to fulfill the spirit of urban renewal on display in the image of Riff leaping from this conflagration of destruction and rebirth. Spearheaded by Robert Moses and John D. Rockefeller III, the project featured not only the performing arts center and luxury housing complex, but also a campus for Fordham University and a headquarters building for the Red Cross. It has commonly been seen as the crowning achievement of renewal under Moses, a high-minded culmination of the process by which cities could, in Nelson's words, "continually and constantly renew themselves by casting off the old and taking on the new."[4]

In large part, this was because Lincoln Square was no mere nuts-and-bolts slum clearance operation. It provided that prosaic urban ideal with its most visionary content since the United Nations went up on Turtle Bay a decade earlier. With Lincoln Center as its centerpiece, Lincoln Square represented the fulfillment of the project of urban rebirth and international visibility, confirming New York's status as the so-called capital of the world. By the mid-1950s, when

4.1. "Explosion on the West Side," *Life,* October 20, 1961. This promotional image—
staged for the camera to advertise the upcoming film version of *West Side Story*—reveals
the mingling of hope and violence at the heart of urban renewal's intervention in the
cityscape. Gjon Mili/Time & Life Pictures/Getty Images.

the project got under way, this triumphal endeavor had acquired a more strategic mission as well, and Lincoln Center was called on to provide a symbol of national cultural maturity and urban resurgence that could be brandished in the Cold War with the Soviet Union. In a time when both urban renewal and the performing arts were envisioned as resources for shoring up the nation's internal cultural defenses, Lincoln Center brought these two cultural and urban missions together in one shining symbol and gave them concrete form in the cityscape. Rockefeller and his allies hoped that it would prove that Americans living in what he called the "affluent society" valued "spiritual" as much as material goods; they sought to symbolize these linked missions by providing Lincoln Center with a setting on a par with classical European models of urban planning. Intended as an American update of a Venetian piazza, Lincoln Center offered what Rockefeller envisioned as "a new kind of city therapy" that made culture and the arts the cornerstone of modernist superblock and open space urban renewal efforts. As in the cinematic world of *West Side Story*, it was the vitality of culture that would save the city.[5] ★

Cold War Urban Renewal

At a time when tomorrow may bring atomic death and destruction, it is hard to concentrate on planning and building for a better world.... Yet, the free society which we are willing to defend with our lives from aggression from without is in danger of crumbling from within unless each individual and each community nurtures the will to freedom and accepts the responsibilities which are incumbent on us as citizens.
—David Rockefeller, "Morningside Heights—The Institutions and the People," 1950

Lincoln Square was the most celebrated in a series of urban renewal collaborations between Robert Moses and a diverse cast of urban liberals from the private sector. Long before the 1949 Housing Act provided federal support and subsidies for slum clearance, urban redevelopment, and further public housing, Moses was working to get an ambitious program of clearance and rebuilding under way. Throughout the 1930s and '40s, Fiorello La Guardia had resisted giving Moses control over public housing and renewal. But Moses had convinced La Guardia's successor, William O'Dwyer, to grant him the newly created post of city construction coordinator and, in 1948, in anticipation of the 1949 Housing Act, a new title, head of the Committee on Slum Clearance (CSC). While the projects at the United Nations and Stuyvesant Town were under way, Moses tried to interest other insurance companies and various city banks in redevelopment projects, but none of these institutions was willing to risk money on slum sites and projects where they might face pressure to admit blacks as tenants. So Moses turned instead to a varied group of other interests, whose ties to city land and life gave them an urgent need to stem the tide of urban deterioration and shore up their investments. These included labor unions, hospital and university officials, builders and real estate developers, civic organizations, and various representatives of New York's financial and political elite, particularly members of the Rockefeller family, who worked through nonprofits, foundations, and other public-minded urban organizations. Over the course of the 1950s, Moses and his allies worked to bring the combined powers of public authority and private munificence to bear on the old nineteenth-century street grid, with its dense thickets of rowhouses, tenements, warehouses, commercial buildings, and factories. In clearing away this older urban world, they pursued both local and global ambitions. They looked to restore profitability to urban land, but they also, increasingly, hoped to give Manhattan a cityscape to match its growing global status and its emerging role as a symbol of American power in the Cold War. These paired concerns motivated a series of projects in the early 1950s all across the city, culminating in the Rockefeller-backed project on Morningside Heights, which served as a dress rehearsal for Cold War urban renewal at Lincoln Square.[6]

None of this, however, would have been possible without the federal Housing Act of 1949. Title I of the act funded urban redevelopment, giving localities federal money to offset the costs of assembling and clearing overpriced urban land.[7] The law's framers imagined that local redevelopment authorities would acquire land through eminent domain laws, clear it, and auction it to the highest bidder. But by the time Congress passed the 1949 Housing Act, Moses had already hashed out his own approach to redevelopment. His experience with Stuyvesant Town—along with the failure to attract banks or other insurance companies to rebuilding—led him to trust only iron-clad agreements with committed private backers. He made what amounted to backroom deals with sponsors he knew he could trust, offering them negotiated, fixed prices for land acquired by eminent domain, prearranged sales of the land with no competitive public auction, and control over clearance and tenant relocation. Securing developers before clearing the land, he said, was the only way to guarantee workable and successful projects.[8]

As head of the CSC, Moses identified patches of city land he deemed fit for clearance and determined whether they would support private investment, public rebuilding, or a combination of the two. He reserved for private sponsors tracts that were either too expensive for the New York City Housing Authority to acquire or too valuable as areas that might attract private investment for white-collar residents or institutions. He favored mixed redevelopments that combined public and private projects, but since federal law did not require blending the two, and private sponsors were often unwilling to have public housing nearby, he did not force the issue unless he could convince sponsors that nearby public housing would ease any controversy over relocation. This aroused the criticism of some housing advocates who, awakened by Stuyvesant Town, worried that private monies would further underwrite class inequality and racial segregation. Still, Moses persevered, preferring workable slum clearance projects to what he saw as pie-in-the-sky social engineering for urban social justice. Moses also favored slum clearance over any efforts at housing rehabilitation. Even after the 1954 Housing Act offered money for tenement rehabilitation to go along with clearance and rebuilding (the basis for the switch in terminology to "renewal"), Moses stuck to his initial procedure, maintaining that only full clearance and rebuilding were cost effective. Only with full clearance and an inside track for favored private partners, Moses maintained, could urban redevelopment deliver what he saw as its chief reward: a city cleansed of slums and ready to attract investment and general prosperity.

redevelopment not renewal

Most important, Moses took advantage of the 1949 act's vague wording to find space in Manhattan for more than just housing. The act restricted federal aid to "slums and blighted areas" that were "predominantly residential" or would be redeveloped for predominantly residential use. But this stricture was not specific enough to guarantee that rundown areas would be rebuilt with housing alone, much less low-income housing. While some city officials interpreted the 1949 act by its title, as explicitly a "housing act" designed to provide much-needed residential developments, Moses always maintained that it was simply another mechanism for slum clearance. Indeed, the terms of the law made it possible to demolish residential neighborhoods and replace them with largely commercial or institutional projects. Most of these included some housing, and some, particularly those built by union-backed cooperative organizations, were almost all housing. But New York and other cities took advantage of this ambiguity in the law, using urban renewal projects to build complexes for universities, hospitals, and civic institutions like Lincoln Center. In order to attract sources of private money and renew neighborhoods, Moses had to loosely interpret the "predominantly residential" clause. These kinds of projects confirmed that the primary objective of redevelopment had become keeping white and middle-class residents, shoppers, and, in the case of Lincoln Center, audiences in town, thereby offsetting suburbanization, propping up central business districts, and easing the fiscal troubles of cities. This was the ultimate endgame for the ethic of city rebuilding. Urban renewal, in the end, made up a key plank in a postwar politics of growth that funneled public subsidies to private entities in order to underwrite increased levels of production, consumption, and economic growth. It was the chief urban accomplishment of the "business welfare state" that housing reformer Charles Abrams had discovered a few years earlier at Stuyvesant Town.[9]

Moses's streamlined renewal practices helped New York to establish the largest Title I portfolio in the country. Between 1949 and 1961, roughly the period in which Moses controlled the redevelopment bureaucracy, New York City alone accounted for 32 percent of all construction activity under the federal law. He proposed 20 Title I projects across Manhattan, near downtown Brooklyn, and in Rockaway, Queens. The 16 of these that ultimately went up rebuilt 314 acres of old city by the early 1960s, displacing more than 28,000 families at a combined cost of $722 million to the city, federal government, and private sponsors. While other cities struggled with federal and local bureaucracies and site selection, Moses quickly identified sites and potential sponsors, made arrangements with city officials, brought bankers on board, directed NYCHA to make units available for relocation, and negotiated for federal funds.[10]

Moses cultivated a wide array of allies from New York's liberal political circles. These activists, drawn from various civic organizations, labor groups, chambers of commerce, local planning bodies, neighborhood groups, hospital and university boards, and elite nonprofit community betterment organizations, were determined to save their immediate areas from slums and blight. They worried about the displacement that rebuilding would cause, but reassured themselves with a larger vision of their neighborhoods cleared of slums and rebuilt along modern, discrimination-free lines. If their ally Robert Moses emphasized practical, achievable goals, they often imbued slum clearance and rebuilding with lofty ideals. Urban renewal appeared to them as a domestic calling congruent with the two great liberal crusades of the age. On the one hand, they drew strength from the memory of the fight against fascism in World War II; on the other, they envisioned rebuilt neighborhoods as internal bulwarks of freedom that were necessary for the struggle against Communism in the newly emerging Cold War. The contradictions between these high-minded visions and the realities of slum clearance would do much to determine not only the shape of rebuilding at Lincoln Square, but also the overall character of urban renewal in New York.[11]

Anxious to preserve their communities and restore profits in urban land, neighborhood leaders in late 1940s and early '50s New York faced a complicated situation. Industrial mobilization for war had unleashed a second great migration of blacks from the South and a new migration of Puerto Ricans, bringing many thousands of newcomers into the old tenement neighborhoods. At the same time, the struggle against fascism had brought new urgency to efforts to dissolve the domestic color line. Many of these leaders took the promise of the "open city" seriously. They embraced social science research heralding the

dissolve color line ⟶ today's "Immigrant Friendly City"

success of planned interracial housing, supported local antidiscrimination laws, and committed themselves to the idea of equal access to housing and public accommodations. They believed that, as historian Joel Schwartz has put it, "the postwar metropolis was to be created not only with brick and mortar, but also with a social structure born of a new racial etiquette."[12]

But in a series of neighborhoods across Manhattan in the early '50s—places like Greenwich Village, Morningside Heights, the Upper West Side, and the Lower East Side—neighborhood leaders worried most about the declining state of their actual bricks and mortar. Faced with the need to clear buildings and displace people, they reassured themselves with postwar liberalism's legislative progress toward formal racial equality and Moses's assurances that the New York City Housing Authority stood ready to absorb the uprooted. But the progress they most wanted required hard and brutal choices on the ground. Their campaigns to knock down tenement and warehouse districts and put up privately backed superblock and tower redevelopment projects fell heavily on working-class neighborhoods, particularly those available to urban newcomers of color from the South and Puerto Rico. At most renewal sites in the early 1950s—Corlears Hook, Manhattantown, Morningside Gardens, NYU-Bellevue, Washington Square Southeast, Columbus Circle—neighborhood leaders collaborated with Moses to remake working-class neighborhoods as white-collar preserves. A number of these areas were rearranged along racial lines as well. For instance, Corlears Hook, Manhattantown, Columbus Circle, and Morningside replaced areas that were between 24 and 65 percent nonwhite with primarily white, middle- or upper middle-class residential developments.[13]

Neighborhood boosters and civic leaders kept their focus on the new cityscape they hoped to usher in, smoothing out the complexities of class and race with an expansive vision of urban renewal's importance for the postwar world. Those who saw the fortunes of their immediate areas as intimately tied to national and international interests struck this note most explicitly. As Rockefeller Institute chief Detlev Bronk told David Rockefeller, he was determined to make the famed research institution's vision of expansion on the East Side help to serve the task of stemming decline and promoting rebuilding. "I want more than ever," he wrote, "to throw myself into the undertaking to make New York the glowing pattern for the future of urban living." Nearby, Winthrop Rockefeller and his deputies claimed that their NYU-Bellevue Hospital Title I project was of utmost importance "as New York City becomes preeminent as an International Medical Center and through the United Nations Center—the Capital of the World."[14]

With the coming of the Cold War, urban renewal's proponents also used this rhetoric to embrace a more specific set of geopolitical implications, which would culminate at Lincoln Square with the building of Lincoln Center. The rhetorical back and forth between free and unfree that governed the Cold War's competition of images and ideas gave neighborhood leaders the opportunity to make reclaiming Manhattan from decay not only part of a "glowing pattern for the future of urban living," but a measure of the nation's ability to meet the threat of Communism. Making common cause with domestic Cold Warriors, renewal boosters aligned particular neighborhood objectives with the abstract goal of preserving a free society. Of course, signing on to this combined mission turned out to be of practical use as well, because it allowed renewal's boosters to assuage the worries about tenant relocation by painting leftist opponents of clearance and displacement as enemies of national progress, unity, and urban purpose.[15]

The Rockefeller family pursued these lofty goals assiduously, becoming the most celebrated and active proponent of this Cold War urban renewal vision. The Rockefeller brothers—Winthrop, Laurance, David, and John III—saw involvement in urban renewal, like their other political, cultural, philanthropic, and business pursuits, as an opportunity to make their wealth and influence work for what they considered to be the "public good." It gave them a way to support particular public-minded urban institutions like hospitals, universities, and cultural centers; to invest in the long-term rebuilding of Manhattan as a world-class center for white-collar residents, workplaces, and attractions; and to address the immediate need for symbolic capital in the looming Cold War contest. Winthrop and Laurance, aided by David, concentrated on the East Side research and hospital complexes, while David set the precedent for John III's efforts at Lincoln Center with his campaign to roll back urban decay on Morningside Heights.[16]

Urban renewal on the "Cold War Acropolis" of Morningside Heights was carried out by a phalanx of educational, religious, and cultural institutions clustered around Columbia University. Officials at these institutions, particularly Columbia, Barnard College, Riverside Church, and International House, were troubled by the deterioration of the area just north of their campuses. Wartime migration had expanded the borders of Harlem, and in the postwar years more and more African Americans and Puerto Ricans were moving south across 125th Street to settle in the blocks of tenements between Riverside Drive and Convent Avenue. Tension between town and gown was rising; neighborhood leaders fretted about a seeming increase in gangs and crime. They worried that the world-class reputations that these institutions enjoyed would be jeopardized by the decline of their immediate surroundings. At the same time, they were concerned to protect their organizations' special roles as beacons of public-spirited education, tolerance, enlightenment, and international understanding. They wanted to stem the tide of blight, but they also wanted to preserve what they saw as a neighborhood that was open to all.[17]

In 1946, David Rockefeller, acting as chair of the boards of Riverside Church and International House, hired Wilbur C. Munnecke, a social scientist and vice president of the University of Chicago, to study the community's options. Munnecke's report rejected past methods of community protection as undemocratic, suggesting that the restrictive covenants customarily used to keep out blacks, Jews, and other "undesirables" were both unproductive and "wrong in principle" for a community that prided itself on tolerance and international understanding. In an era of expanding democracy and pluralism, he recommended that the institutions of Morningside Heights employ "positive actions." City and state programs for redevelopment backed by tax incentives and mortgage subsidies, he wrote, would attract desirable neighbors, discourage undesirable ones, and generally stabilize the area by reclaiming the fringes of the Heights from Harlem's advance. If the community embraced a plan for redevelopment and stuck with it, Munnecke advised, the institutions on the hill could retain their role as liberalism's Acropolis. A 25-year effort, he said, would result in "a self-sustaining Community which is the spiritual, cultural and intellectual center of the world." In late 1946 and early 1947, a panel of Columbia faculty likewise urged a course of "constructive action." Perhaps inspired by the announcement in those same months that the UN headquarters would go up in Manhattan, the group hoped that redevelopment would make Morningside Heights "the educational and cultural counterpart of the political Capitol [*sic*] of the World" and "a community whose facilities can be available without restrictions as to race, color, or creed."[18]

Rockefeller and other neighborhood officials could not face the idea of either abandoning the area or simply carrying on in the face of spreading blight. Not wanting to stain the collective reputations of the institutions on the Heights, they set up an institutional consortium to plan redevelopment efforts. In July 1947, they founded Morningside Heights, Inc. (MHI), with David Rockefeller as president, New York Life head and later Lincoln Center official Otto Nelson serving as a trustee, Wallace Harrison on board as an advisor and architect, and, in a blatant but denied conflict of interest, city planning commissioner Lawrence Orton as director of planning. For almost two years, the group lobbied the various institutional interests around the idea of clearance and rebuilding, gathered information on demographics and land use patterns, and looked for ways to finance the clearing of as much land as possible south of 122nd Street and north of 113th for new institutional buildings and housing. Knowing that high prices and the housing shortage made sufficient clearing impossible without significant public investment, Orton brought Moses to the table, and the construction coordinator made a Morningside Heights redevelopment part of his official plans in March 1949. In June, Rockefeller himself went to Capitol Hill to help speed passage of the Housing Act, and after several more years of

surveys, planning, and design, Moses and MHI announced plans for the Morn-
ingside-Manhattanville clearance area in September 1951. The plan featured the
Morningside Gardens Title I redevelopment (six 21-story modern slab-block
buildings housing 972 middle-income families just north of 123rd Street between
Broadway and Amsterdam) and two massive NYCHA public housing projects,
General Grant Houses and Manhattanville Houses, which would house about
3,200 families in 15 slab-block buildings of 21, 20, and 13 stories in a great swath
stretching from Convent Avenue to Broadway along 125th Street and beyond.[19]

Local opposition to the potential displacement and Title I rents was fierce,
but liberal supporters branded the protestors as either Communist dupes or
agitators and heralded MHI's plans for integration on the Heights. MHI's careful social outreach efforts in the neighborhood convinced many of the Heights'
liberal groups and city officials that the redevelopment would produce advances
in what Rockefeller called the "field of interracial living" as well as a "well-
rounded" housing program for various income levels and plenty of rooms for
those displaced by clearance. As Gertrude Samuels put it in the *Times,* both
the Title I and public projects "will be nonsegregated and 'mixed-up' housing
in the best sense. With no barriers between the buildings—when landscaped,
they will flow naturally into one another—the fairly comfortable and the poor,
intellectuals, white-collar workers, truck drivers, porters, will be living side by
side." In early 1953, the Board of Estimate ignored several hundred protestors
and approved the project. In "a community such as this," Rockefeller told a gathering at Riverside Church, "where a premium is placed on civil liberties and the
rights of man, it should not be an impossible task to make mixed tenancy housing projects profitable and successful ventures."[20]

In fact, through sophisticated administrative controls and recruitment efforts,
Morningside Gardens did become one of the more integrated Title I housing
developments. The project had no trouble attracting middle-class blacks, and
the management assiduously pursued Asian Americans from MHI's member
institutions and white families wherever it could find them in order to keep the
black minority at 20 percent. Any more than that, MHI officials believed, and
the project would reach a tipping point, disrupting the carefully sought balance
and resulting in a more or less black project. The NYCHA projects, on the other
hand, never really achieved that balance, despite similar efforts to recruit white
residents. As in other NYCHA projects carved from black and Puerto Rican
ghettos, the project population reflected the population of the original area.[21]

The controversy over Morningside Heights may have shaken liberal neighborhood leaders' confidence, but it did not dim their faith in the fitness of urban
renewal as a response to the pressures of the age. "Freedom and democracy,"
Rockefeller said in his address at Riverside Church, "can exist in a society only

when there is vitality in its roots." In the "war-torn world in which we live," he warned, it would be "perhaps natural that we should try to find an escape from the grim realities which face our free society by losing ourselves in our work or plunging into a frantic effort to find enjoyment." Any moment might bring "atomic death and destruction," making it "hard to concentrate on planning and building for a better world." But responsibility to freedom, Rockefeller told his audience, required the same kind of dedication at home that it did abroad. The rebuilding of imperiled neighborhoods was on par with fighting Communism abroad, he suggested, because "the free society which we are willing to defend with our lives from aggression from without is in danger of crumbling from within unless each individual and each community nurtures the will to freedom and accepts the responsibilities which are incumbent on us as citizens." It was this sense of mission that David Rockefeller's oldest brother embraced in heading the sponsorship of the city's most heralded urban renewal effort, Lincoln Center for the Performing Arts at Lincoln Square.[22]

The Cultural Burden

Lincoln Center for the Performing Arts symbolizes an increasing interest in America in cultural matters as well as a stimulating approach to one of the nation's pressing problems—urban blight. Here in the heart of our greatest metropolitan center men of vision are executing a redevelopment of purpose, utility and taste.
—President Dwight D. Eisenhower at Lincoln Center groundbreaking, May 1959

Urban renewal at Lincoln Square began as a grand vista in the mind's eye of Robert Moses. The construction coordinator was not ordinarily given to flights of fancy, but the passage of Title I in 1949 gave him a chance to think ahead, to survey new fields for his slum clearance work. Here, he realized, was an opportunity to expand the job begun at the United Nations, Stuyvesant Town, East Harlem, and his other ongoing rebuilding projects along what he called "the whole overcrowded and malodorous East Side." Federal funding would allow him to bring the clean sweep of renewal across the island to the West Side, where slums and blight were, if anything, even more entrenched and recalcitrant. Title I, he would later recall, had unleashed in him a "vision of a reborn West Side, marching north from Columbus Circle, and eventually spreading over the entire dismal and decayed West Side." He launched those efforts in 1951 and 1952 with the Manhattantown Title I project, a 26-acre middle-income housing complex in the 90s along Central Park, the Morningside redevelopment, and the Coliseum Title I project, a 6-acre job on Columbus Circle that featured a hall for trade shows and conventions, an office tower, and 600 units of housing.[23]

Moses renewed his "march" in earnest two years later, when he began to cast about for sponsors for an extension of the Coliseum project. He identified an irregular tract of tenements and warehouses northwest of Columbus Circle between 60th and 70th streets and between Columbus Avenue and the New York Central railyards. The site formed an upside-down and backward L-shape wrapped around the superblock of NYCHA's 1947 project, the Amsterdam Houses. An area of almost 53 acres on 18 city blocks, he designated it section M-8 on the City Planning Commission's revised map of clearance areas, thus officially declaring it a slum. During 1955, Moses considered a number of possible institutional sponsors for the project, eventually lining up commitments from Fordham University for its law, business, education, and social work schools; the New York chapter of the American Red Cross for a new headquarters building; a commercial theater development; Lincoln Center; and developer William Zeckendorf, whose firm, Webb and Knapp, promised to deliver the Lincoln Towers apartments. Later, protests over the high rents planned for Lincoln Towers persuaded Moses to add a middle-income housing cooperative called Lincoln House, and a dispute over land prices with the federal government forced him to drop the commercial theater plan, reducing the area to 14 blocks and 48 acres.

Moses officially designated the site a renewal area in late 1955. The City Planning Commission (CPC) bestowed its initial blessing on the project in the summer of 1956, but bureaucratic struggles with federal urban renewal officials over land prices and write-down values, internal wrangling over the composition of the plan, and protests and court cases launched by local resistance caused innumerable delays. In July 1956, the Board of Estimate, unhappy with the opposition and the disarray, postponed the project. Moses and his staff spent the next year smoothing out the wrinkles: they arranged the middle-income cooperative housing, cultivated the support of editors and writers at the major daily newspapers, ensured the support of city officials like Manhattan Borough president Hulan Jack by accepting a liberal West Side watchdog committee to oversee the relocations, went back and forth with sponsors and federal officials over land prices, and urged John D. Rockefeller III to curry favor with the Eisenhower administration and to bring federal urban renewal administrators in line. With all these delays, the project did not clear the CPC and the Board of Estimate again until September and October 1957, and the city could not acquire the land by eminent domain and resell it to the various sponsors until March 1, 1958. Despite continuing opposition, demolition began in August 1959, and the sponsors hurried tenant relocation to a finish by the end of that year. President Eisenhower presided over the Lincoln Center groundbreaking ceremonies on May 14, 1959, and in 1961 and 1962, six years after Moses announced the project, the first buildings began opening at Fordham, Lincoln Center, and Lincoln Towers.

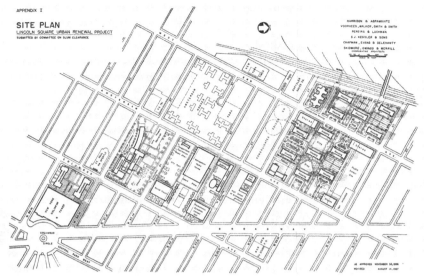

APPENDIX I

SITE PLAN
LINCOLN SQUARE URBAN RENEWAL PROJECT
SUBMITTED BY COMMITTEE ON SLUM CLEARANCE

HARRISON & ABRAMOVITZ
VOORHEES, WALKER, SMITH & SMITH
PEREIRA & LUCKMAN
S.J. KESSLER & SONS
CHAPMAN, EVANS & DELEHANTY
SKIDMORE, OWINGS & MERRILL
COORDINATING ARCHITECTS

4.2. An early map of the Lincoln Square Urban Renewal Plan. Lincoln Towers is at top right, Lincoln Center in the middle, and the Fordham campus to the left. The New York Coliseum, an earlier Title I project, is at lower left. New York City Planning Commission, "Report, Lincoln Square Urban Renewal Plan and Project: Site Plan" (1957). Used with permission of the New York City Department of City Planning. All rights reserved.

4.3. A rendering of the proposed Lincoln Square Urban Renewal Plan looking across Broadway from the northeast, as envisioned by the developers of the Lincoln Towers housing development, Webb and Knapp. Lincoln Towers is to the right in this depiction, with Lincoln Center and Fordham in the center left. New York World-Telegram Photograph Collection, Library of Congress.

Construction continued at Lincoln Square for years after that, however, as the various constituents of Lincoln Center—Philharmonic Hall, the Metropolitan Opera, the New York State Theater, the Vivian Beaumont Theater, the New York Public Library for the Performing Arts, and the Juilliard School—opened their doors over the course of the entire decade, culminating in the Met's debut performance in 1966 and Juilliard's first semester at Lincoln Center in 1969.[24]

Lincoln Center was the centerpiece of the Lincoln Square plan. Despite the fact that Robert Moses initiated the project and would have carried on without the performing arts center—most likely making Fordham the anchor and filling in the balance with more housing—it was ultimately Lincoln Center that imbued Moses's vision of a remade West Side with added national and international value. Lincoln Center represented the ultimate imaginative yoke between the drive to physically rebuild the old city and the effort to prepare the metropolis for its role as the capital of modernity and a bulwark in the Cold War. It served, on the one hand, as confirmation of the effort to remake Manhattan's cityscape for global leadership and, on the other, as the most dramatic instrument yet unveiled in the campaign to shore up Manhattan's national centrality in a time of suburbanization and metropolitan decentralization. Finally, it introduced the idea of culture and the arts as instruments for urban transformation and resurgence, and in so doing ironically helped to provide the terms by which urban renewal's program of modern rebuilding would be questioned and undone.

A series of coincidences brought the performing arts complex to Lincoln Square. Moses knew that the Metropolitan Opera had long been looking for a new home; its old house at Broadway and 39th was cramped, outdated, and in a deteriorating neighborhood. Moses wondered if the opera might not be the linchpin in his vision of a reborn West Side. He had offered it a place in the Coliseum project in 1951, but negotiations with the Met's board had stalled, and he had withdrawn the proposal. In early 1954, Moses again offered the opera a role in his renewal operations, this time in the Lincoln Square project. His initial pitch to the Met's executive committee earned an ambivalent response, so he arranged personal conferences with the committee's chair, Charles M. Spofford, and Wallace K. Harrison, the Rockefeller confidant, UN coordinating architect, and Met architectural consultant. Spofford pushed the Met committee to accept Moses's offer, and in April 1955 it signed on for at least three acres. Meanwhile, Arthur Houghton Jr., the chair of the board of the New York Philharmonic Society, learned that the owners of its home, Carnegie Hall, intended to demolish the grand old theater and put up an office building. He, too, turned to Harrison for advice about a new building. Harrison connected Houghton with Spofford and Moses, and soon the Philharmonic was bidding for space at Lincoln Square as well. Moses hesitated at first, but then agreed, tentatively making four acres available for the two institutions.

Spofford, Houghton, and Harrison, together with C. D. Jackson, publisher of *Fortune* magazine and another Met trustee, began to realize that these two projects would require extravagant sums of money. Not only that, but they would be competing with each other for dollars from the same group of foundations and wealthy donors. With this in mind, they began to think in larger terms, pondering a joint campaign perhaps, or even a single center that would bring all the performing arts under one roof. The organization and planning of such an undertaking would be an immense task—the fundraising effort itself would be unprecedented—and would require a unique and independent coordinating body headed by someone with considerable connections. The obvious choice for such a drive was one of the Rockefeller brothers. Harrison suggested John D. Rockefeller III, chair of the Rockefeller Foundation and eldest of the sons of John D. Rockefeller Jr. Dean Rusk, president of the foundation, seconded the idea, and Spofford approached Rockefeller at a meeting of the Council on Foreign Relations in September 1955. Taking a few moments between sessions, Spofford briefly outlined the predicaments of the Met and Philharmonic as well as Moses's offer of land, and invited Rockefeller to join the deliberations.

Rockefeller was enthusiastic about the fledgling efforts to create a cultural center at Lincoln Square, having already talked it over informally with his assistant Edgar Young and Harrison. During the autumn, Rockefeller joined Spofford, Harrison, Houghton, Jackson, Young, and Anthony Bliss, president of the Metropolitan Opera, in a series of meetings to explore plans for a "musical arts center." With $50,000 in start-up funds from the Rockefeller Foundation, this exploratory committee worked to put together an organization capable of funding, building, and running a cultural center. Over the next year, with Rockefeller serving as chair, the committee expanded to include Devereux C. Josephs of New York Life; Robert E. Blum of Abraham and Straus department stores; Lincoln Kirstein of the New York City Ballet; William Schuman of Juilliard; Laurence J. McGinley of Fordham; Clarence Francis, retired chair of General Foods; and Major General Otto Nelson, also of New York Life, to consult on urban renewal issues.

In June 1956, the group officially incorporated as a nonprofit, taking the name Lincoln Center for the Performing Arts, Inc. This body had an immense list of responsibilities, chief among them raising money. By 1969, when the center was finished, this group had overcome a succession of startling cost overruns and raised the unprecedented sum of more than $140 million from private sources; with government funds included, the final price tag of Lincoln Center was just under $185 million. Beyond finding ways to pay for the complex, the group had to sort out the relations between the various parts and the whole. Recruiting the center's constituents, negotiating with them, determining their space needs, and setting up the complicated financial deals that would ensure both their autonomy and their fealty to the concept of the center took up much of the members' energies. They had to smooth out potential conflicts and suspicions between constituents, overseeing in particular a long series of tortuous and sometimes rancorous negotiations between the Metropolitan Opera, with its elite, upper-crust audience, and the City Center of Music and Drama, with its lower ticket prices and roots in the New Deal people's theater and opera. They created a new repertory theater company out of whole cloth; arranged with Moses for an expanded 13-acre, three-block site; supervised architectural and planning studies for the new complex; negotiated with the city and federal governments over land prices; and oversaw tenant relocation, site clearance, and construction.[25]

Drawn from the highest echelons of Manhattan's financial, corporate, legal, and cultural communities, the committee members were simultaneously the most exalted of Robert Moses's liberal urban renewal partners and a quintessential distillation of the pattern. They commanded a wide array of connections and influence. They had access to deep financial resources and links to the military, the foreign policy elite, major charitable foundations, Wall Street, the liberal wings of both the Democratic and Republican parties, and major media, like the *Times* and Henry Luce's magazine empire. They represented not only the classic WASP American establishment, but Jewish and Catholic power centers as well; theirs was a kind of semi-democratic elite, internationalist in outlook, familiar with the workings of the federal government, unsurprisingly male and white, and self-consciously placed in what they thought of as the leadership of New York's WASP and major white ethnic communities. Fearing for the fate of New York's global influence in an era of suburbanization, they turned their high-minded, munificent civic pride toward making the campaign against decentralization and decay serve even higher national and international goals.

John D. Rockefeller III stood at the head of this group. Thinking over his conversation with Charles Spofford, Rockefeller realized that the three coincidences Spofford had outlined—two major cultural institutions looking for new homes and Moses's patch of available land—represented a major opportunity to expand his life's work in voluntary and philanthropic affairs. Although he was not a connoisseur of dance, opera, or drama, Rockefeller was inspired by the idea of Lincoln Center. The opportunity, he would later remember, allowed him to combine his interests in international affairs, his experience with what the Rockefeller family thought of as "public-spirited work," and the family's long-standing role in the life of New York City. He had recently begun to think a great deal about the role of culture in national life, even going so far as to address the

Council on Foreign Relations—at the same meeting during which he and Spofford had conferred—about the urgent need to improve the unfortunate image of American culture abroad. Lincoln Center rested comfortably at the junction of all of these interests and responsibilities; he saw it as a way to boost America's cultural reputation, to give more Americans access to the edifying effects of high culture, and to make a public-spirited contribution to New York life. It could not hurt, either, that Lincoln Center would represent one more in a string of Rockefeller family projects—those completed, under way, and still to come—that would help to save New York from supposed obsolescence by underwriting the growth of white-collar life in Manhattan.[26]

These relationships among culture, foreign affairs, and urban resurgence would be central to Rockefeller's role over the next decade. Beyond the myriad details of planning, building, and running a new cultural center, Rockefeller and his colleagues had to play the leading role in explaining Lincoln Center to the public and to potential donors. Why should the rich give millions? Why should regular people in New York and across the country donate their hard-won dollars, or feel that they somehow shared in the glory and glamour of the undertakings at Lincoln Square? With these questions in mind, Rockefeller made sure that Lincoln Center became more than a fundraising machine, real estate developer, or auditorium landlord. It was important to him that Lincoln Center have a special role in promoting culture and the performing arts, one that went beyond what any of the individual constituents could do, but did not directly compete with their programming. It was essential that Lincoln Center give people—donors, potential audiences, New Yorkers, other Americans, and foreigners—the sense that the building of Lincoln Center was a response to the great questions of the age. Under Rockefeller's leadership, this effort took the form of an attempt to explain the importance of culture for national life during a time of affluence, for the country's international reputation in an era of Cold War, and for urban resurgence.

Rockefeller and his allies pitched Lincoln Center to audiences and donors as both the product of an age of affluence and newly plentiful leisure and a potential balm for the perils this new age offered to Americans. By the mid-1950s, technological progress, rising incomes, consumer plenty, and growing purchasing power had convinced many observers that the middle-class expansion of the previous decade was a semi-permanent condition, productive of a new kind of American freedom. "American technology, labor, industry and business are responsible for the twentieth-century freedom of the individual" was how President Eisenhower put it in his remarks at the Lincoln Center groundbreaking ceremonies. The happy consequence of freedom through prosperity, he said, was "a greater portion" of "time in which to improve the mind, the body and the spirit." And yet, this new freedom presented a series of challenges. Taking their cues from popular depictions of the postwar era like John Kenneth Galbraith's *The Affluent Society*—where he argued that "when man has satisfied his physical needs, the psychological desires take over"—Lincoln Center's sponsors offered the project as a ready solution to both the possibilities and problems of an age in which "the nation's economic growth has brought Americans higher living standards, more education, more leisure time." The center, they said, was conceptualized as a way to provide the cultural resources needed to fulfill the era's opportunities and to offset its dangers.[27]

On the one hand, the surfeit of education, time, and leisure opened a new world of possibility. Americans, Rockefeller and his colleagues said, were using their newly discovered free time to "enjoy concerts, plays, opera, ballet, and other musical and theater arts." They claimed, for instance, that sales of classical music recordings were "at an all-time high." "Americans," they said, "now are spending five million dollars *more* every year to attend *concerts* than to watch professional baseball." Lincoln Center's plan to collect all the performing arts in one modern complex, they told potential donors, was "a bold and timely answer to the 'cultural explosion' taking place in America today." Or, as Robert Moses summed up the issue for readers of the *New York Times Magazine*:

> Here we are—approximately two hundred million people with too few mental ambitions and resources, more or less indifferent to threats of war and bitter, foreign economic competition, gaily demanding a four day week, less responsibility and more leisure. What shall we do with the 136 non-working hours?…This is where the arts come marching in—over the air, on the screen, the stage, in the picture, and the printed word. Here is the challenge which in time will be met at the Performing Arts and similar ambitious centers.[28]

Growing numbers of Americans, it was said, enjoyed unprecedented supplies of leisure time. They would expect, historian Alice Goldfarb Marquis writes, "to collect a special dividend of psychic income from the arts." In response, high culture took on a specific and crucial social role. More than simply entertainment, the arts were, as a *Life* magazine editorial put it, "equipped to impose form and meaning on the increasing complexities of human experience." High culture's abstract and universal appeal to the "complexities" of the human condition could give "form and meaning" to lives lived beyond the old cares, worries, and meaningless toil. Here was Lincoln Center's highest calling. It was designed, Rockefeller said, to help meet a crucial "responsibility to man's spirit, to his humanness…to all the spiritual, emotional, artistic, and aesthetic qualities that set man above the animal." This melding of art's high-minded appeal with a can-do American spirit, C. D. Jackson observed, would show that "this country, which has licked its quantitative problems will also lick its qualitative ones."[29]

In keeping with this mission, the sponsors pitched the center to a broad public they thought to be "in need" of the "spiritual" and "universal" qualities of the arts and high culture. They were in need of it not only individually, but collectively, as a whole. "The refinement" offered by the arts, *Life*'s editors opined, "must be public and general if our civilization is to be democratic as well as great." Since art was "one of the basic things people are striving for," Rockefeller wrote, the center intended to "go just as far as possible economically in making opera, drama, and ballet broadly available." Lincoln Center was a "necessary part" of the "answer to our modern need," Rockefeller remarked, because "it is an exciting new kind of institution dedicated to the enjoyment of the finest art by the greatest number of people." Or, as the *Saturday Evening Post* put it, Lincoln Center was "based on the theory that, in the future, grand opera must be for the masses, and not merely for the 'carriage trade.'"[30]

Of course, the center's sponsors found American mass culture to be distasteful. Their efforts to democratize the arts amounted to a kind of controlled release, an attempt to guide, supervise, and guarantee its munificent effects from on high, not an attempt to inject high culture into the mass marketplace. Lincoln Center's great gift to a newly affluent American society was to be a curious and novel blend of elitism and democratization, far more open to the public than earlier models of cultural hierarchy rooted in nineteenth-century class antagonism, but still controlled from above. Writing in a special *Times Magazine* issue heralding the coming of Lincoln Center, President John F. Kennedy's special consultant on the arts, August Heckscher, made public the concerns of many of his peers, wondering "whether excellence can be transmitted to a vast population without debasing it." "We actually do not know," he continued, "whether a society such as our own, with its material abundance and its growing leisure for all parts of the population, can attain to a true appreciation of fineness and excellence in the esthetic sphere." It was, Heckscher thought, an "open question," the very one Rockefeller and his colleagues intended Lincoln Center to answer.[31]

Postwar prosperity, Rockefeller and others observed, was as much "peril" as "opportunity." "We will have to learn how to fill the time we have literally manufactured in our factories," worried Rockefeller's Lincoln Center colleague Devereux Josephs. The failure to do so, and do so properly, could result in psychological and societal crises. One Lincoln Center constituent, a New York Public Library executive, wrote that Americans were threatened more by "mass boredom than by atomic bombs." The surfeit of newly available leisure time in an affluent but materialistic society could reveal a void in people's lives, a kind of existential breach easily filled by the psychological meaninglessness and drift of what Rockefeller called "this age of anxiety." Of course, the plentiful and democratized cultural resources of the sort Lincoln Center intended to provide could mitigate "the problems of mental health which are so serious today." And yet, if "the need of modern man for creative fulfillment" was "made more immediate by the pressures that weigh upon him in this age of anxiety," perhaps the most serious problem for Rockefeller went beyond the purely psychological to the broadly social or cultural, resting in the sense that Americans also lived in "an age where our moral and spiritual attainments have not kept pace with our material advances." In such a time, he and his colleagues noted, the dangers surpassed the crises of the individual psyche to become social and political liabilities.[32]

If these dangers were of national and domestic concern, the perils were also profoundly international in scope. Lincoln Center's sponsors were most concerned about the issue that had originally sparked Rockefeller's interest in a cultural center: the image of the United States abroad. "In the eye [sic] of the world," the sponsors wrote in soliciting contributions from a select group of "insiders," "America's cultural attainment is too often overshadowed by our material wealth. Our nation needs Lincoln Center as a symbol of our cultural maturity." In response to the all-too-frequent charge that "Americans are interested only in making and spending money," they suggested, Lincoln Center could stand as a symbol of the nation's coming of age, of its readiness to stand with Europe at the head of civilization.[33]

Lincoln Center's public relations staff—aided in great part by the connections of the board—had considerable success in winning influential support for this idea. The *Times,* for instance, endorsed the project in an editorial, saying that it would go a long way toward proving "that the modern American wants the things of the mind and heart as well as material substances." Even the newspaper's music critic got on board, hailing Lincoln Center as an "answer to a challenge of our times" and, in language more or less cribbed from official Lincoln Center materials, a "symbol of America's cultural maturity, affirming for the entire world our nation's faith in the life of the spirit."[34]

Of course, this talk of noble purpose was intended not only as cultural affirmation, but as a calculated bit of political public relations as well. "Lincoln Center," Wallace Harrison suggested, "is a symbol to the world that we so-called monopolistic, imperialistic degenerates are capable of building the greatest cultural center in the world." Perhaps the chief "anxiety" demonstrated by the "peril" of unprecedented leisure was that it would reveal a nation unfit to meet its commitment to the Cold War struggle for hearts and minds. "Misuse of leisure time can destroy us," a New York Public Library executive warned. If the new quantities of free time were "wastefully and frivolously used, America will grow constantly weaker in its struggle with those who would overturn our way of life." In this context, Lincoln Center became "a symbol to the world" because culture itself took on increasingly weighty symbolic significance.[35]

In a speech to the University Club promoting Lincoln Center, C. D. Jackson announced that culture had acquired a new public role. "Culture," he said, "is no longer a sissy word." Once the province of Victorian matrons, unkempt bohemians, or society wives, culture had stepped out of its feminized, cloistered shroud, shed its association with the insular sphere of private expression, and assumed a role in the manly world of public affairs. World events had conscripted it into service on the frontlines of the era's great struggle, to be deployed by the very sort of men who had come together around the cause of building Lincoln Center. "Today," Jackson continued, "it is a word of immense worldwide political significance. It is absolutely fantastic that, from out of the seething postwar world, it is culture that should have emerged as a dynamic concept, an aspiration of whole nations, a force capable of swaying the masses, an element of decisions in the minds of the uncommitted." Those many thousands around the world who were still "uncommitted" to one side or the other in the Cold War, Jackson suggested, could be swayed by the proper deployment of cultural resources. Here was reason enough for the United States to beef up its "cultural maturity."

The "cultural offensive," Jackson said, was equal in importance to the arms race or the race to secure the highest standard of living. As "a great element of East-West competition," culture had become a "beautiful status symbol" in "vast under-developed areas of the world," as important in its own way as the "steel mill." Having culture, knowing what was "gross," "bad," or "not attractive," and thus "uncultured," had become as worthy of respect in these "uncommitted" lands as having the "new altar" of manufacturing. The postwar world, Jackson suggested, was "stirred" by "immense expectations for good or evil," and Americans had so far failed to capitalize on the ways that achievements in the cultural field could help the nation appear as a force for good rather than evil in the Cold War's simple binary logic. "We haven't thought of [cultural achievements]," Jackson said, "as positive, dynamic, and essential assets in the great and dangerous international game that we must play today." Lincoln Center, he assured his listeners, would be just such a "new, visible, artistically impeccable, majestic, cultural asset."[36]

If Lincoln Center served as a manly "cultural asset" in the campaign to win the allegiance of "uncommitted" millions, it also demonstrated that culture could drive what Lincoln Center construction chief Otto Nelson called a "virile and vast program of urban renewal." The language of gender that Lincoln Center's backers used to describe both fighting on the cultural front of the Cold War and reclaiming New York from slums and blight suggested the shared vision of masculine public effort at the heart of each of these endeavors. Pairing culture with urban renewal, they rescued culture from its "sissy" status and yoked public efforts in urban reclamation and the Cold War struggle to familiar understandings of the postwar gender order. Such gestures contributed to the sense that Lincoln Center was at the heart of its times, reassuring elite audiences that it would exalt rather than trouble the distinctions between public and private roles on which that order was based.[37]

Of course, Lincoln Center also took on such importance because it appeared at a charged moment in the history of the Cold War. Lincoln Square was pitched just after the height of the McCarthy era, but final approval from the city and federal government came in November 1957, just over a month after the Soviets had launched the communications satellite *Sputnik,* which sent Americans into a tailspin of doubt and consternation over the state of U.S. accomplishments in science and technology. While the primary effect of the Soviet satellite launch was to jump-start new investments in engineering and scientific research, *Sputnik* also fueled more general American fears about the fitness of national resolve.

As Roberta Chalmers of Wellesley, Massachusetts, told Rockefeller in a 1958 letter, she was sure that the "entire nation" would find the plans for Lincoln Center "exciting and cheering." Ever since *Sputnik,* she wrote, the alarm had been raised about the need for greater investment in "studies in science," but

> it would be a matter of grave concern if we should try to imitate and compete with a dictator nation principally and almost exclusively in this field, since the great ideas of a free society, and of a people governed by themselves, have proceeded from the humanities and the arts....Any thoughtful citizen will see in Lincoln Center a support not merely of these studies, but of freedom itself.

The cultural complex, she told Rockefeller, echoing his own concerns, "will help immeasureably [*sic*] to reveal to the world...that we are not a philistine and materialistic society." More than that, though, "since our artists are not the minions of the state, the Center should be an equal revelation of the particular excellence of the fruits of unshackled minds."[38]

The idea that Lincoln Center could stand for the freedom of "unshackled minds" appealed to its backers as well. For instance, in their efforts to give the center more democratic appeal, the sponsors reached out to organized labor. They appealed to labor leaders' recent successes in providing union members with job security, higher standards of living, and the unprecedented leisure time supplied by American prosperity, suggesting that supporting Lincoln Center would allow them to be seen as civic leaders rather than simply as parochial labor bosses. Labor responded enthusiastically, pitching in financially and ideologically. Calling on union members to support the center, George Meany, head of the AFL-CIO, stressed its role in the fight against what he called "inhuman totalitarianism" with its "artists in uniform" and its "perversion of the humanistic purposes of art and literature." If "the breath of one-party control blights the growth of genuine culture," then Lincoln Center's "complex of buildings" not only would clear urban blight, but would inoculate the nation against cultural and ideological "blight" by providing the foremost example of freedom's benefits. The buildings themselves, Meany concluded, "symbolize what free men can do in a free society in the interests of advancing a free culture," offering "the American people the possibility of witnessing and tasting the pleasures of a free and democratic culture."[39]

Rockefeller and his colleagues embraced this message, although they played the note with less vigor than Meany did. Rockefeller himself did not broadcast

4.4. President Dwight D. Eisenhower speaking at the groundbreaking for Lincoln Center, heralding the complex's role in underwriting the nation's interest in "cultural matters" and turning back the tide of "urban blight." The podium is hung with an early rendering of the complex (the designs were later modified), and the president is flanked by John D. Rockefeller III (*left*) and Mayor Robert Wagner (*right*). New York World-Telegram Photograph Collection, Library of Congress.

the center's role as a weapon in the Cold War struggle. He preferred less overt appeals, ones more in keeping with the character of his assumed station. He suggested in a letter to Eisenhower's advisor Sherman Adams that more federal funding for Lincoln Square should be freed up because the project was "in harmony with the President's program to strengthen the cultural position of the United States around the world." Still, during the opening week in 1961, he did announce to the public that "Lincoln Center is many things, but before all others it is a living monument to the will of free men acting together on the basis of their own initiative and idealism."[40]

New Culture Cities

Two phenomena of American city life—a cultural explosion and the diminishing vitality, in some cities, of the downtown—offer a twin opportunity for a dimension of city rebuilding never before envisioned.
—*Action Reporter,* November–December 1959

Lincoln Center's sponsors hoped that their bid to prove America's cultural maturity and to advertise American freedoms would be expressed in the center's unique and particularly refined place-remaking opportunities. They pitched it as a melding of new and old, an unprecedented space in the Manhattan cityscape, but also an urban place on par with classical European models. The architects and planners designed it as one part modern "utopia" for the arts—as a *New York Times Magazine* article called it—complete with superblock open spaces and a Robert Moses–designed park, and one part updated Venetian plaza with monumental, classically inspired modern edifices arrayed around a public square and fountain. If they hoped that Lincoln Center itself would marshal the universal balm of high culture to give the newly affluent United States meaning and "spiritual" purpose, they envisioned an analogous role for the complex's intervention in the urban landscape. It would clear away the old tenement grid for a modern, yet classic and refined, urban place. The center at Lincoln Square confirmed in the realm of culture what the UN headquarters complex on Turtle Bay had announced in the realm of diplomacy and world affairs: New York had become the capital of the postwar world.[41]

"We are interested," Rockefeller told a reporter for *Architectural Forum,* "in a new kind of city therapy." Other eras had their needs, Rockefeller and his colleagues opined, but "the advancement of public appreciation of the arts" was the chief "social need" of the current time. Just as improving the community's health and physical welfare had served as the ostensible goal of Metropolitan Life's intervention in the Gas House District, Lincoln Center's sponsors promoted culture and the arts as the chief medium for urban revitalization. "Medicine, museums, experimental housing—each one was the most pressing problem of its own time. But we believe that this is the time for a more active form of help— a time for art." Other forms of "city therapy," Rockefeller implied, were fundamentally passive. They could not equal art's universal capabilities; they did not have its ability to cater to "man's spirit" and to what Rockefeller called "his humanness...to all the spiritual, emotional, artistic, and aesthetic qualities that set man above the animal." This lofty rhetoric served to bring Lincoln Center in line with the ambitious and idealistic goals at the heart of urban renewal. Despite his casual dismissal of "experimental housing," Rockefeller had made his vision of culture-backed urban resurgence congruent with the vision of urban renewal originally spurred by the drive for modern experimental housing. Lincoln Center, Rockefeller and his colleagues thought, would fulfill that promise by new and more appropriate means, serving as a model for how to restore spiritual and human wholeness to what Juilliard head and Lincoln Center president William Schuman called the "artistically underdeveloped areas" of cities.[42]

The power of culture and the arts in urban renewal, Lincoln Center's sponsors and supporters believed, would be nowhere so apparent as in the way that the complex physically transformed the old cityscape. Lincoln Center, they determined, would boast new urban places to equal those of classical Europe. Although they never publicly acknowledged it, they believed that it might preserve the influence in the United States of a threatened European culture. Listed in an early set of notes for a public statement on "the Lincoln Center" was the idea that the performing arts "help to keep alive and meaningful our cultural and blood ties to Great Britain and the Continent." The language of "blood ties" suggests the way that these urban elites were responding to their changing world. In a postwar city transformed by suburbanization, deindustrialization, and new immigration flows from the black South and Puerto Rico, the traditional markers of elite stewardship, influence, and power were slowly eroding. Lincoln Center promised some symbolic support for this endangered social infrastructure. The force of culture and the arts, newly rescued from feminized inertia and recruited for manly duty in the Cold War, would also be deployed to offset the threat to racial purity and stable cultural lineage looming in an era of urban transformation. Of course, Rockefeller and his colleagues would no doubt have denied that those more Manichean visions propelled their efforts. In any case, they quickly abandoned this language, leaving the notion only as a kind of passive undercurrent, less an active motive than an unspoken assumption.[43]

Rockefeller and the others preferred a positive outlook on Lincoln Center's impact, replacing the fear of cultural and racial decline with an emphasis on a boosterish vision of Lincoln Center's inevitable status as a new landmark. "Future generations of visitors from America and abroad," they suggested, "will come to Lincoln Center as they now visit great landmarks in Venice, Athens and Rome: just for the joy of being there." Lincoln Center's backers in the press picked up on this theme and amplified it, depicting the center as a monument to the power of high culture to spur both national vitality and urban resurgence. A 1957 article in *Interiors,* an architecture and design magazine, suggested that New York in the twentieth century was like France in the seventeenth century. The city was enjoying a "cultural boom" the likes of which had not been seen since Paris in the Age of Enlightenment, and Lincoln Center was to be New York's Versailles. The *Herald Tribune* offered a more direct ancestor from Europe's pantheon of great urban places. "Already," the editors remarked in May 1958, "Lincoln Square is being likened to the Piazza San Marco in Venice." It was, of course, the proposed "great plaza in front of the opera house" that inspired such comparisons, "for here will be an open square where New Yorkers may congregate and admire the great buildings."[44]

Lincoln Center's architects and site planners were charged with finding a way to meet these expectations. From the beginning, they looked to reconcile modern site-planning and city-remaking principles with an architectural and design idiom befitting the grandeur they assumed was necessary for the high arts of opera, ballet, and symphony. They saw Lincoln Center as the central element in the Lincoln Square redevelopment plan, which meant that it was responsible for providing the neighborhood with an updated, thoroughly modern site. It had to disrupt the nineteenth-century street grid, rationalize the neighborhood's mixed-use tangle of traffic and commerce, clear away blocks of tenements and warehouses, and provide a fitting complement for the nearby superblocks that would house Fordham's campus and Lincoln Towers' cluster of Corbusian high-rise slab apartment buildings. An early press release—and corresponding *Times* article—even assured the public that the complex's buildings "will stand free in an area of green lawns." But they believed that the center had to evoke more than just faith in avant-garde progress. The planning and architecture also had to deliver a space equal in majesty to the vision of Lincoln Center's purpose that Rockefeller and his colleagues had outlined. It had to naturally evoke the idea that the fine arts were universal and spiritual endeavors of the highest order, bearers of eternal verities that could save an affluent society from itself.[45]

The course they took was the easiest and most prudent available to them. Why risk offending generous employers? Rather than push for a forward-looking scheme that could have been accused of sacrificing dignity for visionary élan, they struck a compromise between modernist shapes and classical ornamentation and iconography. The result—labeled "monumental modern" by the *Times*—earned the approval of arts patrons, Lincoln Center's backers, and much of the public at large, but the disapproval of many architects, planners, and aficionados of both modernism and everyday urban life. With their towering, arched façades and Venetian-inspired plaza, the designs had something of the international style's austerity, but more generally recalled the refined spirit of City Beautiful era civic urbanism and eschewed modernism's pure, abstract forms. Some said the buildings were ponderous and clumsy, too redolent of an overweening classicism last seen in the fascist architecture of Nazi Germany or Italy under Mussolini. Others argued that they represented the somnolent institutionalization of New York's twentieth-century modernist vigor by the very Beaux Arts traditions modernism had once rejected.[46]

Designing and building Lincoln Center was an unprecedented task, best handled by someone with experience in coordinating large jobs. Very soon after incorporating, the Lincoln Center board appointed Wallace Harrison to be the leader and coordinator of the design efforts and gave his firm, Harrison and Abramovitz, the ultimate responsibility for site planning. This was the same position he had held in the building of the United Nations, but the challenges at Lincoln Square were in many ways greater than those he had faced a decade earlier. His first task was to convene a panel of architects and planners for a preliminary advisory committee that would help Harrison and Abramovitz to prepare an urban plan for the complex. This group met twice in 1956 and 1957, and it featured some of the world's most illustrious modern architects, including Alvar Aalto, Pietro Belluschi, Marcel Breuer, Philip Johnson, and Sven Markelius, as well as one more traditional designer, Henry R. Shepley, and a number of consultants on acoustics and stage and theater design.

Sorting through a variety of competing ideas for the three-block site, they decided to emphasize open space by pursuing a group of individual buildings rather than one "megastructure." However, they agreed that what was needed was not "merely an aggregate of buildings," but a "real music center of related units." In keeping with this decision, they also discarded the possibility of an asymmetrical grouping of buildings, choosing instead to create what they hoped would be a harmonious cluster of edifices in symmetrical array around "an enclosed plaza with the main entrance of each building on it." They felt that, since these were public buildings, designed for display, performance, and symbolic evocation of the arts they would showcase, they should not adhere to modern site-planning ideals. The performance halls were not to be arranged by their relation to the sun or the prevailing breezes, but with regard to traditional conceptions of order and symmetry, the very Beaux Arts principles that modernism had arisen to confront. The designers' chief inspirations were, as the newspapers had reported, classical. They thought most often of the San Marco in Venice or Rome's Piazza del Campidoglio, both graceful examples of broad open spaces enclosed by harmonious ensembles of public buildings opening to a vista at one end. One initial scheme, drawn up by Robert Moses's planners, had featured a north-south axis connecting the plaza to the Fordham site to the south. The advisory group rejected this in favor of a plan featuring an east-west axis with a broad opening on the intersection of Columbus and Broadway to the east.[47]

Moses, however, insisted that the southwest corner of the site be preserved as a park. This made for cramped conditions, as all six of the center's main constituents—the Metropolitan Opera, the Philharmonic, the dance theater, Juilliard, the performing arts library, and the repertory theater—jockeyed for space in the superblock. In early 1958, when the additional half-block between 65th and 66th streets was added to the site, the planners were able to move Juilliard across 65th Street, freeing up space for Moses's park and allowing the other constituents to fall in around the plaza. The Metropolitan Opera took pride of place, facing out over the plaza toward Columbus and Broadway beyond. The Philharmonic and the dance theater (soon to be claimed by the City Center of Music and Drama) flanked the Met, while the library and repertory theater were combined in one building and placed in the northwest corner, fronted by their own auxiliary plaza.

This solution offered a reconciliation between the impulse to create a great public space and the need to fulfill the grid-disrupting qualities of the superblock, resolving the contradiction in favor of a sense of ordered remove from the streets. On the one hand, the plan opened to the city all along its broad eastern front, welcoming crowds in the same manner as its classical models. On the other, it was lifted out of its urban context like any other superblock urban renewal plan. The ordered ensemble, symmetrically grouped around an internal plaza, self-consciously and ceremoniously turned its back on the block frontage, presenting high blank walls to 62nd, 65th, and Amsterdam Avenue. "With the realization that for the arts and for music one needs to get out of the maelstrom and into a quiet place," wrote Harrison, "the consultants were unanimous in agreeing that the Lincoln Center for the Performing Arts be an area isolated from the hubbub of New York City." The plaza's open entrance, raised from street level by a broad set of steps, would not offset the sense that the plan was "concentrated upon an inner space and inward-looking." One of the group's members, an acoustician, even suggested that a contemporary "home for the Muses" had to be "a fortress." If Lincoln Center was not quite destined to resemble a fortress, it did combine the city-disrupting tools of the modern superblock and the refined, removed grandeur of the classical plaza to great effect. Or, as Metropolitan Opera president Anthony Bliss put it in a radio broadcast promoting the complex: "The Center will not be just a row of buildings—side by side—which is so typical of much New York architecture. The buildings will all be separate units—divided by spacious plazas planted with trees and, we hope, even gardens." At the same time, what gave the complex its claim to the title of "cultural capital of the world,"

Bliss felt, was not merely the modern abstraction of its superblock, but the fact that it would "give you a feeling that you are entering a special world." This world was separated from the streets not merely by planning principles, but by a spatial vision equal to the grandeur of the center's artistic mission. The arts, the complex said, could rescue the city, but they were not of it.[48]

Architectural work began in 1958, even before the site-planning process was complete. As coordinator, Harrison suggested to the Lincoln Center board that it hire architects from the advisory group for the individual buildings. Due to his long interest and experience with the Met, Harrison himself took on the opera house design. His partner, Max Abramovitz, was given Philharmonic Hall. Lincoln Kirstein personally chose Philip Johnson, the old partisan of the international style, to design the dance theater. The Juilliard design went to Pietro Belluschi, but the board ruled against the two non-Americans, Alvar Aalto and Sven Markelius. Henry Shepley was judged too conservative, and nobody considered the rigid Marcel Breuer to be the right personality for a group effort. Harrison then brought in two younger, but equally prestigious architects, Eero Saarinen and Gordon Bunshaft, for the repertory theater and the library building.

These six made up an uneasy and sometimes discordant alliance. Harrison, still fresh from the struggle over the United Nations, was reluctant to take the sort of active role he had pursued at Turtle Bay. He offered to "coordinate" and promptly

4.5. In late 1959, photographer Arnold Newman posed John D. Rockefeller III with some of Lincoln Center's architects and designers in an oversized mock-up of their vision for the complex that had been erected in the basement of Rockefeller Center. *Left to right:* Edward J. Mathews, Philip Johnson, stage designer Jo Mielziner, Rockefeller, Wallace K. Harrison (*standing at center*), Eero Saarinen, Gordon Bunshaft, Max Abramovitz, and Pietro Belluschi. Arnold Newman Collection/Getty Images.

hired René d'Harnoncourt, the director of the Museum of Modern Art, to serve as an aesthetic advisor and liaison between the architects and the Lincoln Center board. Meanwhile, the architects faced a daunting array of issues: they had to design auditoriums, including seating arrangements, stages, and grand entrances. They each had to think about sight lines, acoustical properties, efficient circulation flows, backstage requirements, office and rehearsal spaces, heating and cooling systems, and very tight budgets. And yet, perhaps the most difficult decisions had to be made collectively: how would these buildings complement one another? How would they form a cohesive unit around the central plaza? The architects were able to settle on a number of "unifying elements" fairly quickly. The plaza was to be raised off the street. The halls facing the plaza would have matching second-floor promenades behind glass façades. All would be finished in Roman travertine from the same source that supplied Rome's Coliseum in ancient times. The opera was to be housed in the predominant structure, while the dance theater and Philharmonic would have similar massing. The other buildings were to be removed from the main plaza, but Belluschi's Juilliard building would be connected at the plaza level by a pedestrian bridge. Belluschi, Saarinen, and Bunshaft, by virtue of their buildings' distance from the central plaza, had more freedom than the others, and as a result produced forward-looking designs less restricted by the center's appeal to classical tradition.[49]

Harrison, Johnson, and Abramovitz, on the other hand, had to agree upon complementary visions for their individual buildings. While they each suffered a long process of trial, error, and dispute in adapting their individual sensibilities to the center's demand for harmony, they were relatively eager to follow the precedent established in the overall space planning and find a way to blend the modern with the monumental. "After all," said Philip Johnson, "we're on the same side of the fence. We have come up through the modern movement together, and we're looking away from the Puritanism of the International Style toward enriched forms." In part, what Johnson called their "extraordinary agreement" over a search for "enriched forms" was a result of critiques of modernism circulating in avant-garde architectural circles at the time. Experimentation with modern ideas could produce buildings like those that Belluschi delivered for Juilliard—great slab-like expanses of travertine and glass with complex articulated window openings labeled "brutalist"—or it could go the opposite way, toward the incorporation of historical forms in the manner pursued by the other Lincoln Center architects. At the time, this tendency was labeled neoclassicism or formalism; it now appears to be an early example of the historically referential postmodernism that swept architecture a generation later.[50]

All three of the designs for the main halls followed a similar logic, blending modern forms with exalted façade treatments adapted from historical models. Each architect began with a minimalist box, provided a glass façade, and encased that façade in pared-down, streamlined takes on classic columns topped by simplified arches. The results were, as the *Times* put it, "monumental without being old-fashioned." The paper thought they had "clean lines, graceful proportions, and a minimum of nonfunctional decoration," but it was really only their minimal detail and abstract bulk that gestured toward modernism. As Johnson reflected, "[T]he idea of the arch is, of course, contrary to 'modern' design, the modern age of usefulness, because it is obvious these arches are not truly structural—not honest. But to me they are handsome and comforting." Harrison, who with the UN designs had claimed to deliver not a symbol of peace, but a functional "workshop for peace," here hoped merely for what he called "convenient and distinguished buildings." For the Lincoln Center board, the architects' "comforting" and "distinguished" buildings were entirely satisfactory, providing just the right touch of what Rockefeller's aide Edgar Young called "architectural variety within a framework of harmony and unity." C. D. Jackson praised the opera's "aesthetic virility" and its ability to create the "atmosphere of a great temple."[51]

The buildings were, if not "virile," at the very least imposing. And while they were not lacking in scale and dignity, some observers felt that they overwhelmed the plaza. This was largely due to the fact that the cramped conditions on the site had reduced the plaza to roughly the same footprint as each of the buildings. In the formal array around the plaza, the architectural historian Kathleen Randall has written, "the effect was rather like three cubes facing an equal cubic volume of void, making a very static plan." Or, as one critic put it, "space does not flow here. It sits—in giant chunks." In general, reactions to the buildings' "monumental modern" style were mixed. Many people found the buildings handsome and inviting when lit up at night, but most critics found the scale clumsy and the mixing of new and old a hackneyed bid for dignity and authority. Ada Louise Huxtable, the *Times*'s architecture critic, approved of the repertory theater and Philharmonic Hall as individual buildings, but she likened the complex as a whole to an "overdressed dowager." She judged the opera hall to be "a sterile throwback" and "a curiously unresolved collision of past and present of which the best that can be said is that it is consistently cautious in décor, art, and atmosphere." Siegfried Giedion, the philosopher of modernism, simply called the entire center "a disappointing retreat to the customs of the late nineteenth century."[52]

These were sensitive aesthetic critiques—and, to this day, Lincoln Center's architectural defenders remain few and far between—but they did not change the fact that Lincoln Center's melding of the monumental and the modern was particularly successful in carrying out the goals of the center's sponsors. This compromise provided a traditional yet contemporary blueprint for high culture's intervention in the New York cityscape. Lincoln Center was not forward-look-ing. It did not advance the cause of modern design. But, if it domesticated the avant-garde, it also facilitated one of modernism's most successful interventions in urban space. It used classic forms to give modern planning ideals a new aes-thetic vision, one that allowed abstract modernism to adapt to the challenges of representing public buildings, the exclusive prestige of the high arts, and the national and international cultural mission Lincoln Center claimed for itself. Lincoln Center's blending of the modern and the monumental provided the most obvious and visible symbol of its city-redeeming powers. This was the aes-thetic vocabulary of John D. Rockefeller's "new kind of city therapy."

With this monumental and modern style in the offing, Lincoln Center's sup-porters could hail the complex as the key to the most significant urban renewal undertaking yet launched. Robert Moses, for instance, commented that Lincoln Center provided the "noblest expression" of the aims of Title I. At the cornerstone ceremonies for Lincoln Towers, William Zeckendorf predicted that the perform-ing arts center would "make New York the modern Athens of the western world." With Lincoln Center as its nucleus, Lincoln Square, he said, "gave its name to the greatest of all efforts in this city to breathe new life into land burdened by blight and to point the way to the promise of a better life for all citizens.…At Lincoln Square, urban renewal in New York City has reached its highest use."[53]

These triumphalist sentiments ultimately rested on the fact that Lincoln Center marshaled the restorative powers of high culture to complement more prosaic city-remaking tools. The project's superblock not only displaced the old cityscape, but its plaza and neoclassical façades introduced a sense of order and prestige. The plan refigured the modern arts of tenement replacement and open space provision with a new aura of refinement supplied by visual connection to a long lineage of classical places. On the one hand, the whole point of modern slum clearance and rebuilding, Otto Nelson told a gathering of building prod-ucts executives, was that "the old" was "giving way to the new in a very complete sense." It was not enough to tear down "a few slum buildings" and put up "some new housing in its place, with no change in the street or traffic patterns," nor to merely replace "an old and outdated theatrical hall" with a new one. "Replacing a part of New York City of the horse-car days" called for the modern planner's neighborhood-unit principles. "The minimum requirement," Nelson continued, "is to select an area big enough to maintain its own social and economic cli-mate and to provide its own neighborhood atmosphere and pattern." However, if modern planning could supply a new superblock-sized neighborhood pattern, it took culture and the high arts to alter the "atmosphere" of the old neighborhood. As the *New York Journal-American* editorialized, "[T]his great new cultural cen-ter will give new impetus and added value to the area north of Columbus Square

4.6. Lincoln Center in the mid-1960s, with Max Abramovitz's Philharmonic Hall
(*right*), Philip Johnson's New York State Theater (*left*), and the central plaza complete.
Wallace Harrison's Metropolitan Opera House is under construction at top left, Gordon
Bunshaft and Eero Saarinen's repertory theater and library building is under way just
to the right of the opera house, and Pietro Belluschi's building for the Juilliard School
of Music has not yet gone up. Lincoln Towers hovers in the background. Photograph by
Bob Serating. Lincoln Center for the Performing Arts, Inc.

[*sic*]," and it would also supply some supplementary, less quantifiable advantage, a more generalized spirit of uplift. "Culture," the editorial continued, "is not an affair of rules, but of atmosphere." Lincoln Center, these accounts implied, offered the ideal medium for replacing one kind of "neighborhood atmosphere" with another.[54]

Paul Henry Lang, a musicologist and critic for the *Herald Tribune* and one of Lincoln Center's most committed supporters, seconded the quest for a new atmosphere with a spirited defense of the arts' role in reclaiming the city. He knew that there was a "tug of war" surrounding the project, a political battle between Lincoln Square's sponsors and those tenants and businesspeople who stood to lose their homes and livelihoods. He claimed to understand "the plight of the dispossessed" and granted that their needs "merit[ed] sympathetic consideration." But dwelling too much on their plight would confuse the issue and obscure the project's "far-reaching importance." Allowing such parochial concerns to slow the course of progress was not only imprudent, but also ultimately impossible. "Urban progress in a growing civilization," Lang asserted, "is inexorable." Any remaining "roadblocks" were simply due to "misconceptions." The sites for most public improvements—highways, railroads, or playgrounds— were condemned "without undue uproar," he wrote, because (no matter that this was not at all true) everyone realized that "the few must yield to the needs of the multitude." But now, when "cultural-artistic institutions" claimed a built-up urban site, "the going is much tougher and indignation sweeps the affected area at such 'frivolity.'" But this was missing the point altogether, he said. Any narrow-minded politicians feeling susceptible to that line of reasoning, Lang importuned, had to understand that music and dance were not mere frivolities. In fact, they were even more important than basic public infrastructure. "Being closest to our sensory life," Lang wrote, echoing Rockefeller and his Lincoln Center colleagues, these high arts "have been ever since the dawn of humanity among the great factors affecting human existence." They influenced "our whole life." Here was a clear case in which what he called "urban progress in a growing civilization" required that "the few must yield to the needs of the multitude."

Besides, he implied, Lincoln Center would benefit both the few and the multitude. "Those of us who have this venture at heart," he wrote, "are not taking the supercilious attitude of 'candy store versus opera house'; the humblest citizen deserves just as much consideration as anyone else." But "New York should be known as a proud center of culture," Lang urged, "and not a metropolis teeming with people whose idea of the pursuit of happiness stops at the limits of a safe and comfortable existence enlivened by television spectaculars." Lincoln Center, Lang implied, was an antidote to blight of both the urban and mental sorts. It could provide the kind of atmosphere needed to dispel the stultifying effects of the mass media and the spread of slums. If the "opera house" replaced the "candy store," the result would be an impetus for both urban and society-wide resurgence, as the universal balm of high art would roll back the influence of the mass media and the slums in which it festered.[55]

The idea that high art was needed to rescue the city from the mass culture of the slums appeared in an even more visible forum when August Heckscher and William Schuman hailed the center's arrival in the *New York Times Magazine*'s 1962 special Lincoln Center issue. Heckscher, the Kennedy administration arts official, observed that Lincoln Center's great opportunity was to capitalize on efforts to both revive cities and spread the balm of high culture. The impulse to "decry 'mass culture,'" he said, assuming a like-minded audience for his thoughts, "recurs almost every time we sit for any length of time before a television set or subject ourselves to the kind of vulgarity spawned by the 'gray areas' of the modern city." Like Lang, he equated the growing threat of mass culture with the spread of similar "vulgarity" in the city's built environment. But Heckscher chose to focus instead on the possibilities of the coming age, a time "without...unremitting toil" that would open up "new universes of knowledge and action." It was an era in which "men and women" were "building themselves new forms of human habitation—cities on a scale never hitherto believed practicable." The arts, he said, would "play a crucial role" in this dawning world, because they alone could "humanize the great community of tomorrow." And yet, not everyone, it seemed, would share in these grand visions. The "we" he addressed necessarily spoke for those who could opt out of "subjecting" themselves to the "vulgarity" of the city; it excluded those who were instead subjected *to* life in the "gray areas" of the city. The residents of the "gray areas," reading their Sunday *Times Magazine,* might have wondered why they seemed to have been written out of this bright new future.[56]

Schuman, the president of Lincoln Center, gave them an indirect hint, implying that they would not benefit because this new world was designed to replace their old, supposedly outmoded one. He remarked, "[A]t a time when so much attention is being given to urban renewal, we should remind ourselves that the arts are not merely ornaments to the great communities of the world...but central to their appeal." The problem, he said, following Lang and Heckscher, was that many cities suffered equally from both the "evil" of "physical slums" and "malnutrition of the spirit—neglect of the cultural diet." Lincoln Center was the answer to both, a solution to the "physical slums" of Lincoln Square and, he implied, to the "underprivileged" community life of the area. For Schuman, Lincoln Square before renewal was a place "in which the spirit is not fed" and "where it does not often enough encounter the perfections of the arts." Schuman, no doubt, meant merely to suggest that the lives of all—slum-dwellers included—might be improved by what he and his colleagues saw as the universal "perfections" of the arts. But in equating the malnourished "spirit" of the people in the neighborhood to the "evil" conditions of their neighborhood—the very kind of place his institution had just bulldozed—he was delivering an implicit judgment on the value of that kind of community and its rightful replacement by the arts institution he directed.[57]

This vision surfaced in a rather more benign fashion in another popular venue of the day. The January 19, 1960, issue of *Look* magazine carried a full-page spread on the building of Lincoln Center. Given the headline "Culture City," the piece featured a panoramic photograph juxtaposing the old and the new. In a vacant Lincoln Square lot, recently cleared of demolished tenements, the magazine had set up a model of the latest designs for Lincoln Center. The model was flanked by a group of what the caption called "talented personalities" from the world of the arts, including the dancer Martha Graham; the Philharmonic's "maestro," Leonard Bernstein; and a number of Lincoln Center officials, including Juilliard's William Schuman and the Metropolitan Opera's Rudolf Bing. The notables stare out at the viewer with looks of dignified contentment, serious and self-assured in their mission. A ballerina and a soprano strike dramatic poses. In the background, shooting to the top of the frame, stand a row of dark tenement fronts with blank windows. The model, painted a stark white to give the impression of travertine, occupies the cleared ground, visually demonstrating by clear contrast the coming fate of the buildings in the background. While the tenements to the rear loom overhead, their dark threat is dispelled by the light-filled foreground, where the simple and clean shapes of Lincoln Center's "monumental modern" design promise to sweep away the dark past. This image is the inverse of the *West Side Story* promotional picture; the hope of a new world has moved to the bright foreground here, signifying not the revivifying violence of slum clearance but the calm, assured, and natural result of culture-backed city remaking. Here, the "virility" of urban renewal is mastered, almost suppressed, and turned toward generating an air of confident inevitability. The necessary violence of clearance and renewal is occluded, subsumed by this serene yet orderly tableau displaying the seemingly natural progression from one cityscape to another.[58]

Lincoln Center's backers found that this vision of a city remade by the arts gave them a way to stress the linked local, national, and international significance of the project. For instance, Harry Rogers, head of the West Side Chamber of Commerce and the project's leading local proponent, hailed the groundbreaking at Lincoln Center as the "dawn of a new era." He deployed all the tropes favored by the center's supporters to herald its beginning and to urge its completion. To the citizens of the West Side, Rogers announced, "this center is a symbol of victory in a great war—a war against disease, darkness, filth and vermin infested

4.7. For *Look* magazine, photographer Arnold Newman posed luminaries from the world of the performing arts and Lincoln Center officials with a model of the new "culture city" that was sweeping away the tenements. This image is a slight variation on the one that ran in *Look* with an article called "Culture City" on January 19, 1960. Arnold Newman Collection/Getty Images.

homes. A fight to give children born and reared in basements the right to sunshine, fresh air and healthful surroundings." In an era of "rockets shooting to the moon and men shooting at each other," he and his allies could also be "proud to participate in fostering nurture for the mind and spirit of man so sorely needed when materialistic concepts threaten to engulf us in a slough of despond that sees no hope for a better world." No doubt, the "leadership of the world, both friend and foe, takes cognizance of the significance of the work now beginning." If it were not for "the men who planned this World Cultural Center"—if they had been "satisfied to allow the slums which occupied the Lincoln Square site to remain" or if they had remained "rooted in the rut that held no hope for a brighter future"—then "this area would have remained a blight on the City of New York, a disgrace to the West Side and a cancer gnawing at the very desire for a better society." Lincoln Center's contribution to that "better society," he testified, would be felt in the way that the arts would lift the "spirits" of audiences "above the commonplace," ease the "tensions of modern living," and give many "hope and inspiration to face the future." Rogers demonstrated that the center's ultimate meaning to "the community, the city, the nation and the entire world" lay in the symbolic influence that the example and experience of culture could wield in overcoming the nation's interlinked spiritual challenges: materialism, the Cold War, and urban renewal.[59]

Perhaps the greatest measure of the project's cultural capital was the frequency with which supporters compared it to the United Nations. For them, Lincoln Center confirmed in the realm of culture what the United Nations had announced in the realm of diplomacy and world affairs. "Now the diplomatic capitol [*sic*] of the world," Rogers wrote, "New York will become its cultural capitol [*sic*] with the completion of the Lincoln Center." Others struck the same note. With its unprecedented importance to the life of the city, nation, and world, Lincoln Center was the "most significant civic improvement in New York City since the completion of the United Nations headquarters on the East River," announced Otto Nelson. It would "make New York the cultural capital of the world in much the same way that the United Nations headquarters has made it [the] capital of world affairs." With its "concentration of the performing arts in new, modern buildings" and its "wide-open plazas and spaces," Robert Moses's aide William Lebwohl told the City Planning Commission, the center would, like the United Nations, "add to the city a great nationwide and even worldwide improvement."[60]

If Lincoln Center was a symbol of how culture had been drafted for duty in the Cold War, and also a symbol of how culture became a means for urban renewal, it ultimately became a concrete representation of how a city aiming to meet Cold War cultural challenges should be redesigned and rebuilt—a physical manifestation of the particular urban qualities that the new cultural bulwark required. Accordingly, Lincoln Center's very form—its design and planning principles—articulated these linked goals. The center's blend of new and old, its neoclassical refinement of austere modern superblock-and-tower planning practices, not only offered the necessary platform for high culture's city-remaking efforts, it gave physical form to the city's cultural Cold War bulwark by clearing away the internal weakness of the slums and replacing them with a monumental modern symbol of American power and New York's rise to world influence. Robert Moses summed up the impact of the new project on the occasion of its groundbreaking: "At Lincoln Square Government marches with the University, the Performing Arts and Shelter to rebuild the heart of no mean city. Let those who say our town has no soul look at Lincoln Square and forever hold their peace."[61]

And yet, in taking up all these exalted missions, Lincoln Center and its sponsors were perhaps too assured in the rightness of their benevolent intervention in the "slums" of Lincoln Square. Descending from on high and fixated on their world historical mandate, Lincoln Center's backers never imagined that they might be forced to reckon with another, more local conception of urban culture.

CHAPTER 5

THE BATTLE OF
LINCOLN SQUARE

The View from Lincoln Arcade

Lincoln Center is possibly the most important architectural project in the world
today.... We Americans are writing our cultural history in stone and steel.
—Wallace Harrison, speech at the University Club, 1959

In the spring of 1959, the painter Raphael Soyer began work on a new canvas.
He called the picture *Farewell to Lincoln Square*. A personal elegy for both a
neighborhood and a building, the painting was his way of saying goodbye to
the world he had come to know in the years he rented a one-room studio in
the Lincoln Arcade building on Broadway between 65th and 66th streets. The
arcade, a five-story warren of shops, offices, and studios spanning the entire
western front of Broadway, housed a motley variety of tenants. Downstairs,
there was a bowling alley, a theater, and jewelry, millinery, and dressmakers'
shops; upstairs, there were lawyers, dentists, fortune-tellers, detective agencies, and dance studios. A number of prominent artists had studios there as
well, from Soyer and his painter friend Joseph Floch to the sculptor Alexander
Archipenko and, a few years before, the famed muralist Thomas Hart Benton. In
the early twentieth century, the arcade had been a gathering spot for the Ashcan
School of realists. George Bellows had a studio there, and John Sloan stopped
by frequently. Robert Henri gave classes in his studio, guiding the early efforts
of future luminaries Rockwell Kent, Stuart Davis, and Edward Hopper. Much
of the artists' affection for this uptown outpost of bohemia was due to the fact
that the building itself seemed to encourage the scenes of urban mixture that
the Ashcan artists and their descendants favored. Soyer, for instance, borrowed
dummies and sewing machines from his dressmaker neighbors, and a number
of young seamstresses served as his models over the years. He and his neighbors called the place, with amused affection, the Dog Kennel. But now, Lincoln
Arcade was slated to go under the wrecking ball. Destined only to be remembered as the most colorful casualty of the Lincoln Square urban renewal plan,
the Arcade's site was to be the future home of the northernmost constituent of
Lincoln Center, the Juilliard School of the Arts.[1]

Several years earlier, when the plans for Lincoln Square had been announced, Soyer, Floch, and Archipenko had hoped to stay in the area. They mounted an effort to either save the arcade or, at the very least, induce the sponsors of Lincoln Center to include studio space for painters and sculptors in the project. Theirs was a small, largely unheralded, and comparatively timid wing of a larger campaign by the residents and businesspeople of Lincoln Square to save the neighborhood. The artists wrote to the editors of the *Times* and the *Herald Tribune,* petitioned Robert Moses, and appealed to John D. Rockefeller III, asking for consideration of their plight, but all to no avail. In June 1959, a judge signed eviction orders for the last remaining Lincoln Arcade tenants, and demolition was scheduled to begin September 1.[2]

Farewell to Lincoln Square is often seen as a "protest" against the displacement of Lincoln Square residents, but the painting appears mournful rather than aggrieved. The actual details of Lincoln Square remain indistinct. Traffic signs, a vague façade, the statue of Dante that graces the square itself—all these hover in disembodied drift over a sketchy, distressed, and hazy background of muddy yellow, wan beige, and grayish green. Even the arcade itself is only dimly apparent in the background. Soyer foregrounds the people of the arcade instead, depicting them as a tight phalanx of men and women wandering out and away from the sparse cityscape. "It shows a crowd of people walking aimlessly," he later explained, "dispossessed people. Joseph Floch is there, and a couple of young women. I even painted the demolition man, very small, in the back, and I'm there too, waving goodbye to the building." Soyer's melancholy parade of "dispossessed" artists, seamstresses, and students drift toward the viewer, all of them save Soyer looking solemnly away or down at their feet. He stares straight out from the middle of the cluster, one hand raised in silent farewell, a gesture that seems simultaneously directed at both the building itself—a goodbye to a place he loved—and to the viewer, a forlorn announcement that we will all lose something under the bulldozer.[3]

If *Farewell to Lincoln Square* betrays little of the actual anger or organized resistance that accompanied the progress of urban renewal at Lincoln Square, it does give a sense of what the neighborhood's residents and businesspeople were fighting *for.* Soyer's old colleague and friend Reginald Marsh had been unable to find human drama in the results of urban renewal at Stuyvesant Town, but Soyer himself discovered that the proper source material for their realist canvases lay not in the triumphant rise of a new kind of cityscape but in the dispersal and loss of an older urban order. Just as abstraction had displaced realism in postwar art, the blocky, abstract forms of modern architecture and city planning had scattered the messy realism of old urban neighborhoods. But in depicting that loss, Soyer had perhaps unwittingly discovered the

5.1. Raphael Soyer, *Farewell to Lincoln Square (Pedestrians)*, 1959. Soyer's painting depicts various tenants of the Lincoln Square Arcade drifting away from the condemned building. The arcade was demolished for the Juilliard School of the Arts; the painting imagines the motley world of the arcade as a symbol for the loss of the entire Lincoln Square neighborhood. Hirshhorn Museum and Sculpture Garden, Smithsonian Institution, Gift of the Joseph H. Hirshhorn Foundation, 1966. Photograph by Lee Stalsworth.

ingredients of a new kind of urbanism. More than just a generic street scene—a realist depiction of a group of pedestrians—the painting displays the world of Lincoln Arcade as a symbolic stand-in for the neighborhood around it; it represents the building's qualities of social mixture and fortuitous adjacency as a microcosm of the possibilities inherent in the old cityscape outside its doors. Ultimately, the painting serves as an early intimation of a new way to see the city, one that the larger resistance to urban renewal at Lincoln Square would begin to articulate.[4]

The insurgency against the Lincoln Square plan was not an isolated outbreak of hostility toward urban renewal's bulldozer. By 1955, when it began, it was the latest and perhaps most well known of a number of campaigns by neighborhood groups to turn back redevelopment plans and luxury high-rise building efforts in working-class enclaves across the city during the '50s. The Lincoln Square effort, which was spearheaded by a lawyer and housing activist named Harris Present, did not stop Lincoln Towers, Fordham University, or Lincoln Center, much less end Robert Moses's full-clearance-or-nothing brand of redevelopment. But it did give the resistance to urban renewal a new kind of language, a new way to articulate the fact that the pain brought on by clearance and rebuilding extended beyond the losses of individual homes and shops to the loss of a whole urban world, an informal system of connections that would disappear along with the tenements, factories, and corner stores. What had begun in the early 1950s as a campaign to save individual homes was, by the end of the decade, contributing to the development of a loose and informal movement and a new urban philosophy dedicated to protecting the intricate mesh of urban interactions hidden in the purported chaos of old neighborhoods.

If, as Wallace Harrison put it, Lincoln Center was an opportunity to write the nation's "cultural history in stone and steel," the neighborhood resistance heralded the emerging discovery of a vision of urban culture imperiled rather than saved by the monumental modern superblocks of Lincoln Center. For Rockefeller, Harrison, Moses, and the other backers of Lincoln Center, the project's cultural legacy was rendered in the grand gestures of modern planning and neoclassical architecture; its city-remaking significance sprang from an aesthetic program inspired by the high art of the Renaissance piazza and a cultural mission attuned to the calling of national purpose in an era of Cold War. The resistance offered a local, neighborhood-level rejoinder to this top-down model, proposing a bottom-up brand of city culture that would, in time, displace Cold War urban renewal as the commonsense understanding of how cities should grow, prosper, and renew themselves.[5]

Roots of the Resistance

We are living there very happily, Puerto Ricans, Negroes, Japanese-Americans and other minorities.... We don't want these communities broken up, but the city wants to have what are called "better class people" there. Title I housing...has come to New York City to "clean up" minority groups.

—Pedro Quinones, Save Our Homes, Morningside Heights, 1953

We have cleared slums. Wonderful. And we have created more extensive
slums because of this overcrowding. The West Side of Manhattan, north of
Greenwich Village up to Columbia University, has been damaged by what we
have done, and it is not the addition of the Puerto Rican population to this city.
It is the slum population whom we have displaced without caring that they are
overcrowding these tiny private homes on the West Side.
—Stanley Isaacs, testimony before the City Planning Commission, 1957

The campaign to stop the Lincoln Square plan was an important, high-profile episode in a larger, loosely coordinated battle to save neighborhoods and homes from the urban renewal bulldozer all across the city. These efforts, which grew in ferocity and desperation over the course of the 1950s, had their roots in two linked but mutually suspicious impulses within the broad front of urban left-liberalism during the immediate postwar years. First were the many neighborhood organizations and individual building councils that made up the tenant movement of the 1930s and 1940s. Second was the strain of dissident liberalism, pioneered by City Council member Stanley Isaacs and housing reformer Charles Abrams, that, while believing in the ethic of city rebuilding, had become increasingly disillusioned with the ways that Robert Moses was putting that ethic to work. Isaacs and Abrams first raised the alarm at Stuyvesant Town. Their concerns over Moses's activities only deepened in the late '40s and early '50s as they campaigned for desegregated housing and humane relocation practices for tenants threatened with removal from the sites of the construction coordinator's many Title I, highway, and other clearance projects.[6]

These two constituencies, initially aligned in support of the ethic of city rebuilding, had traveled separate roads to similar dire conclusions by the mid- to late 1950s. Their concerns first began to merge at Lincoln Square, where the campaign to stop urban renewal transcended the tenant movement's roots in the left wing and brought that movement's tenacious defense of neighborhood life to a broad metropolitan audience, one used to hearing only vague reports that tenants were protesting clearance or that various liberal critics of Moses were unsatisfied with the details of relocation on one or another of the city's many renewal sites. If liberal dissidents like Isaacs, Abrams, and other civic-minded reformers had first noticed the abuses of Stuyvesant Town and the troubles with relocation, it was the tenant movement's long-standing commitment to neighborhood life that allowed liberal critics like Harris Present to move beyond simply asking for better relocation practices to trying to stop projects altogether. This growing resistance joined a mounting tide of public scandal in Moses's Title I operations, setting the stage for the end of Moses-style urban renewal in New York and eventually for the intellectual and philosophical demolition of urban renewal itself.

The tenant movement had deep roots in New York's neighborhoods. Its proudly local groups—organized into a series of citywide leagues staffed predominantly by local women who were often left-wing radicals from the American Labor Party or the Communist Party—were primarily concerned with the lives and fortunes of renters in the city's vast stock of private housing. They ran "rent clinics" to advise tenants of their legal rights, mobilized rent strikes against offending landlords, and tried to prevent evictions. They campaigned for rent control during the Depression and then—after the federal Office of Price Administration (OPA) instituted it in late 1943 as an emergency wartime measure—worked to preserve and extend controls for New York's renters in the postwar era of widening prosperity and suburbanization. Active across the city, they were strongest in those neighborhoods with a history of working-class and socialist activism, particularly East Harlem, portions of the West Side, the Lower East Side, scattered enclaves of Brooklyn, and vast swaths of the Bronx.

At the same time, however, the tenant movement joined the broad front of urban liberalism in supporting the drive for public housing and slum clearance. Tenant groups made up the left flank of a loose array of politicians, settlement workers, housing reformers, architects, labor union officials, civil rights groups, city planners, downtown business interests, civic organizations, and bureaucratic strivers like Robert Moses, all of whom were concerned to tear down tenements, factories, and warehouses and rebuild the slums with planned modern housing for the working and middle classes. If these alliances tempered the tenants' radicalism somewhat—many tenant groups by the late '40s and early '50s found themselves so busy facilitating clients' OPA rent complaints or applications to public and limited-dividend housing projects that they had little time or inclination for mass mobilization or rent strikes—their support for the ethic of city rebuilding eventually brought them face to face with the way that ethic was implemented and the hardships it was causing.[7]

New York tenant groups were initially quiescent in the face of the dislocations caused by slum clearance. At Stuyvesant Town, the Gas House District's tenant leaders, careful not to disrupt the wartime unity of the leftist-liberal Popular Front alliance, chose to support orderly relocation rather than jeopardize the further advancement of slum clearance. The United Tenants League, for instance, saw federally aided private redevelopment as "essential to meet our postwar needs." Like its other allies in the campaign to realize the ethic of city rebuilding, the group saw the contributions of private capital to clearance and rebuilding efforts as "part of the overall housing program" designed to rehouse all New Yorkers in modern dwellings. Gas House District residents relied on their elected leaders in Washington and Albany to speak for them, and it was left to civil rights activists and a few dissident liberals—led by Stanley Isaacs and Charles Abrams—to attack the project as a segregated "walled city" and a product of the "business welfare state." Of course, in the late '40s, Isaacs and Abrams were in the minority among their fellow white liberals on this issue. Most—particularly those on the neighborhood level eager to see their neighborhoods rejuvenated—rallied behind Moses and redevelopment.[8]

Despite growing Cold War tensions, this wary alliance between liberals and leftists continued on two key topics: desegregation and passage of the 1949 Housing Act. Both leftists and liberals believed in the vision of an open city, with equal access for all to both public and private housing. Radical and liberal organizations had a largely symbiotic but mutually suspicious relationship, working on parallel tracks to force Metropolitan Life to admit blacks and to win citywide antidiscrimination legislation. Ironically, these efforts—which resulted in a series of municipal laws banning racial discrimination in publicly assisted housing—ultimately helped to legitimize the practice of urban redevelopment in the eyes of most critics, for whom the chief stumbling block to supporting clearance and private rebuilding had been racial segregation, not the displacement of working-class communities. In the five years after World War II, the tenant movement was still warily supportive of redevelopment, provided that Congress did not bow to the pressures of the private real estate lobby and gut public housing funds. Throughout the congressional deliberations over the 1949 act, tenant activists, led by East Harlem congressman Vito Marcantonio, worked tirelessly, though unsuccessfully, to get funding for enough public housing for the ill-housed working and middle classes of New York.[9]

However, during this same period, rising Cold War political tensions were dividing leftists from liberals of both the pro- and anti-redevelopment stripes, cleaving open the façade of wartime unity and mutual support for New Deal ideals. Leftist campaigns to preserve rent control and back Henry Wallace's 1948 third-party presidential bid, for example, alienated Truman liberals who worried that Communists were trying to discredit the president's domestic policies. In the late 1940s and '50s, many liberals actively disassociated themselves from leftist groups pursuing like-minded goals, fearing that charges of subversion might rub off on them. Leftists, meanwhile, claimed that Truman's Fair Deal and Mayor William O'Dwyer's postwar regime were pale imitations of the heady Roosevelt and La Guardia years. Even after the tenant movement began to see that the policies it had championed were having unexpected consequences, Cold War suspicions hindered the development of unified resistance to the dislocation of urban renewal. Liberals concerned to institute humane relocation practices on renewal sites often used the specter of Communist sway over tenant resistance to urge the city and Moses to adopt better programs for moving site tenants, warning that without humane relocation leftist agitation would threaten the success of Title I. Without the Left's organized constituency, however, the power of liberals' criticism was considerably reduced, and what influence they did have was largely directed toward winning nondiscriminatory housing laws. During the late '40s and early '50s, Moses took Title I urban renewal unhindered through this Cold War divide, offering vague reassurances of more public housing to the liberals while largely ignoring the tenant activists.[10]

Of course, Moses's tactics only worked for so long. By the early 1950s, many tenant groups, particularly those backed by American Labor Party neighborhood organizations, could no longer ignore the displacement caused by redevelopment. In the course of their day-to-day advocacy work, tenant activists began to hear more and more complaints from their clients about looming urban renewal projects and the impending loss of homes. They began to see that the results of the ethic of city rebuilding might be a post-industrial, middle-class metropolis, a city rebuilt without them. Their change of heart about urban renewal was almost immediate, and finding this new enemy helped to rejuvenate the movement.

The first flare-up came in 1950 on the Lower East Side, where the ALP and a citywide umbrella organization called the Manhattan Tenants Council organized a futile attempt to resist the ouster of 878 families from the site of the needle trades unions' Corlears Hook Title I project. Sporadic protests erupted in Harlem in 1951 and 1952 on the sites of the Godfrey Nurse and North Harlem Title I sites, but they did not last in the face of support for redevelopment and new housing among Harlem's political establishment.[11]

ALP tenant activists made their most resolute stand on the Upper West Side, where they met threatened removals for the Manhattantown and Morningside Title I projects with determined and organized resistance. The Manhattan Tenants Council, led by Manhattantown residents, organized the United Committee to Save Our Homes, which brought together potential evictees from sites across northern Manhattan. Save Our Homes became the brand name around which a citywide movement of otherwise isolated protestors rallied. A nonpartisan outfit in name only, Save Our Homes was backed and run by ALP members and Manhattan Tenants Council activists. Branches popped up across the city in areas where renewal loomed and an ailing ALP—hampered by mounting red-baiting—could still claim influence. Leaders like Elizabeth Barker on Morningside Heights and Jane Benedict in Yorkville (where luxury apartment house construction was squeezing out older working- and middle-class buildings) offered an aggressive, confrontational brand of advocacy politics designed to wring concessions of more public housing from Moses and Title I sponsors or, better yet, to stop projects altogether. They picketed public meetings and renewal sites, agitated for alternative housing plans, advised relocatees of their rights, gathered signatures for petitions, and tried to organize site tenants into an effective mass movement.[12]

This new movement won few overt victories. Their campaigns are not well remembered, in large part because Cold War–inspired historical amnesia still obscures their contribution to the story of urban renewal's downfall and the rise of a new brand of urbanism. Indeed, Save Our Homes committees were largely ignored or dismissed by "respectable" opinion in their own day; the fact that only the Communist press carried regular notices of their activities in the Red Scare years of the early 1950s gives a sense of their particular isolation. And yet the significance of the Save Our Homes movement cannot be measured in terms of visibility, absolute influence, battles won, or even numbers of people organized.

What Save Our Homes activists did was expose the first stabs of pain suffered by urban renewal relocatees. Their street-, block-, and neighborhood-level connections made it impossible for them to see the situation in the same terms as liberal critics of renewal did, as simply a technical matter of creating more "humane relocation practices." They saw instead families uprooted, communities scattered, neighborhoods destroyed, an entire panorama of spreading loss and devastation in the cityscape. For them, the places that Moses's bulldozers targeted were not "slums" or "blight." Where official planning surveys, press accounts, and Committee on Slum Clearance brochures found physical decay and social turmoil, tenant activists saw, as one Manhattan Tenants Council fact sheet put it, "old established neighborhoods of 30–50 years" with low rents and close to workplaces. The real problem, they claimed, was clearance itself, which by moving tenants into nearby neighborhoods caused further overcrowding and more slums.[13]

Perhaps most important, their efforts to analyze the human fallout of clearance and to organize the victims of renewal provided some initial glimmerings of a new kind of urbanism, one that would be given wider exposure at Lincoln Square. Like many other critics of urban renewal, they knew that the vast majority of the site's existing tenants would not be able to afford the middle-income or luxury rents of the housing that would be built with Title I subsidies. But due to their concentration in neighborhoods across northern Manhattan, Save Our Homes activists were also among the first to notice that, on many urban renewal sites, the burden of clearance was falling disproportionately on blacks and Puerto Ricans. The populations at the Manhattantown and Morningside sites were each over 50 percent nonwhite; the North Harlem site was 100 percent nonwhite. Tenant activists claimed that 16 percent of residents at Morningside

SAVE OUR HOMES!

Hundreds of Yorkville families are being forced out of homes in which they have lived for twenty years or more.

WHY? So old homes can be torn down to make way for luxury apartment houses.

WHERE? Most recently at:

3rd Ave. & 76–77th Sts.	70th St. between 1st & 2nd Aves.
2nd Ave. & 72nd St.	2nd Ave. & 79–80th Sts.
2nd Ave. & 75–76th Sts.	York Ave. & 75–76th Sts.

WHAT'S WRONG WITH THIS?

These evicted long-time residents can find *no* apartments in the area at rent they can afford. There is a critical housing shortage everywhere. *No* one is helping them. They need new *low-rent* apartments to take the place of their old homes — *not* $60-$100 a room luxury apartments.

WHAT CAN BE DONE?

1. We need a new law to make landlords responsible for finding other apartments at a similar rent for tenants whose buildings are going to be torn down.
2. The city must establish a Relocation Bureau to help find these new homes and to guarantee that landlords obey the new law.
3. A low-rent public housing project must be started in Yorkville.
4. All Yorkville residents should write TODAY to *Mayor Robert F. Wagner,* City Hall, New York, and to *State Housing Commissioner Charles Abrams,* 280 Broadway, urging them to press for these things immediately:
5. All tenants should get together with their neighbors to save their homes.

ACT NOW! THE HOME YOU SAVE MAY BE YOUR OWN!

The AMERICAN LABOR PARTY will gladly give free expert advice on tenants' rights to anyone who visits our clubs in this area:

8th A.D. Club	*9th & 10th A.D. Clubs*
319 East 70th Street	1128 Lexington Avenue
RE 4-6370	LE 5-3366

Open Monday, Wednesday and Thursday evenings: 8:30 to 10:30 p.m.

◄◄◄ 269

5.2. This flyer was distributed around Yorkville on Manhattan's Upper East Side, where luxury housing construction was displacing old neighborhoods in the 1950s. Save Our Homes groups, many affiliated with the American Labor Party, organized across the city to fight displacement, particularly from Robert Moses's renewal projects. Stanley M. Isaacs Papers, Manuscripts and Archives Division, New York Public Library, Astor, Lenox and Tilden Foundations.

and 34 percent at Manhattantown were Puerto Rican. Overall, at the 17 proposed Title I sites across the city—not all of which would eventually go forward—they claimed that there were approximately 50,000 families or 200,000 people under the gun, about half of whom were black and Puerto Rican. Due to the prevalence of racial discrimination in the housing market, displaced minorities had nowhere to go but to already segregated neighborhoods like "walled-in Harlem." Urban renewal, the activists charged, was simultaneously uprooting blacks from neighborhoods that were "old," "stable," and somewhat integrated, and reinforcing the boundaries of the ghetto. Urban renewal was earning the popular sobriquet "Negro removal" among blacks in these years, and tenant activists, reflecting their roots in the Popular Front, added their own version of the critique. They renamed slum clearance "people clearance" and proposed the dense multiracial communities they were defending as an alternative to the vision of urban renewal. "We don't want these communities broken up," said Save Our Homes' Pedro Quinones, "but the city wants to have what are called 'better class' people there." Title I, he charged, was designed to "'clean up' minority groups." "We are living there very happily," Quinones said of his own Morningside Heights neighborhood, "Puerto Ricans, Negroes, Japanese-Americans and other minorities."[14]

In addition, the women activists who led the resistance to Title I mobilized this embrace of urban density and diversity to defy what the historian Roberta Gold has called the prevalent postwar "geography of gender." Women like Jane Benedict and Elizabeth Barker of Save Our Homes resisted the dominant gender arrangements of the era by claiming the right to speak out in public about politics and planning. They also spoke up for a particular model of cityscape and community—the dense urban neighborhood—that made possible this crossing of gender boundaries in the first place. With minimal physical differences and distances between houses and streets and residential and commercial areas, the city of blocks, stoops, and local streets allowed for an easy mixing between social roles and spheres. It provided a model of a place beyond "the suburban geography of gendered space." Furthermore, Benedict, Barker, and their allies defended their neighborhoods in the name of their working-class stability and racial diversity, implicitly arguing for this older urban world as a more just cityscape than that offered by urban renewal.[15]

In the short term, Save Our Homes' agitation at Manhattantown and Morningside embarrassed urban renewal sponsors and helped to raise questions about Moses's slum clearance machine. The ensuing turmoil goaded liberals to question their faith in Title I. On Morningside Heights, Save Our Homes pushed the Rockefeller-backed renewal sponsors to delay their plans several times between 1951 and 1953. Tenants' picket lines, testimony at hearings, and petitions forced Moses to provide 1,600 NYCHA apartments near the Title I site. At Manhattantown, tenant radicals filed suit against Title I in the state supreme court, organized opposition rallies, and shouted down officials at pro-redevelopment meetings. They condemned "Negro removal" in one of the oldest and most stable black neighborhoods outside Harlem and charged that Manhattantown would institute new racial divides in the cityscape by erecting a "wall of Title One houses to bar the West Side and the River Front to Negroes and Puerto Ricans." In the spring of 1952, this chorus of resistance reached a fever pitch, as a citywide housing conference of more than 60 tenant groups and their allies applauded Save Our Homes' accounts of the hardships faced by black and Puerto Rican tenants on urban renewal sites and announced their opposition to Title I and racial discrimination in city housing.[16]

All of this furor unsettled housing liberals. Some, like members of the American Jewish Committee of New York, supported pairing public housing with non-discriminatory Title I projects, but dismissed radical critics of Manhattantown, preferring to let qualified experts handle the difficult relocation issues. The AJC's Israel Laster claimed to see little problem with the plan:

[T]he fact that some Communists support low-rent developments is not disturbing. Yet, when they rant, holler and rave only about the fact that there will be high-cost housing and ignore completely the fact that there will also be balanced housing, which will include low-cost, cooperative, middle-income and high-cost housing, then it is important to separate ourselves completely and decisively from such rantings.

Of course, Laster's conception of a "balanced" approach to housing included the public project planned for Morningside's Title I site, a development that was more than a mile away and already more than spoken for by relocatees from the Morningside site itself.[17]

Other housing liberals were more upset by the seeming indifference to "adequate, humane relocation" on the part of Moses and project sponsors. The Citizens Housing and Planning Council (CHPC) and other liberal civic organizations warned federal redevelopment officials and Morningside sponsors that lax relocation practices would jeopardize all of Title I. "Communist dominated groups," wrote the CHPC's Ira Robbins, "are piling misrepresentations and falsehoods on top of the weak relocation structure presented by the Committee on Slum Clearance Plans. The racial and political tensions that can be stimulated by an ill-advised rehousing program are too dangerous to be ignored." When their behind-the-scenes appeal for a go-slow approach to Title I failed, Robbins and his allies in the NAACP, the United Neighborhood Houses, and the New York chapter of Americans for Democratic Action went public with their concerns, warning Mayor Vincent Impellitteri of the threat to Title I posed by "Communist dominated groups" if relocation continued to be "improperly handled." Moses simply responded with more hardball politics. He hinted that he might have to drop Morningside altogether, then urged the Rockefeller-backed sponsors to use their influence in Washington and make a better case for the deterioration of the area. This last-minute blitz secured federal write-down funds and Board of Estimate approval for Morningside early in 1953, leaving liberal hopes for a fix to the relocation mess in the lurch. Many observers—Save Our Homes excepted— concluded that relocation at Morningside was handled reasonably well, in large part because Rockefeller and the other sponsors had hired Lawrence Orton, the city planning commissioner, to direct the efforts. Whether they found relocation practices sufficient or wanting, liberals remained cautiously supportive of Title I as a whole. Most were not yet willing to jeopardize the benefits of modern city rebuilding to save working-class and minority tenants.[18]

To be sure, some liberal urbanists had been troubled by Moses's high-handed techniques ever since Stuyvesant Town. After the war, Stanley Isaacs, Charles Abrams, and their colleagues in the New York branch of Americans for Democratic Action hoped to realize the city-rebuilding ethic at the core of postwar liberal urbanism: federal monies for public housing; slum clearance and private redevelopment; state and city monies for low-income projects; the full implementation of the City Planning Commission's master plan for rehousing and clearance; and an open city worthy of the United Nations. They envisioned a rebuilt regional metropolis with superblocks, towers, and open space downtown and rings of new highways on the periphery. But they were discouraged by Moses's backroom deals, his piecemeal approach to city remaking, and his cavalier attitude toward working-class tenants and the city's growing population of African American and Puerto Rican migrants. The answer, they thought, was not more grand walled towns; Stuyvesant Town's isolated, antidemocratic brand of renewal would be a mistake in the long run. Only a more systematic approach to rebuilding guided by modern city-planning principles could yoke redevelopment to desegregation and create the just city. At planning and housing conferences in 1946 and 1948, housing liberals railed against Moses and called for a reinvigorated City Planning Commission and neighborhood planning boards. Isaacs even lambasted the "so-called coordinator," who, he said, had become "an octopus sprawling all over the city." But divorced from the left wing's mobilized tenants by growing Cold War tensions and jousting with Moses over methods and not fundamental concepts, liberal critics could only take comfort in the fact that nondiscrimination legislation was moving forward.[19]

By the early '50s, two city laws, the Wicks-Austin and Brown-Isaacs bills, had outlawed discrimination in publicly assisted housing. These laws, though as yet untested, convinced many observers that enough housing could be found for tenants at Morningside, Manhattantown, and other clearance and highway sites. A few others remained disturbed by the conditions on these sites and the trouble stirred up by Save Our Homes protests. They struggled to find a technocratic fix for displacement's mounting toll. Isaacs, for instance, supported adding more low-income public housing to Title I packages. Having different income developments "built side by side," he said, was "socially sound and progressive." But he and others also advocated more public housing on vacant sites at the fringes of the city. They also suggested that New York abandon the Moses method of sponsor selection and give to a central municipal office the responsibility of relocating tenants on renewal sites before the land was sold to private developers.[20]

Moses, for his part, was perfectly willing to bundle NYCHA projects with his Title I endeavors if it meant winning approval for a renewal project that cleared slums. Of course, he was also more than happy to leave public housing out if it would endanger a project. He was cool toward investing too much in public housing on vacant land, in part because it risked stirring up outer borough resistance, but largely because he thought those resources could be better spent clearing slums. And he refused to consider reforming the sponsor selection process or having the city take over relocation; New York's unequaled success in getting Title I out of the gate depended on his ability to give contracts to "responsible" sponsors who would farm out relocation to efficient, business-minded real estate contractors.

Moses's continuing intransigence on these key issues pushed some critics over the edge. In Greenwich Village in 1953, Charles Abrams and other dissenters broke with their erstwhile allies from several local civic organizations and New York University to oppose clearance for a Title I project south of Washington Square Park. A few years earlier, Villagers' uneasiness with relocation and large-scale rebuilding had combined with local working-class Italian resistance to public housing to scuttle two Moses plans for the manufacturing and loft district; the 1953 Washington Square Southeast plan went through only after Moses discarded a planned NYCHA low-income component and put off his long-held vision of a roadway through Washington Square Park. Still, most liberals hoped that Moses would listen to reason, fix relocation, and get Title I back on track.[21]

Struggling to come to grips with the relocation crisis, liberal housers worked to get a full picture of the situation at sites across the city. Between early 1953 and 1956, liberals in various public and private agencies issued a slew of reports on tenant relocation. These efforts began with a report by the New York State Committee on Discrimination in Housing. An explicitly anti-Communist open-housing group formed during the battle over Stuyvesant Town by several liberal groups, including the Citizens Housing and Planning Council and the American Jewish Committee, NYSCDH's report suggested that the seven Title I projects proposed or under way threatened 9,604 families, 45 percent of whom were black. The Committee believed that only 15 percent of those displaced could afford Title I rents, while just 35 percent would be eligible for public housing. The committee warned the mayor that, all told, some 45,000 families were facing removal for Title I developments, NYCHA projects, Port Authority tunnel approaches, school construction, highway building, and the clearance of remaining temporary war housing. The mounting tide of refugees—some 60 percent of whom were black or Puerto Rican—would create more slums and unleash political turmoil. When Committee on Slum Clearance officials and several Title I sponsors tried to avoid NYSCDH's questions, Stanley Isaacs proposed a City Council resolution requesting an official City Planning Commission investigation of relocation. The Board of Estimate agreed and ordered a comprehensive study in March 1953.[22]

Commissioner Lawrence Orton, head of the City Planning Commission's "Master Plan unit" and a cautious Moses skeptic, oversaw the study. Orton was eager to prove that the kind of "humane" relocation procedures he had pioneered at Morningside could be used citywide. In fact, he had directed his staff to begin the research in secret a year or two earlier. They discovered that, in the seven years since the war, public works in New York City had dislodged some 63,000 families or 170,000 people from their homes. They estimated that Title I had so far displaced 800 families in its three-year career, 55 percent of them black, Puerto Rican, or otherwise nonwhite. But the greatest shock came in the estimated totals for the upcoming three years: 150,000 more people would be uprooted through public works by 1956, almost a third of them, or 15,020 families, from Title I operations. About half of these were likely to be black or Puerto Rican. Urban renewal projects, the report claimed, would cause the rate of displacement to more than double, from an average of about 23,500 to 50,000 people a year.

Statistics on what was happening to all these people were harder to come by. By 1953, only 21 percent of tenants cleared from Title I sites had been relocated to public housing. NYCHA, which had been responsible for more than half of the clearance of the previous seven years, had the best records. Its samplings indicated that just under a third of the residents from NYCHA clearance sites had been able to move into public projects, about 10 percent had moved into other areas already slated for potential redevelopment and clearance, and another 11 percent had found places in neighborhoods not officially seen as slums. So, 10 percent were forced back into other slums, and 11 percent might be contributing to overcrowding in nearby neighborhoods or, more hopefully, might have escaped the slums altogether. But this only accounted for people the agency knew about. The largest group, 42 percent of the sample, had disappeared without a trace. Optimists like Moses and his relocation consultants interpreted such findings hopefully. These people, they said, had "self-relocated" and found perfectly good accommodations, moving on with their lives. Moses's critics had a darker reading. They figured that most of these people—roomers, single people, and the very poor or working-class families whose incomes were just above NYCHA income ceilings and thus not eligible for public projects—had simply melted back into tenement neighborhoods around clearance sites or found whatever marginal accommodations they could in other declining areas. The majority of that 42 percent, they worried, should be added to the 10 percent crowding into other slums or to that unknown number whose presence in marginal areas was tipping them into decline.[23]

Surveying this scene, Orton and his staff concluded that the city was not prepared to handle the volume of coming Title I relocations and that the political and human turmoil caused by clearance would only worsen. They recommended that New York aim to make 44,000 new housing units available yearly for the next decade and establish a central municipal relocation bureau to take over from private sponsors. Unfortunately, Moses—wearing his city planning commissioner hat—marshaled his allies on the commission and blocked the report's release for nine months, during which time he significantly toned down its central conclusions and softened its recommendations. Perhaps most shocking to the liberals was the fact that the report's figures did nothing to change Moses's apparent confidence about the city's ability to absorb so many Title I refugees. Every time the issue was raised at a particular site, Moses was ready with statistics proving that NYCHA could shelter the dispossessed. Orton had long suspected that Moses was rhetorically recycling the same unchanging stock of NYCHA vacancies in order to dispel fears—and any careful examination of NYCHA's planned housing starts made that all too clear. Now, Orton and his staff had the numbers to prove it, but Moses had watered down their report. Orton and two other commissioners were able to append a minority report to the final sanitized version, but Moses's whitewash had done its job. Few people ever heard about the report.[24]

Still, more and more of the liberals and reformers were starting to see the reality behind Moses's renewal machine. Reports by the city administrator and the Community Service Society reinforced the City Planning Commission's basic findings. A Women's City Club investigation of the Manhattantown project—now being called West Park—surveyed the deplorable conditions on the site. Although the project had been approved and demolition begun, continuous delays in clearance had left thousands of site tenants—the majority of them African American—in an inhumane state of limbo. These tenants were living in the midst of ruins, neglected by the private developer who now owned the tenements but invested almost nothing in upkeep. Some of the families, it turned out, had been moved to two or more different places on the site. As one building's demolition date approached, the developer would shuffle the remaining tenants to vacant apartments in other sections of the site, collecting and sometimes increasing their rent all the while. Almost none of the families would be able to afford the rents in the new development, and they were barred from most non-slum housing by informal racial discrimination or their own poverty. Only 50 out of 300 families who applied for public housing, a follow-up report discovered, were accepted. And now the neighborhoods around the site were more overcrowded than ever, packed with refugees from the Manhattantown clearance. Moses's relocation scheme, the Women's City Club concluded, did "not adequately meet" the demands of the law or "human decency." The conditions at Manhattantown, a 1954 congressional investigation revealed, were the result of a corrupt developer—one of Moses's hand-picked, reliable sponsors— who was milking the site and its tenants for profits, feeding bogus contracts to specious vendors, and siphoning off money for friends and relatives. And yet the problems, as Save Our Homes had long maintained, were not limited to one site. Even Stanley Isaacs, upset with Moses but still not ready to abandon redevelopment, noted in his 1955 report for the relocation subcommittee of the Mayor's Committee for Better Housing that Title I was in danger of making new slums faster than it wiped out the old ones.[25]

All these challenges to business as usual had begun to dislodge a good portion of Moses's support among liberals in the housing, reform, and planning fields. Many civic groups had now joined Abrams and Isaacs on the anti-Moses barricades. Few of them were ready to abandon privately backed urban renewal altogether—save Abrams, perhaps—but their persistent worries and questions were beginning to have an effect on renewal. Moses could still bury or rewrite their reports—as he did with the final report of the Mayor's Committee for Better Housing—stymie investigative reporters, woo editors, and convince Mayor Robert F. Wagner Jr. and the political bosses of the Democratic machine that the city was better off with him than without him. Gradually, however, Moses's façade was beginning to crack. Over the last half of the decade, a group of influential Upper West Side mothers successfully resisted his plan to bulldoze a Central Park playground for a Tavern on the Green parking lot; Greenwich Villagers stopped his plans for a highway through Washington Square; and a phalanx of reporters at the *World-Telegram* and the *Post* began to break stories exposing the way that Moses's Committee on Slum Clearance delivered Title I contracts to favored sponsors backed by Tammany politicians.[26]

These stories began to lift the veil on Moses himself, but it took other developments to loosen his grip over urban renewal, much less undermine the vision of modern clearance and superblock city rebuilding. In Washington in 1954, the dissonance created by tenant agitation, liberal criticisms, and the stench of scandal at Manhattantown helped to push through a revision of the 1949 Housing Act that provided federal subsidies for rehabilitation and spot clearance to go along with the bulldozer clearance methods already in place. Moses disdained these new methods and never used them, but this reform—which pioneered the term *urban renewal* as a less intrusive approach than *urban redevelopment*—gave critics an alternative policy model to the Moses approach. In later years, a group of reformers would take over renewal from Moses by assuring Mayor Wagner that the 1954 precepts would ensure less disruption of tenants and less political turmoil. Meanwhile, liberal critics of Moses had agreed to coordinate their efforts to reform relocation by forming a City Wide Committee on Housing Relocation Problems. They named attorney Harris Present to be chair of the new group, and he immediately began lobbying for reforms. This is where things stood in 1955, when Moses announced the Lincoln Square plan and the residents of the neighborhood began to look for ways to stop the project.[27]

Fighting for a Neighborhood Culture

It was wonderful to hear those gentlemen speak about culture and music and education.... But what about our homes? Aren't our homes beauty and culture?
—Mary Aitken, resident of Lincoln Square, at City Planning Commission hearings, 1957

Robert Moses's announcement that he was adding Lincoln Square to the Committee on Slum Clearance's docket touched off a fervent effort to defend the neighborhood. The resistance was launched by two neighborhood committees, one representing residents and the other local businesses. As with Save Our Homes, women organized and led the residents' committee. The first two chairs were Ella Root and Margaret Hedman, and the secretary simply called herself "Mrs. Philips" in official correspondence. They were not, however, tenant movement radicals. They had their headquarters in Riverside Community House, a local social service agency, not an ALP club or tenant council headquarters. In fact, early on, the Lincoln Square Residents' Committee and the Lincoln Square Businessmen's Committee refrained from challenging the renewal apparatus at all. "Our program does not oppose slum clearance," the residents' committee wrote to Stanley Isaacs, seeking his help in August 1955. Inspired by Isaacs's recent subcommittee report to the mayor on relocation, they simply felt that "clearance of a site should be accompanied by the building of low-cost housing for the tenants." They knew that the $45-a-room figure floated for the housing portion of the project was far out of reach for the vast majority of neighborhood residents and that, as recent projects had demonstrated, there was "no adequate machinery to safeguard displaced residents against the abuses of unfair relocation practices." They called for "immediate postponement" of the Lincoln Square plan until the city could present "a specific rehousing program" for area residents or have the project reclassified as an urban renewal and rehabilitation area under the 1954 reform of the 1949 Housing Act. In order to press their demands, they collected 1,800 signatures from local residents, petitioned the mayor for a meeting, and tried, with no success, to meet with John D. Rockefeller III and the Lincoln Center Exploratory Committee.[28]

In late 1955, the two committees sought out Harris Present for help in getting the attention of Mayor Wagner and city officials. It turned out that they were bringing him in at a propitious moment in his career, just as he was looking for new answers to the relocation problem. Present had become involved with housing issues through his work as pro bono counsel for the Spanish American Youth Bureau, an organization that was active with the growing Puerto Rican population of Lincoln Square and other Upper West Side neighborhoods. But he had become frustrated with the cautious approach of his colleagues on the City Wide Committee on Housing Relocation Problems, clashing with them over fundamental matters of strategy. They favored the sort of independent studies and reports that had recently aroused liberal concern over the relocation crisis. They worried that more aggressive tactics would fail to respect the proper channels of municipal influence and might embarrass the mayor. Present felt that these respectable and conservative methods could only do so much; the time had come, he argued, to bring direct pressure to bear on the mayor through demonstrations, petitions, letter writing campaigns, and other forms of direct action. When the Lincoln Square residents contacted him, he had recently resigned as chair of the committee to form a new group—the New York City Council on Housing Relocation Practices—dedicated to more proactive approaches to helping threatened tenants.[29]

Present's involvement in Lincoln Square confirmed his growing dissatisfaction with conventional liberal tactics. Faced with the lives and struggles of actual people threatened by displacement, he saw firsthand what more radical tenant activists like Save Our Homes had long been saying: the problem was not with relocation but with urban redevelopment itself. Through advocating for the people of Lincoln Square and their threatened world, he moved from seeing the issue as a technical problem of humanely shuffling people about the city in order to facilitate progress to seeing the progress itself as an inhumane imposition on the lives of the people of the city. Over the course of the two to three years that Present and the Lincoln Square resisters fought Moses, they migrated from asking for a better rehousing plan to demanding that the project be killed altogether. Present was able to use his influence to help the neighborhood put its plight before a much larger audience than any previous tenant movement had enjoyed. At Lincoln Square, tenant resistance went from rarely getting coverage in most major dailies to earning regular notice in the *Times* and ample, often favorable coverage in some of the other papers.[30]

Before the project was approved in late 1957, a diverse array of interests coalesced around the movement to stop Lincoln Square and attracted considerable press attention. Besides those who stood to lose their homes and businesses, there were opponents of further municipal tax exemption, who claimed that urban renewal by nonprofit, tax-exempt bodies would put a future strain on the city's treasury; there were groups that believed that the federal and city funds used to help Fordham build a new campus represented a violation of the separation of church and state; there were those who objected to all public subsidies for profit-making ventures like luxury housing; and there were even those who simply wanted to stop the building of a new concert hall and bring the Philharmonic back to the endangered Carnegie Hall. Present and the Lincoln Square defenders tapped into all of these objections, but the lion's share of their attention went to the jeopardized neighborhood. In the course of their efforts, futile though they turned out to be, the Lincoln Square resistance brought a citywide audience face to face with the outcomes that the muffled liberal reports and studies had already predicted: renewal scattered a diverse working- and lower middle-class community and pushed the growing Puerto Rican population of Lincoln Square into a shrinking pool of housing, thus furthering the growth of slums and intensifying racial segregation.[31]

Most important, the tenants and businesspeople of Lincoln Square delivered an alternative urbanism based in the informal connections of neighborhood culture. Tenant activists may have pioneered the defense of diverse, dense urban communities and pushed liberals to act against Moses—and those distraught liberals and their allies in the press may have brought an end to Moses's reign over slum clearance—but it was at Lincoln Square that the resistance began to outline a new vision. If the Lincoln Square residents and businesspeople failed in their immediate goals, and if their efforts were overwhelmed by public acclaim for Lincoln Center's new model of urban and national culture, they still brought this emerging ideal to a citywide audience, where it contributed not just to the downfall of Moses but also to the emergence of a city beyond urban renewal.

During most of 1956, Present and the Lincoln Square resisters pursued parallel courses of protest. Residents and businesspeople collected petition signatures, recruited local people, and sent pickets to public appearances by Moses and Lincoln Square project sponsors. Meanwhile, Present worked to place the people of Lincoln Square's case before the public and Mayor Wagner. He assumed—quite rightly, it turned out—that he would appear as a reasonable and responsible alternative to picketers and that residents' agitation would increase his own access to city officials rather than decrease it. In a series of letters to the *Times* editor and some well-placed quotes in *Times* stories, he outlined the case for the neighborhood. He told reporters that he was not opposed to the project and wanted simply to postpone it until adequate housing was provided for the victims of clearance. "Although all serious-minded citizens" wanted to see slums eradicated, Present wrote, "many of us would oppose such demolition unless convinced that better housing facilities would be created for the dislocated tenants." The 1949 Housing Act, he reminded *Times* readers, required that site tenants be "relocated in decent, safe and sanitary dwellings," and many believed that "the prime responsibility" of redevelopment was "to provide improved housing for the people living there." After all, "the whole theory of the redevelopment of the Lincoln Square area is that people there are living in bad housing." But their "bad housing" had become an opportunity for a real estate deal, rather than for improved housing conditions.[32]

The Lincoln Square project, Present pointed out, promised to displace more families than any previous redevelopment had. He predicted that it would "be made the issue upon which all responsible individuals and organizations who are opposed to the way our city government has been handling slum clearance will be asked to rally and fight for a change." At a meeting with the mayor in May, the *Times* reported, Present told Wagner that, "unless the city administration began thinking of people first and improvements second the 'Battle of Lincoln Square' would dwarf the 'Battle of the Tavern-on-the-Green' in civic ferocity." Combining appeals to "serious minded citizens" with threats of "civic ferocity," Present courted respectable opinion while simultaneously warning that, if officials failed to act, it would bring greater disruption and chaos. The problem, however, was that the battle would not be won by pointing out the city's failure to meet the requirements of abstruse housing policy. Present and his neighborhood allies could continue to tell the public that there was not enough new housing to go around, but Moses would continue to say that there was while arranging the numbers to make it appear to be true. With or without protests, the resistance would only be able to reach those who already distrusted Moses or urban renewal. This was still a relatively small group. In order to win over the bulk of the public and convince officials that the project was a political liability, they had to take a more difficult but potentially more effective tack: they had to portray the demolition of Lincoln Square as a loss more tragic to the city than the gain of Lincoln Center was triumphant.[33]

This would not be easy to do. Not only was Lincoln Center enjoying mounting public anticipation and glowing praise in the press, but almost nobody in the public at large thought Lincoln Square was anything more than a slum, and certainly not worth saving if it meant derailing the advance of urban renewal's highest calling. Many residents even admitted that the neighborhood had been in decline for some time. Once the southern end of the fashionable residential district that stretched from 59th Street to 125th Street between Central Park and the Hudson River, the Lincoln Square area had always had a more diverse social character than areas north of 72nd Street. The southern half of the neighborhood, known as San Juan Hill since the turn of the century, had been home to a large, mixed-income black population. By the Depression, however, most well-to-do blacks had moved to Harlem, marking the first blow to the neighborhood's fortunes. All of Lincoln Square felt the West Side's postwar decline. Middle- and working-class families moving to the other boroughs or to the suburbs abandoned the neighborhood's stock of single-family rowhouses to speculative landlords, who chopped them up into smaller apartments or rooming houses and rented them to poorer white migrants from Hell's Kitchen, Chelsea, and the Lower East Side or, increasingly, to recently arrived Puerto Rican families.

Outside of the defense that residents and businesspeople mounted to save the neighborhood, little information about the character of life in Lincoln Square has survived. Perhaps it was, like the similarly threatened West End of Boston that Herbert Gans and others studied in the late 1950s, an "urban village" with close-knit ethnic and kin structures despite its overall heterogeneity, hierarchies of class and occupation, local intrigue, prejudices, and gossip. This much is clear: in 1950, Lincoln Square was a mixed working- and lower middle-class neighborhood with a largely white and native-born population and a small but growing Puerto Rican minority. Foreign-born residents traced their heritage to a host of European sources—Italy, Ireland, Germany, Russia, and Greece topped the list—but no group predominated and none made up more than 5 percent of the total population, while about 69 percent of the total were native-born. Most residents had been in the neighborhood for at least 10 years; their median incomes hovered around the median Manhattan income, and they worked at a wide range of white- and blue-collar trades across the skill and educational spectrum. The lion's share were factory operatives and service workers, but there were also sizable numbers of professionals, managers, shop proprietors, clerks, craftspeople, and foremen and a significantly smaller number of unskilled laborers. The neighborhood had not appeared on the City Planning Commission's initial map of Sections Containing Areas Suitable for Clearance, Replanning, and Low-rent Housing in 1940, but Moses had it added to his late 1954 revision of the map, thus officially classifying it as a slum.[34]

In pitching the project, Moses mustered his usual array of facts, figures, maps, images, and seemingly foregone conclusions to drive home the impression that Lincoln Square had suffered irretrievable decline. Committee on Slum Clearance documents, focusing on the actual tenants, painted a picture of acute distress that made it hard to dispute the need for slum clearance. Moses's figures showed that 62.6 percent of the site's families earned less than $4,000 a year, and about 53 percent earned less than the overall New York City median income of $3,526 a year. Twenty-four percent, or 1,250 families, were minorities, 18 percent of whom were Puerto Rican, 4 percent black, and 2 percent listed as "other," most likely of "Oriental" descent. Moses's people counted 6,018 families to be relocated, while the tenant groups put the number closer to 7,000. The official number included only a partial count of the 4,507 dwelling units in 97 rooming houses, because the CSC's real estate firm judged that they sheltered only 750 "cohesive families" requiring relocation under the law. The absolute number of people living on the 48-acre site, while difficult to know for certain, was more than 13,000 and possibly as high as 15,000.[35]

Most damning was the area's state of physical deterioration. Of the 482 three- to six-story residential structures on the site, the vast majority—452—were "old law tenements" built before 1901. These buildings covered, on average, 66–88 percent of their sites. Of these, 134 had "incompatible conversions" from residential to business uses, most of which were apartments converted to rooming houses. This, the report said, was evidence of "economic blight." There were 386 stores in these residential buildings, "all of which are basically in a deteriorating state, similar to the buildings which house them." A "house to house survey" conducted by a real estate firm hired by the CSC concluded that 98 percent of the buildings were "either badly rundown, deteriorated, or deteriorating," and most of them required "major repairs." A "high percent" were said to be "deficient in central heating and/or plumbing facilities," although a closer look at the figures would have revealed that 54 percent had complete bathrooms with central heat and hot water, and only about 5 percent were cold-water flats with baths in the hallways. Still, all these findings amounted to one startling conclusion: by the economic logic of the day, only 4 of the 482 residential structures were "standard" and worth the owners' investment in bringing them up to code. Not surprisingly, there had been very little investment or new construction in the area in some time. The blocks west of Broadway and south of 70th Street over to West End Avenue and down to 60th Street—the entire redevelopment site—had been awarded a "D" rating by the federal Home Owners Loan Corporation 20 years before, ensuring that banks would avoid loaning money for new mortgages or improvements there. The motley culture of social mixture and

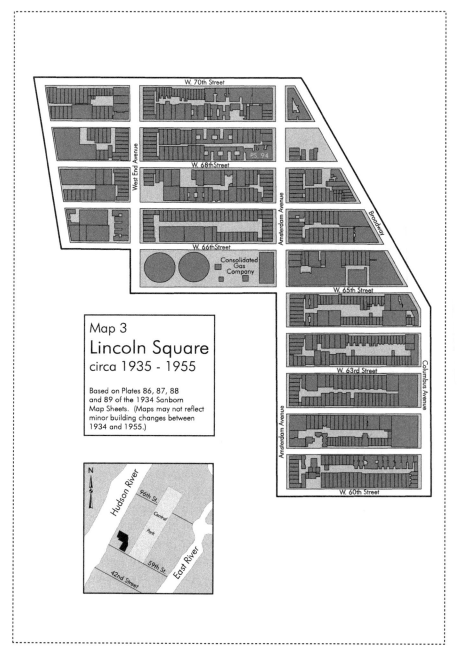

W. 70th Street

West End Avenue

W. 68thStreet

Amsterdam Avenue

Broadway

85, 94

W. 66thStreet

Consolidated
Gas
Company

W. 65th Street

Columbus Avenue

W. 63rd Street

Amsterdam Avenue

W. 60th Street

Map 3
Lincoln Square
circa 1935 - 1955

Based on Plates 86, 87, 88
and 89 of the 1934 Sanborn
Map Sheets. (Maps may not reflect
minor building changes between
1934 and 1955.)

N

Hudson River

96th St.

Central

Park

59th St.

East River

42nd Street

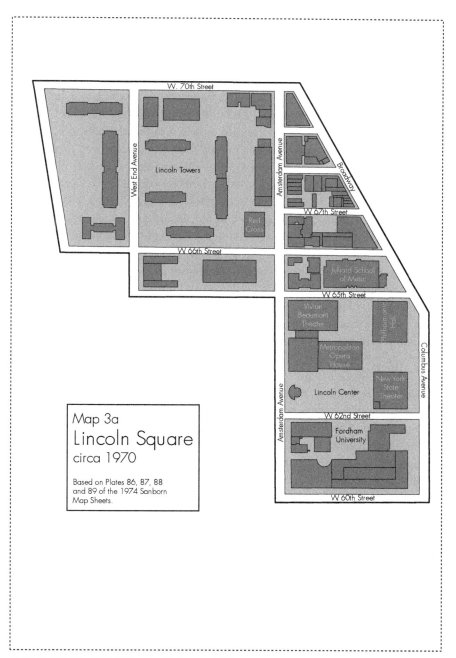

Map 3a
Lincoln Square
circa 1970

Based on Plates 86, 87, 88
and 89 of the 1974 Sanborn
Map Sheets.

W. 70th Street

West End Avenue

Lincoln Towers

Amsterdam Avenue

Broadway

W. 67th Street

Red
Cross

W. 66th Street

Juilliard School
of Music

W. 65th Street

Vivian
Beaumont
Theater

Philharmonic
Hall

Metropolitan
Opera
House

Columbus Avenue

New York
State
Theater

Amsterdam Avenue

Lincoln Center

W. 62nd Street

Fordham
University

W. 60th Street

Maps 3 and 3a. Lincoln Square Before and After.

physical decay that in 1956 attracted Moses's bulldozers had in 1936 guaranteed those bulldozers' eventual arrival.[36]

Moses, the project's sponsors, and other supporters backed up all of these figures with more subjective depictions of the neighborhood's condition. Perhaps most effective were the stark black-and-white photos in the CSC's brochure. Like the images that Metropolitan Life picked for public display from its Gas House District archive, these images were chosen to put the neighborhood in shadow. They hit all the touchstones of tenement horror deployed in the hundreds of slum reports that had preceded them over the years: kids playing in rubble-strewn tenement yards; clothesline laundry collages over dark, empty-paned windows; filthy hallway toilets; dim, low-ceilinged garrets with exposed plumbing and piles of broken plaster and plinth; jerry-rigged electrical sockets spurting wires and bulbs; broken façades, crumbling lintels, and dark rooming houses with sullen tenants loitering out front. The few people depicted, however, were mere afterthoughts. The images did not even bother to construct the usual connection between broken buildings and lost souls that reform-minded image makers had long used to signify urban degradation. The people were there for pure counterpoint: nonspecific, uncaptioned evidence of conditions on the brink of being swept away by the new perfunctory, businesslike modernity evoked in the report's glossy pages, sans serif typefaces, simple design, and authoritative, austere maps.

By 1956, depictions of a doomed tenement district proceeded according to a well-practiced script, one that had been developed at the United Nations and Stuyvesant Town and perfected over the years at numerous clearance sites. Moses, the project's sponsors, and other supporters stuck to the script in the press and in their public speeches. The old neighborhood, it went, was just what flipping through the CSC brochure made it seem: a relic of the past, an inevitable casualty of progress. As Lincoln Center construction chief Otto Nelson had it, Lincoln Square was "a part of New York City of the horse-car days." Surveying this outmoded world, planners added their technical judgments, observing that the neighborhood's dense social and physical fabric, the result of years of historical accretion, was a grave liability to the city. The planner Frederick Gutheim lamented the "curiously divided" nature of the neighborhood. It wasn't just the physical deterioration that made the neighborhood a slum. It was its "thoroughly mixed" character and the "overcongestion, disease, delinquency, crime, and other attendant ills of a cramped and scrambled population." About a quarter of the people there were "Negro and Puerto Rican," he reported. There was heavy truck traffic—pounding "north and south day and night, on Columbus and Amsterdam Avenues"—too many parked cars, and too many languages on the newsstands. All of it was evidence of the fatal problems

LINCOLN SQUARE

SLUM CLEARANCE PLAN
UNDER TITLE I OF THE
HOUSING ACT OF 1949 AS AMENDED

LAND USE

The deteriorated character of the properties in the area can be seen throughout the site.

The area is predominantly residential in character. The residential buildings are mostly "Old Law Tenements" ranging in height from three to six stories, with a high percentage deficient in central heating and/or plumbing facilities. There are 134 incompatible conversions within the 482 residential structures. Many of these have been converted to rooming houses where toilet and bath are a common facility, and others have been converted to commercial purposes. There are 386 stores of various types in residential structures, scattered throughout the area, all of which are basically in a deteriorating state, similar to the buildings which house them.

Existing Distribution of Land use

Residential, Institutional & Public	28.91 Acres
Commercial	16.99 "
Vacant Land	2.09 "
Total	47.99 "

LAND COVERAGE AND AGE OF EXISTING STRUCTURES

The present land coverage varies throughout the project. Blocks 1132 to 1141 and 1158 to 1161 which constitute the majority of residential structures varies from 66% to 88% coverage and blocks 1178 to 1181 consisting of predominantly commercial structures varies from 70% to 81% coverage.

The coverage of residential structures on lots is very dense and tends toward many interior rooms. The stairwells are narrow and basically of wood construction, all creating fire hazards.

Of the 583 structures within this area, 452 residential and 13 non-residential structures were built in 1901 or before:—13 residential and 57 non-residential from 1902–1914:—12 residential and 39 non-residential from 1915–1929:—5 residential and 4 non-residential 1930–1953. The absence of new construction and the conversion of residential to business uses indicate economic blight.

STRUCTURES NEEDING MAJOR AND MINOR REPAIRS

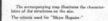

The accompanying map illustrates the characteristics of the structures on the site.

The criteria used for "Major Repairs:"
1. Serious disrepair
2. Lack of proper means of egress
3. Deficiency in sanitary conditions
4. Inadequate original construction

The criteria for "Minor Repairs:"
1. Lack of maintenance
2. Requires minor structural repairs
3. Construction before 1901

The characteristics were determined during a house-to-house survey by Wood, Dolson Company, Inc. and checked by Skidmore, Owings and Merrill.

The analysis of this survey shows that only four residential structures and six commercial structures were in such a state that the owners of these properties would be justified in investing a substantial amount of money to bring them to a condition where they would be acceptable to the present-day New York City Building Codes.

42

5.3. Excerpts from the Lincoln Square Slum Clearance Plan, released by Robert Moses's Committee on Slum Clearance in 1956. Moses's brochures were persuasive devices in and of themselves. The clean, orderly feeling of the designs—bold titles, plenty of white space, seemingly objective amassing of data, photographs bled to the edges of the pages—made for a heightened sense of contrast with the dark, seemingly all-pervasive decay on display in the uncaptioned photos. Committee on Slum Clearance of New York City, *Lincoln Square: Slum Clearance Plan Under Title I of the Housing Act of 1949 As Amended* (New York: City of New York, May 28, 1956). Images courtesy of Lincoln Center for the Performing Arts, Inc., Archives.

of "overcentralization, overconcentration, and overcongestion." Or, as *Architectural Forum* put it, dispensing with the descriptions, the neighborhood was "one of New York City's most traffic-tangled socially polyglot renewal-ready areas."[37]

This corrosive mixing of peoples and uses, the script continued, had resulted in a depleted cityscape, one that seemed depressed in an emotional as well as economic sense. Lincoln Square, a *Times Magazine* piece observed, was a "barren urban waste" where "tenements stand, blowsy and run-down, in silent shoulder-to-shoulder misery, full of filth and vermin." The neighborhood's distress, the script suggested, was not to be found in its people's poverty but in the deterioration that the symptoms and signs of poverty—"overcongestion, disease, delinquency, crime, and other attendant ills of a cramped and scrambled population"—had unleashed on the built environment and its economic well-being. In objecting to the Lincoln Square plan, Harris Present claimed that the plight of ill-housed citizens originally motivated the drive for slum clearance. But his faith in the kernel of reform-minded progressivism at the heart of the ethic of city rebuilding seemed almost naïve in the face of an urban renewal script that positioned slum-dwellers not as victims of urban decay, but as evidence of that deterioration. The social conditions that signaled "slums," the script

5.4. Lincoln Square streetscape (probably West 64th Street) not long before the demolition for Lincoln Center began. Lincoln Center for the Performing Arts, Inc., Archives.

5.5. Lincoln Square aerial view, c. 1957, looking southeast with Amsterdam Avenue on the right and Columbus Avenue and Broadway in the upper left. The New York City Housing Authority's Amsterdam Houses peek out from the bottom right corner. East of Amsterdam Avenue are the Lincoln Center and Fordham sites. Lincoln Center for the Performing Arts, Inc., Archives.

prompted, were troubling because they were also, and most important, evidence of an outmoded cityscape plagued by economic "blight." The cityscape itself was suffering, and the ills of its people were mere evidence of that greater civic pain and disease.[38]

With the neighborhood's problems relegated to the economic sphere—and those economic issues given emotional and civic resonance by planners' judgments—there seemed to be no question that the Lincoln Square plan was a step forward into the future and out of a painful past. As the *Herald Tribune* put it in an editorial, "[A] whole lost neighborhood will be brought back to life" by the renewal plan. The new project, its supporters assured the public, would transform civic depression into national glory. Without Lincoln Center and its assured advance over the old neighborhood, wrote Harry Rogers, publisher of the *West Side News* and one of the biggest local backers of the project, the neighborhood would have remained not just "a blight on the City of New York," or "a disgrace to the West Side," but a "cancer gnawing at the very desire for a better society."[39]

For his part in the play, Moses emphasized the fact that, while this progress might be inevitable, it would not and should not be easy or painless. On the one hand, Moses's pronouncements on the project echoed the tenor of his brochures. He was assured and brash, and in his own inimitable way he signaled the sense of fait accompli and air of inevitability around the project. But he also revealed his vision of necessary and revivifying violence at the heart of the simple urban renewal practice he had carved out of the ethic of city rebuilding. "The Columbus Circle improvements are not enough," he told an audience of builders in a widely noted 1956 luncheon speech. "The scythe of progress must move north. No plasters, nostrums and palliatives will save this part of town," he proclaimed, referring obliquely to the less invasive, rehabilitation-minded schemes on offer in the 1954 revision of Title I. "It calls for bold and aseptic surgery," he continued, echoing Harry Rogers's use of the familiar medical language long employed to naturalize the growth of slums and justify the rooting out of their "cancerous" effect on the municipal and national body politic. Then, however, he interjected a note of warning into this strident jeremiad, admonishing his audience that doubts would not only disrupt the necessary sense of resolve but jeopardize the project altogether. "Delay," he said, "is dangerous, if not fatal." Delay, of course, might give opponents time to gather their strength. As for the people in the way, the ostensible source of any meaningful opposition, he wrote them off with one of his most notorious quips about the violence necessary to spark urban renewal's rejuvenatory powers. "You cannot rebuild a city without moving people," he would say at the Lincoln Square groundbreaking a few years later. "You cannot make an omelet without breaking eggs."[40]

The combined effect of this array of facts, figures, images, and seemingly commonsense judgment was to leave the people of Lincoln Square almost invisible. In the official urban renewal script, they were simply passive ingredients of economic blight, so many eggs to be broken for omelets. In order to render the people of Lincoln Square visible, Harris Present and his clients had to prepare their own bit of political theater, guided by an alternative script to that offered by Moses and the promise of Lincoln Center. Throughout 1956 and 1957, as the project made its way through the regular round of municipal hearings, the Lincoln Square groups threw up a gauntlet of pickets and demonstrators around City Hall, besieged the mayor with petitions and letters, and packed the hearings to decry the project's impact on their lives and community. Their version of the story was at first focused on forcing the city to provide humane relocation, but it soon evolved into an attempt to make city officials, project sponsors, and the public see a different view of the threatened world of Lincoln Square. Their attempt to reframe the reigning conception of the neighborhood came to center not only on demonstrating that there were homes and a functioning community at Lincoln Square, but on showing that preserving that particular neighborhood culture was as important to city life as promoting the version of culture offered by the vision of Lincoln Center. Throwing Lincoln Center's brief for urban rejuvenation through ennobling culture into stark relief, the neighborhood resistance asked the public which was the more "humane" model for urban life: a superblock cultural center that increased racial and economic segregation by wiping out a striving, polyglot, working-class community or that community itself, a dense, interconnected weave of peoples, traditions, and livelihoods?

During the summer and fall of 1956, the Lincoln Square committees sent pickets to City Hall for several preliminary hearings before the Board of Estimate. They hired a sound truck to go through the neighborhood the day before each hearing, urging residents to make the trip downtown. As many as 50 protestors—many of them women and children—appeared each time, carrying signs that read "Humane Progress Means Decent Relocation," "Shelter before Culture," and "No Homes, No Culture." On one occasion, they pitched a tent on a rented trailer and towed it downtown with three kids inside. The tent wore a sign that read, "Mr. Moses, Board of Estimate Members: Is This the Future Home for 7000 Lincoln Square Families?" At a follow-up hearing, Richard Schuckman, owner of a print shop and co-chair of the Lincoln Square Businessmen's Committee, traveled downtown in a horse-drawn carriage adorned with "Battle of Lincoln Square" posters and petition forms. Clad in a colonial frock coat and tricorner hat to emphasize the fundamental loss of liberty at hand, Schuckman swung a bell above his head and delivered a sheaf of petitions bearing 6,501 anti–Lincoln Square signatures to the board. "People must come before culture," Present told the *Herald Tribune* outside City Hall. Inside the closed-door hearings, debate went on for five hours, with 22 speakers opposing the project and only 2 supporting it.[41]

Meanwhile, Present held meetings with other tenant groups facing displacement around the city. They resolved to increase the pressure. Much to the dismay of Stanley Isaacs and the CHPC's Ira Robbins, the protestors launched an election-year mass mail protest. Residents sent thousands of postcards to Mayor Wagner and Manhattan Borough president Hulan Jack, urging the two officials to vote no on the project. The message on the postcards concluded with a stark warning: "You will need our votes in November." The mail protests and angry picket lines earned the protestors headlines and pictures in the press, but they also seemed to have some effect. The *Times* went from uncritically reproducing Moses's estimate of some 6,000 families needing relocation to accepting the tenants' number of 7,000 displaced families. The vociferous resistance also caught Moses off guard. In order to defuse the situation, he hastily added a 420-unit middle-income cooperative—later called Lincoln House—to the plans and

5.6. Lincoln Square Residents Committee members and their allies picket in front of City Hall. The sign "Shelter before Culture" argued that Moses, Rockefeller, and Wagner should value the basic necessity of shelter over the luxury of culture. Eventually, the protestors developed a more subtle argument about their "shelter": that their neighborhood was a form of valuable culture as well. New York World-Telegram Photograph Collection, Library of Congress.

5.7. Lincoln Square Businessmen's Committee head Richard Schuckman, dressed in tricorner hat and colonial frock coat, led a Lincoln Square delegation to City Hall to protest outside municipal hearings on the project. Here, he looks on while a police officer writes his driver a ticket for unauthorized use of a horse-drawn taxicab. New York World-Telegram Photograph Collection, Library of Congress.

made vague promises about building more public housing nearby. The Board of Estimate deferred action on the plan twice, but in September, convinced that Moses and the project's sponsors had the situation in hand, permitted them to file an application for federal Title I funds. This ended most of the wrangling for the time being, as both sides regrouped and prepared to press their cases in the new year.[42]

The year 1957 was a watershed in the history of Title I in New York. Robert Moses spent much of the year mired in a bitter feud with Albert Cole, the federal Housing and Home Finance Agency administrator responsible for approving Title I funds. Upset with Moses's method of preselecting sponsors and the furor over relocation, Cole questioned Moses's appraisals of the land at Lincoln Square and held up approval and federal monies for purchasing the land. But in August, faced with public and behind-the-scenes support for Moses—made up of a mixture of editorials in the major newspapers and an onslaught of calls from the Catholic archdiocese, union leaders, bankers, and John D. Rockefeller III himself—Cole backed down and released the federal write-down funds. On the surface, Moses's reputation was untarnished. But the scandal at Manhattantown made headlines that summer, and in the inside pages of the *World-Telegram* and the *Post,* reporters Gene Gleason, Fred Cook, and William Haddad were beginning to gather and present further evidence of financial and political scandal, evidence that would bring Moses's Title I reign to an end two years later.[43]

Meanwhile, the Lincoln Square resistance began 1957 by declaring that its members were no longer interested in delaying the project in hopes of winning a better relocation plan. They now aimed to kill it. That winter, they signaled their rejection of mere relocation by picketing the newly opened project relocation office. They also unveiled a new strategy. In December, Present had filed suit in state court, claiming that using eminent domain powers and federal funds for a Manhattan campus of Fordham violated the First Amendment of the Constitution. This case and several related spin-offs—all of them eventually unsuccessful—made their way through state and federal courts over the next two years, contributing to the various delays that Moses and the Lincoln Square sponsors faced. Of course, as Present later admitted, it was never likely that the cases would actually stop the project. They were simply legal maneuvers designed to tie up the project in court and to draw public attention to the movement's larger message. No longer content to be simply relocated, the people of Lincoln Square began to focus more concretely on the implications of their poster slogan "No Homes, No Culture." The problem with the bulldozer approach to urban renewal at Lincoln Square and other sites around the city, Present told the *Daily Mirror* and the *Post,* was not only that it destroyed homes, but that it destroyed "the culture, mores and friendships of the residents." There was a slight double entendre in the poster's slogan: without their homes, the residents would lose their own "culture," but the loss would not be theirs alone. The monumental superblock for the performing arts was no equal, they suggested, to the lived "culture" and "mores" of the neighborhood, and the loss of these commonplace values would be a blow to the city's overall culture.[44]

Present and his colleagues got their best chance to offer this alternative urbanism in the late summer when the city announced that the plan would go before the City Planning Commission and the Board of Estimate for final approval. Between 350 and 400 people attended a rally in late August to hear Present exhort them to telephone their friends and neighbors and "make a crusade out of this." He hoped that they could "overwhelm" the planning commission with pickets and speakers. "A Huge Turnout at the Hearing Can Defeat It," trumpeted a flyer that went around the auditorium. On September 11, the day of the hearing, the resistance sent 20 pickets to City Hall bearing signs that read "Moses Is Clearing People Not Slums," "Our Children Need Housing Not Promises," and "We Refuse to Move until Homes for Us Are Made Part of the Plan." One elderly businessman, the proprietor of an auto parts shop in the district for 50 years, sat in an armchair on the sidewalk in front of City Hall with placards that read, "My 50 Year Old Store Is Being Closed by Robert Moses," and "For Hire. 68 Years Old. Small Businessman. Apply Robert Moses." Inside, the hearing lasted almost 11 hours, with 36 speakers opposing the project and 24 favoring it.[45]

Testimony at the public meeting provided a recap of all the issues surrounding relocation. Stanley Isaacs admitted that he found the project "a terribly attractive center for the arts in the city." But Moses, he charged, was still offering the same finite body of available public housing units to every Title I project. Unfortunately, the number of refugees had long outstripped the city's ability to provide new housing. There just wasn't enough decent housing for everybody. Perhaps the worst part of it was that so many of the displaced were minorities. Isaacs reminded the commission that, while New York had some of the most advanced antidiscrimination legislation in the nation—and, as he put it, "I helped to draw and put on the statute books every one of these statutes"— those laws targeted publicly assisted housing and thus reached only 5 percent of the total stock. The growing Puerto Rican population of the clearance area—24 percent of the total on the performing arts site and 18 percent overall—had nowhere to go but other neighborhoods where Puerto Ricans already lived, many of which were facing clearance themselves. The effect would be to increase overcrowding in already stressed areas like East Harlem and ultimately to make more racially segregated slums by clearing slums. "Is it any wonder," asked neighborhood resident Aramis Gomez, why the Puerto Rican people of Lincoln Square oppose the project, when it would "only offer more suffering and

This is a Summons to you

to appear at the
PUBLIC HEARING
of the City Planning Commission
on the
LINCOLN SQUARE PROJECT

WED., SEPT. 11, 9:30 A.M. AT CITY HALL
Public pressure forced delay of the plan until now.

A HUGE TURNOUT AT THE HEARING CAN DEFEAT IT

LINCOLN SQUARE RESIDENTS—LET'S TELL CITY HALL:

- That a plan which doesn't provide housing for the people it uproots is not good for our City. It will cause great hardship.
- We will have to hunt for apartments in the midst of a housing shortage—We will be forced to pay higher rents—Many of us will have to take smaller and poorer apartments—We will have to travel longer distances to our jobs — Many will be forced to move into worse slums, as has been the experience of displaced families in other areas.
- The storekeeper will lose his business and life's savings.

IF YOU DON'T WANT THIS TO HAPPEN —
COME AND TELL THE CITY PLANNING COMMISSION:

- Not to tear down our homes until new ones are built.
- That houses MUST be built for us and people like us at rents WE CAN AFFORD.
- That Businessmen must get paid for goodwill and full moving expenses.

Bring your families — Bring your neighbors
BRING FRIENDS FROM EVERYWHERE

Meet at: Commerce High School, West 65th St. at 9 A.M. or take IRT to Chambers Street and MEET US AT CITY HALL

LINCOLN SQUARE RESIDENTS COMMITTEE
c/o RIVERSIDE COMMUNITY HOUSE
239 WEST 69th ST., NEW YORK 23, N. Y.

LINCOLN SQUARE CHAMBER OF COMMERCE
109 WEST 64th STREET — SU. 7-7405

PACK CITY HALL!
SHOW YOUR SUPPORT FOR OUR SPEAKERS!

no housing for us?" Gomez drew an analogy between slum clearance and the most egregious example of racialized displacement in American history. "Why, this is more like the Old West, where we, the poor people, are the Indians with valuable land that the settlers want. So, like long ago, they take the Indians and put them on a reservation." The Lincoln Square groups picked up on Gomez's rhetoric; later demonstrations featured pickets dressed in buckskin, beads, and feathers, carrying signs reading, "Don't Throw Us Out of Our Tepees" and "Help! Pale Face Moses Scalping Us Indians." If Schuckman had positioned the neighborhood as a repository of American Revolution era virtue, freemen threatened by despotism, this tactic allowed the residents to go him one better, summoning a spirit of authenticity and making themselves into even more "original" Americans: Boston Tea Partyers, perhaps, or underdogs in a contemporary western who were on the verge of losing the very place that made them who they were. Overall, they suggested, their removal would reverberate across the city. In an age of white flight, Lincoln Square was that rare bird: a mixed-race and -class neighborhood, one the liberals behind Lincoln Center should have appreciated. Right now, testified Isabelle Manes, a resident of West 66th Street, Lincoln Square was a "well-integrated, racially and economically balanced neighborhood." If the project went through, however, it would become "an entirely high-income and professional neighborhood," while other neighborhoods became poorer, more overcrowded, and more segregated.[46]

But what was perhaps most notable about the City Planning Commission hearings was that they gave the Lincoln Square resistance the opportunity to more fully articulate what the loss of this "well-integrated, racially and economically balanced neighborhood" might mean for the city. The hearings became the stage for what Present called "a basic battle in philosophy" between the project's backers and the people of Lincoln Square. If Rockefeller and the other Lincoln Center officials favored culture-backed redevelopment for both city and nation, Lincoln Square's residents responded with a defense of particularly local virtues and connections. They questioned how those who claimed to be supporting the human and universal values of the arts and culture could ignore the endangered human culture of their neighborhood. In doing so, they subtly shifted the mean-

5.8. Flyer distributed in Lincoln Square summoning protestors to attend City Planning Commission hearings on the Lincoln Square plan in September 1957. The flyer reflects the fact that the movement began by demanding "decent relocation" practices—this is still one of their talking points. By this time, however, many people, including Harris Present, the main spokesperson for the opposition, had come to believe in the goal outlined in boldface here: defeating the project altogether. Lincoln Center for the Performing Arts, Inc., Archives.

5.9. Outside the City Planning Commission hearings on the Lincoln Square project, Abraham Halikman, 68, a store owner on the Lincoln Square site, protests the loss of customer good will caused by clearance. The idea of "good will" expressed the ineffable and incalculable value found in the relations between the public and private halves of the Lincoln Square neighborhood. Published in the *New York World-Telegram,* September 12, 1957. New York World-Telegram Photograph Collection, Library of Congress.

ing of the term *culture* from a notion that signified solely the higher virtues of the arts to one that embraced the entire way of life of a community. What was more truly "human," they asked the commission, the privilege to be able to appreciate what one resident called "the better things in life," or to have established a complex and interconnected way of life in a difficult urban world? Which should be underwritten, subsidized, and protected in the cityscape? Which was indicative of true "progress"?[47]

They pursued this theme on two fronts. First, the residents located their own human values—their own culture—in an imperiled domestic sphere, in homes and family lives threatened by the overwhelming imposition of an outside force that would scatter and disrupt cherished and long-lasting stability. Then, the businesspeople of Lincoln Square showed that an elaborate, and also imperiled, public world complemented this endangered domestic space. This local public sphere was to be found, they claimed, in the multitudinous informal commercial connections between the neighborhood's residents and its businesspeople. This mesh of relations was based in economic exchange, but the logic of commerce, of exchange between customer and proprietor, could not express the full extent of its reach into the life of the neighborhood. It was the medium by which the two halves of this world—public and private—formed one whole community.

"Why should we give up our homes for this conglomeration of culture?" demanded Lincoln Square resident Vincent Radighieri. This was the fundamental question, one that had seemed unutterable two or three years earlier, before he and his compatriots began to organize. Who was to say which was more valuable or which better represented progress, Lincoln Center or the homes of neighborhood residents? How should that value be measured? "I believe," said Harris Present, "if we are going to talk about progress, we have to talk about human progress first…. I say no matter how impressive any cultural institution may be, or educational institution, there is nothing more important in a democracy than the human beings involved." Louis Okin, the City Council member for the threatened district, agreed: "The human beings must come first." Of course, the Lincoln Square residents were not immune to the appeal of high culture. Just because Robert Moses said their neighborhood was a slum did not mean they were ignorant of the world beyond their few blocks. "I think we want the better things in life," said Cyril Heath, "but certainly not at the expense of human comfort and human life as such." Other residents were less accommodating, questioning who in this conflict could truly be counted as sympathetic to human virtues. "I think it is a disgrace," remarked the current residents' committee chair, Hubert Lewis, "if anybody that professed to love the arts…could at the same time ignore human beings." Aramis Gomez asked sarcastically, "But who cares for the little shopkeeper so long as we have culture? Who cares whether we have a home so long as the Philharmonic and the Metropolitan Opera have one?" With all the evidence presented, he thought the judgment on Lincoln Center was self-evident: "I think you all know how inhuman the project is."[48]

In questioning the humanity of Lincoln Center, they also called into question the true definition of culture. Why couldn't they also claim to be living in an authentic, fully realized world? Or, as elderly resident Mary Aitken put it, "what about our homes? Aren't our homes beauty and culture?" "You must have a home for your family life," remarked a sympathetic outsider, the Brooklynite Josephine Montrose, but "you must have a home for some culture. Culture is not just in a center, a large center located at Lincoln Square. Culture is also something in the home, in the place where the family lives." For some of the protestors, the project's threat to the culture of domestic life was foremost in their minds. "The prime consideration of the fathers of this City right now," Lincoln Square resident Rina Garst told the commissioners, should be "the mothers of this City. We must think of the children....it is essential that they remain in their neighborhoods where they have developed friendships, where they have their family lives." Stanley Isaacs offered a word of warning. "Nobody can reckon the effect on city life," he said, "of the reckless destruction of family life on such an extensive scale as this last decade has witnessed." Lincoln Square was the most extensive example yet of a continuing and as yet unrecognized pattern of dislocation of stable family life. "These uprooted families have been driven far from their friends, their relatives, their children's friends. The children have to go to new schools. The church connections are severed." Homes and families, these comments suggested, were at the core of an entire neighborhood culture, one marked not by the artistic achievement and hierarchy celebrated in Lincoln Center's austere and monumental vision of city remaking, but by the ordinary, everyday neighborhood network. Aitken summed it up: "We don't want to be taken away from our church, [the] wonderful hospital we have near us, [our] wonderful neighbors, and the little children we have known from infancy. We want to be left with those." If Lincoln Center's backers had depicted the project as a masculine weapon in the Cold War, a manly asset in a high-stakes game of diplomacy, the neighborhood's defenders stood up for the domestic realm, the typically feminized private sphere of home and hearth.[49]

Of course, the imperiled connections were not simply private in nature. What Present had called the "culture, mores, and friendships" of the neighborhood had a public dimension as well. At Lincoln Square, public and private were yoked together by the commercial life of the community. There were more than 600 places of business in the project footprint, ranging from hundreds of simple storefronts to a 10-story building that housed offices and light manufacturing. The sheer diversity of going concerns was staggering, although hardly unusual for a bustling working-class neighborhood. There were the usual luncheonettes and delicatessens, corner grocers and fruit stands, fish and meat markets, bars and liquor stores, candy stores, beauty parlors, barbers, laundromats, and corner pharmacies. There were hardware stores, print shops, shoe stores and shoe repair places, men's and women's clothing stores, and tailors. There were furniture stores, toy stores, a bike shop, radio and television repair shops, a record store, newsstands, auto parts stores, a "Chinese goods" store, and a driving school. There were the tradespeople: upholsterers, sign painters, electricians, house painters, plumbers, glaziers, and auto mechanics. There was an interior decorator, photography studios, a Girl Scouts office, a funeral parlor and an embalming academy, a motion picture warehouse, a detective agency, a magazine publisher, a caterer, a breeder of animals for research, at least two ball bearing shops, two advertising agencies, and one sanitarium for birds. There were companies making dresses, carbon brushes, "chromalloys" and "diffusion alloys," machine parts, tape measures, and sprinklers. There were churches of all Christian denominations, a police station, a library, a school, an ambulance service, a Democratic clubhouse, and a social and cultural center. On just the second floor of the 10-story office building at 109 West 64th Street, a business dealing in carburetors shared a hallway with a television studio, an unidentified warehouse, and a concern dealing in "polychrome sales." About half of the neighborhood businesses were storefronts in residential buildings. While only 7 of the 318 stores in residential buildings were owner-occupied in September 1955, when the CSC's real estate firm filed its report, there were also only 12 vacant storefronts, suggesting that the commercial culture of the neighborhood was a healthy one.[50]

If Lincoln Center were approved, this entire commercial landscape and the thousands of jobs it supplied would disappear. Urban renewal sponsors were not required to provide relocation services for displaced businesses, and while federal laws offered a $2,500 reimbursement for moving and fixtures, most businesspeople reported that it would cost many times that to move, pay initial rent, and install their fixtures. One laundryman thought it would cost $6,000–8,000 to move; a pharmacist believed it would take $20,000; and the head of a plastics firm claimed it would cost him $35,000. One merchant, a fire extinguisher salesman named Michael Walpin, even went so far as to personally beg John D. Rockefeller III to make available a $3 million moving fund for the merchants of Lincoln Square. As the World-Telegram put it, "One man's culture is another man's pain in the billfold." A great many of the Lincoln Square businesses, however, would never get a chance to relocate. They would simply go under.[51]

Most of these small businesspeople operated on slim margins. They had little capital and could not easily get loans. Their businesses weren't intended as investments or profit-making endeavors but simply as means of making a living.

Unlike the great urban renewal development schemes, they did not enjoy public subsidies nor great reservoirs of private capital; their commitments were not to a balance sheet nor to the abstract, nonprofit affiliations guiding Lincoln Center. Their primary investments—and this was particularly true of the most local and fragile of them—were actually in the neighborhood itself. Their ultimate value was in large part determined by the "good will" of their neighbors. No municipal, federal, or private urban renewal sponsor would pay business owners for it—but without the symbolic capital that intimate acquaintance with a customer base delivered, the businesses themselves would be worthless. This long, painstaking accretion of local connections stood at the heart of each business and at the heart of the entire community. Urban renewal threatened not only jobs and livelihoods, but the informal web of ostensibly commercial connections strung across the divide between the public and private spheres. Urban renewal policies not only discounted the significance of small businesses to the overall city economy—carelessly destroying the portions of the job and tax base these enterprises represented—but ignored their value in fostering the ineffable connections of a neighborhood culture. It was, in the end, the accumulated good will that the people of Lincoln Square had for one another that would crumble and disappear under the treads of the urban renewal bulldozer.[52]

This depiction was no doubt intended to assure the commission that Lincoln Square was a traditional, old-fashioned community, not a slum. And yet, ironically, if the neighborhood appeared old-fashioned, this registered with the planners as a failing not a virtue. As Save Our Homes had shown, the lines between public and private were thin and often blurry in this older cityscape. If Lincoln Square represented a considerably more democratic and dispersed conception of culture than that on offer in Lincoln Center, it also seemed decidedly retrograde in light of the ostensibly forward-looking spaces of superblock urban renewal, where the lines between the residential, commercial, and monumental spheres were carefully delineated. The world that the people of Lincoln Square defended appeared out of step with both the suburban geography of gender and the pure, abstract visions of superblock-and-tower urban renewal. For the planners, the threat of Lincoln Square lay in both the effects of its socially and physically mixed character—outmoded and hazardous, according to contemporary planning theory—and the challenge that the intermingling of spheres, uses, and peoples posed to the dominant models of urban place remaking. They could not vote to preserve this world; it still appeared to them as both an artifact of an outmoded city and a threat to the full emergence of a modern urban vision.

Despite the varied challenges from residents and businesspeople, the City Planning Commission approved the project, basing its final acceptance on the assurances offered by Moses and Rockefeller that homes could be found for all and that relocation would be handled in what the commission called a "decent and proper manner." The commission found the plan to be "eminently suitable" and far too important in the overall effort to renew the city to delay further. They reassured themselves with the general estimation that, in the next three years, only 75,000 families would be displaced across the city, while it could be expected that 93,500 new private and public housing units would go up in that same period. A month later, in closed-door proceedings before the Board of Estimate, the scenes of protest were repeated. Sixty-nine people spoke—most in opposition—over the course of an 18-hour hearing that went until 4:30 in the morning. Despite the fact that Board of Estimate members were subjected to the longest single session in City Hall history, the board followed the planning commission, unanimously approving the project in late November 1957.[53]

In later years, Harris Present would say that he felt these meetings were "shams," that the "decisions were made behind closed doors," and that the meetings were held simply to fulfill the letter, not the intent, of the law. It was certainly clear that the power brought to bear against the neighborhood was too great and the promise of a gleaming cultural center too seductive. Fighting Moses, Rockefeller's influential board of directors, the editorial writers of the most prestigious papers, the Roman Catholic archdiocese, and the major labor unions all at once, he said, was far too tall a task for the neighborhood forces. The defenders of Lincoln Square were unable to turn back Moses and Rockefeller. The overwhelming appeal of redeeming the city through culture proved too alluring, while their new conception of neighborhood-level urban culture failed to command a comparable following. And yet, they had brought that vision to a citywide audience for the first time. They had moved the debate beyond the question of "humane" relocation practices. In the short term, the question now was whether or not Moses's bulldozer approach to clearance should continue. In the long term, the urban vision that germinated in the Save Our Homes campaigns and bloomed at Lincoln Square would underwrite the effort to unseat urban renewal as the dominant philosophy of progressive urbanism.[54]

Making Way for Culture

Culture is a precious symbol of progress. But it becomes barbarism when we trample roughshod over the simple rights of life, liberty and the pursuit of happiness, which are the heritage of every American citizen.
—John A. Ward, letter to the *New York Times*, 1957

According to conventional wisdom, the actual process of relocation at Lincoln Square unfolded with little of the overt drama kicked up by the campaign to win approval for the project. And yet that surface impression concealed hidden strife. Project sponsors claimed that it involved less difficulty than expected, while Present and the uprooted residents complained of abuses and inhumane treatment. On the face of it, the job did seem to go smoothly, particularly when compared to the debacles at Manhattantown and some of the earlier renewal sites. Even though move-outs were delayed by legal challenges until the summer of 1958, the entire process was completed on all parts of the site by early 1960, well ahead of schedule. Project officials tried to minimize both actual hardships and the appearance of hardships, releasing figures that showed that the average site family had moved to a larger apartment at a lower rent. When newspaper reporters discovered relocated site families living in buildings with no heat or hot water, the management firm hired by the project sponsors claimed ignorance and rushed to make repairs. These efforts earned them kudos on some editorial pages and the widely repeated sense that, as the *Daily News* put it, "resistance is on the wane" and "there had been few, if any, complaints from relocated tenants." The situation at Lincoln Square was taken as evidence that the knotty "relocation hassle" was easing.[55]

But Harris Present and the neighborhood groups disagreed. They accused Moses and the project's sponsors of waging "psychological warfare" on site tenants by trying to scare them into moving out as quickly as possible. While some residents moved hurriedly and with little hassle, many others, particularly Puerto Rican families with limited English, found themselves trapped in the doomed buildings with few prospects. Some reported feeling that they had received little help in finding an apartment they could afford; others felt bitter at the management agents, who they said had threatened to turn off their hot water, gas, and electricity if they didn't get out soon. There were stories of rampant basement fires, a lack of repairs in many buildings, and residents going without heat in the midst of a cold snap in early December. When they complained, residents told reporters, the management simply told them to move out; it took front-page exposés to get the management firm moving on repairs. These divergent perspectives on the same events revealed the gulf between urban renewal's supporters and its opponents.[56]

Most troubling to opponents was the ultimate fate of the uprooted. Some of those who had difficulty finding apartments on their own had hoped to find a place in public housing, but Present claimed—rightly—that only about 10 percent of the site population, or about 540 families, ever made it into NYCHA projects, despite the fact that estimates had suggested that anywhere from 25 to 55 percent of them would be eligible. The authority, it turned out, actually only took applications from 21 percent of the overall site population, or about 1,200 families, and only processed applications from 16 percent, or about 900 families.

A great many people, it appeared, opted out of public housing altogether when they learned that, due to the scarcity of vacancies in nearby West Side projects, they would have to accept assignments wherever NYCHA could find them housing. If sponsors were pleased to see that better than half of the site families had taken advantage of cash bonuses and relocated themselves without help, Present claimed that this was simply evidence that most people had been left to fend for themselves. Available statistics from the Lincoln Center and Fordham sites showed that 55 percent of site families stayed in Manhattan, and a plurality of those—60 percent—found new homes on the Upper West Side or in "midtown West," the neighborhood just south of the site, which was better known as Hell's Kitchen. The next most-common destinations were Washington Heights, East Harlem, and Harlem. While Rockefeller and his colleagues saw the numbers as evidence of orderly dispersal, these findings did little to assuage one of the protestors' central objections to clearance: it would add to overcrowding in the already taxed neighborhoods surrounding the site and would increase segregation and overcrowding in minority neighborhoods like East Harlem and Harlem. Besides, as their testimony made clear, residents loved their neighborhood; the lost home for which they grieved was the neighborhood and its institutions, not necessarily their actual houses. One neighborhood priest, who had lost a third of his flock, reported that the "exodus" from Lincoln Square had been a "heart-rending experience."[57]

These disputes over the process of relocation extended the contest over the meaning of urban renewal at Lincoln Square, providing another example of the divergent conceptions of the effects of modern city-remaking practices. Proponents of the project took a removed and paternal approach to the process of moving residents, trusting that their good intentions, liberal credentials, and technocratic methods would ensure a humane process. For instance, Manhattan Borough president Hulan Jack, wary of the political implications of presiding over another relocation debacle, organized locally influential "civic-minded individuals" into the Citizens Watchdog Committee. The body was chaired by West Side Chamber of Commerce head Harry Rogers and directed by local businessman Leonard X. Farbman, but as Jack told protestor and resident Aramis Gomez, "it would not be suitable for residents to be on the committee." This committee, Jack demonstrated, was designed to be *for* but not *of* the community; it was "in no sense an arbitration committee." It would stand above the fray, managing the flow of refugees from a safe distance.[58]

In all their dealings with aggrieved residents, the project sponsors maintained a carefully composed sense of removed sympathy. They displayed concern for residents and professed to understand the hardships they were undergoing, but nevertheless assumed that even those who were losing their homes or businesses would feel that their sacrifices had been contributions to making a better city. Unable to allow themselves to close the gap between sympathy and action—because to do so risked admitting the true effects of clearance on actual people's lives—they tried to reassure themselves and the displaced that everyone would share in the sense of larger civic glory that the new performing arts center promised. They knew that Moses's "scythe of progress" would cause pain, and they felt sorry to have caused it. But real progress required the liberal application of cleansing violence to clear the ground for a collective reward. Or, as city planning commissioner and former Stuyvesant Town relocation chief James Felt said of Lincoln Center construction head Otto Nelson, "We can't have a city rebuild itself without pain. Otto will feel that pain, will work with it, will be able to turn it into something that brings new life." The wrenching loss of particular streets and neighborhoods could be transformed, they said, into a shared, redemptive sense of collective gain. Belief in the arcane powers of this new urban alchemy served Nelson well in dealing with the most immediate victims of the revivifying violence of slum clearance. For instance, he made a distraught letter from a Lincoln Square rooming house resident named Basil Fellrath into an opportunity for a sermon on the glories of their mutual civic endeavor. Nelson wrote to Fellrath:

> I know, irrespective of what can be done, the pain and sadness you will feel in moving from a place where you have lived for so many years. I am sorry this is necessary but hope that when you see the completed Lincoln Center for the Performing Arts, you will feel that the inconvenience has been for a good cause. You should feel a sense of satisfaction and participation in that you too have helped in bringing about what we believe will be a great civic improvement that will be enjoyed by many thousands of people over the next hundred years.[59]

Lincoln Center's backers embraced the spirit of "creative destruction" that had underpinned so many previous New York place-remaking campaigns. This faith in the redemptive power of modernity's cycles of destruction and rebirth—and their sense that they were directing those energies toward their highest achievement to date—provided a useful rationale by which to dismiss the particular grievances of the uprooted while simultaneously incorporating their losses into a reassuring lesson about how individual sacrifice would underwrite collective gain. This story was not only grist for the public relations mill or a fitting way to display somber, hopeful concern for the fate of displaced residents like Basil Fellrath. It was also, and perhaps most important, the way that the project sponsors explained to themselves the role of displaced lives and communities in the larger drama of destruction and rebirth.[60]

This was most evident in a particular piece of drama staged by employees of Braislin, Porter and Wheelock, the real estate firm hired by Lincoln Center and Fordham to manage relocation on their sites. As an homage to the role of the performing arts in the project, one of the real estate men, Charles D. Atkinson, wrote a one-act musical comedy called "A Day at Lincoln Square" for the company's 1958 Christmas dinner. The play was intended as a lighthearted tale about the recalcitrance of Lincoln Square tenants, little more than a bit of comic relief about their unwillingness to face the inevitability of change. It was based on a simple conceit: no matter how opulent or dignified the new homes the firm found for them, they clung stubbornly to their familiar surroundings. This little drama was bookended by an introduction and conclusion that framed the joke with a reassuring lesson about the collective benefit of culture's displacement of ordinary neighborhood life.[61]

The curtain opened on Atkinson, playing the narrator, and a three-man chorus who introduced "the story." "Well, what kind of a day has it been?" asked the narrator. "A day, like any other day," he responded, answering his own question. It was, the chorus intoned, "a day to try the patience of a Landlord's soul. A day when ten families stopped doing their washing on the future stage of the Metropolitan Opera....A day when Bach and Beethoven evicted Harvey's Bar and Grill." It was, the narrator concluded, "A day when ten hoola hoops circled Sixty-fourth Street no more. A day in which history was made at Lincoln Square and YOU...ARE...THERE!" Then, the chorus began to sing, delivering the theme in a mocking tone that signaled the shared sense of exasperation that they all had with tenant recalcitrance: "It's a terrible, terrible, terrible crisis. No one will move uptown, no one will move down. The brokers are charging impossible prices and some of the tenants are starting to frown." Next, a "tenant" entered, singing, "I will move anywhere, anywhere, anywhere. If you'll be reasonable, I'm not hard to please." But then he reeled off a list of places he wouldn't go: Queens is "too aristocratic"; the Bronx is a "zoo, you can't fool me"; Kings— meaning Kings County, or Brooklyn—are "undemocratic"; and Jersey is "too far under the sea." Besides, Brooklyn is "much like Siberia." It's almost as far away, and "barren and cold since the Dodgers went West." So, he sang, he'll move "anywhere, anywhere, anywhere," as long as anywhere is in the "Fifties, The Sixties, The Seventies indeed." "My dog has asthma, won't let him climb a stair," he concluded. "A home like my old one is just what I need." The chorus responded, reprising the original theme and following it with a comment that echoed the tenant's complaint: "He will move anywhere, anywhere, anywhere, Fifties, the Sixties, the Seventies indeed. His dog has asthma, won't let him climb a stair." But then they altered the last line to remind themselves who truly had the tenants' best interests at heart: "A home like his old one is *not* what he needs!!"

With the overall theme delivered, the narrator introduced the setting—"137 West 64th Street, an old brownstone 4 stories high," which is about to be "immortalized in the annals of relocation"—and the main character, one "Esplanado Di Santiago, an old man 4 stories high." The conflation of man with building, each "4 stories high," revealed the way that the tenants appeared only as an inert feature of the cityscape to their handlers, one more in a series of technical problems to be overcome on the road to demolition and rebuilding. Di Santiago came on with a Braislin, Porter and Wheelock agent, a character called, in a gesture of self-deprecation signifying both his job as relocation coordinator for the block and the dogged, self-defeating perseverance with which he pursued his duties, the "BPW Blockhead." The two went through an absurdist back and forth in which the Blockhead tried to get Di Santiago into a taxi to go over to the new apartment the firm had found for him. Di Santiago stalled by asking about a birdcage he couldn't move without. He was hoping that his 38-year-old canary, "Simon Bolivar," would one day return to him, and he wanted to be ready. Finally, though, he said goodbye to "the home of [his] youth" and got in the cab. Twenty minutes later, however, the narrator informed the audience, Di Santiago returned, unhappy with his new home. "I don't like the neighborhood. It ain't my style! It ain't my class!" The Blockhead was stunned. Did he go to the right place? "Sure I did," replied Di Santiago. "Sure I went to the right place—where you sent me—over to the East Side near the River. The building is over a hundred years old and there's no one living within a hundred yards of the place. The cops have got it surrounded, and besides, I don't like the name—Gracie Mansion."

With the punch line delivered—even the chance to live in the mayor's official residence was not enough to overcome tenant bullheadedness and ignorance—the chorus swept back in to end the play, summing up the triumphant endeavor in which all would share: "Lincoln Center for the Performing Arts, Fordham University, will be built here in many parts, surmounting all adversity. Tenants are living much closer to Paradise, theatre, symphony, opera, ballet, millions of lives will be filled with zest and spice, a wonderful sight for us to display." These dramatic contents were reinforced by the accompanying handmade program, which included the script, score, and a series of cartoonish drawings illustrating the story. The most notable illustration depicted Di Santiago as a perplexed, disgruntled, and mustachioed man squatting barefoot inside his own birdcage like a trapped animal or a traveling curiosity. He was labeled "To Gracie Mansion," but the cage and posture suggested resonances with disturbing traditions of racial and exotic display rather than orderly removal. Here, the image almost seemed to suggest, was the last remnant of a disappearing race, the Lincoln Square Puerto Rican. Other images were less provocative, displaying not suppressed disdain for the residents, but the shared sense of collective endeavor with which Nelson and the sponsors believed the residents should identify. The title page was decorated with a ceremonial drawing of a crossed pick and violin—the implements of destruction and rebirth at Lincoln Square—while the cover and closing page depicted the way in which the tenants, despite their own recalcitrance, would be transformed from bitter displaced persons into joyful participants in the pageant of urban resurgence. On the cover, a desultory family of six lined up with packed bags, ready to make way for the opera house and the great open plaza sketched in behind them. By the end of the play, however, the family had themselves become performers in the drama, celebrating their move that "much closer to Paradise." The two youngest kids portrayed Romeo and Juliet; the eldest son banged on a drum kit; Mother sang an aria; Dad tooted on a horn; and the eldest daughter held up a banner wishing Braislin, Porter and Wheelock employees a Happy New Year. Here, then, in this combination of haughty disdain and munificent paternalism, was the story the project sponsors wanted to tell themselves about relocation: when all was said and done, the dislocated would thank the sponsors and their agents for helping them to play a small part in a great drama of civic splendor, national triumph, and urban rejuvenation.

Not surprisingly, the residents and businesspeople of Lincoln Square viewed the situation somewhat differently. They and their few supporters across the city and in the press were more likely to see resistance as not mere mule-headed recalcitrance or ignorance about the larger world, but attachment to a particular community. They also refused to take a passive role in a drama of civic sacrifice for culture-backed urban renewal. They chose instead to ask what truly constituted "progress," and whether progress achieved in this manner could actually be counted as a credit to the nation. "Culture," wrote a neighborhood defender to the *Times,* "is a precious symbol of progress. But it becomes barbarism when we trample roughshod over the simple rights of life, liberty and the pursuit of happiness, which are the heritage of every American citizen....At stake here is the very essence of democracy." Lincoln Square was not the only project to be labeled antidemocratic; as one resident of the Washington Square Southeast site put it in a letter to the *Herald Tribune,* the relocation practices used there and at Lincoln Square "certainly smack[ed] of totalitarianism." If Lincoln Square's backers envisioned the project as a vital symbol of American freedom and an emblem of Cold War preparedness, the project's opponents came to see the struggle over relocation in terms drawn from the opposite pole of the Cold War's binary logic. "In a dictatorship," the *Post* editorialized about the "Quiet Uprooting" at Lincoln Square, "there could be no argument about these matters; the displaced persons would simply be written off as casualties of 'progress.'" The tragedy, of course, was that this was more or less what was already happening.[62]

Even those who did not explicitly resort to language drawn from the political culture of the Cold War depicted the project's impact in terms that suggested urban renewal's one-dimensional, mass replacement of neighborhood complexity and culture and the total and top-down intervention of its spatial vision. "Hundreds of businesses were actually steamrolled out of existence," a fire extinguisher salesman, Michael Walpin, reminded Otto Nelson in a letter on the occasion of Lincoln Center's groundbreaking. Now that the center was being launched "in all its glory and splendor," he wondered "if those responsible for the desired advancement of culture can hold their heads in equal glory and pride when they see the wide open spaces that mark the death and destruction of the hundreds of what were once real live and profitable business establishments. Lincoln Center shall ever remain their tombstone." For some, the monumental modern façades of Lincoln Center would be monuments only to the lost community of Lincoln Square, the "wide open spaces" of its plaza only a blank and feeble replacement for the interconnected web of neighborhood life.[63]

Indeed, the legacy of the community's uprooting lingered in the streets of the new Lincoln Square. Accounts of the changed neighborhood were quick to note that Lincoln Center had "spark[ed] vast renewal" in the area or given it a "new tone." They noted all of the new stores and restaurants, the new luxury apartment buildings, and the new "class" of people. Moses's original "vision of a reborn West Side, marching north from Columbus Circle," seemed to be on the brink of fruition. The old seemed to have completely given way for the new. And yet, the scars of clearance had not fully faded; they lurked on the fringes of the newly reborn neighborhood. Community leaders worried about divisions between the newcomers and the remaining old-timers, between the luxury towers and the red-brick public housing. Residents of the Amsterdam Houses, the NYCHA project that sat across Amsterdam Avenue from Lincoln Center, appreciated the chance to take in concerts and plays. Lincoln Center helped to underwrite the community center in the project, and as part of its attempt to open the performing arts to everyone the administration brought children from the center (and across the city) to performances and classes. And yet, this sense of liberal munificence could not entirely dispel the feeling that Lincoln Center was an interloper dropped in from on high. Along Amsterdam Avenue, where the center turned its back on the public project with a great expanse of blank white stone, people simply called it the "Chinese Wall." Joseph DiLauros, a butcher whose shop had been relocated from the footprint of Lincoln Towers to West 67th near Broadway, was, according to a *World-Telegram* reporter, "discouraged" but accepted the situation "philosophically." His father had started the business in 1904, but the move and the subsequent transformation of the neighborhood, he said, had "ruined" him. All of his old customers had been scattered to the wind and the "good will" on which he made his living had dissolved. "These people in the big houses," he said of the new luxury apartment-dwellers, "they don't eat. I guess they just pay rent. I got a few customers but they want a small steak, a couple of chops."[64]

In 1965, *Times* reporter Bernard Weinraub visited Lincoln Towers. He found the place to be cosmopolitan and vibrant. It had an air of culture, luxury, and refinement that only an address around the corner from Lincoln Center could provide. Restaurants advertised that they stood "in the midst of the new cultural capital of the world." He interviewed a number of the housing complex's "affluent and successful" residents, many of whom had moved there from the suburbs or other countries. There were, he wrote, "a sprinkling of widows, businessmen, prosperous young couples with children, groups of two or three girls living together, African diplomats and interracial couples." And yet, Weinraub reported, there was a "virtual obsession with protection." Doormen checked identification in the luxury towers; new buildings advertised their state-of-the-art security systems. "Everyone who moves in," a hardware store owner told him, "wants a new lock. Everyone's afraid." People kept a wary eye on the remaining tenements and rooming houses in the surrounding blocks—many of them no doubt packed to more than capacity with Lincoln Square refugees—where old women still stared silently from windows and teenagers clustered on stoops with radios blaring rock'n'roll. "You walk two blocks up, it's terrible," said the owner of a new stationery store in Lincoln Towers. "Here it's beautiful. You don't want a better class of people than these." This, said one new resident of Lincoln Towers' Corbusian slab-block towers, "is the new 'West Side Story.'"[65]

The original *West Side Story*, as it happened, came home to Lincoln Square a few years later, going up at Lincoln Center in 1968 on the stage of Philip Johnson's New York State Theater. The revival of the original Broadway play, reviewers noted, already seemed a bit dated, as the ethnic clashes of 1957 paled in comparison to "the black-white confrontation staring us in the face today." Of course, it was not only the play's original topical thrill that had passed into history; so had the actual lives and cityscape that once motivated its drama. Whatever its failure to capture the tensions of the contemporary moment, the 1968 performance could not fail to provide some opportunity for reflection, however oblique or underappreciated, on the particular loss of the urban world from which its fundamental conflicts originally sprang. As the Jets and Sharks danced across the stage of Johnson's modern temple for the arts, they danced also over the ruins of the very landscape from which their performance had been conjured. Now more than ever, their songs and cries stood in for the silence of the actual voices from which their lines had been cribbed. If the play's original appeal had been its romantic appropriation of the "actual" world of gangs and neighborhood-level ethnic skirmishes, it had now been transformed into a memorial to the disappearance of that world, to the very lives and landscape of Lincoln Square that had been uprooted and bulldozed for the stage on which the play now unfolded.[66]

West Side Story's revival at Lincoln Center offered an unprecedented opportunity to grasp the play's subtle commentary on the entire career of urban renewal itself. At its heart, *West Side Story* tells the tale of Tony and Maria, the two star-crossed lovers who try to escape the world in which the warring factions have trapped them. But their love story is also the story of urban renewal; the play's narrative arc parallels the historical progress of urban renewal's aspirations. If the conflict between the gangs provides some rationalization for the negative impetus for urban renewal, the play's central love story illuminates its utopian hopes and tragic fall. The promise of love in the story acts like the promise of renewal in postwar New York: it offers to deliver the people from worry, want, and danger and to usher in possibility. But, of course, *West Side Story* is a tragedy, and the collapse of the lovers' hopes mirrors the corruption and decline of urban renewal's city-remaking visions.

Consider "Somewhere," the song that Tony and Maria sing together in her bedroom late in the drama. Riff and Bernardo—the Jets' and Sharks' leaders—are already dead in the big rumble, but Tony persuades Maria that her love for him overwhelms the fact that he has killed her brother. The scene expresses the heart of the play's tragic vision—two lovers trapped by bigotry and prejudice or, as Maria puts it, by "everything around us"—as well as its essentially liberal hope: they will break out alone and run away together. Before they make any plans, however, they deliver in song their vision of a new world. They sing, "Somewhere there must be a place we can feel we're free / Somewhere there's got to be some place for you and me … / Peace and quiet and room and air / Wait for us / Somewhere … / We'll find a new way of living / We'll find a new way of forgiving / Somewhere." During the song, the room and the city fall away, revealing a "world of space and air and sun" where they are joined by both gangs and their girls, all hostility and suspicion vanished.

The play's staging makes this utopian vision a social one: they will forgive each other and the gangs; they will find "a new way of living" with each other and with the others in a transformed world unlike the streets and tenements. The scene bounces between escape from the city and its total transformation, between realizing a perfect city of "quiet and room and air" and finding those conditions outside the city altogether. Like the film version's opening shots, this scene sums up the "structure of feeling"—in Raymond Williams's phrase—that lay behind the attempts of urban liberals to rejuvenate the central city in the age of suburbanization and Cold War. This conflicted vision, the lure of an urban ideal that must replace the actual city in order to succeed, encapsulated urban renewal's social and spatial vision of saving the city by knocking it down and replacing it with Stuyvesant Town's "suburb in the city" or Lincoln Center's "cultural fairyland."[67]

And yet this vision is a fleeting one; just as urban renewal was compromised by the violence at the heart of its city-remaking ideals, the vision of "Somewhere" cannot survive the violence that Tony and Maria's romance has called up. The "world of space and air and sun" suddenly dissolves and the city returns. The "dream becomes a nightmare," and the lovers are pulled apart in the "chaotic confusion" of the rumble, a split that foreshadows the play's tragic denouement, in which Maria loses Tony for good to a bullet. Ultimately, *West Side Story* was the most popular dramatic reflection on the power and tragedy of urban renewal. Unlike Robert Moses's slum clearance script, the project sponsors' soliloquies heralding arts-led city remaking, neighborhood residents' ensemble piece touting the culture of community, or Braislin, Porter and Wheelock's relocation pageant, the musical offered no partisan argument, only an opportunity to grapple with the promise and loss of modern urbanism.

By 1968, when *West Side Story* returned home to a transformed Lincoln Square, the original vision of urban renewal had been all but discredited. The struggle over neighborhood culture at Lincoln Square helped to precipitate that downfall, but it would not have been possible without the development of a new vision to supplant it. And that new vision would be created not only out of grief for the losses that urban renewal entailed, but also out of dissatisfaction with the new landscape of urban renewal itself. That critique arrived in the same years that Lincoln Center was proposed and resisted, but it first took shape in the efforts of New Yorkers to come to grips with the new tower-and-superblock landscape of public housing.

CHAPTER 6

COLD WAR PUBLIC HOUSING IN THE AGE OF URBAN RENEWAL

A World Transformed

New brick towers rise along the right-of-way of the New York Central and the New Haven as the commuting trains sweep down from Connecticut and Westchester. The men from Wall Street sometimes talk about it as they fold away the *Times* and the *Tribune* and prepare to get off at Grand Central. It is remarkable, they say, the progress which is being made in the city. You can hardly recognize Harlem. The East Side has been transformed.
—Harrison Salisbury, *The Shook-Up Generation*, 1958

Harrison Salisbury came home to New York in 1954. He had been the *Times*'s man in Moscow since just after the war, covering the rise of the Cold War and the end of the Stalin era. Now, he went to work on the city desk in a New York he felt he hardly knew. He filed stories on mounting garbage problems, the last train on the doomed Third Avenue Elevated, and the "parade" of new office towers, "glass and aluminum palazzos of soap and booze," rising in "the man-made cordillera that is Manhattan." Just as impressive as the new "headquarters area for blue-chip corporations," though, were the vast belts of slums that had gone under the wrecking ball and been replaced by phalanxes of boxy, modern housing towers. All along the East Side waterfront, in particular, tenements and warehouses had fallen and new construction had sprung up in the years since the armistice. First, there was the red-brick cluster of Stuyvesant Town, which brought pastoral ease to the once-shabby precinct of the Gas House District. Then, the pattern had been given noble purpose by the great green-glass and marble slab of the UN Secretariat rising over the ruins of "Abattoir Alley." All told, $750 million in new improvements had gone up between 14th Street and 105th Street. Down in the Lower East Side and up into East Harlem, bulldozers rumbled and rivet guns hammered, erecting sheaves of new buildings to match Stuyvesant Town and the United Nations, and all of them, Salisbury's *Times* colleague Meyer Berger wrote, were "clean and bright by day, jeweled palaces by night."[1]

"The great experiment in public housing launched during the Roosevelt administration seemed to have paid off," wrote Salisbury, recalling his early impressions of this new cityscape. "I was amazed at the changes. Whole areas of the city had given way to fine new construction." He couldn't help but agree with the voyeurs taking in the new East Harlem from passing commuter trains. Like these "men from Wall Street," he too was impressed with the progress made in housing for the poor since the war. Of course, the more conservative among the businessmen were suspicious of Washington's coddling of the poor, suspecting that "it just encourages more of them to come up from Puerto Rico and the Deep South," but they had to "admit that people are better taken care of than in the old days." Even for these guardians of an older order, it was reassuring that their idle glances over the once-benighted slums revealed a new era of urban justice and plenty, one that would fulfill not only the New Deal's social welfare goals, but also more abstract visions dating back to the founding of the republic and forward into the new age of modernity and Cold War.

"At long last," Salisbury would later remember of this period, it seemed that "we were turning our imagination and energy to resolving our social ills and cleaning out the dark, festering corners to try to bring the city on a hill to life on this earth." Twenty years after the first public housing arrived on U.S. shores, New York's experiment in modern housing not only endured, it appeared to make New York's embrace of Roosevelt's New Deal ideals congruent with the highest national myths of providence and destiny. And, at the same time, this chance to perfect the national experiment also arrived at a propitious moment, one in which the city was presented with new international symbolic opportunities to display the evidence of its fulfillment of the national calling. If the UN headquarters had heralded the city's and the nation's rise to global influence, this new domestic cityscape was giving everyday New Yorkers a share in that status. And if the new public housing was a sign that the "city on a hill" had been reached, that would serve the nation well in its mounting Cold War with the Soviet Union. Or, as Salisbury put it: "I wished that I could take a delegation of Russians around and show them what a magnificent job we were doing in the field of public housing."

The new cityscape reassured Salisbury and the "men from Wall Street" that their market system, faced with a mounting challenge from Communism, could achieve freedom, justice, and material security. The new thickets of towers, Salisbury suggested, were evidence of the United States' prowess in the quest for social welfare, a fitting display of capitalism's superiority for any visiting "delegation of Russians." They were also evidence of the fact that the United States was taking strides toward founding a new kind of city in a new time. The Wall Streeters, Salisbury wrote, "admire the rectangular patterns" of the new projects, and say that "it makes you feel good…to live in a country where progress happens almost overnight." Here was the ethic of city rebuilding at work.

This commuter's panorama of East Harlem suggested that European modernist visions could only be realized by the United States and its absolute commitment to technology and "progress." The new projects were fragments of a potential new cityscape, one that could be transformed so absolutely that it would redraw one's sense of the fundamental dimensions of urban time and space. Modernity's progress, happening "almost overnight," seemed to be effacing an older marker of urban time—the slow creep of urban decay—and dissolving its spatial reach: the heretofore inevitable ooze of slums. The new towers now stood as witnesses that this could be accomplished in the near future, their very newness and precision both banner and evidence of a novel and fundamental urban form and the spatial shaping of the passage of urban time. They announced a new urban era, one inaugurated by the replacing of outmoded city spaces.[2]

These impressions are traces of a lost period in the history of public housing: its hopeful prospects just after the war and in the 1950s.[3] Public housing was charged with solving the whole host of social ills that reformers, social workers, and their allies in government believed plagued life in the slums. But for many in the New Deal and immediate postwar years, housing projects represented more than this. They were also vehicles of modernity and progress by which the poor of the United States' slums would be brought into the affluence and prosperity that appeared to be the natural right of the postwar era. The towers themselves appeared as icons of modernization, symbols of a development program for inner-city America analogous to that offered to Third World countries in those years. Machines for slum removal, their standardized construction made them cheap, while their forward-thinking architectural forms and planning ideals seemed guaranteed to sweep away the unhealthful tenement grids and replace them with open space, light, air, and a new neighborhood plan.

During the first decade after World War II, the people of the neighborhood over which the "men from Wall Street" glided in to Grand Central Station welcomed and even demanded new, modern, tower-block housing. Between 1941 and 1961, fully 10 percent of all the public housing built in New York was put down in East Harlem, a few square miles of tenements above 96th Street and east of Fifth Avenue.[4] With arguably the greatest concentration of public housing of any neighborhood in the city, East Harlem became a laboratory of sorts, closely watched by residents and outsiders alike for the effects that the benign intervention of public housing would have on the area.[5] For a few years, it appeared that the promise that Salisbury and the men from Wall Street discerned in the new spread of towers would be fulfilled. And yet, by the mid-1950s, East Harlemites began to endure rather than welcome the continuing and intensifying restructuring of their neighborhood by superblocks, open space, and modern high-rise housing.

Despite the constant demand for New York's public housing—the New York City Housing Authority (NYCHA) has had massive waiting lists for its affordable housing ever since it was founded in 1934—public housing's initial promise has, by most accounts, long since been squandered. In fact, its reputation has undergone a complete reversal. Since at least the 1960s, tower-block public housing has been accused of deepening the problems it was created to solve, and its mainstream public image has been mixed at best, ranging from an unfortunate but unavoidable stain on the cityscape to a racist, inhuman poorhouse. Nowhere is this contradiction more vividly displayed than in East Harlem, where the rise and fall of public housing during the age of urban renewal reveals public housing's complex fate as a both needed and reviled intervention in the cityscape of postwar New York. Looking at the particular ways that public housing remade the physical and social landscape of the neighborhood, and how those changes were received and ultimately reinvented by residents and those who spoke for them, will reveal how public housing in its high modernist mode was made and unmade as a vision of city rebuilding for the poor.

This chapter will tell the first part of that story, tracing how the housing developments with which NYCHA redrew the map of East Harlem in the late 1940s and '50s were formed by a complex collision of aesthetic and planning ideals, political struggles and compromises, economic possibilities and constraints. Cold War–influenced housing debates—in Congress and in the court of public opinion—propelled and limited NYCHA's work in this period. Should the government underwrite mass housing? Or only single-family homes? Struggles over the "social shape of shelter" made public housing a poor stepchild to urban renewal in the 1949 Housing Act and encouraged the high-rise, tower-in-the-park design profile so often associated with the very idea of public housing. Ultimately, this familiar, even notorious, planning solution was a response to contradictory conditions: it arose from the social and technological possibilities of modern housing idealism and the political constraints imposed by the need to rehouse evacuees from the mass tenement destruction of Cold War urban renewal. The transformed world of East Harlem was the archetypal—one might say stereotypical—cityscape of the urban renewal era for the poor.[6]

The story of postwar public housing has often been told as simply the betrayal of prewar modernism. High-minded social modernism, this story goes, was corrupted on American shores by cost-cutting and political expediencies. The 1937 Wagner Act, which split public housing from support for the private mortgage market, was the endgame in the history of social housing. Its low budgets and restrictive income policies for tenants betrayed the true spirit of modernism, dooming later efforts at public housing with rigid, formulaic designs and sparse amenities. Troubles with postwar public housing were not rooted in the modern ideals themselves, but in the problems of maintenance and management created by building big, routinized, debased versions of these ideals. There's no doubt that these accounts are generally persuasive; they do describe things that happened and developments that contributed to the shape and effect of postwar public housing. And yet, they do not tell the entire story.[7]

These accounts condemn the possibilities and struggles of the postwar years to a mere afterthought, leaving us with no understanding of what the officials of a local agency like NYCHA believed themselves to be doing after the war. The assumption of a debilitating and preordained fall from grace obscures the changes in NYCHA's postwar practices and character. If public housing seemed to some of its original boosters, like Catherine Bauer, to be hamstrung and stigmatized from the very beginning, others, like those in NYCHA, had faith in the aesthetic and social program of their version of modern housing. They believed that they could build affordable, sanitary, community-friendly developments. They thought they could deliver a built environment in which the "worthy poor" could extract themselves from poverty. In the postwar years, NYCHA embraced a more socially limited, business-inspired, and ends-oriented approach to modern housing production, which nevertheless retained a far-reaching commitment to slum clearance, neighborhood reclamation, community redesign, and benevolent intervention in the cityscape.

At the same time, these accounts cannot help us to understand the particular possibilities and constraints forced upon NYCHA by the need to negotiate among its modest social goals, the vast slum clearance aspirations of Robert Moses, the Cold War politics of housing and urban redevelopment, and the social difficulties and consequences of shaping housing for a working class transformed by migration from the black South and Puerto Rico in a city experiencing the first shocks of deindustrialization. Understanding public housing's postwar crises and difficulties, as well as its modest successes, requires that we recognize the collision of NYCHA's modern ideals with Cold War–influenced struggles over the social shape of shelter during the federal debates that led to the 1949 Housing Act. It was this subtle and conjoined history that created the symbiotic yet tragic relationship between public housing and postwar urban renewal.

Ultimately, the familiar judgments on postwar public housing can only partially account for the agency's considerable failures and modest successes in making this ethic benefit low-income New Yorkers. If public housing in New York, in its postwar, high modernist, superblock-and-tower phase must be considered a failure, it was not the disaster it was in other cities, which have spent the last generation finding ways to tear down their public housing stock. If this is in part because of the long tradition of high-rise living in New York, or

NYCHA's relative managerial competence compared with other cities' housing agencies, it is also because residents of public housing worked fairly successfully to adapt to life in the new projects. The usual narratives of immediate decline ignore an entire history of efforts on the part of public housing residents, social workers, and NYCHA officials to come to grips with and to transform the new cityscape that NYCHA was creating in neighborhoods like East Harlem.

Like Stuyvesant Town, the new world of East Harlem was an experiment in mass living, but for the working poor rather than the incipient middle class. The high-rise towers and abstract superblocks of high modernist urbanism appeared to many as the perfect design expression of the city-rebuilding ethic's social aims: a rational updating of social modernism that would rehouse low-income slum-dwellers and help to convert the outmoded nineteenth-century industrial city into the core of a modern metropolis. Ultimately, however, the 1949 Housing Act favored Stuyvesant Town's vision of privately subsidized urban redevelopment. The bill hobbled public housing by restricting its numbers, further narrowing design guidelines, and making it the catch basin for the thousands whom slum clearance for urban renewal would displace. In the wake of the massive problems caused by the deluge of displaced urban renewal site tenants, public housing's advocates were put on the defensive. They were hard-pressed to show how public housing represented a continuing, vibrant vision for a new, modern, and total living environment when it seemed to be reinforcing poverty, eroding neighborhood life, and reinstituting with federal support a more brutal form of the racial and class segregation already so well known in New York. Doubts and misgivings about the remaking of East Harlem would combine with the trauma over clearance and relocation in Lincoln Square, leading to a rethinking of the entire project of urban renewal.

Remaking East Harlem

Let us hope that one day we can help the people get more than the run-around. —Percival Goodman to Vito Marcantonio, February 1947

Between 1941 and 1965, NYCHA built 15 new housing projects in or on the immediate fringes of East Harlem. Even a cursory account of the projects themselves gives a sense of their massive impression on the neighborhood. East River Houses—the last of the New Deal era projects in the city—had begun the wave in 1941, with its 1,169 federally backed apartments for a population of close to 4,000. New federal funding did not become available until after the 1949 Housing Act, but the state and city put up 4 more projects in the area while they waited for federal monies to clear Congress. The state-funded James Weldon Johnson Houses arrived in 1948 with 1,310 units for almost 6,000 people, demapping six blocks of tenements and stores between Park and Third and 112th and 115th streets. Lexington Houses, built with city money, followed in 1951 with 448 units for about 1,500 people on two blocks between 98th and 99th, Park and Third. The state-funded Stephen Foster Houses were completed in 1954 on the periphery of the neighborhood, west of Fifth Avenue at 112th Street, with 1,379 apartments. Throughout these same years the state-sponsored Carver Houses were going up along the Park Avenue railroad tracks between 99th and 103rd streets and Madison Avenue. When they were finished in 1958, they provided another 1,246 units for 4,698 people.

Meanwhile, with the federal funds available after 1949, NYCHA produced three massive projects in quick succession: George Washington Houses, Senator Robert F. Wagner Houses, and Thomas Jefferson Houses. Each boasted more than 1,400 units and a combined population of about 20,500 people when they opened in 1957, 1958, and 1959, respectively. Wagner Houses, named for the sponsor of the 1937 Housing Act, featured 2,162 units and a population approaching 8,500 in the far northeastern corner of the neighborhood at Second Avenue and 120th Street. Jefferson ran along both sides of Second Avenue between 112th and 114th streets, while Washington Houses cut a great swath through the very middle of East Harlem, leaving only two out of six cross streets open from 97th to 104th streets between Second and Third avenues. When the city-funded Taft Houses, with its 1,470 apartments, was finished in 1962, it completed a great wall of public housing from Lenox Avenue on the east to First Avenue and Thomas Jefferson Park on the west. The Foster, Taft, Johnson, and Jefferson Houses left all north-south arteries open, but erased 113th and 114th streets from Lenox almost to the East River.

State funds backed two more projects in the early '60s. The Woodrow Wilson Houses, a northern addition to East River, specialized in larger apartments for bigger families. Its 398 units held just over 2,000 people by 1961. The Gaylord White Houses was a smaller infill project for about 375 senior citizens across 104th Street from the northern end of Washington Houses. Federal funds provided for two further efforts along Park Avenue—the James Madison Houses (later renamed Lehman Village) and the DeWitt Clinton Houses—and one on the neighborhood's southern border, the Gerard Swope (later Stanley Isaacs) Houses; their combined 2,000 units housed over 6,000 people by 1965. Finally, in 1965, construction was finished on Franklin Plaza between 103rd and 106th streets and First and Third avenues. Originally planned as a city-backed public project in the early '60s—Benjamin Franklin Houses—it was converted to private co-op status during construction and renamed; it had 1,635 apartments for almost 5,700 people. (See map on page 309.)

When the smoke cleared, 164 acres of the nineteenth-century speculative city grid had been obliterated, and hundreds of tenements, factories, warehouses,

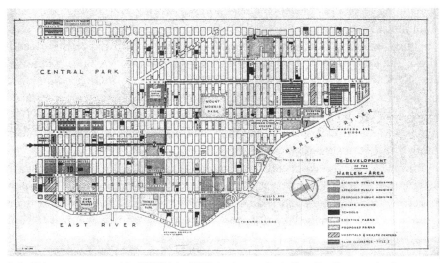

6.1. This map, prepared by NYCHA in 1952 to demonstrate its effectiveness in slum clearance and public housing construction for a group of visiting architects, shows the sudden surge of public housing in East Harlem. The neighborhood was well on its way to becoming one of the densest districts of public housing in the city. New York City Housing Authority Records, La Guardia and Wagner Archives.

stores, and other artifacts of the private, incremental urban fabric had disappeared. In their place stood a new superblocked landscape of 141 modern housing towers that sprang up amid parks, playgrounds, parking lots, and open spaces, a public residential cityscape built with a combination of federal, state, and city funds. All told, these 15 great chunks and ribbons of modern housing had apartments for 16,475 families and an estimated population of 62,400 people, which, by the '60s, was more than a quarter of the neighborhood's population.[8]

In 1961, New York mayor Robert Wagner heralded this $260 million undertaking as "one of the greatest advances made in neighborhood redevelopment in the United States." But where had this program come from? And why did it concentrate so heavily on East Harlem, imagining it could remake an entire neighborhood? In part, these ambitions had roots in the social modernism of the prewar years. But the new cityscape of East Harlem was not the simple fulfillment of a modernist social utopia. It took its shape from the push and pull between the possibilities and optimism surrounding postwar urban modernization through slum clearance—the ethic of city rebuilding—and the limitations and constraints placed on public housing in the era of Cold War and urban renewal.[9]

In New York in the period right after World War II, public housing was still seen by all but the most hostile real estate interests as a forward-looking way to clear slums, build decent housing for the poor and working classes, foster community, and create a new and modern total living environment for remaking cities. In a neighborhood like East Harlem, a whole range of groups, institutions, and powers from across the political and social spectrum favored knocking down tenements and putting up public housing. Motives and interests differed—some of these groups agreed on little else—but a significant array of tenant groups, politicians, housing reformers, social workers, planners, architects, federal housing officials, and real estate interests supported expanding the investment in public housing that began in 1941 with the East River Houses. Some of them also wanted to see private redevelopment, but the different approaches this rough chorus of city-rebuilding boosters took to the neighborhood and its housing conditions supported "neighborhood redevelopment" by way of public housing.

For some, the need for public housing was based on close, local dedication to the people of the neighborhood. For instance, when the modern architect Percival Goodman wrote to Vito Marcantonio, East Harlem's congressman, in 1947 with his salute to "the people" quoted above, he was not simply expressing his personal solidarity with Marcantonio's well-known leftist populism. They were engaged in a partnership to promote, design, and build new low-income housing for East Harlem. Just after the war, Marcantonio had Goodman help him to produce ideas and designs for a campaign of slum clearance and housing construction. The architect, who was just then writing the well-known utopian urban manifesto *Communitas* with his brother Paul, brought state-of-the-art modern housing ideals to Marcantonio's passion for serving his constituency. Goodman suggested that Marcantonio call for the immediate construction of 10,000 low-rent apartments on cleared land in his district. These were to be "decent, safe apartments" of fireproof construction with "modern plumbing and heating, cross-ventilation in each apartment, sunlight, and a room for each member of the family." Goodman provided Marcantonio with a map of likely sites "selected on the basis of a minimum destruction of useful buildings." He also offered illustrations of the new developments and how they would be built, stressing that the combination of "tall buildings and also some lower walk-up types" would go up in stages to reduce displacement, and many of the tenements would be replaced with parks and playgrounds.[10]

Vito Marcantonio was a brash American Labor Party leader and protégé of Fiorello La Guardia whose congressional district—the 20th—covered most of East Harlem. He had crafted a unique and particularly effective power base by careful and dedicated service to a neighborhood undergoing immense change. East Harlem was a polyglot combination of white ethnics and migrants from the South and Puerto Rico, 37 percent of whom were foreign-born in the late 1930s. The eastern reaches of the neighborhood, beyond Third Avenue and up to 125th

Street, held the heart of Italian Harlem, a community that had migrated from the crowded blocks of the Lower East Side and Little Italy over the previous three-quarters of a century. But by 1945, many Italians were looking for easier living outside Manhattan, many in the Bronx, some in the suburbs.[11] Meanwhile, by the late 1930s, about 30,000 African Americans had spilled over into the northwestern corner of the district from Harlem proper, joining a new group of immigrants that began to arrive in large numbers in the 1920s and 1930s. Puerto Ricans, many uprooted by unemployment stemming from mainland corporatization of the island's rural and artisanal economy, began to migrate to New York during the early twentieth century. They settled in numerous neighborhoods in Manhattan and Brooklyn, but by the 1930s the largest *colonia*, known as Spanish Harlem, or El Barrio, had solidified along Third and Madison avenues between the Italian and black communities. By 1945, there were more than 20,000 Puerto Ricans in El Barrio, and by 1950 the number had reached 63,000, while the number of Italians had decreased significantly, to about 50,000.[12]

By the late '40s, Marcantonio had served this mix of peoples for more than a decade. His political organization, although always under fire from anti-Communists and other conservatives in both the Republican and Democratic parties, was the most powerful political entity in East Harlem. But Marc, as his constituents called him, was not a cynical political boss. He brought an older system of ward boss patronage into the age of the New Deal welfare state by funneling government services and benefits to the working class and poor of East Harlem. One part savvy politician, one part idealist, he keyed his political activities to the demands of his constituents and his own left-wing radicalism. As a former tenant organizer, his major response to the militant tenant activism of the Depression and war years was to make new public housing one of his top priorities. Time and time again, Marcantonio joined other East Harlem and Harlem politicians in demanding better housing for slum-dwellers. He had joined La Guardia in urging NYCHA to build the East River Houses, and he consistently supported more public housing on the House floor, excoriating those who would dispense "housing with an eyedropper."[13]

Marcantonio continued to back public housing even as Cold War pressures closed in on him in the conservative Congress of the immediate postwar era. One of his campaign films, the 1948 short *People's Congressman*, linked public housing to securing a diverse, democratic city for all workers. The film shows him standing in front of a sign for NYCHA's newly built James Weldon Johnson Houses as the voice-over stumps for better housing, schools, swimming pools, and playgrounds to offset the hazards of the streets and to protect the neighborhood from juvenile delinquency. Marcantonio, the narrator assures viewers, believes that the fruits of social democracy—and the film makes it clear that

6.2. Vito Marcantonio, East Harlem's congressman, speaks at a rally for the East Harlem Houses, 1941. Marcantonio, a former tenant organizer, consistently pushed for more public housing for East Harlem and argued that urban renewal legislation without sufficient provision for public housing was counterproductive. Historical Society of Pennsylvania, Leonard Covello Collection.

among those must be counted the James Weldon Johnson Houses themselves—"should be commonplace in our rich country." He is "a fighting Progressive candidate" who won't bow down to "all the corrupt errand-boys of Wall Street" in his drive to bring workers "the living wage of the American Dream."[14]

Throughout the '40s, a diverse array of interests, many of whom did not share Marcantonio's radicalism, Popular Front sympathies, or mistrust of unfettered private enterprise, ratified his leadership on the housing issue. They echoed the basic sentiments of his campaign, making slum clearance and public housing in East Harlem a widely demanded and popular postwar expectation. For instance, representatives of the Women's City Club and the Union Settlement House—East Harlem's oldest community institution—called for a democratic planning effort to assist NYCHA's efforts in the area. The New Harlem Tenants League congratulated NYCHA on its efforts and demanded more houses. Leonard S. Gans, a local realtor, identified 15 blocks along the East River above 96th Street that were "available and begging for redevelopment." He urged the City Planning Commission, the housing authority, and private capital to take notice. The Liberal Party announced in a political ad, "We Can Get Rid of the Slums of New York in Our Time!" It demanded that the city "stop treating public housing as a stunt, an experiment or a demonstration" and work with the state and federal governments to provide a $45 million subsidy for low-income housing. The leftist-liberal tabloid *PM* called for public housing "on the grand scale" with "no race test for occupancy" to "get rid of our crumbling ghettoes." And in 1948, the more conservative *World-Telegram* hailed the Johnson Houses, "rising like a shining mountain from lower Harlem," but worried that funds were drying up and supply would never meet the increasing demand.[15]

In general, across the country in the immediate postwar years of upheaval and housing shortages, new housing was a celebrated cause. Public and private projects were portrayed and understood as linked, complementary efforts to clear slums, house the homeless, and usher in postwar prosperity. Forty-eight percent of respondents to a 1946 Roper poll—and 58 percent of veterans—said that the government should "start building houses on a large scale for sale or rent to the public." Public housing, the poll showed, had more support among the public than it did in Congress.[16]

This was particularly true in New York, where low-income housing appeared as both a social good and an economic boon. The *Times* reported that the East River Houses represented "a vast new potential market" that was attracting real estate investment to the neighborhood before the project was even finished. NYCHA's projects and incipient urban renewal projects were seen as linked undertakings. For instance, the James Weldon Johnson Houses and Stuyvesant Town were both featured, along with several other private and public projects, in the ad for the department store Ludwig Baumann's Housing Center, where project residents could get design tips and do furniture planning (see figure 3.4). NYCHA studied the tastes of project residents to show their fitness for the home decoration market and set up programs in their community centers to encourage residents' full participation in the domestic wing of the renewed postwar consumption economy. New tenants of East Harlem's Carver Houses described their apartments as "like a palace," and delighted in their new ranges and refrigerators. In the immediate postwar years and into the early '50s, public housing's new forms still evoked the spirit and intent of the European moderns, while simultaneously appearing as part of the American mass market for housing. To a broad swath of the public, the projects appeared as a goad to economic growth and prosperity, a benevolent intervention in the cityscape. Many, it seemed, would have sympathized with reporter Alan Keller's flight of fancy in the *World-Telegram*: "To the slum dweller a public housing development is a dream world he aspires to as he does to life after death."[17]

Of course, the desires of the prototypical "slum-dweller" were not the only and probably not even the chief motivation behind the massive influx of public housing in East Harlem. As much as a broad spectrum of the public could sympathize with the need for a public housing program, a more pressing and decisive factor was the long-standing public demand for slum clearance in neighborhoods like East Harlem. Conditions in the neighborhood were certainly less than ideal. Even in the 1930s, when migration to the outer boroughs had reduced the pressure on Manhattan's housing stock, East Harlem was significantly overcrowded. A 1937 mayoral committee reported that more than 10 percent of the population of Manhattan lived in the neighborhood, despite the fact that it included only 6.6 percent of the island's total area. The neighborhood had about 201,000 people living on 947 acres, for an average population density of 212 persons per square acre. This was more than 50 percent in excess of the prevailing average for the entire borough. Even more distressing was the fact that 60 percent of the blocks in East Harlem housed more than 90 percent of the population. The more crowded blocks had over 300 persons per square acre, and one block boasted 2,460 residents. Even worse, the vast majority of this congestion was in dilapidated or illegal tenements, 90 percent of which dated from the turn of the century. Despite all the congestion, there was a high vacancy rate, about 21.5 percent. East Harlemites lived in family groups or other communal situations not because there was no housing available (although some unknown percentage of the vacant apartments were illegal tenements that had been boarded up by the city), but because they could afford little else. The vast majority of East Harlem families fell into the "lower or lower medium rent" category, paying a total of less than $30 a month for their apartments.[18]

East Harlem had seen little new private investment in its housing stock during the 1920s and '30s. This situation was perpetuated by the federal government's guidelines for residential desirability and investment. Investigators from the Home Owners Loan Corporation (HOLC) gave the entire district above 96th Street a red or "hazardous" rating on their preliminary 1933 survey. They followed that up with a more definitive rating of "fourth grade" or "D" on the residential security maps of 1937, thereby guaranteeing that the private real estate market would see the area as an unwise investment. The HOLC found that East Harlem was a "slum district" with "mostly low grade tenements." One section— the northwest—was a "Negro slum district." The "major part" of its rentals was in the "low bracket," and in most of the neighborhood, "extensive demolition of existing housing" was "desirable." With the district so decisively redlined, it is no surprise that area social workers would claim, 15–20 years later, that there had been no mortgage money available for the improvement of property since at least 1941.[19]

New York housing and planning officials agreed with the federal government's final assessment of East Harlem. The neighborhood fit all the criteria for "extensive demolition." According to the series of maps produced in 1933 by the Slum Clearance Committee—forerunner to NYCHA and not to be confused with Robert Moses's later Committee on Slum Clearance—it was a "deteriorated area" suitable for clearance. It appeared as a "black area" on these maps, with high density and vacancies, low rental rates, and high concentrations of black and immigrant populations, deaths by car accidents, fatal fires, infant mortality, tuberculosis, juvenile delinquency, felonies, diphtheria, and venereal disease. When NYCHA emerged in 1934, it took over these results and issued a new round of reports covering similar phenomenon. One, entitled "The Slum and Crime," demonstrated that juvenile delinquency and adult petty crime, misdemeanors, and felonies were all linked to one another and to the persistence of slum conditions, particularly in East Harlem. The entire Harlem area was considered so maladjusted by this point that NYCHA issued an entire report dedicated to both central and East Harlem. With all this federal and municipal evidence at hand, city officials felt sure that what was required was not piecemeal rehabilitation of "deteriorated areas," but wide-scale demolition and slum clearance of the "black areas" on their maps. The 1937 mayoral committee felt that much of East Harlem "is to be looked upon as particularly eligible for demolition and such future development as can be managed by and for a relatively low income population." It concluded that "it is unrealistic to think of any considerable part of the area as destined for higher rentals. The great central portion will stand or fall as the home of modest income families. The question is what can be done to provide accommodations suitable for them."[20]

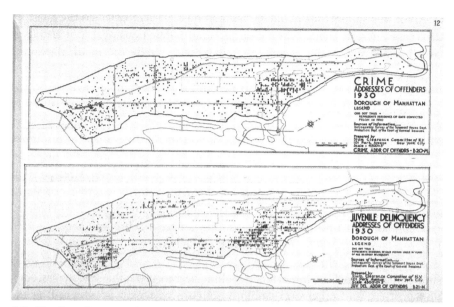

6.3. The Slum Clearance Committee of New York, a 1930s precursor to the New York City Housing Authority headed by housing reformers, compiled and published a series of maps like this one, which plotted the residences of criminals and juvenile delinquents in Manhattan. The visual density of social disorder and physical deterioration in particular neighborhoods like Harlem and East Harlem confirmed the reformers' belief that these "slums and dilapidated areas" were fit for clearance and new modern housing. These judgments merged with more progressive interest in providing low-cost housing for working people to underwrite the ethic of city rebuilding.

In 1940, East Harlem appeared as area M-3 in the City Planning Commission's "Master Plan…Sections Containing Areas for Clearance, Replanning and Low Rent Housing." As we have seen, this master plan was never formally adopted, but still provided a malleable guide for the coming generation of redevelopment and public housing efforts. The term "replanning" in its title was vague enough to allow for privately sponsored redevelopment projects; in essence, the plan simply showed where the city thought it should rebuild and did not prescribe how, thus effectively sealing the neighborhood's fate as a target of redevelopment at whatever level the market would bear. Although some speculative plans to redevelop East Harlem with private capital appeared during the war, no sponsors emerged, and it appeared that the judgment rendered by the mayor's committee would hold. When Robert Moses gained control of public housing, he followed the informal master plan's prescriptions for the neighborhood, finally consigning redevelopment of East Harlem entirely to the public sector.[21]

All of this support for public housing in East Harlem reflected the fact that divergent interests backed slum clearance and public housing, but it also concealed some conflicts that such agreement masked. On the one hand, Marcantonio and Goodman agreed with city officials and federal and municipal planners; East Harlem was in desperate need of slum clearance and new low-income housing. But Marcantonio and Goodman saw clearance as primarily a way to provide the people of East Harlem with modern, sanitary housing. They worried about the appropriate replacement of housing stock, wanted to minimize destruction, and designed their redevelopment scheme to reduce the displacement of residents. City planners and officials, particularly Moses, stressed slum clearance as much as public housing. For them, the priority was to excise slums and restore property values; improving housing opportunities for East Harlem's residents was not a primary goal, but simply a necessity brought about by East Harlem's lack of appeal to the private real estate market.

NYCHA tried to bridge the gap between these two demands. Its initial 1930s studies had stressed the importance of slum clearance, but the rent strikes, eviction protests, and other anti-landlord activism of tenant groups during the Depression and war years pushed the authority to make building new housing for slum-dwellers its primary goal. After the war, NYCHA capitalized on the widespread optimism about public housing and the fear that slums might jeopardize postwar prosperity to launch an extensive campaign of clearance and rehousing in neighborhoods like East Harlem.

Of course, there were also those for whom East Harlem was not a problem to be solved but a threat to be contained. In the choice words of a 1946 *Time* magazine article, East Harlem was "a verminous, crime-ridden slum" whose Communist-sympathizing congressman represented "hordes of Italians, Puerto Ricans, Jews, and Negroes." Such sentiments swam close to the surface of national debates over slum clearance and public housing. With the onset of the Cold War, slums appeared as a particular kind of domestic liability—a dissolvent of national resolve, an international embarrassment, and a breeding ground for impressionable discontent. President Harry Truman, campaigning for reelection in 1948, gave voice to the liberal version of *Time*'s scare tactics, warning a crowd of the dangers of slums to America's image: "How can we expect to sell democracy to Europe until we prove that within the democratic system we can provide decent homes for our people?" Likewise, 10 years later, the liberal leader Adlai Stevenson worried that the fact that the United States had "still fallen far short of even arresting the spread of blight and decay in our cities" would hamper the ability to meet "the communist economic offensive." Public housing's supporters hoped that it would cure the ills of the slums and allay these fears. But public housing's foreign profile, its social democratic roots, and its nominally collectivist ideals stoked suspicions of its potentially subversive qualities.[22]

The emerging Cold War cast a long shadow over public housing. We cannot account for the shape and extent of the superblock towers that transformed the landscape of East Harlem without understanding how public housing was itself transformed by Cold War–influenced struggles over the 1949 Housing Act. In fact, the 1949 act, best remembered for its Title I urban redevelopment provisions, was at its core a referendum on the role of public housing in American life. Real estate interests made resistance to an expanded federal commitment to public housing their primary opposition to the act. They saw the fight as a struggle over the social shape of shelter, a showdown between the private, individualist, single-family home and mortgage, on one side, and the public, New York born and bred, "socialist" vision of mass modern housing reform, on the other. They were not ultimately able to scuttle the Housing Act, but they did succeed in restricting and hampering federal public housing provisions.

The Cold War Shape of Shelter

I do not say this is a socialistic program. The Socialists themselves say this is a socialistic program.
—Jesse Wolcott, congressman from Mississippi, June 1948

In the years immediately following the war, NYCHA acted quickly to help ease the local ramifications of the chronic nationwide housing shortage. In 1947, the authority estimated that 300,000 apartments were needed in the city to end the shortage and restore the housing market to a sane vacancy rate of 5 percent. But this did not spell the end of New York's housing need. An additional 600,000 apartments would be required, NYCHA planners believed, to wipe out old law tenements and "other unsafe and unsanitary dwellings." There was no danger of overbuilding as long as the new housing was made affordable. By late 1947, the authority had 16 new projects completed, under way, or on the drawing boards. Four years later, that number had risen to 18, providing homes for about 24,000 families. In addition, NYCHA built 20 middle-income projects, most in the outer boroughs on less expensive land, through a city-financed "no cash subsidy" program. All but one of these projects were built with state or city funds, and they served mostly veterans and the middle-income tenants who could find no housing during the shortage. Significant as their impact on the city was, these projects did not reach low-income slum-dwellers. The authority could not begin to make a dent in the slums nor do its part in easing the housing shortage without federal aid.[23]

New federal monies for public housing were long in coming. The unequal two-tier approach to housing established during the Depression continued in the immediate postwar years. Loans, tax credits, mortgage insurance, and veterans' benefits for the private, suburban, single-family home market expanded, while public housing was put on hold. In the postwar Congress, any extension of New Deal programs was controversial, and public housing proved to be the most explosive. New funds were first introduced in 1945 as part of an omnibus housing bill, the Taft-Ellender-Wagner Act. This bill meandered through conferences, committees, hearings, and a storm of political controversy surrounding its public housing provisions. When it was eventually passed and signed by President Truman in 1949, as the U.S. Housing Act, the bill did supply federal subsidies for public housing. Of course, the bill's primary goal, contained in Title I, was to provide federal money to local redevelopment agencies to help them acquire, clear, and sell land to developers at reduced costs. Most of this subsidy would go to private developers, but Congress did underwrite the land accumulation and clearance activities of local housing authorities like NYCHA under Title I, while also extending the 1937 Housing Act by authorizing up to 810,000 new public housing units nationwide under Title III.

This new structure, which separated the process of clearing slums from that of building housing, appeared to be a new opportunity for supporters of public housing to undo the limitations of the 1937 act. Freeing public housing authorities from the financial burden of clearing high-priced slum sites, the act could in theory provide more low-income housing in a variety of locations, not just the former slum sites served by the 1937 act. Public housing could now be sited according to the provisions of a comprehensive city plan and in a harmonious relationship with new, private, middle-income projects, rather than in reaction to the immediate, piecemeal demands of slum clearance.[24]

However, public housing only narrowly survived the legislative flak thrown up around the 1949 act; the damage done to its image and philosophical integrity would do much to limit its effectiveness, leaving its supporters powerless to fully control how it would be paired with its more powerful partner, publicly subsidized private redevelopment. Real estate and banking interests lobbied hard against the bill, concentrating their fire on public housing. They put little effort into opposing subsidies for slum clearance and redevelopment, because those measures opened urban areas for private investment. Public housing, however, was unfair competition that endangered the building industry. In truth, of course, public housing operated in a low-income market that private builders had never pretended to serve. It didn't pay. But builders, mortgage lenders, and real estate interests worried that, if public housing were successful as a low-income enterprise, it might catch on and endanger their ability to profit from the buying and selling of land. These same groups had worked to narrow the provisions of the 1937 act; in the late '40s and into the '50s, through two administrations and two housing acts, these lobbies redoubled their federal and local efforts, hoping to kill public housing altogether.

During the late '40s, as the Taft-Ellender-Wagner Bill made its way through Congress, deepening tension between the United States and the Soviet Union began to figure not only as a question of foreign relations and international diplomacy, but as a domestic, internal problem as well. This was nowhere more apparent than in the debate over federal housing legislation, a contest that brought into sharp relief the role of public housing in the culture of abundance promised to Americans after the defeat of fascism.

Postwar recovery depended on the real estate market. A new, affordable, modern, fully equipped home was the purchase upon which so many others depended, stoking demand for a host of other big-ticket items, from cars and refrigerators to furniture and televisions. From 1945 to the early 1950s, housing concerns consistently ranked high in opinion polls and commanded a disproportionate share of headline inches. In fact, the single-family house emerged as a symbol of the new postwar world. Potently blending the pursuit of property values with the pull of domestic virtue, the single-family house captured perfectly the marriage of public striving and private repose, manly enterprise and feminine caretaking to which the consumption economy catered. So when the housing shortage persisted into the late '40s, many feared that it was delaying or preventing the promised consumer boom. Housing, *Fortune* magazine's editors remarked, was "the industry capitalism forgot." Failure to produce homes for Americans, they opined, "will do more to undermine free institutions than ten thousand Union Square orators." Housing, in other words, seemed to be the beam on which prosperity and abundance precariously balanced; with the Cold War, these appeared as not merely economic concerns but matters of national security.[25]

Material abundance became an all-encompassing symbol in these years, an ideal around which the new global contest between capitalism and Communism turned. The very idea of ever-increasing prosperity became a bulwark of national identity, a shared pursuit expected to gather diverse peoples into a secular faith, a communal belief in which, ironically, the raw materials of belonging were individualism, self-reliance, and the freedom of consumer choice. With the Cold War, material abundance became a medium in which the war by other means was joined. First, it was the armament with which the gathered American people could confront the growing threat of Communism, an ideology that appeared to offer collectivity in place of nationalism as a form of solidarity. And it was simultaneously an endangered right, which Americans were called, as a people, to defend against Communist aggression abroad and subversion at home. The commercial building market could not help but find itself at the center of this concatenation of hopes and fears; prosperity, it appeared, depended on a hidebound, conservative industry organized for piecework revamping itself to allow for mass-produced Levittowns.[26] But public housing remained something of a question mark. Was it a further prop for prosperity and abundance, a guarantor of a better life for working-class and poor Americans? Or was it a socialist plot, an internal threat to the American way of life?

For President Truman and the drafters of the Housing Act, public housing was both a way to jump-start economic growth and a social welfare measure. Truman made housing a central Fair Deal program, railing against conservative legislators of both parties who dragged their heels during the housing shortage. He also refused to shy away from public housing's roots in the labor and reform wings of urban liberalism, championing it as an extension of Progressive Era and New Deal traditions. In housing policy, at least, Truman honored Roosevelt's ideals. He saw housing as a comprehensive and vital resource for modern living—"the heart of a community" in the president's words—and public housing as a cure for the ills of poverty and urban disorder, the solution for what Roosevelt had famously called the "one third of a nation" living in slums. "A decent standard of housing for all is one of the irreducible obligations of modern civilization," Truman told Congress in September 1945. "The people of the United States, so far ahead in wealth and production capacity, deserve to be the best housed in the world. We must begin to meet that challenge at once." But resistance to Truman's Fair Deal was fierce and bipartisan, and that resistance would eventually force Truman to back away from his early eager support and his allies to modify their hopes for reinvigorated public housing.[27]

Public housing's opponents formed predictable lines of battle. Southern Democrats joined conservative Republicans from the West and Midwest in attacking public housing. Rural legislators called it unfair and reported that their constituents were loath to contribute tax dollars to programs intended only for big cities. Conservatives bemoaned government meddling in the private market. But the legislative back and forth was not just another routine big government versus states' rights squabble; it quickly went beyond pork-barrel politics. Real estate interests and their congressional allies made the debate into a referendum on the fate of the New Deal's urban social provisions and the social shape of shelter, a struggle over what form of living arrangements the U.S. political economy should endorse and underwrite in the dawning Cold War. They set out to defend the private housing market from New York–style public housing and to protect the social ideal of single-family homeownership from the incursion of mass-produced modern housing with its communal amenities and collectivist spirit.

Ultimately, when legislators joined real estate and building interests in attacking state-run housing as a residue of the New Deal, an invitation to socialism, and a grave threat to the American nation, they were setting the terms by which cities could be remade, splitting urban renewal and modern housing ideals into related, but distinct and ultimately unequal, fiefdoms. The struggle revealed the role of Cold War conflicts in shaping the unequal fabric of the postwar city and the arrangement by which the private housing market, public/private urban renewal, and public housing would be separately deployed to make modern residential metropolises out of old nineteenth-century industrial cities.[28]

To the Housing Act's opponents, public housing was "creeping socialism," and its dangers came from both inside and outside the nation. "Congress has before it a proposal to corrupt permanently our free political system with all the evils in subsidized housing inherited from the New Deal," charged Congressman Ralph Gwinn of New York in 1948. To Gwinn and other lawmakers, it was, of course, only "our free political system" that separated the United States from the old nations of Europe with their entrenched ideological and class divides. The New Deal and its heirs threatened to lead the United States away from global leadership and capitalist prosperity and toward socialism. "It is significant," remarked the National Association of Real Estate Boards (NAREB) in its newsletter, *Headlines*, "that in every country where economic planning and dictatorship have arisen in the last two decades, public housing on a large scale has been one of their first concerns." Public housing was, as Herbert Nelson of NAREB had it, "European socialism in its most insidious form." It was the link between New Deal planning ideals and European socialism, both of which posed a danger to free enterprise and, by extension, the prosperity and global leadership that the "American way" promised to usher in. If the housing industry failed to do its part, or if lawmakers were not vigilant, it should be no surprise what would happen. "The very basis of socialism is that the Government shall take over when private enterprise has failed to meet a demand or a production program," said Mississippi congressman Jesse Wolcott. Ultimately, opponents charged, the bill would make the United States no different from European countries, where social welfare ideals underwrote national life. As Thomas S. Holden of the F. W. Dodge Corporation put it, public housing was "cunningly devised as an instrument for transposing the American free society into a blurred carbon copy of the socialist and semi-socialist states of Europe."[29]

For some lawmakers and budding Cold Warriors, however, European socialism was only the first step on a slippery slope. Public housing, NAREB president Morton Fitch announced in 1947, is "the cutting edge of the Communist front." Later that year, Senator Joseph McCarthy made a visit to the Rego Park Veterans Project in Queens, one of several temporary housing developments that NYCHA had built for returning servicemen and their families. Incensed by the difficult conditions in the slapdash temporary project, he called public housing "breeding grounds for communism" and launched hearings designed to smear public housing and to push the private housing industry into action. Still some years away from his prime red-baiting efforts, McCarthy nevertheless made public housing the opening gambit in his attempt to end New Deal social provisions, foreshadowing his campaign against the Communist-inspired or -affiliated Left. In McCarthy's committee, as well as in other legislative hearings on the 1949 act, public housing was pilloried as a threat to American institutions and the wedge by which Communism might prop open the door to economic and political influence.[30]

For the first few years of its career as a bill, the Housing Act faced hostile Republican majorities in one or both houses of Congress. By 1949, however, Democrats had recaptured the legislature. Some opponents of the bill, seeing that it was likely to pass, stepped up their rhetoric. The 1949 act, they claimed, was a watershed moment, one in which Americans themselves threatened to undermine their own way of life. "All the fellow travelers are for the bill," real estate lobbyists warned, "as the most subtle means of breaking down American self-reliance and American self-rule." Communism was "the enemy," they said, and they feared that the housing bill's success meant that "gradually it seems to be winning some of our leaders from within." Frederick C. Smith, an Ohio congressman, joined them, calling the bill "a sweeping advance on the part of the power planners toward their goal of complete regimentation, Russian style."[31]

Rodney Lockwood, president of the National Association of Home Builders, summed up the opposition's position. Public housing, they felt, was a danger to "free American institutions and a free economy based on individual initiative and responsibility." It threatened not merely to centralize government, but to erode "our traditional social and political concepts which are founded upon the family unit sheltered in its own dwelling." For Lockwood and his allies, public housing was "socialistic" precisely because it would, they charged, undermine "independent home ownership." They were defending a particular conception of the social shape of shelter, one that was, in Lockwood's words, "peculiarly the province of the private citizen." The Housing Act, Lockwood said, "proposes to substitute something we have never had in this country for our traditional method of basing our democratic form of government upon the economic basis of the family unit owning its own home, owning a piece of America, if you please, and living in its dwelling on that piece of land." Public housing, he suggested, was an entirely foreign way to organize living arrangements, a collectivist stain on "independent" American soil and its proper role as the essential commodity of individualism and liberty.[32]

By this measure, public housing presented a grave threat to basic American freedoms. Robert Gerholz, head of the National Association of Real Estate

Boards' Washington lobby, claimed that the bill would "destroy what we think probably is the last frontier in the world where free men still have a chance to work out their own destiny." Congressman Smith painted the Housing Act in the starkest light possible, calling it "a bill to further enslave the people of the United States." Smith and Gerholz were picking up on the rhetoric that would drive American Cold War strategy, a vision laid out in a National Security Council paper, number 68, a year later. The NSC 68 report saw a sharp division between a "free society"—the United States—and a "slave state," the Soviet Union. Delivered as a top-secret prod to policymakers, its Manichean message was intended to encourage a campaign of massive, worldwide military resistance to inevitable Soviet aggression. However, its binary rhetoric of slave and free societies legitimated an already prevalent and widely accepted view of the emerging tensions between the superpowers as a struggle between darkness and light. Any statist ideals, whether of the social democratic or Communist variety, could be portrayed as evil burrowing from within. Cast in that light, public housing could not fail to appear as a dark threat to American ideals.[33]

Despite their venom, the anti–public housing forces were not able to eliminate state-subsidized housing from the 1949 Housing Act. Encouraged by Truman's bully pulpit, the Fair Deal coalition of Democrats (less quite a few southerners) and urban liberal Republicans narrowly carried the day for urban renewal and public housing. Of course, the implementation of public housing required local initiative, and it was carried out with little federal oversight beyond funding and guidelines for design and building. Over the next few years, real estate and building interests launched a centrally organized campaign to discredit public housing, encourage local resistance, and dissuade cities and towns from setting up housing agencies. Supplying their member organizations with ideas and materials for media campaigns, they deployed the same arguments in trying to win local referendums and sway city councils as they had in lobbying Congress.

Truman's "political public housing" program, NAREB claimed in 1952, was "contrary to the spirit of American institutions" and "takes a long step towards communism." To this, it added the looming threat of spreading subsidization, a kind of domino theory of public housing. New York was particularly instructive in this regard. "The outstanding experience shown by New York City public housing," warned the National Association of Home Builders, "is that once a full fledged public housing program is adopted, public housing grows, and *grows*, and GROWS. One project leads to another. Every thousand units of public housing completed opens demand for another thousand."[34]

This industry campaign against proliferating socialized housing dovetailed profitably with an already fierce local resistance drawn along lines of race.

In a number of places, the specter of New York–style public housing inspired neighborhood associations and citizen groups to protect white neighborhoods against public housing. They protested its building and, on many occasions, resorted to violence and intimidation to try to prevent blacks from moving into newly built projects. These attacks on public housing were part of a larger attempt by whites in cities and suburbs across the country to prevent blacks from moving out of ghettos into neighboring white areas. Cold War politics and this widespread racial conflict over urban space combined to make public housing appear doubly threatening. Advocated by liberals, leftists, and the federal government, public housing seemed to some to be nothing short of a conspiracy to overthrow property rights and democracy and to enforce race mixing. Not only did it threaten to "enslave" Americans politically and economically, and to confer upon whites the unfree status historically forced upon blacks, but it also promised to profoundly underscore this sense of unfreedom by making whites live on the same streets and in the same buildings as blacks. Nationwide, resistance to public housing and black mobility emerged as the most profound and lasting legacy of Cold War housing politics. It erected public housing and urban renewal as bulwarks of segregation and reinforced the divisive power of race—which had been on the wane as a marker of biological difference in these years—by perpetuating and strengthening its spatial and economic power.[35]

In New York, however, things were a bit more complex. The city's postwar social democracy—with its powerful leftist unions, expansive rent control laws, labor-backed cooperative builders, municipal housing subsidy programs, and series of laws banning discrimination in housing—provided little fertile ground for these protests. New York suffered from no shortage of de facto segregation, but organized campaigns against housing projects in the immediate postwar years were less coordinated or sustained than they were elsewhere or than they would become in later years.[36] Although isolated, such sentiment was by no means quiescent. Many people worried that public housing was attracting Communists as residents and that "reds" had fatally infiltrated the housing authority itself. As one letter writer, calling himself "An American Born," complained to the head of NYCHA in 1951:

> Stalin and the Russians are said to believe that it is not necessary to go to war to defeat the US. They believe they can defeat us by ruining our economy, and are fast accomplishing this. Never has a communist uttered a word against public housing, and the Commies are well satisfied with the way that we have almost socialized housing, and must be more than satisfied with the part you have taken in it.

Calling for the chair's immediate resignation, the writer accused him of "bringing us closer to socialism every day by allowing the crowd that stuck to Alger

Hiss to use you....Every time I look at one of your projects they remind me of 'tombstones of democracy.'" As the letter writer's pen name indicated, there were those who considered public housing to be a foreign influence full of peoples who were outside American tradition by way of birth, color, or political inclination. From the perspective of this Cold War–style nativism, public housing was outside the accepted and legitimate bounds of American life. A handy tool for a foreign enemy, it sprang from the minds of irresponsible and elitist experimenters or gullible dupes, operatives akin to those who "stuck to" the Brahmin subversive Alger Hiss. Ultimately, it was the source of a potential economic and social catastrophe that would result in socialism and race mixing. A challenge to the entire culture, public housing's visual appearance, its blocky, rigid forms, gave away its true role as a "tombstone" marking the grave of democracy.[37]

If nothing else, right-wing attacks served to expose public housing's roots in modern housing ideals. In a sense, public housing's most extreme opponents agreed with its most idealistic proponents on one fundamental proposition. Modern housing ideals *were* a challenge to the established parameters of capitalist American political culture. They *did* mark a pervasive intervention in the entire form of American cities and the fundamental social shape of shelter. Or, as Mississippi Democrat Jesse Wolcott put it, there was no need to question whether public housing was a threat: "The Socialists themselves say this is a socialistic program." And yet, these attacks forced supporters to be increasingly careful with their claims. Wolcott and his allies used rhetoric with powerful public appeal and scare tactics that proved persuasive. Their constant red-baiting threatened to paint public housing as outside the national consensus and to send it into permanent exile. Supporters could not allow it to be written out of American tradition and politics altogether. Too much was at stake. Getting public housing passed and then built on any meaningful scale would require downplaying the more visionary aspects of modern housing ideals.

Throughout the late 1940s and early '50s, supporters felt constantly embattled. Even in New York, where public housing enjoyed widespread support and NYCHA actively pursued a comprehensive, community-focused clearance and building program, housing officials never felt that their programs were safe from legislative attack. This was in no small part due to the almost negligible rhetorical difference—measured only in tone—between local extremist attacks like those leveled by "An American Born" and resistance on the floor of Congress. The frequency and viciousness of the attacks made public housing's prospects perpetually unstable. Even after the 1949 act was passed, public housing did not enjoy guaranteed appropriations. Localities had to apply for federal monies, and funding was always in jeopardy; ultimately, the number of units permitted each year was determined by political deals at both the state and federal levels.

These fears pushed advocates back onto safer rhetorical ground. Retreating from public housing's roots in European social democracy, supporters adapted to the new Cold War conditions and planted their ambitions squarely in the American grain. Abandoning the communal vision that gave their opponents such potent ammunition, they tried to cast their programs in a reassuring, capital-friendly, nationalist light. As they worked both to pass the 1949 act and then to insulate its public housing provisions from Cold War legislative fallout in the early '50s, they took the safest course, emphasizing first public housing's contributions to democracy and prosperity, and then its role as not liability but weapon in the struggle between free and unfree.

The raw material for these defenses had been available for some years, particularly in the rhetoric of New York's militant tenant leagues. "Housing projects," declared the City-Wide Tenants Council in 1940, "represent the promise of a better life, of the American way." Removing people from the "social apathy" of the slums, they provided "for their residents the means for expressing themselves in community activities—meeting rooms, club facilities, newspapers, etc." Far from being the tombstones of democracy prophesied by "An American Born," projects were "laboratories of democracy" that "should lead the way in translating democracy from theory into actual everyday practice." In other words, public housing was not where democracy went to die, but where it went to be tested and perfected. These expressions of Popular Front affirmation—public housing as true Americanism, not as training grounds for collectivism—survived the diminishing life expectancy of left-wing politics because liberal advocates adopted them during the Cold War housing struggles. However, supporters also adapted this rhetoric, transforming it for a new era. They first claimed that public housing's democratic promise underpinned an expansive vision of postwar prosperity and abundance. But as conflicts over public housing grew, they largely abandoned even that market-minded utopian promise and cast public housing as a practical program of temporary housing for the poor and a defensive bid for Cold War security.[38]

Near the end of World War II, Philip J. Klutznick, a commissioner of the federal Public Housing Administration, suggested that public housing was a central front in the quest to secure the "peacetime economy of abundance" that all Americans expected. "Good housing is not a luxury," he said, and a nation that allows housing to be seen only as a "scarce commodity" accepts slums. The United States "cannot continue to permit the ebbing of its strength through the broken windows and shattered walls, through the airless and lightless coops of its slums." That would betray the ideals of the war the country was fighting "to save humanity." "Not with this jagged chink in our shining armor," he concluded, "can we realize the destiny of a people who must lead the world to peace and security, happiness and contentment." Slum clearance and public housing, then, carried an immense burden of expectation as the postwar era dawned, enjoying a place in the exceptionalist assumptions with which American policymakers looked to usher in American dominance over the globe. Public housing retained the utopian façade imagined for it by modernists, but in the Cold War era that vision was now more and more subordinated to its emerging role as a by-product of urban renewal, the other part that Klutznick prescribed for it in the growth politics of the times: a nationalist prop for the emerging American century.[39]

Public housing remained a challenge to business as usual in the real estate market, yet supporters more often now sought to align it with the emerging era of prosperity and American power. New Deal housing economist and Truman aide Leon Keyserling called public housing "one of our great American social and economic reforms" that "stimulated a complete reorientation of the private builder's ideas about suitable housing accommodations." Its design, including standards of light and air, community facilities, and infusion of hope, "not only transforms the slums; it transforms popular attitudes about the kind of housing that the American nation needs, deserves, and can afford." Public housing had raised the bar and made new visions of urban transformation possible. Now, in 1946, when Keyserling wrote, the Housing Act and its public provisions looked to extend that promise to all, giving the United States' global sway a more democratic footing. The bill, he said, was "founded upon the abundance which is part of the birthright of every American family" and "at the core of the struggle to realize in our time the full promise of a peaceful America." But with great expectations came great dangers. The housing bill was necessary for full employment, and if the United States failed to act upon it, the contrast with other "more rigorous, though less free, systems" would be "held up for all to see." That "would imperil our influence in world affairs at the very time when it may be needed most."[40]

As competition with the "more rigorous, though less free, systems" increased, however, and public housing came under attack as a form of internal subversion, advocates shifted to meet the charge. They agreed with their antagonists that the Cold War was a struggle between light and dark, good and evil. And they agreed that public housing would be a central battleground in the domestic front of the Cold War. But they hoped to show that public housing's attackers were the real danger to democracy and the American way. Public housing could demonstrate the United States' drive for internal social cohesion—if only the Right would stop attacking it and encouraging the spread of slums. The "unholy alliance" between real estate and insurance groups, said Herbert Stichman, the New York State housing commissioner, was "working hand in glove with the fifth column elements and Communists" to further private interests over the public good and the national cause. It was unchecked capitalism that was subversive, Stichman implied, not public housing. Such craven behavior from lobbyists and legislators was demoralizing, one letter writer to the *New York Times* suggested in mid-1948. Congress's failure to enact the housing bill "has done much to encourage Communism," wrote the curiously monikered Phelps Phelps. Jesse Wolcott's attempts to eliminate "low cost and public housing," Phelps continued, have "done more to turn disgusted GI's to communism than any single act of Joe Stalin."[41]

Passing the housing bill, congressional supporters argued, would actually prevent Communism. Public housing, said Representative Scott Lucas of Illinois, is "a challenge to the menace of communism which breeds easily in some of the slum-blighted areas throughout the country." Preventing Communism from raising its ugly head in the festering slums was as important as fighting it abroad. "We are spending billions across the water to curtail the spread of communism," said Congressman Ray Madden of Indiana, and "this legislation will be of untold value in curtailing the communistic agitators in the industrial centers throughout America."[42]

Lingering New Deal commitment in a newly Democratic Congress joined with near-total agreement on the need for urban redevelopment to push the 1949 Housing Act over the top, but in the years afterward the Cold War rhetorical context would reveal the weakness of public housing's position. Faced with mounting opposition, Truman's early enthusiasm for public housing faded, and while he continued to officially support it, he also took pains to assure the real estate and housing industries that he would not endanger their business. Meanwhile, the act's supporters, forced to emphasize public housing's adherence to national ideals and slum clearance's usefulness as a deterrent to Communism, found themselves boxed into a defensive mode and hard-pressed to stop the attacks, much less push an active public housing vision. As opponents rolled out their aggressive, top-down, local and national anti–public housing campaigns, supporters struggled to defend the ground they had won in 1949. Searching for language to counter the "wild charges" of the opposition, the nonprofit National Housing Conference announced in 1950 that public housing was a "truly American objective." It was not socialism, but "responsible democracy," an investment in "a basic minimum of shelter for low-income families" that "strengthens the morale and confidence of the people in the American democratic processes and in the private enterprise system." Slums, supporters said, were a "blot on America" that tarnished the United States' image abroad; they were a source of "national welfare sabotage" and "creeping crime, corruption and social rebellion" where Communism might take root. These "cancers" could be excised with "clean, decent housing" that would give American citizens "a fair chance to bring up their families in godly cleanliness, healthful happiness and patriotic loyalty."[43]

Public housing, supporters began to argue, was vital to what Gerald J. Carey, executive director of NYCHA, called "the basic fabric of our society." In a speech before the National Association of Housing Officials critiquing legislative cuts in housing funds, he observed that the Cold War "struggle is one not alone of force, but of ideologies." Public housing might not be "the one weapon, or even the most important weapon, with which we will defeat Communism in general, or the Soviet Union in particular," but "the strength that comes from unity of purpose and equality of sacrifice is needlessly sapped" when public housing is endangered. "We have been told that we must gather our strength for the long pull," he continued. "Why then do we casually decimate a program that not only helps provide the decent shelter so necessary to our long-term strength and well being, but that also demonstrates our ability to democratically solve a difficult social problem?" Public housing, Carey argued in another speech to a New York civic group, "does help to cut the ground from under the communist arguments," and that is "a source of satisfaction" to reformers. But the main reason for public housing was "the essential dignity of all people" and "the right of every American family to live in a decent home."[44]

Unfortunately, by the early '50s, few Americans believed that public housing was crucial to the basic fabric of American society. Some may have supported it in principle, or as a means to alleviate the postwar housing shortage, but after years of attacks by the real estate industry, support for public housing began to evaporate. The idea that, as John Sparkman, Democratic senator from Alabama, put it, "any home-community investigation would show public housing to be true Americanism" was confounded by already existing, widespread notions of how American "homes" and "communities" should be built and what they should look like. Suburban homeownership—underwritten by cultural ideals, public policy, government subsidies, and the powerful real estate lobby—made urban public housing seem foreign, cramped, uncomfortable, and disconcertingly collectivist. State-run housing, already suspicious, could easily be seen as downright seditious in an era of rejuvenated capitalism, reestablished American power, and Communist threat at home and abroad. Red-baiting made good press in the McCarthy years, and charges of statist subversion stuck in the public mind more vividly than defensive Americanism or appeals to equality for the poor.[45]

Advocates could always fall back on the pragmatic idiom of the 1949 act—Carey's "right of every American family to a decent home"—or abstract appeals to "the dignity of all people," but they could muster no positive and expansive vision of public housing's contribution. No doubt, the rhetoric of Americanism and democracy helped to pass the 1949 act, but afterward supporters were put on the defensive, hoping to guard and preserve the appropriations they had narrowly won. Title III's 810,000 units of public housing was actually a reduction from an initial figure of 1,050,000, and even the smaller amount came within five votes of elimination.

Over the next 5 years, continued attacks on public housing at the local and federal levels took their toll. At the outbreak of hostilities on the Korean peninsula, less than a year after the 1949 act had passed, the Truman administration reduced the annual maximum number of units to 50,000 from 135,000; by 1954, President Eisenhower had reduced that number to 35,000 a year. In the 11 years after the 1949 act, only 322,000 new units were started nationwide. Of course, public housing was not discontinued altogether, and amounts did pick up somewhat later in the '60s. But public housing never truly recovered. It was, as Catherine Bauer put it in her late '50s lament over the "Dreary Deadlock of Public Housing," always in "a kind of limbo, continuously controversial, not dead but never more than half alive."[46]

Public housing never escaped the legacy of the Cold War struggles that finally sealed the second-tier status conceived for it by the 1937 Housing Act. The polarized rhetoric that propelled the Cold War debate—was public housing prosperity or ruin, democracy's incubator or its death knell, weapon or danger in the struggle with the Soviet Union?—was resolved at the national level by the early 1950s. Charges of Communist subversion had dovetailed with market-minded ideals of individualism and private property to exile public housing from the culture of postwar prosperity. The real estate industry's aggressive public relations campaign across the country had the desired effect. The Cold War struggles over federal and local housing policy confirmed, renewed, and perpetuated a postwar cultural and political compact: house-minded Americans would not accept public housing as part of an ideal of democratic abundance for the American century. As a result, in most of the country its possibilities were restricted and its social vision curtailed; more and more, it became the province of individual failure that its detractors claimed it was, the place where those who couldn't make it on their own were forced to live rather than a stepping-stone to prosperity or a new infrastructure for communal life.

With its power reduced, public housing's promised independence was damaged too. Public housing did have its own program, run by the Public Housing Administration, but it never enjoyed the power necessary to use its supposed freedom. Public/private redevelopment was given the true freedom, measured chiefly in the flexibility given it to incorporate or reject low-income housing. Redevelopment projects were enjoined to be "predominantly residential," but there was no mention or oversight of what kind of housing should be built. As a result, public housing was given not freedom, but unequal, junior partner status in the urban renewal compact. Most important, the 1949 act required that adequate housing had to be supplied for all families displaced by Title I projects and that those displaced from redevelopment be given first preference in public housing. This seemingly benign, even necessary provision virtually guaranteed that relocatees from urban renewal clearance sites would overwhelm low-income projects. With their numbers and status reduced by Cold War struggles, public housing programs were hard-pressed to handle the tide of displaced people and to establish their own independence. Ultimately, the 1949 Housing Act and its 1954 successor made public housing useful merely as a way to salve the wounds of slum clearance and redevelopment. Here was the ethic of city rebuilding completely transformed into the practice of urban renewal. These were the business-friendly ideals at the heart of Cold War urbanism and the final and lasting legacy of the accord between European modern housing visions and American slum clearance policies.

Cold War Modern in East Harlem

We have decided now to clean out the whole overcrowded and malodorous East Side. We are building here not only for the poor but for people of many income groups. This is not socialism. We see here progressive government working with progressive private capital.
—Robert Moses, Baruch Houses dedication, 1953

And finally, the sheer volume and extent of public housing, past, present, and anticipated is so great that it is becoming a vital feature in the physiognomy of the City. What we do, I mean you architects and we bureaucrats, in the way of design, is of grave concern not only to the citizens who live or hope to live in housing projects, but to all the citizens who cannot escape them as they go about their daily lives, and are in one way or another affected by the pattern of their city. —Samuel Ratensky, NYCHA chief of planning, 1949

New York's housing officials struggled mightily to resist the mounting evidence of public housing's demise. They were aided by the fact that public housing's fortunes were, in part, a local matter. New York's liberal political culture and labor-backed social democracy provided a largely hospitable and optimistic milieu for public housing. For 20 years after the war, NYCHA's planners and officers attempted to advance what they believed to be a progressive housing policy, one that paired slum clearance and tower construction at the core of the city's old industrial districts with building on vacant land at the edges of the outer boroughs. They built modern apartments in larger numbers than did any other city and often included space for childcare, nursery programs, health stations, and other community facilities run by outside agencies. They continually tried to modify their design parameters to produce neighborhood- and people-friendly projects, updating what they called their "blueprint for living" as they discovered what worked and what did not. They constantly worried that their funding would evaporate, but tried hard to improve their program in the face of high land costs, slowly dwindling funds, and strict federal regulations. If the insecurity and penury brought on by these hardships fixed public housing, as historian Leonard Freedman has put it, in a "sterile and inflexible mold," they tried hard to resist that fate. They insisted, as Samuel Ratensky put it in his 1949 speech to New York architects, that the authority try to keep its "concepts flexible" and to "respect [the] individuality of solution[s]" within "a general framework of standards." Ultimately, they aimed to fulfill the letter and spirit of the 1949 Housing Act—"decent and sanitary dwellings suitable for American family life"—by trying to find ways to build what Ratensky called "humane communities where people want to live, with domestic character and scale, and some gratification, however simple, for the human spirit." It was an uphill battle. National politics and new federal restrictions found echoes in local developments; together, they would have a marked effect on public housing in New York, transforming NYCHA's design and planning efforts.[47]

NYCHA faced significant changes and challenges. In the decade after the war, the authority slowly lost its original focus on housing reform and social work. This loss, however, did not spell an absolute retreat from the idealism of modern housing. Instead, NYCHA was embracing a new, practical, business-oriented modernism that paired a reduced version of the ideals and goals of the older authority with a new focus on achieving pragmatic accomplishments on a massive, citywide scale. "The purposes of public housing," NYCHA's annual report for 1952 suggested, "are better carried out by providing good housing for many rather than ideal housing for a few." This new emphasis on quantity adhered to the post-1949, redevelopment-friendly atmosphere of national policy. But it also had sources in changing local political conditions, particularly the growing influence of Robert Moses over housing policy. These local and national pressures had significant impact on NYCHA's building program, paving the way for an ideologically limited but ambitious campaign of utilitarian, standardized, mass housing production. Idealism was not entirely bred out; the new conditions made for a refined set of design parameters that seemed to promise even greater accomplishments in slum clearance and project building. With this in mind, NYCHA chair Philip Cruise could close his 20th anniversary annual report to Mayor Robert Wagner and the public with the "confident" assertion that "New York will one day be a city without slums."[48]

The authority's utilitarian, standardized approach to slum clearance and modern mass housing production was influenced, in part, by a new relationship with Robert Moses. Although the authority never admitted it, and it was rarely if ever recognized in the press at the time, Moses gained significant control over NYCHA's overall operations in the years immediately after the war. From the mid-1940s until 1958, when the authority was reorganized in the wake of a number of scandals, Moses shaped the NYCHA board through mayoral appointees he suggested or approved. The extent of his control is difficult to measure, but throughout this period—the core years in which urban renewal visions remade the city—Moses had significant influence over when and where NYCHA built. He did not control how it built, but his influence with Mayors William O'Dwyer and Vincent Impellitteri steadily weaned NYCHA away from its roots in housing reform and social work. He made sure that the original housing reformers on the board were replaced by men he could trust to support his urban renewal plans. By the late '40s, he had handpicked a majority of the NYCHA board. Thomas Farrell and Philip Cruise, NYCHA's chairmen between 1947 and 1958, were confirmed Moses men. Even if board members did not always see eye to eye with Moses, they were often won over by his ability to get apartments built, or they sympathized with his preference for conservative business practices rather than supposedly airy reform ideals.[49]

NYCHA's gradual abandonment of its roots in housing reform masked an emerging rapport between Moses's business-minded slum clearance and redevelopment aims and the straitened, but still forward-looking, goals of modern housing idealism. This rapport made itself felt in the way Moses and NYCHA reconstructed significant swaths of the city with extensive, pragmatically selected belts of modern, tower-block public housing. NYCHA's postwar projects were a practical refinement of modern housing ideals, an adaptation of the European visionary tradition to the era of Cold War urban redevelopment. With less funding and more political hostility than any social housing vision imagined, NYCHA still forged an expansive, if aesthetically limited, program. Even as the authority's social ideals calcified, and it turned more and more toward the immediate goal of building apartments, its spatial ambitions multiplied. NYCHA planners embraced slum clearance and neighborhood reclamation, hoping that the new federal and municipal goal of redevelopment would inevitably mean more public housing and an increased role for their benevolent intervention in the cityscape.

Moses summed up the refined urban renewal ethic quite succinctly at the dedication ceremonies for NYCHA's Baruch Houses on the Lower East Side in the late summer of 1953. Speaking to an audience that included President Eisenhower, he defended public housing against the administration's cuts but celebrated redevelopment for its ability to restore the city "for a variety of suitable purposes." Reviewing the combined public and private efforts begun a decade earlier at Stuyvesant Town, he celebrated his mixed approach to redevelopment economics: building "not only for the poor but for people of many income groups" ensured that it was "not socialism," but "progressive government working with progressive private capital." In general, Moses drew up plans to guide the authority's site selection procedures, while NYCHA's designers, planners, and subcontracted architects drafted plans for the projects themselves. What resulted was a pragmatic, hardheaded housing program that sought to knock down slums and put up decent, no-frills housing for the poor, and to do that on as large a scale as possible within the constraints enforced by Cold War politics and the public/private vision of urban renewal.[50]

As construction coordinator and head of the mayor's Committee on Slum Clearance, Moses administered New York's Title I programs and controlled much of the decision making over the siting of public housing. In keeping with the drift of national practice, he made public housing subservient to urban renewal. For him, this meant that the two enterprises should be interdependent. Business-minded redevelopment could not depend on a low-income housing practice that was overly inhibited by the social implications of its work. In general, Moses was a pragmatist and an opportunist. He wanted to clear slums and replace them with combinations of modern public housing and middle-class neighborhoods, but he did not believe that the city should rely on rebuilding by public housing alone and never in a spot that might attract a sponsor for a private Title I project. He insisted on sound, conservative business practices like those he had arranged in attracting Met Life to build Stuyvesant Town. He looked for results in the form of finished projects rather than what he considered idealistic social engineering, and he particularly distrusted city planners. The Housing Act did require that all redevelopment happen in accordance with a city master plan that designated areas for clearance, but the only plan Moses used was the malleable guide to redevelopment areas first introduced in 1940. He had it updated to include the Gas House District for Stuyvesant Town, and then again in 1949 to make way for his redevelopment goals. But his main guide was circumstance and opportunity. Where could he interest a private redevelopment sponsor? Where could he find land prices low enough and housing stock degraded enough to warrant public housing? Would the promise of nearby public housing ensure a redevelopment project's acceptance by city and federal authorities, or would local resistance to public housing doom his plans?[51]

Moses's expedient site decisions had uneven effects on the city. In some neighborhoods, he put public projects and Title I renewal sites near each other, making for mixed-income neighborhoods where only slums had stood before. But many other neighborhoods, particularly those he figured would be hardpressed to attract private investment, he slated for rebuilding by NYCHA alone.

Ratifying a generation of city-planning precedents by municipal and federal agencies, Moses believed that East Harlem, like the South Bronx, the bulk of the Lower East Side, central and eastern Brooklyn, and most of the rest of Harlem, could not attract private redevelopment and was therefore fit only for public rebuilding. Beginning in the mid-1940s, Moses repeatedly rejected the idea—floated by East Harlem community leaders—that the neighborhood could support middle-income housing, and he designated East Harlem a low-income zone. Moses's decisions had fateful implications for these neighborhoods; throughout the '50s, he used their expanding swaths of public housing to house populations displaced by renewal and other infrastructure projects, which ultimately reinforced, with federal and state imprimatur, the racial and economic ghettos that had previously formed by way of the private real estate market.[52]

But what did NYCHA do with these concentrated areas Moses had turned over to public housing? The agency was not simply following Moses's lead; its own particular planning responses to the conditions, restrictions, and possibilities of the post-1949 era determined the fate of East Harlem as well. During the late 1940s and early '50s, NYCHA was building on an unprecedented scale. It completed nearly three times as many projects between 1946 and 1952 as it had in its entire previous history and, as a result, transformed from a small reformer-led social housing operation into an unwieldy bureaucratic city agency with its own police force and nascent social programs. Of course, budget restrictions kept the authority from building as widely and quickly as it would have liked—one 1949 NYCHA projection had 80,000 new apartments and a half million New Yorkers in public housing by 1957—but by the end of 1965, it had completed 146,653 apartments in 152 projects; 129,900 of them had been built since the war, and almost 50,000 of these went up in Manhattan. The income of public housing residents averaged about $3,500 per year in 1962. Rents, which ranged from about $12 to $14 per room per month in federal projects to $16 per room per month in state-funded developments to upward of $20 per room in city-funded projects, including utilities, were pegged to residents' incomes and family sizes. By the 1960s, about 13,434 households paid their rent with a welfare check.[53]

As the authority's residential population grew and refugee flows from redevelopment multiplied, its planning and design efforts transformed as well. The 1949 Housing Act instituted new design guidelines, which made the previous minimum standards for apartment size and amenities into the new maximum standards. The act required that projects cost no more than $2,500 per room. The authority, following architectural and design fashions, had already begun to experiment with a more strictly continental-inspired, international style design profile, but the new regulations pushed it even further toward cheaper, simpler, and taller plans. NYCHA planners had to find a way to house more people with less money, while still preserving the original social goals of benevolent intervention: light, air, and open space. Chicago, St. Louis, and other cities had already adopted new, more austere styles, trying to find ways to outperform New York. In response, NYCHA began to phase out what its 1951 Annual Report called "red-brick elevator buildings, of six and fourteen stories," arrayed in "variations of the cross-shaped building," retooling the pre- and immediate postwar period NYCHA modernism with the "strip-shaped" building laid out in in-line, slab forms. The older cruciform plans had provided a measure of economy by clustering apartments, elevators, and other services around a central core. But the new slab forms featured one long hallway with "double loaded" corridors of rooms on either side. This shape, authority architects argued, could be even cheaper than the cruciform style if the authority made the hallways long enough to get more apartments on each floor.[54]

NYCHA planners found that building higher and reducing building footprints multiplied savings. Walk-ups went by the boards entirely (except in a few outer borough locations). Combinations of 6-, 11-, and 14-story buildings remained, but most towers began at 10 or 11 floors, and many went to 15 or 18. By the late '50s, there were numerous 20-story towers and even a few that went to 30. Ground coverage in the old cross style was low, almost always coming in under 25 percent of the site area, but the slabs pushed that figure even lower, often down to between 12 and 18 percent, leaving the vast majority of the site for, as NYCHA put it, "landscaping, lawns, playgrounds, walks, benches, and off-street parking." Gains in these traditional amenities were expected to offset the inevitably high population density. Double-loaded corridors made cross-ventilation in all but corner apartments impossible, but with east-west orientations and the benefit of no shadow-casting wings, all apartments could be situated to catch breezes and either afternoon or morning sun. NYCHA maintained that the strip buildings, sometimes combined in Y and X shapes, allowed for larger public lobbies on the ground floor and more apartments with living room privacy, "so that it is not necessary to walk past or through the living room from the front door to the kitchen and bedrooms." *Architectural Forum* called this new style "a major revolution in the housing field." In the new era of urban redevelopment refugees, federal budget cuts, business-minded operations, and modernist austerity, these designs appeared to be state of the art. NYCHA, the American Institute of Architects said in 1949, was "instrumental in introducing a new concept of city-living."[55]

These changes were nowhere more apparent than in East Harlem, where the full elaboration of these developments could be tracked in the newly rebuilt cityscape. The earliest projects, East River and James Weldon Johnson Houses, with their 6-, 11-, and 14-story, red-brick cruciform buildings and 21 and 19 percent site coverage, looked almost quaint by the mid-1950s. Carver Houses retained

6.4. The James Weldon Johnson Houses in East Harlem during the 1950s. When they went up in the late 1940s, the Johnson Houses were a prime example of NYCHA's traditional red-brick modernism and laid out in the cruciform shape the authority had been using since the 1930s. Only a few years later, these designs would be phased out for more advanced variations on the slab form, which offered less ground coverage and greater cost savings. New York City Housing Authority Records, La Guardia and Wagner Archives.

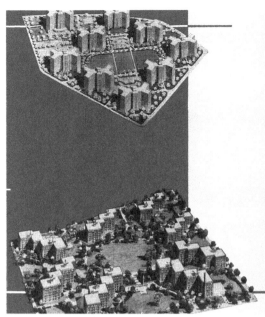

DESIGN

The Site

There are a number of objectives in planning the layout of a site. Perhaps foremost is that of making the project a physical part of the community, not an island set apart by itself. Buildings are placed, if at all feasible, so that the project seems to open into the surrounding neighborhood. The person on the outside can look into the broad landscaped areas within; and he is not shut out by a wall of buildings. On the average only fifteen to twenty percent of a site is covered by buildings, the open areas being left for landscaping, play, and rest. Buildings are located so far as practicable to provide each apartment with sunlight sometime during the day. Advantage is taken of the natural features of the site: its terrain, its views, even old trees worth saving.

6.5. "Design: The Site," NYCHA, Annual Report, 1950. This excerpt shows NYCHA's newer improvisations on the slab form with less ground coverage and more open space than previous cruciform designs. Ironically, the text here describes the authority's efforts to make the projects be more a part of the surrounding communities, a goal at odds with the more abstract designs. New York City Housing Authority Records, La Guardia and Wagner Archives.

the cross style, but reduced coverage to 15 percent in its 6- and 15-story buildings. Federally backed George Washington and Jefferson Houses were the first in East Harlem to adopt the slab style. Washington had 12- and 14-story buildings with 14 percent coverage; Jefferson, while employing a variation on the in-line slab, remained more old-fashioned, combining 7-, 13-, and 14-story towers on 20 percent of its site. Wagner Houses had its 2,162 apartments in 7- and 16-story in-line slab and slab-X formations; the buildings covered just 12.9 percent of their sites. At Taft Houses, the slabs went to 19 stories with 17 percent coverage. DeWitt Clinton Houses had 9- and 18-story buildings, and the Woodrow Wilson Houses and the James Madison Houses both topped off at 20 stories in 1961, covering 17 percent of their sites.[56]

NYCHA planners stressed the low coverage of their projects because they knew that they could do little to lower the high population densities when they built on pricey in-town land. The average population density of residential New York in the late 1930s was 190 people to the acre. East Harlem's was, of course,

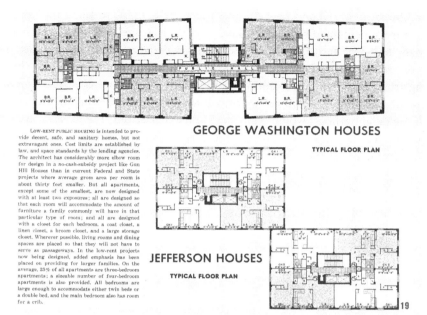

GEORGE WASHINGTON HOUSES

TYPICAL FLOOR PLAN

JEFFERSON HOUSES

TYPICAL FLOOR PLAN

6.6. Floor Plans of George Washington Houses and Jefferson Houses, NYCHA, Annual Report, 1950. Two versions of the new slab style in East Harlem, showing the layouts of the apartments. They are, the authority tells the reader, "decent, safe, and sanitary homes, but not extravagant ones." New York City Housing Authority Records, La Guardia and Wagner Archives.

somewhat higher, coming in at about 212 persons per acre. NYCHA's earliest projects exceeded this figure, but not by much: the first seven projects had an average density of 235 persons an acre. As the authority built taller, the number of people sharing the land increased apace. East River was built on 21 acres and had a population density of 338 people to each acre. Johnson and Carver were built on 12- and 13-acre superblocks; they had population densities of 428 and 406 persons per acre, respectively. Some of the federal slab-block projects brought these figures down somewhat—Washington Houses had 311 persons per square acre on a 12-acre site, and Jefferson had 325 persons per acre on a 19-acre site—but they could never bring densities below the levels of the tenement districts they replaced. Lexington Houses reached 449 persons per acre on its small 3.5-acre site; as NYCHA built higher and higher, it accepted greater and greater densities.[57]

By the mid-1950s, clearance had begun for many of these second-generation projects, and by the early '60s all of them were at least partially occupied. This blooming spread of towers and superblocks made East Harlem a peculiar combination of old and new. All over the ancient, familiar, ailing nineteenth-century tenement district, a new vanguard cityscape sprouted, seeming to many to be the fully developed and finally realized product of a decades-old promise. Several generations of housing reform and slum removal were bearing fruit. This great intervention in the fabric of postwar East Harlem was creating not simply a new urban form, but a new mode in which the social life of the neighborhood would be formed and experienced. The new towers and superblocks appeared to some as progressive forces of order and modernization come to put the city's wrongs right. "Before, I lived in the jungle," said Miguel Ruiz, a garment worker relocated from a demolished brownstone to a Harlem project. "Now I live in New York." And yet, the new towers could seem less a step up on the evolutionary scale from the "jungle" of the tenements to the modern world of "New York" than a cruel inversion of that promise of pro-

6.7. By the early 1960s, East Harlem had undergone two decades of intense slum clearance and public housing construction. The urban fabric of the neighborhood had been completely transformed. This panorama, looking east from 106th Street and Park Avenue in 1962, shows Franklin Plaza on the left, Woodrow Wilson Houses straight ahead, East River Houses in the right background, and George Washington Houses on the right. In the right foreground, clearance for one section of the DeWitt Clinton Houses is under way. New York World-Telegram Photograph Collection, Library of Congress.

gressive order. With their great densities, vast heights, and stark features, the towers could seem less like homes than warehouses, systems for storing people rather than organic landscapes created by people themselves. This ambiguous new order stood at the heart of public housing and urban renewal's Cold War profile.[58]

The Cold War Culture of Public Housing

The new housing villages are scattered and largely unconnected, with as yet no general pattern. They are high, boxlike, and institutional, but they are also sanitary, clean, open to air and sunshine, covering usually less than a fourth of the land.... Perhaps New York can go on to finish the job and provide decent housing for the masses. —Robert Moses, 1952, quoted in *Public Works*, 1970

We had possessed the dream, we had prepared our foundations, but the gap between ideal and reality was growing. Benign attempts to cure one social ill sowed the seeds of another. The architects of the bright future could not—even with computers—predict what new disease might be born in the cure of the old. —Harrison Salisbury, *A Time of Change*, 1988

The housing project tower blocks that transformed East Harlem loomed even larger in the public imagination than their imposing height or their superblocked acreage. Tensions over the meaning of public housing's supposedly benevolent intervention had lasting effects on the fate of urban liberalism's embrace of modernist city building and social engineering. Housing was the era's chief consumer item, and public housing towers were, in an important sense, just as much a kind of "mass culture" of the 1950s as the tract houses of Levittown or television, tailfins, and the photography in *Life* magazine. As a product of the Cold War era, public housing necessarily became an iconic representation in the war of images between East and West, like a version of the famous Nixon-Khrushchev kitchen debate with its domestic implications writ large in the urban landscape rather than in the suburban appliance-scape. Just as Cold War politics had influenced how public housing was built, Cold War cultural tensions helped to determine how public housing's benevolent intervention in the cityscape was received and understood. Public housing's reputation and prospects reflected the bifurcated, polarized logic of that struggle. If it appeared to some a munificent support for American equality and security, it seemed to others, in its foreign inspiration and aspirations to mass impact, reminiscent of the very subversive powers some claimed it would preempt.

On the one hand, the towers' simple, precise geometry spoke for a frank and assuredly progressive vision of how capitalist democracy, flush with unprecedented economic growth, would solve the problem of housing the masses. The product of a rapprochement between European modern housing theory and U.S. tenement reform brought up to date for an era of widespread urban modernization, the new towers appeared to satisfy all the requirements of economy and progressive idealism. Monuments to universalism and modernization's clean sweep over the past, housing towers were icons of liberal internationalism. They were symbols of the orderly, technocratic rationalism that would bring prosperity and modernity to underdeveloped areas of both the First and Third worlds, while showing the Second World that capitalism could solve urban problems better than centralized planning could.

The towers' sleek lines and profiles—so distinct from the jumbled, haphazard urban fabric they replaced—made an obvious visual contrast between the future city and the outmoded past. Their very forms seemed to reveal their power as the most efficient and ruthless means of destroying tenements yet devised. Slums, the new towers seemed to say, were of another era, foreordained to be swept away by the new forms of city building. Or, as one *New York Times* reporter put it in a 1954 story about the particularly impoverished stretch of East 101st between the Washington and East River Houses, slums were an "Atom Age anachronism" of "decayed rookeries" destined to give way to modern housing. Architects, planners, housing reformers, crusaders against slums, construction companies, labor leaders, social workers, liberal politicians, city officials—all could embrace the simple, repeatable forms as a universal tool for slum eradication anywhere in the city. Ultimately, they provided more housing and more light and air for less money; they were the manifestation in concrete, steel, and glass of New York's urban renewal compact: business-savvy social vision put to work to redeem the city.[59]

This was the conventional wisdom up until the mid-1950s. Almost everyone, save some public housing residents and some of those whose neighborhoods had been invaded by projects—people, in other words, who had little access to the press or other public mouthpieces—thought the slums were melting away. But then, some reporters, social workers, planners, and architects began to look a little closer at the new housing developments. Architects were among the first to quail; the traditionalists among them had never liked public housing, but by the mid- to late 1950s quite a few modernists began to see the new towers as monolithic and regimented, largely as a result of inflexible federal design guidelines. And then, reporters and social workers began to investigate conditions in the projects.

Harrison Salisbury, for instance, didn't linger on that East Harlem train trestle from which he and the "men from Wall Street" had admired the bold new "rectangular patterns" of the tower-block arrays. In 1958, he came down from those removed heights to examine the new developments for a series of *Times* pieces on youth gangs. He was surprised by what he found. NYCHA projects were anything but "sanitary" and "clean." There were broken windows, cracked plaster, muddy playgrounds, graffiti, vandalism, crime, dark urine-stained hallways and elevators. But more alarming than the physical deterioration of the housing itself was what the reality did to his former optimism. By the time he sat down to write, he had been shaken out of his earlier naïveté. Now, he saw that public housing had "institutionalized our slums." He had seen, he would later remember, "how man transformed a utopia into a caricature, a bizarre Orwellian nightmare." The "benign attempts" to end slums had "sowed the seeds" of even worse deprivation. "The architects of the bright future could not," he wrote, "predict what new disease might be born in the cure of the old." The "new disease" had brought an element of regimentation to the old squalor that was, for Salisbury, immediately reminiscent of Soviet housing schemes. He had seen "shoddy housing in Moscow," but he "never imagined" that he "could find the equivalent of Moscow's newly built slums in the United States." "Nowhere this side of Moscow," he wrote in the *Times*, "are you likely to find public housing so closely duplicating the squalor it was designed to supplant." In its form and intent—and its failures—it was too close to the Soviet social welfare housing models. "Orwellian" public housing, with its "gigantic masses of brick, of concrete, of asphalt" and its "planned absence of art, beauty or taste" was a new mass landscape that threatened individualism, community, and American national promise.[60]

While Harrison Salisbury had considerable sympathy for the "shook" kids of the projects he met while doing his reporting, this sort of judgment on the mass character of public housing could easily become a judgment on the character of public housing's residents as well. The unspoken assumption behind this view was that public housing was like the theaters, arcades, parks, and other arenas that symbolized and shaped earlier moments in urban development. It was a space in which people congregated, and reproduced themselves, and through which they understood themselves as a collectivity selected by social and municipal forces over which they had little immediate control. In this sense, public housing represented an opportunity for organization and directed social action. But, simultaneously and more pervasively, it represented a way of seeing people *as* masses, as lump sums of humanity as undifferentiated and standardized as the architecture of the buildings in which they lived. This notion attached to suburban tract housing developments as well—Organization Man's hometown, the built environment of the Lonely Crowd—but it took on particularly menacing connotations when it was discovered in the city and could thus be joined to older suspicions of city life.[61]

The literary critic Leslie Fiedler gave voice to this strain of massification panic in 1953 when he observed that Julius and Ethel Rosenberg, recently executed for espionage, had once lived in a "melancholy block of identical dwelling units that seem the visible manifestation of the Stalinized petty-bourgeois mind: rigid, conventional, hopelessly self-righteous." The Rosenbergs had lived in Knickerbocker Village, a New Deal–era project on the Lower East Side, not one of the new postwar towers. But Fiedler's intimation of what cultural critic Andrew Ross calls "guilt by housing" was telling in that it established a one-to-one correspondence between housing and individual character that fully emerged as a pervasive threat in the Cold War era. The experiment of New Deal liberalism faltered, he implied, when it employed the kind of social engineering that had been programmatically embraced by Communism or its agents in this country. Fiedler appeared equally motivated by elite disdain for petit bourgeois ways of thinking and by the bitterness that comes of mortally wounded faith in the surety of liberal progress. His response to the built representation of those ideals of progress was to cast the project as the dark inverse of its supposed promise and as an incubator of the Stalinist mind its architecture visibly displayed. Mass housing, Fiedler implied, would produce the sorts of drones needed to fulfill the busy work of a "mass society." And worst of all, it was liberalism's impulse toward perfectibility that ensured its disheartening congruence with the ideologically blinkered, yet self-assured attitude of the duped Communist who would never know real freedom.[62]

This kind of doubt continuously dogged public housing. The legislative battles of the '40s and '50s confirmed the single-family house as the ideal American shape of shelter. Condemning mass housing as suspiciously un-American, they lastingly constricted its design parameters, social amenities, and economic fortunes. Meanwhile, the architecture of public housing seemed uncomfortably similar to that on offer in the Soviet Union. This was an often unspoken aspect of public housing's threat, but it moved beneath the surface of opinion, an assumption as much as a declaration. It appeared in minor ways—Lewis Mumford's offhand comment that NYCHA's modernism traded in a regrettable "Leningrad formalism" ensuring "unnecessary monotony"—and in extreme versions, including the "tombstones of democracy" that "An American Born" saw in the visual profile of NYCHA's projects. Most of all, it was said that the new fields of public housing remaking New York's inner-city neighborhoods sapped their residents of their initiative. This seemed to be the case on a purely practical level—as even NYCHA chair Thomas Farrell admitted, income limits for residents meant that economic advancement could lead to eviction—but it colored the entire idea of public housing as well. Despite the history of New Deal housing reform and the active campaigns waged by working people to attract public housing to their ailing neighborhoods, the new towers, with their formal, abstract geometry and planned simplicity, seemed to represent a bureaucratic, top-down, un-American solution to urban ills. A true solution to the problems of East Harlem, wrote sociologist Patricia Cayo-Sexton in 1965, would not

> resemble the endless blocks of symmetrical and identical brick towers that are now found in East Harlem (and—even more so—in Moscow and other Russian cities where the city planners have taken over); it will look like a community where the people who have to live in a building have had some say about the building's plan, and a chance to put their own personal mark on it.[63]

Ultimately, Cayo-Sexton's fear that this was an impersonal, imposed landscape merged with Fiedler's claim that its rigidity shaped the character of its residents. Public housing more and more came to be seen as an alien and bureaucratic response to urban ills that did nothing to help pull its residents up from poverty, much less remake them as new community-minded citizens of little superblock democracies. The darkest implication of public housing seemed to be that it reinforced and amplified the feelings of helplessness that often accompanied poverty. Handicapped and stigmatized by these residues of Cold War political culture, public housing was not only legislated into penurious, second-class citizen status. Its image as a threat to capitalism also dovetailed with its emerging role as a poorhouse, ensuring that it would be seen as a place fit only for those deemed lazy or irretrievably poor, a place to put those who could not make it on their own or, even more ominously, those whom society had determined, because of their race and supposed social habits, should not be allowed to make it out of poverty. The Cold War concerns that helped to birth the urban renewal age also helped to foster the segregation and spatial underdevelopment of inner cities, some of the very conditions underpinning the "urban crisis" that urban renewal and public housing had sought to offset.

In the decade after the war, NYCHA officials, planners, and architects had defended their plans on practical grounds; this was the quickest and most efficient way to provide mass housing and clear slums. They had not junked the more visionary aspects of European social housing ideals, but whether or not they were building the infrastructure of a social democratic city, they were forced to filter their idealism through the hard lenses of real estate deals, urban land prices, the economics of housing production, the social complexities of managing and maintaining housing stock in a city transformed by black and Puerto Rican migration, and the perils of Cold War hostility. Seeking a compromise to stay alive, they stuck fast to a basic program geared toward fulfilling the limited terms by which the Cold War urban renewal compact interpreted modern housing ideals. By the mid-1960s, however, the fields of towers built across East Harlem appeared to many as an impoverished mirror image of midtown's glass skyscraper rows or a suspicious cousin to Moscow's housing blocks. These new landscapes seemed to have been built by ideologues who had forsaken any human considerations in city building for a rigid adherence to the demands of a rationalist, modernist aesthetic, or by tragic racists whose utopian visions had blinded them to the suffering of the displaced populations being shuttled around the city from one doomed neighborhood to another.

If Cold War conflicts contributed to a widespread national disillusionment with public housing and urban renewal, they also informed, in oblique terms, similar currents of dissent surging through the local landscapes of East Harlem and neighborhoods like it. Challenges to the impact of public housing on East Harlem would be launched not only in response to the brutal social costs of slum clearance or around questions of racial and economic segregation, but on the grounds that public housing and urban renewal had altered fundamental properties of city and neighborhood life. These critics claimed that these interventions in the cityscape and in the fabric of East Harlem were not advancements, but violations of a previous, neglected, and cherished urban sensibility. They wanted new, sanitary housing, but not at the expense of their sedimented and rooted experiences of the time and space of neighborhood life. In effect, the new towers had disrupted an older urban world and replaced it with what some saw as a rootless, unsure world of drifting anomie. Progress had led to disruption and fear, not abundance and prosperity. The specter of what came to be called the "federal bulldozer" constantly loomed over the old tenement districts, while people transplanted to new project towers grieved for the severed bonds of community life. In East Harlem, small groups of concerned social workers and committed urbanists joined forces with public housing residents to try to remake the urban renewal vision that was fast remaking their neighborhood.

CHAPTER 7

CONFRONTING THE "MASS WAY OF LIFE"

Surveying the Public Landscape

When blocks and blocks of tenements were razed to put up a new City Housing Project, no one could deny that it was all to the good. The housing projects perhaps represent the greatest "abstract good" in the neighborhood, and almost by definition then, one of the people's most complex and frustrating problems.
—Dan Wakefield, *Island in the City,* 1959

In 1955, Ellen Lurie began visiting the recently completed first section of the George Washington Houses. Assisted by a team of volunteer interviewers— Lurie was herself a volunteer social worker at East Harlem's Union Settlement House—she walked around the first six open buildings, riding the elevators 14 stories up, knocking on doors along the long slab-block interior hallways, and talking to residents in their new, clean kitchens and living rooms, trying to understand how the proliferating projects were changing the lives of tenants and the East Harlem community at large. What she found dismayed her and challenged her assumptions about the neighborhood she was coming to love.

Lurie and her Union Settlement colleagues had been hearing complaints and rumors of complaints about the new projects for some time. They were alarmed, and not a little confused. They regarded the new housing as fruits of their own long efforts to better the lives of East Harlemites. As recently as five or eight years earlier, the new projects rising around town were seen as beacons of hope, their precise geometry, clean lines, and modern fittings seeming to represent in mortar, brick, concrete, and glass the clean, ordered urban future they would bequeath to city life. The social workers had mostly believed the eager pronouncements made by housing reformers, architects, tenant organizers, and other allies in the broad movement that had been mustered to win public housing over the last 20–30 years. Slum clearance and public housing, it had been said, would spell an end to the social and personal ills of slum life. With enough clearance and new housing—and East Harlem was slated to receive more than its share of what journalist Dan Wakefield called this "abstract good"—slums would melt away. Crime, juvenile delinquency, disease, infant mortality, broken families, fires—all the traditional perils to conventional family life that reformers had long identified in the city's poorer districts—would dissipate and recede. Settlement houses and social service agencies would be put out of business.[1]

It was said that the new "machines for living" made the settlements' relief work unnecessary; they already incorporated social goals into their very design. They had light, air, open space, and modern kitchens, of course, but they also provided the proper grounds for real community life. The new "neighborhood units" carved from the tenement jumble by superblocks and housing towers disrupted the city grid, freeing the poor from the clutches of slumlords and real estate speculation. These units were sized not only to displace slums, but to keep negative influences at bay by encouraging tenants to turn inward and invest in new community centers and other shared amenities. This new public landscape was open to all, regardless of creed or color, and efforts at fostering racial integration seemed to be working; public housing heralded the beginning of the end of racial and economic ghettos.

By the mid-1950s, however, those hopes appeared to be in jeopardy. There had always been doubters, but now the social workers could discern a gathering chorus of voices, all clamoring to reveal this supposed utopia as nothing but a false dream. Residents had begun to complain about the towers' dispiriting monotony, while those displaced from housing project and Title I urban renewal sites overwhelmed nearby tenement neighborhoods and NYCHA waiting lists.[2] These rumblings were echoed and embellished by occasional newspaper reports describing project-fed jumps in crime and juvenile delinquency, charges that public housing was merely cladding persistent slums in modern architectural fashions, and objections to the fact that income ceilings squelched initiative and turned projects into monolithic reserves for the poor. A whole array of troubles had started to collect and fester. When Lurie and her team returned with their report, the social workers realized not only that these complaints hit home, but also that they were literally hitting *home,* right there in East Harlem.

Washington Houses and other new East Harlem projects, Lurie discovered, did not resemble the ideal communities of the reformers' hopes. There were, of course, many tenants who appreciated their new housing; the majority, probably, welcomed the chance to leave the overcrowded tenements behind. Those few who had lived on the site beforehand and now lived in the project were generally satisfied. But for many others, the new world of the towers was confusing and dispiriting. Many had been imported from other clearance sites in distant neighborhoods. They felt isolated, anonymous, and apathetic. They didn't care to try to make new friends. Some never unpacked, as if they hoped they would be moving again at any moment. Others stayed indoors with their shades drawn at all hours. Some arrived with intractable personal or family problems, which compounded the effects of their poverty. Some found it difficult to tear themselves away from their old neighborhoods and made long, inconvenient journeys to do their shopping or visit friends and family in other tenement districts soon to face the wrecking ball. Racial tension was growing as blacks, whites, and Puerto Ricans were thrown together into new proximity in a new landscape. Few seemed to have a feeling of ownership over the project, and thus lacked what Lurie called a "sense of civic responsibility" for the project's welfare. Residents exhausted their energy trying to deal with crowded schools, inadequate police protection, and increased vandalism and crime. The projects were what the Puerto Rican lawyer and activist Herman Badillo called "islands of hope," but they remained just that, islands unto themselves, cut off from the neighborhoods from which they had been carved. And if the intricate social infrastructure of the old neighborhoods had been supplanted, the new public landscape of the towers seemed to offer little connective tissue as compensation.[3]

Ten or so blocks uptown from the Washington Houses, Mildred Zucker and the staff of the James Weldon Johnson Community Center (JWJCC) were seeing similar problems and coming to similar conclusions. The JWJCC had been initiated in 1948 by the East Harlem Council for Community Planning (EHCCP)—a local civic and business group—and other area social organizations to serve the newly built James Weldon Johnson Houses. But the "promise" of "a new life of cleanliness, open space and hope" the projects had offered appeared to be going unfulfilled. The projects "left much to be desired as structures for a human community," the Johnson Center staff wrote, and provided few resources for former slum-dwellers "inaugurating a new mass way of life."[4]

Confronted with this "new mass way of life," Lurie realized that they had been "much too wistful, too wishful." In the "good old days," they "always knew exactly what to do: Press for better housing." That had been the way to end slums. Now, they had to reexamine their assumptions. In the words of Preston Wilcox, another East Harlem social worker, modern project housing had served to "whet our appetites for the good life." It had seemed to be analogous in aim and effect to the complementary experiment in mass housing under way in the suburbs. Few of them used exactly these terms, but the social workers' brand of faith underwrote the broad sense that public housing was a benevolent intervention in the cityscape, one which promised to provide America's working poor with the infrastructure of prosperity, modernity, and freedom for which the peace had been won and the new ideological struggle with the Soviet Union joined. But a few years of experience had turned such assumptions inside out. Now, the social workers talked about the projects in language that inadvertently echoed some darker implications of the Cold War–influenced urban renewal compact.[5]

East Harlem amid urban renewal was becoming a "civic and social wasteland." The "mammoth housing program," the JWJCC said, "provided air and plumbing but destroyed the social structure that largely held the community together. Stores disappeared, neighbors scattered, and the traditional gathering places vanished. With old ties gone, an estimated 60,000 strangers rattle around thirteen hygienic developments—lonely, rootless, apathetic and hostile." This new mass way of life was grim, ordered, and routinized in spirit; it seemed to embody the emerging "mass society" of contemporary sociologists' nightmares. Despite the sometimes haughty or imperious tone of their judgments on the character of project life, the social workers blamed these ills not on the people themselves but on the process of top-down clearance and rebuilding. If New York mayor Robert Wagner hailed East Harlem's fields of towers as "one of the greatest advances made in neighborhood redevelopment in the United States," Union Settlement House headworker William Kirk responded that what had happened should rightly be called "superimposed neighborhood renewal." East Harlem, he said, had $250 million of public housing, more than any other neighborhood in the country. That was a high price to pay for the losses they were seeing.[6]

For the next decade, these social workers grasped the political and social initiative in East Harlem. Aiming to "reclaim" the "wasteland" of public housing and "rebuild the shattered human fabric" of East Harlem, Union Settlement and the JWJCC joined forces in 1957 to found the East Harlem Project. Before federal War on Poverty funds and programs arrived in the mid-1960s, giving explicitly Puerto Rican political networks access to power and community leadership, the East Harlem Project undertook a series of efforts to build indigenous community organizations, confront city authorities, and remake the public landscape. It worked to undo the practice of all-or-nothing bulldozer renewal, to encourage the redesign of public housing in a more community-friendly mold, to ease racial tension by bringing groups together in community organizations and redesigned urban spaces, and to foster economic diversity by attracting private investment and middle-income co-op housing.[7]

Ultimately, the East Harlem Project hoped to forge a link between the residents on the ground and the planners at their drawing boards and to remake public housing in the image and spirit of the old neighborhoods the social workers saw slipping away all around them. It sought to restore the democratic element of East Harlem life that it believed had been eroded by what it called "absentee decision making," so that residents of the public landscape could regain a measure of control over their own lives and achieve the prosperity and abundance expected from postwar life. The organization hoped, in other words, to realize the original ideals of postwar public housing: a social and physical infrastructure that would encourage "the potential of people to help themselves, to choose their own destinies and to enjoy the social, physical and economic benefits of an affluent society."[8]

These efforts had uneven results. There was no shortage of unrealized plans, sparsely attended meetings, and strained relations with project residents. But the East Harlem Project also produced a series of redesigned plazas, middle-income co-ops, and renewal plans set into rather than on top of the urban fabric of the neighborhood. However, the greatest impact of its efforts was not immediate or limited to East Harlem alone. The social workers pursued connections with various planners, architects, and other urban thinkers, soliciting plans, designs, speeches, and advice from experts like the writer Jane Jacobs and the architect Albert Mayer. In so doing, they made the East Harlem experience a major source of inspiration for an informal, but ultimately effective, movement to dislodge modernist urbanism from its reigning influence over the practice of architecture and planning, an effort that made up one part of the revolt against urban renewal. Of course, that process was made possible by the fact that the East Harlem social workers were some of the first outsiders to recognize the beginnings of an uprising against public housing and urban renewal–fed displacement on the part of public housing residents themselves. Faced with this trouble, the social workers did not reject public housing and renewal; they looked to modify its modernizing impulse and reclaim the spirit of community endangered by absentee decision making and the new public landscape. But their discontent with the all-or-nothing bulldozer approach to renewal and the abstract visions of modern housing refined already-percolating objections to the new cityscape that urban renewal offered and the losses it entailed. When the uprising against urban renewal was fully joined, it proceeded along paths blazed in East Harlem.

The New Mass Way of Life

Thus far, George Washington Houses is merely a shelter for a large number of families more or less forced by necessity to accept project conditions; until these families feel themselves as part of a neighborhood in which they have importance as well as responsibility, the project will be not more than a sterile, sanitary slum.
—Ellen Lurie, Washington Houses Study, 1956

Ellen Lurie and her team of social workers went into George Washington Houses in 1955 and 1956. Two or three years later, the judgments they made about public housing would be on the way to entirely unseating earlier optimism as the reigning commonsense understanding of publicly subsidized housing. By 1965 at the very latest, the newspaper reports and rumors cataloging public housing's decline would solidify into a new conventional wisdom that was as narrow in its horror over the effects of public housing as modernism's initial enthusiasts had been in their grand expectations for its city-changing powers.[9] But in the mid-1950s, as they visited the towers and drew up their report, Lurie and her team were ahead of the curve, reporting only to their colleagues in a handful of social service agencies and participating in a conversation that did not extend far beyond those residents, housers, architects, planners, and city officials who had championed public housing and urban renewal in the first place. George Washington Houses provided them with both a starting point and a microcosm; it encapsulated the entire range of problems facing East Harlem after the public housing deluge and launched the social workers into an effort to reform the public landscape. Their findings and programs, while never intended to undermine public housing, did much to guide the terms of the debate that ultimately doomed the reputations of public housing and urban renewal.

George Washington Houses, Lurie reported, was producing a wholesale transformation of its immediate neighborhood. Only the first section had opened, but the project, when completed, would swallow seven city blocks. Its three superblocks demapped four cross streets between 97th Street and 104th Street, between Second Avenue and Third Avenue, replacing the thick tenement and storefront cluster with green lawns, winding paths, parking lots, and playgrounds. The project's 1,515 apartments replaced 1,826 tenement apartments. Only 14 percent of the site was given over to buildings: 14 of the new, avant-garde slab-block towers of 12 and 14 stories. Rents in the new towers were low, averaging about $44, but that was still double the average rent of the old tenement district. Many of the old 5-story walk-ups the project replaced had no private toilet, heat, or running water, and the project considerably reduced population density from 444 to 273 persons per acre. Two schools on the site were saved and modernized, and the project featured laundry rooms, a community center, a child health station, and a day care center. But this new public landscape, ironically, was devoted almost entirely to domestic life. More than 200 stores, cafes, churches, clubs, and other commercial ventures went under the wrecking ball. Such losses suggested that Washington Houses was introducing social changes equal to its sweeping physical intervention in the cityscape.[10]

Lurie and her colleagues concluded that the troubles collecting around Washington Houses could be traced to its isolation from the older neighborhood around the project. Of course, this was no accident. In keeping with modern housing's neighborhood-unit principles, the project was designed to be a world unto itself, socially segregated from the rest of East Harlem. What was alarming, however, was that Washington Houses suggested that the new "islands of hope" would keep at bay much that was vital and positive about the old tenement neighborhood, replacing its diversity and unplanned—if forced and sometimes

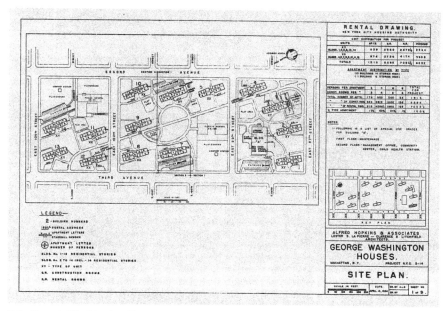

7.1. George Washington Houses was one of the authority's newer slab-block projects. Its 14 towers, arranged to catch the morning and evening sun, were 12 and 14 stories high and covered 14 percent of their site on three superblocks. New York City Housing Authority Records, La Guardia and Wagner Archives.

tense—mixtures of peoples, classes, ages, and genders with a community that appeared to be more homogeneous, one-dimensional, and divided.

This was immediately apparent in the age, family, and class makeup of the new project. The social workers compared 1950 Census figures and 1956 project statistics, finding that the project had more than doubled the number of children under 5 living in the area, while cutting the number of people over the age of 45 in half. In 1950, there had been 3,255 families and 1,420 "unrelated individuals" living on their own in the census area. The project was only open to family units of two or more persons, so a large group of single adults had been eliminated. The widows and widowers; bachelors and spinsters; single aunts, uncles, and cousins of neighborhood families; boarders, transients, and other "free-floating" people who had made up a significant portion of the neighborhood were not eligible for the project. The old area had been a middle-aged community with as many teenagers as babies, while the project was a young, child-bearing community in which childless couples were a distinct minority, and single people (unless they were parents) nonexistent. Only 15 percent of the women Lurie and her colleagues interviewed were in paid employment.

7.2. George Washington Houses' technological advancement came to be seen as a liability. In 1955, not long after the first buildings opened, the social worker Ellen Lurie discovered that the new housing was not solving the ills it had been designed to assuage. Lurie argued that much of the problem was the avant-garde design itself, which she thought provided no context for community life to flower. New York City Housing Authority Records, La Guardia and Wagner Archives.

This narrowing in age profile and family structure was echoed in the project's loss of economic diversity. A small but significant minority of the residents of the old neighborhood—7 percent, or 335 out of 4,675 family units—earned more than the $4,000 income limit for admission to public housing. These people—many of whom were neighborhood business proprietors, schoolteachers, doctors, or other professionals—were not eligible for the project. Lurie found that the project population featured an increased number of laborers and clerical workers and a decreased number of proprietors, professionals, and service workers. The largest group in both the project and the old neighborhood were semi-skilled workers, but at the two extreme ends of the income scale—proprietors or professionals and laborers—there had been a winnowing at the top and an increase at the bottom. The number of laborers had more than doubled—from 6 percent in the census area to 14 percent of the project—while professionals and proprietors had all but disappeared, going from 6 percent of the old area to only 1.5 percent of the new high-rise population. In a pattern playing out all around East Harlem in areas where NYCHA projects were built, a mixed community of all ages with a small but crucial middle class was being replaced by a collection of young and poor families. In 1959, the median family income of East Harlem as a whole was $3,765 a year. In 1961, the average net income in all the projects was $3,070, less than the neighborhood median two years earlier. At Washington Houses and other clearance sites around the neighborhood, a new concern was rising. Rose Carrafiello, for instance, was a site tenant removed from the footprint of Jefferson Houses, but her income priced her out of public housing. She put it this way to the Board of Estimate in 1956: "Are we getting too many low income projects in East Harlem? Are you going to make it an economic ghetto?"[11]

These demographic transformations were echoed by a corresponding loss in the commercial landscape of the old neighborhood. NYCHA projects of the postwar period were entirely residential. Prewar designs that included rentable space for stores (a practice adopted and expanded by Metropolitan Life at Stuyvesant Town) had been largely abandoned so that public projects would not further raise the ire of powerful anti–public housing forces by appearing to "compete" with private enterprise. When blocks of tenements were cleared for these residential monocultures, all the commercial and industrial space knit into the fabric of the old blocks disappeared as well. Unless they owned their building and received a condemnation award from the city sufficient to finance a move, owners of small neighborhood businesses in the path of the wrecking ball were given no funds to assist with a move, save a reimbursement fee for "unmovable fixtures." Just as at Lincoln Square, many went out of business or relocated in unfamiliar terrain. The people of East Harlem, whether they were new project residents or not, lost familiar landmarks, community institutions, sources of jobs, and the modestly affluent business proprietors who had provided a measure of economic diversity for the area.

If the loss of housing stock made further overcrowding in the remaining tenements inevitable—and by 1961, 8 new projects in the neighborhood resulted in a net loss of 2,043 dwelling units—East Harlemites were most aggrieved by commercial losses.[12] Responding to local concerns, the social workers and other neighborhood advocates tracked the losses throughout the '50s. In the early 1950s, Union Settlement conducted a study of 70 square blocks of the neighborhood, a third of which had been redeveloped and was thus unavailable to stores or other commercial concerns. The study found that East Harlem had an average of more than 20 stores—sometimes many more—in each of the 45 blocks that did have stores. In 1955, the social workers and their allies launched another survey and found that 10 projects built or planned in East Harlem to date had destroyed about 1,569 retail stores, at least 1,500 of which had been put out of business altogether, taking with them about 4,500 jobs.

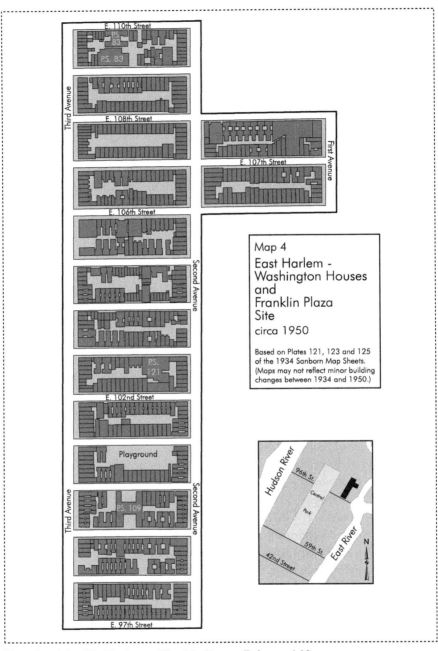

Maps 4 and 4a. Washington and Franklin Houses Before and After.

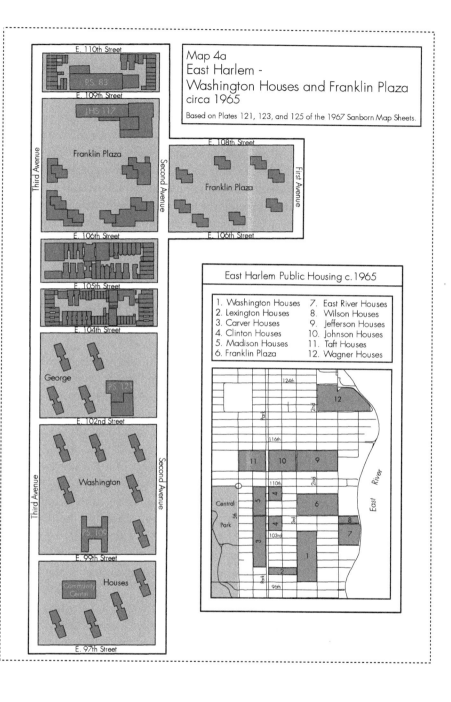

Map 4a
East Harlem -
Washington Houses and Franklin Plaza
circa 1965

Based on Plates 121, 123, and 125 of the 1967 Sanborn Map Sheets.

E. 110th Street
P.S. 83
E. 109th Street
JHS 117
Third Avenue
Franklin Plaza
Second Avenue
E. 108th Street
Franklin Plaza
First Avenue
E. 106th Street
E. 106th Street
E. 105th Street
E. 104th Street
George
P.S. 121
E. 102nd Street
Third Avenue
Washington
Second Avenue
P.S. 109
E. 99th Street
Community Center
Houses
E. 97th Street

East Harlem Public Housing c. 1965

1. Washington Houses
2. Lexington Houses
3. Carver Houses
4. Clinton Houses
5. Madison Houses
6. Franklin Plaza
7. East River Houses
8. Wilson Houses
9. Jefferson Houses
10. Johnson Houses
11. Taft Houses
12. Wagner Houses

Central Park
East River
124th
116th
110th
103rd
96th

The situation on the site of the middle-income Benjamin Franklin Houses was particularly dire. Clearance threatened 169 merchants and craftspeople engaged in over 40 lines of work, including 14 groceries, 14 candy stores, 11 clothing stores, 11 bakeries, 10 dry cleaners, 8 barber shops, 4 bars, a bike shop, 7 restaurants, 2 liquor stores, a couple of hardware stores, toy stores, 2 travel agencies, 4 print shops, 2 drugstores, 4 butchers, 3 cheese shops, a plumber, a couple of contractors, a pet shop, and a fortune-teller. There were also 28 factories and warehouses, 11 storefront offices for social, political, and labor organizations, and 3 churches, making for a total of 211 threatened commercial establishments employing at least 530 people. The study determined that most of those businesses had deep roots in the neighborhood, estimating the average tenure to be about 17 years. Faced with this situation, NYCHA admitted that the loss of stores (although not industrial or job losses) was a problem—its estimate of overall store losses in East Harlem was even higher, at 1,800 establishments—and announced that it would put stores into two new middle-income developments still on the boards, Taft and Franklin Houses. Unfortunately, the handful of stores offered there did little to stem the tide, and commercial losses continued unabated. In the early '60s, when all the dust had settled, the East Harlem Project estimated that more than 2,000 businesses had disappeared.[13]

The effects of these losses were felt inside and outside of the new housing towers. Project residents, learning to deal with life in these residential monocultures, often faced long walks to the new supermarkets or old stores and a weakened community fabric. Marta Valle was an activist with a Puerto Rican youth group that provided volunteers for Lurie's study and worked for the East Harlem Project and Union Settlement. She later remembered that the lack of commercial space in the projects contributed to a "high degree of isolation" among the new residents. "There didn't seem to be any centers where people could gather," she said, "any natural centers of activity the way the old neighborhood had the businesses, the natural gathering places, the grocery stores, the barber shops, social clubs, which were completely done away with when the very antiseptic housing projects came in." The community centers were largely for kids, and so residents met fleetingly in the elevators, on park benches, and in the laundry rooms.[14]

Architectural Forum editor Jane Jacobs, reflecting on what she had learned about disappearing storefronts during her time as a Union Settlement board member, called these lost stores "the missing link in city redevelopment." Everyone in the area felt their loss, she believed, because they made "an urban neighborhood a community instead of a dormitory." They supplied the space for the "institutions that people create, themselves"; the stores and meeting places were the functional equivalent of "the plaza, the market place, and the forum, all very

7.3. This 1955 NYCHA photo shows a stretch of East 106th Street in East Harlem, not long before clearance for the Franklin Houses (later, Franklin Plaza) began. The loss of local businesses like the Supreme Food Market worried neighborhood residents and East Harlem social workers. NYCHA projects were too often residential monocultures and, as the Lincoln Square protestors and Jane Jacobs pointed out, the loss of neighborhood stores eroded a neighborhood's vitality. New York City Housing Authority Records, La Guardia and Wagner Archives.

ugly and makeshift but very much belonging to the inhabitants, very intimate and informal." Jacobs, already beginning to rehearse the ideas that would later inform both her own struggles against renewal in Greenwich Village and her famous attack on modern planning, *The Death and Life of Great American Cities,* called the lost storefronts of East Harlem "strips of chaos that have a weird wisdom of their own not yet encompassed in our concept of urban order." In general, the social workers and their allies found that all the residents of East Harlem mourned the loss of their own familiar "strips of chaos," whether they featured Puerto Rican bodegas and *cuchifritos* stands, Italian meat markets, or all-purpose barber shops, candy stores, and army-navy stores.[15]

In addition to ushering in a loss of economic and social diversity, public housing appeared to be escalating white flight and heightening racial tension. Washington Houses was going up along Third Avenue, the traditional border

7.4. Another view of the site of Franklin Plaza in East Harlem, this time showing the corner of Third Avenue and East 107th Street and the B. Chaplan Co. Hardware store. A NYCHA official stands in the foreground holding a placard identifying the project name and the photograph number. New York City Housing Authority Records, La Guardia and Wagner Archives.

between the Italian side of the neighborhood to the east and the increasingly Puerto Rican side to the west. Even though the traditional divisions among blacks, Puerto Ricans, and Italians had always been recognized and even policed, they were porous, particularly along the borders these communities shared. Before 1960, East Harlem could not be considered a "ghetto" like Harlem because it was not monolithic in either income or race; many of its blocks featured a mix of peoples and classes.[16] Public housing began to erode these traditional frontiers, but with results that were less salubrious than the mixture offered by the old block-and-tenement cityscape. The social workers found that the projects seemed to be hastening the departure of Italian families from East Harlem while increasing the number of black families. Rather than offering a new, fully integrated landscape in place of the fluid but recognized racial and ethnic enclaves, NYCHA housing was solidifying the segregation of low-income blacks and Puerto Ricans from whites.

Washington Houses served as an early barometer of these changes. First, there appeared to have been a precipitous decline in the number of white families in Washington Houses as compared to the blocks it replaced. The 1950 Census showed that the white population had been on the decline throughout the 1940s as Puerto Ricans began to arrive in large numbers. Still, more than half of the people in the old neighborhood described themselves as "white" in 1950. When demolition began for the project in the early '50s, somewhere between 33 and 43 percent of the tenants on the immediate site, depending on the source, were considered white. By 1956, though, NYCHA figures for Washington Houses showed that only 12.5 percent of the tenants were white, while 87.5 percent were nonwhite, a group that was split almost evenly between blacks and Puerto Ricans. By 1959, the white population had decreased to 7.5 percent.[17]

Across the neighborhood, a similar pattern seemed to be taking hold. By 1956, despite NYCHA's open admissions policy, whites were an absolute minority in all but one of East Harlem's public projects, Jefferson Houses, where NYCHA and a diligent manager had worked to attract white families and create a balanced tenantry.[18] (Even there, though, where whites had been between 60 and 80 percent of the original site tenants, whites were only 49 percent of the residents in 1956.) Whites were outnumbered by blacks in all other projects and outnumbered Puerto Ricans in only two. Whites made up less than 25 percent of the population in four out of six projects the social workers surveyed, and less than 15 percent in three of those. Even in East River Houses, deep in Italian East Harlem, where the original tenantry of the project in 1941 had been 89 percent white, the white population was only 36 percent in 1956. By 1959, this pattern had accelerated, with none of the projects having more than a 30 percent white population. By 1965, it had solidified in the older developments and metastasized in the new projects going up. Jefferson stabilized at about a third white, East River dipped to 27 percent white, and even newer projects like Wagner Houses and Wilson Houses, built on the northern and southern fringes of East Harlem, where the population was still around 80 percent white in the late '50s, had small white populations of 21 percent and 25 percent, respectively. The James Weldon Johnson Houses went from 7 percent white in 1956 to 5 percent in 1959 to zero in 1965. The average white population across nine projects was 19 percent in 1965. Even in 1956, Lurie and her colleagues observed, there was only one project in which there was more than a token white population in comparison to the black and Puerto Rican populations. This mirrored the corresponding decline in East Harlem's overall white population, which reached a low of 21.4 percent in 1960.

Indeed, the rise of public housing dovetailed with larger demographic shifts, propelling a profound reshaping of the entire neighborhood's racial and ethnic geography. In the postwar era, as the last of East Harlem's Jews and Irish and a majority of its Italians withdrew to the outer boroughs and suburbs, white flight was compounded by intensifying black migration from the South and an entirely new phenomenon: the airborne migration of thousands upon thousands of Puerto Ricans from the island commonwealth to the mainland in the 20 years after World War II. The majority landed in New York: between 1940 and 1950, Puerto Rican migration to the city increased 206 percent. Between 1950 and 1960, more than 200,000 Puerto Ricans came to the city, and by 1960 the Puerto Rican population of New York was about 612,000. While they settled all over the city, most came to Manhattan, and many to East Harlem. This influx expanded the boundaries of Spanish Harlem, or El Barrio, eastward into what had traditionally been Italian East Harlem; by 1960, Puerto Ricans constituted about 40 percent of the overall neighborhood. Public housing intensified this transformation, both by the fact that absolute numbers of Puerto Ricans increased in most East Harlem projects over the years and by the fact that NYCHA housing brought great numbers of Puerto Ricans into areas that had been largely white only 10 years before. Wagner and Jefferson Houses, for instance, cleared blocks that had been between 60 and 80 percent white; by 1959, the projects had Puerto Rican populations of 44 and 39 percent, respectively. Washington Houses completely breached the Third Avenue line between El Barrio and Italian East Harlem. In an area that had been at least 34 percent white before demolition, the project had a 53 percent Puerto Rican population in 1959 and 49 percent in 1965.

At the same time, public housing brought into East Harlem an unprecedented number of African Americans, many of whom were refugees from various slum clearance projects in Harlem proper, not recent arrivals from the South.

Developments that went up in the northwest corner of East Harlem, like Taft and Johnson Houses, cleared blocks that were mostly Puerto Rican and black, with small white minorities. By 1965, both projects had black majorities of 57 and 75 percent, with significant Puerto Rican populations and few, if any, whites. At East River Houses, which was largely white in the 40s and early 50s, blacks constituted 41 percent of the population by 1959 and 43 percent by 1965. Wilson and Lexington Houses, both located in traditionally Italian and Puerto Rican areas, had black populations of 45 and 55 percent, respectively, by 1965. Overall, by 1965, almost half of the population of East Harlem's public housing was black, a third was Puerto Rican, and a fifth was white. These changes were mirrored in the overall black population of East Harlem, which climbed to 38 percent in 1960, just under the Puerto Rican population at 40 percent.[19]

Looking at these statistics frozen in time—say in 1955 or 1960—East Harlem's public housing could appear to be a model of integration, or at least more so than any comparable private housing at the time. Viewed *over* time, however, the pattern is unmistakable. As early as 1950, the Citizens Housing and Planning Council had warned that the unplanned influx of public housing in East Harlem would destroy the interracial nature of the neighborhood and "freeze" it into a traditional ghetto. By the mid- to late 1950s, the social workers discovered that this process was well under way. At Washington Houses, for instance, Lurie and her team discovered right away that the project was doing little to break up the concentration of blacks and Puerto Ricans in Harlem and East Harlem. Over half of the black and Puerto Rican project tenants had been moved from other parts of Harlem—the majority from West Harlem or other parts of East Harlem, where they had been uprooted from various clearance sites. In addition, few whites who lived on the site had wanted to move into Washington Houses; indeed, only 9 percent of the project tenants formerly lived on the site, and most of them were Puerto Rican. At the same time, 41 percent were people uprooted from other renewal sites. The project seemed to be having a dual effect: it was simultaneously uprooting people's lives and consolidating a nonwhite ghetto. Washington Houses displaced clusters of Italians, while at the same time increasing and spreading a residential monoculture of primarily low-income blacks and Puerto Ricans segregated from whites and the neighborhood in which the project had intervened. Despite an open admissions policy and NYCHA's concerted attempts to attract white families, public housing was reinforcing and even perpetuating white flight from East Harlem.[20]

The social workers discovered that these changes were taking their toll inside the projects, where people were thrown together in a disorienting new landscape. First, many of the new residents did not even want to be there. Sixty percent of the new residents had not chosen Washington Houses and had been forced to move there against their will. Black families, Lurie and her team reported, were having a hard time adapting because they had been forced into an unfamiliar neighborhood, away from the churches, clubs, cafes, and political organizations central to Harlem's black life. Interviews revealed that if they appreciated the amenities of project living, they still found themselves in a place with, as Lurie put it, "all of the disadvantages of Harlem and none of its benefits." They found Puerto Rican customs and food to be strange and worried about the hostile white neighborhoods to the south and east.

Many of the Puerto Ricans, having moved from nearby, were more or less content. Few were from the site itself, so most did not actively miss the world the project had replaced. On the other hand, the Puerto Rican families, Lurie found, were divided among themselves. A significant minority had been relocated from the Bronx—some whisked out of the path of Robert Moses's Cross-Bronx Expressway—and they tended, on average, to be slightly wealthier, lighter-skinned, and further removed from Puerto Rico than some of their neighbors. Some had grown up in East Harlem and seen the move to the Bronx as a step up. Now, they had been forced back and felt superior to the neighborhood and people they had earlier left behind. Other Puerto Ricans knew less English, were darker-skinned, or still longed to return to the island. They did not see project life as a long-term proposition and had no reason to try to make common cause with neighbors who acted superior.

Worst of all were the small minority of white families, who, Lurie reported, were a "pretty unhappy lot to interview." While there were some who wanted to make the best of it and try to "improve" the situation in the project, others were ashamed, resentful, and angry "at the world for allowing them to live in such a situation." They seemed to be embarrassed to live in a housing project and "uncomfortable" surrounded by a "poor class of people" whom they did not "consider their equals." Some of their children had been ganged up on by black and Puerto Rican kids; one mother, who wouldn't let her kids go to the community center for fear of how they would be treated, suggested that all the white parents should get together to form a social group. She suggested an interracial committee to oversee separate "white and colored" social groups.

All across East Harlem, in and out of the projects, public housing was perpetuating a crisis among the shrinking Italian population. Many of the remaining Italian families had incomes that put them just beyond eligibility for public housing. As one East Harlem Project memo put it, they were now "confronted with an expanding colored population, better housed at lower rentals than they themselves were paying. They were not only outraged at the apparently favored position of the migrants but terrified by their alien customs and color." Public housing was, for white East Harlemites, a forcible intrusion on their world, one that facilitated the encroachment of outsiders who threatened to displace them and their neighborhood.[21]

The social workers' efforts to improve what they called "intergroup relations" across the neighborhood as a whole were made infinitely more difficult by an overall decline in the quality of life inside the projects themselves. Ever since the 1949 Housing Act had given the displaced tenants of urban renewal sites priority in public housing, NYCHA had been faced with a growing number of what the social workers called "problem families." According to housing officials and social workers, these families, many of which would have been screened out in the era before mass displacement put such a strain on public housing rolls, had a range of difficulties with varying degrees of severity—from broken families, intense marital discord, bad housekeeping, and rent delinquency to criminal children, mental illness, alcoholism, prostitution, and drug use or peddling. This "small hard core," as social worker and houser Elizabeth Wood's influential 1957 study of Harlem's St. Nicholas Houses called them, not only had problems of their own, but also could be a source of serious problems for an entire project. One such family on a floor or hallway, social workers claimed, could make life unbearable for all of their neighbors. Several could ruin a whole building. As one tenant organizer in East Harlem's James Weldon Johnson Houses discovered, "the sincere efforts of a majority of the tenants could be defeated by the bad living habits and destructiveness of a minority of problem families." The "small hard core" was said to be behind the recent jumps in crime and vandalism many residents were reporting, the rising costs of project maintenance, and the general tendency of "normal families" to increasingly leave or reject public housing in the first place.[22]

Ten or so years later, the emphasis on "problem families" would harden into the widespread public, national consensus that the "pathological" behavior of nonwhite residents, mired in a "culture of poverty," was to blame for public housing's woes. The roots of that judgment can be seen in the social workers' shock over the new, disturbing conditions in public housing. Wood admitted that she and her colleagues had slightly revised their previous environmentalist faith in the idea that slum conditions created antisocial behavior. Now, they believed that "there are some slum dwellers" with "very unsavory habits...who can and do help make slums." Or, as one anonymous "close student of New York's slums" told a *Fortune* reporter in 1957:

> Once upon a time we thought that if we could only get our problem families out of those dreadful slums, then papa would stop taking dope, mama would stop chasing around, and Junior would stop carrying a knife. Well, we've got

them in a nice new apartment with modern kitchens and a recreation center. And they're the same bunch of bastards they always were.

Despite this kind of cynicism and condescension, in the late 1950s the social workers, including Wood and the East Harlemites, did not take the "problem families" issue as an opportunity to entirely reject the capacities of public housing residents. On the contrary, it inspired them to redouble their efforts to organize tenants for campaigns to win better welfare, maintenance, and police services from the housing authority.[23]

In the end, the social workers' greatest fear was that the vast majority of "normal" families would abandon public housing altogether. Then, the projects would be left as reserves for those problem families—like papa, mama, and Junior—whose behavior appeared to make them the exact opposite of the social workers' traditional conception of a normal family. They noted that many people were already leery of public housing, because its rules and image seemed rigid, institutional, and restrictive. Families whose incomes increased above the NYCHA-mandated ceiling would be evicted and often have to return to the slums they had previously escaped. This deprived the project of its highest-income families and forced many others to make an odious moral choice between hiding increased income from the authorities or stifling opportunities to better their prospects. Residents also worried that their neighbors were spying on them and might report any change in income—or merely the arrival of new appliances or clothes that might signal good fortune—to a watchful management. They also noted NYCHA's increasing tendency to mimic the private real estate market. Since the late '40s, the authority had shifted away from providing extensive in-house welfare services toward simply housing construction, rent collection, and maintenance. This made the authority seem little more than what its name implied, a removed and distant power unresponsive to tenant needs. None of this made for a cohesive or active community life in the projects, instead breeding a sense of paternalism, impersonal authority, suspicion, and capitulation to fate. As Ellen Lurie described the situation in the George Washington Houses, "the management list of do's and don't's have taken over for the more informal sanctions of a real community."[24]

Ultimately, the social workers worried that the "abstract good" of public housing's benign intervention had not helped at all, but instead brought the neighborhood full circle. In "morale and spirit," Lurie concluded of George Washington Houses, "the people in the project have not been emancipated from the slums." She left this somber verdict out of the final version of her report, but it represented her hardest, most clear-eyed look at the perils and promises of public housing. For all its technological advances, George Washington

Houses was "merely a shelter" for those "more or less forced by necessity to accept project conditions." Until its residents "feel themselves as part of a neighborhood in which they have importance as well as responsibility, the project will be not more than a sterile, sanitary slum."[25]

In order to avoid this fate, Ellen Lurie and her successor, Preston Wilcox, led the East Harlem Project in an ambitious organizing effort. They looked to find ways to bring "antagonistic groups together" and spark "community development" from the ground up rather than the top down. They tried to find indigenous leadership drawn from East Harlem itself, nurture what they called its "self-confidence" and "self-worth," and encourage the neighborhood to mobilize to seek answers to community problems. In order to deal with the impact of

7.5. Design for Living Revisited? This undated picture, taken for Union Settlement and used in its promotional literature, recalls the documentary photography of an earlier era, which was designed to expose the ills of the slums. Like "Design for Living?" the frontispiece of Edith Elmer Wood's *Slums and Blighted Areas in the United States*, this image also shows children endangered by their environment, right down to the burning refuse (see figure I.1). Of course, here, housing projects have replaced tenements as the new slums and the new threat to traditional domestic life. Union Settlement Association Records, Rare Book and Manuscript Library, Columbia University in the City of New York.

"early irrational public housing," the East Harlem Project set out to intervene in the decision-making processes reshaping the landscape of East Harlem by bringing the experiences of the residents themselves to bear on the problems of public housing. They began to organize tenant associations in many of the new projects, bringing them all together under an umbrella group called the East Harlem Public Housing Association. These groups addressed the basic conditions of everyday life in public housing by organizing parties, social events, meetings, and summer camp programs and working to get better police protection, stepped-up maintenance, and vandalism prevention. They pressured NYCHA to provide better welfare services for problem families, to raise income ceilings, to offer better amenities, and to simplify regulations. In general, the East Harlem Public Housing Association claimed to offer a living rebuke to the idea that "low income" was a "sign of delinquency or second class citizenship." Despite the fact that "life in the project leaves little privacy, freedom and opportunity for initiative," the organization demanded "respect for the dignity of the tenant," "sympathy" for the tenant's problems, and the opportunity to "appeal" to "his intelligence, sense of fair play, cooperation," and "natural desire to improve his environment."[26]

At the same time, the social workers also intended these groups to be sources of ideas, inspiration, and pressure for their larger effort to rethink the monolithic public landscape. So, while they wanted to organize tenants and influence the management of current projects, they also launched an extensive program to influence the overall direction, planning, and design of future rebuilding efforts in the neighborhood. For this effort, the East Harlem Project worked to revive the largely dormant East Harlem Council for Community Planning, turning the civic and business organization's focus toward community development. Together, the two organizations—led by this core of activist social workers— embarked on a mission to force the city government, NYCHA, and the urban renewal authorities to plan "with us not for us," as their ally Herman Badillo put it to Mayor Wagner at a 1960 town meeting in East Harlem.[27]

In order to begin this effort, however, the social workers had to make sense of what they were seeing. They had to name the phenomenon and provide terms and reference points for the transformations remaking their world. After all, Lurie and her colleagues found themselves just as bewildered by this new cityscape as they judged the residents of public housing to be. For more than 10 years, the bulldozers and construction cranes had been swarming over East Harlem like an invading army or a precision bombing and rebuilding campaign. In the wake of this swarm of demolition and building, the social workers said, the new physical order concealed social wreckage, devastation that they began to describe in terms that inverted the very hope they had once invested in public

THE LITTLE FOXES

THE RED DEVILS

JR. COUNSELOR STAFF

COUNSELOR STAFF

THE DIAMONDS

THE FALCONS

7.6. Summer camp photos, 1960, Washington Houses Community Center. The social workers' organizing activities attempted to bring a measure of interracial community to the new tower-and-superblock landscape. These posed photos, carefully arranged on the project plazas with the towers in the background, give a sense of the social workers' ambitions and visions: orderly happiness in a new modern cityscape. Union Settlement Association Records, Rare Book and Manuscript Library, Columbia University in the City of New York.

housing. The new fields of towers had created a "civic and social wasteland." They were home to a "rootless, urban community" adrift in a "social and community vacuum." Life in the new "wasteland," while sanitary and potentially efficient, was routinized and poor in spirit. It endangered self-sufficiency and community life alike, the social workers said, and bred a disengaged, cowed populace. These were "abstract" communities that bred fear, anomie, and hopelessness for too many. Unchecked public housing construction had subsumed the community in a new, alienating way of life.[28]

For the social workers, East Harlem amid urban renewal was a paranoid landscape overrun by fear, resentment, racial conflict, and suspicion of authority. The anomie they discerned in the new "mass way of life" led them to see a Cold War dystopia emerging from utopian plans, a manifestation in brick, glass, and steel of the "mass society" that preoccupied so many contemporary social critics. What the social workers called the "mass way of life" in public housing appeared as an urban counterpart to the much maligned conformity and regimentation now being seen as taking root in the new suburban housing developments. Of course, this had been a challenge for the new residents of Stuyvesant Town, too; they were forced to use their relative affluence and cultural capital to make Metropolitan Life live up to the project's middle-class ideals. Here, though, in East Harlem, residents not only were thought to be stripped of both initiative and belonging, but also were forced to cope with the hopelessness of urban poverty. For the social workers, the ordered, universalist, neighborhood-unit ideals of superblock modern housing were a bust. Of course, they hadn't failed. They had succeeded all too well in disrupting and scattering the patterns of an older life. Public projects, they said, offered only removed, "superimposed" authority and vertical, distant allegiance in place of horizontal, neighborhood connections.

The social workers believed that the people of East Harlem—new migrants, urban renewal relocatees, and long-time residents alike—were victims of absentee decision making that left them adrift in the new alienating landscape. Removed and distant forces—residents used the shorthand "City Hall"—had ordered entire neighborhoods bulldozed and an old, recognizable landscape interrupted and intermittently displaced by a new urban fabric. In the imposed renewal zones, the city had replaced the familiar evil of the landlord with its own distant, abstract power—the "authority" or "housing"—which seemed to control and regulate the new space with an impersonality and bureaucracy that made the old life of the slums seem positively understandable. The resulting confusion was both individual and collective. The social workers claimed that project residents felt that they no longer had control of their own lives in this new abstract space and thus felt no need to take any responsibility for their surroundings or the well-being of their neighbors. Many retreated into seclusion or into the isolated family units that NYCHA mandated as the fundamental building blocks of its apartment communities.[29]

At the same time, renewal destroyed the intangible ties that had bound disparate individuals together. "What feeling and mutual identity a community had before the bulldozer came in is shattered" by relocation and uprooting, wrote one social worker. The new cityscape itself confused and scrambled basic patterns of meaning and disrupted well-established paths to power. Vito Marcantonio was gone, red-baited away, and slum clearance, although largely supported by East Harlem's Democratic leaders, initially appeared to vitiate traditional sources of neighborhood political and social leadership by scattering constituencies and subjugating the leadership's authority to the imperatives of federally backed rebuilding. As unhappiness with the new housing grew, the politicians who had supported it could offer little constructive response. In some ways, this power vacuum gave the social workers room to operate. But more than an opportunity, it supplied the problem. It left many project residents unsure of how to represent themselves in the public bureaucracy. "The very impressiveness of these solid institutional gigantic buildings," Lurie later reflected, "seemed to be imbuing their new tenants with a sense of their own unimpressiveness." They no longer knew where to turn for help, guidance, or authority in the new landscape.[30]

Lurie and her colleagues called this new arrangement of powers and effects the "public quality of life" or the new "mass way of life." They suggested that it was mirrored and compounded by the physical properties of the new tower-block projects themselves. The projects seemed to have created their own culture, reordering past patterns, affiliations, and possibilities and replacing them with a sense of confusion that had yet to cohere into a new order. The new spaces of the projects, wiped clean of the familiar markers of neighborhood and ethnic ties, were not only big, they were bewildering and dispiriting, and "the poverty of the human equation" that the social workers were seeing in the "vast new structures" was intimately bound up with the buildings' physical impact on the landscape. Like the flummoxed local political leadership, residents were "left standing in the midst of such overwhelmingly complex newness" that they felt even less able to control their own destinies than they had in the private slums. If this "overwhelmingly complex newness" could be found in the maze of bureaucracy and removed power that built the projects, it also echoed in the maze of towers that had replaced the familiar grid of the tenement district. Designs that had appeared so simple, transparent, and functional on the drawing board produced a bewildering landscape on the ground, which made physically and overwhelmingly concrete the removed and distant benevolence—the "abstract" sense of "good," in Dan Wakefield's words—from which such designs arose. As much as they were concerned with management and other day-to-day issues, the social workers were "convinced that a great part of the poor social showing of East Harlem's projects is owing to the physical design of the buildings themselves and their grounds. They are ill suited in design to the needs of the families who must live in them and to the neighborhoods of which they are a part." In fact, this new cityscape seemed so overwhelming that Ellen Lurie could be sure that the "project design effects [*sic*] the essence of the daily lives" of public housing residents.[31]

However, even as the social workers set out to reform and rethink the public housing landscape, they made sure not to abandon the promise of public housing altogether. They did not want their criticisms to undermine or jeopardize already weak and underfunded public efforts to rehouse the poor. Over the years, they continued to ask for more, not less, public housing. "Before any of this is read," wrote Lurie in a short preface to her report on Washington Houses:

> let this, above all, be understood: WE BELIEVE IN PUBLIC HOUSING, AND WE BELIEVE IN IT STRONGLY....But, if those of us who desire it most keenly tear at it and examine it and rework its parts—then, and only then, will this most necessary plant receive the light and air it so desperately needs in order to grow.

Ellen Lurie, Mildred Zucker, Preston Wilcox, William Kirk, and the other workers and volunteers at Union Settlement and the JWJCC, like most of the residents of public housing they tried to represent, did not want to knock down the towers and start over, nor did they have the power to do so. Instead, their particular position—in the neighborhood but not entirely of it, outside the offices of city housing and redevelopment powers, but with the professional and social resources to make connections to those authorities—gave the social workers the opportunity to have more subtle and long-lasting effects on the city-rebuilding practices of the era of urban renewal. Ironically, these effects would begin in the odd fact that they found themselves almost pining for a world they had worked to eradicate. The old tenement blocks now seemed sources of community and belonging, their "strips of chaos" supplying intangible connective powers and the stage for the mixture between classes and races, while the new housing they had championed and hoped for seemed to be becoming monolithic slums. This sudden and unexpected sense of nostalgia would propel their efforts to move forward.[32]

Every Superblock a Village

Public housing has not brought neighborhood renewal. Too much of the cultural richness inherent in the slum neighborhood was destroyed....Planners are needed—and not only architects. Sociologists, psychologists, clergymen,

educators and the people of the neighborhood themselves must study the social as well as the physical needs of the neighborhood. Those who do this must be humble, for even the poorest, most unsavory-appearing community has elements of unique vitality which must be recognized, ferreted out, and saved.
—Ellen Lurie, *Architectural Forum*, June 1957

Faced with deepening racial tension, income inequality, and social disloca-tion, the social workers looked to return some of the human scale of the old neighborhood to the new project landscape and to restore economic diversity to all of East Harlem. They followed two courses of action, both of which comple-mented the tenant organizing they were undertaking in already existing public housing. First, they launched a campaign to influence the design and planning of the project landscape, and second, they lobbied the city to provide more mid-dle-income housing in the neighborhood.

The social workers' efforts to rethink the monolithic public landscape were joined and propelled by a mounting chorus of doubts about the overall profile of tower-in-the-park public housing. Throughout the '50s, architects, planners, and other urbanists had complained about the monotony, standardization, rigid-ity, and general dreariness of public housing. Lewis Mumford blamed excessive "formalism"—the "inflexible carrying out of a system that has no regard for the site or the needs of its inhabitants." The Citizens Housing and Planning Council worried that the city was building "vertical sardine cans." Some of this clamor was not new; many older, established design professionals had never signed on with modern housing and planning in the first place. Still, even as committed a modernist as Percival Goodman, the architect who had corresponded with Vito Marcantonio about rebuilding East Harlem, considered much contemporary housing design to be "shelter engineering," not architecture. Architects were given a "hard-boiled program" that they "translated into concrete and brick." "The result," he wrote, "can hardly be other than thoughtless, mechanical— a design for robots, by robots." By the mid-1950s, these doubts had begun to spread beyond professional circles, as newspapers and magazines from the *New York Daily News* to *Newsweek* focused on the declining conditions in New York's public housing. They called it "a brick and steel Tobacco Road" and a "million-dollar barracks," thereby cementing the impression that public housing was the new atomic-age version of the old slum.[33]

Perhaps the most surprising and encouraging development was that NYCHA was beginning, however slowly, to take note of these criticisms. In the early 1950s, the agency began to make its design standards and guidelines more flexible, a process that led to a broader range of façade colors and arrange-ments, new building footprints, new window and entrance treatments, and the increased use of balconies and public galleries. It even announced a plan, which was rolled out incrementally and at a pace befitting the ponderous bureaucracy NYCHA had become, to build some "vest-pocket" projects to offset the overweening scale of the clearance and disruption caused by superblock neighborhood units. Then, in May 1958, following a municipal investigation of NYCHA conditions, policies, and practices, Mayor Wagner reorganized the authority, replacing Robert Moses's ally Philip Cruise with William Reid and the Citizens Housing and Planning Council's Ira Robbins. After that, the authority began to raise income limits, offer more social service programs, and further reconsider design and planning.[34]

While these currents of dissent and change spread, some of public housing's original boosters were simultaneously undertaking an even more fundamental rethinking of its design and planning. If the East Harlem social workers had reversed their earlier optimism about the impact of public housing, describing its failures with rhetoric inspired and informed by the Cold War language of alienation and anxiety, other housers went even further, reneging on the earlier faith in European-inspired collective and progressive housing visions and tacitly embracing the language of individuality and American nationalism that was used to attack funding for public housing at the national and local levels. Even they had begun to abandon the neighborhood-unit ideals of modern housing and grudgingly admitted that what Americans "wanted" was a free-standing house and a yard. Architect and planner Henry Whitney sounded the first note in this reversal as early as 1950, but mindful of the high regard in which public housing still stood among housers, he wrote under the sardonic pseudonym "Maxim Duplex." Most public housing in the United States, he said, featured living units that were too small, grouped in communities that were "too institutional and too paternalistic in character to measure up to any true native standard for a permanent home environment." It had too little private garden area outdoors and too little private recreational room indoors, and it offered too few opportunities for tenants to take responsibility for their own spaces. In short, public housing was "not a home in the normal American sense."[35]

A year later, Catherine Bauer, who had done more than almost anyone to bring modern housing to U.S. shores in the 1930s, offered her own doubts. Public housing design, with its "system of standards and mass production," could achieve what she called "urbanity," or "the balancing of mass and space for formal beauty," but it could not achieve what most Americans wanted, which was "individuality," which she identified as "the sense of unique and personal qualities pertaining to each dwelling, or the quaint charm that results from historic accretion and personal craftsmanship." In 1957, Bauer summed up this line of reasoning in an influential *Architectural Forum* article surveying the "premature ossification" at the heart of the "dreary deadlock of public housing." She noted the resistance of the real estate lobby, the shortages in funding, the various problems with policy and management, and the bifurcated structure of overall housing policy, which segregated public, low-income, "charity case" housing from the middle- and upper-income, Federal Housing Administration–supported suburban mortgage market. She hailed Whitney's judgments and argued that this "machinery" of policy and design had produced residential development that was not only unpopular, but also "quite alien to any American ideal of community." Modern "large-scale community design," while rightfully critiquing "chaotic individualism" and "the wasteful crudity of the ubiquitous gridiron street pattern," too quickly embraced "functionalist and collectivist architectural theories that tended to ignore certain subtler esthetic values and basic social needs." The "rigid formulas" of this policy and practice prevented the chance to "adapt and humanize these principles in suitable terms for the American scene." The "bleak symbols of productive efficiency and 'minimum standards'" associated with public housing were "hardly an adequate expression of the values associated with American home life." Echoing the East Harlemites' discovery that vertical authority was replacing horizontal affiliation, she wrote that "management domination" was "built in, a necessary corollary of architectural form." The "technocratic architectural sculptors" who designed housing towers forced residents "into a highly organized, beehive type of community life for which most American families have no desire and little aptitude."[36]

The East Harlem social workers took a different tack. They did not deploy the same rhetoric of Americanism, and they felt no need to scrap apartment living and demand that public housing be conceived as a series of "individual homes." They knew that public housing could not be further individualized. It still had to provide thousands of apartments for the ill housed. With their newfound nostalgia for what Bauer called the "historic accretion" of the old street grid, they thought that public housing was not collective enough; it had traded the communal life of the old neighborhoods for the isolation of tower-block living. The real problem was that project designs, policies, and regulations created an artificial community where a real one had stood before. Intent on focusing on local conditions, they incorporated the reformist impulses gathering around them and looked for ways to modify project design by respecting what Ellen Lurie, in a response to Bauer's article, called the "cultural richness" and "elements of unique vitality" inherent in old neighborhoods.[37]

Their first opportunity came in the summer and fall of 1958, when they learned that the authority was willing to consider alternative design proposals for the DeWitt Clinton Houses, soon to go up south of 110th Street between Lexington and Park avenues. Jane Jacobs, Ellen Lurie, Mildred Zucker, and William

Kirk, representing the East Harlem Project and the Housing Committee of the East Harlem Council for Community Planning, began meeting with chair William Reid of NYCHA, with members of the City Planning Commission, and with tenant organizations in East Harlem projects to discuss new ways of seeing public housing. In December, the group secured the pro bono aid of the architectural firm Perkins and Will, which agreed to take on an alternative design for the project.[38]

The social workers set out to emulate rather than replace the fabric of the old block-and-tenement cityscape. First, they rejected the still-prominent idea that high population density led to "socially unfit project design." Instead they argued that public housing's troubles stemmed from its disregard for what they called "the social structure of city neighborhoods, particularly poor neighborhoods," where density had underwritten not simply poverty, but a complex collective life. Public housing design ignored the cooperative and communal society of city neighborhoods, creating instead spaces that offered not privacy, but a brand of isolation they called "sophisticated family individualism." The new public landscape provided few of the social connections that the old neighborhoods offered on every stoop and corner, leaving tenants to fall back on their own meager financial resources and the authority's "artificial, institutional, and impersonal" substitutes. Public spaces in the projects—stairwells, lobbies, hallways, and open spaces—were "extensions of the street," but they discouraged the "casual and varied human contacts" that provided informal social controls as well as opportunities for mutual assistance and social and commercial contact. The results were predictable: high crime rates, vandalism, and a pervasive sense of alienation.

DeWitt Clinton Houses threatened to repeat these failures. It was, they said, a "bankrupt stereotype." Intended to be one of the authority's new vest-pocket projects, its current design—several 18-story towers on a cleared block—looked "precisely as if it were a fragment of a large project." Even without the disruption of a superblock, it offered a similar intervention in the fabric of the neighborhood, providing no integration with the surrounding area and no alleviation of tower-fed "institutionalism or anonymity." Clinton functioned just like the traditional tower-in-the-park designs, showing no sensitivity to local knowledge or concerns. This was betrayed in something as simple as the fact that the authority listed Jefferson Park as a community amenity, even though the park was four long avenue blocks away in the heart of Italian East Harlem, too far to be convenient and too dangerous for the Puerto Ricans and blacks who would form the majority of the new project's population.[39]

The East Harlem group focused its alternative schemes on diminishing the planned physical separation between the neighborhood and the project. The first step was to provide a more congenial environment for family and social life by reducing the size of the typical high-rise towers. Surveying the social dislocation she found at Washington Houses, Ellen Lurie had wondered if one of the reasons that "a socially-conscious, responsible group of project adults" had so far failed to appear was that the project was just too overwhelming. Fourteen buildings of 12 and 14 stories, she felt, forced a large group of strangers to "suddenly, impersonally start to live together." The scale caused difficulties for administration and maintenance, while families made social connections only on their floor, if at all. In their old neighborhoods, parents were near the stoops and sidewalks where kids played. Here, parents told Lurie, they might be 10 or a dozen flights up, around the corner, or a building away from the designated playgrounds; they could no longer do housework while the children played within sight or earshot.[40]

For the redesigned Clinton Houses, Lurie, Jacobs, and the others proposed instead a combination of high-rise buildings with small apartments for childless, older residents and low-rise, four-story buildings with large apartments for families with children. This experiment in the "more creative use of land coverage" made all of the low-rise buildings walk-ups—an acknowledged violation of what they considered to be specious federal public housing codes—so that kids would have no reason to use the elevators, which would now only serve the smaller apartments on the upper floors of the high-rises. The first four floors of even the high-rises were walk-ups; they also had larger apartments and entrances separated from the elevator lobbies. Perkins and Will designed the low-rise buildings as courtyard blocks of 30 families each, a figure the social workers had determined was the maximum number possible to both preserve privacy and facilitate easy social connections between families around the interior courtyards. The low-rises featured open interior corridors on all floors above the courtyards, so that mothers could easily supervise children below.[41]

They also reimagined the role of open space in project design. Public housing codes had derived their open space requirements from modern housing principles, which made nature the absolute determination of all design decisions by orienting buildings to the sun and the wind. The East Harlem group abandoned this principle, making the life and character of the streets around the project the inspiration for their design decisions. They appreciated the light and air that modern housing principles created, but questioned the ultimate utility of all the open space. Ultimately, they said, project open space was just "a means to keep buildings separated." Much of it was unusable, simply a series of parking lots or "broad untouched lawns" strewn with litter and guarded by Keep Off the Grass signs. Jane Jacobs suggested that the low-rise buildings and the streets themselves could be figured as "open space" when calculating the amount of light and air a project needed. This would allow the architects to put buildings closer to the streets themselves and forgo the usual sterile, useless buffer of grass or concrete between building and sidewalk, while returning "casual recreational and social" encounters to sidewalks, where they had always occurred in the old neighborhoods. At the same time, Perkins and Will preserved the privacy these buffers had offered by putting the first floor of each building not at ground level, but a half-floor up, just above eye level.[42]

The East Harlem group also suggested that there should be a more natural relationship between the project grounds and the surrounding streets. They knew that the streets and sidewalks of East Harlem were alive with strollers and sitters, with men playing dominoes and drinking beer, with street vendors plying their wares and people listening to music and watching television outdoors. Jacobs and the social workers aimed to "bleed" this street life into the project by combining open, inviting entrances to the project grounds with a series of planted and paved sitting and play spaces that would weave in and out of the courtyards, under the raised buildings, and up to the sidewalk. Throughout, there would be built-in niches and nooks offering continuations of the stoops and sidewalks outside the project. Perkins and Will also provided spaces for vendors to set up booths, gave the health and community centers active street frontages, and provided space in which future stores, social clubs, or other elements of commercial life could find a home in the project.[43]

The final plans that Perkins and Will drew up did not mimic the tenement streetscape. They were, instead, an effort to adapt the social infrastructure of the old neighborhood to the demand for new housing, a brief for rendering the qualities of dense urbanism in a modern architectural idiom. Indeed, they were architecturally forward-looking and even proposed closing 109th Street to make a superblock, something that NYCHA had not planned to do. Ultimately, they demonstrated what had come to be an unfortunate reality for architects and planners: the real problem with public housing design was not the power of orthodox modernism in architectural and planning circles but the layers of rules and policies that the orthodoxy had deposited in federal and local public housing codes over the years. Perkins and Will knowingly thwarted the city and federal codes to make their point. Not surprisingly, NYCHA responded to the plans by throwing up its hands and declaring them impossible to implement. Clinton Houses went ahead as originally planned: four 18-story towers amid lawns and parking lots. Still, the experience reinforced the social workers' belief that, as Mildred Zucker put it, "functional design based on knowledge gained from low-income tenants" was "the best way to produce [public] housing that would serve its purposes as originally conceived by those who fought so long and hard for it."[44]

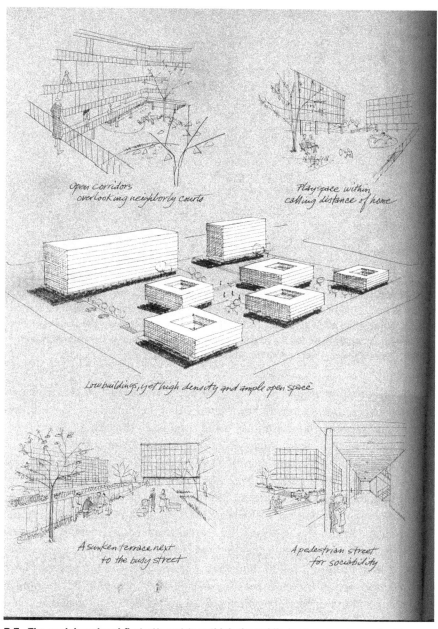

Open corridors
overlooking neighborly courts

Playspace within
calling distance of home

Low buildings, yet high density and ample open space

A sunken terrace next
to the busy street

A pedestrian street
for sociability

7.7. The social workers' first attempt to rethink the public landscape—in a redesign of the DeWitt Clinton Houses—tried to adapt modern design idioms to the principles of street-level interaction. It featured a combination of low and high buildings, open courts overlooked by interior walkways, a pedestrian street, and a free-flowing relationship between the project grounds and the surrounding streets. The design was rejected by NYCHA for its violations of federal housing codes. This drawing was published in *Architectural Forum* in April 1959. Perkins and Will.

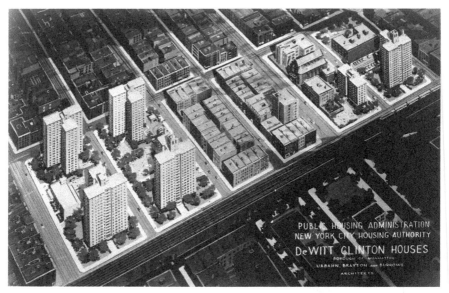

PUBLIC HOUSING ADMINISTRATION
NEW YORK CITY HOUSING AUTHORITY
DeWITT CLINTON HOUSES
BOROUGH OF MANHATTAN
URBAHN, BRAYTON AND BURROWS
ARCHITECTS

7.8. DeWitt Clinton Houses as it was eventually constructed on two separate slivers of available land. (The two blocks at left and the two towers at upper right make up the project.) One of the authority's first vest-pocket projects, it respected the street grid but still looked to supply light and air to residents with tower-in-the-park designs. New York World-Telegram Photograph Collection, Library of Congress.

The disappointment that Jacobs and the social workers felt at NYCHA's per-functory rejection was tempered by the sense that their ideas were gaining credence and that other opportunities would soon be in the offing. They did not have to wait long. In 1959, Mildred Zucker proposed a new playground and public space in the Jefferson Houses. After getting NYCHA officials on board by assuring them that the $40,000 bill would be picked up by foundation grants (eventually, the Federal Housing Administration chipped in too), she and the Johnson Community Center staff engaged the pro bono services of the planner and architect Albert Mayer. Mayer and Zucker resolved that, even if they were unable to get NYCHA to alter the uniform profile of its high-rise towers, they could at least propose ways to reinvent the spaces between the towers. Mayer found Perkins and Will's design for Clinton Houses encouraging, but he thought they had failed to provide a "convincing relationship" between the high and low buildings. Like the social workers, he was guided by the idea that, as Jane Jacobs put it, the "outdoor space" of the housing project "should be at least as vital as the slum sidewalk." Still, he felt that Perkins and Will's design lacked a sense of "community" and "focus." Mayer's efforts to provide these necessary intangibles at Jefferson Houses, and a year later in nearby Franklin Plaza, had immediate effects. They inspired a series of open space redesigns at other NYCHA projects and a widespread set of visions and plans for humanizing sterile project environments by other planners and architects.[45]

Mayer was a committed but unorthodox modernist. He was one of the founders, with Henry Wright and Lewis Mumford, of the Housing Study Guild, whose work in the 1930s had influenced Catherine Bauer and the campaign to bring modern housing ideals to the United States. He was also the original master planner for Chandigarh, a new town in India, but he lost the job after the more famous Le Corbusier stepped in. But, like Jacobs and the social workers, he had grown restless with the calcified state of public housing design and particularly with its vision of open space. "Superblocks are wonderful things," Mayer said during a radio interview with NYCHA's Ira Robbins, "because you keep the traffic out, the kids can run around." However, they caused two problems. First, their interior grounds were often inert and lifeless. A "feeling of too much incidentalness about landscaping, about the internal street structure," had simply left project grounds as open space without "life and vitality." Second, as the social workers had discovered, the superblock's neighborhood-unit ideals had overwhelmed and blotted out the surrounding community. Its blank open space was entirely disconnected from the surrounding street life. Mayer believed that public housing should not be treated as a separate "enclave" or a municipal afterthought. In fact, he thought that public housing could serve as the key to proper urban and regional development and as a source for replacing urban "anomie" with "local democratic action." But those possibilities, contingent upon a number of technical and social issues, were impossible without an effort to erase public housing's "separation from the neighborhood" and make it "more a culmination of the neighborhood—something that belongs to the neighborhood as well as to the people who live in [public] housing."[46]

Mayer believed that this goal could be reached through the design of project open space. The key was to strike a balance between establishing the identity of the project space and offering an invitation to the larger neighborhood. Well-crafted public spaces both welcomed outsiders and, "in the face of the city's overwhelming anonymity," delivered a sense of identity to project residents. His designs for Jefferson Houses and Franklin Plaza were intended to offer "some sense of entrance or symbolic enclosure that says 'here we are.'" These entrances led to what he called, "in quotation marks," an internal pedestrian "Main Street" that, as "in small towns and in villages," provided gathering places, recreation, planned events, and a "festive" atmosphere. The Main Street idea accomplished two goals. First, it preserved "the best essence of *street*" by creating an environment for spontaneous mixing and planned events without the usual danger of traffic. If carried out with some style and grace, Mayer claimed, this effort could link "the development to its adjacent world and transmute the so-frequent enclave feeling into a feeling of being part of a larger world." Second, with the right kinds of spaces for meeting, greeting, and talking, it could supply the built infrastructure needed to incubate "small and fairly intimate sub-communities" within the larger project culture. This would bring a sense of much-needed "intimacy" to project life and offset the difficulty of creating "'face-to-face' neighborhood contacts" in the anonymous, mass world of public housing. Ultimately, Mayer's vision of superblock villages hoped to provide "a neighborhood climax, not a neighborhood vacuum."[47]

At Jefferson Houses, Mayer created a multipurpose landscape called the Gala East Harlem Plaza. At first intended to be only a playground, Mayer eventually designed a plaza complex that combined playgrounds, a bandstand, picnic areas, a fountain, and a children's sprinkler with a number of removed, quiet sitting areas. Built as a series of clustered circles grouped around the central fountain, wading pool, and bandstand, the scheme offered informal groups of what *Architectural Forum* called "scalloped seating shells" rather than the usual rows of benches along project walks. These provided the sense of intimacy that Mayer desired, while the concrete furniture and metal light fixtures and umbrellas made for durable, if somewhat unyielding fittings. The East Harlem Plaza, as it was more informally called, debuted in May 1960 and soon began hosting cultural events and performances. Mayer often compared the East Harlem Plaza to Lincoln Center, remarking that all of the citizens of New York deserved the "decentralization of excellence" in design that neighborhood-level versions of the massive urban renewal–supported arts center would deliver. He hoped, he said, to have created "something exciting visually and useful functionally."[48]

Mayer got the chance to realize the full scope of his ideas soon after the East Harlem Plaza opened, when the social workers helped him to secure the contract to design the landscaping for Franklin Plaza. Franklin Plaza, 1,635 apartments on 14 acres between 106th and 109th streets and First and Third avenues, was the first realization of the social workers' efforts to offset the deepening economic ghettoization of East Harlem by attracting more private, middle-income housing to the area. The project was initially planned as a middle-income, city-aided NYCHA development called the Benjamin Franklin Houses, but in 1960, while it was already under construction, NYCHA agreed to sell it to a private "co-oporation" created by Union Settlement and a group of local clergy and businesspeople. This group, organized by the EHCCP, managed it as a private co-op under the New York State Limited-Profit Housing Companies, or Mitchell-Lama, law. By the early 1960s, attracting middle-income families to

You are cordially invited

Free Community Arts, Crafts, Photography Show

East Harlem Plaza, 114th between 2nd and 3rd

Sunday, June 10, 1962, 2 p.m. to 5 p.m.

Rain Date, Next Clear Sunday

Sponsored by The Cultural Committee of the

East Harlem Council for Community Planning

7.9. The East Harlem Plaza was Albert Mayer's first attempt to remake the blank open spaces of the project yards. He and the East Harlem social workers hoped that the plaza would provide a space in which East Harlemites could come together across racial and ethnic lines to participate in events like the 1962 arts and crafts show advertised here. Manuscripts, Archives and Rare Books Division, Schomburg Center for Research in Black Culture, New York Public Library, Astor, Lenox and Tilden Foundations.

the middle of East Harlem was not easy, so the social workers and the management company used the project design as an amenity. Unfortunately, they had no opportunity to control the project's overall design profile. Its 14 20-story, modified-slab towers were standard-issue NYCHA fare and looked, as the *Herald Tribune* put it, like the "sad afterthoughts of Mies van der Rohe." But Mayer's design offered a chance to enliven the grounds and make them an attraction not only for the new residents of Franklin Plaza, but for the surrounding neighborhood as well.[49]

At Franklin Plaza, Mayer had the entire grounds at his disposal, with ample room to develop his Main Street idea. In place of the blank, unvaried openness of the usual project yard, Mayer offered a dense, varied landscape that tried to translate the spontaneous possibilities of the urban streetscape into a new kind of superblock environment. He began by bisecting the grounds

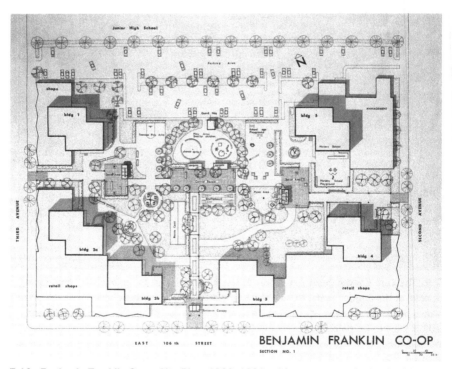

7.10. Benjamin Franklin Co-op Site Plan, 1960–1961, with open space design by Albert Mayer. Mayer created a complex new landscape featuring a series of different spaces linked by pathways. The central avenue bisecting the site from east to west (*left to right*) functioned as a kind of Main Street for the project. Union Settlement Association Records, Rare Book and Manuscript Library, Columbia University in the City of New York.

with a central avenue running east to west across the site. This avenue was broad and straight, but not directly continuous. It was interrupted and slightly redirected by several open squares, which he called "social areas," and then bisected at its midpoint in each block by a formal walkway from the south leading to 106th Street. The central avenue formed the axis around which clustered a complex series of interrelated squares, age-specific playgrounds, lawns, tree groves, picnic areas, ball courts, and smaller pergola-shaded plazas, all connected by variously direct and winding pathways. Moving through the grounds gave the sense of an unfolding experience, a series of discrete but related encounters or possibilities, enlivened by what Mayer called a "counterpoint between activity centers, quiet areas, and green planted areas." Mixing areas whose uses were programmed and those that were open to interpretation, he provided places for gathering, playing, and meeting, as well as spots for solitary or intimate sitting.[50]

Mayer's designs won accolades and awards in architecture and planning circles, and a number of commentators gave them credit for providing new centers of community life in East Harlem. At the same time, the work he and the social workers did in the neighborhood inspired an outpouring of similar

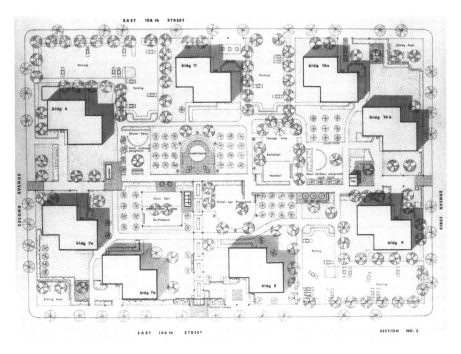

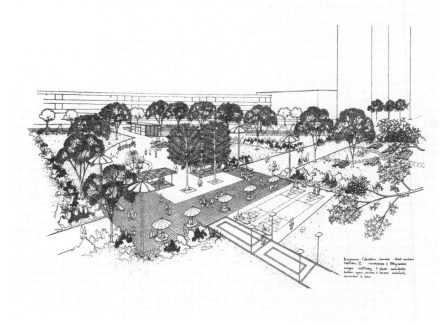

7.11. Benjamin Franklin Co-op Plaza Design Views, 1960–1961, open space design by Albert Mayer. These renderings of views from building windows show the intimate scale Mayer tried to foster within the vast open spaces of mass housing. Union Settlement Association Records, Rare Book and Manuscript Library, Columbia University in the City of New York.

efforts at humanizing public housing and restoring economic diversity to the neighborhood. Mayer proposed a similar open space redesign for Washington Houses, the architects Pomerance and Breines offered their own version of the community square in 1965 at Carver Houses, and in 1963 the Lavanburg Foundation funded an ambitious blueprint for modular, mass-produced "village" or "commons" plans to be installed in project grounds citywide.

Meanwhile, Franklin Plaza was the first of several middle-income, infill, and urban renewal projects that came to East Harlem over the next 10 years, including 1199 Plaza, a 12-acre Mitchell-Lama development sponsored by the Drug and Hospital Workers Union that went up above 107th Street along the river, and Metro North Plaza, first designed for a site between 99th Street and 104th Street between the river and Second Avenue. Hired by a local group calling itself the Metro North Citizens Committee, Mayer's partners, Whittlesey and Conklin, designed a site-specific rehabilitation that used spot demolition, vest-pocket parks, and selective building to open up the tenement blocks but not level them. Their designs made Mayer's ideas the guiding ideals of an entire project; they were an explicit attempt to preserve the social and built infrastructure of the tenement streetscape while upgrading the housing stock and providing new amenities. Unfortunately, the project ran into difficulties, and only a reduced version was built on the two blocks of the site that fronted the river.[51]

Elizabeth Wood's 1961 book, *Housing Design: A Social Theory*, gave this emerging set of ideals an influential manifesto. Like Mayer and the social workers, she thought it unwise to abandon large-scale planning and dense urban environments, but if new projects were to "compete with the suburbs for social desirability," designers would have to offer a "richer and more fulfilling environment." Most open space design in high-rise projects, she said, prevented or minimized "accidental or casual communication between people." In order to encourage informal contacts between strangers and neighbors—the sort of design for "social structure" out of which tenant organizations might grow— she encouraged the implementation of four interrelated, productive design principles that echoed Mayer's and Perkins and Will's efforts but turned them toward the practical goal of establishing safe projects. The four principles were design for increased visibility so that people could see and be seen; design for loitering; design for activity spaces for informal adult groups; and design for the planned presence of people so that informal social controls would take hold. Wood also urged policymakers to allow more commercial establishments onto project grounds, including, somewhat controversially, "a native counterpart to the English pub." Wood observed that housing administrators and the "critical public" wanted their "poor to be pure" and "protected from temptation," but that

7.12. Franklin Plaza from above, showing Mayer's designs completed. The project was built by NYCHA, but the social workers and their allies, fearing that the influx of public housing was making East Harlem into a ghetto, convinced the authority to sell the project to a neighborhood co-op association. New York City Housing Authority Records, La Guardia and Wagner Archives.

didn't change the fact that "drinking beer in company" was a popular form of recreation and a prime source of informal social contacts. Despite—or maybe because of—this advice, Wood's pamphlet attracted a good deal of attention. NYCHA even bought copies for its design staff and project architects. Eventually, over a number of years, these efforts to bring the "street" and neighborhood back into the project made their way into official public housing design strategies nationwide, completely unseating tower-in-the-park modernism with its superblocks and slab buildings in favor of smaller low-rise and townhouse

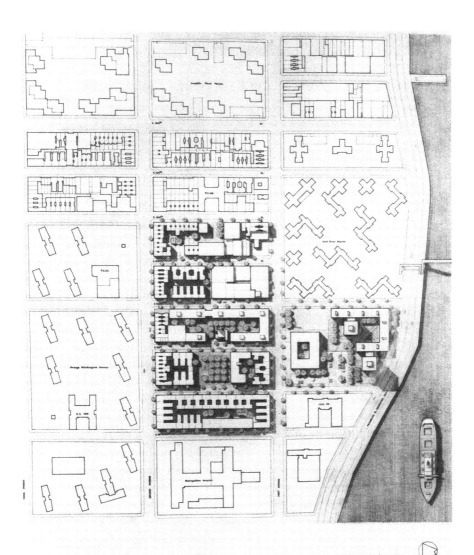

PROPOSED REDEVELOPMENT
METRO NORTH

WHITTLESEY & CONKLIN Architects & Planners
October 1965   Scale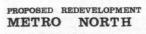

7.13. Proposed Metro North Redevelopment, by Whittlesey and Conklin, October 1965. In keeping with the various critiques of urban renewal and modernist urbanism leveled by the mid-1960s, the Metro North plan offered a more neighborhood-friendly design, including spot demolition and rehabilitation, vest-pocket parks, and no street closures. Due to financial problems, the entire eastern portion was never built. Only the block by the river saw the light of day. Union Settlement Association Records, Rare Book and Manuscript Library, Columbia University in the City of New York.

developments with rear courts fronting on streets and sidewalks. The roots of this turnaround are in East Harlem.[52]

Authority and Culture in the New Village Superblocks

These groups flowed to the Plaza, each Monday night, with regularity, in a holiday mood. . . . In the jostling open air crowd, jests and gallantries were exchanged. It was evident that here was a sense of belonging, quite different than being swallowed up in the dark cavern of a movie theater, or escaping for a brief time in the 20 inch screen in the confines of one's apartment.
—Sam Rand of the JWJCC, on concerts at the East Harlem Plaza, 1962

If these efforts to build the neighborhood and the street back into public housing received a lot of attention among professional urbanists—ultimately laying the groundwork for a culture-wide rethinking of tower-in-the-park public housing and renewal ideals—it was somewhat less clear how they were received by public housing residents themselves. Albert Mayer and the social workers did know that East Harlem Plaza and the grounds at Franklin Plaza saw active and prolonged use by a cross-section of the community; from their periodic observations, it is clear that they thought the spaces were enjoyed and properly used. For instance, William Kirk noticed the "innumerable small semi-autonomous areas" at Franklin Plaza, with their sense of "independence, if not quasi-privacy." Mayer was gratified that his designs "were being used by those for whom they had been intended, and in much the same way as visualized." He hoped that some of the "small kids" he saw—a number of whom were "quite poorly dressed"—had been welcomed in the middle-income project and worried that there was some "ethnic concentration" among the various gatherings. In general, the social workers interpreted the use of these new spaces first, like Mayer, as confirmation of their initial impulse to return the vitality of street life to project grounds, and second, as evidence that their efforts were beginning to undo the alienation and anomie bred by the mass way of life in the public landscape.[53]

This was particularly true at the East Harlem Plaza, where the social workers hoped that their cultural programming would both bring "antagonistic groups" together and give project tenants some sense of identity among the mass society of public housing. They saw the plaza as a space in which to forge explicitly multicultural and neighborly bonds between previously disparate and potentially hostile peoples. The plaza was "a place where neighbors with different cultural background[s] and heritage[s] would sit together, plan together and enjoy the cultural programs representing the many forms of art—music, dance, songs and paintings that have contributed to America by the vast variety of peoples who settled here." They hoped that it would facilitate the sharing of what they called "both our common bonds and our differences" in an effort to "live together in harmony and goodwill." The plaza fostered a sense of community belonging, a feeling that, as Mayer put it, "this is our part of town." At the same time, they saw the plaza as a source of individuation, a way to restore what Mayer called an imperiled "sense of identity" or wholeness for public housing residents faced with "the city's overwhelming anonymity."[54]

During the early '6os, the JWJCC put on an annual summer series of concerts and performances at the plaza, bringing opera, ballet, symphonic music, Italian folk dances, African drumming and dancers, and folk singers to East Harlem. Like the little Lincoln Center Mayer imagined, the plaza typically favored high art and folk authenticity over popular or commercial music. Sam Rand, the JWJCC's summer concert series program director, carefully monitored these performances, interpreting audience reaction through the lens of contemporary social science thinking on the role of the arts in a time of mass media and mass culture. In fact, he explicitly credited the power of the arts to undo the forces of alienation and anomie that he and his colleagues found in both project living and the larger mass society the projects seemed to mirror and perpetuate. Quoting from East Harlem Project literature, Rand was pleased to see that audiences drawn from "lonely, rootless, apathetic, and hostile" project populations, those "strangers" that "rattle around 13 hygienic developments," appeared to react with a "proper attitude" to high culture. "Despite the saturation bombing" of mass cultural influences, these audiences "ran contrary to the prevailing zeitgeist and came to see, hear and wonder at performances of a high cultural level." Even with the "continuous bombardment of the vast industry selling Elvises," which kept teenagers "from the competition of more specialized appeals," a ballet performance had the audience "as transfixed as a Wagnerian audience during a performance of the Ring."[55]

In some of the audiences, Rand found that special character he called "the hush of quiet contemplative communion with the divine life." In this "communion," he could see evidence of both healthy individuation and increased communal fellowship. On the one hand, the audiences were in touch with what José Ortega y Gasset—whom Rand quoted at length in an epigraph to his report—called the "faculty of wonder" that, while "refused to your football 'fan,'" leads "the intellectual man through life in the perpetual ecstasy of the visionary." On the other hand, even as plaza audiences were becoming a gathering of visionary intellectuals, they were also discovering what Rand called "a sense of belonging," an experience he hoped would supplant the less salubrious influence of "the dark cavern of a movie theater" or "the 20 inch screen in the confines of one's apartment." East Harlem Plaza, Rand claimed, was undoing both the isolating and massifying effects of the alienated world of public housing, restoring individual identity and community spirit to souls damaged by what his colleagues had called the "mass way of life." As the little Lincoln Center Mayer had envisioned, the Plaza appeared both democratic and high-minded, a simultaneous source of collective belonging and cultural instruction for neighborhood residents disoriented by the mass culture of urban renewal and commercial entertainments.[56]

Rand did notice some resistance to his cultural programming. Audience members, he recognized, brought particular "social and cultural context[s]" to their plaza experiences, but rather than interpreting these as evidence of autonomous alternatives to his vision, he treated them as contained anomalies, "improper" attitudes that the plaza and those who accepted it could incorporate or smooth out. For instance, some parents remarked that, as Rand put it, even if they "didn't dig this high class music," they still pushed their kids forward to, as one was overheard to say, "get down front and get that good music." When a "man in a fez" came through the crowd telling everyone to leave before they got "poisoned by this junk" and to "throw the 'whites, the hell out of here,'" he was confronted by Teddy, a "long-time member of Johnson Center and former leader of one of the neighborhood gangs." When the man in the fez said he was "going back to Africa to escape this contamination," Teddy defused the situation with a quick joke—"Man, you don't even have the fare to Staten Island"— and told him that, as Rand put it, "folks loved the Plaza, and that's where they planned to stay."[57]

East Harlem Plaza served as confirmation of the social workers' conception of their role in helping East Harlem. By the mid-1960s, with the new plaza, new open spaces, new middle-income housing, new schools, new community-friendly urban renewal projects, and a host of other improvements, the social workers believed they had served as midwives to a small renaissance in East Harlem. "When deep commitment is coupled with local initiative," the EHCCP said in an announcement for a 1965 exhibit called "The Changing Face of East Harlem," "physical improvement brings with it social vitality and growth."[58]

At the heart of this optimism was the sense that what they had understood to be wrong with East Harlem *was* what was truly wrong with it. There was still much work to do, but they had found a means to undo the alienation and rootlessness that plagued the new public housing spaces. They felt they had found a way to restore the tissues of identity and connectivity severed by the overweening universalism of Cold War era planning and architecture. They had undone their earlier faith in the promise of modern city-rebuilding ideals and found a language and shape for a new kind of urbanism, one that would address the faults their previous faith had obscured. Of course, at the same time, they believed that their reforms were helping public housing to achieve the original postwar goals they had imagined for it—providing a means through which those with low income could, as they had put it, "enjoy the social, physical, and economic benefits of an affluent society." If they sensed that public housing in the age of urban renewal was little more than a dumping ground for "surplus populations" unable to be incorporated into the postwar consumer economy, they still hoped that their reforms and programs could provide the physical and social infrastructure to withstand that tendency.

The social workers also intended to attract a new middle class to East Harlem. Bringing a measure of middle-class influence back to the area, they believed, would provide examples for emulation in both culture and income. This, they blithely assumed, would forge a connection between public housing residents and the larger society, and also restore economic diversity and growth to the area. The height of this effort was a campaign to attract buyers at Franklin Plaza, which symbolically relocated the co-op out of East Harlem and into what they called "The New Upper East Side." Their map of East Harlem based on this new vision offered a new geography for the neighborhood. "The New Upper East Side" put Franklin Plaza (between 106th and 109th streets) at the heart of a neighborhood that began at 90th Street rather than the traditional southern border of 96th Street and went only as far north as 116th Street rather than 125th Street, the usual northern frontier. Symbolically resituating East Harlem as a northern precinct of the Upper East Side not only suited the co-op's pragmatic goals by making Franklin Plaza seem less isolated from familiar middle-class regions of the city, but it also expressed the social workers' larger ambitions for the area's revitalization by placing the plaza at the center of a world of new improvements and programs about to launch or already under way. The new map was a form of visual assurance, a document that suggested both how revitalization had already proceeded and would go forward and who was responsible for the upgrade. Of course, this surety was also evidence of a growing rift between the social workers and the people of the neighborhood they served.[59]

Preston Wilcox once remarked that the goal of the East Harlem Project was to give the people of the neighborhood the resources to represent themselves, to help them create a local system that would confront the "distant social system which has traditionally pre-ordained their destinies." But by the early to mid-1960s, the social workers were finding that they themselves were increasingly identified with that dictatorial "distant social system." There had always been an imperfect match between the middle-class social work organizations and their clientele. But in a neighborhood that was becoming poorer and more black and Puerto Rican, the Anglo-led social work, community center, and settlement house network was increasingly seen as "the establishment," bent on pacifying and disciplining unrest rather than championing it. Echoing a common critique of his profession, Wilcox

The New Upper East Side and the Franklin Plaza Cooperative

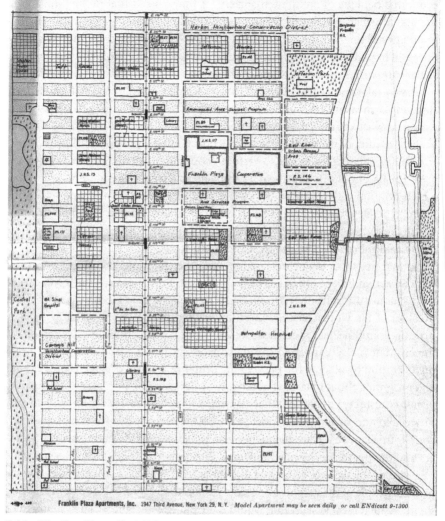

7.14. "The New Upper East Side and the Franklin Plaza Cooperative." This map, intended to help attract buyers to the Franklin Plaza Co-op, symbolically resituated East Harlem as a northern quadrant of the Upper East Side in the hope of making the co-op more attractive to middle-class buyers. Union Settlement Association Records, Rare Book and Manuscript Library, Columbia University in the City of New York.

said that social workers too often saw "their jobs as a sedative for social ills rather than a good hard push for change." For a growing number of activists and community organizers, Wilcox included, the traditional focus on individual casework and family therapy had little to offer a world in need of massive intervention to reverse the spread of poverty and deindustrialization.[60]

In truth, the social workers were themselves divided, simultaneously offering the active, participatory vision of the East Harlem Project, the paternalist vision of the cultural programming at East Harlem Plaza, and the rebranding of the neighborhood as the New Upper East Side. Even the East Harlem Project never intended to organize East Harlemites to mount explicitly political challenges to the distant social system. The organizers tried instead to encourage local capacity, motivation, and organization for efforts to attract government services and attention. Their efforts were an attempt to encourage public housing residents to join a bureaucratic, organizational age, a way to give them the tools and confidence to participate in the distant social system and feel a sense of belonging amid an alienating technocracy. This was a significant step away from individual casework, but in the context of deepening poverty and growing urban unrest, the distinction began to pale. Like other settlement house workers around the country in these years, the East Harlem workers were finding that their traditional attempts to direct and manage the upward mobility and assimilation of their clients—efforts, really, to control errant and antisocial tendencies—had not entirely dissipated with their newer interest in cross-class and multiracial tenant organization. Ultimately, the long-time class and cultural divides, as well as deepening generational and racial splits between the social workers and the neighborhood, began to assume as much importance as matters of professional social work strategy. The social workers tended to favor order over disruption, preferring what they saw as the proper attitude and a positive spirit of uplift to the seemingly rowdy conviviality of working-class popular culture. Even their attempt to bring the energy of the street back into the sterile project grounds— and it's clear that they were serious in this effort—resulted in new environments that, while complex and engaging, were still contained and canned versions of urban spaces. The fact that Union Settlement had been in the neighborhood since 1896 counted against the social workers as much as for them. Some residents, Cayo-Sexton reported, saw them as out of touch and aloof, "alien emissaries of the middle class world," or a "cabal" that stifled development and progress in an increasingly black and Puerto Rican working-class neighborhood. Many young East Harlemites, particularly, saw them as untrustworthy, "do-gooder" nuisances, or "rat-fink types" with nothing to offer. To the rising generation, the neighborhood was no longer the social workers' East Harlem. It was theirs, and they called it Spanish Harlem or, increasingly, El Barrio.[61]

Of course, all establishments, as Patricia Cayo-Sexton observed of East Harlem's political elites, "spawn those who will unseat them." With its emphasis on community participation, the East Harlem Project and its better-known downtown counterpart, Mobilization for Youth, had been early inspirations for the War on Poverty; by the mid-1960s, federal infrastructure and money were helping to undo the social workers' direct influence over the fate of the neighborhood. The power of the social workers' settlement house and community center network was diminishing, making way for a younger generation of explicitly Puerto Rican community organizers and politicians intent on representing themselves. These new politicos were rising in the Democratic Party, establishing new community groups, and tapping into federal funds to start antipoverty projects. They were also shifting away from direct engagement with the physical environment of public housing. With some important exceptions, the groups that struggled with each other to get federal dollars and to represent East Harlem in the mid-1960s, organizations like Massive Economic Neighborhood Development (originally backed by the social workers), the East Harlem Tenants Council, and the grassroots, explicitly Puerto Rican groups like the Real Great Society and the Young Lords, were less interested in planning or public housing issues and more interested in using political power to contest poverty, racism, deindustrialization, and underdevelopment. Some, like the Real Great Society's Urban Planning Studio, protested urban renewal and offered grassroots "advocacy planning," but they were more likely to view conditions in public housing as a symptom rather than a cause of the neighborhood's problems.[62]

By the mid-1960s, public housing had, for better or worse, done its work in East Harlem. A few small infill projects would be built over the next 20 years, but the last of the NYCHA towers went up in 1965. Despite their support for low-income housing, the social workers' efforts had helped to slow and then stop the surge of public projects. Their initial skepticism about the impact of the public landscape had been confirmed by a host of other commentary in the years since they first went into Washington Houses. By the 1960s and '70s, there was no shortage of dismay at the way the dream of better housing had gone wrong. The projects were seen as more dangerous and more crime-ridden than nearby tenement blocks; they were seen as prisons for irredeemable peoples; they were the new vertical ghettos. "Big brick housing projects were all over the place," says the narrator of Piri Thomas's autobiographical novel, *Down These Mean Streets,* upon his return to El Barrio after years in prison; they were "big, alien, intruders" that were "mutilating my turf." In 1960, James Baldwin wrote in *Esquire* that the projects were "lumped all over Harlem, colorless, bleak, high, and revolting." The projects, he reported, were "hated." They were an "an insult to the meanest intelligence." They revealed "unbearably, the real attitude of the white world" toward the people of Harlem, providing "additional proof of how thoroughly the white world despised them." They were evidence of "liberal innocence—or cynicism, which comes out in practice as much the same thing." They were symbols of an arrogance and naïveté that revealed the white world's basic inhumanity toward the black and brown peoples in their midst.[63]

And yet, true as that verdict seems from afar, it is not at all clear that the projects were or are hated, particularly in New York. Many still view public housing as an intrusion on older neighborhoods, or feel unsafe and ill at ease in inhumane towers. Most public housing residents still must cope with crime, drugs, and vandalism. However, into the '70s, polls of public housing residents, both in East Harlem and across the nation, showed some appreciation for the quality of their housing conditions or indicated their feeling that public housing was an improvement over their previous residences. Even now, according to ethnographer Judith Noemi Freidenberg, despite the fear of robberies and muggings, public housing is still often considered the best place to live in East Harlem. Public housing has consistently ranked, in the eyes of those forced to make such choices, as a small but significant step up from the tenements of the neighborhood. Persistent shortages of affordable housing have kept waiting lists for NYCHA housing long, and the authority, despite its troubles, has a reputation for being well managed. New York projects have also been improved by the participatory politics of tenant activism. While many New Yorkers and other Americans have abandoned the idea of public housing, generations of residents have been able, sometimes, to make communities out of places that seemed to outsiders to be landscapes of alienation.[64]

In the end, the most significant effect of the social workers' campaign to bring the neighborhood and the street back into public housing was its influence on the movement to reform the city-remaking visions at the heart of urban renewal. If many accounts of the process by which modern planning ideals were reformed and given a more postmodern, community-oriented, and human-centric profile credit the transforming effect of Jane Jacobs's 1961 book, *The Death and Life of Great American Cities*, the story of East Harlem offers a significant wrinkle on that familiar tale. It is often forgotten that Jacobs's ideas were shaped by the struggle with public housing in East Harlem. In fact, it would not be too extreme to say that the East Harlemites' movement to remake public housing lies at the heart of her book and the effects it undoubtedly had on modernist urbanism. The intellectual and social movement to remake modern urbanism and to imagine cities again from the perspective of streets and stoops rather than towers and plazas had one of its sources not in a book or in any one inspired genius, but in the process by which a neighborhood like East Harlem worked not simply to resist or dismantle modern idealism, but to adapt it to the needs of its people. Nostalgia for lost community in East Harlem was funneled into an effort to manipulate change and modernization for the better and to make the dream of better housing for all both a reality and a success. While Ellen Lurie, Jane Jacobs, Preston Wilcox, and the other East Harlemites grappled with the new mass way of life in public housing, tensions over urban renewal reached their height across the city. The insurgency against public housing and urban renewal would only continue to grow as Title I projects displaced more and more people, swelled public housing waiting lists, taxed already impoverished tenement neighborhoods, and replaced an older world of horizontal affiliations and intimate, cross-class connections with new modern landscapes for a white-collar, cosmopolitan city. By the late-1960s, urban renewal would be all but undone as the reigning vision for urban development.

CONCLUSION
UNDER THE SIGN OF
THE WHITE CROSS

What is marked for death in New York? The little, the old, the malfunctioning; the decayed, the unsightly, the verminous; the impractically spacious and the intimately charming; the unexpected, the irregular, the unorthodox. All these are doomed by the inexorable law of economics: the more valuable the land, the more use must be made of it. Against this no other value has power, least of all sentiment and those smaller human pleasures which have sustained man through his immemorial woes.
—Marya Mannes, *The New York I Know*, 1961

At the end of the 1950s, the writer and arts critic Marya Mannes set out to capture in prose the New York she knew. From the refined perch of her pre-war apartment above Central Park West, she delivered a series of biting essays for the magazine the *Reporter*, surveying the changing moods and mores of Manhattan life.

Collected in a book called *The New York I Know*, the essays charted her mounting dismay over the city's seemingly inexorable decline. She took in the life of her own motley West 70s, where the few "decent people" left hoped that urban renewal at Lincoln Square would "clean up some of the dirt." She visited the rarefied stretches of Park Avenue and walked among the "shodiness [*sic*] and vulgarity" of Broadway. She lamented the increase of "violence" and "perversity" in Central Park and the "joyless self-consciousness" animating her former bohemian haunts in the Village; she tried to listen in on the "impenetrable" chatter of polyglot "City Voices" and took to the island's rivers and harbors in an effort to put some watery distance between herself and the spreading stench of "corruption," "decay," and "venality."

Mannes was an unapologetic mandarin whose parents, Leopold Mannes and Clara Damrosch Mannes, founders of the Mannes College of Music, had given her a classical education liberally salted with visits to the Continent for study and pleasure. An equal opportunity scold, she blamed the city's ongoing fall equally on the cloistered rich, who could "afford to cushion themselves with money" against urban troubles, and on the all-too-visible poor, those black and brown migrants from the South and Puerto Rico whose mounting rage over their lot seemed to her to stain the streets with ugliness. She bemoaned the city's easy embrace of "the limitless pursuit of financial profit" as much as the way that "street children," with their "poor diction and almost total reliance on obscenity" did not so much "speak" as "rape." But she saved her most potent stew of bile and sorrow for the surging tide of demolition and rebuilding that had swept the city in the years since the war.

"New York," she wrote, "is in the throes of the greatest building boom in its history, a convulsion equal to the wrinkling of the earth's skin by interior forces, a transformation so rapid and so immense that the native of New York becomes a stranger in a new city, all landmarks fled." For Mannes, Claude Lévi-Strauss's intimations of doom had proven prophetic. Everywhere, uptown and down, she was haunted by the universal sign of imminent demolition: slapdash white crosses painted across the dark, sooty windows of doomed tenements, brown-stones, old houses, and shops. So much of the old New York she had once known was going under the wrecking ball: "the little restaurant in the side street," the "shoemaker's two blocks up," anything "impractically spacious" or "intimately charming," and, most of all, "the unexpected, the irregular, the unorthodox." "The windows of all," she wrote, "are crossed with white."

Of course, she welcomed the *idea* of slum clearance. In their race to "scrape out . . . places long since unfit for human habitation," the wreckers were opening "great spaces . . . less like a war-blasted city than like a drawing of deep breath" and granting "the balm of distance" to New Yorkers "forever bullied by the imme-diate." Just around the corner from her apartment, "the great space cleared for Lincoln Center was filled with promise, where each could imagine the future." All this, she thought, was in the spirit of the era; it meant "excitement and thrust and power and plenty." It was "impossible to be unmoved by it, or unconscious of the immense will and effort and talent" mustered by the wreckers and build-ers. And yet, the more clearing and building the city endured and the closer that seemingly guaranteed future appeared to be, the more the sense of promise seemed to recede.

"The gain," she thought, "is matched by a definite loss." There was, of course, the plain fact that most of the new building was for the rich. But loss echoed also in the very shape and form of the new city rising amid the old. The brick for-ests of public housing clustered all along the East River shore were "grim cities within themselves." Taking the doubts of the East Harlem social workers to their limit, she found "something not only wrong but sinister in these arbitrary group-ings of human life," calling them "premature tombs in which the human spirit is confined in a rigid and graceless coffin of convenience, identically ventilated by identical windows with its legion of neighbors, refused the small benedictions of decoration or difference." Even in the bright, clean, luxury towers, her "appreci-ation of the new techniques of living, the functional gain, is matched by a sense of poverty." They struck her as being "like filing cabinets for the human species, one to a drawer, equipped with everything needed for living except that mysterious marriage of man and environment called mood." In the new Manhattan, she said, "space has become mechanical rather than mystical."

Ultimately, it was the fundamental "*feeling* of New York" that urban renewal and related upheavals of the urban crust were altering. The "excitement" of Manhattan was "diversity." The "optical" serendipity of mismatched building styles thrown together in the cityscape, the unexpected conglomerations of shops, houses, and workplaces—"this planless variety, this incongruity of accident"— these were New York's singular charm, but were now "steadily threatened by the new homogeneity rising about us everywhere." "For years," she concluded, "change will be the order of Manhattan, upheaval the climate of all New Yorkers." The change weighed heaviest on the old. The "shifting of ground under their feet is spiritual as well as physical" because they lived with the past. "They are part of the doomed buildings, and every attack on these is an assault on them. They feel the cataract of crosses on their eyes, and the blind and empty rooms leave their hearts cavernous and deserted. And when the bulldozers finally grind the old houses to dust, their bones are mixed with it."[1]

Mannes's sorrow song was an early and particularly acidic entry in a genre of complaint that reached its apogee in the mid-1960s and lasted through the '70s. She anticipated the themes and moods of Richard J. Whalen's *A City Destroying Itself,* Norman Mailer's "Why Are We in New York?" and Jason Epstein's "The Last Days of New York"—works that announced New York's irretrievable decline into "urban crisis." But Mannes captures particularly well the intermingled exhilaration and dismay that years of city rebuilding had brought to New York. She offers a vivid—if selective and decidedly elitist—depiction of the "structure of feeling" with which many New Yorkers greeted the age of urban renewal. On the one hand, it was hope, power, newness, the promise of making New York the capital of the world. On the other, and increasingly, it seemed to spell only loss, ruin, and devastation. Her musings bundled the diverse strands of resistance to urban renewal into an impressionistic whole. She captured the sense of tragedy echoing in both the vanished cityscape defended by neighborhood resistance and the spaces of the new superblocks and towers the social workers and new residents struggled to understand. Her lament prepares us to understand how the resistance to urban renewal born at Stuyvesant Town, developed at Lincoln Square, and refined in East Harlem broke out everywhere across the city during the late 1950s and early '60s. New Yorkers of all stripes, most not possessed of Mannes's particular combination of nostalgia, sophisticated racism, and haughty wisdom, began to question the ideals of the planners and renewal officials. Within a few years, urban renewal as both idea and practice would be entirely unseated, no longer the commonsense vision for remaking cities.[2]

Of course, New Yorkers had long noticed the loss of the old city. As early as 1948, one *Times* reporter had recorded his mild sorrow at the "Lost Streets" resulting from the "facelifting operations all over town." The new towers and superblocks, the writer reflected, "pull out of shape" a "pattern of New York" fixed in many citizens' intimate memories of place. For instance:

> a whole row of streets between Twenty-third and Fourteenth lost all of each of them that lay east of First Avenue. They were swallowed up in the towering brickwork and abundant open spaces of Stuyvesant Town and Peter Cooper Village, where many soldiers of our most recent war, now returned to civil employment, are raising families for whatever may happen while we wait for the Parliament of Man to put wars out of business.

The arrival of the United Nations in Manhattan seemed to ease the trauma of losing familiar streets. "All this is progress," the reporter concluded, "but the old friends will be missed." A decade later, the reaction to those sorts of losses was hardly ever so sanguine. The impositions and dislocations of clearance and modern superblock-and-tower rebuilding had unleashed a storm of criticism and the first intellectual and practical revisions of the urban renewal vision.[3]

In the years just after the Lincoln Square controversy and the early activity of the East Harlem critics, this spreading turmoil first made itself known in the political arena, where the mounting tide of controversy over Robert Moses's Title I practices was forcing Mayor Robert Wagner to reevaluate the city's urban renewal programs. Throughout 1959, enterprising reporters continued to ferret out new and embarrassing revelations about the way that Moses's renewal infrastructure delivered contracts, favors, and profits to developers linked to Democratic Party insiders and members of Moses's own renewal staff. As these stories spread from paper to paper and to the front pages, they became harder and harder for Wagner and Moses to ignore. Moses insisted that all the undue and irresponsible criticism of Title I would scare away potential sponsors and jeopardize the city's efforts to continue slum clearance and housing programs. By the summer of 1959, he was calling Title I a "dead duck," hoping to scare liberal critics back into the fold.

Wagner stood by his slum clearance chief, but liberal reformers, tenant activists, and politicians of all parties continued to raise the alarm. Congressman John Lindsay called for a congressional investigation of Moses's Committee on Slum Clearance. Tenant resistance at a proposed renewal site in the Gramercy Park area—along with revelations of favoritism in the choosing of a state assemblyman as a project sponsor—forced the city to abandon the plan. Financial scandal doomed the proposed Soundview project in the Bronx. Resistance by local businesspeople and settlement house workers killed the Delancey Street Title I project. Resistance around the Bellevue Hospital renewal site forced Moses to offer vest-pocket housing rather than full clearance. The Citizens Housing and Planning Council still supported urban renewal, but recommended a series of procedural reforms, including more comprehensive planning, a centralized relocation bureau, better screening of sponsors, and better design. All across the city, community groups of various stripes sprang up to protest clearance.[4]

Samuel Spiegel, a sympathetic state assemblyman, collected the grievances of tenants in his 1959 book, *The Forgotten Man in Housing*. Site tenants, he wrote, were "distressed at the thought of severing their communal and social ties." Their plight had achieved epic proportions, ranking with the postwar refugee crises in Europe. Those facing the bulldozer were, "in effect, living in a 'displaced persons camp,'" awaiting evacuation and relocation. Noting the growing resistance to clearance in neighborhoods across the city ever since the furor at Lincoln Square, he warned his fellow politicians and city officials that it was not the controversy, but the callous treatment of site tenants itself that threatened the city's ability to provide new housing. "They cannot be easily placated. They will not passively submit to eviction merely because someone cries 'Make way for Progress.' Is this progress?"[5]

Tenant radicals from across the city, united by their similar struggles against clearance and renewal, came together in 1959 to form the Metropolitan Council on Housing, an umbrella organization that advocated for tenants' rights, rent control, and community participation in neighborhood renewal. Harris Present was the keynote speaker at its opening meeting. During the 1960s and '70s, Met Council, as it was called, would be instrumental in helping a new generation of "advocacy planners" to win a formal role for communities in neighborhood development. This new movement's first major challenge came at Cooper Square on the Lower East Side. Cooper Square was one of Moses's original Title I projects, but troubles locating a sponsor had forced him to delay its start for years. By 1956, Moses secured a commitment from Abraham Kazan's United Housing Foundation, a union-backed housing nonprofit that built a number of middle-income projects, including Corlears Hook, Seward Park, Penn South, Rochdale Village in Queens, and eventually, Co-op City in the Bronx. Moses and Kazan proposed to raze most of the area commonly known as the Bowery, New York's traditional skid row. Second only in size and potential displacement to Lincoln Square, the Cooper Square project would have cleared 12 blocks of tenements, single-room occupancy hotels, lodging houses, and missions.[6]

In 1959, when it looked like the project would finally go forward, local Met Council activists Frances Goldin and Esther Rand organized a fierce resistance

C.1. By the late 1950s and early '60s, urban renewal was under fire all across the city. In 1962, a group of protestors from downtown Brooklyn neighborhoods marched before City Hall, looking to halt the tide of white crosses appearing in the windows of old buildings and the demolition they heralded. New York World-Telegram Photograph Collection, Library of Congress.

to the plan. Reaching out to neighborhood social workers like Thelma Burdick and the future historian Staughton Lynd, they formed a left-liberal alliance, the Cooper Square Committee, to stop Moses and Kazan. They also recruited Walter Thabit, a New School for Social Research planner and Charles Abrams protégé, to help the community produce an alternative plan. Thabit's plan for Cooper Square offered much less clearance; rehabilitation of sound housing stock; a mixture of low-, moderate-, and middle-income housing; varied design profiles for new construction; and a gradual program of phased demolition that would ease relocation. It consciously honored and protected the diverse fabric of neighborhood life, which tenant activists had long sought to save. The alternative Cooper Square plan—never implemented as originally envisioned—helped to sidetrack the original Title I plan and suggested that a major sea change was under way; resistance to urban renewal's dislocations had teamed with the impulse to revise modernist urbanism's overweening imposition in the cityscape. Business-as-usual bulldozer clearance and superblock-and-tower urban renewal were on the ropes.[7]

All this turmoil revealed that the pro-growth coalition that had backed renewal in New York was coming undone. As more and more liberal reformers and politicians got cold feet, they increasingly turned on Moses and the Democratic Party officials, unions, financial elites, and neighborhood businesspeople with whom they had supported renewal. Moses's public reputation, which had been slowly eroding for several years, was in shambles. Harris Present best summed up the changing tide. Still atop the bully pulpit that his role at Lincoln Square had provided, Present called for Moses's immediate dismissal and a "complete reorganization" of the city's urban renewal bureaucracies. "The continuous disclosure of questionable practices in the Slum Clearance Committee, with its overtones of political favoritism, requires drastic revision of the entire set-up," said Present in a front-page *Times* article. "Mayor Wagner will have to make up his mind. He will have to clean up this mess or go down in the mire with it."[8]

Wagner, shaken by all the controversy, was still hesitant to dump Moses. The mayor did favor more neighborhood-friendly renewal and housing policies, and he had acted before to slightly curtail Moses's power. In 1958, he had appointed a new Urban Renewal Board to carry out a study of a combined rehabilitation and renewal area for the Upper West Side under the provisions of the 1954 federal revision of Title I. That same year, scandal had forced Wagner to reorganize the NYCHA board, thus ending Moses's 13-year reign of indirect influence over public housing. But this was different. Moses controlled hundreds of thousands of dollars of contracts that benefited Democratic Party politicians. Wagner depended on the support of these men. As Robert Caro has put it, "Wagner's power rested on Moses's money." But Wagner could also see that Moses was becoming more trouble than he was worth.

Then, a solution appeared from a somewhat unexpected quarter, Moses himself. The rewards he reaped from orchestrating slum clearance, while attractive, had never equaled the public glories of building parks, bridges, highways, and beaches. Tired of the controversy over Title I, mired in personal financial trouble, and weary of the complex and dispiriting housing and renewal fields, Moses was angling for a way out. He spied one in the as-yet-unfilled presidency of the 1964–1965 World's Fair, a position he hoped could be the capstone to his career. Moses let it be known that he would resign his Committee on Slum Clearance post and his other city jobs if the World's Fair presidency could be his. In August 1959, Wagner, while still publicly backing Moses, quietly helped to secure the World's Fair job for him and appointed an outside consultant, J. Anthony Panuch, to review the city's urban renewal programs and suggest reforms.[9]

Over the course of the fall and winter, Panuch delivered two reports—one on relocation and one on urban renewal as a whole. The relocation report was in many ways a remarkable document. It offered official recognition of the "human problem" of relocation, stating forthrightly what the resistance—from Save Our Homes to Harris Present to Samuel Spiegel—had been saying for years: "Relocation means the uprooting of homes and families. It deprives the small shopkeepers of their means of livelihood. It turns an uncounted number of individuals into displaced persons. It destroys communities." Panuch was in no way sympathetic to the protestors—he called them "professional manipulators of minorities and merchants of discontent"—but he incorporated their concerns nonetheless. The report noted the problems that roomers and lodgers faced, the way that relocation perpetuated racial segregation, the unequal treatment of site businesses, and the sharp increase in "problem families" in public housing.

Most of all, Panuch recognized that "slums, after all, are neighborhoods and communities." They were filled with "people who like the place in which they live for simple but deep rooted reasons.... Because they like being near their family, their friends, their church or the little grocery store that gives them credit when times are bad." Echoing the concerns of the East Harlem social workers, he noted the troubles that residents had in moving from old neighborhoods to new public housing towers. The "institutional" look of public housing could be frightening. "Moving into it," he wrote, "is an emotional shock accompanied by the loss of the feeling of neighborhood, of community, of belonging." Panuch did not think that a central bureau would be enough to solve the deep problems of relocation. He called instead for a "Tenant's Bill of Rights" at the state level, citywide coordination of relocation from all clearance projects, and, in his final report of March 1960, a total reorganization of urban renewal efforts into one

Housing and Redevelopment Board that would take over all ongoing Title I and rehabilitation efforts and place them under one authority.[10]

In the meantime, Moses had readied his official resignation. "The appearance of the Panuch report," he wrote to his Lincoln Square partner the Reverend Laurence J. McGinley, the president of Fordham University, "affords the opportunity my group has sought to retire as gracefully as possible from the Title One picture." For the record, he informed Panuch and the mayor that the Committee on Slum Clearance had "done what it was originally established to do" and that its work was finished. The committee disbanded and Moses's construction coordinator position was abolished, but he retained indirect influence over the Parks Department, control of highway building through his continuing chairmanship of the Triborough Bridge and Tunnel Authority, and responsibility for a host of other state-level jobs. The Moses era of New York urban renewal was over, but urban renewal itself continued.[11]

Wagner appointed a former member of Moses's Committee on Slum Clearance, Department of Real Estate commissioner J. Clarence Davies Jr., to head the new Housing and Redevelopment Board suggested by the Panuch report. Davies, a realtor by trade, had been a dissenting member of Moses's committee. In fact, it was he and his mentor, city planning chair and fellow Committee on Slum Clearance member James Felt, whom Wagner had appointed to head the West Side Urban Renewal Study two years earlier. Felt had come a long way since he ran relocations for Moses at Stuyvesant Town. Like many other liberals, he had grown increasingly troubled by the plight of displaced tenants; he and Davies had originally hoped to show a better way to stop slums with their West Side Urban Renewal Study. Now, they thought they had the power to do so on an even larger scale.[12]

Felt's first priority was to pass a major revision of the city's zoning code, the first thorough overhaul since 1916. This reform, which went into effect in 1961, attempted to translate the visions of modern city-planning ideals into the language of zoning codes. In essence, the new ordinance looked to accomplish what city planners had long hoped to do: separate out supposedly "incompatible" uses—commercial, residential, manufacturing—and give each its own protected zone in the cityscape. "There are no more unrestricted or undetermined districts," Felt said, "everything has a place and shall be protected." The code also encouraged new construction to offer more open space and lower density by adopting modern design and planning strictures. Rather than allowing tall buildings to fill up their entire lot at ground level and step back as they went up—as the 1916 code had done—Felt's ordinance offered a new system of floor area ratios that pegged building sizes to lot sizes and allowed buildings to go higher if they provided proportional open space at their base. Modern towers floating in open plazas would replace the art deco piles and "wedding cakes" of an earlier era.

On the one hand, the new zoning code seemed to represent a modest retreat from the pure orthodoxies of modern site planning. Rather than select an entire neighborhood unit for replanning and guarantee its protection from surrounding blight by closing streets and laying out superblocks, the new zoning codes looked to achieve a revamped downtown cityscape block by block, lot by lot, and building by building. On the other hand, with its strict separation of uses and enshrinement of modern design tenets, the code reflected the influence of modernist architecture and the planning vision associated with urban renewal. In truth, Felt hoped that the zoning overhaul would provide a citywide framework for urban growth and complement the new urban renewal program over which he and Davies would preside.[13]

Davies and Felt's ventures into urban renewal offered a similarly limited revision of modern dogma. In 1960 and 1961, they announced a slate of projects, including the ongoing West Side Urban Renewal Area and a project for Greenwich Village, which would mix rehabilitation with spot clearance and new construction. Doing away with Moses's full-on bulldozer approach, they claimed to want to encourage and facilitate community input on these new projects and find a way to rejuvenate neighborhoods without undue hardship for the people already living there. And yet, they ran headlong into redoubled opposition to any urban renewal efforts at all. As a result, their efforts turned out to be short-lived and their accomplishments few. The rethinking of urban renewal, Davies and Felt discovered, was leaping ahead of them.

The most far-ranging, persuasive, and influential critique of urban renewal launched during this moment of flux has also had the greatest staying power in the public's memory. Fresh from her experiences with William Kirk, Ellen Lurie, Mildred Zucker, and the other dissident social workers of East Harlem, Jane Jacobs took a leave from her editorial position at *Architectural Forum,* won a grant from the Rockefeller Foundation, and retired to her house in Greenwich Village to write a book about modern city planning. The result, *The Death and Life of Great American Cities,* arguably did more than any other single force to unseat urban renewal as the commonsense ideal for city rebuilding.

Looking back, it might seem like Jacobs and her book came almost out of nowhere. In 1961, when *Death and Life* appeared, she was a largely unheralded editor, known among a small circle of writers and urbanists as the author of a few articles advocating better urban design and an iconoclast who had helped a group of her Villager neighbors thwart Robert Moses's plans to run a road through Washington Square. The plainspoken literary power of *Death and Life,* however, was bracing, and the book had a far-reaching influence on a rising generation of architects, planners, community activists, and city lovers of all stripes. As the writer Jane Kramer put it in a 1962 *Village Voice* profile, "Overnight she became a prophet and leader of a great neighborhood revival and, just as quickly, the scourge of nearly every city planner in the United States." Jacobs seemed to materialize from the streets, storefronts, and cafes of Greenwich Village like an urban Rachel Carson, a prophetic amateur whose commonsense wisdom alerted the world to an organic neighborhood ecosystem imperiled by the cataclysmic forces of progress and modernization. And yet, it would be a mistake to imagine, as most accounts of these events do, that the ideas Jacobs championed arose solely out of the mind of one *Architectural Forum* editor concerned to preserve the quaint bonhomie of Greenwich Village. If one easily dispelled myth is that Jacobs was just a housewife who cherished her neighborhood butcher and corner store, rather than a committed writer and urbanist, another, stickier one is that the sole source of the revolt against modern planning was simply one inspired writer's love affair with the lanes, brownstones, and "public characters" of the Village.[14]

In truth, Jacobs's book was an intellectual culmination of the resistance to urban renewal, a summation of all the tumult of the 1950s. She provided no direct account of this history, but the echoes of those struggles collected in her work. Jacobs surveyed neighborhoods and renewal efforts in a number of cities across the country, including Philadelphia, Boston, Pittsburgh, Baltimore, Washington, St. Louis, Chicago, and San Francisco, and drew on the work of a number of rising urbanists—Kevin Lynch and his studies of the images of cities, William H. Whyte and his thinking on "the exploding metropolis," Grady Clay and his irreverent looks at cityscapes, Herbert Gans and his ethnography of the clearance-threatened West End of Boston—but a great deal of the book sprang from her attention to the struggles over renewal and public housing in New York. She had consulted with Harris Present and Samuel Spiegel; she knew Charles Abrams from the Village; she had read Harrison Salisbury's early critiques of the effects of clearance; she had worked closely with the social workers of East Harlem. Many of her most trenchant observations about the impact of urban renewal were drawn from direct observation in the new superblock-and-tower spaces of Manhattan, particularly in the three iconic spaces where renewal had been idealized and criticized: Stuyvesant Town, Lincoln Square, and East Harlem. If much of the inspiration for her urban prescriptions came from her immediate environs on Hudson Street in the Village, it did not originate only there. Jacobs remarked that "the basic idea, to try to begin understanding the intricate social and economic order under the seeming disorder of cities," was not her idea at all, but came from William Kirk. By showing her East Harlem, Kirk had shown Jacobs "a way of seeing other neighborhoods, and downtowns too."[15]

Jacobs's great talent was to sum up all the rising discord and loosely connected laments over urban renewal—its losses and dislocations, its impositions and its new monotonous spaces—and translate them into a rich, unique idiom all her own, one that suggested equal parts wisdom, common sense, and subtlety. Capitalizing on the citywide unease that Marya Mannes had so vividly captured, Jacobs gave Mannes's bitter despair a much-needed jolt of practical, can-do polemicism. *Death and Life,* she wrote, in its opening paragraph, was an "attack…on the principles and aims that have shaped modern, orthodox city planning and rebuilding." The "principles and aims" of city rebuilding, Jacobs claimed, were a form of "unurban urbanization." Just as Met Life had promised for Stuyvesant Town, urban renewal brought "the suburb into the city." Of course, for Jacobs, this meant that the company had tried to "beat it into some inadequate imitation of the noncity." She traced an informal, and rather imprecise, history of modern planning ideals, charging that they were an unholy amalgam of Ebenezer Howard's Garden City visions, Le Corbusier's Radiant City plans, and formalistic City Beautiful civic centers—all of which were hostile to the real life of the city. The result was "a sort of Radiant Garden City Beautiful, such as the immense Lincoln Square project for New York, in which a monumental City Beautiful cultural center is one among a series of adjoining Radiant City and Radiant Garden City housing, shopping, and campus centers." The planners of such places, she charged, had trusted too much in their "symbolic and abstracted" technique, rather than in the "literally endless intricacy of life." To approach a neighborhood "as if it were a larger architectural problem, capable of being given order by converting it into a disciplined work of art, is to make the mistake of attempting to substitute art for life." The results were "neither life nor art"; they were "taxidermy." Modern planning put on "exhibitions of dead, stuffed cities." "This is not the rebuilding of cities," she famously charged, "this is the sacking of cities."[16]

Jacobs concentrated her fire on the simultaneously divisive and monolithic character of the new superblock-and-tower projects. Just as Stanley Isaacs had dubbed Stuyvesant Town a "walled town" almost 20 years earlier, Jacobs suggested that places like Stuyvesant Town and Park West Village (the final name for Manhattantown) were protected outposts that residents inhabited "like pioneer life in a stockaded village." These projects were dropped down into a neighborhood and immediately divided it into a series of "turfs" that were isolated, mentally and physically, from the city around it. The basic idea at the heart of "orthodox planning theory"—the neighborhood unit—was "deeply committed to the ideal of supposedly cozy, inward-turned city neighborhoods." But all the careful calculations of ideal community size and the attention to large-scale intervention had simply resulted in a vision of "the city neighborhood as an island, turned inward on itself." Clearance and rebuilding were converting the city "into a parcel of mutually suspicious and hostile Turfs." Functionally severed—"decontaminated," as she put it—from the surrounding city, these turfs were also largely monolithic within themselves, dedicated to housing, entertainment, education, or some other single-use program. The greatest and most tragic example of this was, of course, "the planning island called Lincoln Center for the Performing Arts," which removed halls from other parts of the city that needed them to underwrite vitality and isolated them in one area. As she had put it in a 1958 speech, Lincoln Center was "so planned and so bounded that there is no possible place for variety, convenience, and urbanity to work itself in or alongside." The result was "built-in rigor mortis."[17]

Perhaps the most disturbing thing about these supremely rational schemes was the way they treated people. In order "to house people in this planned fashion," Jacobs wrote in her typically irreverent way, "price tags are fastened on the population, and each sorted-out chunk of price-tagged populace lives in growing suspicion and tension against the surrounding city." Planners looked at people like commodities, quantifiable units, or assortments of average populations that could be moved across the city at will and grouped in monolithic island turfs. Picking up on the kind of unease that new residents of Stuyvesant Town felt about the regimented landscape of towers and superblocks and refining and expanding her initial impressions of the public landscape of East Harlem, she claimed that planners had forgotten that people "live rather than just exist." They made spaces for "fixed, bodiless, statistical people." If other commentators had noticed the monotonous nature of project design—Albert Mayer, for instance, was by this point condemning the similar "endlessness and institutionalism" of both Lincoln Towers and Stuyvesant Town—Jacobs revealed the greater conceptual system of machine-like people sorting that resulted in bland, repetitive towers.[18]

Of course, this impulse also underwrote and rationalized the scourge of displacement. The "people who get marked with the planners' hex signs," she wrote, "are pushed about, expropriated, and uprooted much as if they were the subjects of a conquering power." The problem—as those displaced from Lincoln Square had articulated—was that "real people are unique." People in neighborhoods "invest years of their lives in significant relationships with other unique people, and are not interchangeable in the least. Severed from their relationships, they are destroyed as effective social beings—sometimes for a little while, sometimes forever." The rebuilders had refused to understand that the "slowly grown public relationships" of everyday life made up a series of "neighborhood networks." Like the Lincoln Square resisters, Jacobs argued that it was these networks—not renewed districts, modern towers, or cultural centers—that made up a "city's irreplaceable social capital."[19]

Jacobs described urban renewal as akin to the foreign aid that the United States doled out to encourage "deprived and backward" countries to take on massive development projects. In the spirit of Cold War era modernization theory, these funds were poured in from on high "according to decisions by absentee experts from the remote continent inhabited by housers and planners." This was what she called "cataclysmic money"—investment designed to produce a violent upheaval that could then be mastered and directed toward progress. In a neighborhood like East Harlem, it produced only more "trouble and turmoil." In essence, Jacobs showed that urban renewal was undermined by a fundamental contradiction at its very heart. Its effort to improve city life was doomed by the form of its own endeavor. Like the U.S. military in that other great American modernization campaign of the Cold War era, the Vietnam War, urban renewal's boosters found themselves in the tragic and ugly position of having to destroy the city to save it. What was needed instead, Jacobs said, was "gradual money" that would encourage local residents to bring troubled neighborhoods back themselves.[20]

As clear as all these objections were in Jacobs's telling, they were for her perhaps best summed up by a resident of Washington Houses in East Harlem. Explaining why project residents despised the great open lawn at the center of the project, she had said:

> Nobody cared what we wanted when they built this place. They threw our houses down and pushed us here and pushed our friends somewhere else. We don't even have a place around here to get a cup of coffee or a newspaper even, or borrow fifty cents. Nobody cared what we need. But the big men come and look at the grass and say, "Isn't it wonderful! Now the poor have everything they need."

This was the summation of the accumulated grievances that had been gathering across the city for 15 years.[21]

Ultimately, Jacobs revealed—as did Mannes, the new residents of Stuyvesant Town, the protestors at Lincoln Square, and the insurgent social workers of East Harlem—that urban renewal's drive for modernization from on high was shared across ideological boundaries in the Cold War years. Modernization in the form of capitalist urban renewal and public housing, her attack implied, was no different from modernism of a more socialist stripe. One was charged with making property profitable, while the other made material the social leveling required by collectivist ideals. Both, however, were imagined by their backers as symbols of readiness in the Cold War struggle. And both required disposing of an older, more nuanced cityscape with great cascades of "cataclysmic money" dropped in from above. Jacobs did not explicitly invoke these terms, but her attacks crystallized urban renewal's shifting fortunes: once aid in the Cold War struggle, the results of its interventions more and more appeared uncomfortably akin to the mass society Americans feared from Communism.

The greatest hurdle facing the resistance to urban renewal, Jacobs noted, was not so much the effects of modern planning ideals, but the sway they held over so many minds. "By now," she wrote, "these orthodox ideas are part of our folklore. They harm us because we take them for granted." So pervasive was their influence that they were "taught in everything from schools of architecture and planning to the Sunday supplements and women's magazines." Of course, their decades-long grip over the public imagination had been loosening lately, but the gathering insurgency still needed new ways to see the city and a new language with which to suggest alternatives. This was perhaps the most important of Jacobs's accomplishments. She delivered a new paradigm for measuring and encouraging city vitality, a new urban common sense.[22]

In Jacobs's mind, her East Harlem informant had offered more than a condemnation of urban renewal; she also had provided a primer on how to deal with cities as they were. If her informant was lamenting the loss of her old neighborhood and the monotony in her new project landscape, she was also explaining, in her own way, the very thing that Jacobs had learned from her work in the neighborhood and that she put at the heart of her book. "There is a quality even meaner than outright ugliness or disorder," Jacobs wrote, "and this meaner quality is the dishonest mask of pretended order, achieved by ignoring or suppressing the real order that is struggling to exist and be served." Modern planning principles had focused on the perceived disorder and chaos of old cities—creating terms like "slums" and "blight" to categorize it—while missing an entirely different set of connections and relationships that gave shape to city life in these kinds of places. Cities posed what she called "a problem in handling organized complexity." The particular landscape of nineteenth-century cities, she thought, was well suited to handle this problem. This was the case in a number of ways, but it was most so at the level that urban renewal ideals most abhorred: the streets and sidewalks. She made an informal study of street-level interactions and discovered what she famously called an "intricate sidewalk ballet." This dance, easily observed outside her front door on Hudson Street, was an improvisatory "complex order" beneath the seeming disorder of everyday back and forth. With its "intricacy of sidewalk use" and "constant succession of eyes," this order maintained "the safety of the streets and the freedom of the city."[23]

The key words here were "intricacy" and "complexity," in no small measure because these were the chief characteristics of street life that superblock-and-tower rebuilding sought to winnow out. With their monocultural uses, the new spaces of urban renewal eschewed complexity for simplicity, replacing mixed-use streetscapes with single-use superblocks. "Intricate minglings of different uses in cities are not a form of chaos," Jacobs reported. "On the contrary, they represent a complex and highly developed form of order." Human efforts that hindered or destroyed that difference and complexity in cities rather than encouraged it would also destroy the cities. The entire book, Jacobs wrote, hinged on this concept. It was one that the resistance at Lincoln Square, with its defense of the web of public and private life, would have recognized as an interpretation of the residents' imperiled world.[24]

In the short term, Jacobs hoped that the complexity of street and sidewalk life could be knitted back into the fabric of renewal zones. She had teamed with Perkins and Will to "bleed" street life into their redesign of Clinton Houses in East Harlem; Albert Mayer had followed suit by trying to extend the street into his redesigned plazas. In general, however, she hoped that planners would reorient themselves totally toward encouraging the "intricate mutual support" that lay beneath the seeming disorder of city neighborhoods. She thought that "the science of city planning and the art of city design, in real life for real cities, must become the science and art of catalyzing and nourishing those close-grained working relationships" already at the functioning heart of city life.[25]

The first test of Jacobs's ideas was not long in coming. In early 1961, a few weeks after she finished writing *Death and Life,* Davies and Felt announced their intention to study a renewal plan for the West Village. Jacobs and her neighborhood allies immediately formed the Committee to Save the West Village and organized to turn it back. The irony here was that *Death and Life* had been written as a response to the era of Moses-led clearance and rebuilding while Davies's new Housing and Redevelopment Board had been intended as a reform of Moses-style clearance as well. No matter. Jacobs had once held out some hope for what she called "spot renewal," but by the time she came to write her book she saw it as "largely the trick of seeing how many old buildings can be left standing and the area still converted into a passable version of Radiant Garden City." The problem, of course, went deeper than that. Jacobs and the new renewal bureaucracy were at loggerheads over the very nature of the Village. For Davies and Felt, despite all their interest in reforming urban renewal, the neighborhood may have been charming, but its patchwork of shops, factories, rowhouses, and apartments was anathema. For Jacobs, the jumble was precious; it needed protecting at all costs. She and her neighbors put everything they had into defeating Felt and Davies, refusing to compromise just because the city officials claimed to want to represent the neighborhood's wishes in their plans. After close to a year of bitter confrontation, Mayor Wagner was forced to step in and advise Felt and Davies to drop the plan. Davies resigned not long after, and within a year Felt had stepped down from the chairmanship of the City Planning Commission.[26]

C.2. Jane Jacobs speaking at an anti–urban renewal rally in 1966. The sign on the podium opposes the construction of a new library for New York University. The university partnered with Robert Moses to use Title I funds to rebuild several blocks south of Washington Square in Greenwich Village with faculty housing and other university buildings. Fred W. McDarrah/Getty Images.

James Felt called Jacobs's approach "the *laissez faire* theory of urban renewal." For him, it was simply a return to the bad old days, a failure of will that would lead to "abandon[ing] our cities to the very process which created the slums of the past." Perhaps it should have been no surprise, then, that Jacobs and the neighborhood forces were joined on the anti-renewal barricades by an unexpected ally, the conservative policy analyst Martin Anderson, whose 1964 book,

The Federal Bulldozer, attacked urban renewal from the right as a colossal waste of taxpayer money. Anderson, whose book caused almost as much of a stir as Jacobs's had, suggested that only "free enterprise" could rebuild cities. It gave the Right renewed ammunition for its long-held belief that, as Ronald Reagan put it in 1964, urban renewal was an "assault on freedom." Anderson went on to prominent positions in the Nixon and Reagan administrations as a chief strategist of conservative efforts to roll back the New Deal. Jacobs advocated careful attention to the existing patterns of city life and gradual, from the ground up transformation—or "unslumming"—of ailing neighborhoods without massive governmental intervention. If the grassroots and conservative oppositions to urban renewal had different aims—one wanted to return power to neighborhoods, the other wanted to privatize or do away with public efforts to aid cities—they dovetailed in their condemnations of the power of the state.[27]

Urban renewal, it turns out, was one of the roots of the great ideological divide that marked the era we call the '60s. On one side, the neighborhood groups represented, in embryonic form, a movement for a new kind of humanistic social transformation, which sought to make political change not through parties, petitions, and elections but by remaking the conditions of everyday life. They offered an early inkling of the New Left and counterculture's efforts to lead a permanent revolution in culture, social life, and consciousness. On the other, the attack from the right foreshadowed the extent to which all liberal reforms would come to be tarred with the brush of "big government" and rendered a threat to individual freedom. In the early '60s, both sides joined in uneasy alliance to defend imperiled freedom against the "federal bulldozer"; a decade later, they had diverged, and the currents of dissent each captured were seen as hopelessly at odds.

By the early '60s, urban renewal and its modern planning visions were under fire across New York and in other cities such as Boston, San Francisco, Philadelphia, Chicago, and New Haven. Jacobs's book was the most visible representative of a building chorus of dissent that joined the various neighborhood laboratories for anti-renewal sentiment into one loosely connected, but widely shared spirit of resistance to clearance, superblocks, modern towers, and urban expressways. In New York, Puerto Rican resistance to the West Side Urban Renewal Plan stalled it and limited the scope of its rebuilding. East Harlem's social workers took an active role in shaping Felt's urban renewal plans for the area, guiding them away from too much clearance. The historic preservation movement, which had for years been determined to save the city's declining roster of historic structures, added its voice to the clamor against mass demolition. Jacobs and other Villagers led a successful campaign against Moses's long-hoped-for Lower Manhattan Expressway. Some post-Moses urban renewal chiefs, like Edward Logue, who worked in Boston and New York in the '60s, tried to incorporate community wishes. Other planners and architects—often affiliated with activist groups like Met Council, the Architects Renewal Committee in Harlem, or the Real Great Society's Urban Planning Studio in East Harlem—began to see themselves as "advocacy planners" and tried to turn their skills toward working for neighborhoods rather than for planning agencies. They began to recognize what had long eluded the proponents of urban renewal: slums were symptoms not causes of urban poverty. All over the country, a new generation of urbanists—and even city officials—began to declare themselves disciples of Jacobs and tried to find ways to build her precepts into city development schemes. Individual renewal projects continued into the 1970s, but with the intellectual underpinnings of renewal more or less dismantled by the mid-1960s, they were often embattled affairs with less clearance and more community input. Overall, as the planner David R. Hill put it, looking back on Jacobs's influence from the perspective of the 1980s: "old style federal urban renewal has ended; huge project-scale urban demolition has slowed; infill strategies have been instituted; greater flexibility and diversity in zoning has been attempted; mixed-use projects are more common; freeway building has sometimes been stopped."[28]

In the wake of all these proliferating critiques, it appeared to many that there could be no doubt that urban renewal had done just what all of the dissenters and critics had been saying it was doing: it had destroyed neighborhoods. It had cleared away commerce and spurred deindustrialization. It had erected new divisions of class and race in the cityscape and perpetuated, with federal imprimatur, old patterns of racial segregation. It had destroyed working-class Manhattan to save it for the white middle class, which was leaving for the outer boroughs and suburbs. It was the first move in a decades-long transfer of all sense of locality to the boroughs, one that continues to this day and more and more leaves the island as the home of white-collar, cosmopolitan, corporate culture. Across the city, it had dropped great stretches of inhuman space over the ruins of a vital cityscape. Its vision may have been undone, but it left a physical legacy in concrete, steel, brick, and glass. In its wake was a newly bifurcated urban environment: on the one hand, a landscape of loss and ruin, the first and earliest marker of the trouble that by the mid-1960s was called the "urban crisis"; on the other, the new expanses of modern city for white-collar uses: the new superblock-and-tower housing and university, hospital, and cultural centers that represented the vast transformation of New York from an industrial city to a global and post-industrial metropolis. This was the legacy of urban renewal: a city simultaneously rising to become the capital of the world and falling into urban crisis.

Of course, this split legacy should prompt us to appreciate urban renewal's complex history. Along with destruction and alienation, it left a new cityscape, one that has—in Manhattan, at least—not always been the urban scourge we've been given to understand. Modern superblocks, plazas, lawns, and towers—while fatal to smaller or less dense cities and certainly no blueprint for future urban design—have in Manhattan provided some relief from the strict regularity of the street grid and opened new vistas and green spaces. They were often too big, or unwisely sited, or clumsily connected to the grid, but Stuyvesant Town, Lincoln Center, and the grounds of East Harlem's public housing also supply the quasi-Jacobsean virtue of variation in the streetscape. Claude Lévi-Strauss may have found prewar New York to be "a city where one could breathe easily," but urban renewal and public housing also sometimes fulfilled Marya Mannes's hopes: entering from the street into the sun-dappled walks and ovals of Stuyvesant Town can feel akin to a drawing of deep breath. Like Central Park, these sorts of places offer "the balm of distance" to New Yorkers "forever bullied by the immediate." Even Jacobs was not entirely prescient, and not all of her contentions have stood the test of time. Her organic model of urban life, dependent as it was on a view of cities as naturally developing organisms, limited her understanding of the ways that public and private power had conjoined to make racial division a persistent and lasting feature of the divided postwar metropolis. At the same time, she underestimated how city life would, haphazardly and unevenly perhaps, find its way back into the area around Lincoln Center, or how people could find a way to make a life in public housing, or how the workings of time, which so ennobled the cityscape of Greenwich Village, could also soften and domesticate the regimented order of Stuyvesant Town.

But the greatest accomplishment of public housing and urban renewal is far more prosaic. After decades of ups and downs in New York's real estate markets, the projects built by Robert Moses and NYCHA look like ever more irreplaceable and rare resources. Supplying working- and middle-class New Yorkers with thousands of affordable apartments in one of the most expensive places on the planet, the unloved projects have managed to fulfill, on a small scale, one of the central tenets of the modern housing movement: to remove housing from the block-and-lot grid and preserve it as shelter for ordinary people rather than as raw material in a speculative market in land.[29]

By now, the language of Jacobs's alternative urban vision has become as dominant as urban renewal once was. What Marshall Berman calls Jacobs's "modernism of the street" is no longer an insurgent movement, but the lingua franca of planners and city lovers everywhere. No big development project can go forward without at least the appearance of community review. "Mixed-use" planning has acquired the same level of untroubled acceptance that superblocks and towers enjoyed 60 years ago. And yet, the revolt against urban renewal ultimately did little to dislodge the power of private real estate developers—the heirs of Moses's "responsible" project sponsors—over the prospects for urban development in New York and in many other places. They may do less clearance, but they still enjoy substantial public subsidies for white-collar office and luxury housing construction. Almost no new public housing has been built in a generation, and since the fall of urban renewal concerted society-wide attempts to break up ghettos, house the poor, and plan cities have all but gone by the wayside. On the plus side, the philosophies that Jacobs and the advocacy planners pioneered have helped formerly abandoned neighborhoods in cities nationwide to find innovative ways to renew themselves. Sometimes, these market-fed strategies simply spur real estate development or feed unchecked gentrification, a form of displacement that, while less dramatic than that put in motion by slum clearance, can be just as hard on the working-class and poor populations of these neighborhoods. Sometimes, it allows these people to invest in their own homes and neighborhoods and be a part of the revitalization. But in a world of hyper-urbanization, where more and more people in developing nations across the globe are leaving rural areas and moving to cities, the world is facing, on a global scale, the same problems of industrialization and urban decay that European and North American cities faced in the nineteenth and twentieth centuries. Can these market strategies reclaim cities worldwide? Maybe. It is hard to imagine, however, that the problem will be bested without collective public commitment. Perhaps the greatest tragedy of urban renewal is that its failure left us with no comprehensive vision for how to deal with the perils of global urbanization and little political will to develop one.[30]

NOTES

Abbreviations

ARCHIVES

Avery	Avery Architectural and Fine Arts Library, Columbia University, New York
CHPC	Citizens Housing and Planning Council Archives, New York
Columbia	Central files, Columbiana Library, Columbia University Archives, New York
EBYoung	Edgar B. Young Collection, Record Group 17, series 1.9, E. B. Young Papers and Photographs, Rockefeller Archive Center, Sleepy Hollow, NY
Hutchins	Office of the President, Hutchins Administration Collection, Special Collections Research Center, University of Chicago Library, Chicago, IL
Isaacs	Stanley Isaacs Papers, Manuscripts and Archives, New York Public Library, New York
JDR3	Rockefeller Family Archives, Record Group 5, John D. Rockefeller III Papers, series 1, subseries 4, Rockefeller Archive Center, Sleepy Hollow, NY
JWJCC	James Weldon Johnson Community Center Papers, Schomburg Center for Research in Black Culture, New York Public Library, New York
LCPA	Lincoln Center for the Performing Arts, Inc., Archives, New York
Marc	Vito Marcantonio Papers, Manuscripts and Archives, New York Public Library, New York
MLA	Metropolitan Life Archives, New York
MosesNYPL	Robert Moses Papers, Manuscripts and Archives, New York Public Library, New York
MosesYale	Moses Collection, Manuscripts and Archives, Sterling Memorial Library, Yale University, New Haven, CT
NARA	National Archives and Records Administration, College Park, MD
NYCHA	New York City Housing Authority Records, La Guardia and Wagner Archives, La Guardia Community College, City University of New York, Long Island City, Queens, NY
ParksGen	Parks Department—General Files, Municipal Archives, New York
ParksMoses	Parks Department—Moses Files, Municipal Archives, New York
RockCult	Rockefeller Family Archives, Record Group 2, Cultural Interests series, Rockefeller Archive Center, Sleepy Hollow, NY
UNArch	United Nations Archives and Records Management Section, New York
UnSett	Union Settlement Papers, Columbia University Rare Book and Manuscript Library, New York

NEWSPAPERS AND MAGAZINES

AF   *Architectural Forum*
AR   *Architectural Record*
DC   *Daily Compass*
DW   *Daily Worker*
NYAN   *New York Amsterdam News*
NYDM   *New York Daily Mirror*
NYDN   *New York Daily News*
NYHT   *New York Herald Tribune*
NYJA   *New York Journal-American*
NYP   *New York Post*
NYS   *New York Sun*
NYT   *New York Times*
NYTM   *New York Times Magazine*
NYWT   *New York World-Telegram*
NYWTS   *New York World-Telegram and Sun*
TV   *Town and Village*

Introduction

1. Claude Lévi-Strauss, "New York in 1941," in *The View from Afar*, trans. Joachim Neugroschel and Phoebe Hoss (New York: Basic, 1985), 258–267. Lévi-Strauss was able to leave France under the auspices of a program for "endangered intellectuals" organized by the Rockefeller Foundation. See Didier Eribon and Claude Lévi-Strauss, *Conversations with Claude Levi-Strauss*, trans. Paula Wissing (Chicago: University of Chicago Press, 1991), 25–46.

2. See Carlo Rotella, *October Cities: The Redevelopment of Urban Literature* (Berkeley: University of California Press, 1998), 1–16. Or, as historian Eric Darton puts it, a building or public space "embodies in its particular form the social imagination that gave it license." Eric Darton, *Divided We Stand: A Biography of New York's World Trade Center* (New York: Basic, 1999), 6. As critic Beatriz Colomina puts it:

> [Architecture] is a system of representation.... The building should be understood in the same terms as drawings, photographs, writing, films, and advertisements; not only because these are media in which more often we encounter it, but because the building is a mechanism of representation in its own right. The building is, after all, a "construction," in all senses of the word.

See Beatriz Colomina, *Privacy and Publicity: Modern Architecture as Mass Media* (Cambridge, MA: MIT Press, 1994), 13–14. These formulations are all indebted to the fundamental insight that space is "socially produced." See Henri Lefebvre, *The Production of Space* (Cambridge: Blackwell, 1991); David Harvey, *The Condition of Postmodernity* (Cambridge: Blackwell, 1990); and Edward Soja, *Postmodern Geographies* (New York: Verso, 1989). Of course, these ideas go back a long way. As Lewis Mumford put it, "Mind takes form in the city, and in turn, urban forms condition mind." Mumford, *The Culture of Cities* (New York: Harcourt, Brace, 1938), 5. My interest in the ongoing struggle for "symbolic hegemony" between various groups trying to shape both understandings of urban renewal and the social and built environment of the city itself is indebted to the ideas of Antonio Gramsci. See Stuart Hall, "Gramsci's Relevance for the Study of Race and Ethnicity," in David Morley and Kuan-Hsing Chen, eds., *Stuart Hall: Critical Dialogues in Cultural Studies* (New York: Routledge, 1996), 411–440 and Raymond Williams, "Hegemony" and "Structures of Feeling," in *Marxism and Literature* (New York: Oxford University Press, 1977) 108–114, 128–135.

3. See Paul E. Peterson, *City Limits* (Chicago: University of Chicago Press, 1981). See also Gregory J. Crowley, *The Politics of Place: Contentious Urban Redevelopment in Pittsburgh* (Pittsburgh: University of Pittsburgh Press, 2005), 7–57. My remarks here also draw from the account of urban renewal in Robert O. Self, *American Babylon: Race and the Struggle for Postwar Oakland* (Princeton, NJ: Princeton University Press, 2003), 17–20, 135–137, particularly his treatment of the way that city officials continually strove to "make property profitable." On city officials' campaigns to upgrade infrastructure, see Jon C. Teaford, *The Rough Road to Urban Renaissance: Urban Revitalization in America, 1940–1985* (Baltimore, MD: Johns Hopkins University Press, 1990), 83.

4. See Alison Isenberg, *Downtown America: A History of the Place and the People Who Made It* (Chicago: University of Chicago Press, 2004), 166–202.

5. The literature on the policy of urban renewal is quite vast. See Peter Marris, "A Report on Urban Renewal in the United States," in Leonard J. Duhl, ed., *The Urban Condition: People and Policy in the Metropolis* (New York: Basic, 1963), 113–134; Martin Anderson, *The Federal Bulldozer: A Critical Analysis of Urban Renewal, 1949–1962* (Cambridge, MA: MIT Press, 1964); Scott Greer, *Urban Renewal and American Cities: The Dilemma of Democratic Intervention* (New York: Bobbs-Merrill, 1965); Charles Abrams, *The City Is the Frontier* (New York: Harper and Row, 1965); the essays, particularly Herbert J. Gans, "The Failure of Urban Renewal," in James Q. Wilson, ed., *Urban Renewal: The Record and the Controversy* (Cambridge, MA: MIT Press, 1966); Jeanne R. Lowe, *Cities in a Race with Time: Progress and Poverty in America's Renewing Cities* (New York: Random House, 1967); Lawrence Friedman, *Government and Slum Housing: A Century of Frustration* (Chicago: Rand McNally, 1968), 147–172; Mark I. Gelfand, *A Nation of Cities: The Federal Government and Urban America, 1933–1965* (New York: Oxford University Press, 1975), 105–156; John H. Mollenkopf, *The Contested City* (Princeton, NJ: Princeton University Press, 1983); Teaford, *Rough Road to Urban Renaissance*; Robert Halpern, *Rebuilding the Inner City: A History of Neighborhood Initiatives to Address Poverty in the United States* (New York: Columbia University Press, 1995), 57–82; Mindy Thompson Fullilove, *Root Shock: How Tearing Up City Neighborhoods Hurts America and What We Can Do about It* (New York: Ballantine, 2004). For studies of particular cities, see Herbert J. Gans, *The Urban Villagers* (New York: Free Press, 1962), 281–335 (on Boston); Peter Rossi and Robert Dentler, *The Politics of Urban Renewal* (New York: Free Press, 1961) (on Chicago); Harold Kaplan, *Urban Renewal Politics: Slum Clearance in Newark* (New York: Columbia University Press, 1968); John F. Bauman, *Public Housing, Race, and Renewal: Urban Planning in Philadelphia, 1920–1974* (Philadelphia: Temple University Press, 1987); Joel Schwartz, *The New York Approach: Robert Moses, Urban Liberals, and Redevelopment of the Inner City* (Columbus: Ohio State University Press, 1993); Howard Gillette Jr., *Between Justice and Beauty: Race, Planning, and the Failure of Urban Policy in*

Washington, DC (Baltimore, MD: Johns Hopkins University Press, 1995), 151–189; June Manning Thomas, *Redevelopment and Race: Planning a Finer City in Postwar Detroit* (Baltimore, MD: Johns Hopkins University Press, 1997); Arnold R. Hirsch, *Making the Second Ghetto: Race and Housing in Chicago, 1940–1960,* 2nd ed. (Chicago: University of Chicago Press, 1998); Dana Cuff, *The Provisional City: Los Angeles Stories of Architecture and Urbanism* (Cambridge, MA: MIT Press, 2000); David Schuyler, *A City Transformed: Redevelopment, Race, and Suburbanization in Lancaster, Pennsylvania, 1940–1980* (University Park: Penn State University Press, 2002).

6. As Marshall Berman has remarked, "the city has become not merely a theater but itself a production, a multimedia presentation whose audience is the whole world." New York's "construction and development," he continues, is a form of "symbolic action and communication." See Marshall Berman, *All That Is Solid Melts into Air* (New York: Simon and Schuster, 1982), 288–289. On New York's postwar reign as "cultural capital of the world," see Leonard Wallock, ed., *New York: Culture Capital of the World, 1940–1965* (New York: Rizzoli, 1988); and William B. Scott and Peter Rutkoff, *New York Modern: The Arts and the City* (Baltimore, MD: Johns Hopkins University Press, 1999).

7. Byron G. Rogers, "A Domestic Point 4," reprinted from the *Congressional Record,* April 21, 1953, by the Labor Housing Conference, in box 71C7, folder 1, NYCHA. On modernization and modernism, see Nils Gilman, *Mandarins of the Future: Modernization Theory in Cold War America* (Baltimore, MD: Johns Hopkins University Press, 2003). On modernity and "creative destruction," see Peter Osborne, *The Politics of Time* (New York: Verso, 1995); Berman, *All That Is Solid;* and Max Page, *The Creative Destruction of Manhattan, 1900–1940* (Chicago: University of Chicago Press, 1998).

8. As historian David Reynolds puts it, across the globe modern architecture and planning "created the essential framework for daily living, rather than its ancillary pleasures." See David Reynolds, *One World Divisible: A Global History since 1945* (New York: Norton, 2000), 148.

9. See Jane Jacobs, *The Death and Life of Great American Cities* (New York: Random House, 1961; New York: Modern Library, 1993). See also Robert Goodman, *After the Planners* (New York: Simon and Schuster, 1971); Martin Pawley, *Architecture versus Housing* (New York: Praeger, 1971).

10. Some urban historians have challenged the idea that modern planning and architecture could be the sole evil at the root of public housing's social ills. For the most succinct summary of this position, see Robert Fishman, "Rethinking Public Housing," *Places* 16, no. 2 (Spring 2004): 26–33. Some architectural and design historians, on the other hand, are more likely to argue that American practitioners and conditions undermined, cheapened, or diverted the original genius of modern design. See, for instance, Friedman, *Government and Slum Housing,* 145; Richard Plunz, *A History of Housing in New York City* (New York: Columbia University Press, 1990); and Eric Mumford, "The 'Tower in the Park' in America: Theory and Practice, 1920–1960," *Planning Perspectives* 10 (January 1995), 17–41. Others, particularly lately, when modernism has been undergoing a growing revival in design circles, hope to insulate the European modern masters from the design failures of modern tower-block public housing. See Mardges Bacon, *Le Corbusier in America: Travels in the Land of the Timid* (Cambridge, MA: MIT Press, 2001).

11. See James C. Scott, *Seeing Like a State: How Certain Schemes to Improve the Human Condition Have Failed* (New Haven, CT: Yale University Press, 1998), 85–104. The most influential conception of the "planners" and the "walkers" is Michel de Certeau, "Walking in the City," in his *The Practice of Everyday Life* (Berkeley: University of California Press, 1984), 91–110.

12. I see this term as a successor to the "ethic of tenement destruction" identified by Max Page. See Page, *Creative Destruction*, 71–75. The literature on the history of slum clearance and housing reform is vast. See, in addition to Page, Schwartz, *The New York Approach*; John D. Fairfield, *The Mysteries of the Great City: The Politics of Urban Design, 1877–1937* (Columbus: Ohio State University Press, 1993); Robert Fogelson, *Downtown: Its Rise and Fall, 1880–1950* (New Haven, CT: Yale University Press, 2001); Roy Lubove, *The Progressives and the Slums: Tenement House Reform in New York City, 1890–1917* (Pittsburgh: University of Pittsburgh Press, 1962); John F. Bauman, Roger Biles, and Kristin M. Szylvain, eds., *From Tenements to the Taylor Homes: In Search of an Urban Housing Policy in Twentieth-Century America* (University Park: Penn State University Press, 2000); Paul Boyer, *Urban Masses and Moral Order in America, 1820–1920* (Cambridge, MA: Harvard University Press, 1978); Plunz, *History of Housing*; Daniel Rodgers, *Atlantic Crossings: Social Politics in a Progressive Age* (Cambridge, MA: Harvard University Press, 1998), 367–408; Anthony Jackson, *A Place Called Home: A History of Low Cost Housing in Manhattan* (Cambridge, MA: MIT Press, 1976); Gail Radford, *Modern Housing for America: Policy Struggles in the New Deal Era* (Chicago: University of Chicago Press, 1996); M. Christine Boyer, *Dreaming the Rational City: The Myth of American City Planning* (Cambridge, MA: MIT Press, 1983); Mark Gelfand, *A Nation of Cities*; Marc Weiss, "The Origins and Legacy of Urban Renewal," in J. Paul Mitchell, ed., *Federal Housing Policy and Programs, Past and Present* (New Brunswick, NJ: Rutgers University Press, 1985), 265–266; Hubert-Jan Henket and Hilde Heynen, eds., *Back from Utopia: The Challenge of the Modern Movement* (Rotterdam: 010 Publishers, 2002); Hilde Heynen, *Architecture and Modernity* (Cambridge, MA: MIT Press, 1999); William J. Curtis, *Modern Architecture since 1900* (London: Phaidon, 1996); Bacon, *Le Corbusier in America*; Rosalie Genevro, "Site Selection and the New York City Housing Authority, 1934–1939," *Journal of Urban History* 12, no. 4 (August 1986): 334–352. See also Peter Marcuse, "The Beginnings of Public Housing in New York," *Journal of Urban History* 12, no. 4 (August 1986): 353–390; Howard Gillette, "The Evolution of Neighborhood Planning: From the Progressive Era to the 1949 Housing Act," *Journal of Urban History* 9, no. 4 (August 1983): 421–444; Robert Fairbanks, *Making Better Citizens: Housing Reform and Community Development Strategy in Cincinnati, 1890–1960* (Urbana: University of Illinois Press, 1988).

13. Leon Keyserling, "Homes for All—and How," *Survey Graphic* (February 1946): 37–41, 63. Keyserling was New York senator Robert Wagner's chief aide in 1937 and was primarily responsible for drafting the 1937 Housing Act that bears Wagner's name. On wartime planning, see Donald Albrecht, ed., *World War II and the American Dream: How Wartime Building Changed a Nation* (Washington, DC, and Cambridge, MA: National Building Museum and MIT Press, 1995).

14. New York City, City Planning Commission, City-wide Map Showing Sections Containing Areas for Clearance, Replanning and Low Rent Housing, January 3, 1940, 4–6. See also Schwartz, *The New York Approach*, 75.

15. The best accounts of this process are Fogelson, *Downtown*, 317–380; and, in the legal and policy sphere, Wendell E. Pritchett, "The 'Public Menace' of Blight: Urban Renewal and the Private Uses of Eminent Domain," *Yale Law and Policy Review* 21, no. 1 (2003): 1–52.

16. See Henry R. Luce, "The American Century," reprinted in *Diplomatic History* 23, no. 2 (Spring 1999): 159–171.

17. Wolfe calls it an attempt to produce the good society through "growth and empire," not "dissent and reform." See Alan Wolfe, *America's Impasse: The Rise and Fall of the Politics of Growth* (New York: Pantheon, 1981), 23. Historians have used a range of terms to describe this postwar political economy and the political culture it produced: corporate liberalism, military Keynesianism, the politics of growth, pro-growth politics, economic growthmanship. See Robert M. Collins, *More: The Politics of Economic Growth in Postwar America* (New York: Oxford University Press, 2000), 17–67; John Mollenkopf, *The Contested City* (Princeton, NJ: Princeton University Press, 1983); George Lipsitz, *Rainbow at Midnight: Labor and Culture in the 1940s* (Urbana: University of Illinois Press, 1994); Tom Engelhardt, *The End of Victory Culture: Cold War America and the Disillusioning of a Generation* (New York: Basic, 1995). The classic account of postwar prosperity is David M. Potter, *People of Plenty: Economic Abundance and the American Character* (Chicago: University of Chicago Press, 1954).

18. Lizabeth Cohen, *A Consumer's Republic: The Politics of Mass Consumption* (New York: Knopf, 2003); Dolores Hayden, *Building Suburbia: Green Fields and Urban Growth, 1820–2000* (New York: Pantheon, 2003). Robert A. Beauregard, *When America Became Suburban* (Minneapolis: University of Minnesota Press, 2006), 18.

19. Elizabeth Wood, quoted in Lurie, "The Dreary Deadlock of Public Housing— How to Break It," *Architectural Forum* 106 (June 1957): 224. See also Mollenkopf, *The Contested City*.

20. George Kennan, "The Long Telegram," excerpted in Jussi Hanhimaki and Odd Arne Westad, *The Cold War: A History in Documents and Eyewitness Accounts* (New York: Oxford University Press, 2003), 111. On NSC 68, see Ernest R. May, *American Cold War Strategy: Interpreting NSC 68* (New York: St. Martin's, 1993). See also Wolfe, *America's Impasse,* 116.

21. Gerald J. Carey, "Priorities for Construction and Maintenance," May 11, 1951, in box 59D2, folder 05, NYCHA.

22. James Bryant Conant, *Slums and Suburbs* (New York: McGraw-Hill, 1961), 34. I am indebted here to Louis Menand, "The Long Shadow of James B. Conant," in his *American Studies* (New York: Farrar, Straus, and Giroux, 2002), 91–111.

23. Nicholas Dagen Bloom, *Merchant of Illusion: James Rouse, America's Salesman of the Businessman's Utopia* (Columbus: Ohio State University Press, 2004), xiii, 1–26.

24. See Mary Dudziak, *Cold War Civil Rights: Race and the Image of American Democracy* (Princeton, NJ: Princeton University Press, 2000). On "containment," see Elaine Tyler May, *Homeward Bound: American Families in the Cold War Era* (New York: Basic, 1988); Alan Nadel, *Containment Culture: American Narratives, Postmodernism, and the Atomic Age* (Durham, NC: Duke University Press, 1995); Engelhardt, *End of Victory Culture*. Also see Arnold Hirsch, "'Containment' on the Home Front: Race and Federal Housing Policy from the New Deal to the Cold War," *Journal of Urban*

History 26, no. 2 (January 2000): 158–189. On the critique of "mass society" during the Cold War see, for example, Andrew Jamison and Ron Eyerman, *Seeds of the Sixties* (Berkeley, University of California Press, 1994), 30–63; Richard Pells, *The Liberal Mind in A Conservative Age: American Intellectuals in the 1940s and 1950s* (New York: Harper and Row, 1985), 183–261; Andrew Ross, *No Respect: Intellectuals and Popular Culture* (New York: Routledge, 1989), 42–64.

25. See Joshua Freeman, *Working-Class New York: Life and Labor since World War II* (New York: New Press, 2000); Edgar M. Hoover and Raymond Vernon, *Anatomy of a Metropolis: The Changing Distribution of People and Jobs within the New York Metropolitan Region* (Cambridge, MA: Harvard University Press, 1959); John Mollenkopf and Manuel Castells, "Introduction," and Richard Harris, "The Geography of Employment and Residence in New York since 1950," both in Mollenkopf and Castells, eds., *Dual City: Restructuring New York* (New York: Russell Sage Foundation, 1991), 3–22, 129–152; Robert Fitch, *The Assassination of New York* (New York: Verso, 1993); Schwartz, *The New York Approach,* 229–260. Schwartz tells the story of the one economic study to question the effects of deindustrialization: John I. Griffin, *Industrial Location in the New York Area* (New York: City College Press, 1956). On the effects of Moses's highways, see Leonard Wallock, "The Myth of the Master Builder: Robert Moses, New York, and the Dynamics of Metropolitan Development since World War II," *Journal of Urban History* 17, no. 4 (August 1991), 339–362. On suburbanization and federal subsidies, see Rosalyn Baxandall and Elizabeth Ewen, *Picture Windows: How the Suburbs Happened* (New York: Basic, 2000); Kenneth T. Jackson, *Crabgrass Frontier: The Suburbanization of the United States* (New York: Oxford University Press, 1985); Thomas Hanchett, "U.S. Tax Policy and the Shopping Center Boom of the 1950s and '60s," *American Historical Review* 101 (October 1996): 1082–1110; Lizabeth Cohen, "From Town Center to Shopping Center: The Reconfiguration of Community Marketplaces in Postwar America," *American Historical Review* 101 (October 1996): 1050–1081. For the effects of these policies on the city, see Craig Steven Wilder, *A Covenant with Color: Race and Social Power in Brooklyn* (New York: Columbia University Press, 2000), 175–218. On migration to New York, see Nancy Foner, *From Ellis Island to JFK: New York's Two Great Waves of Immigration* (New Haven, CT: Yale University Press, 2000); and Frederick M. Binder and David M. Reimers, *All the Nations under Heaven: An Ethnic and Racial History of New York City* (New York: Columbia University Press, 1995).

26. The literature on New York's decline is extensive. See Roger Starr, *The Rise and Fall of New York City* (New York: Basic, 1985); Fitch, *The Assassination of New York;* and Ken Auletta, *The Streets Were Paved with Gold* (New York: Random House, 1975). For the national picture, see Robert Beauregard, *Voices of Decline: The Postwar Fate of US Cities* (Cambridge: Blackwell, 1993), and the book that alerted a national academic audience to the "urban crisis": Edward Banfield, *The Unheavenly City: The Nature and Future of Our Urban Crisis* (Boston: Little, Brown, 1965). For another contemporary account, see Richard Whalen, *A City Destroying Itself* (New York: Morrow, 1965).

27. Other scholarship also argues that the origins of the urban crisis lie in the 1940s and 1950s rather than the 1960s. See Thomas Sugrue, *The Origins of the Urban Crisis:*

Race and Inequality in Postwar Detroit (Princeton, NJ: Princeton University Press, 1996); and Arnold Hirsch, *Making the Second Ghetto*. For New York, see Eric C. Schneider, *Vampires, Dragons and Egyptian Kings: Youth Gangs in Postwar New York* (Princeton, NJ: Princeton University Press, 1999), ch. 2. For the opposing argument, see Fred Siegel, *The Future Once Happened Here: New York, D.C., L.A. and the Fate of America's Big Cities* (New York: Free Press, 1997). On urban renewal and the overall crisis of urban liberalism, see Christopher J. Klemek, "Urbanism as Reform: Modernist Planning and the Crisis of Urban Liberalism in Europe and North America, 1945–1975," Ph.D. diss., University of Pennsylvania, 2004.

28. See Serge Guilbaut, *How New York Stole the Idea of Modern Art: Abstract Expressionism, Freedom, and the Cold War,* trans. Arthur Goldhammer (Chicago: University of Chicago Press, 1983); Leonard Wallock, ed., *New York 1940–1965: Culture Capital of the World* (New York: Rizzoli, 1988); Saskia Sassen, *The Global City* (Princeton, NJ: Princeton University Press, 1991); Martin Shefter, ed., *Capital of the American Century: The National and International Influence of New York City* (New York: Russell Sage, 1993); Robert A. M. Stern, Thomas Mellins, and David Fishman, eds., *New York 1960* (New York: Monacelli, 1995); William B. Scott and Peter M. Rutkoff, *New York Modern*; Martha Biondi, *To Stand and Fight: The Struggle for Civil Rights in Postwar New York City* (Cambridge, MA: Harvard University Press, 2003). My account of New York's role in the Cold War is indebted to comments made by Mike Wallace, "The Cold War City," Gotham Center Seminar on Postwar New York City History, City University of New York, October 22, 2003.

29. Stern et al., *New York 1960,* 13.

Chapter 1

1. E. B. White, *Here Is New York* (New York: Little Bookroom, 1999), 54–56; Thomas J. Hamilton, "Buildings Plotted in U.N. Site Here," *NYT,* March 24, 1947, 1, 2.

2. O'Dwyer quoted in Robert Caro, *The Power Broker: Robert Moses and the Fall of New York* (New York: Knopf, 1974), 771.

3. Robert Moses is quoted in "Work on U.N. Site behind Schedule," *NYT,* November 25, 1948, 3.

4. The story of how Manhattan claimed the United Nations has been told many times. My account is assembled from Robert A. M. Stern, Thomas Mellins, and David Fishman, eds., *New York 1960: Architecture and Urbanism between the Second World War and the Bicentennial* (New York: Monacelli, 1995), 601–609; Samuel E. Bleecker, *The Politics of Architecture: A Perspective on Nelson A. Rockefeller* (New York: Rutledge, 1981), 71–79; Victoria Newhouse, *Wallace K. Harrison, Architect* (New York: Rizzoli, 1989), 104–113; William Zeckendorf, with Edward McCreary, *Zeckendorf: The Autobiography of William Zeckendorf* (New York: Holt, Rinehart and Winston, 1970), 63–71; Robert Moses, *Public Works: A Dangerous Trade* (New York: McGraw-Hill, 1970), 486–489; James Monahan, "How the U.N. Found Its Home at Last," *Reader's Digest,* May 1947, 16–20. See also George Barrett, "New Skyscraper Home Now Possible as U.N. Center," *NYT,* December 8, 1946, 1, 11; and George Barrett, "City Tract Chosen," *NYT,* December 13, 1946, 1, 4.

5. George R. Leighton, "Fifty Nations in Search of a Capital," *NYTM*, July 8, 1945, 9, 32–33; and "The Capital of the World," *NYT*, February 4, 1946, 21.

6. State of New York, Senate, Albany, January 8, 1947, in series 0472, box 36, file 21, Central Registry, SG-HQ Planning—Co-operation and Support—NY State Legislature with UN, February 24, 1947–April 19, 1947, UNArch; John D. Rockefeller to Eduardo Zuleta Angel, December 10, 1946, in roll 25, box 102733, ParksGen; "A Sacred Ceremony," *NYT*, April 13, 1947, 110. See also Robert Moses, "Remarks of Robert Moses at the Opening of the United Nations Exhibit, Brooklyn Museum," September 15, 1947, in roll 49, box 107888, folder 50-UN, 1, ParksMoses.

7. Trygve Lie, "General Arguments for New York," December 12, 1946, in series 186, box 1, file 10, Permanent Site, July 1946–December 1946, UNArch. A handwritten note on the document reads "For Mr. Lie's personal file." See also Lie's deputy Benjamin Cohen quoted in Morris Kaplan, "U.N. Breaks Ground for Its Capital," *NYT*, September 15, 1948, 1, 3. See also Glen Bennett, secretary of the UN Headquarters Planning Office, in "Broadcast over WHLI, Hempstead," May 21, 1948, in series 0472, box 33, file 7, Central Registry, SG-HQ Planning-Publicity-Radio-Approval of Scripts, February 7, 1948–June 4, 1951, UNArch.

8. O'Dwyer forwarded Werner's letter to Moses, who dismissed it in a letter to Deputy Mayor John J. Bennett. While Werner's complaints may have been minor or relatively inconsequential, the response indicates the offhand and habitual dismissal that black concerns received at the highest level of New York government. See Ludlow W. Werner to William O'Dwyer, April 14, 1947; O'Dwyer to Robert Moses, April 18, 1947; Moses to John J. Bennett, April 22, 1947, all in roll 25, box 102763, ParksGen. On race in postwar New York, see Martha Biondi, *To Stand and Fight: The Struggle for Civil Rights in Postwar New York City* (Cambridge, MA: Harvard University Press, 2003).

9. The Haitian UN staff member is quoted in George Barrett, "Life in the U.S. as Seen by the U.N. Staff," *NYTM*, May 2, 1948, 54. On the United Nations in New York, see Thomas Borstelmann, *The Cold War and the Color Line: American Race Relations in the Global Arena* (Cambridge, MA: Harvard University Press, 2001), 79; and Mary L. Dudziak, *Cold War Civil Rights: Race and the Image of American Democracy* (Princeton, NJ: Princeton University Press, 2000), 229–230.

10. For Truman's Tennyson keepsake, see David McCullough, *Truman* (New York: Simon and Schuster, 1992), 64–65. For Acheson's feelings on the United Nations, see Dean Acheson, *Present at the Creation: My Years at the State Department* (New York: Norton, 1969), 111–112.

11. On New York's postwar social idealism, see Joshua Freeman, *Working-Class New York* (New York: New Press, 2000). For race, ethnicity, and pluralist ideals during the war and in the postwar years, see Nikhil Pal Singh, *Black Is a Country: Race and the Unfinished Struggle for Democracy* (Cambridge, MA: Harvard University Press, 2004), 103–105, 136; and Singh, "Culture/Wars: Recoding Empire in an Age of Democracy," *American Quarterly* 50, no. 3 (September 1998): 474; Manning Marable, *Race, Reform and Rebellion: The Second Reconstruction in Black America, 1945–1982* (Jackson: University of Mississippi Press, 1984), 14–17; Gary Gerstle, *American Crucible: Race and Nation in the Twentieth Century* (Princeton, NJ: Princeton University Press, 2001), 187–237; Richard Polenberg, *One Nation Divisible: Class, Race and Ethnicity in*

the United States since 1938 (New York: Penguin, 1980), 46–86; Carol Anderson, *Eyes Off the Prize: The United Nations and the African-American Struggle for Human Rights, 1944–1955* (New York: Cambridge University Press, 2003).

12. "A Sacred Ceremony," *NYT,* April 13, 1947; Lie, "General Arguments for New York"; and "The Capital of the World," *NYT,* February 2, 1946.

13. The definitive account of the design of the UN headquarters has been delivered by one of the participants, Wallace Harrison's deputy George Dudley. My take on the story is indebted to his work. See George A. Dudley, *A Workshop for Peace: Designing the United Nations Headquarters* (New York, and Cambridge, MA: Architectural History Foundation, and MIT Press, 1994). On Harrison's selection and the basic timeline, see also Newhouse, *Wallace K. Harrison,* 112–115, 140; Moses, *Public Works,* 491–500; Stern et al., *New York 1960,* 609–613. Harrison quoted in Dudley, *Workshop for Peace,* 342; and Arthur Massolo, "Skyscraper U.N. Plan Practically Discarded," *NYP,* February 7, 1947, 24. The headline of this article proved to be a false alarm, the product of overeager reporting on Massolo's part that Harrison denied the next day.

14. See Dudley, *Workshop for Peace,* 342–343. For Le Corbusier's suggestion of "a single office building" with an "entirely definable" and "exact biology," see Le Corbusier, "Report to the Secretary General, Trygve Lie," July 9, 1946, 25–26, in series 186, box 1, file 9, Permanent Site, 1/1947–6/1947, UNArch. This description was accompanied by a sketch of a slab-block office tower standing in an open plain. It featured a cross-hatched, glass façade and stood on Corbusier's trademark stilt-like *pilotis.* This report was later published as the first part of Le Corbusier, *UN Headquarters* (New York: Reinhold, 1947), 28–32. For more on Corbusier's influence, see Mardges Bacon, *Le Corbusier in America: Travels in the Land of the Timid* (Cambridge, MA: MIT Press, 2001), 304–309; and Peter Blake, *The Master Builders: Le Corbusier, Mies van der Rohe, Frank Lloyd Wright* (1960; rpt., New York: Norton, 1976), 125–132.

15. The "bold thrust into the future" quote comes from "The U.N. Plans Its Home," *NYT,* August 10, 1947, E10. The "massive vitreous structure" quote comes from George Barrett, "U.N. Capital Shows Much Glass," *NYT,* September 17, 1947, 2. Also see "The Secretariat: A Campanile, a Cliff of Glass, a Great Debate," *AF* (November 1950): 93–112. On the United Nations' significance, see Bleecker, *Politics of Architecture,* 39; and Stern et al., *New York 1960,* 613–619. Stern and his colleagues call it "the long-awaited, tri-umphant realization of interwar-era Modernist architecture and urbanism" (613). See also Hasan-Uddin Khan, *International Style: Modernist Architecture from 1925 to 1965* (Cologne, Germany: Taschen, 2001), 124. Popular reaction in New York focused on the glass façades. See "World Capital Built of Glass," *NYS,* September 17, 1947; Fendall Yerxa, "U.N. Headquarters Model Shows Its Façade as One Vast Window," *NYHT,* September 17, 1947, 1, 7. On modernist opinion, see Stern et al., *New York 1960,* 619–621; and see other architects' verdicts in "The Secretariat," 101–105.

16. For Austin quote, see George Barrett, "Top U.N. Site Post to W. K. Harrison," *NYT,* January 1, 1947, 6.

17. Gertrude Samuels, "What Kind of Capitol for the U.N.?" *NYTM,* April 20, 1947, 9, 55–57, 59; Barrett, "Top U.N. Site Post to W. K. Harrison," 6.

18. Harrison quoted in Fendall Yerxa, "Design of U.N. 'Workshop for Peace' Revealed," *NYHT,* May 22, 1947, 1, 13. See also George Barrett, "U.N. Capital Plans Stress Function,"

NYT, May 22, 1947, 19. Bassov and Le Corbusier quoted in Samuels, "What Kind of Capitol for the U.N.?" 56.

19. "U.N. Site Plan Dazes Architects; One Calls It a 'Diabolical Dream,'" *NYHT,* May 23, 1947; Lewis Mumford, "Buildings as Symbols," in his *From the Ground Up* (New York: Harcourt, Brace, 1956), 31, 35. See also Ada Louise Huxtable, "Buildings That Are Symbols, Too," *NYTM,* April 5, 1959, 18–19, 103, in which Huxtable charges that, "according to many critics," the Secretariat is "no more than a glorified office building" and has "neither the architectural force nor the distinction appropriate to the expression of an important ideal." Or, as one later critic put it, "the UN building should have been symbolic of the universal hopes of man for world peace, but our architects were unequal to this vision and aspiration." See Donald McDonald, interview with Allan Temko, in *The City* (Santa Barbara, CA: Center for the Study of Democratic Institutions and Fund for the Republic, 1962), 22–23.

20. "The Secretariat," 94–97. For one influential account of the postwar office building, see Paul Goldberger, *The Skyscraper* (New York: Knopf, 1986), 103–113. See also Benjamin Flowers, *Skyscraper: The Politics and Power of Building New York City in the Twentieth Century* (Philadelphia: Penn Press, 2009).

21. "Warren of bureaucratic offices" is from McDonald, interview with Temko, 22. See also Henry Stern Churchill, "United Nations Headquarters: A Description and Appraisal," *AR* 111, no. 7 (July 1952): 103–124 and "The Secretariat," 94–97. Interestingly, this verdict may have accurately reflected political reality. The structure and agenda of the United Nations were, from its very founding in San Francisco during the war, in many ways driven by the United States' geopolitical needs. See Stephen Schlesinger, *Act of Creation: The Founding of the United Nations* (New York: Westview, 2004). This would change somewhat in later years as questions surrounding decolonization took center stage, but the United Nations' actions were always deeply influenced, and some would say its goals and principles often hampered and compromised, by the Cold War conflict between the United States and the Soviet Union. See Stanley Meisler, *United Nations: The First Fifty Years* (Boston: Atlantic Monthly Press, 1997); and Paul Kennedy, *The Parliament of Man: The Past, Present, and Future of the United Nations* (New York: Random House, 2006).

22. Liang quoted in Samuels, "What Kind of Capitol for the U.N.?" 56. Linda Sue Phipps, "Constructing the United Nations Headquarters: Modern Architecture as Public Diplomacy," Ph.D. diss., Harvard University, 1998; Le Corbusier, "Declaration, Headquarters Planning Office," New York, April 18, 1947, in series 0472, box 3, file 6, Central Registry, SG-HQ Planning Board of Design Consultants—General, UNArch. See also comments by Trygve Lie, addressing the General Assembly, in which he finds hope for the "men of politics" in the fact that the "men of art and science" were able to reach "common agreement." See General Assembly Second Session, Verbatim Record of the One Hundred and Twenty First Plenary Meeting, November 20, 1947, 2, in roll 25, box 102763, UN-Site, ParksGen.

23. Harrison quoted in Samuels, "What Kind of Capitol for the U.N.?" 59. A Chicago architect also commented, "The UN buildings, by showing men can work together, promise us a world in which all men *could* function together in peace." See "The Secretariat," 105.

24. For the Carnarvon quote, see "The Secretariat," 95.

25. As Max Abramovitz, Harrison's architectural partner, put it, "the feeling in all our plans reflected his indirect influence via his past works and writings, especially among the younger men." See Dudley, *Workshop for Peace,* 342.

26. Lewis Mumford, "UN Model and Model UN," in *From the Ground Up,* 22–23. On the provisions for the site made by New York City, see United Nations, General Assembly, "Headquarters Advisory Committee, Summary Record of the Third Meeting, Held in the Arsenal Building, New York City, New York, on Friday, 7 March 1947, at 11:00 a.m.," March 15, 1947, 1–8, in roll 25, box 102763, UN-Meetings, ParksGen; Robert Moses, "The United Nations in New York," March 10, 1947, draft copy in roll 26, box 102763, folder 5, UN-Site, ParksGen; "List of Actions Proposed to Be Taken by the United Nations and by the City to Carry Out the Complete Development Program in and Adjacent to the United Nations Site," attached to Robert Moses to William O'Dwyer, March 24, 1947, in roll 26, box 102763, folder 5, UN-Site, ParksGen. Ironically, Moses was personally against "a series of buildings in midtown Manhattan" as not a "proper or dignified setting for the U.N." See Robert Moses, "Memo to Grover Whalen on U.N. Permanent Site," September 12, 1946, in roll 41, box 107884, folder 4, UN-3, ParksMoses. Moses continued to assert that his Flushing Meadows site was the happy medium between country and city. See Moses, *Public Works,* 489.

27. My account of the site and the removals is drawn from Chief Inspector Morris Goldfinger, Division of Housing, to Commissioner N. Thomas Saxl, City of New York, intradepartmental memorandum, "Proposed U.N. Site," December 16, 1946, in roll 25, box 102733, ParksGen; William M. Ellard to Robert Moses, In Re: United Nations Site, Borough of Manhattan, June 20, 1947, copy in series 0472, box 36, file 24, Central Registry, SG-HQ Planning-Legal-Termination of Occupancy, April 8, 1947–September 17, 1948, UNArch; William M. Ellard, Director of Real Estate, to Byron Price, City of New York, intradepartmental memorandum, Re: Relocation of Residential Tenants Residing on UN Site, July 9, 1947, in series 0472, box 36, file 10, Central Registry, SG-HQ Planning-Redevelopment and Planning-Relocation of Resident Tenants on Site, April 9, 1947–July 9, 1947, UNArch; "Schedule for Relocation of Tenants Affected by Street Improvements around the United Nations Site," September 8, 1947; and James Felt to Robert Moses, November 12, 1947, copies of both in roll 26, box 102763, Relocation, ParksGen; Joseph Seif to Glen E. Bennett, Executive Officer, United Nations interoffice memorandum, "Interim Report on the Evacuation of the Commercial Tenants," February 19, 1948, in series 0472, box 36, file 11, Central Registry, SG-HQ Planning-Redevelopment and Planning-Relocation of Resident Tenants on Site 120–127 2nd Ave., July 29, 1947–May 15, 1951, UNArch; William J. McCurdy, Acting Director of Real Estate, to Robert Moses, City Construction Co-ordinator, In Re: Street Widenings, Etc. Adjoining United Nations Site, Borough of Manhattan, August 13, 1948, roll 26, box 102792, UN-Tenant Relocation, ParksGen; William M. Ellard to Glenn Bennett, In Re: United Nations Headquarters Site Rehabilitation Work, 1021/1027, Second Avenue, Block 1327, Lots 25/28, Borough of Manhattan, February 3, 1949, copy in series 0472, box 36, file 11, Central Registry, UNArch.

28. On "job clearance" at the UN site, see Joel Schwartz, *The New York Approach* (Columbus: Ohio State University Press, 1993), 238–239. Schwartz's estimates

are based on the 1934 Real Property Inventory, which recorded 155 industrial or commercial structures. This is at odds with the 51 commercial buildings recorded by the Division of Housing in late 1946, so Schwartz's estimate may be high. However, the Real Property Inventory does not include the jobs lost in the small stores that lined the ground floors of many residential structures. Whatever the total, it appears that industry had been abandoning the area even before the United Nations arrived on the scene. On the halting resistance to clearance and the official response to these entreaties, see A. M. Rosenthal, "Plan to Tear Down Church for U.N. Stirs People of 47th Street Area," *NYT,* March 28, 1947; Robert Moses to Colonel Dawson, April 1, 1947; Peter Albano to William O'Dwyer, April 3, 1947; John J. Bennett to Peter Albano, April 17, 1947, all in roll 49, box 107888, ParksMoses; George Barrett, "Occupant of Site Delays U.N. Start," *NYT,* June 15, 1947, 27; "Priest Sues to Bar UN from Midtown Site," *NYDN,* October 10, 1947, 24; "2 Tenants Fight Eviction, Delay U.N. Site Work," *NYHT,* December 20, 1947.

29. See "New York: U.N. in Turtle Bay," *NYT,* December 15, 1946, E2. See also William Zeckendorf's reminiscences of the "odor zone" created by the site's "1890 Chicago-in-miniature complete with cattle pens, packing plants, and an all-pervasive, stomach-turning stench!" Zeckendorf with McCreary, *Autobiography,* 63–64.

30. See "UN Site—Symbol of UN Job," *United Nations World* 1, no. 3 (April 1947): n.p.

31. Joel Schwartz estimates that clearance of the UN site was just the first salvo in a war against the "factory economy" that would claim between 18,000 and 30,000 jobs along the Brooklyn and Manhattan East River waterfront between 1945 and 1955. See Schwartz, *The New York Approach,* 229–260, statistics on 239.

32. See Le Corbusier, "Report to the Secretary General, Trygve Lie," July 9, 1946, 36; Jules Korchien and Maxfield Vogel, "Statement Presented by Greater New York CIO Council to the City Planning Commission," January 22, 1947, in roll 26, box 102763, UN-Zoning, ParksGen. See also G. E. Kidder Smith to Editor, "Setting for the U.N.," *NYT,* June 17, 1947.

33. Mumford quoted in Stern et al., *New York 1960,* 604; and Lewis Mumford, "Stop and Think," *Progressive Architecture-Pencil Points* 27 (April 1946), 10. During their entire search in rural, urban, and suburban areas, UN officials continually expressed their interest in using "modern city planning with a low density of population." See "Proposed Press Release (Submitted by Site Committee)," August 5, 1946, in series 186, box 1, file 4, Headquarters Commission, June 1946–August 1946, UNArch.

34. Le Corbusier's newfound enthusiasm for the New York site was included in the appendix that he added to his earlier report to Lie when he published it as a book in 1947. See Le Corbusier, *UN Headquarters,* 77, 68, 72. Also see Corbusier quoted in Dudley, *Workshop for Peace,* 21; and George Barrett, "3 Tall Buildings in U.N. Plan for a Mechanized Capital," *NYT,* March 27, 1947, 1, 21. Corbusier's early doubts about New York were first recorded in his report to Lie and then included in the book as well. See Le Corbusier, *UN Headquarters,* 18. Corbusier had long had misgivings about New York. See Bacon, *Le Corbusier in America;* and Le Corbusier, *When the Cathedrals Were White: A Journey to the Country of Timid People* (New York: Reynal and Hitchcock, 1947), his account of his journey to the United States in 1935.

35. Harrison quoted in "East Side Site of U.N. Forecast as Garden City," *NYT*, January 14, 1947; and in Louise Levitas, "World Capital's Architect-in-Chief," *NYP Magazine*, February 23, 1947, 9.

36. Bennett quoted in "U.N. 'Dream City' to Stand by Itself," *NYT*, June 24, 1947, 40. See also "Harmony Is Stressed by U.N. Site Planners," *NYT*, August 10, 1947, 21.

37. Trygve Lie, *Report to the General Assembly of the United Nations by the Secretary General on the Permanent Headquarters of the United Nations* (New York: United Nations, 1947), 11, 74, 79. See also George Barrett, "Superb Park Site Projected for U.N. in Proposal by Lie," *NYT*, 1, 20.

38. See "United Nations Headquarters, New York," *Architects' Journal* (August 21, 1947): 164. Also see Ketchum and Morris quoted in "Planners and Architects Praise U.N. Headquarters Proposals," *NYT*, August 13, 1947, 25; Hugh R. Pomeroy, "The Permanent Headquarters of the United Nations," *Survey Graphic* (October 1947): 531–533; William Zeckendorf to Robert F. Wagner Jr., April 9, 1948, and Zeckendorf to Robert Moses, November 17, 1948, copies of both in roll 26, box 102792, UN-Approach, ParksGen. See also Zeckendorf's own account in Zeckendorf with McCreary, *Autobiography*, 72–78; New York Chapter of the American Institute of Architects, "East Midtown Manhattan," 1947–1948, in roll 26, box 102792, UN-East Mid-Manhattan Development, ParksGen; City Planning Commission, "Addition of United Nations Replanning and Redevelopment Section," May 10, 1950, copy in series 0472, box 2, folder 5, UNArch. See also "U.N. Site Plan Backed," *NYT*, April 8, 1950, 9. Robert Moses opposed this change to the master plan. Ever practical, he thought that upgrading of the area should be left to the private market. In his memoir, he showed how that happened, as the assessed property valuation of the UN area went up 245 percent from 1946 to 1967, while the values of all Manhattan real estate went up 88 percent. See Moses, *Public Works*, 505. Still, without the goad of the United Nations, Moses thought that the area would have needed clearance for public housing or a Title I project. See Robert F. Wagner Jr. and Robert Moses, *The United Nations and the City of New York* (New York: Borough of Manhattan President, 1951), 4.

39. See Hugh R. Pomeroy, "Squalid Surroundings for U.N. Splendor?" 11–12, draft in series 0472, box 2, file 5, Central Registry, SG-HQ Planning-General-Surrounding Development, February 10, 1947–July 25, 1950, UNArch; "For a Worthy World Headquarters," in Citizens Housing Council, "Housing Is Everybody's Business," pamphlet in box 73C5, folder 5, NYCHA.

40. Cleveland Rodgers and Rebecca Rankin, *New York: The World's Capital City, Its Development and Contributions to Progress* (New York: Harper, 1948), 282, 352, 362–365.

41. See "New York in 1999—Five Predictions: Architects and City Planners Look into the Crystal Ball and Tell What They See," *NYTM*, February 6, 1949, 18–19, 51, 53.

42. See Herblock, "Did They Fool You on Housing, Too?" *Washington Post*, June 28, 1948. On the stalled UN loan, see Fendall Yerxa, "U.N. Building Plans Upset as House Fails to Act on Loan," *NYHT*, June 21, 1948, 1.

43. White, *Here Is New York*, 19.

Chapter 2

1. A. L. Kirkpatrick, "Along the Row: Facts and Comment," *Chicago Journal of Commerce* (April 24, 1943). In the 1940s and '50s, Metropolitan Life was commonly called "the Metropolitan" by journalists, company officials, politicians, and the public. For the sake of variation, I will alternate between this name and the common and official abbreviation that the company uses in its histories and press releases: Met Life.

2. See untitled Metropolitan press release, Stuyvesant Town History and Plans, 1943–1967, S14, MLA.

3. "Topics of the Times," *NYT*, January 6, 1945; "One Way to Invest," *Business Week*, May 8, 1943, 105. For the most explicit and succinct formulation of these principles, see Frederick H. Ecker, "Housing (with Particular Reference to New York City)," address to the Annual Conference of Mayors, New York, February 16, 1948, 11, Uncatalogued Stuyvesant Town Materials, MLA. As a mutual company, Met Life had no stockholders. Its policyholders were technically owners of the company and received as dividends any profit the company made on its investments. See Metropolitan Life Insurance Company, "What Is a Mutual Company?" in Uncatalogued Stuyvesant Town Materials, MLA.

4. See Olivier Zunz, *Making America Corporate, 1870–1920* (Chicago: University of Chicago Press, 1989), 114. On the internal organization of Metropolitan's tower, see ibid., 114–121; and Roberta Moudry, "The Corporate and the Civic: Metropolitan Life's Home Office Building," in Moudry, ed., *The American Skyscraper: Cultural Histories* (New York: Cambridge University Press, 2005), 120–146. On the gender implications of Met Life's corporate structure, see also Roland Marchand, *Creating the Corporate Soul: The Rise of Public Relations and Corporate Imagery in American Big Business* (Berkeley: University of California Press, 1998), 38–39, 104–105, 184–185; and Angel Kwolek-Folland, *Engendering Business: Men and Women in the Corporate Office, 1870–1930* (Baltimore, MD: Johns Hopkins University Press, 1994), 129–135.

5. Joel Schwartz, *The New York Approach: Robert Moses, Urban Liberals, and Redevelopment of the Inner City* (Columbus: Ohio State University Press, 1993), xvii.

6. See "Metropolitan's Housing Plans Hit at Hearing," *NYT*, May 20, 1943, 23.

7. For Met Life's size and postwar investment outlook, see Henry Reed, "Investment Policy of the Metropolitan Life," *Task* 4 (1944): 38–40. Also see Richard L. Stokes, "Way Set for Low-Cost Housing Built and Managed Privately," *Washington Star*, August 8, 1943. By 1947, Metropolitan had assets of more than $8 billion. "Metropolitan Life Assets Now Exceed Eight Billions," *NYWT*, February 13, 1947.

8. Thomas C. Cochran, "Largest Private Corporation," review of *The Metropolitan Life: A Study in Business Growth*, by Marquis James, in *NYHT*, March 7, 1947.

9. See untitled typescript (history of Metropolitan housing efforts up to Parkchester), n.d., 1, Uncatalogued ST Materials, Zismer-All Communities folder, MLA. Met Life's housing vision was an updated, large-scale descendant of the ideals of the model tenement movement. This small group of turn-of-the-century patricians—a well-heeled, business-minded branch of the early housing reform movement—believed in market solutions to housing the poor.

10. By 1943, Metropolitan had projects planned or under way in Los Angeles, San Francisco, and Alexandria and Fairfax, Virginia, both outside Washington, DC. See

Business Week, May 8, 1943, 105. For more on those communities and Metropolitan's three interlinked goals—writing insurance, investing funds, and providing for social welfare—see "Metropolitan Life Makes Housing Pay: How to Order a City," *Fortune* 33, no. 4 (April 1946): 134; Gretta Palmer, "Middletown-on-the-Subway," *Christian Science Monitor,* November 1, 1941 (republished and condensed in *Reader's Digest,* December 1941, 132–134). For more on Parkchester, see untitled typescript (history of Metropolitan housing efforts to Parkchester), Uncatalogued ST Materials, MLA. See also "Metropolitan's Parkchester: Private Enterprise Builds a City for 42,000 People, Trades Modern Living for Low Rents, Crooks a Finger at Idle Investment Millions," *AF* (December 1939): 412–422.

11. Schwartz, *The New York Approach,* 26; Robert Fogelson, *Downtown: Its Rise and Fall, 1880–1950* (New Haven, CT: Yale University Press, 2001), 334; Max Page, *The Creative Destruction of Manhattan* (Chicago: University of Chicago Press, 1998), 100; for statistics, see Community Service Society, "The Rehousing Needs of the Families on the Stuyvesant Town Site," June 14, 1945; Anthony Jackson, *A Place Called Home: A History of Low-Cost Housing in Manhattan* (Cambridge, MA: MIT Press, 1976), 208.

12. Moses to Thomas E. Dewey, March 22, 1943, roll 17, folder 010, ParksMoses; Fogelson, *Downtown,* 340–342; Schwartz, *The New York Approach,* 70–72.

13. Ecker quoted in Schwartz, *The New York Approach,* 92. Moses claimed, "I induced the Metropolitan Life Insurance Company to build Stuyvesant Town," while George Gove, former vice president and director of housing for Met Life, told Arthur Simon that "it was the company's idea." See Robert Moses, *Public Works: A Dangerous Trade* (New York: McGraw-Hill, 1970), 431; and Arthur Simon, *Stuyvesant Town, USA: Pattern for Two Americas* (New York: New York University Press, 1970), 41n5.

14. For a good discussion of the concepts of "slum" and "blight," see Mark Gelfand, *A Nation of Cities: The Federal Government and Urban America, 1933–1965* (New York: Oxford University Press, 1975), 106–110:

> Although often used interchangeably in popular literature, the terms "slums" and "blight" came to have distinctly different meanings....Slums connoted poor housing conditions and all the attendant social evils; blight, on the other hand had economic significance. To say that a district was blighted meant that the area was unprofitable, both to private investors and the municipal government. (110)

Some urbanists considered the slum an "advanced case of blight." See Fogelson, *Downtown,* 346–350. However, few officials with the power to transform the cityscape worried too much about distinguishing between these concepts. Moses called the Gas House District a slum, and Met Life had no reason to question his judgment if it aided the company's cause. See also Wendell E. Pritchett, "The 'Public Menace' of Blight: Urban Renewal and the Private Uses of Eminent Domain," *Yale Law and Policy Review* 21, no. 1 (2003): 17–19. See also Robert A. Beauregard, *Voices of Decline: The Postwar Fate of US Cities* (Cambridge: Blackwell, 1993), 137–138, which highlights the role of real estate speculation in causing both slums and blight.

15. Untitled agreement, February 1, 1943, Stuyvesant Town, History and Plans, 1943–1967 folder, S14, MLA.

16. "Suggested Letter from Mr. Ecker to Assemblyman Mitchell," roll 17, folder 010, ParksMoses; Moses to Jeremiah Evarts, March 2, 1943; Moses to Ecker, March 5, 1943; Moses to Dewey, March 22, 1943 (see also letters from La Guardia and state insurance superintendent Louis Pink to Dewey, urging action), all in roll 17, folder 010, ParksMoses.

17. See Moses to La Guardia, April 21, 1943; memorandum to the Board of Estimate from Robert Moses as to Objections to the Stuyvesant Town Contract, Friday, May 28, 1943, 10–11; Moses to Dewey, March 22, 1943, all in roll 17, folder 010, ParksMoses.

18. The exceptions were several private efforts in the 1920s and '30s, made possible by the string of state laws granting eminent domain and partial tax exemption to builders, to clear tenements and build nonpublic housing on the Lower East Side, most notably the Amalgamated Dwellings built by the Amalgamated Clothing Workers of America and developer Fred French's federally assisted Knickerbocker Village. Before the 1949 Housing Act went into effect, Stuyvesant Town was the only privately sponsored postwar project in the city.

19. On the "superior public use" clause, see Pritchett, "The 'Public Menace' of Blight," 33. (He misidentifies the date as 1942.) See also A. Scott Henderson, *Housing and the Democratic Ideal: The Life and Thought of Charles Abrams* (New York: Columbia University Press, 2000), 126; Thomas E. Dewey, "For Release in the Afternoon Papers of Saturday, April 3, 1943," copy of March 30, 1943, memorandum, roll 17, folder 010, ParksMoses.

20. Oliver Ramsay, "Governor Fails to Protect Public in New Slum Clearance Projects," *New Leader*, May 8, 1943. See also Oliver Pilat's three-part series on the Hampton-Mitchell bill, *NYP*, April 7, 8, and 9, 1943; and Schwartz, *The New York Approach*, 93.

21. Untitled Metropolitan press release, 1, MLA; "East Side 'Suburb in City' to House 30,000 after War," *NYT*, April 19, 1943 1, 9; "18-Block East Side 'Suburbia' for 30,000 to Be Built after War," *NYWT*, April 19, 1943, 3. See also Moses to La Guardia, April 16, 1943, with attached "Data for Mayor's Talk on Metropolitan Housing Project," roll 17, folder 010, ParksMoses; and Dominic J. Capeci Jr., "Fiorello H. La Guardia and the Stuyvesant Town Controversy of 1943," *New-York Historical Society Quarterly* 62, no. 4 (October 1978): 289–310.

22. See untitled Metropolitan press release, MLA, 2–3; "One Way to Invest," *Business Week*, May 8, 1943, 105; Boyden Sparkes, "Can the Cities Come Back?" *Saturday Evening Post*, November 4, 1944, 29; Fogelson, *Downtown*, 319–320, 342–357.

23. See Tom O'Connor, "The End of the Gashouse District," *PM*, March 1, 1945; M. V. Casey, "Gas House District Set for Oblivion," *NYHT*, April 18, 1943; Erwin Savelson, "Gas House Gang Down, but Not Out," *NYDM*, March 3, 1945; "Stuyvesant Town," *NAHO News*, July 16, 1943; Gene Gleason, "N.Y. Gashouse District Is Being Razed," *Owensboro Messenger*, March 28, 1945; James Treverton, "Metropolitan Life Has Gotham Housing Plans," *St. Louis Globe Democrat*, October 10, 1945.

24. Denis Sneigr, "Tenements Tumble for Stuyvesant Town," *NYWT*, March 7, 1946; Savelson, "Gas House Gang Down, but Not Out"; Casey, "Gas House District Set for Oblivion." According to the Community Service Society, in the 1940 Census, the district was 59 percent foreign-born. However, the numbers they give add up to something closer to 65 percent. The society claimed that 20.7 percent of the foreign born were

Italians, 6.5 percent were Polish, 5.9 percent each were Germans and Russians; Austrians were at 4.7 percent, Hungarians, 3.5 percent, Czechs, 2.4, and the remaining 15 percent included Spanish, Latin Americans, Greeks, Romanians, Slavs, Swiss, French, and Scandinavians. The Irish, mostly second or third generation, do not make it into these figures, but accounted for a substantial minority of the neighborhood population. The census listed only 10 blacks. See Community Service Society, "The Rehousing Needs of the Families on the Stuyvesant Town Site," June 14, 1945, 54–55.

25. Lewis Mumford, *The Culture of Cities* (New York: Harcourt, Brace, 1938), 192; Thomas Wolfe quoted in O'Connor, "The End of the Gashouse District."

26. See Community Service Society, "Rehousing Needs of the Families"; Edwin S. Burdell, "Rehousing Needs of the Families on the Stuyvesant Town Site," *Journal of the American Institute of Planners* (Autumn 1945): 15–19; "Explanation of Security Area Map" and "Area Descriptions," both in Manhattan—New York Security Map and Area Description Folder, Records of the Federal Home Loan Bank Board, Home Owners Loan Corporation, Records Relating to the City Survey file, 1935–40, New York, RG195, box 59, NARA.

27. "Where Stuyvesant Town Will Transform Area," *NYWT*, January 29, 1945, 20. The editors borrowed liberally from an untitled Metropolitan press release announcing the beginning of the clearance program, January 12, 1945; see also George Gove to Jeremiah Evarts, January 11, 1945, both in Uncatalogued ST Materials, MLA.

28. Ecker quoted in Savelson, "Gas House Gang Down, but Not Out"; Frederick H. Ecker, "Housing (with Particular Reference to New York City)," address to the Annual Conference of Mayors, February 16, 1948, 8. See Alison Isenberg, *Downtown America: A History of the Place and the People Who Made It* (Chicago: University of Chicago Press, 2004), 192–199.

29. The photographs are organized according to the block numbers on New York City ward maps. Thus, the photos include blocks 946–951, 972–977, and 982–987. Block 982 is missing, but there are multiple copies of some blocks. See boxes 1–3, RG11, MLA.

30. Metropolitan Life Insurance Company, *Stuyvesant Town: This Is Your Home* (New York: Metropolitan Life, 1952), 4–5, in S12, 4/11, MLA. The *Philadelphia Inquirer* put three of these images to work in a 1945 article designed to get its city moving on urban redevelopment. See Frederic V. Lewis, "From Slums to Paradise: Firm to Build Homes for 8000 Families," *Philadelphia Inquirer,* March 1, 1945. One of the photos is 949–39, in RG11, box 1, MLA. The *St. Louis Globe Democrat* used a Met Life image, juxtaposed with a photograph of Parkchester, for similar ends in Treverton, "Metropolitan Life Has Gotham Housing Plans." The photos were captioned "Slum Clearance Before and After."

31. The photo is 946–69, RG11, box 1.

32. "These Must Give Way when 'Walled City' Moves In," *PM,* May 28, 1943. Four days later, *PM* followed this up with another article on the neighborhood. See "10,000 Housing 'Evictions' Feared: Realty Owners Deny That Gas House District Is a Slum Area," *PM,* June 1, 1943.

33. Joseph Newman, "Gas-House District Dismayed as Housing Plan Dooms Homes," *NYHT,* April 19, 1943.

34. Amy Abraham, "City Has Its Displaced Persons as Stuyvesant Town Aftermath," *NYHT*, December 16, 1945, 1, 5.

35. Newman, "Gas-House District Dismayed"; "East Side Tenants Resigned to Evictions," *NYWT,* March 27, 1945; "East River Slums to Go—He'll Stay," *NYJA,* December 5, 1944; Community Service Society, "Attitudes about Moving and about Stuyvesant Town," June 6, 1945, in Uncatalogued ST Materials, MLA; Community Service Society, "Rehousing Needs of the Families," 49–52. See also Lee E. Cooper, "Uprooted Thousands Starting Trek from Site for Stuyvesant Town, Vans Rumble through Lower East Side in City's Greatest Mass Movement, with New Quarters a Problem," *NYT,* March 3, 1945, 15, 26.

36. "10,000 Housing 'Evictions' Feared: Realty Owners Deny That Gas House District Is a Slum Area," *PM,* June 1, 1943; Fay Seabrook, Executive Secretary, Stuyvesant Tenants League, to Vito Marcantonio, April 24, 1945, in box 50, Marc; Thomas Hope, Chairman, Stuyvesant Tenants League to Fiorello La Guardia, February 13, 1945; memo, C. H. Huebner, Stuyvesant Town Corporation to George Gove, Re: Meeting at Stuyvesant Housing Corp., February 27, 1945, 2, both in Uncatalogued ST Materials, MLA; Cooper, "Uprooted Thousands"; Joel Schwartz, "Tenant Power in the Liberal City, 1943–1971," in Ronald Lawson, ed., *The Tenant Movement in New York City, 1904–1984* (New Brunswick, NJ: Rutgers University Press, 1986), 138–141; Schwartz, *The New York Approach,* 97–99.

37. "Metropolitan Life Makes Housing Pay," *Fortune* (April 1946): 209. Met Life paid $2,133,985 for properties worth $3,064,400 and got mortgages worth $1,329,500 for $722,674. See "List of Properties Purchased Up to October 27, 1943," and "List of Mortgages Purchased Up to October 27, 1943," both in ST-Contract with the City folder, MLA. Also see "Stuyvesant Town Gets Title to 135 Properties," *NYT,* May 9, 1944, and other articles in RG12, Printed Materials, Scrapbooks, Housing-ST, book 1, MLA.

38. George Gove to Sub-Committee of the Joint Legislative Committee to Recodify the Multiple Dwellings Law, March 12, 1945; Fiorello La Guardia to Frederick H. Ecker, February 19, 1945; Frederick H. Ecker to La Guardia, February 23, 1945; Ecker to Moses, January 12, 1945; Revised Vacate Schedule is in Moses to La Guardia, February 26, 1945; memo, Stuyvesant Town: Residential Tenants, January 17, 1945; "To the Tenants in the Stuyvesant Town Area," January 17, 1945, all in Uncatalogued ST Materials, MLA.

39. Naomi Jolles, "Old Flats to Go—Where Will Tenants Go?" *NYP,* December 1, 1944; Betsy Luce, "Move Out, a Notice Reads; But Where To? a Mother Asks," *NYP,* January 30, 1945; James Parlatore, "Stuyvesant Site Folks Feel Like Refugees," *PM,* February 28, 1945; James Felt to John Scofield, Regional Rent Director, Office of Price Administration, March 15, 1945; State of New York Report of the Sub-Committee to the Joint Legislative Committee to Recodify the Multiple Dwelling Law, in Respect to Stuyvesant Town, March 17, 1945, 3, both in Uncatalogued ST Materials, MLA; Rosamond G. Roberts, *3000 Families Move to Make Way for Stuyvesant Town: A Story of Tenant Relocation Bureau, Inc.* (New York: Felt, 1946), 9, 17, 6; I. L. Kalish, Carb, Reichman, and Luria to Churchill Rodgers, June 15, 1945, in Uncatalogued ST Materials, MLA.

40. Joseph Platzker to William Wilson, November 21, 1944; Moses to Wilson, November 22, 1944; Moses to Walter Binger, November 20, 1944, all in folder 002, 1944, Parks-Gen; James Felt, "A Justifiable 'Bulge,'" March 20, 1946, 4, in ST-Statistics folder, MLA;

and Leon Leighton, "Study of Rehabilitation of Substandard Tenements to Provide Accommodations for Displaced Stuyvesant Town Tenants," December 7, 1945, 45, in Uncatalogued ST Materials, MLA.

41. Burdell, "Rehousing Needs of the Families," 17, 19; Roberts, *3000 Families Move*, 19, 20, 22. See also Malcolm Logan, "Metropolitan's Rents for East Side Double What Tenements Ask," *NYP*, April 19, 1943. James Felt believed that his policy of avoiding substandard dwellings as destinations meant that 90 percent of the families moved into better quarters than those they left and at equivalent rents. From the statistics presented here, it seems that the first claim is possible, while the second is unlikely. See Burdell, "Rehousing Needs of the Families," 16.

42. For even-handed approval, see "Stuyvesant Town Plans," *NYHT*, June 3, 1943. But the *World-Telegram* claimed that "words like gargantuan, titanic and epoch-making rest easily on the stout shoulders of the East Side housing development." It was a "show window example of what private capital can do." See Allan Keller, "Stuyvesant Town: Where Hard Heads Made Dream True: Giant Housing Project Which Wiped Out Slum a Masterpiece of Capital," *NYWT*, June 11, 1948, 23. Likewise, see Leslie Gould, "City Talks Housing, but Private Firms Produce," *NYJA*, March 24, 1948. On recentralization, see "Suburb in a City," *Adirondack-Enterprise*, June 23, 1943. It is hard to exaggerate how much of a national media event Stuyvesant Town was. I counted about 60 towns and cities where there was at least one and sometimes multiple articles about Stuyvesant Town. See Housing-Stuyvesant Town, book 1, and Housing-General, book 1, in RG12, Printed Materials, Scrapbooks, MLA.

43. See Radio Reports, "Some of the Lighter Aspects of Town and Village," on Bill Leonard, *This Is New York*, WCBS, June 29, 1951, 2; "The City under the Bomb," *Time*, October 2, 1950, 12; "Single Flight Films U.S., Coast to Coast," *NYHT*, September 12, 1948. Met Life had inquiries about Stuyvesant Town, Peter Cooper Village, and its other housing developments from around the world. See "International Inquiry…from Africa, Belgium, and Brazil," *Home Office*, November 1948, 17.

44. Charles Abrams, "The Walls of Stuyvesant Town," *Nation*, March 24, 1945, 328. Abrams uses the term "business welfare state" to describe Stuyvesant Town in "Stuyvesant Town's Threat to Our Liberties: Government Waives the Constitution for Private Enterprise," *Commentary*, November 1949, 426–433. See also Henderson, *Housing and the Democratic Ideal*, 99–145. Abrams used the idea of the business welfare state to critique much of the New Deal's housing policy for its offering of subsidies to businesses rather than direct aid to citizens.

45. "Stuyvesant Town," hand-dated March 15, 1948, in ST-Statistics folder, Uncatalogued ST Materials, MLA; "Stuyvesant Town: Rebuilding a Blighted City Area," *Engineering News and Record*, February 5, 1948, 76. For Gas House District coverage, see Stuyvesant Town Corporation to City Planning Commission, May 12, 1943, 4, in roll 18, folder 14, 1943, ParksGen.

46. See Peter G. Rowe, *Modernity and Housing* (Cambridge, MA: MIT Press, 1995), 34, for more on this tendency in much American mass-housing production.

47. Richard Plunz, *A History of Housing in New York City* (New York: Columbia University Press, 1990), 255; Lewis Mumford, "The Sky Line: Prefabricated Blight," *New Yorker*, October 30, 1948, 49–54.

48. William Lescaze to Editor, "An Architect Believes Better Design Will Improve Stuyvesant Town," *NYS*, June 5, 1943. Lescaze favored a more open, vaguely Corbusian design; he would have put the buildings on columns, provided balconies, and varied their heights. Mumford, "Prefabricated Blight," 54. See also Tracy B. Augur, "An Analysis of the Plan of Stuyvesant Town," *Journal of the American Institute of Planners* (Autumn 1944): 8–13.

49. Lewis Mumford, "The Sky Line: Stuyvesant Town Revisited," *New Yorker*, November 27, 1948, 65–72. Mumford predicted that Stuyvesant residents, inured to "cramped, sunless, dusty, and even garbagy [*sic*] blighted areas" and thus unfit to judge the project, would view "their new homes through a rosy haze." Not surprisingly, residents of Stuyvesant Town were less than happy with Mumford's pronouncements. The local community newspaper, *Town and Village*, led off its next issue with "An Open Letter to the *New Yorker*." Editor Mark A. Stuart defended the project and its residents' judgment; he felt "constrained to doubt [Mumford's] human sentiments." See Stuart, "An Open Letter to the *New Yorker*," *TV*, November 18, 1948, 4; and Mrs. C. C. Robinson to Editor, "Hey, Mr. Mumford," *TV*, December 9, 1948, 4.

50. See Leopold Arnaud et al. to City Planning Commission, May 3, 1943, in ST-1943 folder, CHPC; City Planning Commission, "Approval, as Required by the Redevelopment Companies Law as Amended by Chapter 234 of the Laws of 1943, of a 'Plan of a Project' Proposed by the Stuyvesant Town Corporation," report no. 2765, adopted May 20, 1943, 5–7, in ST-Contract with the City folder, Uncatalogued ST Materials, MLA. See also "Proposed Postwar Housing Project," *AR* (June 1943): 16.

51. The city donated, by the CHC's calculations, 739,861 square feet in streets to Met Life for the project. The company gave 235,412 square feet of that back to widen First Avenue, 20th Street, and 14th Street, meaning that the city had given a net gift of 504,449 square feet. Population density calculations commonly did not include streets and other public areas, but because the company owned the streets inside the project it included them in its calculations. See "'Stuyvesant Town'—Must a Challenging Opportunity Be Lost?" *CHC Housing News*, June–July 1943, 1–2, in ST-1943 folder, CHPC. For Isaacs's statement, see untitled Statement of Hon. Stanley Isaacs, May 27, 1943, 9, in ST-Briefs folder, CHPC.

52. Community Service Society, "The Rehousing Needs of the Families on the Stuyvesant Town Site," June 14, 1945, 24, in ST-1943 folder, CHPC. Metropolitan, meanwhile, reported that the area had a population of 27,000 in 1920. Stuyvesant Town Corporation to City Planning Commission, May 12, 1943, 2, in roll 18, folder 14, 1943, ParksGen. Moses quoted in Mumford, "Stuyvesant Town Revisited," 65; and see memorandum to the Board of Estimate from Robert Moses as to Objections to the Stuyvesant Town Contract, Friday, May 28, 1943, 3, in roll 17, folder 010, ParksMoses.

53. "'Stuyvesant Town'—Must a Challenging Opportunity Be Lost?" *CHC Housing News*, June–July 1943, 2, in ST-1943 folder, CHPC; "Metropolitan's Housing Plans Hit at Hearing," *NYT*, May 20, 1943, 23. Moses hoped to get the company to put smaller towers at the edges of the project. See Moses to George Spargo, Re: Metropolitan Housing Project, March 31, 1943; also Moses to Richmond Shreve, April 8, 1943; Moses to Ecker, April 20, 1943; and Moses, "Important Matters to Be Included in the Contract," April 21, 1943, all in roll 17, folder 010, ParksMoses.

54. See "No Holds Barred," *AF* (June 1943), where it was reported that at the City Planning Commission hearings, "as if by prearrangement many of the speakers" opposing immediate approval "referred to Stuyvesant Town as a 'medieval walled town in the middle of the city.'" Whether they had conferred ahead of time or not, the phrase was at least informally agreed upon as the rhetorical way to link Stuyvesant Town's social, aesthetic, and economic faults. See also Henry S. Churchill to Editors, "Met Gits the Mostest," *AF* (June 1943). He writes, "However, look! Stuyvesant Town is to be a walled city, a medieval enclave!" The editors of *Architectural Forum,* however, had little patience with the opposition, doubting that a better scheme for the real problem—high urban land costs—could be produced. See also "CIO Rallies 500,000 against 'Walled City': City's Headlong Rush to Approve Met Life Plan Assailed," *PM,* May 27, 1943; "Public Indignation Mounts over 'Walled City' Housing: Civil Liberties Union Joins Fight on Race-Biased Project," *PM,* May 30, 1943; "Citizens Make Protest against Metropolitan 'Walled City,'" *NYAN,* June 5, 1943.

55. "Metropolitan Life Makes Housing Pay: How to Order a City," *Fortune* 33, no. 4 (April 1946): 210, 242; Ecker, "Housing (with Particular Reference to New York City)," 6.

56. Keller, "Stuyvesant Town: Where Hard Heads Made Dream True," 23.

57. See Fogelson, *Downtown,* 336–337; Augur, "Analysis of the Plan of Stuyvesant Town," 9; and Harold Buttenheim, "The City That Might Be," *United States Investor,* May 20, 1944, 40. On the "neighborhood unit," see John Fairfield, *The Mysteries of the Great City: The Politics of Urban Design, 1877–1937* (Columbus: Ohio State University Press, 1993), 208–214.

58. Ecker, "Housing (with Particular Reference to New York City)," 6; Joseph McGoldrick, "The Super-Block Instead of Slums," *NYTM,* November 19, 1944, 10–11, 53–55.

59. Simon Breines, "Stuyvesant Town: A Life Insurance Company Plans a Post-War World," *Task* 4 (1944): 38. Ecker's affidavit in the *Dorsey v. Stuyvesant Town* case (discussed below) quoted in Simon, *Stuyvesant Town, USA,* 59–61. Of course, Moses realized that fighting for redevelopment on "social" grounds was a losing battle. He claimed that those interested in making redevelopment serve "social objectives" jeopardized further slum clearance and new housing. As the controversy went on, Ecker more and more refused to be drawn into a debate about social objectives, which the company stood only to lose. Instead of emphasizing the company's long-standing interest in the health and welfare of New Yorkers, he stuck to depicting Stuyvesant Town as a commonsense fiscal deal.

60. Charles Abrams, "Here's the Meat of the Moses-Mumford Mix-Up," *NYP,* December 15, 1948. The rhetorical scuffle between Moses and Mumford in the pages of the *New Yorker* had attracted enough attention that *Time* ran a short piece summarizing it. See "New Nightmares for Old?" *Time,* December 13, 1948. Abrams viewed the subsidy as far-reaching. In 1945, Abrams put the figure for the tax exemption at $25 million. Later, in a 1947 series of articles for the *New York Post* and *Bronx Home News,* he said the project would cost taxpayers $53 million. A year later, *Survey Graphic* estimated that the "gift of the city" would "amount over the years to some $50,000,000 in uncollected taxes for Stuyvesant Town alone." See Charles Abrams, "The Walls of Stuyvesant Town," *Nation,* March 24, 1945, 328; Abrams, "City Lost $36 Million in Stuyvesant Town Subsidy," *Bronx Home News,* August 22, 1947; Abrams, "Stuyvesant

Town Makes 8½% at Taxpayers' Expense," *NYP,* August 22, 1947; Abrams, "Stuyvesant Town Symbol of Freebooting Realty Lobbies," *NYP,* August 25, 1947; Kathryn Close, "New Homes with Insurance Dollars," *Survey Graphic* 37, no. 11 (November 1948): 454.

61. See Abrams, "Stuyvesant Town's Threat to Our Liberties," 430. See also Henderson, *Housing and the Democratic Ideal,* 99–122.

62. See Abrams, "The Walls of Stuyvesant Town," 329; and Abrams, "Stuyvesant Town's Threat to Our Liberties," 429, 433, 427.

63. Gelfand, *Nation of Cities,* 148; Freeman, *Working-Class New York,* 105; Plunz, *History of Housing,* 274; "Stuyvesant Town Starting Rentals," *NYT,* June 4, 1946; "7,000 Rush Pleas for Housing in '47," *NYT,* June 6, 1947; Joseph Platzker, "100,000 Families Want to Live in Stuyvesant Town," *East Side Chamber News* 19, no. 4 (October 1946): 1; untitled typescript on renting ST apartments, n.d., ST-Statistics, MLA. By August 1946, Met Life had more than 75,000 letters on file, and by October the tally had topped 100,000.

Chapter 3

1. "Topics of the Times," *NYT,* April 20, 1943.

2. Stanley M. Isaacs, untitled statement, May 27, 1943, 7, in ST-Briefs folder, CHPC.

3. Corinne Demas, *Eleven Stories High: Growing Up in Stuyvesant Town, 1948–1968* (Albany: State University of New York Press, 2000), xiii, xiv.

4. Hettie Jones, *How I Became Hettie Jones* (New York: Dutton, 1990), 124.

5. Quoted in Jane Jacobs, *The Death and Life of Great American Cities* (New York: Random House, 1961; New York: Modern Library, 1993), 63–64.

6. Hettie Jones labels Stuyvesant Town an "island of middle class, segregated housing" in 1960. See Jones, *How I Became,* 120. In 1956, the National Committee against Discrimination in Housing counted 30 black families in Stuyvesant Town. See NCADH, "Open Occupancy Grows in Apartment Housing," *Trends in Housing* 1, no. 3 (December 1956): 2.

7. Naomi Jolles, a reporter for the *Post,* approached Ecker after the City Planning Commission hearings to ask whether "Negroes" would be permitted to live in Stuyvesant Town, at which point Ecker made his soon to be notorious statement. See Simon, *Stuyvesant Town, USA,* 32. Much like Isaacs's "walled town" comment, Ecker's words were widely reproduced, particularly in the black press. See, for instance, "Metropolitan True to Form," *Pittsburgh Courier,* May 29, 1943.

8. For an account of this early postwar context, see Lizabeth Cohen, *A Consumer's Republic: The Politics of Mass Consumption in Postwar America* (New York: Knopf, 2003), 112–129. On desegregation as a "Cold War imperative," see Mary L. Dudziak, *Cold War Civil Rights: Race and the Image of American Democracy* (Princeton, NJ: Princeton University Press, 2000).

9. See Roberta Gold, "City of Tenants: New York's Housing Struggles and the Challenge to Postwar America, 1945–1974," Ph.D. diss., University of Washington, 2004, 52–53. For considerations of the various and unpredictable political commitments of the middle class, see Burton J. Bledstein and Robert D. Johnston, eds., *The Middling Sorts: Explorations in the History of the American Middle Class* (New York: Routledge, 2001). On white flight, see Eric Avila, *Popular Culture in the Age of White Flight: Fear and Fantasy in Suburban Los Angeles* (Berkeley: University of California Press, 2006);

and Kevin Kruse, *White Flight: Atlanta and the Making of Modern Conservatism* (Princeton, NJ: Princeton University Press, 2007).

10. Cohen, *Consumer's Republic*, 181, 185. See also Martha Biondi, *To Stand and Fight: The Struggle for Civil Rights in Postwar New York City* (Cambridge, MA: Harvard University Press, 2003); and Thomas Sugrue, *Sweet Land of Liberty: The Forgotten Struggle for Civil Rights in the North* (New York: Random House, 2008). The New York State Committee against Discrimination in Housing (NYSCDH)—launched in 1949 to pressure Met Life—helped to pass the 1950 Wicks-Austin law that banned discrimination in any housing built under Title I of the 1949 Housing Act, the 1951 Brown-Isaacs law that made discrimination in all publicly supported private housing illegal, and a 1963 state law banning discrimination in all private housing. The national organization that helped to secure the 1968 Fair Housing Act was an early offshoot of NYSCDH. See Biondi, *To Stand and Fight*, 131–135, 280.

11. See Nikhil Pal Singh, "Culture/Wars: Recoding Empire in an Age of Democracy," *American Quarterly* 50, no. 3 (September 1998); Manning Marable, *Race, Reform and Rebellion: The Second Reconstruction in Black America, 1945–1982* (Jackson: University of Mississippi Press, 1984); Gary Gerstle, *American Crucible: Race and Nation in the Twentieth Century* (Princeton, NJ: Princeton University Press, 2001), 187–237. On New York's particularly resilient, antiracist, class-conscious forces, see Joshua Freeman, *Working-Class New York: Life and Labor since World War II* (New York: New Press, 2000), 78–79, 90–95; and Biondi, *To Stand and Fight*, 137–190.

12. Simon, *Stuyvesant Town, USA*, 31–38. Met Life never made segregation official policy. It simply claimed the right to control tenant selection. In order to prove that segregation was the intent, Councilman Isaacs directly asked Ecker at the Board of Estimate hearings whether it was true that blacks would be barred. Ecker did not reply. Then, State Assemblyman William T. Andrews, who represented Harlem, read a letter from George Gove, housing director of Metropolitan, which stipulated, "no provision had been made for Negro families." See also "City Approves Metropolitan's Housing Plan," *NYHT*, June 4, 1943; "Citizens Make Protest against Metropolitan 'Walled City': Plans Bar Negroes as Undesirables," *NYAN*, June 5, 1943; Algernon D. Black, "Negro Families in Stuyvesant Town," *Survey* 86 (November 1950): 502–503; and Joseph B. Robison, "The Story of Stuyvesant Town," *Nation* 172 (June 2, 1951): 514–516.

13. *Amsterdam News* editorial quoted in Simon, *Stuyvesant Town, USA*, 38–39; Abrams, "The Walls of Stuyvesant Town," 328.

14. The first of these was the municipal zoning ordinance forbidding occupancy by certain races. When this was found to be unconstitutional, the real estate industry popularized the private racial restrictive covenant. The U.S. Supreme Court had recently outlawed these arrangements in real estate deeds, but now urban redevelopment, Abrams argued, was poised to do much more. It would authorize cities to displace minorities in the name of the "superior public use" of slum clearance. See Simon, *Stuyvesant Town, USA*, 57–60; and A. Scott Henderson, *Housing and the Democratic Ideal: The Life and Thought of Charles Abrams* (New York: Columbia University Press, 2000), 134.

15. Simon, *Stuyvesant Town, USA*, 57–60. The *Dorsey* case was sponsored by the American Civil Liberties Union, the American Jewish Congress, and the National

Association for the Advancement of Colored People. See Robison, "The Story of Stuyvesant Town," 515. For the AJC, see Shad Polier to Editors, "Racial Policies in Housing," *NYT,* August 6, 1947. For the NAACP, see Thurgood Marshall to Friend, NAACP Legal Defense and Educational Fund, Inc., November 5, 1948, in ST-Briefs folder, CHPC; Abrams, "Stuyvesant Town's Threat to Our Liberties," 427; Tom O'Connor, "Stuyvesant Town Vital Bias Test," *DC,* May 17, 1949.

16. Simon, *Stuyvesant Town, USA,* 57–69; Henderson, *Housing and the Democratic Ideal,* 139–145. As planner Tracy Augur put it, "[A] public subsidy is being granted not to get something that the public wants so much as to get rid of something that the public considers disadvantageous." See Augur, "Analysis of the Plan of Stuyvesant Town," 11. On the rejection of the case, see "Stuyvesant Town Upheld on Appeal," *NYT,* December 21, 1948; "White Stuyvesant," *Survey* 85 (January 1949): 56; "Discrimination Upheld for Stuyvesant Town," *Survey* 85 (August 1949): 442; Charles Abrams, "Slum Clearance Boomerangs," *Nation* (July 29, 1950): 106.

17. Simon, *Stuyvesant Town, USA,* 73–77; "Mayor Assails Color Line in Project Lease," *NYDN,* December 3, 1948; Paul L. Ross to Friends, T&V Tenants' Committee to End Discrimination in Stuyvesant Town, January 13, 1949, in ST after 1943 folder, CHPC; "Petition to Require the Metropolitan Life Insurance Company to Abolish Discrimination against Negroes and to Rent Them Apartments in Stuyvesant Town," n.d., in ST after 1943 folder, CHPC.

18. Lee Lorch had been dismissed from CCNY without explanation, despite the fact that he was highly recommended for promotion by a faculty committee. Lorch believed it was due to his activism with the tenants committee. A year later, Penn State refused to reappoint him as well, after a university official had been assigned by the trustees to probe Lorch's activities at Stuyvesant Town. Albert Einstein and the American Association of University Professors intervened on Lorch's behalf, but by then Lorch had moved on to Fisk University. Despite consistently excellent peer reviews, Lorch became unemployable in the United States and, as of this writing, lives in Canada, where he is a professor emeritus at York University. See Simon, *Stuyvesant Town, USA,* 79–82, 100; Biondi, *To Stand and Fight,* 278; Lee Lorch to author, emails, November 6, 2006, and May 1, 2009.

19. Simon, *Stuyvesant Town, USA,* 77–82; Biondi, *To Stand and Fight,* 129; Richard Carter, "Negro Couple Living in Stuyvesant—No Thanks to Metropolitan Life," *DC,* August 11, 1949; Carter, "Stuyvesant Welcomes Negro Neighbors," *DC,* August 12, 1949; Art Shields, "1st Negro 'Tenants' at Stuyvesant Town Tell Their Story," *DW,* August 12, 1949; "First Negro Family in Stuyvesant Town Gets Respite on Move as Hosts Delay Return," *NYT,* September 7, 1949; Dan Gillmor, "Hendrixes Stay in Stuyvesant Town," *DC,* September 12, 1949.

20. Simon, *Stuyvesant Town, USA,* 85–91; Biondi, *To Stand and Fight,* 131–133. On the 1944 bill, see "Board Accepts Discrimination Ban in Housing," *NYHT,* June 9, 1944. On Brown-Isaacs, see Robison, "The Story of Stuyvesant Town," 515–516; Charles Abrams to Editors, "Brown-Isaacs Ordinances Barring Racial Discrimination Favored," *NYT,* February 9, 1951; "Estimate Board Votes Anti-Bias Bill on Housing," *NYHT,* March 2, 1951; and untitled handscript, chronicle, and summary of *New York Times* articles on Brown-Isaacs, in Stuyvesant Town folder, Uncatalogued ST Materials, MLA.

21. Simon, *Stuyvesant Town, USA,* 91–100; Biondi, *To Stand and Fight,* 133–135; Roberta Gold, "City of Tenants: New York's Housing Struggles and the Challenge to Postwar America, 1945–1974," Ph.D. diss., University of Washington, 2004, 56–59. See also Hortense W. Gabel to Emanuel Redfield, August 14, 1950, in ST after 1943 folder, CHPC; Marjorie McKenzie, "Pursuit of Democracy: Stuyvesant Town Tenants Committee Working Out a Method to Fight Race Bias," *Pittsburgh Courier,* August 19, 1950; "Stuyvesant Town Lifts Race Ban," *NYHT,* August 25, 1950; Ira Robbins, CHC memo, "Stuyvesant Town Evictions," September 20, 1950; and Hortense W. Gabel to Cooperating Organizations of the NYSCDH, September 26, 1950, both in ST after 1943 folder, CHPC. Efforts to defend the tenants also found sympathizers in Harlem, where a federation of organizations, looking to both fight the evictions and open the project formed the Continuations Committee of the Harlem Conference to Defend the "31" and Enforce the Brown-Isaacs Law. None other than Raphael Hendrix served as the executive secretary. See Announcement, Conference to Defend the "31" and End Discrimination in Stuyvesant Town, May 3, 1951; and "Harlem Residents Renew Fight on Stuyvesant Bias," *DW,* June 29, 1951. For efforts by the tenants committee itself, see T&V Tenants Committee to End Discrimination in Stuyvesant Town, memo, "To Bring You Up to Date," September 1951; Esther Smith, "Urgent Open Letter," October 28, 1951; Esther Smith to Friend, "Emergency Memorandum," January 10, 1952, all in ST after 1943 folder, CHPC; Radio Reports, "Barry Gray Reports Staying of Stuyvesant Town Evictions," January 18, 1952, WMCA-NY, in Uncatalogued ST Materials, MLA.

22. See Biondi, *To Stand and Fight,* 128.

23. Moses told Adam Clayton Powell, "I make no apologies for being a middle-of-the-road fellow who believes in reaching limited objectives and not in preaching the instant realization of the millennium. I am convinced that sure and steady progress is only made in this way." See Moses to Powell, August 10, 1943, and Powell to Moses, August 16, 1943, both in roll 17, folder 010, ParksMoses. On the racial makeup of the Gas House District, see Robert Moses to H. A. Overstreet, August 30, 1943, also in roll 17, folder 010, ParksMoses. Moses and Met Life were right, in a limited sense, that private funds were leery of redevelopment; in 1948, *Survey* reported that, with all the uproar over discrimination, insurance executives no longer saw housing as a sound investment. It would take the powers of the federal government and the 1949 Housing Act to draw private capital back to the center cities in a significant way. See Kathryn Close, "New Homes with Insurance Dollars," *Survey* (November 1948): 487. Still, the opposition was able to show that, as Joel Schwartz puts it, Moses and Ecker had "spurned the moral message of the war." See Schwartz, *The New York Approach,* 96.

24. "Post-War Planning for Discrimination," *New Republic,* June 21, 1943; Simon Breines, "Stuyvesant Town: A Life Insurance Company Plans a Post-War World," *Task* 4 (1944): 35, 38; Dominic J. Capeci Jr., "Fiorello H. La Guardia and the Stuyvesant Town Controversy of 1943," *New-York Historical Society Quarterly* 62, no. 4 (October 1978): 295.

25. "First Negro Family in Stuyvesant Town Gets Respite on Move as Hosts Delay Return," *NYT,* September 7, 1949; Carter, "Negro Couple Living in Stuyvesant"; United Office and Professional Workers of America, flyer, "Help Us Stop Metropolitan Life's Un-American Activities!" hand-dated September 15, 1949, in Uncatalogued Materials, MLA; Carter, "Stuyvesant Welcomes Negro Neighbors."

26. S. Kasper to Editor, and Isidore Sapir to Editor, *TV*, September 8, 1949, 10; Simon, *Stuyvesant Town, USA*, 74. Annie Mae McKay, a black domestic who worked in both town and village, wrote in to say that she thought it unfortunate "that the group that is pushing this issue are using the Negro Race to further their own political ambitions." See Annie Mae McKay to Editor, "A Domestic Speaks," *TV*, September 15, 1949, 4. For many, ALP activity in Stuyvesant Town became overwhelming evidence that the Communists had taken over the desegregation campaign. See A Resident, "They Took Me Like a Baby, Dupe of Packed Meeting Says," *TV*, January 25, 1951, 2, 20.

27. Daniel B. English to Churchill Rodgers, memo, "Meeting: 'The East Side Welcomes First Negro Family to Stuyvesant Town,'" August 29, 1949, in S12, 3/11, MLA. The tenants committee, and desegregation efforts in general, had long had the support of various CIO unions, Vito Marcantonio, and the ALP. See "Housing Plan Opposed: 'Walled City for Privileged' Is Seen by Union Council," *NYT*, May 27, 1943; "Local 65 Proud of Stuyvesant Tenant's Bid to Negro Couple," *DW*, August 15, 1949; "Marcantonio to O'D: End Tax Exemption to Stuyvesant Town," *DW*, July 21, 1949.

28. See "The Color Line," *TV*, November 11, 1948, 4; "The Leases," *TV*, June 15, 1950, 4.

29. For instance, on November 26, Barry Gray, a radio host on WMCA who was sympathetic to the protestors, had Jesse Kessler and Milt Roseman, another tenants committee member, on his show. He continually tried to get Kessler and Roseman to talk about how they had been called Communists. Both either denied that they had or downplayed its importance. See Radio Reports, "Barry Gray and Lazarus Joseph Discuss Stuyvesant Town," WMCA, November 25–26, 1951; "Called Communists, Because They Took Negroes into Stuyvesant Town," WMCA, December 5, 1951; "Judge Delaney Comments on Stuyvesant Town Policy," WMCA, January 16–17, 1952, all in Uncatalogued ST Materials, MLA. Talbot quoted in Ted Poston, "New York, NY," *NYP*, January 16, 1952.

30. Abrams to Editor, "Brown-Isaacs Ordinances."

31. Arthur Simon charged that the company provided the papers with "a collection of clippings which linked the integration struggle with Communist and left-wing support" but gives no direct source for the claim. See Simon, *Stuyvesant Town, USA*, 90–91; "Estimate Board Votes Anti-Bias Bill on Housing," *NYHT*, March 2, 1951.

32. Robison, "The Story of Stuyvesant Town," 516; Black, "Negro Families in Stuyvesant Town," 503; Hortense Gabel to Vincent Impellitteri, September 22, 1950, 2, in ST after 1943 folder, CHPC.

33. Gabel to Impellitteri, September 22, 1950, 2.

34. Simon, *Stuyvesant Town, USA*, 104, 127–132; Biondi, *To Stand and Fight*, 135.

35. See Biondi, *To Stand and Fight*, 2. There were exceptions to these tendencies. In Manhattan's dense urban fabric, public housing could be found cheek by jowl with other housing stock in upscaling neighborhoods, but the bulk of it went into Harlem, East Harlem, the Lower East Side, and out in the Bronx or Brooklyn, where it helped to create new concentrations of Puerto Rican and black poverty. See chapters 6 and 7, below.

36. See "Stuyvesant Town," memo on costs, May 8, 1947, in ST after 1943 folder, CHPC. See also memorandum, Stuyvesant Town Corporation, "Analysis of Cost of Tenant Removals at Stuyvesant Town Site," October 23, 1945, in Uncatalogued ST

Materials, MLA, which found that removals of residential, commercial, and industrial tenants cost $214,604. Gustave Zismer to Mr. Goldstein, May 28, 1952, 3, in Zismer-Miscellaneous folder, MLA; Zismer, untitled typescript, n.d., in Zismer-All Communities folder, MLA.

37. The income statistics are calculated from Met Life, "Supplementary Statistical Data Relating to Stuyvesant Town Residential Tenants," November 28, 1950, in ST-Statistics folder, MLA. This memo is based on a survey of 3,349 families (38 percent of the project) that had renewed their leases since moving in. Manhattan median income from *United States Census: New York City, Manhattan Borough* (Washington, DC: U.S. Government Printing Office, 1950), 85. Demas, *Eleven Stories High*, 3; Martha Seidman and Pamela Long, interviews with author, August 2, 2009, New York. According to a 1950 study of 400 Jewish families in Stuyvesant Town, 49 percent of the Jews–and 63 percent of the Jewish men—had graduated from college. 41 percent of the men were professionals and there were no semi-skilled or unskilled workers among the Jewish population. See Joshua M. Zeitz, *White Ethnic New York: Jews, Catholics, and the Shaping of Postwar Politics* (Chapel Hill: University of North Carolina Press, 2007) 34, 237 n. 55.

38. Zismer, untitled typescript, n.d.; Edward A. Stevens to Editor, "Perplexed Veteran: Caught in Housing Emergency, He Has Cause for Concern," *NYS*, April 1948, in RG12, Printed Materials, Scrapbooks, Housing-General, book 3, MLA.

39. Ecker, "Housing (with Particular Reference to New York City)," 3; Mrs. C. C. Robinson to Editor, *TV*, December 9, 1945, 4. See also Gilmore D. Clarke to Gustave Zismer, December 1, 1949, in ST-Landscaping folder, MLA; Metropolitan Life Insurance Company, "45 Acres of Breathing Space," August 16, 1951, *TV* ad text, in Uncatalogued ST Materials, MLA; Pamela Long and Martha Seidman, interviews, 2009. For praise of the project's pastoral character, see Edda Belle Smith to Arthur Wilson, May 7, 1963, in Uncatalogued ST Materials, MLA.

40. This ideological compact was never fully successful in everyday life—women struggled to maintain their independence; some suburbs were more working class in character; suburbs often preserved ethnic and particularly racial division as much as resolved it—but, as part of what May suggests was a domestic containment strategy, the suburban home as an ideal did serve as a source of imagined national unity for the Cold War homefront. See Elaine Tyler May, *Homeward Bound: American Families in the Cold War Era* (New York: Basic, 1988), 89; Dolores Hayden, *Redesigning the American Dream: The Future of Housing, Work, and Family Life* (New York: Norton, 1984), 17–18; Clifford E. Clark Jr., "Ranch House Suburbia: Ideals and Realities," in Lary May, ed., *Recasting America: Culture and Politics in the Age of Cold War* (Chicago: University of Chicago Press, 1989); Rosalyn Baxandall and Elizabeth Ewen, *Picture Windows: How the Suburbs Happened* (New York: Basic, 2000), 148–149; Dolores Hayden, *Building Suburbia: Green Fields and Urban Growth, 1820–2000* (New York: Pantheon, 2003), 128–153.

41. Metropolitan Life, *Stuyvesant Town: This Is Your Home*, 1951, 24, in Stuyvesant Town-Booklet, MLA. See "'Rabbit Town' Honors a Friend," *NYT*, January 24, 1983, B3; memorandum, Breakdown of Families with Children as of October 1, 1948, n.d.; memorandum, Peter E. Sheridan to Carl Huebner, Breakdown of Families with Children as of

June 1, 1949, dated June 7, 1949; memo, Stuyvesant Town: Approximate Child Population, 1952; Met Life, "When They Counted Heads," n.d., all in ST-Children, MLA.

42. The data on income differentials are indicative rather than conclusive, considering that the "other income" category is general rather than specific, and it's impossible to know precisely whether women's incomes went up or down in the period. Met Life, "Supplementary Statistical Data Relating to Stuyvesant Town Residential Tenants," November 28, 1950; Demas, *Eleven Stories High,* 3, 101–102. On the patterns of women's work, see William H. Chafe, *The American Woman: Her Changing Social, Economic and Political Roles, 1920–1970* (New York: Oxford University Press, 1972). Despite— or because of—the pressure to stay home, Electra Demas's ambivalence about giving up her paid employment was fairly typical of women nationwide. See May, *Recasting America,* 75–91, 202–207. This ambivalence was, of course, one of the major revelations of Betty Friedan's exposé *The Feminine Mystique* (New York: Norton, 1963). Joanne Meyerowitz has shown that postwar women's magazines celebrated not just house-wives but career "superwomen" as well. See Meyerowitz, "Beyond *The Feminine Mystique*: A Reassessment of Postwar Mass Culture, 1946–1958," in Joanne Meyerowitz, ed., *Not June Cleaver: Women and Gender in Postwar America, 1945–1960* (Philadelphia: Temple University Press, 1994). Martha Seidman, interview, 2009.

43. For a good discussion of the complexities of marketers' appeals to both men and women, see Lizabeth Cohen, *A Consumers' Republic: The Politics of Mass Consumption in Postwar America* (New York: Knopf, 2003), 146–150; Demas, *Eleven Stories High,* 81.

44. Sachs Quality Stores advertisement, *NYDN,* May 12, 1946, 31, in S12, 1/11, MLA.

45. *NYJA* advertisement, *Advertising Age,* April 7, 1947, in RG12, Printed Materials, Scrapbooks, Housing, General, book 2, 138, MLA.

46. "Have You Studied the New Mass Homes?" *Home Furnishings Merchandiser,* July 1947, 47–48; "What Housing Projects Offer Retailers," *Fashion Trades* 1, no. 34 (November 8, 1946): 1. This article suggested that the new housing projects would be ideal locations for chain store branches.

47. See Cohen, *Consumer's Republic.* On the attraction of the single-family home, see Kenneth T. Jackson, *Crabgrass Frontier: The Suburbanization of the United States* (New York: Oxford University Press, 1985), 45–72.

48. Milton Lewis and Mildred Lewis, "We Live in a 'Barracks'—and Like It!" *NYHT,* December 9, 1956, 4–5.

49. Eugenia Sheppard, "An Apartment of Stuyvesant Town Is Shown," *NYHT,* June 6, 1947; Ann Pringle, "Hearns Caters to Stuyvesant Town Tenants," *NYHT,* November 18, 1947.

50. Hearns advertisement, *TV,* November 20, 1947, 5–6.

51. "Have You Studied the New Mass Homes?" *Home Furnishings Merchandiser,* July 1947, 47–48.

52. Ludwig Baumann Housing Center ad, *NYJA,* October 1947, in RG12, Printed Materials, Scrapbooks, Housing-General, book 3, MLA.

53. Ann Pringle, "New Ideas Seen in Stuyvesant Town Dwelling," *NYHT,* April 16, 1948. Gimbels intended to carry out its redecoration for $1,618; see the April 1948 issue of *McCall's*; Lee Bowman, "$1406 Furnished Our T&V Apartment," *TV,* February 24, 1949.

54. "They Live in Stuyvesant Town," *House and Garden* 94 (September 1948): 118–121, 163, 166. Met Life was also concerned to individualize the enormity of Stuyvesant Town. In its first tenant booklet, the company tried to "personalize every illustration as much as possible" and developed "techniques" to overcome the "bigness and magnitude of the project." Specifically, it made sure to avoid photos of the "vastness" of the project. See Mr. William J. Barrett, Third Vice-President, Re: Proposed Booklet, "Stuyvesant Town—This Is Your Home," n.d., in Stuyvesant Town-Booklet, MLA.

55. I examined a selection of 30 columns from the period 1947–1951. Many of the published columns, close to half, took Peter Cooper Village as their subject. I did not use those in my sample. The column began as an unsigned piece. Later, it was written by two interior decorators, Selma Zane and Rhoda Sande.

56. On "The House I Live In" and Sinatra's left-wing politics, see Michael Denning, *The Cultural Front* (New York: Verso, 1996), 335. Also see Jon Wiener, "His Way," *Nation*, June 8, 1998.

57. Metropolitan Life Insurance Company, "Is It Reasonable to Increase Rents of Stuyvesant Town?" July 12, 1951, *TV* ad text, in Uncatalogued ST Materials, MLA. See also Shad Polier to Editor, "Racial Policies in Housing," *NYT*, August 6, 1947.

58. Frederick Ecker to Charles T. Andrews, August 17, 1948, in ST-Construction folder, MLA; "Private Management vs. Public Mismanagement," *TV*, March 7, 1957.

59. Demas, *Eleven Stories High*, 8, 19–20; "Corlear's Column," *TV*, September 15, 1949, 2.

60. Seymour Roman to Editor, "Not in a Vacuum," *TV*, July 1, 1948, 4. Martha Seidman's husband, Al, for instance, grew up on Eldredge and Houston on the Lower East Side and was "slightly nostalgic" for his childhood there. Martha Seidman, interview, 2009.

61. Lewis and Lewis, "We Live in a Barracks," 4; Mumford, "Prefabricated Blight," 50; See also Demas, *Eleven Stories High*, 182.

62. Cole quoted in Christine Lyons, "Stuyvesant Town: Tranquility at Center of Things," *New York Newsday*, October 4, 1986, 26; also see William Cole, "Conformity," *New Yorker*, September 9, 1967; Demas, *Eleven Stories High*, 28.

63. Mumford, "Prefabricated Blight," 49; Martha Seidman and Pamela Long, interviews, 2009; Demas, *Eleven Stories High*, 28; Radio Reports, June 26, 1951, 4.

64. Radio Reports, "Metropolitan Life's Town and Village Less Neighborly than at First," Bill Leonard, *This Is New York*, WCBS, June 25, 1951.

65. I have a sample of 20 of these pamphlets from the years 1952, 1953, 1954, 1956, 1963, and 1964. They are signed by resident managers Carl Huebner and Arthur Wilson. They are found in ST-History and Plans folder, 1943–1967, S14, MLA.

66. The earliest available tenant reports are for the year 1963. I selected a sample of 34 representative reports, and 20 of those were reports made by the management directly against residents. They are in Uncatalogued ST Materials, MLA.

67. See ISR [Ira Robbins], memorandum, "Stuyvesant Town Evictions," September 20, 1950, in ST after 1943 folder, CHPC.

68. Of the 34 tenant reports I selected from 1963, 14 involve tenants making complaints to management. The quoted report is Anonymous to Arthur Wilson, March 22, 1963, in Uncatalogued ST Materials, MLA.

69. See Radio Reports, "Leonard Explores Some of Stuyvesant Town Gripes," Bill Leonard, *This Is New York,* WCBS, June 27, 1951, 2–4; Radio Reports, June 26, 1951, 4.

70. "600 at City Hall Win Fight to Bar Stuyvesant Rise," *NYHT,* May 20, 1952; "City Board Bans Stuyvesant Town Rent Rise; Metropolitan Life to Appeal to the Courts," *NYT,* May 20, 1952; Lotte N. Doverman to Editor, "Middle Income Housing," *NYT,* May 24, 1952. All the papers agreed that Met Life would eventually get its increase, because by the terms of its contract with the city it was illegal not to give the raise to it. This was the first of a series of rent increases in the '50s, as the company worked to keep profits in line with inflation.

71. On the conflict between community and bureaucracy—"*Gemeinschaft* ends with *Gesellschaft* means"—in planned superblock housing projects inspired by neighborhood-unit ideals, see John D. Fairfield, *The Mysteries of the Great City: The Politics of Urban Design, 1877–1937* (Columbus: Ohio State University Press, 1993), 208–218.

72. See "T and V Is Fine, but Gas House District Was Better Painting, Noted Artist Says," *TV,* November 30, 1950, 6. On Marsh, see Marilyn Cohen, *Reginald Marsh's New York: Paintings, Prints, Drawings, Photographs* (New York: Dover, 1983).

Chapter 4

1. Arthur Laurents, *West Side Story: A Musical* (New York: Random House, 1958). The film version is Jerome Robbins and Arthur Laurents, dirs., *West Side Story,* United Artists, 1961.

2. Keith Garebian, *The Making of West Side Story* (Buffalo, NY: Mosaic, 1995), 143; "Small Rumble," *New Yorker,* April 2, 1960, 34–35; Howard Thompson, "At Work on 'West Side,'" *NYT,* August 14, 1960, X5; "West Side Story," *NYTM,* October 2, 1960, 27. See also Greg Lawrence, *Dance with Demons: The Life of Jerome Robbins* (New York: Putnam's, 2001), 289–290.

3. See "Explosion on the West Side," *Life,* October 20, 1961, 80–87+; photo on 81.

4. Otto Nelson, "Investments in Urban Renewal," address before the 20th Annual Building Products Executives Conference, Washington, DC, November 7, 1958, 10, 14, in box 117, Committee on Slum Clearance, 1958 folder, MosesNYPL.

5. John D. Rockefeller III quoted in "The Rockefeller Touch in Building," *AF* 108, no. 3 (March 1958): 90–91. Lincoln Center pioneered the still-ongoing attempts by cities to use cultural centers as catalysts for revitalization. See Elizabeth Strom, "Converting Pork into Porcelain: Cultural Institutions and Downtown Development," *Urban Affairs Review* 38, no. 1 (September 2002): 3–21.

6. Joel Schwartz, *The New York Approach: Robert Moses, Urban Liberals, and Redevelopment of the Inner City* (Columbus: Ohio State University Press, 1993), 108–109, 125–130. Moses often used the threat that "responsible" interests would be scared away from renewal as a way to motivate municipal allies and embarrass critics. See, for instance, Moses, address at Conference of Federal Housing and Home Finance Agency, Region I, New York, April 17, 1958, in box 117, MosesNYPL.

7. The policy mechanism for this effort, first suggested by the economists Alvin Hansen and Guy Greer in 1941, took government intervention in the urban real estate market beyond the eminent domain and tax exemptions that had thus far been offered to private interests. Called the "write-down," this provision allowed the federal

government to subsidize "net project cost." Title I intended that local redevelopment authorities would acquire land, clear it, and auction it off at "fair value" to a private developer. Of course, the "fair value" for open land cleared of income-producing property was much less than the authority had paid for it, so the local authority could use the public monies to "write-down" the value of the land to the point where a developer would consider it to have fair value. The federal government paid two-thirds of the difference between the local authority's purchase price and fair value, while local governments supplied the rest. On the write-down, see Ashley Foard and Hilbert Fefferman, "Federal Urban Renewal Legislation," in James Q. Wilson, ed., *Urban Renewal: The Record and the Controversy* (Cambridge, MA: MIT Press, 1966), 71–125; Lawrence Friedman, *Government and Slum Housing: A Century of Frustration* (Chicago: Rand McNally, 1968), 148; Jeanne R. Lowe, *Cities in a Race with Time: Progress and Poverty in America's Renewing Cities* (New York: Random House, 1967), 28–29; Robert Fogelson, *Downtown: Its Rise and Fall, 1880–1920* (New Haven, CT: Yale University Press, 2001), 357–371; Schwartz, *The New York Approach*, 81, 131–132.

8. On the New York method, see Lowe, "The Man Who Got Things Done for New York: Robert Moses Tackles Slum Clearance," in her *Cities in a Race with Time*, 68–72; and Schwartz, *The New York Approach*, 129–131 and 171–174. See also Moses to Norman Mason, April 15, 1959, in roll 14, box 103019, folder 1, ParksGen.

9. On the "predominantly residential" clause and Moses's application of it, see Friedman, *Government and Slum Housing*,150–152. See also Fogelson, *Downtown*, 377–378. For one example of Moses's insistence that Title I was about slum clearance, not about building housing, see Moses to Lee B. Wood, November 13, 1958, box 117, Committee on Slum Clearance, 1958 folder, MosesNYPL. See also Robert Moses, *Public Works: A Dangerous Trade* (New York: McGraw-Hill, 1970), 459–460. On urban renewal and the politics of growth, see Alan Wolfe, *America's Impasse: The Rise and Fall of the Politics of Growth* (New York: Pantheon, 1981), 82–88. On Charles Abrams and the idea of the business welfare state, see chapter 3 above; and A. Scott Henderson, *Housing and the Democratic Ideal: The Life and Thought of Charles Abrams* (New York: Columbia University Press, 2000), 99–122.

10. For New York's Title I accomplishments, see Martin Anderson, *The Federal Bulldozer* (Cambridge, MA: MIT Press, 1964), 95–97; Lowe, *Cities in a Race with Time*, 66–68; Moses, *Public Works*, 441–442; Schwartz, *The New York Approach*, 175. See also Hilary Ballon, "Robert Moses and Urban Renewal: The Title I Program," and the other essays in Ballon and Kenneth T. Jackson, eds., *Robert Moses and the Modern City: The Transformation of New York* (New York: Norton, 2007). After the Moses era various New York planning and redevelopment agencies took advantage of several modifications to the original 1949 Housing Act and added many more "urban renewal areas" to the city's docket, but these were quite different than the original projects launched by Moses. Reflecting the struggles of the Moses era, most of these featured far less demolition, more in-fill construction, and greater community consultation. By the middle of the 1980s, depending on how one counts, there were about 58 areas in Manhattan and approximately 148 in the city overall. See *New York Urban Renewal Atlas* (New York: City of New York, 1984).

11. See Schwartz, *The New York Approach*, 108–109, 133–134, 144–145, 164–165, 170–171.

12. Ibid., 145; see also 164–169.

13. See ibid., 133–203. Corlears Hook replaced an area that was 24 percent nonwhite, Manhattantown 52 percent, Columbus Circle 54 percent, and Morningside 65 percent. See Schwartz, *The New York Approach*, 175.

14. Bronk quoted in Schwartz, *The New York Approach*, 222; and Winthrop Rockefeller in Schwartz, *The New York Approach*, 224.

15. See ibid., 192–196.

16. On the Rockefellers, their involvement in New York, and their interest in urban renewal, see Robert Fitch, *The Assassination of New York* (New York: Verso, 1993), 28–30, 100–101, and 206–229; Schwartz, *The New York Approach*, 300–301; Wesley Janz, "Theaters of Power: Architectural and Cultural Productions," *Journal of Architectural Education* 50, no. 4 (May 1997): 232 and 242n21. See also, more generally, John Ensor Harr and Peter J. Johnson, *The Rockefeller Century* (New York: Scribner's, 1988), 430–452; and John Ensor Harr and Peter J. Johnson, *The Rockefeller Conscience* (New York: Scribner's, 1991).

17. Juilliard School of Music, Barnard College, Corpus Christi Church, Teachers College, Union Theological Seminary, Jewish Theological Seminary, Cathedral of St. John the Divine, and two Rockefeller-backed organizations, Riverside Church and International House, joined Columbia in an effort to protect their existence on the Heights. See Gertrude Samuels, "Rebirth of a Community," *NYT*, September 25, 1955, 26–27, 37, 39, 42, 44; Charles Grutzner, "City's 'Acropolis' Combating Slums," *NYT*, May 21, 1957, 37, 40; Schwartz, *The New York Approach*, 151–159, 185–189, 195–197, 200–203; Andrew S. Dolkart, *Morningside Heights: A History of Its Architecture and Development* (New York: Columbia University Press, 1998), 325–332. See Schwartz, *The New York Approach*, 151, for his coining of the phrase "Cold War Acropolis."

18. See "International House, New York, Second Interim Report and Recommendations," August 30, 1946, 9; and "International House, New York, Final Report of Wilbur C. Munnecke, the University of Chicago," October 30, 1946, both in box 121, folder 6, Hutchins. See also Samuels, "Rebirth of a Community," 26; and Schwartz, *The New York Approach*, 152–153. On the faculty panel, see Schwartz, *The New York Approach*, 155.

19. Schwartz, *The New York Approach*, 155–159, 185–189; Grutzner, "City's Acropolis," 37, 40.

20. Samuels, "Rebirth of a Community," 37; and David Rockefeller, "Morningside Heights—The Institutions and the People," speech delivered at the Homecoming Dinner, Riverside Church, October 4, 1950, 10, in MHI folder, Columbia.

21. See Schwartz, *The New York Approach*, 196–197, 203.

22. Rockefeller, "Morningside Heights," 1.

23. Robert Moses, *Public Works: A Dangerous Trade* (New York: McGraw-Hill, 1970), 440; Moses quoted in Robert Caro, *The Power Broker* (New York: Knopf, 1974), 1013.

24. For the details of Lincoln Square, see Moses, *Public Works*, 449, 513–533; Caro, *The Power Broker*, 1013–1016; Schwartz, *The New York Approach*, 276–277; Robert A. M. Stern, Thomas Mellins, and David Fishman, eds., *New York 1960: Architecture and Urbanism between the Second World War and the Bicentennial* (New York: Monacelli, 1995), 677–680, 717; Michael Thanner, "Lincoln Square: The Dramatic Transformation of a New York Neighborhood," M.S. thesis, Columbia University, 1994. On Fordham's

involvement, see John T. McGreevey, *Parish Boundaries: The Catholic Encounter with Race in the Twentieth Century Urban North* (Chicago: University of Chicago Press, 1996), 111–132. See also Committee on Slum Clearance, *Lincoln Square: Slum Clearance Plan under Title I of the Housing Act of 1949 as Amended* (May 28, 1956); Robert A Poteete, "Vast Plan for Lincoln Square Spread before Parley Here," *NYHT,* April 16, 1956, 1; Charles Grutzner, "Moses Outlines City within City for Lincoln Square," *NYT,* May 28, 1956, 1, 21; Robert Moses to Robert Wagner, September 12, 1956, in box 57, folder 508, JDR3; Frederick W. Roevekamp, "Lincoln Square Project: 'Big, Bold, and Beautiful,'" *Christian Science Monitor,* October 9, 1957, 1; Grutzner, "Lincoln Square Sites Acquired by City, Sold to Sponsors," *NYT,* March 1, 1958, 1, 17; Grutzner, "Plans Enlarged for Lincoln Square," *NYT,* April 9, 1958, 35; "Co-op Takes Last of Lincoln Area," *NYT,* August 2, 1958, 19; Grutzner, "Work Is Speeded on Red Cross Site," *NYT,* February 18, 1959, 26; Otto Nelson Jr. to John D. Rockefeller III, "Summary of Activities, July 1, 1959, to December 31, 1959," January 27, 1960, in box 43, folder 428, RockCult; Lincoln Center, Inc., "Housing Near Center to Start," *Performing Arts* 11, no. 3 (May 6, 1960); "Cornerstone Is Laid for Lincoln Tower Apartments," *NYT,* June 28, 1961.

25. The general story of Lincoln Center's founding and building has been told a number of times. My account relies on these sources: Martin Mayer, *Bricks, Mortar and the Performing Arts: Report of the Twentieth Century Fund Task Force on Performing Arts Centers* (New York: Twentieth Century Fund, 1970); Edgar B. Young, *Lincoln Center: The Building of an Institution* (New York: New York University Press, 1980); Victoria Newhouse, *Wallace K. Harrison, Architect* (New York: Rizzoli, 1989), 186–197; Harr and Johnson, *The Rockefeller Conscience,* 120–157; Kathleen Randall, "Lincoln Center for the Performing Arts: Cultural Visibility and Postwar Urbanism," M.S. thesis, Columbia University, 1992; Stern et al., *New York 1960,* 677–716; Alice Goldfarb Marquis, *Art Lessons: Learning from the Rise and Fall of Public Arts Funding* (New York: Basic, 1995), 9–51; Janz, "Theaters of Power."

26. See Young, *Lincoln Center,* 16–18; and Harr and Johnson, *The Rockefeller Conscience,* 124. For Rockefeller's own account, see John D. Rockefeller III, "The Evolution: Birth of a Great Center," *NYTM,* September 23, 1962, 14, 30–33.

27. President Eisenhower quoted in "Addresses Given at the Ceremony," *Performing Arts* 1, no. 6 (May 22, 1959): 2; Galbraith quoted in Marquis, *Art Lessons,* 2; Lincoln Center, Inc., *Lincoln Center: "A Mighty Influence,"* May 14, 1959, 4–5, in box 40, folder 404, RockCult. See also John D. Rockefeller III, "The Arts and American Business," *Music Journal,* February 1959, copy in box 75, folder 647, JDR3. On the role that culture and the public funding of culture played in postwar American life generally, see Alvin Toffler, *The Culture Consumers* (New York: St. Martin's, 1964); and Howard Brick, *Age of Contradiction: American Thought and Culture in the 1960s* (New York: Twayne, 1998), 11–13.

28. Rockefeller, "The Arts and American Business"; Lincoln Center, *Lincoln Center: "A Mighty Influence,"* 4; Robert Moses, "New York as the Cultural Capital of the Nation: We Break Ground for the Performing Arts at Lincoln Square," *NYTM,* May 10, 1959.

29. *Life* editorial quoted in Marquis, *Art Lessons,* 2; John D. Rockefeller III, press release, November 9, 1958, in box 73, folder 635, JDR3; Jackson quoted in Action, Inc., "Action Theme: Commerce-Culture Centers," *Action Reporter* 4, no. 2 (November–December 1959): 2–3.

30. Marquis, *Art Lessons,* 2; John D. Rockefeller III quoted in Seymour Peck, "A Rockefeller Enters 'Show Biz,'" *NYTM,* November 18, 1956, 62; Rockefeller, "The Arts and American Business"; Joe Alex Morris, "Colossus on Broadway," *Saturday Evening Post,* July 19, 1958, 77.

31. August Heckscher, "The Nation's Culture: New Age for the Arts," *NYTM,* Lincoln Center supplement, September 23, 1962, 15.

32. Devereux Josephs, "Josephs Foresees New Conflicts as Result of Cultural Lag," *NYJA,* October 4, 1959, 16; Marquis, *Art Lessons,* 24; Rockefeller, "The Arts and American Business."

33. Lincoln Center, Inc., Lincoln Center for the Performing Arts, "Insider's Statement, July 1957," 10–11, in box 42, folder 420, RockCult; "Notes for a Public Statement on the Lincoln Center," n.d., in box 42, folder 419, RockCult.

34. "Symbol of U.S. Culture," *NYT,* July 23, 1956; Harold Taubman, "Third Draft of a Public Statement on Lincoln Center," August 31, 1956, in box 36, folder 419, RockCult. Even Moses got in on the act, writing in the *Times* that Lincoln Center would provide "a fit stage for the spreading panorama of the lively arts to demonstrate to all the world that in New York we do not live by bread alone." Moses, "Significance: What the City Means," *NYTM,* April 29, 1956, 48.

35. Harrison quoted in Wesley R. Janz, "Building Nations by Designing Buildings: Corporatism, Eero Saarinen, and the Lincoln Center for the Performing Arts," Working Monographs in Architecture and Urban Planning, University of Wisconsin-Milwaukee, August 1995, 6; Marquis, *Art Lessons,* 24–25.

36. C. D. Jackson, "Culture: Status Symbol for the World," *Performing Arts* 1, no. 1 (March 12, 1959): 2.

37. Nelson, "Investments in Urban Renewal," 10, 14.

38. See Roberta Chalmers to John D. Rockefeller III, July 17, 1958, in box 37, folder 380, RockCult. On the impact of *Sputnik,* see Paul Dickson, *Sputnik: The Shock of the Century* (New York: Walker, 2001).

39. Lincoln Center for the Performing Arts, Inc., minutes, March 14, 1960, 7, in box 103058, folder 6, roll 15, ParksGen; Meany quoted in "Labor Chiefs Urge Support of Fund Campaign," *Performing Arts* 2, no. 16 (March 17, 1961): 4.

40. See John D. Rockefeller III to Sherman Adams, n.d., box 58, folder 518, JDR3; Rockefeller quoted in Young, *Lincoln Center,* 172.

41. Action, Inc., "Action Theme: Commerce-Culture Centers," *Action Reporter,* November–December 1959, 2–3; Harold Schonberg, "The Lincoln Center Vision Takes Form," *NYTM,* December 11, 1960, 7.

42. Rockefeller quoted in "The Rockefeller Touch in Building," *AF* 108, no. 3 (March 1958): 90–91; John D. Rockefeller III, press release, November 9, 1958, box 73, folder 635, JDR3; Lincoln Center, "Insider's Statement, July 1957," 4; Rockefeller, "The Arts and American Business"; William Schuman, "The Arts and a Great City," *Performing Arts* 3, no. 13 (January 26, 1962).

43. See "Notes for a Public Statement on the Lincoln Center." This hidden subtext lends weight to the judgment made by historian Karene Grad that Lincoln Center was, in effect, a kind of second coming of the White City at the World's Columbian Exposition of 1893 in Chicago. Like the White City, Lincoln Center was built along with a world's

fair—the 1964–1965 World's Fair in New York (although it was not a prime exhibit in that fair)—and spoke to a similar concern with purity, order, and social control in a world torn by class and racial divisions. Karene Grad, "Lincoln Center; or, The Cultural Politics of Urban Renewal," paper given at the Center for Study of Race, Inequality, and Poverty, April 2002, Yale University. For another take on Lincoln Center's urban mission, see Julia L. Foulkes, "The Other West Side Story: Urbanization and the Arts Meet at Lincoln Center," *Amerikastudien/American Studies* 52, no. 2 (2007): 227–241.

44. Lincoln Center, *Lincoln Center: "A Mighty Influence,"* 4; "Building for Culture: Shades of Versailles?" *Interiors,* March 1957; Editors, "Lincoln Square on the Way," *NYHT,* May 26, 1958.

45. See Lincoln Center, Inc., press release, October 11, 1956; and Harold C. Schonberg, "Architects Join on Center Plans," *NYT,* October 22, 1956, both in box 37, folder 377, RockCult.

46. Ross Parmenter, "Lincoln Square Plan Developing toward World Cultural Center," *NYT,* July 23, 1956, 1; for critiques of Lincoln Center's planning, see Randall, "Lincoln Center for the Performing Arts," 87–102; Stern et al., *New York 1960,* 677–716; William B. Scott and Peter M. Rutkoff, *New York Modern: The Arts and the City* (Baltimore, MD: Johns Hopkins University Press, 1999), 351–361.

47. Randall, "Lincoln Center for the Performing Arts," 61–62, 67–68.

48. Harrison quoted in Janz, "Theaters of Power," 233; Anthony A. Bliss, "Cultural Capital of the World," *Performing Arts* 2, no. 17 (March 31, 1961).

49. On Lincoln Center's architecture and planning in general, see Randall, "Lincoln Center for the Performing Arts," 60–102; Stern et al., *New York 1960,* 677–716; Young, *Lincoln Center,* 79–95; Newhouse, *Wallace K. Harrison,* 186–197.

50. Johnson quoted in Harold C. Schonberg, "Six Architects in Search of a Center," *NYTM,* February 8, 1959, 22. On Lincoln Center as brutalist and as a preview of postmodernism, see Stern et al., *New York 1960,* quoting Paul Goldberger, 716.

51. See Schonberg, "Lincoln Center Vision Takes Form," 7; Randall, "Lincoln Center for the Performing Arts," 78; Young, *Lincoln Center,* 79. Jackson quoted in Lincoln Center for the Performing Arts, Inc., "Minutes of Meeting—Board of Directors and Members," November 9, 1959, 6, in roll 14, box 103019, folder 5, ParksGen.

52. Randall, "Lincoln Center for the Performing Arts," 65–66; Huxtable quoted in Stern et al., *New York 1960,* 716; and Young, *Lincoln Center,* 257; Giedion quoted in Randall, "Lincoln Center for the Performing Arts," 69.

53. Robert Moses to Charles Spofford, February 2, 1960, in roll 15, box 103058, folder 5, ParksGen; William Zeckendorf quoted in Webb and Knapp, *Lincoln Square Progress, June 27, 1961: Lincoln Towers Cornerstone Ceremony* (New York: Webb and Knapp, 1961), 5, in box 74, folder 640, JDR3.

54. Nelson, "Investments in Urban Renewal," 6, 10; "Cultural Center," *NYJA,* July 22, 1957.

55. Paul Henry Lang, "Music and Musicians: The Lincoln Square Art Center," *NYHT,* June 2, 1957.

56. Heckscher, "The Nation's Culture," 15.

57. William Schuman, "The Idea: 'A Creative, Dynamic Force,'" *NYTM,* September 23, 1962, Lincoln Center supplement, 36.

58. See "Culture City: New U.S. Capital for the Performing Arts," *Look,* January 19, 1960, 40–41. See also box 84, folder 6, EBYoung.

59. Harry Rogers, "The Dawn of a New Era," *West Side News,* May 14, 1959, 15.

60. Ibid., 15; Otto Nelson to William Reid, November 12, 1958, in box 73B4, folder 6, NYCHA; Otto L. Nelson, "Rebuilding Districts to Recapture Values: Lincoln Center for the Performing Arts," address at the Real Estate Board of New York luncheon, January 21, 1959, in box 75, folder 647, JDR3; William Lebwohl quoted in New York City, City Planning Commission (CPC), "Public Hearing before the City Planning Commission," September 11, 1957, City Hall, Manhattan, Master Plan, Borough of Manhattan, 5–6, Avery. Rockefeller maintained that the center "would be a focal point for the performing arts as the U.N. is for international interests." See John D. Rockefeller III, New York Building Congress Address, October 26, 1956, in box 76, folder 655, JDR3. Overall, the *Herald Tribune* editorialized, Lincoln Square and Lincoln Center offered a "tremendous physical and economic transformation…for metropolitan renewal" and "a cultural vision that should develop a new world capital of the arts." See "Get Moving on Lincoln Square," *NYHT,* November 16, 1957.

61. See Robert Moses, "New York as the Cultural Capital of the Nation: We Break Ground for the Performing Arts at Lincoln Square," *NYTM,* May 10, 1959.

Chapter 5

1. On the history of the Lincoln Arcade building, see Owen Johnson, "Owen Johnson Discovers a New Bohemia Here," *NYTM,* October 22, 1916, 9; Peter Salwen, *Upper West Side Story* (New York: Abbeville, 1989), 202–204, 272.

2. See Joseph Floch et al. to Robert Moses, April 4, 1956, in box 116, 1956 Library Correspondence, folder 1 of 3, MosesNYPL; Alexander Archipenko, Raphael Soyer, Joseph Floch to Editor, "Space for Artists," *NYHT,* May 1, 1956; Joseph Floch, Alexander Archipenko, Raphael Soyer to Editor, "Artists' Studios in Lincoln Square," *NYT,* May 3, 1956; Joseph Floch to John D. Rockefeller III, June 5, 1956, in box 40, folder 409, RockCult; "33 Ordered Evicted at Arts Center Site," *NYT,* June 18, 1959, 25.

3. See Salwen, *Upper West Side Story,* 272. See also Abram Lerner, ed., *The Hirshhorn Museum and Sculpture Garden* (New York: Abrams, 1974), 750.

4. On Soyer's relationship with Reginald Marsh, see Raphael Soyer, *Diary of an Artist* (Washington, DC: New Republic, 1977), 156–160. The inheritors of Soyer's vision were the younger generation of artists coming of age in the late '50s and early '60s, artists like Jim Dine, Red Grooms, Robert Rauschenberg, and Claes Oldenburg, who embraced abstraction but divorced themselves from the reigning orthodoxy of abstract expressionism by focusing on urban street life and the material reality of the city as subject matter. See Joshua Shannon, "Claes Oldenburg's *The Street* and Urban Renewal in Greenwich Village, 1960," *Art Bulletin* 84, no. 1 (March 2004): 136–162.

5. Wallace Harrison, "Talk Given by WKH, Jan. 7, 1959 at University Club Dinner for Lincoln Center Fund Raising," quoted in Kathleen Randall, "Lincoln Center for the Performing Arts: Cultural Visibility and Postwar Urbanism," M.S. thesis, Columbia University, 1992, 77.

6. The first recorded attempts to save neighborhoods threatened with postwar clearance and to stop projects altogether were launched by local residents unaffiliated

with the organized tenant movements at Stuyvesant Town in New York, at the Lake Meadows site in Chicago in 1948, and at several sites in Pittsburgh in the late '40s. Residents of the Highland Park neighborhood in Pittsburgh may have been the first community group that succeeded in stopping a project, in the summer of 1949. On Chicago, see Arnold R. Hirsch, *Making the Second Ghetto: Race and Housing in Chicago, 1940–1960*, 2nd ed. (Chicago: University of Chicago Press, 1998), 125–127. On Pittsburgh, see Gregory J. Crowley, *The Politics of Place: Contentious Urban Redevelopment in Pittsburgh* (Pittsburgh: University of Pittsburgh Press, 2005), 58–89.

7. On the tenant movement's fraught relationship with liberal housers and urbanists, see Roberta Gold, "City of Tenants: New York's Housing Struggles and the Challenge to Postwar America, 1945–1974," Ph.D. diss., University of Washington, 2004, 13, 14, 38; Joel Schwartz, "Tenant Power in the Liberal City, 1943–1971," in Ronald Lawson, ed., *The Tenant Movement in New York City, 1904–1984* (New Brunswick, NJ: Rutgers University Press, 1986).

8. On tenants organizations at Stuyvesant Town and the United Tenants League approach to renewal, see Schwartz, "Tenant Power," 139–140. The UTL did join other organizations in the critique of the project itself, but it refrained from mobilizing to help tenants. See Gold, "City of Tenants," 48; Joel Schwartz, *The New York Approach* (Columbus: Ohio State University Press, 1993), 98–99.

9. Schwartz, *The New York Approach*, 164–169. On Vito Marcantonio, housing, and renewal, see Gerald Meyer, *Vito Marcantonio, Radical Politician, 1902–1954* (Albany: State University of New York Press, 1989); Annette T. Rubinstein, ed., *I Vote My Conscience: Debates, Speeches and Writings of Vito Marcantonio, 1935–1950* (New York: Vito Marcantonio Memorial, 1956), 271, 302–303, 307. See particularly Marcantonio's testimony before Congress during the debate over the 1949 Housing Act. Marcantonio pressed lawmakers to adopt a bill with more public housing and saw the bill that was finally passed as compromised by the real estate lobby. See *Housing Act of 1949, Hearings before the Committee on Banking and Currency, House of Representatives, Eighty-first Congress, First Session on H.R. 4009, April 7, etc.* (Washington, DC: U.S. Government Printing Office, 1949), 664–666.

10. Schwartz, "Tenant Power," 154–155; Schwartz, *The New York Approach*, 108–109.

11. Gold, "City of Tenants," 93; Schwartz, "Tenant Power," 155; and Schwartz, *The New York Approach*, 177.

12. On the ostensibly nonpartisan character of Save Our Homes, see Gold, "City of Tenants," 93. As Gold notes, the Yorkville committee had to make alliances with more "conservative" neighbors. On activities in Yorkville, see "Yorkville Tenants Demand Protection," *NYT,* January 18, 1956, 33; and Jane Benedict to Stanley M. Isaacs, April 25, 1955, in box 25, 1955-ALP folder, Isaacs.

13. Manhattan Tenants Council, "Slum Clearance or People Clearance? (Fact Sheet on Title I Urban Redevelopment)," June 1955, 1, in box 68C1, folder 2, NYCHA. The tenant activists' defense of these neighborhoods crossed the line into exaggeration when they claimed that "many" of the threatened apartments were "large" with "elevators, steam heat, hot water, and other modern conveniences."

14. There is no definite source for the Manhattan Tenants Council's numbers, so they are difficult to interpret and can only be taken as rough estimates and predictions.

By comparison, Joel Schwartz estimates that the 16 completed Title I projects displaced 100,000 people, about half as many as the Manhattan Tenants Council estimated might lose their homes from 17 proposed projects. Susan and Norman Fainstein show figures of 65 percent nonwhite at Morningside and 52 percent nonwhite at Manhattantown. These figures are also difficult to interpret as some percentage of these people were Puerto Rican, and a significant portion of the "white" population would have been Puerto Rican as well. Because census data did not include accurate counts of Puerto Rican migrants—counting some as white and some as nonwhite in these years—it's difficult to know exactly who was on the sites without explicit statistics on Puerto Rican populations. See Manhattan Tenants Council, "Slum Clearance or People Clearance?" 1–2; Schwartz, *The New York Approach,* xv and 175; Norman I. Fainstein and Susan S. Fainstein, "Governing Regimes and the Political Economy of Development in New York City, 1946–1984," in John Hull Mollenkopf, ed., *Power, Culture and Place: Essays on New York City* (New York: Russell Sage, 1988), 166; Michael Singer, "Eviction Project Blocked for Second Time by Tenants," *DW,* November 16, 1951, 1, 6; Schwartz, "Tenant Power," 157; Virginia Gardner, "Housing Conference Votes Mass Albany Visit Feb. 3," *DW,* January 19, 1953, 3, 6.

15. On gender in the tenant activist–led anti-renewal movement, see Gold, "City of Tenants," 80, 85, 124–125.

16. See Schwartz, *The New York Approach,* 191–192; Schwartz, "Tenant Power," 155–159; Gold, "City of Tenants," 91–92; John Howard Jones, "City Meet Backs Fight on Bias at Knickerbocker," *DW,* May 5, 1952, 1, 6. See also "Manhattan Tenants Council Raps Proposed High-Rent Housing Project," *DW,* September 28, 1951, 8; Abner W. Berry, "City's White Fathers Plan Bigger Negro Ghettos," *DW,* December 18, 1951, 4; Martha Biondi, *To Stand and Fight: The Struggle for Civil Rights in Postwar New York City* (Cambridge, MA: Harvard University Press, 2003), 224–225.

17. Laster quoted in Schwartz, *The New York Approach,* 193.

18. Ibid., 194–195; Schwartz, "Tenant Power," 158.

19. Isaacs quoted in Schwartz, *The New York Approach,* 109–111.

20. Isaacs quoted ibid., 188.

21. Ibid., 138–143, 145–151, 179–184; Schwartz, "Tenant Power," 155, 161. On the Village, see Robert Fishman, "Revolt of the Urbs," in Hilary Ballon and Kenneth Jackson, eds., *Robert Moses and the Modern City: The Transformation of New York* (New York: Norton, 2007).

22. Schwartz, *The New York Approach,* 199. See also Jeanne Lowe, *Cities in a Race with Time: Progress and Poverty in America's Renewing Cities* (New York: Random House, 1967), 82.

23. City Planning Commission, *Tenant Relocation Report* (New York: City of New York, January 20, 1954).

24. For the story of the report and its suppression, see Robert Caro, *The Power Broker: Robert Moses and the Fall of New York* (New York: Knopf, 1974), 966–969, 976–979. The only newspaper to give the report adequate coverage, Caro notes, was the liberal *New York Post.*

25. See Caro, *The Power Broker,* 969–976, 979–983; Gold, "City of Tenants," 104–108. On the various reports, see Lowe, *Cities in a Race with Time,* 83; Algernon Black and

Frances Levenson to Cooperating Organizations, September 30, 1955, and State Committee on Discrimination in Housing, Statement for House Investigation Subcommittee of the House Committee on Banking and Currency Sitting in New York City, October 5, 6, and 7, 1955, 2, both in box 26, NYS Committee on Discrimination in Housing folder, Isaacs. See also Office of City Administration, City of New York, "Tenant Relocation and the Housing Program," May 20, 1954; Community Service Society, Committee on Housing, "Relocation of Residential Site Tenants in New York City, with Special Reference to Title I of the Housing Act of 1949: A Report and Recommendations," February 1956; Mayor's Committee for Better Housing of the City of New York, "Report of Subcommittee on Problems of Relocation of Persons Displaced by New Housing and Other Public Improvements," n.d.; Stanley Isaacs, "Problems of Relocation," November 1955, all in box 26, Speeches folder, Isaacs. See also "50% Added Space Is Housing Goal," *NYT,* August 1, 1955, 38. For some early press coverage of the relocation problem, see Bernard Nossiter, "What Happens to Displaced Slum Tenants?" *NYWTS,* May 9, 1955; and Nossiter, "City Slum Evictees 'Intimidated,'" *NYWTS,* May 10, 1955.

26. See Caro, *The Power Broker,* 984–1025, 1042–1060. For a summary of the results of the press investigations, see Fred J. Cook and Gene Gleason, "The Shame of New York," *Nation,* October 31, 1959.

27. On the effect of Title I scandals on the 1954 Housing Act, see Schwartz, "Tenant Power," 160–161. See Lowe, *Cities in a Race with Time,* 34–37, on the intentions of the new bill. For some of the thinking at the federal level that motivated the reform, see Albert M. Cole, address before the National Housing Conference, Washington, DC, May 11, 1953, in box 71C7, folder 1, NYCHA. Unlike Moses and Congress, Cole, the head of the Housing and Home Finance Agency, viewed the primary objective of the 1949 act as the "improvement of the housing conditions of American families," not merely slum clearance. For an example of Harris Present's activities on the new committee, see Present to Editor, "Relocating Tenants," *NYT,* July 21, 1954, 26, in which he critiques the city administrator's review of the CPC relocation report and asks the Board of Estimate to schedule a public hearing on relocation. The origin of the City Wide Committee on Housing Relocation Problems is somewhat murky. Joel Schwartz dates it at 1953. See Schwartz, *The New York Approach,* 199. However, Present remembers it as starting up in 1949, as a direct reaction to the 1949 Housing Act. Harris Present, interview with author, March 28, 2008, New York.

28. Mrs. Philips, Secretary, Lincoln Square Residents Committee to Stanley Isaacs, August 18, 1955, in box 26, folder 1, Mayor's Committee for Better Housing folder 1, Isaacs; Margaret Hedman to Philip J. Cruise, June 27, 1956, and attached Lincoln Square Residents Committee Statement, 1955, in box 73B7, folder 08, NYCHA; Ella Root to Herman Weinkrantz, November 11, 1955, and attached Lincoln Square Residents Committee, memorandum to Mayor Wagner on Lincoln Square Development, n.d., in box 116, Housing Correspondence folder, MosesNYPL; Willard Keefe, memorandum to Mr. Rockefeller, Mr. Fowler, Mr. Jamieson, Subject: Lincoln Square Residents Committee, March 21, 1956, in box 43, folder 428, RockCult.

29. Present, interview, 2008; Harris Present, oral history, February 15, 1991, 17–24, LCPA. See also Harris Present to the Editor, "To Study City's Housing," *NYT,* November 8, 1954, 20; Harris Present to the Editor, "Composition of Housing Committee," *NYT,*

November 12, 1954, 20; Harris Present to the Editor, "Puerto Ricans in New York," *NYT*, April 27, 1955, 30.

30. Present was also deeply affected by a trip he took to Puerto Rico around the time he learned of the troubles at Lincoln Square. There, he saw a housing project designed for low-income tenants. It was being put up *before* the future tenants' nearby neighborhood was demolished. They would move in and then their old homes would meet the wrecking ball. This initiated his fundamental doubts about the concept of relocation. Present, interview, 2008. Contrary to Robert Caro's assertion that the New York press was not interested in the story of displacement, the sheer volume of coverage cited here, particularly in the *Times,* suggests otherwise. Caro is certainly correct that newspaper editors and publishers still backed Moses, but they gave ample and unprecedented space, in both the news and letters pages, to Present and the Lincoln Square organizations. See Caro, *The Power Broker,* 1014.

31. For a summary of the various issues motivating the multiple strands of resistance to Lincoln Square, see Charles Grutzner, "Lincoln Project Facing New Fight," *NYT*, February 23, 1957, 19.

32. See Present, interview, 2008; Present, oral history, 25; Harris Present to Editor, "Relocating Slum Residents," *NYT*, February 18, 1956, 18; Present to Editor, "Plans for Lincoln Square: Lack of Provision and Compensation Charged," *NYT*, August 16, 1956, 24.

33. Charles Grutzner, "Lincoln Square Near Subsidy Stage; Groups Map Displacement Fight," *NYT*, April 25, 1956, 37; "Lincoln Square Delay Urged on Mayor," *NYT*, May 5, 1956, 21.

34. Robert A. M. Stern, Thomas Mellins, and David Fishman, eds., *New York 1960: Architecture and Urbanism between the Second World War and the Bicentennial* (New York: Monacelli, 1995), 661–666, 674–675. On the early history of San Juan Hill, see Marcy Sacks, *Before Harlem: The Black Experience in New York City before World War I* (Philadelphia: Penn Press, 2006). The portrait of the neighborhood was drawn from *United States Census, New York City, Manhattan Borough* (Washington, DC: U.S. Government Printing Office, 1950), 93, 316–317. New York City, City Planning Commission, City-wide Map of Sections Containing Areas Suitable for Clearance, Replanning and Low Rent Housing, January 3, 1940; New York City, City Planning Commission, Plan of Sections Containing Areas Suitable for Development and Redevelopment, December 30, 1954. Note that the map was renamed in the 1954 revision, signifying the new emphasis on private redevelopment. On the West End of Boston, see Herbert Gans, *The Urban Villagers: Group and Class in the Life of Italian-Americans* (New York: Free Press, 1962); Marc Fried, *The World of the Urban Working Class* (Cambridge, MA: Harvard University Press, 1973); and essays by Gans, Fried, and others in Sean M. Fisher and Carolyn Hughes, eds., *The Last Tenement: Confronting Community and Urban Renewal in Boston's West End* (Boston: Bostonian Society, 1992).

35. New York City, Committee on Slum Clearance, *Lincoln Square: Slum Clearance Plan under Title 1 of the Housing Act of 1949 as Amended* (May 28, 1956), 50; Milton Saslow to Philip J. Cruise, April 13, 1956; and Frederick E. Marx, Wood, Dolson, Inc., to Robert Moses, "Tenant Relocation Report," September 30, 1955, both in box 73B7, folder 08, NYCHA. On the three-block Lincoln Center site, the proportion of

Puerto Ricans was slightly higher: 75 percent white, 24.5 percent Puerto Rican, and 0.5 percent black. See memorandum, Willard Keefe to Mr. Rockefeller et al., April 20, 1956, in box 76, folder 655, JDR3. The figure for the median income was taken from City Planning Commission, *Tenant Relocation Report* (New York: City of New York, January 20, 1954), 62.

36. See Marx to Moses, "Tenant Relocation Report," 2; Committee on Slum Clearance, *Lincoln Square*, 38–49; Protestant Council of the City of New York, Department of Christian Social Relations, Statement on Lincoln Square, June 4, 1957, in box 73B7, folder 8, NYCHA; "Manhattan—New York Security Map and Area Description Folder," Records of the federal Home Loan Bank Board, Home Owners Loan Corporation, Records Relating to the City Survey file, 1935–1940, New York, RG195, box 59, NARA.

37. Otto Nelson, "Investments in Urban Renewal," speech before the 20th Annual Building Products Executives Conference, November 7, 1958, in box 117, Committee on Slum Clearance, 1958 folder, MosesNYPL; Frederick Gutheim, "Athens on the Subway," *Harper's* 217 (October 1958): 66–67; Russell Bourne, "Building's Two-Star General," *AF* (June 1958).

38. Harold C. Schonberg, "Progress Report on the New Arts Center," *NYTM*, May 28, 1958, 38. For other expectant accounts of the wonders that Lincoln Center would bring, see Kitty Hanson, "The New West Side Story: Slum Scarred Area Is Slowly Returning to Grandeur of Past," *NYDN*, March 2, 1959, 26; and Hanson, "The New West Side Story: Once-Bleak Area to Glow with Art," *NYDN*, March 3, 1959, 26.

39. Editors, "Lincoln Center Is Born," *NYHT*, May 14, 1959, 18; Harry Rogers, "The Dawn of a New Era," *West Side News*, May 14, 1959, 15.

40. See Robert Moses, "Lincoln Square," talk at a luncheon of the New York Building Congress, October 26, 1956, 1, in box 1, 1956, vol. 2 folder, MosesYale; "Moses Asks Lincoln Square Action Now, Urges 'Surgery' to Restore Area," *NYHT*, October 27, 1956; "Moses Pushes Lincoln Square," *NYDN*, October 27, 1956; Robert Moses, "Remarks on the Groundbreaking at Lincoln Square," in Kenneth T. Jackson and David S. Dunbar, eds., *Empire City: New York through the Centuries* (New York: Columbia University Press, 2002), 736–738.

41. "Displaced Tenants to Picket City Hall," *NYT*, June 15, 1956, 26; Charles G. Bennett, "New Park Fight Embroils Moses," *NYT*, June 16, 1956, 21; "Lincoln Square Residents Protest against Threatened Loss of Homes," *NYT*, June 16, 1956, 21; "Gerosa Cautions on Nuisance Tax," *NYT*, July 27, 1956, 23; Charles Grutzner, "Two Housing Projects Proposed to Ease Lincoln Square Relocation," *NYT*, August 31, 1956, 1; Richard C. Wald, "Lincoln Sq. Project Put Off a Month; 23 Assail It," *NYHT*, August 31, 1956; Richard Schuckman and Michael Walpin, Co-Chairmen, Lincoln Square Businessmen's Committee, to Editors, *NYT*, September 29, 1956.

42. Charles Grutzner, "Lincoln Sq. Plans Disturb Tenants," *NYT*, August 28, 1956, 29; "Mail Protests Assailed in Lincoln Square Dispute," *NYHT*, September 9, 1956; Charles Grutzner, "Foes Threaten a Political Fight against Lincoln Square Project," *NYT*, September 8, 1956, 19; Grutzner, "Lincoln Sq. Plans to Get U.S. Study," *NYT*, September 29, 1956, 21.

43. See Caro, *The Power Broker*, 1014–1016, 1006–1013 for details of newspaper coverage. Albert Cole was aware of the controversy at Lincoln Square in part because the

Lincoln Square groups had petitioned the Housing and Home Finance Agency. See "New Fight on Lincoln Sq. Project; Violation of Constitution Charged," *NYP*, November 14, 1956; "Opponents Bid U.S. Call It Off at Lincoln Square," *NYDN*, November 14, 1956; Charles Grutzner, "U.S. Asked to Kill Lincoln Sq. Project as Unconstitutional," *NYT*, November 14, 1956; "Lincoln Sq. Group Gets U.S. Promise," *NYT*, February 5, 1957.

44. See Present, interview, 2008; Charles Grutzner, "Lincoln Project Facing New Fight," *NYT*, February 23, 1957, 19; Harris L. Present to Editor, "Lincoln Square Project—The People's Burden," *NYDM*, June 9, 1957; Grutzner, "Lincoln Tenants Advised to Delay," *NYT*, March 2, 1957, 23; "Lincoln Square Rally Held," *NYT*, May 10, 1957, 38. For another instance in which Present discussed the "culture, mores, friendships, and associates of the residents involved," see "City Planners Get Pros, Cons on Seward Park," *NYP*, July 17, 1957. The legal campaign to have Lincoln Square declared a violation of the Constitution earned significant coverage over a period of two years in several newspapers, making the front page of the *Times* three times in that period. See *NYT*, February 22, 1957; December 25, 1957; and June 10, 1958.

45. "Lincoln Square Rally Tonight," *NYDN*, August 28, 1957; "Fordham Plan Fought," *NYT*, August 29, 1957, 27; "Fight to Block Square Project," *NYJA*, August 29, 1957; A. K. Holding and John McNulty to Edgar B. Young, "Report on Lincoln Square Rally," August 28, 1957, and attached flyer, in Urban Renewal 1957–1969 folder, RGA Organization, LCPA; Paul Crowell, "Foes of Lincoln Sq. to Picket City Hall," *NYT*, September 11, 1957, 26; Ted Poston, "Isaacs Urges City Delay OK of Lincoln Square," *NYP*, September 11, 1957; "Where Can He Go?" *NYP Daily Magazine*, September 11, 1957; "Relocation Asked before Lincoln Square OK," *NYDN*, September 11, 1957, 5; Thomas Furey, "Isaacs Asks Delay at Lincoln Square," *NYWTS*, September 11, 1957, 6; "Plans for Lincoln Center Revealed amid Picketing," *NYJA*, September 11, 1957, 12; Paul Crowell, "Lincoln Sq. Rivals Clash at Hearing before Planners," *NYT*, September 12, 1957, 1; David Wise, "Lincoln Sq. Project Debated at Planning Board Hearing," *NYHT*, September 12, 1957, 1; "Want Relocation First in Lincoln Square," *NYDN*, September 12, 1957; Harry Raymond, "Lincoln Square Residents Picket City Hall to Save Homes, Stores," *DW*, September 12, 1957.

46. CPC, "Public Hearing," 30, 38, 102–103, 174–175, in Avery. On Puerto Rican displacement and the perpetuation of racial segregation, see "Translation—Editorial in *El Diario de Nueva York*," December 7, 1955, in box 36, folder 373, RockCult; "League Hits Plans for Lincoln Square," *NYAN*, June 29, 1957; I. D. Robbins to Editor, "Housing Lincoln Square: Present Plans Said to Create Non-Integrated Neighborhood," *NYT*, September 15, 1957; Marcus Heyman to John D. Rockefeller III, October 28, 1957, and November 29, 1957, both in box 37, folder 379, RockCult; Murray Illson, "Puerto Ricans Told of Dispersal in City by Realty Pressure," *NYT*, March 20, 1960, 64. For the "Indian" pickets, see photos accompanying Gene Gleason, "Moses MCs Talk for Lincoln Center," *NYWTS*, October 25, 1957; and Paul Crowell, "Lincoln Square Vote Deferred by City," *NYT*, October 26, 1957. On the historical significance of "playing Indian" as a cultural and political strategy, see Philip J. Deloria, *Playing Indian* (New Haven, CT: Yale University Press, 1998).

47. Present quoted in CPC, "Public Hearing," 8.

48. Quotes from CPC, "Public Hearing," 148, 10–11, 91, 261, 178, 102, 99. See also Mrs. Philip B. Sheridan to Editor, *NYWTS*, October 4, 1957, in which she congratulated the paper for its "concern for human values versus culture."

49. Quotes from CPC, "Public Hearing," 225, 219, 254, 41–42, 226.

50. See Marx to Moses, "Tenant Relocation Report," 6–19, for a full list of the businesses on the site.

51. See Joseph Kahn, "Lincoln Sq. Launderette Man Fears He'll Be Washed Up," *NYP,* June 2, 1958; CPC, "Public Hearing," 261; William Longgood, "Don't Say Art to Lincoln Sq. Merchant," *NYWT,* July 7, 1958; Michael Walpin to John D. Rockefeller III, May 27, 1958; Edgar B. Young to Michael Walpin, June 3, 1958; Michael Walpin to John D. Rockefeller III, June 20, 1958; Michael Walpin to Otto Nelson, May 14, 1959; Leo Stein to John D. Rockefeller, May 15, 1958; Otto Nelson to Stein, May 20, 1958; Augusta Koenig to John D. Rockefeller III, April 19, 1960, all in box 43, folder 428, RockCult.

52. On the business resistance to Lincoln Square, see "Lincoln Sq. Trade Group Joins Residents Fighting Relocation," *NYT,* May 10, 1956, 33; Richard Schuckman and Michael Walpin to Robert Moses, May 31, 1956; Moses to Walpin, June 14, 1958, both in box 116, 1956 Library Correspondence, folder 1 of 3, MosesNYPL; "The Banished Shopkeeper," *NYT,* February 16, 1957, 15. See also CPC, "Public Hearing," 14, 31, 95–99, 141–147, 188, 261–262, particularly for the use of the term "good will."

53. On the City Planning Commission's judgments and housing unit calculations, see City of New York, City Planning Commission, "Report, Lincoln Square Urban Renewal Plan and Project," October 2, 1957, 8–9, 18–21; Thomas W. Ennis, "75,000 Families Here Must Move," *NYT,* October 27, 1957, 1, 12; "City Says Housing Is Adequate to '60," *NYT,* November 25, 1957, 33. These statistics were more misleading than revealing. Of the 93,500 new units, about 56,000 would be private, Title I, or middle-income units, all of which would be out of reach for the typical site tenant, while 36,000 units would be public housing. In addition, 9,000 or so already built apartments would be available in NYCHA turnover. Even if all of these 45,000 public units went to displaced site residents—which was highly unlikely given the long waiting lists and other restrictions involved in public housing—that still left almost 30,000 of the original 75,000 displaced families looking for homes in those remaining 56,000 housing units, the vast majority of which would be far too expensive for the vast majority of home seekers. No matter how the numbers were presented, nothing could change the fact that they did not take into account the inability of dislocated families to pay for most available new housing. On the results of the hearings, see Crowell, "Lincoln Square Vote Deferred by City," *NYT,* October 26, 1957, 23; Robert A. Poteete, "Lincoln Square Hearing on for Eighteen Hours," *NYHT,* October 27, 1957, 1, 25; "Sponsors Rushing Lincoln Square Plans," *NYT,* November 28, 1957.

54. See Present, oral history, 52–53.

55. On the move-out process, see Charles Grutzner, "First Lincoln Square Tenants Will Begin Moving Out Today," *NYT,* June 10, 1958, 56; Murray Illson, "Exodus Starting from Lincoln Square," *NYT,* June 11, 1958, 37; Illson, "9 at Lincoln Sq. Get Moving Bonus," *NYT,* June 12, 1958, 33; Grutzner, "Wreckers Start Lincoln Sq. Job," *NYT,* July 29, 1958, 25. For the various reports of successful relocation, see Lincoln Center for the

Performing Arts, press release, July 29, 1958, in box 73, folder 635, JDR3; Braislin, Porter and Wheelock, Inc., "The First 742 Families: A Mid-Program Analysis of the Relocation Program of Lincoln Center for the Performing Arts," November 1, 1958, in box 73B4, folder 6, NYCHA; Braislin, Porter and Wheelock, Inc., "Final Report," November 30, 1959, in box 43, folder 428, RockCult; "Relocation Completed Ahead of Schedule; 1647 Families Moved," *Performing Arts* 1, no. 13 (December 4, 1959): 1, 4; Editors, "The Lincoln Square Story: Better Homes—Lower Rents," *West Side News,* November 13, 1958; Edmond J. Barnett, "Tenants' Exodus Shown in Survey," *NYT,* March 6, 1960, 1, 5. See also Editors, "Improvement in Relocation," *NYWTS,* n.d., and "Man of the Week: General Relocation's Philip Schorr Sees Work as Sociological Effort," *Real Estate Weekly,* n.d., both clippings in Relocation and Management Associates brochure in box 70A7, folder 25, NYCHA. Also see Kitty Hanson, "The New West Side Story: Slums Go Fast, People Go Slower," *NYDN,* March 5, 1959, 40.

56. See "Moses Is Criticized on Lincoln Sq. Plans," *NYT,* July 18, 1958, 12; Charles Grutzner and Fern Marja, "Lincoln Sq.—A Dream for the Future but a Nightmare for Present Tenants," *NYP,* July 25, 1958; "Leaflets Advise Lincoln Sq. Tenants to Delay Eviction by Filing Protests," *NYT,* August 1, 1958, 42; Gene Gleason, "Families Shiver in Heatless Flats," *NYWTS,* December 1, 1958, 1, 3; Thomas Furey, "Lincoln Square Families to Get Heat at Last," *NYWTS,* December 2, 1958, 23; Charles Grutzner, "13 Families Defy City in Lincoln Sq.," *NYT,* April 20, 1961. In practice, on the Lincoln Center and Fordham sites, the management filed 25 motions to dispossess in court and evicted only 3 tenants. See Braislin, Porter and Wheelock, "Final Report," 25.

57. See "Relocation Attacked, Present Charges Only 10% in Lincoln Sq. Get Help," *NYT,* November 9, 1959, 26; Editors, "Monuments and People," *NYP,* July 8, 1958; NYCHA, Site Management Division, James W. Loughlin to Alexander J. Moffat, "Title I Program—Housing Participation," May 14, 1959, 2; December 16, 1959, 2; February 15, 1960, 1, all in box 73B8, folder 2, NYCHA; NYCHA, Albert Morgan to Ira Robbins, "Lincoln Square Relocation," November 9, 1959; Ira S. Robbins to Leonard X. Farbman, November 10, 1959, in box 73B7, folder 8, NYCHA; Braislin, Porter and Wheelock, "Final Report," 27–34; John O. Wicklein, "Project Depletes West Side Parish," *NYT,* January 3, 1960, 38. On grief for the loss of neighborhoods over actual houses, see Marc Fried's work on the development of a "spatial identity" in working-class neighborhoods: Marc Fried, "Grieving for a Lost Home," in Leonard J. Duhl, ed., *The Urban Condition* (New York: Basic, 1963), 151–171; Fried, *World of the Urban Working Class*; and Fried, "Grief and Adaptation: The Impact of Relocation in Boston's West End," in Fisher and Hughes, *The Last Tenement,* 80–93.

58. See James Loughlin to Philip J. Cruise, January 27, 1958, Meeting at Borough President's Office, January 24, 1958, at 5:30 P.M.; Lincoln Square Tenant Groups—Re: Watchdog Committee and Hulan Jack to William Reid, March 24, 1959, with attached press release, both in box 73B7, folder 8, NYCHA; Charles Grutzner, "Jack Undertakes Relocation Tasks," *NYT,* March 19, 1958, 33. See also Leonard Farbman, oral history, January 7, 1991, 48–50, LCPA.

59. Felt on Nelson quoted in Bourne, "Building's Two-Star General," *AF* (June 1958); Basil Fellrath to John D. Rockefeller, August 27, 1958, and Otto L. Nelson to Fellrath, September 8, 1958, both in box 43, folder 428, RockCult.

60. Max Page, *The Creative Destruction of Manhattan, 1900–1940* (Chicago: University of Chicago Press, 1998).

61. Charles D. Atkinson, "A Day at Lincoln Square," Braislin, Porter and Wheelock, Christmas Dinner, 1958, 1–6, in box 59, folder 757, EBYoung. Emphasis and punctuation is in the original script.

62. John A. Ward to Editor, "For Lincoln Square Delay," *NYT*, September 27, 1957; Diana Hansen Lesser to Editor, "Tenant Relocation," *NYHT*, November 26, 1956; Editors, "Quiet Uprooting," *NYP*, July 25, 1958, 5.

63. Michael Walpin to General Otto Nelson, May 14, 1959, in box 43, folder 428, RockCult.

64. Glenn Fowler, "Lincoln Center Sparks Vast Renewal on the West Side," *NYT*, September 16, 1962, 374; Carol Taylor, "Lincoln Center's Magic Act," *NYWTS*, October 22, 1964, 21; "Small City Rising in Lincoln Square," *NYT*, January 3, 1965, B1; Moses quoted in Caro, *The Power Broker*, 1013; Carlos Morales, oral history, April 24, 1991, 30, LCPA.

65. Bernard Weinraub, "A Neighborhood Grows at Lincoln Square," *NYT*, January 22, 1965, 15. See also Don Ross, "Upper West Side—Squalor, Culture Side by Side," *NYHT*, June 25, 1961, 1, 17.

66. On the 1968 revival, see Dan Sullivan, "Theater: Jets vs. Sharks," *NYT*, June 25, 1968, 32; and Clive Barnes, "A New Look at 'West Side Story,'" *NYT*, September 1, 1968, D20.

67. For the *West Side Story* stage directions, see Norris Houghton, ed., *Romeo and Juliet and West Side Story* (New York: Bantam Doubleday Dell, 1965), 201–202. On the "cultural fairyland," see Harold C. Schonberg, "Progress Report on the New Arts Center," *NYT*, May 25, 1958, 38. On "structures of feeling," see Raymond Williams, *Marxism and Literature* (New York: Oxford University Press, 1977) 128–135.

Chapter 6

1. Harrison Salisbury, *The Shook-Up Generation* (New York: Harper and Row, 1958), 73; Salisbury, *A Time of Change* (New York: Harper and Row, 1988), 8–29; Salisbury, "Our Changing City: The Manhattan Midtown Area, New Buildings Climb Skyward in Districts Already Congested," *NYT*, June 27, 1955, 23; Meyer Berger, "Our Changing City: Social and Economic Shifts Reshape New York's Face," *NYT*, June 20, 1955, 1, 23. See also Murray Schumach, "The East River Shore Regains Its Glory," *NYTM*, January 19, 1947, 8–9, 38; "East River Slum Areas Clearing Fast," *NYHT*, January 25, 1948, 1; Joseph C. Ingraham, "Our Changing City: Old Lower Manhattan Area, New East Side Housing Provides Most of Difference in the Last 25 Years," *NYT*, June 24, 1955, 23; Peter Kihss, "Our Changing City: Upper and Middle East Side, U.N. Buildings and Big Apartments Remake Face of Four-Square-Mile District," *NYT*, July 1, 1955, 23; Laymhond Robinson Jr., "Our Changing City: Harlem Now on the Upswing," *NYT*, July 8, 1955, 25.

2. Salisbury, *A Time of Change*, 37; and Salisbury, *Shook-Up Generation*, 73–74.

3. On the early history of public housing, see Anthony Jackson, *A Place Called Home: A History of Low Cost Housing in Manhattan* (Cambridge, MA: MIT Press, 1976), 225–231; J. S. Fuerst, *When Public Housing Was Paradise: Building Community in Chicago* (Westport, CT: Praeger, 2003). See also the recollections of "Jose," whose family moved

to East Harlem's Jefferson Houses in 1957 and who remembered what Russell Sharman calls "a welcome sense of order." See Sharman, *The Tenants of East Harlem* (Berkeley: University of California Press, 2005), 56. See also "'It Takes a Village to Raise a Child': Growing Up in the Patterson Houses in the 1950s and Early 1960s," an interview with Victoria Archibald-Good by Mark Naison, *Bronx County Historical Society Journal* 40, no. 1 (Spring 2003): 4–22; and Sudhir Alladi Venkatesh, *American Project: The Rise and Fall of a Modern Ghetto* (Cambridge, MA: Harvard University Press, 2000).

4. James Weldon Johnson Community Center, "A Statement on Public Housing in East Harlem," March 8, 1961, box 1, folder 19, JWJCC.

5. East Harlem's main competitors for the title were the Lower East Side of Manhattan, the South Bronx, and Brownsville and East New York in Brooklyn. For a brief account of the events detailed here, see Nathan Glazer, "What Happened in East Harlem," in his *From a Cause to a Style: Modernist Architecture's Encounter with the American City* (Princeton, NJ: Princeton University Press, 2007), 165–191.

6. This account is adapted from Peter Marcuse's seven-part periodization of public housing history in Marcuse, "Interpreting 'Public Housing' History," *Journal of Architectural and Planning Research* 12, no. 3 (Autumn 1995): 240–258. Marcuse argues that there were seven "separate programs." I am addressing here the fourth of his programs, "The Redevelopment Program," and suggesting that it was a refinement for new conditions of the first of his programs, "The Reformers Program." The two periods in between— "The War Program" of temporary housing for war workers and "The Middle Class and Veterans Program" of state- and city-funded housing for veterans and higher-income workers are less germane to the history of East Harlem. For a full history of NYCHA, see Nicholas Dagen Bloom, *Public Housing That Worked* (Philadelphia: Penn Press, 2008).

7. See Gail Radford, *Modern Housing for America: Policy Struggles in the New Deal Era* (Chicago: University of Chicago Press, 1996), 191; Daniel Rodgers, *Atlantic Crossings: Social Politics in a Progressive Age* (Cambridge, MA: Harvard University Press, 1998), 477–478; Richard Plunz, *A History of Housing in New York City* (New York: Columbia University Press, 1990), 233–279; John F. Bauman, *Public Housing, Race, and Renewal: Urban Planning in Philadelphia, 1920–1974* (Philadelphia: Temple University Press, 1987). For an argument similar to mine, see Lawrence M. Friedman, *Government and Slum Housing: A Century of Frustration* (Chicago: Rand McNally, 1968), 116.

8. Project information compiled from Thomas W. Ennis, "Harlem Changed by Public Housing," *NYT*, June 23, 1957, 1, 25; JWJCC, "Background Data—Housing, Part III. East Harlem Public Housing Developments," 1960, 8, in box 1, folder 21, JWJCC Papers; NYCHA, news release, March 1, 1961, in 59C8, folder 6, NYCHA; JWJCC, "A Statement on Public Housing in East Harlem," March 8, 1961, in box 1, folder 19, JWJCC; Thomas W. Ennis, "City Lifting Face of East Harlem," *NYT*, March 5, 1961, 1, 8; East Harlem Public Housing Association, "Fact Sheet: Public Housing, East Harlem," May 17, 1963, in box 1, folder 16, JWJCC; NYCHA, "Status of Projects as of December 31, 1966," in box 60D3, folder 1, NYCHA.

9. Wagner quoted in Ennis, "City Lifting Face of East Harlem," 1.

10. Percival Goodman to Vito Marcantonio, February 17, 1947, in box 2, General Correspondence "G," and Goodman to Marcantonio, October 7, 1946, in box 50, Marc.

11. Mayor's Committee on City Planning, "East Harlem Community Study," New York, Mayor's Office, City of New York, 1937, 16. The first Italians made the journey as early as the 1870s, drawn to jobs on the expanding trolley lines or in the building trades putting up Harlem luxury apartments that would later be subdivided for incoming African Americans. By the 1920s, the northeasternmost corner of Manhattan Island, particularly along First Avenue, had become Italian Harlem, a community of about 70,000 souls. A number of Russian Jews remained—many of them merchants in the outdoor market that flourished under the trestle of the New York and New Haven Railroad over Park Avenue—but they were dwindling in number by the war. There were some remaining Irish and Germans about, too. See Robert Orsi, "The Religious Boundaries of an In-Between People: Street Feste and the Problem of the Dark-Skinned Other in Italian Harlem, 1920–2000," in Orsi, ed., *Gods of the City: Religion and the American Urban Landscape* (Bloomington: Indiana University Press, 1999), 262–263.

12. Virginia Sanchez-Korrol, *From Colonia to Community: The History of Puerto Ricans in New York City, 1917–1948* 2nd ed. (Berkeley: University of California Press, 1994), 27–28 and 55–62; Gerald Meyer, *Vito Marcantonio, Radical Politician, 1902–1954* (Albany: State University of New York Press, 1989), 144.

13. See "Housing Project in 1st Ave. Started," *NYT*, March 3, 1940, 1. For Marcantonio's record on housing, see Annette T. Rubinstein, ed., *I Vote My Conscience: Debates, Speeches and Writings of Vito Marcantonio, 1935–1950* (New York: Vito Marcantonio Memorial, 1956), 271, 302–303, 307. See also Alan Schaffer, *Vito Marcantonio, Radical in Congress* (Syracuse, NY: Syracuse University Press, 1966); and John T. Metzger, "Rebuilding Harlem: Public Housing and Urban Renewal, 1920–1960," *Planning Perspectives* 9 (1994): 260–264.

14. See *People's Congressman,* produced by American Labor Party and Union Films Productions, director unknown, c. 1948, Museum of Modern Art Film Archives, New York. Accordingly, the congressman was uneasy with privately backed urban redevelopment, believing that slum clearance without adequate provisions for low-income housing was just a way to bail out property owners with high land costs and to subsidize private developers. See "Memorandum on Title I of H.R. 933," n.d., in box 53, Marc.

15. See "Women Spur Plan for East Harlem," *NYT*, April 22, 1942, 27; Victor C. Gaspar to General Thomas F. Farrell, March 1, 1950, in 70D2, folder 3, NYCHA; "Realty Man Finds 15 East Harlem Blocks Ripe for Realty and Housing Development," *NYT*, November 14, 1948, R1; Liberal Party, "We Can Get Rid of the Slums of New York in Our Time!" advertisement in *NYT*, September 12, 1945, 20; Gerald Blank, "Fresh Meadows—and Harlem," *PM*, September 3, 1947; Allan Keller, "Huge City-in-a-City Not Big Enough," *NYWT*, June 7, 1948.

16. Elmo Roper, "What People Are Thinking: How Veterans View Housing Problem," *NYHT*, March 21, 1946.

17. Lee E. Cooper, "Demand for Store Sites Begins to Appear in Blocks Adjoining the East River Houses," *NYT*, March 23, 1940; Ludwig Baumann, "Come to the New 'LB' Housing Center," advertisement in *NYJA*, October 1947. On the links between public and private projects, see Lee E. Cooper, "Large-Scale Housing Leads Building

Activity in City," *NYT*, August 31, 1947, R1; Cooper, "A Great City Plans Its Housing," *Housing Progress*, Spring 1945, 6–10, 30, 31; "Tastes Are Studied in Housing Project," *NYT*, January 25, 1950, 38; "Tenants Rejoice in Carver Houses," *NYT*, January 26, 1955, 28; Allan Keller, "Housing Projects Break Hearts: Thousands Suffer Bitter Disappointment for Few Who Obtain Apartments," *NYWT*, June 10, 1948. See also "It's Heaven, It's Paradise," *Fortune* (April 1940): 86–89, 114, 116, for an account of residents' satisfaction with their new apartments in Brooklyn's Red Hook Houses.

18. Meyer, *Vito Marcantonio*, 145; and Mayor's Committee on City Planning, "East Harlem Community Study," 16–19.

19. See "Explanation of Security Area Map" and "Area Descriptions," in Manhattan—New York Security Map and Area Description folder, Records of the Federal Home Loan Bank Board, Home Owners Loan Corporation, Records Relating to the City Survey file, 1935–40, New York, RG195, box 59, NARA. See also East Harlem Project, "The East Harlem Project," November 25, 1960, in box 17, folder 2, UnSett.

20. SCC maps reprinted and NYCHA report referenced in Edith Elmer Wood, *Slums and Blighted Areas in the United States* (Washington, DC: U.S. Government Printing Office, 1935), 30–32, 33–34; Mayor's Committee on City Planning, "East Harlem Community Study," 22, 59.

21. Joel Schwartz, *The New York Approach* (Columbus: Ohio State University Press, 1993), 75–77; Plunz, *History of Housing*, 245–246; New York City, City Planning Commission, Adoption as Part of the Master Plan, of a City-wide Map Showing Sections Containing Areas for Clearance, Replanning and Low Rent Housing, January 3, 1940. For visions of East Harlem as redeveloped by private monies, see Schwartz, *The New York Approach*, 102–103; and Manhattan Development Committee, *A Realistic Approach to Private Investment in Urban Redevelopment Applied to East Harlem as a Blighted Area* (New York: Architectural Forum and Time Inc., 1945).

22. *Time* magazine piece quoted in Meyer, *Vito Marcantonio*, 112. Truman and Stevenson quoted in Nicholas Dagen Bloom, *Merchant of Illusion: James Rouse, America's Salesman of the Businessman's Utopia* (Columbus: Ohio State University Press, 2004), xi.

23. NYCHA, 15th Annual Report, 1947, 14–15, in box 98D1, folder 7, NYCHA. Postwar project statistics were calculated from NYCHA, "Status of Projects as of Dec. 31, 1966," in box 60D3, folder 1, NYCHA; Citizens Housing Council of New York, "The New York City Housing Authority," *CHC Housing News* 6, no. 2 (October–November 1947). See also NYCHA, 10th Annual Report, 1944, in box 98D1, folder 5, NYCHA; and Barbara Klaw, "Out of the Slums, into Clean Homes," *NYP*, October 24, 1945.

24. See Warren Jay Vinton, "Public Housing and the Rebuilding of Our Cities," *CHPC Housing News* 8, no. 4 (December 1949): 1, 4; U.S. Housing and Home Finance Agency, *The Relationship between Slum Clearance and Urban Redevelopment and Low-Rent Public Housing* (Washington, DC: U.S. Government Printing Office, November 1950), 11–12; Ashley A. Foard and Hilbert Fefferman, "Federal Urban Renewal Legislation," in James Q. Wilson, ed., *Urban Renewal* (Cambridge, MA: MIT Press, 1966), 71–125. A complete account of the tangled history of housing legislation in the immediate postwar years can be found in Richard O. Davies, *Housing Reform during the Truman Administration* (Columbia: University of Missouri Press, 1966).

25. Leonard Freedman, *Public Housing* (New York: Holt, Rinehart and Winston, 1969), 100–103; Editors, "The Industry Capitalism Forgot," *Fortune* 36 (August 1947): 61–67, 167–170; "Let's Have Ourselves a Housing Industry," *Fortune* (September 1947): 12.

26. Of course, those rows upon rows of boxes seemed an uncomfortably mass solution to the problem and attracted highbrow derision. Still, they were individual homes with yards, bought on time with favorable credit terms. For a contemporary attack on the culture of suburban housing developments, see John Keats, "The Crack in the Picture Window," *Esquire*, January 1957, 70, 72.

27. See Freedman, *Public Housing*, 101–103; Truman quoted in Davies, *Housing Reform*, 31–32.

28. Or, as Warren Vinton put it, "The Act clearly recognizes the distinction between the program of urban redevelopment and the program of low-rent housing. It recognizes also their intimate interrelationship." See Vinton, "Public Housing and the Rebuilding of Our Cities," 1. See also John F. Bauman, Roger Biles, and Kristin M. Szylvain, eds., *From Tenements to the Taylor Homes* (University Park: Penn State University Press, 2000), 140.

29. See testimony of Morton Bodfish in *Housing Act of 1949, Hearings before the Committee on Banking and Currency, House of Representatives, Eighty-first Congress, First Session on H.R. 4009, April 7, etc., 1949* (Washington, DC: U.S. Government Printing Office, 1949), 423. *Headlines* and Nelson quoted in Davies, *Housing Reform*, 18–20. Gwinn quoted in Bloom, *Merchant of Illusion*, 13. Wolcott quoted in NYCHA, Transcript of Congressional Housing Debate for June 18, 1948, 9, in box 71C7, folder 2, NYCHA. Holden quoted in *Housing Act of 1949, Hearings before the Committee on Banking and Currency*, 454.

30. Fitch quoted in *NYT*, March 28, 1947. McCarthy quoted in Bess Furman, "McCarthy Pledges Housing Aid Speed," *NYT*, September 3, 1947. For the activities of the McCarthy housing committee, convened for five months in 1947 and 1948, see Rosalyn Baxandall and Elizabeth Ewen, *Picture Windows* (New York: Basic, 2000), 87–105.

31. Lobbyists quoted in Davies, *Housing Reform*, 18. Smith quoted in Freedman, *Public Housing*, 165.

32. Lockwood quoted in *Housing Act of 1949, Hearings before the Committee on Banking and Currency*, 296, 313, 314.

33. Gerholz quoted in *Housing Act of 1949, Hearings before the Committee on Banking and Currency*, 589. Smith quoted in Freedman, *Public Housing*, 161. On NSC 68, see Ernest R. May, ed., *American Cold War Strategy: Interpreting NSC 68* (New York: St. Martin's, 1993).

34. For details on local campaigns against public housing, see Freedman, *Public Housing*, 43–44 and 67. NAREB quoted in "U.S. Housing Called 'Step to Communism,'" *NYT*, May 10, 1952; National Association of Home Builders quoted in Freedman, *Public Housing*, 169. See also A. Scott Henderson, "'Tarred with the Exceptional Image': Public Housing and Popular Discourse, 1950–1990," *American Studies* 36, no. 1 (Spring 1995): 33–34.

35. See Freedman, *Public Housing*, 140–157; Dominic J. Capeci Jr., *Race Relations in Wartime Detroit: The Sojourner Truth Housing Controversy of 1942* (Philadelphia: Temple University Press, 1984); Thomas J. Sugrue, "Crabgrass-Roots Politics: Race,

Rights, and the Reaction against Liberalism in the Urban North, 1940–1964," *Journal of American History* 82 (September 1995): 551–578; Sugrue, *The Origins of the Urban Crisis* (Princeton, NJ: Princeton University Press, 1996), 55–88; Arnold R. Hirsch, "Massive Resistance in the Urban North: Trumbull Park, Chicago, 1953–1966," *Journal of American History* 82 (September 1995): 522–550; Hirsch, *Making the Second Ghetto,* 2nd ed. (Chicago: University of Chicago Press, 1998), 40–99; Stephen Grant Meyer, *As Long as They Don't Move Next Door* (Lanham, MD: Rowman and Littlefield, 2000). The most complete account of the effect of the Cold War on public housing outside New York comes from Don Parson, *Making a Better World: Public Housing, the Red Scare, and the Direction of Modern Los Angeles* (Minneapolis: University of Minnesota Press, 2005).

36. On New York's social democratic support for housing, see Joshua B. Freeman, *Working-Class New York* (New York: New Press, 2000), 105–124. Isolated incidents did occur. Protestors demonstrating at the construction site for the Elliott Houses in Chelsea in the late '40s accused the authority of Communistic intentions and protested the arrival of blacks in the neighborhood. See Salisbury, *Shook-Up Generation,* 71–72. There were also a few homeowners groups in Queens that protested public housing. Their efforts made little headway in the '40s and '50s. Later, however, in the '60s and early '70s, when NYCHA wanted to build "scatter-site" projects in low-density, homeowning Queens, these protests had much more impact, contributing to increased resistance to the spread of public housing across the city. The classic account of these struggles is Mario M. Cuomo, *Forest Hills Diary* (New York: Vintage, 1974). See also Robert A. M. Stern, Thomas Mellins, and David Fishman, *New York 1960* (New York: Monacelli, 1995), 997–1001; and Vincent J. Cannato, *The Ungovernable City* (New York: Basic, 2001), 504–515.

37. "An American Born" to Frank A. Farrell [*sic*], April 11, 1951, in 70D2, folder 3, NYCHA. The head of NYCHA was named Thomas Farrell, and by 1951 he was no longer chair of the board, having been replaced in 1950 by Philip J. Cruise. These sorts of charges were repeated at various times during the '40s and '50s. See William Henderson, "Thousands of Pro-Reds Live in Housing Projects," *NYDM,* August 2, 1951; Henderson, "Would Bar Reds in Public Housing," *NYDM,* August 3, 1951; Michael T. Abbene, American Legion to Mayor Vincent Impellitteri, August 11, 1951, and John Q. Citizen to Governor, December 21, 1952, both in box 70D2, folder 2, NYCHA. The charges came to a head in early 1957 when the *Daily News* ran a 15-part series charging that a "clique" of Communists had infiltrated NYCHA and were turning the projects into slums. See 15 articles and associated editorials by various authors, "Reds Peril N.Y. City Housing," *NYDN,* February 18–March 8, 1957.

38. City-Wide Tenants Council, "Civil Liberties in Housing Projects," August 6, 1940, in box 54D5, folder 9, NYCHA.

39. Philip J. Klutznick, "Post-War Public Housing," November 18, 1944, in box 73C5, folder 5, NYCHA.

40. Leon H. Keyserling, "Homes for All—and How," *Survey Graphic,* February 1946, 37–41, 63.

41. Stichman quoted in Robert Dwyer, "Stichman Assails Foes for 'Attack' on Housing," *NYDN,* October 15, 1947; and "Stichman Says Housing-Bond Foes Aid Reds," *NYHT,* October 22, 1947; Phelps Phelps to Editor, "Need for Housing Bill," *NYT,* June 23, 1948.

42. Lucas and Madden quoted in Bloom, *Merchant of Illusion,* 14.

43. See Davies, *Housing Reform,* 135; Marc Weiss, "The Origins and Legacy of Urban Renewal," in J. Paul Mitchell, ed., *Federal Housing Policy and Programs, Past and Present* (New Brunswick, NJ: Rutgers University Press, 1985), 265–266; National Housing Conference, "The Truth about Public Housing," April 1, 1950, 1, 8, in box 71C7, folder 1, NYCHA. Supporters are quoted in Bloom, *Merchant of Illusion,* 76–77.

44. Gerald J. Carey, "Priorities for Construction and Maintenance," May 11, 1951, in box 59D2, folder 05, NYCHA; and "Speech by Gerald J. Carey," September 16, 1952, in box 59D2, folder 04, NYCHA.

45. Sparkman quoted in "House GOP Chiefs Plan to Fight Bill for Public Housing," *NYT,* May 18, 1949.

46. Davies, *Housing Reform,* 110–113, 137, 141; Kenneth T. Jackson, *Crabgrass Frontier* (New York: Oxford University Press, 1985), 224; Roger Biles, "Public Housing and the Postwar Urban Renaissance, 1949–1973," in Bauman et al., *From Tenements to the Taylor Homes,* 143–162. See also Bloom, *Merchant of Illusion,* 74–78; Catherine Bauer, "The Dreary Deadlock of Public Housing," *AF* 106 (May 1957): 140–142, 219, 221.

47. On the features of NYCHA apartments and the "blueprint for living," see NYCHA, "How to Make a House Your Home: Tenant's Handbook," n.d., in box 59A7, folder 1, NYCHA. On community facilities, see NYCHA, "Community Facilities and Activities in New York City Public Housing Projects," January 1946, in box 86E5, folder 2, NYCHA; Freedman, *Public Housing,* 56; Samuel Ratensky, speech before New York State Association of Architects, Rochester, NY, October 21, 1949, in box 59D2, folder 7, NYCHA. See also Bloom, *Public Housing That Worked,* 109–198.

48. NYCHA, 19th Annual Report, 1952, 21, in 98D1, folder 13, NYCHA; and NYCHA, 20th Annual Report, 1954, 1, in 98D1, folder 15, NYCHA.

49. See Robert A. Caro, *The Power Broker* (New York: Knopf, 1974), 706–707, 724–727, 768–769, 775, 796–797, 803–805; Schwartz, *The New York Approach,* 122–123; and Metzger, "Rebuilding Harlem," 270–273.

50. Robert Moses, *Public Works* (New York: McGraw-Hill, 1970), 440; *NYT,* August 20, 1953, 16; and Metzger, "Rebuilding Harlem," 273.

51. See Schwartz, *The New York Approach,* 171–172. Overall, Moses supported a limited economic niche for public housing. See Moses to William Lebwohl, June 19, 1943, in roll 17, folder 011, ParksMoses.

52. See Schwartz, *The New York Approach,* 119–124 and 115–117.

53. NYCHA, "Status of Projects as of December 31, 1966"; "80,000 Apartments in City Projected," *NYT,* November 20, 1949, 16; NYCHA, "Housing Supply and Construction in New York City—1965," March 1966, 1–2; and NYCHA, "The Crisis Facing the Housing Program of New York City," September 14, 1962, 3, both in 60D3, folder 1, NYCHA; NYCHA Statistics Division, "Selected Data on Changes in Population and in Housing Conditions in New York City, 1950–1960," January 8, 1963, n.p., in 71E4, folder 9, NYCHA; Thomas W. Ennis, "City Lifting Face of East Harlem," *NYT,* March 5, 1961, 1.

54. See "Slum Surgery in St. Louis," *AF* 94 (April 1951): 128–136; and NYCHA, 18th Annual Report, 1951, 24, in 98D1, folder 13, NYCHA.

55. NYCHA, 18th Annual Report, 1951, 24; NYCHA, 22nd Annual Report, 1955, 26–30, in 98D1, folder 18, NYCHA; Eric Mumford, "The 'Tower in the Park' in America: Theory

and Practice, 1920–1960," *Planning Perspectives* 10 (January 1995): 31–38; Plunz, *History of Housing*, 264–266; "Public Housing, Anticipating New Law, Looks at New York's High Density Planning Innovations," *AF* 90 (June 1949): 87–89; American Institute of Architects, "The Significance of the Work of the New York City Housing Authority," New York, AIA, 1949, 99.

56. Project information was compiled from NYCHA project files, in boxes 65D7, folders 6, 7, 13; 65E5, folders 12 and 14; 65E4, folder 4; 72A6, folder 5; and NYCHA News Release on Madison Houses, March 1, 1961, 1, in box 59C8, folder 6, NYCHA.

57. See Mayor's Committee on City Planning, "East Harlem Community Study," 16; Edwin L. Scanlan, "Public Housing Trends in New York City," M.A. thesis, Rutgers University, 1952, 62–65, and appendix.

58. Ruiz quoted in Thomas C. Wheeler, "New York Tries a New Approach," *Reporter,* June 17, 1965, 18–20.

59. "Project May Rise in Misery Street," *NYT,* October 4, 1954.

60. Salisbury, "Shook Youngsters Spring from Housing Jungles," *NYT,* March 26, 1958, 1; Salisbury, *Shook-Up Generation,* 73–74; Salisbury, *A Time of Change,* 36–37.

61. For the concept of culture as a "way of seeing," see Raymond Williams, *Culture and Society, 1780–1950* (1958; rpt., New York: Columbia University Press, 1983), 300.

62. Leslie Fiedler, "Afterthoughts on the Rosenbergs," in his *An End to Innocence* (Boston: Beacon, 1955), 26; Andrew Ross, *No Respect: Intellectuals and Popular Culture* (New York: Routledge, 1989), 15.

63. Lewis Mumford, "Versailles for the Millions," in Robert Wojtowicz, ed., *Sidewalk Critic: Lewis Mumford's Writings on New York* (New York: Princeton Architectural Press, 1998), 259; Farrell quoted in Allan Keller, "Over the Rainbow—Housing Utopia: City May Never Catch Up with Its Dreams, Says Gen. Thomas F. Farrell," *NYWT,* June 9, 1948; Patricia Cayo-Sexton, *Spanish Harlem* (New York: Harper and Row, 1965), 195.

Chapter 7

1. Dan Wakefield, *Island in the City: Puerto Ricans in New York* (New York: Corinth, 1959), 240–241.

2. See Joel Schwartz, *The New York Approach* (Columbus: Ohio State University Press, 1993), 262. For objections to the locations of new projects in Harlem, see John T. Metzger, "Rebuilding Harlem: Public Housing and Urban Renewal, 1920–1960," *Planning Perspectives* 9 (1994): 276–277.

3. Ellen Lurie, "A Study of George Washington Houses," conducted by Union Settlement Association, 1955–1956, section V, 2, in box 11, folder 13, UnSett; Ellen Lurie, "Community Action in East Harlem," March 1962, in box 35, folder 8, UnSett, later published as Ellen Lurie, "Community Action in East Harlem," in Leonard J. Duhl, ed., *The Urban Condition* (New York: Basic, 1963), 246–258; Herman Badillo, "Housing Statement," presented to Mayor Wagner at East Harlem Town Meeting, June 6, 1960, 2, in box 17, folder 2, UnSett.

4. The JWJCC had even secured initial funding and space in the Johnson Houses from NYCHA. JWJCC, "The Johnson Center Story," December 12, 1950, box 1, folder 30, JWJCC. James Weldon Johnson Community Center, *JWJ Newsletter* 1, no. 2 (March 1962): 2, in box 1, folder 37, JWJCC.

5. Lurie, "Community Action in East Harlem," 5; Preston Wilcox, "Policy Statement on Low-Income Housing," Housing Committee, East Harlem Council for Community Planning, June 26, 1963, 3, in box 27, folder 2, UnSett.

6. See JWJCC, "Reclaiming a Wasteland," 1960, in box 11, folder 14, JWJCC; and "The East Harlem Project," n.d., 1, in box 17, folder 3, UnSett. Wagner quoted in Thomas W. Ennis, "City Lifting Face of East Harlem," *NYT,* March 5, 1961, 1; William Kirk to Editors, "Renewing City Areas," *NYT,* March 7, 1961, 34. For another account of a New York neighborhood where activists demanded public housing and then struggled to cope with the effects of a massive NYCHA building campaign, see Wendell Pritchett, "Race and Community in Postwar Brooklyn: The Brownsville Neighborhood Council and the Politics of Urban Renewal," *Journal of Urban History* 27, no. 4 (May 2001): 445–470; and Pritchett, *Brownsville, Brooklyn: Blacks, Jews, and the Changing Face of the Ghetto* (Chicago: University of Chicago Press, 2002), 105–174.

7. On the complexity of political and social power in East Harlem during the '50s and '60s, as well as the social workers' heyday and influence, see Patricia Cayo-Sexton, *Spanish Harlem* (New York: Harper and Row, 1965), 92–119; JWJCC, "Reclaiming a Wasteland"; "The East Harlem Project," n.d., 1. On the nationwide encounter of settlement houses, public housing, and urban renewal, see Judith Ann Trolander, *Professionalism and Social Change* (New York: Columbia University Press, 1987), 75–91.

8. See East Harlem Project, 1961–62 Program Year, 1, in box 17, folder 2, UnSett.

9. A. Scott Henderson suggests that 1965 was the turning point in public appreciation for public housing. After that, public housing as an idea came to be synonymous with "Negro-occupied high rises" despite the diversity of scale and occupancy in public projects across the country. See A. Scott Henderson, "'Tarred with the Exceptional Image': Public Housing and Popular Discourse, 1950–1990," *American Studies* 36, no. 1 (Spring 1995): 31–52. However, doubts were widespread among those who had pioneered public housing as early as 1956 and 1957. And the splashiest public attack on New York public housing came in 1957, when the *NYDN,* between February 18 and March 8, delivered a 15-part series of articles and editorials on the failings and dangers of public housing. See "Reds Peril N.Y. City Housing," *NYDN,* February 18–March 8, 1957. George Washington Houses was the focus of the 10th article in the series. See Joseph Martin, Dominick Peluso, and Sydney Mirkin, "Project Half-Built—and Shot," *NYDN,* February 28, 1957, 3, 34. Ellen Lurie's experience in East Harlem shows that some ordinary New Yorkers began to have doubts before the housing experts or the scaremongers of the *NYDN.* Lurie claimed that "projects had a bad reputation, status-wise, long before George Washington Houses opened." See Lurie, Washington Houses Study, 1956, III:19, UnSett.

10. Lurie, Washington Houses Study, 1956, I:1–3.

11. Lurie, Washington Houses Study, 1956, I:5–9. Lurie and her assistants interviewed 216 families out of the 637 living in section I(iii). They used data from Census Tract 164, a 10-block area, half of which was included in the area of Washington Houses. The average net income of the projects increased to $4,305 by 1964. See JWJCC, "East Harlem Census Tracts," table I and table X, September 1964, in box 1, folder 19, JWJCC; "Proposed Low Rent Housing Development for Lexington and 105th Street Area, East Harlem, Board of Estimate Hearings, July 26, 1956, Mrs. Rose Carrafiello Speaking, 'Outline of Remarks,'" in box 35, folder 7, UnSett.

12. Despite the fact that NYCHA could claim to be building more apartments than it was destroying citywide, by 1961 three East Harlem projects—East River, Lexington, and Wilson Houses—represented a gain of 1,934 dwelling units, while five others—Carver, Jefferson, Johnson, Wagner, and Washington Houses—resulted in a loss of 3,977 apartments, for a net loss of 2,043 apartments. Calculated from NYCHA, news release, "Slum Dwelling Units Demolished and Public Housing Units Created," June 30, 1961, in box 59D1, folder 1, NYCHA.

13. See "Shops a Problem in East Harlem," *NYT*, May 8, 1955, 46; NYCHA, press release, June 26, 1955, in box 59D2, folder 1, NYCHA; Maurice Foley, "Realtors to Map Store Phase of the City's Housing Program," *NYT*, June 26, 1955, R1; East Harlem Small Business Survey and Planning Committee, "Fact Sheet," January 16, 1956, 1–3, in box 35, folder 7, UnSett; "Tenants Charge Neglect by City," January 17, 1956, 35; Lurie, Washington Houses Study, 1956, I:4, IV:2; JWJCC, "Social Characteristics of East Harlem," January 1, 1957, 1–2, in box 1, folder 19, JWJCC; "Most of Neighborhood Business Men Uprooted by East Harlem Project Complain of Treatment by City," *NYT*, March 18, 1957, 29; "Displaced Business Men," *NYT*, March 25, 1957, 24; JWJCC, "A Statement on Public Housing in East Harlem," March 8, 1961, in box 1, folder 19, JWJCC; Preston Wilcox, "Proposal for Massive Economic Neighborhood Development," 1964, 3, in box 3, folder 10, UnSett. Unfortunately, only 4 out of the 47 spaces in the Franklin project were businesses relocated from the site, and "not more than a dozen," a local businessman reported, had been able to find places "around the edge of the project." See Charles Grutzner, "City's Constant Building Leaves Small Shopkeepers by Wayside," *NYT*, March 23, 1964, 31, 51. The number of projects that had stores stayed relatively small citywide. In 1957, 9 out of 82 projects had stores. By 1964, only 12 out of 120 did. See Charles Grutzner, "Shopping Scarce in City Projects," *NYT*, June 16, 1957; and Grutzner, "City's Constant Building," 51.

14. Valle quoted in Union Settlement, "Listen [to] What People Say," 1973, 3, in box 3, folder 6, UnSett.

15. Jacobs delivered these remarks in a speech at a Harvard University conference on urban design in April 1956. They reflect conversations with William Kirk and Ellen Lurie about their findings in East Harlem, particularly those from the ongoing study of Washington Houses, details of which appear in Jacobs's text. The speech was later published as "The Missing Link in City Redevelopment," *AF* (June 1956): 132–133. See also Jane Jacobs, *The Death and Life of Great American Cities* (New York: Random House, 1961; New York: Modern Library, 1993). My final sampling of lost institutions is adapted from the memories of Ed Vega (also known as the novelist Edgardo Vega Yunque), "The Mythic Village of El Barrio," in his *Spanish Harlem* (Washington, DC: National Museum of American Art, 1994), 14.

16. The best account of this neighborhood on the verge of transformation is Robert Anthony Orsi, *The Madonna of 115th Street* (New Haven, CT: Yale University Press, 1985), esp. 45–49. See also Orsi, "The Religious Boundaries of an In-Between People: Street Feste and the Problem of the Dark-Skinned Other in Italian Harlem, 1920–2000," in Orsi, ed., *Gods of the City* (Bloomington: Indiana University Press, 1999), 262–263; and Virginia Sanchez-Korrol, *From Colonia to Community*, 2nd ed. (Berkeley: University of California Press, 1994), 27–28 and 55–62.

17. Lurie, Washington Houses Study, 1956, I:4, III:22. Accurate figures were hard to come by, the social workers admitted, because before 1960 the census did not have a separate category for Puerto Ricans, instead asking them to count themselves as either "white" or "nonwhite." The figures they used from NYCHA were more accurate. The difference of 10 percent in accounting for the number of whites on the original site reflects a discrepancy in two sources. A NYCHA survey offers 33.9 percent while a City Planning Commission report—compiled from statistics from NYCHA and the Department of City Planning—says that 43 percent of the tenants were "other" than "Puerto Rican and nonwhite," few of whom would have been anything other than "white ethnics" of one sort or another, predominantly Italians. See NYCHA, "Projects Completed in the East Harlem Area," December 15, 1959, box 73C3, folder 13, NYCHA; and New York City Planning Commission, *Tenant Relocation Report* (New York: City of New York, 1954), 44.

18. On the efforts of NYCHA to keep Jefferson Houses integrated, see Charles Grutzner, "City Housing Unit Bars Race Quotas," *NYT,* July 5, 1959, 27.

19. Statistics on racial distribution over time were compiled from Lurie, Washington Houses Study, III:22; NYCHA, "Projects Completed in the East Harlem Area"; NYCHA, "Projects Planned or Under Construction in East Harlem Area," December 15, 1959, in box 73C3, folder 13, NYCHA; NYCHA, Project Resources Information Sheets—East Harlem, 1962, in box 72A6, folder 05, NYCHA; Cayo-Sexton, *Spanish Harlem,* 36; City Planning Commission, *Tenant Relocation Report,* 44; James Weldon Johnson Community Center, "Table C: Population Characteristics for East Harlem: 1960," in box 1, folder 19, JWJCC. Statistics on Puerto Rican migration are from Department of City Planning, "Puerto Rican Population Trends," *Newsletter,* October 1962, 1; and the extensive demographic work done by Judith F. Herbstein in "Rituals and Politics of the Puerto Rican 'Community' in New York City," Ph.D. diss., City University of New York, 1978, 50–54.

20. Citizens Housing and Planning Council, "East Harlem—A Challenge," *CHPC Housing News* 8, no. 9 (July 1950): 1, 4; Citizens Housing and Planning Council, press release, November 19, 1951, in box 73C5, folder 1, NYCHA; Lurie, Washington Houses Study, II:1–4.

21. Lurie, Washington Houses Study, II:6–13; "The East Harlem Project," November 25, 1960, 1, in box 17, folder 2, UnSett. On tensions between the projects and the surrounding neighborhoods, see Jefferson Houses Tenants Association, "End of the Year Evaluation," June 1959, in box 17, folder 1, UnSett.

22. Elizabeth Wood, *The Small Hard Core: The Housing of Problem Families in New York City* (New York: Citizens Housing and Planning Council, 1957); Jeannie Rosoff, "Report of the Work of the Tenants League of the James Weldon Johnson Houses," July 30, 1957, 2, in box 1, folder 33, JWJCC; and Lurie, Washington Houses Study, II:26, III:2 and 14–15.

23. See Henderson, "'Tarred with the Exceptional Image," 40–42; Elizabeth Wood, *Public Housing and Mrs. McGee* (New York: Citizens Housing and Planning Council, 1956), 4; Daniel Seligman, "The Enduring Slums," *Fortune* (December 1957): 216. For more on NYCHA's difficulty with problem families and the role it played in the May 1958 reorganization that freed the authority from Robert Moses's influence, see Schwartz, *The New York Approach,* 290–292.

24. See Lurie, Washington Houses Study, II:29–35, III:11–16, 25, V:2. Lurie's comment about management rules was adopted from a phrase by the housing researcher Anthony Wallace, whose work on Philadelphia public housing influenced the East Harlemites. See Anthony F. C. Wallace, *Housing and Social Structure* (Philadelphia: Philadelphia Housing Authority, 1952), 22–23.

25. Ellen Lurie, "Draft of Conclusions to Washington Houses Study," October 15, 1956, in box 35, folder 7, UnSett.

26. East Harlem Project, untitled typescript, November 25, 1960, in box 17, folder 2, UnSett; "The Case for East Harlem Project," n.d., 1, in box 17, folder 2, UnSett; East Harlem Public Housing Association, "Proposed Statement," n.d., in box 73C3, folder 15, NYCHA. There are only partial records of the activities of the various tenant organizations. More work is needed to get a full picture of their activities and the results of their efforts. For an account of organizing in Baltimore's public housing, see Rhonda Y. Williams, *The Politics of Public Housing: Black Women's Struggles against Urban Inequality* (New York: Oxford University Press, 2004); and in Chicago, see Roberta Feldman and Susan Stall, *The Dignity of Resistance: Women Residents' Activism in Chicago Public Housing* (New York: Cambridge University Press, 2004). The East Harlem Public Housing Association's reflexive assumption that tenants could be summed up with the pronoun "his" ("his intelligence" and "natural desire to improve his environment") was, at the least, misplaced, as Williams and Feldman and Stall show in their studies, because much of the activism in public housing was undertaken by women— the very people who would be scapegoated in later years as the ambitionless "welfare queens" who undermined public housing. From the records available, it appears that quite a few women were involved in East Harlem as well. For an account of tenants in Boston's public housing, see Lawrence J. Vale, *Reclaiming Public Housing: A Half-Century of Struggle in Three Public Neighborhoods* (Cambridge, MA: Harvard University Press, 2002). On St. Louis see Joseph Earl Heathcott, "The City Remade: Public Housing and the Urban Landscape in St. Louis, 1900–1960." Ph.D. diss., Indiana University, 2002. It should also be noted that the East Harlem Project followed a comprehensive approach to neighborhood organization and development. It made efforts in a wide variety of areas besides public housing. Perhaps its most conspicuous success was in organizing parents, who demanded and got more schools in the overcrowded district. It also tried to curb juvenile delinquency and heroin addiction; and the group started programs to attract services as diverse as jobs for youth, credit unions, day care, and cross-town bus service on 116th Street. It also embarked on various consumer advocacy, voter registration, and health and nutrition campaigns. These efforts await their own historians.

27. Badillo, "Housing Statement," 4. See also Cayo-Sexton, *Spanish Harlem,* 120–147.

28. See JWJCC, "Reclaiming a Wasteland"; Walter Lord to David F. Freeman, October 7, 1963, in box 28, folder 9, UnSett; Orville H. Schell Jr., memorandum to William Kirk, etc., March 22, 1961, in box 17, folder 2, UnSett; "The East Harlem Project," n.d., 1, in box 17, folder 3, UnSett.

29. East Harlem Project, 1961–62 Program Year, in box 17, folder 2, UnSett.

30. Dave Borden to William Kirk, n.d., 2, in box 30, folder 6, UnSett; and Lurie, "Community Action in East Harlem," 4.

31. See Lurie, "Community Action in East Harlem," 13, 5; East Harlem Project, Progress Report, June 1961, in box 11, folder 26, JWJCC; William Kirk, Ellen Lurie, Jane Jacobs, and Mildred Zucker, untitled typescript, February 3, 1959, in box 35, folder 8, UnSett; Lurie, Washington Houses Study, III:9.

32. Lurie, Washington Houses Study, frontispiece. This was a contentious issue. Some worried that long-time opponents of federally subsidized housing would use any criticism of public housing, while others wanted to "let the chips fall where they may." According to one account of a housing committee meeting, the "consensus" was that they believed the government should continue to finance low-income housing, "with a view towards innovation and experimentation" and in developments mixed with middle-income units. They should also look to expand subsidies so that private builders could enter the low-income housing market. See East Harlem Council for Community Planning, Housing Committee Minutes, June 25, 1963, in box 28, folder 2, UnSett; East Harlem Council for Community Planning, Meeting on Legislation, December 14, 1964, in box 27, folder 3, UnSett.

33. Lewis Mumford, "The Red Brick Beehives," *New Yorker,* May 6, 1950, 97; Citizens Housing and Planning Council, "Are We Building Vertical Sardine Cans?" *Citizens Housing and Planning News* 16, nos. 8–9 (April–May 1958): 2; Percival Goodman quoted in "What's Wrong with Public Housing? What Architects Think about Public Housing," *AR* (July 1958): 185. For other architectural critiques of public housing from this period, see the other comments in the *AR* article, 183–186; Seligman, "Enduring Slums," 221; Richard Plunz, *A History of Housing in New York City* (New York: Columbia University Press, 1990), 289–295. See also Joseph Marfin, Dominick Peluso, and Sydney Mirkin, "The Housing That Your Jack Built Is Now Tobacco Road," *NYDN,* February 19, 1957, 3, and the other articles in this 15-part series, which ran from February 18 to March 8, 1957; "Metropolis in a Mess," *Newsweek,* July 27, 1959.

34. The authority actually noted at least as early as 1941 that outsiders had described its architectural designs as "mediocre and mechanistic." See NYCHA, William Ballard to Gerard Swope, December 1, 1941, in box 54D5, folder 8, NYCHA. See also Philip J. Cruise to Skidmore, Owings and Merrill, September 5, 1951. This letter, one of 12 sent to major architectural firms, noted that NYCHA had become "increasingly concerned" that architectural professionals thought the authority's work "dull, institutional, uniform, etc." The letter invited the architects to a meeting where they could give the authority their "free and frank opinion." Letters are in box 72D4, folder 4, NYCHA. Also see American Institute of Architects, Eighty-fourth Convention Visit to East Harlem Public Housing Projects, June 25, 1952, in box 74A5, folder 2, NYCHA; NYCHA, Annual Report 1952, 15, 18–21, in box 98D1, folder 13, NYCHA; Philip J. Cruise, Chairman, NYCHA, speech at the annual luncheon, Architects and Engineers Division, Federation of Jewish Philanthropies, November 24, 1953, 2–3, in box 59D2, folder 3, NYCHA; John D. Crist, East Harlem Protestant Parish to Philip J. Cruise, March 24, 1955, in 60D3, folder 1, NYCHA; NYCHA, 22nd Annual Report, 1955, 26–28; NYCHA, 1960 Annual Report; and NYCHA, 1962 Annual Report, all in box 98D1, folders 18, 23, and 24, NYCHA. On the reorganization of NYCHA, see Charles F. Preusse, City Administrator to Mayor Robert F. Wagner, September 16, 1957, in box 71E4, folder 6, NYCHA; Anthony Jackson, *A*

Place Called Home (Cambridge, MA: MIT Press, 1976), 236–237; and Schwartz, *The New York Approach*, 290–291.

35. Maxim Duplex, "The New Issue in Public Housing," *Journal of Housing* 7, no. 6 (June 1950): 202–206. See Friedman, *Government and Slum Housing*, 141–143, for a survey of the housers' doubts.

36. Catherine Bauer, "Social Questions in Housing and Community Planning," *Journal of Social Issues* 8, nos. 1–2 (1951): 20–21; Catherine Bauer, "The Dreary Deadlock of Public Housing," *AF* 106 (May 1957): 140–142, 219, 221. See also CHPC, "Memorandum on Public Housing Design for the Conference of April 28, 1959, Carnegie International Center for Peace," n.d., in box 73C5, folder 1, NYCHA; NYCHA, "Resume of Meeting of April 28, 1959, at Carnegie Center for Peace," May 19, 1959, in box 73B4, folder 2, NYCHA.

37. Ellen Lurie, reply to Catherine Bauer, in "The Dreary Deadlock of Public Housing—How to Break It," *AF* 106 (June 1957): 140–141. See also Lurie, "Architectural Forum," n.d., typescript in box 35, folder 7, UnSett.

38. See Mildred Zucker to William Reid, October 6, 1958, in box 73C3, folder 13, NYCHA; Housing Committee of the EHCCP, Summary of Proposals and Discussions with CPC—October 31, 1958, in box 73C3, folder 11, NYCHA; William Kirk to William Reid, December 30, 1958; and East Harlem Project, Tenant Leaders Meeting re New Design for Clinton Houses, both in box 35, folder 8, UnSett; Mildred Zucker, Report of the Housing Committee of the EHCCP for the Year June 1958 through May 1959, May 19, 1959, in box 73C3, folder 11, NYCHA.

39. See the committee's presentation to NYCHA: William Kirk, Ellen Lurie, Jane Jacobs, and Mildred Zucker, untitled typescript, February 3, 1959, 1–6, in box 35, folder 8, UnSett.

40. Lurie, Washington Houses Study, III:8–9.

41. See Housing Committee of the EHCCP, Statement on Physical Design of Public Housing Projects, July 2, 1958, 1–2, in box 73C3, folder 11, NYCHA; Mildred Zucker to William Reid, October 6, 1958; William Kirk et al., untitled typescript, February 3, 1959, 7; Housing Committee of the EHCCP, press release, February 9, 1959, in box 35, folder 8, UnSett; Richard A. Miller, "Public Housing...for People," *AF* 110 (April 1959): 134–137.

42. See Housing Committee of the EHCCP, Statement on Physical Design of Public Housing, July 2, 1958, 2; Housing Committee of the EHCCP, Summary of Proposals and Discussions with CPC—October 31, 1958, 1; Perkins and Will Architects, Meeting January 8, 1959, Re: DeWitt Clinton Housing Study, January 15, 1959, 1; Perkins and Will Architects, Meeting January 16, 1959, Re: DeWitt Clinton Housing Study, January 20, 1959, 1, both in box 35, folder 8, UnSett; William Kirk et al., untitled typescript, February 3, 1959, 8–10; Mildred Zucker to Perkins and Will Architects, February 6, 1959, in box 35, folder 8, UnSett; Miller, "Public Housing...for People," 136.

43. Perkins and Will Architects, Meeting January 15, 1959, 2; William Kirk et al., untitled typescript, February 3, 1959, 8–10; Miller, "Public Housing...for People," 136.

44. See Miller, "Public Housing...for People," 137; William Reid to Douglass Haskell, March 19, 1959, in box 73B4, folder 2, NYCHA; William Reid to William Kirk, March 17, 1961; and Kirk to Reid, April 4, 1961, both in box 36, folder 10, UnSett; Mildred Zucker, Report of the Housing Committee...June 1958 through May 1959, May 19, 1959, 2.

45. See JWJCC, "The Story of the 'Gala East Harlem Plaza,'" December 1959; JWJCC, "The Gala East Harlem Plaza," n.d., both in box 73C3, folder 13, NYCHA; Jacobs, "Missing Link," 133; Albert Mayer, "Public Housing Design," *Journal of Housing* 20, no. 3 (April 1963): 142.

46. See Paul Goldberger, "Albert Mayer, 83, Architect and Housing Planner, Dies," *NYT*, October 16, 1981, B6; Mayer quoted in NYCHA, *Monthly Housing Report: The New Face of Public Housing* (broadcast over radio station WNYC on October 11, 1962), 2–3, in box 59C8, folder 4, NYCHA; Albert Mayer, *The Urgent Future* (New York: McGraw-Hill, 1967), 20, 28.

47. Albert Mayer, "Public Housing Architecture Evaluated from PWA Days Up to 1962," *Journal of Housing* 19, no. 8 (October 1962): 450, 453–456; NYCHA, *Monthly Housing Report*, October 11, 1962, 3. In 1965, Mayer expanded his Main Street idea, proposing to create a new "Main Street or Pedestrian Promenade" that would cut across East Harlem on an east-west axis, join Jefferson Park on one end and the Park Avenue Market on the other, and pass through Johnson Houses and Jefferson Houses. See Albert Mayer, "For East Harlem: A New 'Main Street' or Pedestrian Promenade," December 28, 1965, 1–2, in box 14, folder 6, JWJCC.

48. Mayer quoted in NYCHA, *Monthly Housing Report: The New Face of Public Housing* (broadcast over radio station WNYC on September 13, 1962), in box 59C8, folder 4, NYCHA; and in "New York City Tries a Just-for-Fun Venture," *Journal of Housing* (August–September 1960): 306. See also JWJCC, "The Story of the 'Gala East Harlem Plaza'"; JWJCC, "The Gala East Harlem Plaza"; NYCHA, press release, "Address of Ira S. Robbins, Vice-Chairman of the New York City Housing Authority, at the Dedication of the East Harlem Plaza, Jefferson Houses, Monday, May 16, 1960," May 17, 1960, in box 59D1, folder 2, NYCHA; "Plaza Dedicated in East Harlem," *NYT*, May 17, 1960, 33; "Harlem's Playful Playground," *AF* 114, no. 3 (March 1961). For Mayer's comparison of the plaza to Lincoln Center, see "Search for Community Comment," n.d., in folder 11, box 13, JWJCC.

49. Anthony Bailey, "Uphill on 106th Street," *NYHT Magazine*, January 26, 1964. See also JWJCC, Report to the Board of Trustees, Re: Benjamin Franklin Houses Cooperative, September 12, 1960, in box 12, folder 14, JWJCC; Martin Arnold, "Prospective Tenants Avoiding 4 Co-op Projects Built by City," *NYT*, November 12, 1961, 84; Sam Kaplan, "New Cooperative Spur to Renewal," *NYT*, October 8, 1961, R1; Cayo-Sexton, *Spanish Harlem*, 155–159; and Donald G. Sullivan, *Cooperative Housing and Community Development: A Comparative Evaluation of Three Housing Projects in East Harlem* (New York: Praeger, 1969), 46–52. Robert A. M. Stern and his colleagues have argued that, contrary to the *Herald Tribune*'s dismissal, "the use of slender towers" rather than the typical slabs "managed to create an environment that conveyed the positive values of the open city in a way few postwar projects had." This design did help to give most apartments corner windows. See Robert A. M. Stern, Thomas Mellins, and David Fishman, *New York 1960* (New York: Monacelli, 1995), 865.

50. Mayer, "Public Housing Architecture Evaluated," 455.

51. Mayer won the National Honor Award from the American Society of Landscape Architects and a Certificate of Merit from New York's Municipal Arts Society for his work. See NYCHA, *Monthly Housing Report: The New Face of Public Housing* (broad-

cast over radio station WNYC on September 13, 1962), 1. For more praise of Mayer's work at Jefferson and Franklin Houses, see Lawrence O'Kane, "Battle of Frills: A Plea for Help, Architects and Others Talk of Project Problems," *NYT,* April 25, 1965, R1. On Mayer's proposed redesign for Washington Houses, see Albert Mayer, "Landscape Renewal 'Sub-community,' George Washington Homes North," July 12, 1962, in series VIII, roll 3, UnSett; and Mayer, "Public Housing Design—Architect Albert Mayer Proposes Design Ideas for Modernizing Old Projects; Improving New," *Journal of Housing* 20, no. 3 (April 1963): 135. On Pomerance and Breines's redesign of Carver Houses, see "Making Public Housing Human," *Progressive Architecture* (January 1965): 177–179; NYCHA, Fact Sheet on Carver Houses Plaza, January 1965; and Simon Breines to Max Schreiber, Re: Carver, January 20, 1965, both in box 69E3, folder 11, NYCHA. See also the fact sheets on designs for Gaylord White Houses in East Harlem (by Mayer's firm, Mayer, Whittlesey, and Glass) and Mott Haven Houses (by Ginsbern Associates), both of which show a concern with creating "really meaningful spaces" in new NYCHA projects, also in box 69E3, folder 11, NYCHA. On Lavanburg's efforts, see Francis Scott Bradford, *The Village in the City* (New York: Lavanburg Foundation, c. 1960), in box 62D1, folder 11, NYCHA; Wolf Von Eckhardt and Charles Goodman, *Life for Dead Spaces: The Development of the Lavanburg Commons* (New York: Harcourt, Brace, 1963); "New Housing Projects Viewed as Destroyers of Urban Life," *NYWTS,* November 14, 1963; Mary Perot Nichols, "Who Will Humanize the Humanizers?" *Village Voice* 9, no. 7 (December 5, 1963): 1, 6; Lawrence O'Kane, "Village Look Sought in the Bronx," *NYT,* March 17, 1965. On 1199 Plaza and its various iterations, see "Contest Gives City Novel Housing Plan," *NYT,* August 23, 1963, 1, 22; Ada Louise Huxtable, "Design for Progress," *NYT,* August 23, 1963, 22; Stern et al., *New York 1960,* 866. On Metro North, see "Housing Planned for 'Worst Block,'" *NYWTS,* January 18, 1965; "Metro-North to Wipe Out 'Worst Block,'" *NYHT,* October 10, 1965.

52. Elizabeth Wood, *Housing Design: A Social Theory* (New York: Citizens Housing and Planning Council, 1961). For NYCHA's interest, see Wolcott E. Andrews and E. J. McGrew Jr., "Housing Design: A Social Theory," July 11, 1961, in which the two officials recommended that the authority should "depart from our previous inflexible standards and stimulate the site and landscape architects to use their imagination," and NYCHA, files, Mary Costa, Administrative Associate, Housing Design: A Social Theory, July 25, 1961, in which Costa records distributing copies of the book to project architects and officials, both in box 73C5, folder 1, NYCHA. Wood's proposals were largely "productive," intended to encourage "positive" behavior rather than prevent "negative" behavior. Within a few years, however, NYCHA and other municipal housing bodies were being urged to implement "defensive" design measures to offset and prevent vandalism and crime. See "U.S. Offers Ideas for Apartments: Housing Agency Consultant Studies the Problems in High-Rise Structures," *NYT,* August 22, 1965. The culmination of this trend was Oscar Newman's influential research, much of it carried out in NYCHA projects. See Newman, *Defensible Space: People and Design in the Violent City* (New York: Macmillan, 1972). For the evolution of public housing design, see Karen A. Franck and Michael Mostoller, "From Courts to Open Space to Streets: Changes in the Site Design of U.S. Public Housing," *Journal of Architectural and Planning Research* 12, no. 3 (Autumn 1995): 186–219.

53. See William Kirk to Albert Mayer, June 27, 1962; and Albert Mayer, handwritten notes, "Visit to Franklin Plaza Outdoors (3rd–2nd Ave. Section), 6:15–6:45 PM, Sat. Aft.," June 15, 1968, both in box 39, folder 3, UnSett. See also Joseph Krois, Observations on Franklin Plaza Outdoor Area, March 18, 1964, in box 39, folder 5, UnSett.

54. JWJCC, Good Neighbor Week Program, April 30, 1962, in box 11, folder 13, JWJCC; Mayer quoted in "Plaza Dedicated in East Harlem," *NYT,* May 17, 1960, 33; and Mayer, "Public Housing Architecture Evaluated," 454–455. See also Muriel Fischer, "East Harlem Can Hardly Wait for the Song and Dance at Plaza," *NYWTS,* May 9, 1961; Marjorie Rubin, "A Shortened 'Barber of Seville' Is Heard Outdoors," *NYT,* August 21, 1963; and JWJCC, "The Arts and East Harlem," n.d., in box 1, folder 19, JWJCC.

55. Sam Rand, "Monday Night Concert Series at the Gala East Harlem Fountain-Plaza, 1962," September 21, 1962, 1–3, in box 8, folder 8, JWJCC.

56. Ibid., 2, 1.

57. Ibid., 3–4.

58. See EHCCP, "The Changing Face of East Harlem," March 31, 1965, in box 16, folder 10, UnSett; JWJCC, "A Report on the Exhibition Known as the Changing Face of East Harlem," July 19, 1965, in box 11, folder 10, JWJCC; East Harlem Project, 1961–62 Program Year, 1, in box 17, folder 2, UnSett.

59. See East Harlem Council for Community Planning, luncheon meeting, "The Revitalization of East Harlem—the New Upper East Side," October 16, 1961, in box 26, folder 2, UnSett.

60. Preston Wilcox to Walter Lord, Chairman of Union Settlement, September 9, 1963, 2, in box 17, folder 4, UnSett. Wilcox quoted in Cayo-Sexton, *Spanish Harlem,* 100.

61. For the quoted reactions to the social workers' influence over the neighborhood, see Cayo-Sexton, *Spanish Harlem,* 99–100 and 167–169; and Patte Vega, "The First 105 Days," May 7, 1965, 15, in box 39, folder 1, UnSett. Historians have amply demonstrated that, in addition to the social work profession's focus on casework and individual upward mobility, the settlement houses' roots in a Victorian ideology of "social control" continued to dampen their ability to help their clients well into the twentieth century. In the years after World War II, middle-class, white social workers, confronted with neighborhoods that were becoming black or Puerto Rican, were accused of hiding their impulse toward social control behind a vision of interracial, cross-class cooperation and harmony. The new generation of professional African American and Latino men and women who began to rise in the ranks of social workers and settlement house administrators (Preston Wilcox is a good example of this trend) made this critique their own, and they soon began replacing the middle-class white women who had long spearheaded the settlement movement. However, the new grassroots organizations of the civil rights and War on Poverty eras eclipsed the settlement house movement's traditional role in low-income neighborhoods, prompting the social workers to fall back on a more limited, professionalized social work role. See Herbert J. Gans, "Redefining the Settlement's Function for the War on Poverty," in his *People and Plans* (New York: Basic, 1968), 249–259; Trolander, *Professionalism and Social Change;* Mina Carson, *Settlement Folk* (Chicago: University of Chicago Press, 1990); Elizabeth Lasch-Quinn, *Black Neighbors* (Chapel Hill: University of

North Carolina Press, 1993); Daniel J. Walkowitz, *Working with Class* (Chapel Hill: University of North Carolina Press, 1998).

62. Cayo-Sexton, *Spanish Harlem,* 99. The politics of East Harlem in the '50s and '60s still await a full history. See Arlene Davila, "Dreams of Place: Housing, Gentrification and the Marketing of Space in El Barrio," *CENTRO Journal* 15, no. 1 (Spring 2003): 116–118; Jose Ramon Sanchez, "Housing Puerto Ricans in New York City, 1945–1984: A Study in Class Powerlessness," Ph.D. diss., City University of New York, 1990; Herbstein, "Rituals and Politics"; Anerris Goris and Pedro Pedraza, "Political Participation of Puerto Ricans in El Barrio," *CENTRO: Boletin del Centro de Estudios Puertorriquenos* 4, no. 2 (1992): 88–97; James Jennings, *Puerto Rican Politics in New York City* (Washington, DC: University Press of America, 1977); Jose Ramon Sanchez, "Puerto Rican Politics in New York: Beyond 'Secondhand' Theory," in G. Haslip-Viera and S. Baver, eds., *Latinos in New York* (South Bend, IN: Notre Dame University Press, 1996), 259–301. On struggles between the Massive Economic Neighborhood Development and the East Harlem Tenants Council, see John Kifner, "Poor to Choose in East Harlem," *NYT,* March 6, 1966, 69; Kifner, "Agency Here Asks U.S. Fund for Poor," *NYT,* April 14, 1966, 30; Kifner, "A Poverty Feud Grows Bitterer," *NYT,* October 14, 1966, 28. On the Real Great Society's efforts in advocacy planning, see Luis Aponte-Pares, "Lessons from El Barrio: The East Harlem Real Great Society/Urban Planning Studio: A Puerto Rican Chapter in the Fight for Urban Self-Determination," in Rodolfo D. Torres and George Katsiaficas, eds., *Latino Social Movements: Historical and Theoretical Perspectives* (New York: Routledge, 1999), 43–77. For another late '60s planning effort, in which a group of tenants hired a planner to develop a scheme to re-knit the Taft Houses back into the fabric of the surrounding neighborhood as part of a proposed urban renewal plan, see Stern et al., *New York 1960,* 866–869; and Roger Katan, "Pueblos for El Barrio," December 21, 1967, in Avery.

63. Piri Thomas, *Down These Mean Streets* (New York: Knopf, 1967), 314; James Baldwin, "Fifth Avenue, Uptown," *Esquire,* July 1960, 72–76. The only project Baldwin mentioned by name was Riverton, Met Life's effort to buy off desegregation pressure for Stuyvesant Town. This drew an angry letter from the chair of the Riverton Tenants Association, who maintained, "we are cut from the same fabric of the American community as are others." See Richard P. Jones to Editors, "Up the Riverton," *Esquire,* September 1960.

64. Donald G. Sullivan found that 40 out of 50 people surveyed in the Jefferson Houses in the late '60s found their residences there to be better than their previous ones. See Sullivan, *Cooperative Housing and Community Development,* 159–161. See also Louis Harris and Associates, Inc., "A Survey of the Attitudes and Experience of Occupants of Urban Federally Subsidized Housing, Prepared for HUD," National Housing Study Review Paper, No. 2331; Housing and Public Affairs, no. PR28, Department of Housing and Urban Development, 1973, 60–61; Judith Noemi Friedenberg, *Growing Old in El Barrio* (New York: NYU Press, 2000), 218–224; Terry Williams and William Kornblum, *The Uptown Kids: Struggle and Hope in the Projects* (New York: Putnam, 1994), 241–244; and Plunz, *History of Housing,* 270. Colette Winkfield, a resident of Jefferson Houses in the early 1960s, reported that her neighbors felt that the "overall potential there is good." They were concerned with "safety, cleanliness, beauty and

recreational facilities" and were not "preoccupied with rats, roaches and mountains of garbage." See Vega, "The First 105 Days," 2. Thomas Webber, who lived in the Washington and Wilson Houses between 1957 and the early '60s, reports that project dwellers were at the top of East Harlem's "social ladder." Among project residents, there was an internal hierarchy as well, based on, according to Webber, "how well your buildings are maintained, who has the best outside gardens, whose lobbies are cleanest and sport the best decorations at Christmastime, whose tenant associations are most sought after by the local politicians." See Thomas L. Webber, *Flying over 96th Street: Memoir of an East Harlem White Boy* (New York: Scribner, 2004), 107. In the late twentieth and early twenty-first centuries, when most cities began to tear down their tower-block public housing, New York renovated and preserved it. In 2003, the city even made one of its first projects, Williamsburg Houses, a city landmark. See Sandy Zipp, "A Landmark Decision: With Public Housing Projects Undergoing Demolition Nationwide, Why Is New York Preserving This One?" *Metropolis*, November 2003, 34–36. For another twenty-first-century appreciation of the projects, this one from an outsider simply passing by, see Philip Lopate, "Ode to the Projects," in his *Waterfront: A Journey around Manhattan* (New York: Crown, 2004), 348–372.

Conclusion

1. Marya Mannes, *The New York I Know* (Philadelphia: Lippincott, 1961), 142, 147–148, 82, 156, 151–152, 159.

2. Richard J. Whalen, *A City Destroying Itself: An Angry View of New York* (New York: Morrow, 1965); Norman Mailer, "Why Are We in New York?" *NYTM*, May 18, 1969; Jason Epstein, "The Last Days of New York," in Roger E. Alcaly and David Mermelstein, eds., *The Fiscal Crises of American Cities* (New York: Vintage, 1976), 59–76. Whalen's book was originally published as a long essay in the September 1964 issue of *Fortune*. In 1965, the *Herald Tribune* popularized the idea of seeing the city as in crisis, devoting several months to a comprehensive series called "New York City in Crisis." See, for instance, Marshall Peck, "Urban Renewal and Human Havoc," *NYHT*, February 19, 1965, 1, 11.

3. "Lost Streets," *NYT*, July 26, 1948.

4. See Charles Grutzner, "Relocation Rule of U.S. Is Opposed," *NYT*, May 2, 1959, 11; Grutzner, "Congress Urged to Study Moses' Housing Actions," *NYT*, June 20, 1959, 1; Richard E. Mooney, "Slum Clearance Hard to Control," *NYT*, June 28, 1959, E8; Wayne Phillips, "Unorthodox Title I Procedures Used by Moses Create Disputes," *NYT*, June 30, 1959, 1; Wayne Phillips, "Title I Slum Clearance Proves Spur to Cooperative Housing in City," *NYT*, July 2, 1959, 13; Grutzner, "Moses Says Title I Is a 'Dead Duck,'" *NYT*, July 4, 1959; Grutzner, "Mayor to Bolster Title I Committee," *NYT*, July 8, 1959, 1; Jewel Bellush and Murray Hausknecht, *Urban Renewal: People, Politics, and Planning* (New York: Anchor, 1967), 189–197; Jeanne Lowe, *Cities in a Race with Time* (New York: Random House, 1967), 96–99; Robert Caro, *The Power Broker* (New York: Knopf, 1974), 1006–1066; Christopher J. Klemek, "Caught between Moses and the Market: Jane Jacobs and Urban Renewal's Lost Middle Way," chapter 4 in "Urbanism as Reform: Modernist Planning and the Crisis of Urban Liberalism in Europe and North America, 1945–1975," Ph.D. diss., University of Pennsylvania, 2004, 164.

5. Samuel A. Spiegel, *The Forgotten Man in Housing* (New York: Spiegel, 1959), 15, 5. See also Kitty Hanson, "Our City's Slum Tenants Are Also Condemned: Many Wind Up D.P.'s as Their Homes Fall," *NYDN,* December 15, 1959, 34; Hanson, "Sometimes It's Relocation, Often It's Just Dislocation," *NYDN,* December 16, 1959, 48.

6. Harris Present, interview with author, March 28, 2008, New York. On the Met Council and Cooper Square, see Roberta Gold, "City of Tenants: New York's Housing Struggles and the Challenge to Postwar America, 1945–1974," Ph.D. diss., University of Washington, 2004. On Kazan and the United Housing Foundation, see Joshua B. Freeman, *Working-Class New York* (New York: New Press, 2000), 105–124; Tony Schuman, "Labor and Housing in New York City: Architect Herman Jessor and the Cooperative Housing Movement," available at http://www.lesonline.org/cv/aboutus.htm, accessed February 26, 2006.

7. On resistance to urban renewal at Cooper Square, see Joel Schwartz, "Tenant Power in the Liberal City, 1943–1971," in Ronald Lawson, ed., *The Tenant Movement in New York City, 1904–1984* (New Brunswick, NJ: Rutgers University Press, 1986), 176; Robert A. M. Stern, Thomas Mellins, and David Fishman, eds., *New York 1960* (New York: Monacelli, 1995), 257; Gold, "City of Tenants," 198–216; Ella Howard, "Urban Renewal, Vagrancy Laws, and the Contested Role of the Homeless in Public Space," Boston University, 2003, paper in author's possession, 9–23; Marci Reaven, "Cooper Square," paper presented at the annual conference of the Organization of American Historians, April 19, 2006, Washington, DC, paper in author's possession; Norman I. Fainstein and Susan S. Fainstein, *Urban Political Movements* (Englewood Cliffs, NJ: Prentice-Hall, 1974), 43–46; Tom Angotti, *New York for Sale* (Cambridge, MA: MIT Press, 2008).

8. Present quoted in Grutzner, "Congress Urged to Study Moses' Housing Actions," 22.

9. Caro, *The Power Broker,* 1055–1066; Murray Illson, "Mayor Stands by Title I Programs," *NYT,* October 28, 1959. Lawrence Kaplan and Carol P. Kaplan have argued, based on the recollections of observers Milton Mollen and Louis Winnick, that, contra Caro, Moses did not leave of his own accord and was forced out by Wagner in 1959 or 1960. See Kaplan and Kaplan, *Between Ocean and City: The Transformation of Rockaway, New York* (New York: Columbia University Press, 2003), 99. It does seem likely that Wagner was desperate to find a way out of the impasse; it still seems hard to say whether he fired Moses or not, without fresh sources from the time. What is clear is that Moses himself did want out; he expressed as much to others at the time. See note 11, below.

10. J. Anthony Panuch, "Relocation in New York City: Special Report to Mayor Robert F. Wagner," (New York: Mayor's Office, City of New York, December 15, 1959), 16–19; J. Anthony Panuch, "Building a Better New York: Final Report to Mayor Robert F. Wagner," (New York: Mayor's Office, City of New York, March 1, 1960).

11. Robert Moses to Rev. Laurence J. McGinley, February 8, 1960; Moses to J. Anthony Panuch, January 28, 1960, both in roll 15, box 103057, folder 1, ParksGen.

12. On Davies and Felt's ascendancy, see J. Clarence Davies III, *Neighborhood Groups and Urban Renewal* (New York: Columbia University Press, 1966), 6–29; Lowe, *Cities in a Race with Time,* 99–103; Klemek, "Caught between Moses and the Market," 145–152.

13. On zoning, see S. J. Makielski, *The Politics of Zoning: The New York Experience* (New York: Columbia University Press, 1966); Roy Strickland, "The 1961 Zoning Revision and the Template of the Ideal City," and Norman Marcus, "Zoning from 1961 to 1991," both in Todd W. Bressi, ed., *Planning and Zoning New York City* (New Brunswick, NJ: Rutgers University Press, 1993), 48–102; Stern et al., *New York 1960*, 128–131; Klemek, "Caught between Moses and the Market," 149–150. See also New York City, Department of City Planning, "Public Hearing before the City Planning Commission in the Matter of a Proposed Comprehensive Amendment Pursuant to Section 200 of the New York City Charter of the Zoning Resolution of the City of New York," (New York: Department of City Planning, March 14, 15, 18, 21, 22, 23, and 25, 1960), 367, 259.

14. Jacobs's influence is widely heralded, and her name has come to stand for the widespread grassroots resistance to modernism and urban renewal. Major examples are Peter Blake, *No Place Like Utopia* (New York: Norton, 1993), 179–180; Marshall Berman, *All That Is Solid Melts into Air* (New York: Simon and Schuster, 1982), 314–319; Stern et al., *New York 1960*, 77–78; Ric Burns and James Sanders, with Lisa Ades, *New York: An Illustrated History* (New York: Knopf, 1999), 514–520; Alice Sparberg Alexiou, *Jane Jacobs: Urban Visionary* (New Brunswick, NJ: Rutgers University Press, 2006); Anthony Flint, *Wrestling with Moses: How Jane Jacobs Took On New York's Master Builder and Transformed the American City* (New York: Random House, 2009). For an account of the end of urban renewal nationwide that relies on Jacobs, see Jon C. Teaford, "Urban Renewal and Its Aftermath," *Housing Policy Debate* 11, no. 2 (2000): 443–465. See also Jane Kramer, "All the Ranks and Rungs of Mrs. Jacobs' Ladder," in Max Allen, ed., *Ideas That Matter: The Worlds of Jane Jacobs* (Owen Sound, ON: Ginger, 1997), 69. For a more fleshed-out account of Jacobs's activities in Greenwich Village, see Robert Fishman, "Revolt of the Urbs," in Hilary Ballon and Kenneth Jackson, eds., *Robert Moses and the Modern City* (New York: Norton, 2007). On the theoretical and architectural debates informing Jacobs's views, see Peter Laurence, "The Death and Life of Urban Design: Jane Jacobs, the Rockefeller Foundation and the New Research in Urbanism, 1955–1965," *Journal of Urban Design* 11, no. 2 (June 2006): 145–172. The Jacobs-as-housewife idea originates with Lewis Mumford's angry review of *Death and Life*, "Mother Jacobs' Home Remedies for Urban Cancer," in Mumford, *The Urban Prospect* (New York: Harcourt, Brace, 1962), 182–207. I owe the phrase "urban Rachel Carson" to Michael Cohen, although Robert Fulford, Howard Husock, and Rebecca Solnit have also suggested the resonances between Jacobs and Carson. See Robert Fulford, "Abattoir for Sacred Cows: Three Decades in the Life of a Classic," excerpted in Allen, *Ideas That Matter*, 5–9; Howard Husock, "Urban Iconoclast: Jane Jacobs Revisited," *City Journal* (Winter 1994); Rebecca Solnit, "Three Who Made a Revolution," *Nation*, April 3, 2006, 29–31.

15. Harris Present remembers meeting with Jacobs. (He also met with and advised the Cooper Square protestors.) See Present, interview, 2008; Harris Present, oral history, February 15, 1991, 42–44, LCPA. Jacobs thanks the others in her acknowledgments or mentions their work in the course of her text. Jane Jacobs, *The Death and Life of Great American Cities* (New York: Random House, 1961; New York: Modern Library, 1993), xxi, 21–22.

16. Jacobs, *Death and Life*, 5, 10, 34, 486, 6; Jacobs, "The Missing Link in City Redevelopment," *AF* (June 6, 1956): 133.

17. Jacobs, *Death and Life,* 64–65, 149–150, 219–221; and Jacobs, "Talk Given April 20, 1958, at a Dinner Panel of the New School Associates, New School for Social Research," in box 37, folder 380, RockCult.

18. Jacobs, *Death and Life,* 6, 182. Mayer quoted in transcript, *The New Face of Public Housing,* WNYC, November 8, 1962, 3, in box 59C8, folder 4, NYCHA.

19. Jacobs, *Death and Life,* 7, 178, 180.

20. Ibid., 401.

21. Ibid., 21.

22. Ibid., 23, 379, 5.

23. Ibid., 65, 21, 20.

24. Ibid., 290, 169, 188, 19.

25. Ibid., 65, 19.

26. Ibid., 32. Earlier, Jacobs had been cautiously optimistic about the reforms. See Jacobs, "Talk Given April 20, 1958," 8. On the battle for the West Village, see Davies, *Neighborhood Groups and Urban Renewal,* 72–109; Klemek, "Caught between Moses and the Market," 180; Klemek, "From Political Outsider to Power Broker in Two 'Great American Cities': Jane Jacobs and the Fall of the Urban Renewal Order in New York and Toronto," *Journal of Urban History* 34, no. 2 (January 2008): 309–332.

27. Felt quoted in Klemek, "Caught between Moses and the Market," 176. See also Jacobs, *Death and Life,* 353, 414; Martin Anderson, *The Federal Bulldozer: A Critical Analysis of Urban Renewal, 1949–1962* (Cambridge, MA: MIT Press, 1964); "After the Bulldozer," *AF* (May 1965). Reagan quoted in Damon Rich, "Big Plans and Little People; or, Who Has the Keys to the Federal Bulldozer?" paper presented at City Legacies: A Symposium on Early Pratt Planning Papers and Street Magazine, October 14, 2005, Pratt Institute, Brooklyn, NY. For another account that notes Jacobs's affinities with conservatism and free market ideals, see Husock, "Urban Iconoclast."

28. David R. Hill, "Jane Jacobs' Ideas on Big, Diverse Cities," *Journal of the American Planning Association* 54, no. 3 (Summer 1988): 312. See also Teaford, "Urban Renewal and Its Aftermath"; Davies, *Neighborhood Groups and Urban Renewal* 206; Stephen Petrus, "From Gritty to Chic: The Transformation of New York City's SoHo, 1962–1976," *New York History* 84 (2003): 50–87; Editors, "Beyond the Modern Movement," *Harvard Architecture Review* 1 (Spring 1980): 4–9; Stern et al., *New York 1960,* 133. One of the great documents of advocacy planning is Robert Goodman, *After the Planners* (New York: Simon and Schuster, 1971). On the Architects Renewal Committee in Harlem, see Stern et al., *New York 1960,* 858–859, 888–891. On the Real Great Society, see Luis Aponte-Pares, "Lessons from El Barrio," in Rodolfo D. Torres and George Katsiaficas, eds., *Latino Social Movements* (New York: Routledge, 1999), 43–77. See also Christopher Klemek, "The Rise and Fall of New Left Urbanism," *Daedalus* (Spring 2009): 73–89. For a history of anti–urban renewal activism in one city, see Mandi Isaacs Jackson, *Model City Blues: Urban Space and Organized Resistance in New Haven* (Philadelphia: Temple University Press, 2008). On Ed Logue, Lizabeth Cohen, "Edward J. Logue and the Politics of Urban Redevelopment in Postwar America," paper given at Robert Moses: New Perspectives on the Master Builder conference, Columbia University, March 3, 2007.

29. For a twenty-first-century appreciation of Moses's work, see Ballon and Jackson, *Robert Moses and the Modern City.* On NYCHA, see Nicholas Dagen Bloom, *Public*

Housing That Worked (Philadelphia: Penn Press, 2008). Perhaps the first commentator to notice Jacobs's blindness on race was Herbert J. Gans in "Urban Vitality and the Fallacy of Physical Determinism," in his *People and Plans* (New York: Basic, 1968).

30. Berman, *All That Is Solid,* 314. There are many accounts of revitalized cities and neighborhoods and the struggles surrounding them. See, for instance, Roberta Brandes Gratz, *The Living City* (New York: Wiley, 1995); John O. Norquist, *The Wealth of Cities* (New York: Perseus, 1999); Roberta Brandes Gratz and Norman Mintz, *Cities Back from the Edge* (New York: Wiley, 2000); Paul S. Grogan and Tony Proscio, *Comeback Cities: A Blueprint for Urban Revival* (New York: Westview, 2001); Alexander von Hoffman, *House by House, Block by Block* (New York: Oxford University Press, 2004); Tom Angotti, *New York for Sale* (Cambridge, MA: MIT Press, 2008). On the rise of the global slum, see Robert Neuwirth, *Shadow Cities* (New York: Routledge, 2004); and Mike Davis, *Planet of Slums* (New York: Verso, 2006). Hernando de Soto argues that slums could be eased by capitalism if only property rights could be extended to urban squatters; see *The Mystery of Capital* (New York: Basic, 2003).

Index

culture and arts
American image abroad, 175, 178
as antidote to mass culture, 193
as chief social need of time, 182
democratization of, 177
depictions of urban renewal in, 8,
153–54, 197, 198–200, 247–49
gender imagery in, 179–80, 183
as instrument for urban
transformation, 172, 182–83, 184,
189–96, 239
J. Rockefeller's reflections on, 174–75
New Deal funding for, 174
as weapon in Cold War, 161, 178–79,
183, 196
See also Lincoln Center for the
Performing Arts; modern art

dance theater, at Lincoln Center, 186, 187
See also City Center of Music and
Drama
Davies, J. Clarence, Jr., 359, 360, 366
Davis, Stuart, 197
"A Day at Lincoln Square" (Atkinson),
243–45
The Death and Life of Great American
Cities (Jacobs), 10, 311, 349, 360–66
deindustrialization
from suburbanization, 20, 26–27
from urban renewal, 10, 21, 369
as welcome intervention in cityscape,
8, 56–59
Delancey Street project, 355
Demas, Corinne, 116, 129–30, 131–32, 147,
149, 150
Demas, Electra, 132
Depression, 14, 202
desegregation. See racial desegregation
Dewey, Thomas, 81, 82
DeWitt Clinton Houses
designs for, 290, 327–30, 331, 332
funding, 259
images of, 292, 332
d'Harnoncourt, René, 188
DiLauros, Joseph, 246–47

Dillon, Marion, 84
Dorsey v. Stuyvesant Town, 121, 122
Double-V campaign, 118
Down These Mean Streets (Thomas), 348
downtowns
diminishing vitality of, 182
shopping in, 5, 7
See also urban renewal
"Dreary Deadlock of Public Housing"
(Bauer), 282, 326–27
Drug and Hospital Workers Union, 339
Dudley, George, 45

East Harlem
African Americans in, 261, 262, 313, 314
crime in, 266, 267, 268
Harlem residents overflowing into,
262
images of, 251, 311, 312
Italians in, 262, 313, 314, 315, 316–17
marketing directed at, 140, 264–65
on Master Plan, 267
middle-income housing in, 11, 287,
302, 303, 310, 325, 334, 336, 339, 345
outdated housing in, 258, 265–66
overcrowding in, 231, 241, 265, 307
population densities, 265, 290–91
Puerto Ricans in, 261, 262, 313, 314, 315
refugees from other clearance areas,
241
social and racial demographics,
261–62, 305–7, 313, 314
tenant movement in, 202
white population in, 313, 314
See also East Harlem public housing;
Harlem
East Harlem Council for Community
Planning (EHCCP), 301, 320, 328,
334, 344
East Harlem Plaza, 334, 335, 342, 343–44
East Harlem Project
as advocacy group, 302–3, 310, 316, 348
community organizing effort, 319–20
and redesign of DeWitt Clinton
Houses, 328–30

East Harlem public housing
  backlash against, 21, 255, 256–57, 258,
    298, 303–4, 326
  bringing street life back into, 324–42,
    349
  built between 1941 and 1965, 21–22, 255,
    258–60, 260, 302
  community organizing in, 319–20, 321,
    345–49
  confronting "mass way of life" in, 21,
    301, 320, 322–24, 342
  creating open spaces to build
    community, 342–45
  cultural programming in, 342–45, 349
  designs and plans for, 288–93, 289, 290,
    300, 308, 309, 324, 325–26
  erosion of community life caused by,
    258, 298, 301, 302, 304, 324
  ethic of city rebuilding in, 258, 260–61
  images of, 260, 289, 292, 306, 319, 321,
    332
  initial optimism about, 5, 202, 253–56,
    257, 258–68, 299–300, 301
  loss of businesses from, 259–60, 302,
    304, 307, 310–11
  loss of housing stock from, 307
  loss of jobs from, 307, 310
  Marya Mannes on, 352–53
  as massive intervention in cityscape,
    258–60, 291–93, 298, 300, 304, 370
  mass marketing to, 140, 264–65
  monotony of, 300
  racial issues in, 311, 313–17
  social worker investigations of,
    299–319
  today, 22
  See also Housing Act of 1949; public
    housing in Cold War America;
    specific public housing projects
East Harlem Public Housing Association,
  320
East Harlem Tenants Council, 348
East River, 18, 62
East River Houses
  building of, 15, 258, 261, 262, 264

design of, 288
images, 16, 292
population densities, 291
racial mix in, 313, 314
East River Park, 80
East Side
  Gas House District relocations to, 99,
    100
  urban renewal in, 169, 253–54
  See also Stuyvesant Town; United
    Nations project
Ecker, Frederick
  announcement of Stuyvesant Town,
    82
  as chairman of Met Life, 74, 75
  development of Stuyvesant Town, 19,
    80–81
  interest in families, 130, 131
  interest in housing, 78, 80
  on Met Life's goals at Stuyvesant
    Town, 74, 109
  public/private collaboration at
    Stuyvesant Town, 19, 20, 76, 80–83,
    103, 111–12, 112, 121, 285–86
  on segregation, 117, 118
Ecker, Frederick, Jr., 77
EHCCP (East Harlem Council for
  Community Planning), 301, 320,
  328, 334, 344
Eisenhower, Dwight D.
  at Baruch Houses dedication, 285
  cultural program, 182
  Lincoln Center groundbreaking, 169,
    170, 175, 181
  support for public housing, 282
El Barrio, 262, 314, 347
1199 Plaza, 339
eminent domain
  doctrine of, 5
  as tool in urban renewal, 5, 8, 78, 162
  use by Fordham University, 230
  use for Stuyvesant Town, 78, 80
Empire State Building, 3, 157
English, Daniel B., 126
Epstein, Jason, 353

446 | INDEX

redesigns of open space in public
    housing, 21, 303, 332–34, *335*, 336,
    339, 342, 366
May, Ernst, 14
Mayor's Committee for Better Housing,
    213
McCall's, 139
McCarthy era, 180, 281
McCarthy, Joseph, 273–74
McGinley, Laurence J., 173, 359
McGoldrick, Joseph, 80, 110
Meany, George, 181
Metro North Redevelopment, 339, *341*
Metropolitan Council on Housing,
    355–56, 369
Metropolitan Life Insurance Company
    "benevolent intervention" of, 80, 81,
        102–3, 106, 112, 182
    financial profile in early 1940s,
        77–78
    interest in housing initiatives, 78–79
    racial segregation policy, 76, 102, 119
    Riverton project, 120–21, 146
    See also Gas House District;
        Stuyvesant Town
Metropolitan Opera House
    architect, 187
    architecture, 188, 189
    early negotiations, 172, 173, 174
    images, *191*
    site plan, 186
    See also Lincoln Center for the
        Performing Arts
middle class
    luring back to city, 5, 7, 163
    marketing to, 132–45
    postwar expansion of, 175–76
    Title I funds used to benefit, 129
    urban redevelopment benefiting,
        19, 165
    See also Stuyvesant Town
Middle East Side, 100
middle-income co-op housing, 11, 287,
    302, 303, 310, 325, 334, 336
Mielziner, Jo, *187*

minorities
    burden of urban renewal on, 205–7
    See also African Americans; Puerto
        Ricans
Mitchell-Lama developments, 334, 339
Mobilization for Youth, 348
modern architecture
    as alienating, 5
    corporate buildings, 28, 50–51
    critique of, 188
    design idioms of, 9–10, 189
    European, 104
    formalism in, 188, 325
    Julliard School as, 188
    leading champion for, 50
    and modern planning theory, 7
    "monumental," 184–85, 189–90
    postmodernism, 188
    remaking cityscapes through, 5, 8, 20
    skyscrapers in, 28, 36, 42, 48
    "tower in a park" form, *16*, 104
    in urban renewal, 5, 8, 9–10, 12
    See also East Harlem public housing;
        Lincoln Square project; public
        housing in New York City;
        Stuyvesant Town; United Nations
        project
modern art
    abstract expressionism, 28
    Ashcan School, 197
    depictions of urban renewal in, 8,
        153–54, 197, 198–200, 247–49
    Manhattan as incubator for, 28
    postwar, 198
    urban realism, 154
    urban renewal's resemblance to, 9
modern housing movement
    architects of, 261
    continental idioms, 104
    impact of World War II on, 15–16
    origins of, 12, 13–14, 333
    public housing roots in, 258, 260,
        277
    in United Nations project, 51
    See also Le Corbusier

modernism
American betrayal of, 256–57
corporate, 50–51
"creative destruction" in, 9
debates over, 22
leading champion of, 50
in public housing towers, 104, 260
in United Nations buildings, 49
in urban renewal, 9, 20, 364
utopian, 20, 104
modernity
"deliberate plans" of, 4
in furnishings and decoration, 132–45
Manhattan as capital of, 5, 26, 27
public housing projects as symbols
of, 255
skyscrapers as symbols of, 28, 36, 48
Stuyvesant Town as emblem of, 119
See also modern architecture; modern
housing movement
modernization
Manhattan as image of, 5
public housing towers as icons of, 255
theory of, 9, 364
modern planning theory
discrediting of, 25–26
influence on urban renewal policies,
7, 9–10
issues of race and gender in, 7
Jane Jacobs's critique of, 362, 365
mixed neighborhoods in, 222, 224–25,
238
neighborhood units in, 15, 190
remaking cityscape through, 5, 12, 20
See also neighborhood units;
superblock planning
Montrose, Josephine, 236
Morningside Gardens, 165, 167, 168, 169
Morningside Heights
African Americans in, 166, 200
blight in, 166, 167
relocation efforts at, 168, 211
tenant activism, 200, 204–5, 207–9
urban redevelopment in, 162, 165,
167–68

Morningside Heights, Inc. (MHI), 167,
168
"Morningside Heights—The Institutions
and the People" (D. Rockefeller), 161
Morris, Newbold, 64
Moses, Robert
Baruch Houses dedication, 283, 285–86
belief in public/private collaboration
to rebuild NYC, 79, 80, 81–82, 111,
112, 161–63, 165, 285–86
building projects between 1949 and
1960, 21, 164, 169–70
bulldozer approach to urban renewal,
21, 239, 360
as city construction coordinator, 161,
286, 359
as Committee on Slum Clearance
head, 5, 161, 162–63, 213, 214, 286, 357,
358, 359
control over New York City Housing
Authority, 284–87, 357
and Cooper Square, 355–56
description of public housing, 293
and East Harlem, 267, 268
East Side renewal efforts, 169
as embattled, 357–58
Gas House District relocations, 99
and highway building projects, 359,
368
and Housing Act of 1949, 163–64, 169
liberals' support for, 203
Lincoln Square project, 20, 159, 169,
170, 172–73, 176, 182, 186, 196, 198,
214, 217, 226, 230, 238–39
and Lincoln Square resistance
movement, 226, 227–28
mixed redevelopment favored by,
162–63, 286
Morningside Heights project, 167, 168,
169, 207–8, 209
and 1940 Master Plan, 16–17, 18, 267,
286
opposition to, 11, 201, 207, 212–14, 354
predictions for 1999 New York, 66
prewar public works program, 79–80

public housing in New York City
  African American and Puerto Rican
    influx into, 27, 297, 313–15
  and antidiscrimination legislation, 122,
    127, 203, 209–10, 231, 276, 304
  architecture, 255, 256, 294, 296
  built between 1941 and 1965, 21–22, 255,
    258–60, 260, 287
  class segregation in, 258
  community-building efforts by social
    workers in, 319–20, 321
  crime in, 300, 301, 317, 318, 320, 328, 349
  designs and plans of, 14–15, 283–84,
    285, 287–91, 289, 297, 300, 325–26,
    358
  discrediting, 26, 256, 298, 303–4
  greatest accomplishment of, 370
  income ceilings in, 287, 318, 320, 326
  income segregation in, 327
  initial optimism about, 5, 202, 253–56,
    257, 258–68, 299–300, 301
  lawlessness in, 146
  linked to "global city" status, 36
  loss of community life in, 258, 301, 302,
    310, 322, 324, 358
  as machines for living, 255, 300
  maintenance and management issues,
    11, 257, 317, 318, 320
  as merger between slum clearance and
    modern housing, 14, 258
  modernity of, 14–15, 104, 255
  morale of residents in, 295, 296–97,
    300, 302, 310, 318–19, 320, 322–24, 328
  new projects in, 371
  in 1930s, 7
  physical deterioration of, 295
  population densities, 291
  poverty reinforced in, 258, 296–97, 301,
    322
  private/public initiatives in, 25, 82
  problem families in, 317–18, 320, 358
  racial discrimination bans in, 203,
    209–10
  racial integration in, 300, 301
  racial mix in, 168
  racial segregation deepened by, 11,
    119–20, 129, 203, 258, 287, 297, 313,
    314
  racial tensions deepened by, 301, 311,
    313
  refugees from urban renewal to,
    210–13, 214–15, 217, 227, 230, 231, 233,
    240–41, 256, 314–15, 317
  remaking cityscape through, 4, 256
  rents in, 287
  separating from slum clearance, 270
  siting of, 286
  "top-down" authority in, 318, 322–23,
    326, 327
  tower-block planning in, 15, 254, 255,
    256, 258
  welfare services in, 318, 320, 326
  See also East Harlem public housing;
    Housing Act of 1949; public housing
    in Cold War America; specific public
    housing projects
Public Works, 293
Puerto Ricans
  displacement by urban renewal, 10,
    165, 205, 207, 211
  in East Harlem, 261, 262
  in East Harlem public housing, 301,
    302
  grass roots groups, 348
  influx into NYC, 27, 164, 183, 257, 261,
    262, 297, 314
  in Lincoln Square neighborhood,
    200, 215, 216, 218, 221, 222, 231–32,
    240
  at Morningside Heights, 166, 200
  as portrayed in West Side Story, 159
  at Stuyvesant Town, 116, 128

Queens
  Met Life housing development in, 78
  postwar housing developments in,
    273–74
  postwar white flight to, 27
  proposed UN site, 37
  Title I projects in, 164

Queensboro Bridge, *55*
Quinones, Pedro, 200

race
  as a special construct, 276
race relations
  in Cold War America, 41, 120, 123, 128
  in postwar New York, 39–40, 41, 164–65
  and public housing debate, 275–76
  United Nations vision for, 41
racial desegregation
  red-baiting as tactic in, 120, 122, 125–27
  at Stuyvesant Town, 19, 76, 77, 116,
    118–29, *124*, *144*, 145, 150, 153, 203
racial discrimination
  banned in Title I projects, 119–20
  in New Deal programs, 103
  in private housing market, 207, 213
  in public housing, 11, 119–20, 203
racial segregation
  in postwar New York, 39–40, 119–20
  in public housing, 11, 119–20, 129, 203,
    258, 287, 297, 313, 314
  reinforced by urban renewal, 7, 10, 25,
    27, 112, 129, 207, 231, 241, 287, 369
  in suburbs, 27, 103, 119
  See also Stuyvesant Town
Radighieri, Vincent, 235
Ramsay, Wyeth, 139
Randall, Kathleen, 189
Rand, Esther, 355
Rand, Sam, 342, 343
Rankin, Rebecca, 42, 64–65, 66
Ratensky, Samuel, 283, 284
Reagan, Ronald, 368
real estate industry
  campaign against public housing, 269,
    275, 279–80, 282
  ongoing power of, 370–71
Real Great Society's Urban Planning
  Studio, 348, 369
red-baiting
  in desegregation attempts, 120, 122,
    125–27
  in McCarthy era, 274, 281

  of tenant activists, 204
  of Vito Marcantonio, 323
Red Cross, 20, 159, 170
Rego Park Veterans Project, 273–74
Reid, William, 326
relocations
  advocacy for humane, 202, 203–4,
    205, 208
  aggressive attitude toward, 56
  of businesses, 237
  investigation by City Planning
    Commission, 210–14
  report by A. Panuch to Mayor Wagner,
    358–59
  under Title, I, 237, 282–83
  See also tenant movements
rent control, 202, 276, 355
repertory theater at Lincoln Center, 186,
  187, 189, *191*
Reporter, 351
the Right, 368
Riis, Jacob, 12, 90
Riverside Church, 166, 167, 168
Riverside Community House, 214
Riverton, 120–21, 146
Robbins, Ira, 208, 227, 326, 333
Robinson, C.C., Mrs., 131
Robinson, Earl, 145
Rochdale Village, 355
Rockefeller Center, 45, 157
Rockefeller, David, 161, 165, 166, 167–69
Rockefeller Foundation, 173, 360
Rockefeller Institute, 165
Rockefeller, John D., III
  Cold War urban renewal vision, 166
  and Lincoln Arcade evictions, 198
  Lincoln Square project, 20, 159, 161,
    166, 170, 173, 174–75, 215, 230, 237,
    238–39
  photos, *181*, *187*
  on role of arts in society, 20, 161,
    174–75, 178, 182–83, 190
  vision for "city therapy," 161, 182–83, 190
Rockefeller, John D., Jr.
  on New York City, 39

sons of, 166, 173
United Nations project, 17–18, 38
Rockefeller, Laurance, 166
Rockefeller, Nelson, 38
Rockefeller, Winthrop, 165, 166
Rodgers, Cleveland, 42, 64–65, 66
Rogers, Byron, 9
Rogers, Harry, 194–95, 196, 225, 226, 241
Roman, Seymour, 147
Roosevelt, Franklin D., 41, 67, 120, 203, 272
Root, Ella, 214
Rosenberg, Julius and Ethel, 128, 296
Rosner, Shirley, 152
Ross, Andrew, 296
Ross, Paul L., 122, 123, 126
Rotella, Carlo, 6
Rotundo, Anthony, 97
Ruiz, Miguel, 292
Rusk, Dean, 173
Russon, John, 100

Saarinen, Eero, 187, *187*, 188
Saarinen, Eliel, 66
Sachs Quality Stores, 132
Salisbury, Harrison, 253–54, 293, 294–95, 361
Samuels, Gertrude, 46, 47, 168
San Juan Hill, 218
Sapir, Isidore, 126
Saturday Evening Post, 83, 177
Save Our Homes
flyer, *206*
historical significance of, 205–8, 239
Manhattantown project, 204, 205, 207–8
methods of, 204–5
Morningside Heights project, 205, 207–8, 209
quotes by, 200, 207
women as leaders of, 204, 207, 214
Yorkville project, 205, *206*
See also tenant movements
Schonberg, Harold C., 157
Schuckman, Richard, 227, 229, 233

Schuman, William, 173, 183, 193–94
Schumpeter, Joseph, 9
Schwartz, Joel, 56, 165
Scott, James, 11
Seagram Building, 51
Secretariat of United Nations
architecture, 36, 42, 46
design, 43, 44–46, 51, 62
images, *31, 35, 45, 63*
opening, 46
symbolism, 48, 49, 51
See also United Nations project
segregation. *See* racial segregation
Seidman, Martha, 130, 131, 132, 146, 148
Senator Robert F. Wagner Houses, 259, 290, 314
Seward Park, 355
Shepley, Henry R., 185, 187
The Shook-Up Generation (Salisbury), 253
shopping
bringing back to city, 5, 7
gender roles in, 132
Shreve, Richmond, *75*, 104
Simkhovitch, Mary, 12
Sinatra, Frank, *144*, 145
single-family homes, 270, 271
skyscrapers
symbolism of, 28, 36, 42, 48
at United Nations, 36, 42, 44–45
Sloan, John, 197
slum clearance
advocates for, 12–13, 14
aggressive attitudes toward, 56
as attempt to preserve profitability of city property, 7, 162
before Housing Act, 7
as "benevolent intervention," 5
burden on minorities, 205–7
creation of new slums through, 10, 21, 27, 201, 205, 211, 216, 231
destruction vs. rebirth in, 153
discrediting of, 25–26
displacement created by, 10, 27, 202, 205–7

Truman, Harry
   and desegregation, 120
   economic policy, 22–23
   and Fair Deal, 7, 68, 203, 272
   and Housing Act of 1949, 7–8, 22–23,
      270, 280, 282
   on international image of U.S., 268
   and United Nations, 40
Tudor City, 56, 63
Turtle Bay. See United Nations project

Union Settlement House, 264, 299, 302,
   307, 324, 334, 347
United Committee to Save Our Homes,
   204
   See also Save Our Homes
United Housing Foundation, 355
The United Nations and the City of
   New York, 61
United Nations Board of Design, 43–45,
   44, 47, 49
United Nations project
   architects, 43–44, 44
   architecture, 19, 35–37, 41, 44–45, 46,
      48, 50–51
   construction, 35, 42
   design process, 42–46, 47, 49–50
   E. B. White on, 33, 34–36, 41, 42, 51, 65, 68
   engineering, 48
   ethic of city rebuilding in, 19, 36, 37, 51,
      59, 66, 67–68
   images, 31, 35, 45, 63, 157
   influence on future urban
      redevelopment, 51, 57–59, 64, 65–66,
      68–69
   as model for geopolitical
      transformation, 34–37, 41, 42–43,
      49–50, 51, 59–60
   as model for urban transformation,
      34–37, 41–42, 43, 50, 51, 59–60,
      64–66, 65, 68–69
   municipal incentives for, 51–52
   not true urban renewal project, 17–18
   prefiguring postwar urban renewal, 36,
      51, 57–59

race relations highlighted by, 37, 39–41
site clearance, 51, 52–59, 222
site plan, 36–37, 44, 51–52, 53–54,
   59–64, 61
site selection, 17–18, 37–39, 46, 55
symbolism of, 18, 19, 35–36, 46–50, 51,
   59, 66
world-capital status of NYC enhanced
   by, 34, 36, 37, 39, 64–65, 66, 165, 254
See also United Nations organization
United Nations Headquarters
   Committee, 38, 43
United Nations organization
   domestic reception for, 40–41
   impact of Cold War on, 68
   search for new site, 37–39
United Nations World, article on
   clearance site for UN, 56–57, 58, 59
United Neighborhood Houses, 208–9
United States
   reception for United Nations, 40–41
   See also postwar America; race
      relations
United States Congress
   investigation into Manhattantown, 213
   See also Housing Act of 1937; Housing
      Act of 1949; Housing Act of 1954
United States Housing and Home
   Finance Agency, 230
United States Supreme Court, 41, 120
United Tenants League (UTL), 97, 202
University Club, 179, 197
University of Chicago, 167
Upper West Side, 165, 213, 241, 357
urban crisis
   literary descriptions of, 351–54
   New York's descent into, 6–7, 12, 26,
      27, 28–29, 353, 369
urbanism, 6, 12, 216, 239
urban liberalism
   broad front of, 5, 77, 201, 202, 272
   high tide of, 23
   See also civil rights groups; labor
      unions; leftists; liberals; social
      workers; tenant movements